VIDEO
re/VIEW

THE (*best*) SOURCE
FOR CRITICAL WRITINGS ON
DIAN ARTISTS' VIDEO
y Gale and Lisa Steele, 1996

OAKVILLE GALLERIES
1306 LAKESHORE ROAD EAST
OAKVILLE, ONTARIO L6J 1L6

Maurie **Alioff** John **Anderson** Renee **Baert**
Marjorie **Beaucage** Jean-Yves **Bégin** Jody **Berland**
Hank **Bull** Eric **Cameron** Daniel **Carrière** Marie-
Hélène **Cousineau** Sara **Diamond** George **Elliott**
Bruce W. **Ferguson** Robert **Forget** Vera **Frenkel**
Richard **Fung** Jean **Gagnon** Peggy **Gale** General
Idea Nicole **Gingras** Michael **Goldberg** John
Greyson Lydia **Haustein** Vern **Hume** Igloolik
Isuma Productions Harold **Innis** Gary **Kibbins**
Larissa **Lai** Monique **Langlois** Françoise **Le Gris**
David **McIntosh** Marshall **McLuhan** Jan **Peacock**
Louise **Poissant** Becki **Ross** Christine **Ross** Susan
Rynard Tom **Sherman** Lisa **Steele** Nell **Tenhaaf**
Dot **Tuer** Elizabeth **Vander Zaag**

VIDEO
re/VIEW

**THE (*best*) SOURCE
FOR CRITICAL WRITINGS ON
CANADIAN ARTISTS' VIDEO**
ed. Peggy Gale and Lisa Steele, 1996

Art Metropole and V tape, Toronto

CONTENTS

CONTENTS

CONTENTS

CONTENTS

PREFACE AND

PEGGY GALE AND LISA STEELE

The present volume is intended as both introduction and historical overview for artists' video in Canada — for those readers generally interested in contemporary art, and also as reference tool for the specialist: for artist, teacher, viewer and critic. It is a project generated originally by Lisa Steele, who proposed the idea for this book to Peggy Gale and then to Art Metropole as a joint endeavour with V tape; nearly four years have elapsed in its preparation.

We are of course especially grateful to the authors for their original efforts, and for their subsequent permission to reprint their writings. Thanks too to the University of Toronto Press for permission to include the work of Harold Innis and from MIT Press for a chapter from Marshall McLuhan's *Understanding Media*, newly released to mark the book's thirtieth anniversary. Just a few documents are published here for the first time, including excerpts from a (successful) funding proposal to Telefilm Canada by Igloolik Isuma Productions, as well as an original memo from Robert Forget to the National Film Board which resulted in the founding of Vidéographe, and the transcript of a video interview between Marjorie Beaucage and Wil Campbell. Note should also be made that three essays included here — Nell Tenhaaf's "Of Monitors and Men ...", Richard Fung's "Colouring the Screen..." and Jean Gagnon's "Entanglement: Video Art and TV" — were commissioned originally by Renee Baert for her book-length *The Video Issue/Propos Vidéo* anthology, sponsored by the Satellite Video Exchange Society (Video In) in Vancouver,which appeared eventually as (part of) an inter-magazine publishing project in 1993. For drawing our attention to the early "Warning to Artists" by George Elliott, we thank the eagle eye and good will of Bob Foley from The Banff Centre.

Given the significant presence of Québécois video both nationally and internationally, it was crucial to include responses to the work and the artists of that province. For assistance in collecting French-language material

ACKNOWLEDGEMENTS

for the bibliography, special mention must be made of the research of Maria Cristina Martinez, as well as the help of Christine Ross, Charles Guilbert and Serge Murphy who contacted individuals and solicited documentation. Of the 49 texts finally chosen for the book, over a quarter were written originally in French. A total of eight articles appear here in English for the first time, with our thanks to Jean-Luc Svoboda for his able and timely assistance as translator. (A further five essays had already been published bilingually, appearing in translation as well as their original French.) Artists' and independents' video in Quebec and the rest of Canada have tended to follow different paths of development, as have avenues of distribution and public response. Video in Canada has many regions and characteristics; it has been our hope to acknowledge that diversity and strength of difference.

Simply locating previously-published materials was no easy task. Many of the magazines and journals cited here as original publishers have long since disappeared, and museum catalogues, even if still available, may be hard to trace. The sheer scale of the bibliography became an increasing surprise during the months this project developed, but its virtual invisibility at the outset of our researches made this collection of information all the more pressing. Undoubtedly, additional entries will come to light after the "final" state settled on for publication here; we can only assert that we have been as thorough as time and resources permitted.

Given the size of the present volume, the sheer numbers of words and entries, it became impossible to consider visual accompaniment for the essays and articles. One is encouraged to seek out the original publications for that. Photographs in **VIDEO re/VIEW: The (best) Source for Critical Writings on Canadian Artists' Video** have been employed more as punctuation — or inspiration — than as illustration for text and ideas. We wish to thank the artists and institutions who have made their images available for use in this book.

For the elegant design solutions to so massive a quantity of text, we thank Christian Morrison and Julie Gibb of GreenStreet Design for their fine and discerning ideas, and their admirable commitment to this project.

Funding for this publication came from the Media section of the Canada Council, from the Toronto Arts Council, the Ontario Ministry of Citizenship, Culture and Recreation, and from the Film/Video/Photography section of the Ontario Arts Council. Assistance through federal and provincial work programs such as Section 25 and Futures was invaluable for inputting text through hiring Judy Mintz, and for assembly of Index information. For the latter, we thank Cheryl Rondeau-Hoekstra for her help. Proofreading was accomplished in large part by Peggy Gale, Lisa Steele, Kim Tomczak and Susan Wheeler, with the professional advice and assistance of Beverley Endersby and Karen MacCormack. The articles and essays have been reprinted as they originally appeared, without modifications beyond those few corrections of fact as requested by the authors. Throughout, the editors have appreciated the support and overall assistance afforded by both Art Metropole and V tape and their staffs.

There *is* a history of artists' and independent video in Canada, but it has remained for too long scattered and ignored. Now, we have a selection of some of the most evocative of the available writings, chosen for their ability to delineate a moment, an issue, a "scene," or for their confirming character, their evidence of exchange, their currency for "then" or "still."

VIDEO re/VIEW is an historical anthology of writings on Canadian video — a portrait and a commentary, made largely from *inside* by individuals long involved with the field. We hope it will find its deserved and desiring audience.

INTRODUCTION | PEGGY GALE

Since the early 1970s artists in Canada have been producing works on and with video — a technology that offered a means, a support, a context that has continued to evolve. One of its most appealing features in the early days was *video's lack of history*: there was no need to take up a position with this new medium, no need to refute a past or establish a hegemony. There was no critical context whatever for video-as-art. Everything seemed eligible, all seemed possible. The only drawbacks were practical ones: back in the early 70s the video production/presentation equipment itself was limited, with half-inch black and white open reels, virtually no editing possible, and with a presumedly brief shelf life. All of that seemed just fine, though.

Much is changed now. There *is* a history of accomplishments, a long list of artists and titles in the field. The equipment is no longer so limited, in that colour and post-production capabilities are to be assumed. The drawbacks now are in the new expense of producing this work, and the still-difficult issues of distributing it, finding and speaking to the right audience. But the work itself has much to offer.

And now we want to know that history, trace those issues and ideas over the first 25 years of artists' video in Canada. This collection of texts offers an overview of a period and a broad range of mindsets, aimed at both general reader and specific researcher or practitioner. Variety as well as depth of information was our goal. But the preparation of the present book brought with it many surprises.

We began with a conviction that this would not be "the" history: we always intended to present *many* voices, many histories, a picture of the field's variety and ambitions. We wanted to show change over the years, and offer a place to compare difference of opinion, of desire, of accomplishment, of audience. We had no idea that quite so much had been written over the years, dispersed as it was in catalogues, journals, magazines and personal files.

The words of artists would be as important as those of critics, historians, curators. A broad landscape was envisaged, dealing with such topics as early performance-based work, autobiography and sexual identity, evolving into more issue-centred and documentary-related considerations of gender and colour, ethnicity, nationalism and language politics, the interaction in general of artistic and social questions, the individual in society. We wanted to search out video's Canadian roots, reassert the intellectual relevance of Harold Innis and Marshall McLuhan as well as the visual arts base in Conceptual Art and Performance of the 60s and 70s.

While the present collection includes all of these elements, their appearance is less programmatic than originally envisaged. Rather than proposing a linear or chronological development, **VIDEO re/VIEW** is arranged in clusters. An opening section offers background material to the developments of artists' video: a chapter from Harold Innis' landmark work in communications that set the stage for conceiving the role of technology in human interaction, along with a fragment from Marshall McLuhan's *Understanding Media* over a decade later, when television became a focus for pop psychology and McLuhan an internationally famous "media guru." The brief "Warning to Artists" published in a 1953 issue of *Canadian Art* underlines the perceived dangers of television in a representation of artists' achievements and ideas — at a time when broadcasting itself was new to Canada, and years before low-cost consumer-grade portable video cameras would make individual use of the medium an easy option.

The second section brings together essays arguing for autonomy and diversity of voice across the regions. Rather than a traditionally narrow view of arts and business as seen from Central Canada, this group of writings records important changes in self-representation by native cultures and prairies artists over a fifteen year span. In Section Three are "origins" of other sorts for video, documents from the founding proposal for Montreal's

Vidéographe in 1970 and descriptions of the organization in development three years later, and a sampling of Michael Goldberg's unique *Accessible Portapack Manual* from the mid-1970s in Vancouver. Eric Cameron's "Notes for Video Art," published in 1973, propose some new possibilities for camera and viewer, a quintessential document from the days of High Conceptual art. Peggy Gale offers an early discussion of video viewing habits, arguing against the medium's reputation for being "boring." Christine Ross and Jody Berland mark out the parameters for language in conceiving video, and artist Vera Frenkel insists on the place of memory and story-telling in living culture, through her evocation of censorship and government control in *The Last Screening Room* from 1984.

The fourth section continues the histories of the video medium and its artists, with a mid-eighties sketch of early Québécois production by Jean Gagnon and Jan Peacock's later re-assessment of early body-based work in Halifax. Sara Diamond traces the complex roots and relationships of Vancouver projects and personalities, dating from the international *Matrix* conference of 1973, and Louise Poissant argues for the place of video as literal recorder of history and geography, a location in time and space. Tom Sherman, Nell Tenhaaf and David McIntosh explore a history of technological components and changing desires, an investigation of how machines mutate along with our needs and attitudes — or vice versa. Elizabeth Vander Zaag sums up ironically, a written "performance" of the artist as accomplice in her own institutionalization, as video establishes its foothold in the public arena.

Section five comprises surveys over theme areas: a place for women, for AIDS activism, for works against racism, for new forms of documentary, video as commentary on television, and the cross-engagements of artists addressing multiple issues. Longer and more complex assessments of exemplary individuals' works appear in the sixth grouping, with essays on Colin Campbell, Vera Frenkel, Daniel Dion, Lisa Steele and Kim Tomczak, Paul Wong, Michèle Waquant and Stan Douglas. Briefer reviews appear in section seven, with commentary on single works of Julian Samuel, Ardele Lister, Chantal duPont, Charles Guilbert and Serge Murphy, Margaret Moores and Almerinda Travassos, Rodney Werden and others, plus a timely assessment of The Gina Show in mid-seventies' Vancouver. The final word returns to the artists themselves: *Adjusting a Colour Television* by Tom Sherman, and *Towards an Audience Vocabulary* by General Idea. **VIDEO re/VIEW** is completed by contributors' biographies, distribution sources, and the full bibliography for Canadian artists' video over more than twenty-five years, assembled here for the first time.

There is no time-line plotted here, for developments have been organic and personal as much as geographical and theoretical. The genealogies are fluid and mixed, inter-generational as well as social and contextual. And "art" itself has a changing face. Problems with censorship as well as funding and distribution, appearing regularly in chameleon form over the years, have been left in the files; somehow too rooted in local factors, no overview appeared that was both specific and illuminating for these contentious constants. Included here are responses to individuals, collectives, communities, and the works they have produced.

Ideas have changed with time. The work included here represents a very long beginning for Canadian video, or more likely, a fascinating middle ground.

Next, a future. ...

ON THE TEACHING OF VIDEO ART | LISA STEELE

Early in the spring of 1991, after over a decade of teaching video at the Ontario College of Art in Toronto, I played a tape in an introductory video class which changed the way I approached teaching and led, ultimately, to the book you're holding. The tape was made in 1972 by a (then) graduating student at Mt. Allison. University in Sackville, N.B. It is a single, unedited shot: the eyes of a male-but-somewhat-androgenous face fill the frame, staring into the camera's eye/our-the-viewer's-eye. In black-and-white, the image is not remarkable — except that it is so still. Not frozen (as when the machine pauses), but preternaturally still (as when a person stops). Still breathing, the image of this young man's eyes catch us, and caught in the headlights of his gaze, we also stop. And then it's a stand-off. As the minutes tick by, the strain within the room is palpable; while some are attentive (if sceptical), other students heave themselves from buttock to buttock, audibly expressing their impatience with this "piece of presumptuous indulgence".

After about 7 minutes, I announced, "We've reached the half-way mark ." Over the next 60 seconds, the feel of the room changed perceptibly, the restlessness giving way to grudging attention, trancelike involvement and genuine interest.

When the tape finished playing, the discussion was amongst the most responsive and perceptive which I have ever experienced as an instructor. The students spoke of their sense of engagement with the student/artist whose work they had just viewed, with his image, his visage, his action (minimal as it was), his body, and finally with his corpus — the mute witness, the testimony of nuance and detail offered to them — across the years. This is not to say that all the students present that day "liked" the early video art piece entitled *Peepers* by John Watt. Some loathed it, thinking it tedious; others were moved almost to tears. But all had something to say and that, in my experience, made the time spent viewing very useful — for them as student/artists and for me as a teacher.

After this, I began to show not just *Peepers* but other works from video art history to my students. I had done this only rarely before being uncertain whether a convincing context for these older works could be stitched together from the fragments of critical discourse, artists' statements and catalogue essays available to me as a teacher. But the reward was too great to resist any longer.

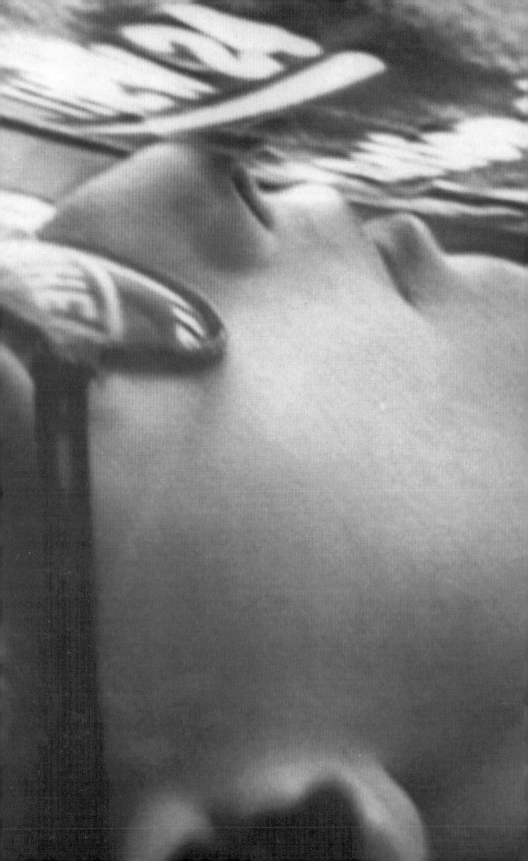

A WARNING TO ARTISTS

by George Elliott

If this were a guide to television for artists, rule number one would be: *Never* let an oil or water colour of yours be televised because it won't look like the work of art you painted.

It has been suggested publicly that one of the benefits of Canada's new television broadcasting service is that it will become an "electronic art gallery", that it will bring the world of fine art into every living-room, that it will banish the complaint of "gallery-foot" for ever. The absurdity of this suggestion was equalled once before when it was claimed the printed word was doomed by the advent of radio. Television and works of art are not compatible.

The only possible meeting-ground for the artist and the television producer is in the field of social documentation. Television can record the way an artist lives and works. Television can report that the artist has some paintings on exhibition. That is all. There are too many drawbacks to television for an artist to permit his works to be televised.

Television is an *entertainment* medium. It is a process that puts the *movement* of people and objects into the home of about one hundred and seventy-five thousand families in Canada. If the moving people make a *noise*, television transmits that too.

Entertainment, movement, noise: stripped of its dreams of glory, television boils down to these three elements. The movement may be as absurd as a hand puppet blowing its nose. The noise may be as divine as a late Beethoven quartet. It remains entertainment.

In passing, television's dreams of glory include the notion that it is a medium of uplift. It is a medium of uplift to the degree of enthusiasm and to the amount of energy given to the broadcasting of drama, television's least understood field.

There is no place for works of art in this mixture of entertainment, drama, movement and noise because the plastic arts depend for their existence on the things that television destroys in its devastatingly cavalier fashion.

Colour, of course, is the first element to be sacrificed if a painting is put in front of the television camera. Can you imagine a Goodridge Roberts landscape without Roberts' very private blues and greens? Binning's subtleties of colours are an important part of his charm. Varley's disturbing palette of piercing greens, blues, cold pinks and earth are essential to the uniqueness of Varley.

Under perfect studio lighting, perfect transmission, perfect reception, perfect camera focus, perfect receiver adjustment, a painting can be televised only about half as successfully as taking a print off a panchromatic negative of the painting. The variables of television cannot be brought under such perfect control.

Texture is next to get rough treatment in front of the image orthicon tube. In a sense, texture is a third dimension in painting, almost a dimension of depth. A characteristic of television is to broadcast near and far things indiscriminately. Therefore such subtleties of textures that depend on minute shadows (as with John Martin's romantic church walls) would be lost.

Where the genius of a painting is in the artist's handling of light, the painting will very likely "wash out" on television because the camera is not as discerning as the human eye. Last year the exhibition "Berthe Morisot and her Circle" was the subject of a television broadcast. Her pale and gentle impressions of light, bathing the people she loved and painted, reflected a pale and contented attitude in a rich, comfortable era. However, on television all was lost. Subtleties of light became anaemic brush strokes.

Finally, spatial movement disappears in the painting. Where the painter has arranged planes of colour to direct the eye "in and out" and around the rectangle, the elements merge, or lose their relative values or even change their values. For example, an ordinary blue shirt or a canary yellow blouse comes out pure white on television.

Painting and sculpture are too intellectual for such a frivolous medium. They are too enduring in their impact for such an ephemeral means of communication. A painting or a statue does not exist until it has been in a room or a gallery with a spectator. A painting needs an intellectual presence before it can work its magic. Placing *anything* between the viewer and the painting kills the viewer. Television not only kills the magic, it prevents the viewer from contributing his sensibility to the process of enjoying a painting.

Television has a voracious appetite for things that move, things that entertain, things that make a noise. This is the prime contradiction: a painting is static, intellectual, coloured, meaningful; television is noise, movement and entertainment.

How has art fared so far on Canadian television? There was a "March of Time" programme about American art museums. There was a three-part question about the Group of Seven on a quiz show which the experts could not answer. There was a thirty minute programme showing the Morisot paintings when they were in Toronto. There was another half-hour show devoted to the Canadian Group of Painters. This latter was moderately stimulating because Eric Newton and Paul Duval were pitted against a Toronto columnist in a strange discussion of some Group painting which the columnist didn't understand and about which Newton made patronizing remarks.

The motion picture, *Canadian Landscape*, has also been telecast and probably illustrates television's best function in this contest: the delivery into the homes of viewers of carefully conceived background material about the artist and his life.

THE BIAS OF COMMUNICATION[1]

by Harold Innis

The appearance of a wide range of cultural phenomena at different periods in the history of Western civilization has been described by Professor A.L. Kroeber in *Configurations of Cultural Growth* (Berkeley, 1946). He makes suggestive comments at various points to explain the relative strength or weakness of cultural elements but refrains from extended discussion. I do not propose to do more than add a footnote to these comments and in this to discuss the possible significance of communication to the rise and decline of cultural traits. A medium of communication has an important influence on the dissemination of knowledge over space and over time and it becomes necessary to study its characteristics in order to appraise its influence in its cultural setting. According to its characteristics it may be better suited to the dissemination of knowledge over time than over space, particularly if the medium is heavy and durable and not suited to transportaion,or to the dissemination of knowledge over space than over time, particularly if the medium is light and easily transported. The relative emphasis on time or space will imply a bias of significance to the culture in which it is imbedded.

Immediately we venture on this inquiry we are compelled to recognize the bias of the period in which we work. An interest in the bias of other civilizations may in itself suggest a bias of our own. Our knowledge of other civilizations depends in large part on the character of the media used by each civilization in so far as it is capable of being preserved or of being made accessible by discovery as in the case of the results of archaeological expeditions.[2] Writing on clay and on stone has been preserved more effectively than that on papyrus. Since durable commodities emphasize time and continuity, studies of civilization such as Toynbee's tend to have a bias toward religion and to show a neglect of problems of space, notably administration and law. The bias of modern civilization incidental to the newspaper and the radio will presume a perspective in consideration of civilizations dominated

---

1. A paper presented at the University of Michigan on April 18, 1949.

2. See the complaint that archaeologists have been unduly concerned with objects of art. S. Clarke and R. Englebach, *Ancient Egyptian Masonry, the Building Craft* (London, 1930), p. vi.

by other media. We can do little more than urge that we must be continually alert to the implications of this bias and perhaps hope that consideration of the implications of other media to various civilizations may enable us to see more clearly the bias of our own. In any case we may become a little more humble as to the characteristics of our civilization. We can perhaps assume that the use of a medium of communication over a long period will to some extent determine the character of knowledge to be communicated and suggest that its pervasive influence will eventually create a civilization in which life and flexibility will become exceedingly difficult to maintain and that the advantages of a new medium will become such as to lead to the emergence of a new civilization.

Egyptian civilization appears to have been powerfully influenced by the character of the Nile. Utilization of its periodic floods depended on the unified control of an absolute authority. It has been claimed that the discovery of the sidereal year as early as 4241 B.C. made it possible to work out a calendar avoiding the difficulties of a year dependent on the moon. The discovery and the adoption of a calendar with the certainty of dates for religious festivals facilitated the establishment of an absolute monarchy and the impositions of the authority of Osiris and Ra, the Nile and the Sun, on upper Egypt. Success of the monarchy in acquiring control over Egypt in terms of space necessitated a concern with problems of continuity or time. The idea of immortality strengthened the position of the monarch. Mummification and construction of the pyramids as devices for emphasizing control over time were accompanied by the development of the art of pictorial representation as part of the funerary ritual and by the emergence of writing. The spoken word, by which the orders of the monarch were given, in itself possessed creative efficiency which in turn was perpetuated in the written word in the tomb. Pictorial decorations became hieroglyphic script. Writing gradually developed toward phoneticism and by the time of Menes (about 3315 B.C.) many picture signs had a purely phonetic value and were regularly spelled out. Autocratic monarchy developed by divine right culminated in the pyramids of about 2850 B.C. Private property disappeared and all arable land became the king's domain.

The monopoly of knowledge centring around stone and hieroglyphics was exposed to competition from papyrus as a new and more efficient medium. Royal authority began to decline after about 2540 B.C. and its decline was possibly coincident with the discovery of the solar year by the priestly class as a device to overcome the deficiencies of the sidereal year in which a day was gained each year. The king was lowered from the status of the Great God to the son of Ra. The chief priest of the Ra cult was exalted to the rank of chief god and Heliopolis became the centre of priestly power. Oligarchy succeeded an absolute monarchy. After about 2000 B.C. the masses were admitted to religious rites and immortality and to political rights. The gates of heaven and the jaws of hell were opened and a "most powerful instrument for the domination over men's unruly wills" devised.[3] The increasing use of papyrus and the brush was accompanied by the development of the hieratic character and the emergence of the profession of scribes. Writing and thought were secularized. Administration was extended following the spread of writing and reading. The social revolution involved in a shift from the use of stone to the use of papyrus and the increased importance of the priestly class imposed enormous strains on Egyptian civilization and left it exposed to the inroads of invaders equipped with effective weapons of attack. The Hyksos or Shepherd Kings captured and held Egypt from 1660 to 1580 B.C. The strength of Egyptian cultural elements facilitated reorganization, and mobilization of resources was directed to expulsion of the invaders. The introduction of the horse and light four-spoked chariots enabled Egyptian rulers not only to expel the Hyksos but also to conquer vast new territories and to build an empire.

An extension of political organization to include peoples of different races and religions reflecting a temporary solution of problems of space in government compelled the king to attempt a solution of problems of continuity. Worship of the solar disc was designed to provide an imperial religion which would overrule distinctions between Egyptians and foreigners. Failure to overcome the hostility of the entrenched priestly class in Egypt was followed by imperial decline and eventually by the subjugation of Egypt by the Assyrians and the Persians. A monopoly of knowledge supported by a difficult script resisted demands for change and brought the Egyptian Empire to an end. With abundant supplies of papyrus and conservative influence of religion on writing, pictographic writing was maintained and the emergence of consonantal signs was largely a result of the introduction of foreign names and words. The spoken word tended to drift away from the written word in spite of the efforts of Ikhnaton to bring them into closer accord.

In contrast with the civilization of the Nile that of the Euphrates and the Tigris lacked the necessity of unity and was characterized in its early development by a number of small theocratic city states in which the chief priest of the temple was direct representative of the god. Rivers were subject to irregular and incalculable flooding. The growth of city states assumed continuity in time and the

3. V. Gordon Childe, *What Happened in History* (New York, 1946), p. 150.

development of writing and reading by which the complex systems of accounting could be made intelligible to individuals and to their successors.

Alluvial clay as the medium for writing had implications for Sumerian civilization in the difficulties of transport and the tendency to encourage the development of a decentralized society. The difficulties of writing on moist clay led to the disappearance of pictographs and the emergence of conventional signs or formal patterns of cuneiform. The stylus was developed in relation to the demands of clay. With a language which was largely monosyllabic, signs were introduced to meet the demands of economy and the necessity of uniformity to establish communication between scattered cities. The administration of temple properties and trade implied an emphasis on mathematics in the early development of writing and in turn an emphasis on abstractions.

Accumulation of wealth in temple organizations involved rivalry, warfare between city states, the emergence of a military leader and an army. The problems of control over space in contrast to the success with which problems of time were met in a religious organization necessitated centralization in the hands of a king. Control over large stretches of territory meant delegation of authority and an emphasis on law as a means of offsetting religious jealousies. To the same end old capitals were destroyed and new capitals were built to strengthen the prestige of the king, and the deities of conquered cities were arranged in hierarchies under the deity of the conqueror. The difficulties of political organization were evident in the ultimate break-down of Sumerian empires and in the success of Semitic invaders, as the advantages of cultural organization were evident in the tenacity of Sumerian institutions under alien rule. Semitic invaders rearranged the position of the chief gods of city states.

The eventual success of Semitic peoples was marked by the ascendancy of Babylon as a new capital and by the reforms of Hammurabi. The centralized power of a monarchy favoured the architecture of palaces, and the use of stone in sculpture as a medium of writing, particularly of laws designed to establish uniformity over vast empires. The language of the conquerors could not be united to that of the conquered but the sign of the latter were used by the former. The Semitic language was made official by Hammurabi. The spoken work was Semitic but the written word was in the non-Semitic forms of the Sumerians. The conventionalization of written language was hastened by the demands of the conquerors. "The basis of the Sumerian system of writing was word-values, while that of the Accadian method was syllable-values."[4] Sumerian became a fossilized sacred language of priests.

4. See G.R. Driver, *Semitic Writing from Pictograph to Alphabet* (London, 1948), p. 59.

Hammurabi developed the territorial state with a centralized system of administration, a common collection of written laws, a common capital, and a common calendar. Trade over a vast territory was facilitated by the use of fixed standards of weights and measures. Mathematics was developed in the use of the sexagesimal system with its enormous advantages in the handling of fractions, advantages still exploited in the currency system of Great Britain, and in the twenty-four hour system which has persisted in the reckoning of time.

A centralized system of administration persisted with modification under peoples speaking Aryan languages. Equipped with more efficient instruments of warfare, particularly the horse and the chariot, the invaders captured and dominated Babylon from about 1740 B.C. to the end of the thirteenth century. Political organizations in northern regions without an abundant supply of writing material such as clay were built up but were unable to find an effective solution to problems of time. The Hittites worked out a highly organized central administration with a strong imperial capital and a system of radiating communications but were unable to capture Babylon in their attack about 1150 B.C. The Assyrians succeeded in disrupting the Hittite federation and eventually dominated the Aramaeans by the use of heavier horses which made possible the introduction of cavalry, and the use of iron which had been developed by the Hittites. Their imperial organization was based on the establishment of provincial governments placed under governors who exacted tribute. Babylonia was captured in 729 B.C. and the religious pantheon subjected to rearrangement under Ashur as the Assyrian god. The power of Babylonian religion and culture was apparent in the difficulties of governing Babylon evident in its destruction on 689 B.C. and in the attempt to develop the prestige of the capital at Nineveh by the building of a library of Sumerian documents. Egypt was invaded and made an Assyrian province in 674 B.C. but the task of governing two powerful and divergent religious centres proved insuperable, and Nineveh was destroyed in 612 B.C.

Expansion of the Assyrian Empire was accompanied by the subjugation of peoples of different languages, races, and cultures, the destruction of Aramaean city states, and the practice of deportation on a large scale to stamp out narrow local cultures. As a result of these measures trade increased greatly. In the twelfth century the camel was domesticated and caravan trade was extended. An enlarged empire facilitated the growth of trade and industry. In turn these developments assumed a more efficient system of writing shown in the increasing dominance of Aramaic.

Monopolies of knowledge to an important extent dominated by priestly organization and protected by complex types of script such as the cuneiform and the hieroglyphic checked the growth of political organization. Escape from these monopolies came from the fringes of Babylonian and Egyptian civilizations in which new languages among primitive peoples demanded simplicity. Semitic peoples in contact with Egypt before 1500 B.C. apparently invented an alphabet in Palestine and perfected it on the Phoenician coast. Access to supplies of papyrus from Egypt and acquaintance with the reed pen enabled marginal peoples to borrow the simplest signs of the Egyptian system and to abandon its complexities. Invasion of the Hyksos apparently created a barrier between the south and the north of Arabia and led to a divergence between Aramaic and Phoenician writing. Aramaic script developed in relation to the demands of an extensive land trade for a concise conventional alphabet and possibly in relation to the use of parchment. The Phoenician script developed as a result of the demands of an extensive maritime trade for an alphabet in relation to the use of papyrus. Sounds of human speech were analysed into primary elements represented by twenty-two consonants.

A flexible alphabet favoured the growth of trade, development of the trading cities of the Phoenicians, and the emergence of smaller nations dependent on distinct languages. Hebrew was probably spoken in Palestine after 1200 B.C. The oral tradition was written down and the sacred character of writing emphasized by the Egyptians was reflected in the writing of the Hebrews. The importance of sculpture to large-scale political and religious organizations was shown in the prohibition of images by the Hebrews. The written letter replaced the graven image. Concentration on the abstract in writing opened the way for an advance from blood relationship to universal ethical standards, to the influence of the prophets in opposition to the absolute power of kings, and to an emphasis on monotheism. Laws were collected and written down in codes. Literature such as is presented in the Old Testament took root and flourished. Destruction of local sanctuaries by Sennacherib was followed by an emphasis on Jerusalem as the single sanctuary after 621 B.C.[5] After the fall of the Assyrian Empire the Babylonians extended their control and captured Jerusalem in 586 B.C.

With the advantage of new instruments of war such as the long bow and the long pike and of an improved alphabet, the Persians rapidly built up an empire to take the place of the empire of the Assyrians. As a result of support from the priests Cyrus became king of Babylon in 536 B.C. Cambyses added Egypt to the Empire in 525 B.C. The problems of the Assyrians in dominating two divergent religious centres were inherited by the Persians. They were solved in part by a policy of toleration in which subject peoples were allowed to keep their gods and their religions. The Jews were released from captivity in Babylonia in 539 B.C. and Judah

5. J.M.P. Smith, *The Origin and History of Hebrew Law* (Chicago, 1931), p. 55.

became the centre of an effective religious organization. The Persians developed an elaborate administration based on a system of roads and the use of horses to maintain communication by post with the capital. Satrapies were created and three officials, a satrap, a military governor, and a secretary of state, each acting independently of the other and directly responsible to the capital, were appointed. But centralization of power in the hands of the king quickly brought to the fore the problem of administrative capacity and of continuity or the problem of time. Difficulties increased with the tenacious religious centres of Babylonia, Egypt, and Jerusalem and with peoples such as the Greeks located on the fringe of the Empire. The introduction of new tactics of warfare enabled Alexander to overthrow the Empire in the decisive battles of 333 B.C. and 331 B.C. Oriental empires succeeded in organizing vast areas and in solving territorial problems but failed to find a solution to problems of continuity and of time. The empires of Assyria and Persia emphasized control over space but were unable to solve the problems of time in the face of the monopolies of religion in Babylonia and Egypt.

The Phoenician Semitic consonantal alphabet was taken over by the Greeks on the north shore of the Mediterranean. Unlike the peoples of Aryan speech in Asia Minor the Greeks escaped the full effect of contact with the civilizations of Egypt and Babylonia. The necessity of crossing water enabled the Greeks to select cultural traits of significance to themselves and to reject others. Without a script they had built up a strong oral tradition centring about the courts of conquering people from the north. The Homeric poems were the work of generations of reciters and minstrels and reflected the demands of generations of audiences to whom they were recited. This powerful oral tradition bent the consonantal alphabet to its demands and used five of the twenty-four letters as vowels. As vowels were equal in value to consonants they were used in each written word. The written language was made into an instrument responsive to the demands of the oral tradition. Introduction of the alphabet meant a concern with sound rather than with sight or with the ear rather than the eye. Empires had been built up on communication based on sight in contrast with Greek political organization which emphasized oral discussion. Greece escaped the problem of worship of the written word which had embarrassed oriental empires. The delay in the introduction of writing until possibly as late as the beginning of the seventh century, the difficulties of securing large and regular supplies of papyrus from Egypt, and the limitations of stone as a medium combined to protect the oral tradition. No energy was lost in learning a second language and monopolies of knowledge could not be built around a complex script.

The significance of the oral tradition and its vitality in Greek civilization became evident in its influence on the later history of the West. Its power has been such that it becomes impossible for modern Europeans who have participated in the heritage to approach it from an objective point of view. The impact of writing and printing on modern civilization increases the difficulties of understanding a civilization based on the oral tradition. We can perhaps remain content in quoting Renan, "Progress will eternally consist in developing what Greece conceived."

The power of oral tradition was evident in the Homeric poems and in the adaptability of the hexameter to a wide variety of content. Hesiod's poetry was in sharp contrast with that of Homer. It facilitated the break of the individual from the minstrel tradition. The demands for greater sensitivity were met by the development of elegiac and iambic poetry. With accessibility to papyrus from Egypt in the late seventh and sixth centuries and the use of the lyre as a musical instrument, the position of professional minstrels was weakened. Lyric poetry developed on an impressive scale.

Not only did the strength of the oral tradition bend the alphabet to suit its needs, it also adapted other contributions of earlier civilizations. In the Homeric poems the gods became anthropomorphic deities. The supernatural was replaced by a concern with nature and science. The Ionian philosopher was able to reject the implications of the word as implying a creative act. "And God said" of the Hebrews ceased to be the symbol of creation. The contributions of the Chaldeans after the introduction of an exact system of chronology in 747 B.C. which facilitated a study of the periodic character of celestial phenomena were apparently used by Thales of Miletus to predict the eclipse of May 28, 585 B.C. The Olympian tradition which assumed fixed limits to the power of gods and men emphasized spatial concepts and in turn geometry. The science of nature dominated by geometry involved a concern with the internal properties of things rather than their relations with other things.

A concern with geometry and spatial relations was reinforced by the place of land and the search for land in colonization in Greek life. The results were evident in the evils which followed attempts to monopolize land. The growth of written laws in the colonies and in Athens in the seventh century threatened to impose a heavy load on debtors. But the power of the oral tradition was evident in the effectiveness of a search for means by which freedom might be achieved. It was possible to give individuals such as Draco, Solon, and Cleisthenes power to set up machinery adapted to continuous adjustment. Solon in the tradition of Ionian philosophy sought for universal truths and expressed the conviction that violation of justice involved disruption of the life of the community. The individual became responsible for his actions and the root of authority was destroyed. The rights of creditors engraved on ward stones erected on property were destroyed and the enslavement of labour as a disruptive force avoided. Solon discovered the secret of democracy in "the constitution of the judicial courts out of the whole people" (Bury).

Solon's reforms reflected the increasing significance of trade in contrast to land but their inadequacy became evident in the rise of a commercial class and in turn of tyrants in the sixth century. The Apollonian religion and Ionian philosophy were offset by encouragement of the worship of Dionysus. The tyrants encouraged the arts and in 537 B.C. assembled a collection of oracles to offset the prestige of the temple of Delphi. Increased trade and a concern with money suggested the limitations of an interest in geometry and spatial relations and the necessity of an interest in arithmetic and time. The philosophy of spatial externality involved discreteness and neglected the importance of continuity. The religion of Dionysus was probably modified by the influence of Mithraism from the East and by the Orphic revival. In turn Pythagoras developed a philosophy of numbers rather than geometry. As a result of these refinements a reconciliation between the Dionysian religion and the Apollonic became possible and the road was opened leading to the overthrow of the tyrants and the reforms of Cleisthenes. Solon had been largely concerned with problems incidental to the importance of land, space, and geometry and Cleisthenes was concerned with problems incidental to the importance of trade, time and arithmetic. He rescued control over time from the nobles and introduced a solar calendar which governed a definite system of rotation in elections to the councils. The family state was replaced by the city state.

The effectiveness of the oral tradition in the development of the state becomes evident in the success with which the Greeks checked the expansions of the Persian Empire and in the cultural flowering of Athens in the fifth century. A powerful stimulus was given to philosophical speculation by the arrival of Ionian refugees from Miletus. The Dionysiac ritual and choral lyric as perfected by Pindar provided the background for the development of the drama[6] under Aeschylus, Sophocles, and Euripides. In the second half of the fifth century writing began to make its encroachments on the oral tradition. Nietzsche has pointed to the significance of music, in which the joy of annihilation of the individual was understood, to tragedy. Disappearance of the spirit of music was followed by the decline of tragedy.[7] An increase in laws reflected an interest in prose. Literature in prose increased rapidly after the beginning of the Peloponnesian War. Plays were widely read in the time of

6. J.E. Harrison, *Prolegomena to the Study of Greek Religion* (Cambridge, 1908), p. 568.
7. F. Nietzsche, *The Birth of Tragedy from the Spirit of Music* (Edinburgh, 1923), pp. 120-7.

Euripides. By the end of the fifth century the *boustrophedon* style had been abandoned and changed to writing from left to right. The Ionic alphabet was adopted in Athens with the codification and republication of the laws in 403-2 B.C.[8]

An increase in writing in Athens created divergences in the Greek community and accentuated differences particularly with Sparta. The Athenian Empire proved unable to meet the strains imposed by diverging cultures. Athenian courts were unable to escape charges of favouritism to democratic states. Interstate co-operation imposed demands which could not be met. The end came with the outbreak of war and the defeat of Athens.

In the fourth century Plato attempted to save the remnants of Greek culture in the style of the Socratic dialogues which in the words of Aristotle stood half way between prose and poetry. In the seventh epistle he wrote, "no intelligent man will ever be so bold as to put into language those things which his reason has contemplated, especially not into a form that is unalterable — which must be the case with what is expressed in written symbols." The interest of Aristotle in science was reflected in prose. But neither Aristotle nor Plato thought of a library as a necessity to the city state. It was significant that a library was founded by Aristotle in 335 B.C and a public library started in 330 B.C. The written tradition had brought the vitality of the oral tradition to an end. In the words of Nietzsche, "Everyone being allowed to read ruineth in the long run not only writing but also thinking."

The role of the oral tradition in providing the milieu for the cultural activity of Greece had a profound significance for the history of the West and immediately for the history of Rome. The success with which the problems of time and space were solved had its implications for Roman culture. Greek culture awakened the native forces of Rome. Greek gods and Greek architecture were introduced in the latter part of the sixth century. The struggles for reform in Greece culminating in the work of Draco, Solon, and Cleisthenes were paralleled at a later date in Rome in the decemvirs' code of the Twelve Tables in 451 and 450 B.C. and in the increasing powers of the plebians culminating in the appointment of the first plebeian pontifex maximus in 253 B.C.

The comparative isolation of Roman culture from Greece in the fifth and fourth centuries was followed by a fresh invasion of Greek influence in which the rich development of Greek culture checked that of Rome and compelled the latter to concentrate on its own capacities notably in law. Flexibility inherent in the oral tradition was evident in the rise of the plebians, and in constitutional changes, in

8. W.S. Ferguson, *The Treasure of Athena* (Cambridge, Mass., 1923), p. 178.

the activity of lawyers, and in the creation of machinery designed to meet the increasing demands for adjustment. In 242 B.C. the position of a second praetor, *peregrinus,* was introduced to reflect the importance of an expanding trade with alien peoples. Formulae were made more flexible in spite of the spread of writing. Praetors issued new edicts at the beginning of their years of office adapted to changing demands. The *patria potestas* was broken down to make way for the individual, and the contract, that "greediest of legal categories," developed. The concept of property was isolated. *Res privata* necessitated a concern with *res publica* and an interest in the legal concept of the state. By the middle of the first century B.C. the influence of writing became evident in the demand for codes. Laws and precedents in the oral tradition had been largely in men's minds to the time of Cicero. In the senate the introduction of an official gazette in 54 B.C. compelled speakers to consider a wide public and created a demand for a matter-of-fact style. Limitation of time for pleas in court in 52 B.C. reinforced the tendency. Latin prose which had developed in relation to the demands of the republic in the speeches of the Gracchi, of Cato, and of Cicero was subjected to the influence of writing.[9] The oral tradition absorbed the philosophy of teachers of Stoicism from the East and law was subjected to the demands of universality. Custom was criticized, the religious and ceremonial character of law was weakened, equality was promoted, harshness mitigated, and the factor of intent emphasized.

The adaptability of Roman law in the oral tradition facilitated the extension of the Roman Empire which followed the success of Roman arms. Wars with Carthage brought Rome into conflict with Hellenistic kingdoms and into contact with Greek culture. The Antigonids who succeeded Alexander in Macedonia gradually changed Greek city states into municipalities but continued difficulties enabled Rome to destroy the Achaean League in 168 B.C. and to dominate Greece and Macedonia. The Ptolemies inherited the problems of political control in Egypt. They created a new capital at Alexandria, a large library, and a new god Serapis to offset the influence of the priestly class at Thebes. The demotic system and the use of the pen were encouraged at the expense of the hieratic system and the brush. As Rome acquired control over Egypt she adopted the policies of the Ptolemies. The Attalids built up a library at Pergamum to offset the prestige of the Ptolemies and, prevented from using papyrus by prohibitions on export, began the use of parchment on a large scale. Friendly relations with Rome were evident in the transfer of the *Magna Mater* in 204 B.C. The Seleucids, inheriting the problems of the Persian Empire of dominating the Persian, Babylonian, and Hebrew religions, attempted to introduce

---

9. "The build of the Roman sentence was but another consequence of Rome's battles which in giving her conquests forced her people as a nation to think administratively." (Spengler)

the city state as an instrument of government but failure was evident in the ultimate collapse of the kingdom. Rome fell heir to the unfortunate legacy.

As a result of expansion to the east Rome felt the full effects of Greek cultural achievements. Libraries were brought from Greece. Supplies of papyrus were available from Egypt. A book trade was developed and public and private libraries constructed. The spread of writing brought an interest in the codification of laws. Bureaucratic administration emerged. The Republic was replaced by the Empire. The emperor began to face the problems of empire which had been faced by earlier civilizations and to rely on solutions which had been developed in the East. Emperor worship gradually became more important. The dynastic problem which had menaced the attempts of former absolute monarchs to establish control over time strengthened the position of the army and a bureaucratic administration. New dynasties relied to an increasing extent on the prestige of Greece.

Under the influence of law the individual had been separated from the family. With the increasing rigidity of codes in the Empire the individual turned to Eastern religions. Efforts to exclude alien religions gradually broke down. The scrupulous fear of the gods which according to Polybius kept the Roman Empire together was no longer adequate.[10] Attempts of the nobility to maintain the traditional religion of the state against new tendencies meant leading a class against the masses and conflict with the "religious feelings of those lacking social privilege" (Max Weber).[11] Military campaigns in the east were followed by the spread of Mithraism and in 274 A.D. Aurelian dedicated a shrine to the god *Sol Invictus*. Recognition of an Eastern religion as a basis of political support brought a revival of the hostility of Hellenism and compelled the emperor to accept the support of a religion more acceptable to Greek demands. Unable to provide a link between Greece and Persia since the Greeks refused to accept an absolute emperor Rome was compelled to set up a model similar to that of Persia in Constantinople. In turn the demands of bureaucracy were reflected in the division of the Empire between the Latin West and the Greek East. The Illyrian mountains prevented the establishment of a capital linking the Latin and the Hellenic provinces as the Alps were later to prevent the establishment of a capital uniting the German and Italian divisions of the Holy Roman Empire.[12]

The bureaucratic development of the Roman Empire and success in solving problems of administration over vast areas were dependent on supplies of papyrus.

10. T.R. Glover, *The Conflict of Religions in the Early Roman Empire* (London, 1932), p. 17.

11. Franz Altheim, *A History of Roman Religion* (London, 1938), p. 330.

12. Vaughan Cornish, *The Great Capitals: An Historical Geography* (London, 1923), p. 140.

The bias of this medium became apparent in the monopoly of bureaucracy and its inability to find a satisfactory solution to the problems of the third dimension of empires, namely time. A new medium emerged to meet the limitations of papyrus. The handicaps of the fragile papyrus roll were offset by the durable parchment codex. With the latter the Christians were able to make effective use of the large Hebrew scriptures and to build up a corpus of Christian writings. The contributions of Alexandrian scholars in translating the Hebrew scriptures into Greek and the development of a Christian centre of learning at Caesarea after 231 A.D. checked the influence of a Babylonian priesthood, which had been encouraged by the Seleucids to check the influence of Persian religion, and which had been reconciled with Persian religion after the fall of Babylon in 125 A.D. Support of these religions for the Sassanid dynasty after 228 A.D hindered the spread of the Roman Empire and compelled Constantine to select a new capital in Constantinople in 330 whence he could command the interest of a Christian population. The problem of the Roman Empire in relation to time was solved by the support of religion in the Christian church. The cumulative bias of papyrus in relation to bureaucratic administration was offset by an appeal to parchment as a medium for a powerful religious organization. Recognition of Christianity was followed by the drastic suppression of competing pagan cults.

The attempt of emperors to build up Constantinople as the centre of the civilized world especially after the fall of the Western Empire in 476 A.D. by establishing a large library and producing a code of civil law created friction with Rome and with Alexandria. Justinian's *Digest* carried in its prefix a description of law identical with that of Demosthenes, namely, an invention and gift of the gods, the opinion of sensible men, the restitution of things done amiss voluntary and involuntary, and a general compact of a state in accordance with which it is proper that all in that state should live.[13] But geographical separation reinforced differences in religion and exposed the Eastern Empire to the attacks of the Persians and in turn of the Arabs.

The spread of Mohammedanism cut off exports of papyrus to the east and to the west. The substitution of parchment in the West coincided roughly with the rise of the Carolingian dynasty and the decline of the Merovingians. Papyrus was produced in a restricted area and met the demands of a centralized administration whereas parchment as the product of an agricultural economy was suited to a decentralized system. The durability of parchment and the convenience of the codex for reference made it particularly suitable for the large books typical of

13. J.L. Myers, *The Political Ideas of the Greeks* (New York, 1927), pp.308-16.

scriptures and legal works. In turn the difficulties of copying a large book limited the numbers produced. Small libraries with a small number of large books could be established over large areas. Since the material of a civilization dominated by the papyrus roll had to be recopied in the parchment codex, a thorough system of censorship was involved. Pagan writing was neglected and Christian writing emphasized. "Never in the world's history has so vast a literature been so radically given over to destruction."[14] "Whatever knowledge man has acquired outside Holy Writ, if it be harmful it is there condemned; if it be wholesome it is there contained" (St . Augustine).[15] The ban on secular learning gave a preponderance to theological studies and made Rome dominant.[16] The monopoly of knowledge centring around parchment emphasized religion at the expense of law.

Parchment as a medium was suited to the spread of monasticism from Egypt throughout western Europe. St. Benedict founded a monastery at Monte Cassino about 520 A.D. and emphasized rules which made the preservation of books a sacred duty. His work followed by that of Cassiodorus gave a "scholarly bent to western monasticism." In spite of these efforts learning declined in Europe. Revival came on the fringes of the West in the independent and self-governing monasteries of Ireland. Missionary zeal led to the establishment of monasteries in Scotland and northern England and early in the seventh century on the Continent. The revival gained impetus with the support of Charlemagne and the migration of Alcuin from York. England and northern France were exposed to Danish raids but European monasteries had acquired transcriptions from English codices and supplemented them with those from Rome. Durable parchment books could be moved over long distances and transferred from regions of danger to regions of safety.

In the Byzantine Empire attempts to check the spread of Mohammedan influence were made by appeals to monophysite influence in the proscription of image worship and in attacks on the drain of monasticism on economic life. Resistance to Mohammedanism in the East strengthened the pressure of Mohammedanism in the West but the dangers were checked by the success of Charles Martel in 732 A.D. The ultimate effects were evident in the division between the East and the West. Encouraged by the success of resistance in the west, the papacy allied itself to the Carolingian line and anathematized the iconoclasts of the East. To recapture the West the Byzantine emperors abandoned the iconoclastic controversy in 775 A.D. In turn Charlemagne forbade the worship of images. The accession of the Empress

14. T.K. Osterreich, *Possession Demoniacal and Other, among Primitive Races, in Antiquity, the Middle Ages, and Modern Times* (London, 1930), p. 160.

15. Benjamin Farrington, *Science and Politics in the Ancient World* (London, 1939), p. 46.

16. P.H. Lang, *Music in Western Civilization* (New York, 1941), p. 46.

Irene to the Byzantine throne in 797 enabled Charlemagne and the papacy to regard the throne as vacant under Salic law. Charlemagne was accordingly crowned emperor. The concern of Charlemagne for an efficient administration was reflected in efforts to improve educational institutions under control of the church and in his success in encouraging the development of an efficient uniform script, the minuscule.[17] His contributions toward the unification of Europe were destroyed by the recognition of the Teutonic principle of equal division among the heirs. A nucleus of power emerged in Paris following attempts to check the influence of the Danes and in Germany following attempts to defeat the Magyars. Encroachments of the Holy Roman Empire on the papacy were followed by reforms in the church and the development of a powerful ecclesiastical organization. Parchment became the medium through which a monopoly of knowledge was built up by religion.

This monopoly of knowledge invited the competition of a new medium, namely paper from China. Discovery of the technique of making paper from textiles provided a medium with which the Chinese, by adaptation of the brush for painting to writing, were able to work out an elaborate system of pictographs. A system of four to five thousand characters was used for ordinary needs "enabling those who speak mutually unintelligible idioms to converse together, using the pencil instead of the tongue."[18] Its effectiveness for this purpose meant the abandonment of an attempt to develop an alphabet system.

An elaborate development of writing supported the position of the scholarly class in administration of the empire. In turn a wide gap between a limited governing class and the mass of the people led to the spread of Buddhism from India. The monopoly of knowledge of the Brahmins in India based on the oral tradition and the limitations of communication had led to the spread of Buddhism with its emphasis on writing and its appeal to the lower classes. After Alexander, Buddhism had been encouraged but decline of Macedonian power brought a revival of the power of the Brahmins and migration of Buddhism to China. Access to supplies of paper in China enabled Buddhists to develop block printing on a large scale. Confucianism gained by the influence of the state and the reproduction of the classics. A script which provided a basis for administration in China and emphasized the organization of an empire in terms of space proved inadequate to meet the demands of time and China was exposed to dynastic problems and to the domination of the Mongols from 1280 to 1368.

17. The minuscule was a descendant of papyrus cursive writing which had been submerged by the vellum uncials after the fourth century. See F.G. Kenyon, *The Palaeography of Greek Papyri* (Oxford, 1899), pp. 124-5.

18. Edward Clodd, *The Story of the Alphabet* (New York, 1913), p. 182.

The spread of Mohammedanism to the east was followed by introduction to the technique of paper production. After establishment of a capital at Baghdad by the Abbasids paper manufacturing expanded and became the basis for an intense interest in learning. The Nestorians excommunicated from the Church had established schools in which Greek and Latin works were translated into Syriac. Closing of the schools in Athens by Justinian in 529 A.D. had been followed by the migration of scholars to Persia. From this background of learning Baghdad became a centre for translators of Greek, Syriac, and Persian works into Arabic.

The prestige of Baghdad provoked a revival of Greek learning in Constantinople and of Latin learning in the West in the ninth century.[19] Revival of Greek learning in Constantinople was followed by the hostility of Rome. Rivalry between the Eastern and the Western church was accompanied by missionary activity and extension of the activities of the Eastern church into Bulgaria. The scriptures were translated into the Slavic vernacular on the one hand in the East, and the translations from Latin into the vernacular were discouraged on the other hand in the West. The Cyrillic and the Glagolitic alphabets were invented to represent the sounds of the Slavonic language and to provide the basis for a richer expression.[20] An emphasis on secular learning in Byzantine education widened the breach with Rome and led to final separation of the churches of the East and West in 1054. Decline of the Abbasids was accompanied by activity of the Seljuk Turks and the capture of Jerusalem in 1070. The papacy refused to meet the requests of the Byzantine emperor for assistance and organized the Crusades. Ultimate failure to maintain control over Jerusalem led Crusaders to turn to Constantinople. It became subject to Latin states from 1204 to 1261 when it was recaptured by the Greeks.

Paper production spread from Baghdad to the West. After the capture of Baghdad by the Mongols in 1258, manufacturing was confined to western centres. With its development in Italy in the latter part of the thirteenth century new processes were introduced and a much better quality of paper produced. The art of paper making spread to France in the fourteenth century. Since linen rags were the chief raw material and the large cities provided the chief market for paper, production was determined to an important extent by proximity to cities with access to supplies of water and power. The commercial revolution beginning about 1275 paralleled increasing production of paper. The activity of the commercial cities of Italy weakened the Byzantine Empire. Religious prejudice against a product of Arabic origin was broken down and the monopoly of knowledge held by monasteries of rural districts was weakened by the growth of cities, cathedrals, and universities.

19. Werner Jaeger, *Humanism and Theology* (Milwaukee, Wisc., 1943), p. 24.
20. D. Diringer, *The Alphabet, a Key to the History of Mankind* (London, n.d.), p. 475.

The effects of the introduction of paper suggested by the rise of Baghdad were evident also in the concern with learning among the Mohammedans in Sicily and Spain. Large libraries were collected in Spain and following the recapture of Moorish cities by the Spaniards their contents in philosophy, mathematics, and medicine were made available to Europe. Acquaintance with the writings of Aristotle led to attempts such as those of St. Thomas Aquinas (1227-74) to reconcile classical with Christian teaching. Aristotle as a creator of formal logic could be absorbed in orthodoxy. Attempts of the church to dominate learning in the universities were paralleled by attempts to check the spread of the scriptures in the vernacular. Persecution of the Waldensians and other heretics and the Albigensian crusades were followed by the creation of new preaching orders, the Dominican and the Franciscan, and the establishment of the Inquisition. Revival of an interest in the study of Roman law in the twelfth century strengthened the position of the emperor but it was offset by the codification of canon law. In spite of this activity the increased use of paper and the growth of trade favoured the development of cities and the position of monarchies. The increasing importance of the vernacular and the rise of lawyers strengthened the position of political at the expense of ecclesiastical organizations. The power of France was evident in the migration of the papacy to Avignon (1308-78) and in the hostility of England. Roman law made little impression in England and the influence of the common law was shown in the jury system and in parliament. Again as a result of the war with France the court encouraged the vernacular. Decline of the monopoly of knowledge based on parchment in which an ecclesiastical organization emphasized control over time followed the competition of paper which supported the growth of trade and of cities, the rise of vernacular, and the increasing importance of lawyers, and emphasized the concept of space in nationalism.

Monopolies of knowledge controlled by monasteries were followed by monopolies of knowledge controlled by copyist guilds in the large cities. The high price for large books led to attempts to develop a system of reproduction by machine and to the invention of printing in Germany which was on the margin of the area dominated by copyists. The centralized control of France was less adapted to evasion than the numerous political divisions of Germany. The coarse brown parchment of Germany led to an interest in the use of paper. The beauty of Gothic script in manuscript[21] and its adaptability to printing were other factors emphasizing an interest in the invention with its numerous problems of ink, production of uniform type of a large scale, and a press capable of quick operation. Abundance of paper in Italy and political division similar to that of Germany led to the migration of printers to

21. A. W. Pollard, *Early Illustrated Books* (New York, 1927), pp. 7-8.

Italian cities and to the development of Roman and italic types. Printing in Paris was delayed until 1469 and in England until even later.

Manuscripts which had accumulated over centuries were reproduced and by the end of the fifteenth century printers became concerned with the possibilities of new markets. Commercialism of the publisher began to displace the craft of the printer. The vernacular offered new authors and new readers. The small book and the pamphlet began to replace the large folios. In England, Caxton avoided the competition of Latin books produced on the Continent and attempted to widen his own market. He wrote in the Prologue to the *Eneydos*: "And that comyn englysshe that is spoken in one shyre varyeth from another....I haue reduced and translated this sayd booke in to our englysshe, not ouer rude ne curyous, but in suche termes as shall be vnderstanden...."[22] In Germany opposition of the German language to scholasticism as it had developed in Paris in the French language implied an emphasis on mystical teaching and the vernacular. The attack on the pride of scholastic philosophy was evident in the words of Thomas à Kempis, "But what is the good of wisdom without the fear of God?"[23] "For lack of training the mind turns to reason" (Henry Adams). German music protected by the Hohenstaufens resisted encroachments from the church. An interest in the vernacular was supplemented by the concern of scholars such as Reuchlin and Erasmus with Hebrew and Greek and led to the translations of Luther and Tyndale of the Bible in German and English. Publication of the scriptures in the vernacular was followed by new interpretations and by the intensive controversies conducted in pamphlets and sheets which ended in the establishment of Protestantism. Biblical literalism become the mother of heresy and of sects.

Printing activity incidental to the Reformation in Germany was accompanied by repressive measures against heretical publications in France. The authority of the University of Paris stood in contrast to the Frankfort Book Fair and the rise of Leipzig as a publishing centre. Printers migrated from France to adjacent countries such as Switzerland and the Netherlands and published books to be smuggled back to France. Learning declined in France in the sixteenth century but the vernacular found fresh support in printers shown in the writings of Montaigne and Rabelais. French became an official language after 1539. Its influence in the Huguenot controversies was evident in the Edict of Nantes of 1598, the first acknowledgement of a Roman Catholic country that heretics should be accorded civil rights. A policy of restrictions on publications paralleled a policy encouraging exports of paper. Countries encouraging a free press were subsidized by French mercantilist policies

22. Cited G.M. Trevelyan, *English Social History* (New York, 1942), p. 82.

23. Jaeger, *Humanism and Theology*, p. 14.

and the difficulties of restricting the smuggling of prohibited literature were increased. In the Empire repression in Antwerp was followed by the migration of printers such as Plantin to Holland and by an intensive development evident in a large-scale type-founding industry. Printing was accompanied by the production of printed sheets and postal services and by the growth of a financial centre at Antwerp. After the destruction of Antwerp in 1576 Amsterdam increased in importance. The Union of Utrecht in 1579 with ample financial resources was able to withstand the demands of the Empire and of France.

In England the absolutism of the Tudors involved suppression of printing but encouragement of the Renaissance and of the Reformation. Abolition of the monasteries and disappearance of clerical celibacy were followed by sweeping educational reforms. The printing press became "a battering-ram to bring abbeys and castles crashing to the ground."[24] Freedom from the Salic law made it possible for women to ascend to the throne and to encourage the literature of the court. Restrictions on printing facilitated an interest in the drama and the flowering of the oral tradition in the plays of Shakespeare.

By the end of the sixteenth century the flexibility of the alphabet and printing had contributed to the growth of diverse vernacular literatures and had provided a basis for divisive nationalism in Europe. In the seventeenth century France continued to implement a mercantilist policy in suppression of publications and encouragement of exports of paper. Revocation of the Edict of Nantes in 1685 was followed by migration of skilled paper makers and the growth of paper making in England and Holland. Inefficiency in paper making incidental to state interference in France was paralleled by the introduction of more efficient methods in Holland. Refugees from France such as Pierre Bayle and Descartes developed a critical literature and a philosophy which had repercussions in the later criticism of the eighteenth century. In Holland type founding became an industrial enterprise and publishing activity by such firms as the Elzevirs built up markets throughout Europe. In England suppression of printing contributed to the outbreak of civil war. Increase in numbers of booksellers who encouraged printers as a means of reducing costs of publication led inevitably to the production of seditious literature, to renewed suppression, and finally to the outburst of controversial literature of the civil war.[25] Emphasis on the Bible accompanied restrictions on printing and facilitated an attack on Aristotelianism and scholastic philosophy and contributed to an interest in the moderns, the emergence of science, and deism. The Royal Society founded in

24. Trevelyan, *English Social History*, p. 58.

25. H.R. Plomer, *A Short History of English Printing, 1476-1900* (New York, 1927), p. 169.

1662 was concerned with the advancement of science and the improvement of the English language as a medium for prose. It demanded a "mathematical plainness of language" and rejection of "all amplifications, digression and swellings of style."[26]

Suppression of printing limited the attention to language which characterized France. Dictionaries were gradually developed but the English language was not adequate to the precision of the law codes of the Continent. Printing and improved communication strengthened a representative system in parliament. Suppression was met by newsletters and the rise of coffee-houses. The absolute power of parliament emerged to offset the absolute power of anarchy and annihilated the claims of common credit which persisted in the colonies. It became the basis of public credit. The revolution of 1689 was followed by establishment of the Bank of England in 1694. Again, the revolution brought an end to the Licensing Act, in 1694. Immediately large numbers of papers were printed and the first daily appeared in 1701. In the Augustan age, Addison and Steele reconciled "wit and virtue, after a long and disastrous separation, during which wit had been led astray by profligacy and virtue by fanaticism." Limitations of the hand press led to a political war of pamphlets and to the imposition of a stamp tax in 1712. The excessive burden of a tax on a commodity selling at a very low price compelled printers to undertake compendious works such as weeklies and monthlies and Ephraim Chambers's *Universal Dictionary of Arts and Sciences* which appeared in 1728. Restrictions on political writing hastened the development of other types of literature such as the novel and children's books and the establishment of circulating libraries. The Copyright Act of 1710 gave protection to publishers but a legal decision of 1774 denying the right to perpetual copyright under common law destroyed control over publications, encouraged large numbers of small publishers to engage in the production of reprints, supported a large second-hand book trade, and compelled large publishers to concentrate on expensive publications. Scottish writers who had not been hampered by the Grub Street of English writing in the early part of the eighteenth century and who had the support of universities and a background of Roman law concentrated on such philosophical speculation as those produced by Hume and Adam Smith. Scottish publishers exploited the limitations of English publishing.[27] Constable was concerned with publication of the work of Sir Walter Scott and the *Edinburgh Review.*

The decline of political censorship after the fall of Walpole, an increase in the production of paper, escape from the monopoly of Dutch type foundries in the work

26. M.M. Lewis, *Language in Society* (London, 1947), p. 38.

27. See L.E. Gates, *Three Studies in Literature* (New York, 1899), pp.50ff.; also J.A. Greig, *Francis Jeffrey of the Edinburgh Review* (Edinburgh, 1948). On the influence of Roman law on Adam Smith see the Rt. Hon. Lord Macmillan, *Two Ways of Thinking* (Cambridge, 1934), pp.28-30.

of Caslon, and increased reliance on advertising following legislation against bill posters were followed by an expansion of newspapers. Resistance of the city of London against the absolute supremacy claimed by parliament supported the activities of Wilkes and Junius in the demand for the right to publish debates. Alderman Oliver, a member of parliament, stated that "whenever King, Lords or Commons assume unlimited power I will oppose that power."[28] The press attacked "the triple union of Crown, Lords and Commons against England." The newspaper article displaced the editorial and the essay in the writings of Junius who chose anonymity as it was "by no means necessary that he should be exposed to the resentment of the worst and most powerful men in the country." In spite of the achievement, taxes and threats of libel suits restricted expansion of newspapers and contributed to an interest in romantic literature. The position of deism which had been strengthened by the problems of the church during the revolution was weakened by the attacks of Hume and the way was opened to romanticism and to the religious revivals of Wesley and Whitefield. ·

The interest in literature which paralleled suppression of newspapers checked the growth of literature in the colonies and compelled an emphasis on newspapers. In the colonies a demand for printers for the publication of laws of the assemblies was followed by an interest in newspapers and in the post office. Printers were concerned with an agitation against restrictions and followed the arguments imported from England. The enormous burden of the stamp tax in 1765 on a low-priced commodity led to successful demands for repeal. Protests of Wilkes and Junius against the supremacy of parliament were elaborated in the colonies and the role of the newspapers in the Revolution was recognized in a bill of rights guaranteeing freedom of the press. Reliance on the common law implied a refusal to accept the principle of supremacy of parliament. Inability to find a middle course between absolute dependence and absolute independence broke the first empire. The influence of Roman law evident in an absolute parliament implied a conflict with an emphasis on common law in the colonies.

In France increasing centralization imposed heavy burdens on the administrative capacity of the monarchy. The increasing disequilibrium which followed attempts to export paper and to restrict publications led to increased development of printing in Holland and Switzerland and to continued smuggling of books into France. Attacks of French writers on restrictions became more aggressive in the writings of Voltaire, Diderot, Montesquieu, Rousseau, and others. The *Encyclopaedia* based on Chambers's work in England became a storehouse of ammunition directed

28. Michael MacDonagh, *The Reporters' Gallery* (London, n.d.), p. 236.

against the monarchy. With the outbreak of revolution newspapers became the artillery of ideas. After the Revolution Napoleon introduced a system of censorship. Throughout the nineteenth century the long struggle for freedom of the press was marked by advance culminating in the revolution of 1830, by recession under Louis Napoleon, and by advance under the republic. Journalists played an active role as politicians with disturbing effects on the political history of France.

Fear of the effects of the French Revolution in England was evident in the severely repressive taxes on the press.[29] Introduction of machinery in the manufacture of paper and in the printing press and restrictions on newspapers led to an emphasis on media concerned with material other than news. Periodicals, magazines, and books increased in importance and brought a demand for the reduction of taxes and cheap postage. The moderation of the French revolution of 1830 preceded the bloodless revolution of the Reform Acts.[30] In the second half of the century the monopoly of *The Times* protected by taxes disappeared and newspapers increased in number and circulation in London and in the provinces. The monopoly of London strengthened by the railway was destroyed by the invention of the telegraph which encouraged provincial competition after 1868.[31] The success of German education, regarded as responsible for the defeat of Austria in 1866 and of France in 1870, led to the Education Act of 1870 and the creation of a large number of new readers. Newnes and Northcliffe exploited the new market in the new journalism. The monopoly of the circulating library disappeared before the new periodicals, cheap editions of novels, and literary agents.

An emphasis on literature in England in the first half of the nineteenth century incidental to the monopoly of the newspaper protected by taxes on knowledge and absence of copyright legislation in the United States compelled American writers to rely on journalism.[32] Publishers in New York such as Harper after the introduction of the steamship line drew on the vast stores of English literature and made them available to the enormous reading public of the United States.[33] Publishers and paper dealers such as Cyrus W. Field and Company opposed proposals for international copyright in 1852.[34] The emphasis on news which consequently

29. See A. Aspinall, *Politics and the Press, c. 1780-1850* (London, 1949); and W.H. Wickwar, *The Struggle for the Freedom of the Press, 1819-1832* (London, 1928).

30. Emery Neff, *A Revolution in European Poetry, 1660-1900* (New York, 1940), p. 110.

31. James Samuelson, ed., *The Civilization of Our Day* (London, 1896), p. 277.

32. E.L. Bradsher, *Mathew Carey, Editor, Author and Publisher: A Study in American Literary Development* (New York, 1912), p. 79; and L.F. Tooker, *The Joys and Tribulations of an Editor* (New York, 1924), pp. 3-10.

33. J.H. Harper, *The House of Harper* (New York, 1912), p. 89.

34. *Ibid., p. 108.*

characterized American journalism protected by the Bill of Rights supported the development of technological inventions in the fast press, the stereotype, the linotype, and the substitution of wood for rags. As in England the telegraph destroyed the monopoly of political centres and contributed, in destroying political power, to the outbreak of the Civil War. Technological development had its effects in the new journalism in England and on the Continent. The varying effects of technological change spreading from the United States destroyed the unity of Europe and contributed to the outbreak of the First World War. The British according to Bismarck were unable to participate in the work of the intimate circle of European diplomacy because of responsibility to parliament, and the inability increased with the new journalism.[35] The attitude of Bismarck expressed in the remark, "Never believe a statement until you see it contradicted,"[36] was in contrast with Anglo-American journalism. The great pioneers of intellectual life in Germany left a legacy of leadership assumed after about 1832 by the state culminating in a deadening officialdom.[37] Northcliffe in the search for news made unprecedented use of cables and private wires and exploited Paris as a vast and cheap source of journalistic wealth with the result that French influence became more powerful.[38] The diplomatic institutions and techniques of an age of dynastic cabinet politics failed to work in a situation characterized by the press, electrical communications, mass literacy, and universal suffrage.[39] The Treaty of Versailles registered the divisive effects of the printing industry in its emphasis on self-determination. The monopoly of knowledge centring around the printing press brought to an end the obsession with space and the neglect of problems of continuity and time. The newspaper with a monopoly over time was limited in its power over space because of its regional character. Its monopoly was characterized by instability and crises. The radio introduced a new phase in the history of Western civilization by emphasizing centralization and the necessity of a concern with continuity. The bias of communication in paper and the printing industry was destined to be offset by the bias of the radio. Democracy which in the words of Guizot sacrificed the past and the future to the present was destined to be offset by planning and bureaucracy.

35. J.A. Spender, *The Public Life* (London, 1925), p. 48.

36. Harold Spender, *The Fire of Life: A Book of Memories* (London, n.d.), p. 36.

37. Viscount Haldane, *Selected Addresses and Essays* (London, 1928), p. 22.

38. Max Pemberton, *Lord Northcliffe: A Memoir* (New York, n.d.), p. 62.

39. O.J. Hale, *Publicity and Diplomacy, with Special Reference to England and Germany, 1890-1914* (New York, 1940), p. 209.

MEDIA HOT AND COLD

by Marshall McLuhan

"The rise of the waltz," explained Curt Sachs in the *World History of the Dance*, "was a result of that longing for truth, simplicity, closeness to nature, and primitivism, which the last two-thirds of the eighteenth century fulfilled." In the century of jazz we are likely to overlook the emergence of the waltz as a hot and explosive human expression that broke through the formal feudal barriers of courtly and choral dance styles.

There is a basic principle that distinguishes a hot medium like radio from a cool one like the telephone, or a hot medium like the movie from a cool one like TV. A hot medium is one that extends one single sense in "high definition." High definition is the state of being well filled with data. A photograph is, visually, "high definition." A cartoon is "low definition," simply because very little information is provided. Telephone is a cool medium, or one of low definition, because the ear is given a meager amount of information. And speech is a cool medium of low definition, because so little is given and so much has to be filled in by the listener. On the other hand, hot media do not leave so much to be filled in or completed by the audience. Hot media are, therefore, low in participation, and cool media are high in participation or completion by the audience. Naturally, therefore, a hot medium like radio has very different effects on the user from a cool medium like the telephone.

A cool medium like hieroglyphic or ideogrammic written characters has very different effects from the hot and explosive medium of the phonetic alphabet. The alphabet, when pushed to a high degree of abstract visual intensity, became typography. The printed word with its specialist intensity burst the bonds of medieval corporate guilds and monasteries, creating extreme individualist patterns of enterprise and monopoly. But the typical reversal occurred when extremes of monopoly brought back the corporation, with its impersonal empire over many lives. The hotting-up of the medium of writing to repeatable print intensity led to nationalism and the religious wars of the sixteenth century. The heavy and unwieldy media, such as stone, are time binders. Used for writing, they are very cool indeed, and serve to unify the ages; whereas paper is a hot medium that serves to unify spaces horizontally, both in political and entertainment empires.

Any hot medium allows for less participation than a cool one, as a lecture makes for less participation than a seminar, and a book for less than dialogue. With print many earlier forms were excluded from life and art, and many were given strange new intensity. But our own time is crowded with examples of the principle that the hot form excludes, and the cool one includes. When ballerinas began to dance on their toes a century ago, it was felt that the art of the ballet had acquired a new "spirituality." With this new intensity, male figures were excluded from ballet. The role of women had also become fragmented with the advent of industrial specialism and the explosion of home functions into laundries, bakeries, and hospitals on the periphery of the community. Intensity or high definition engenders specialism and fragmentation in living as in entertainment, which explains why any intense experience must be "forgotten," "censored," and reduced to a very cool state before it can be "learned" or assimilated. The Freudian "censor" is less of a moral function than an indispensable condition of learning. Were we to accept fully and directly every shock to our various structures of awareness, we would soon be nervous wrecks, doing double-takes and pressing panic buttons every minute. The "censor" protects our central system of values, as it does our physical nervous system by simply cooling off the onset of experience a great deal. For many people, this cooling system brings on a lifelong state of psychic *rigor mortis*, or of somnambulism, particularly observable in periods of new technology.

An example of the disruptive impact of a hot technology succeeding a cool one is given by Robert Theobald in *The Rich and the Poor*. When Australian natives were given steel axes by the missionaries, their culture, based on the stone axe, collapsed. The stone axe had not only been scarce but had always been a basic status symbol of male importance. The missionaries provided quantities of sharp steel axes and gave them to women and children. The men had even to borrow these from the women, causing a collapse of male dignity. A tribal and feudal hierarchy of traditional kind collapses quickly when it meets any hot medium of the mechanical, uniform, and repetitive kind. The medium of money or wheel or writing, or any other form of specialist speed-up of exchange and information, will serve to fragment a tribal structure. Similarly, a very much greater speed-up, such as occurs with electricity, may serve to restore a tribal pattern of intense involvement such as took place with the introduction of radio in Europe, and is now tending to happen as a result of TV in America. Specialist technologies detribalize. The nonspecialist electric technology retribalizes. The process of upset resulting from a new distribution of skills is accompanied by much culture lag in which people feel compelled to look at new situations as if they were old ones, and come up with ideas of "population explosion" in an age of implosion. Newton, in an age of clocks, managed to present the physical universe in the image of a clock. But poets like Blake were far ahead of Newton in their response to the challenge of the clock.

Blake spoke of the need to be delivered "from single vision and Newton's sleep," knowing very well that Newton's response to the challenge of the new mechanism was itself merely a mechanical repetition of the challenge. Blake saw Newton and Locke and others as hypnotized Narcissus types quite unable to meet the challenge of mechanism. W.B. Yeats gave the full Blakean version of Newton and Locke in a famous epigram:

> Locke sank into a swoon;
> The garden died;
> God took the spinning jenny
> Out of his side

Yeats presents Locke, the philosopher of mechanical and lineal associationism, as hypnotized by his own image. The "garden," or unified consciousness, ended. Eighteenth-century man got an extension of himself in the form of the spinning machine that Yeats endows with its full sexual significance. Woman, herself, is thus seen as a technological extension of man's being.

Blake's counterstrategy for his age was to meet mechanism with organic myth. Today, deep in the electric age, organic myth is itself a simple and automatic response capable of mathematical formulation and expression, without any of the imaginative perception of Blake about it. Had he encountered the electric age, Blake would not have met its challenge with a mere repetition of electric form. For myth *is* the instant vision of a complex process that ordinarily extends over a long period. Myth is contraction or implosion of any process, and the instant speed of electricity confers the mythic dimension on ordinary industrial and social action today. We *live* mythically but continue to think fragmentarily and on single planes.

Scholars today are acutely aware of a discrepancy between their ways of treating subjects and the subject itself. Scriptural scholars of both the Old and New Testaments frequently say that while their treatment must be linear, the subject is not. The subject treats of the relations between God and man, and between God and the world, and of the relations between man and his neighbor — all these subsist together, and act and react upon one another at the same time. The Hebrew and Eastern mode of thought tackles problem and resolution, at the outset of a discussion, in a way typical of oral societies in general. The entire message is then traced and retraced, again and again, on the rounds of a concentric spiral with seeming redundancy. One can stop anywhere after the first few sentences and have the full message, if one is prepared to "dig" it. This kind of plan seems to have inspired Frank Lloyd Wright in designing the Guggenheim Art Gallery on a spiral, concentric basis. It is a redundant form inevitable to the electric age, in which the concentric pattern is imposed by the instant quality, and overlay in depth, of electric speed. But the concentric with its endless intersection of planes is necessary for insight. In fact, it is the technique of insight, and as such is necessary for media study, since no medium has its meaning or existence alone, but only in constant interplay with other media.

The new electric structuring and configuring of life more and more encounters the old lineal and fragmentary procedures and tools of analysis from the mechanical age. More and more we turn from the content of messages to study total effect. Kenneth Boulding put this matter in *The Image* by saying, "The meaning of a message is the change which it produces in the image." Concern with *effect* rather than *meaning* is a basic change of our electric time, for effect involves the total situation, and not a single level of information movement. Strangely, there is recognition of this matter of effect rather than information in the British idea of libel: "The greater the truth, the greater the libel."

The effect of electric technology had at first been anxiety. Now it appears to create boredom. We have been through the three stages of alarm, resistance, and exhaustion that occur in every disease or stress of life, whether individual or collective. At least, our exhausted slump after the first encounter with the electric has inclined us to expect new problems. However, backward countries that have experienced little permeation with our own mechanical and specialist culture are much better able to confront and to understand electric technology. Not only have backward and nonindustrial cultures no specialist habits to overcome in their encounter with electromagnetism, but they have still much of their traditional oral culture that has the total, unified "field" character of our new electromagnetism. Our old industrialized areas, having eroded their oral traditions automatically, are in the position of having to rediscover them in order to cope with the electric age.

In terms of the theme of media hot and cold, backward countries are cool, and we are hot. The "city slicker" is hot, and the rustic is cool. But in terms of the reversal of procedures and values in the electric age, the past mechanical time was hot, and we of the TV age are cool. The waltz was a hot, fast mechanical dance suited to the industrial time in its moods of pomp and circumstance. In contrast, the Twist is a cool, involved and chatty form of improvised gesture. The jazz of the period of the hot new media of movie and radio was a hot jazz. Yet jazz of itself tends to be a casual dialogue form of dance quite lacking in the repetitive and mechanical forms of the waltz. Cool jazz came in quite naturally after the first impact of radio and movie had been absorbed.

In the special Russian issue of *Life* magazine for September 13, 1963, it is mentioned in Russian restaurants and night clubs, "though the Charleston is tolerated, the Twist is taboo." All this is to say that a country in the process of industrialization is inclined to regard hot jazz as consistent with its developing programs. The cool and involved form of the Twist, on the other hand, would strike such a culture at once as retrograde and incompatible with its new mechanical stress. The Charleston, with its aspect of a mechanical doll agitated by strings, appears in Russia as an avant-garde form. We, on the other hand, find the *avant-garde* in the cool and the primitive, with its promise of depth involvement and integral expression.

The "hard" sell and the "hot" line become mere comedy in the TV age, and the death of all the salesmen at one stroke of the TV axe has turned the hot American culture into a cool one that is quite unacquainted with itself. America, in fact, would seem to be living through the reverse process that Margaret Mead described in *Time* magazine (September 4, 1954): "There are too many complaints about society having to move too fast to keep up with the machine. There is great advantage in moving fast if you move completely, if social, educational, and recreational changes keep pace. You must change the whole pattern at once and the whole group together - and the people themselves must decide to move."

Margaret Mead is thinking here of change as uniform speed-up of motion or a uniform hotting-up of temperatures in backward societies. We are certainly coming within conceivable range of a world automatically controlled to the point where we could say, "Six hours less radio in Indonesia next week or there will be a great falling off in literary attention." Or, "We can program twenty more hours of TV in South Africa next week to cool down the tribal temperature raised by radio last week." Whole cultures could now be programmed to keep their emotional climate stable in the same way that we have begun to know something about maintaining equilibrium in the commercial economies of the world.

In the merely personal and private sphere we are often reminded of how changes of tone and attitude are demanded of different times and seasons in order to keep situations in hand. British clubmen, for the sake of companionship and amiability, have long excluded the hot topics of religion and politics from mention inside the highly participational club. In the same vein, W.H. Auden wrote, "...this season the man of goodwill will wear his heart up his sleeve, not on it...the honest manly style is today suited only to Iago" (Introduction to John Betjeman's *Slick But Not Streamlined*). In the Renaissance, as print technology hotted up the social *milieu* to a very high point, the gentleman and the courtier (Hamlet-Mercutio style) adopted, in contrast, the casual and cool nonchalance of the playful and superior being. The

Iago allusion of Auden reminds us that Iago was the *alter ego* and assistant of the intensely earnest and very non-nonchalant General Othello. In imitation of the earnest and forthright general, Iago hotted up his own image and wore his heart on his sleeve, until General Othello read him loud and clear as "honest Iago," a man after his own grimly earnest heart.

Throughout *The City in History*, Lewis Mumford favors the cool or casually structured towns over the hot and intensely filled-in cities. The great period of Athens, he feels, was one during which most of the democratic habits of village life and participation still obtained. Then burst forth the full variety of human expression and exploration such as was later impossible in highly developed urban centers. For the highly developed situation is, by definition, low in opportunities of participation, and rigorous in its demands of specialist fragmentation from those who would control it. For example, what is known as "job enlargement" today in business and in management consists in allowing the employee more freedom to discover and define his function. Likewise, in reading a detective story the reader participates as co-author simply because so much has been left out of the narrative. The open-mesh silk stocking is far more sensuous than the smooth nylon, just because the eye must act as hand in filling in and completing the image, exactly as in the mosaic of the TV image.

Douglas Cater in *The Fourth Branch of Government* tells how the men of the Washington press bureaus delighted to complete or fill in the blank of Calvin Coolidge's personality. Because he was so like a mere cartoon, they felt the urge to complete his image for him and his public. It is instructive that the press applied the word "cool" to Cal. In the very sense of a cool medium, Calvin Coolidge was so lacking in any articulation of data in his public image that there was only one word for him. He was real cool. In the hot 1920s, the hot press medium found Cal very cool and rejoiced in his lack of image, since it compelled the participation of the press in filling in an image of him for the public. By contrast, F.D.R. was a hot press agent, himself a rival of the newspaper medium and one who delighted in scoring off the press on the rival hot medium of radio. Quite in contrast, Jack Paar ran a cool show for the cool TV medium, and became a rival for the patrons of the night spots and their allies in the gossip columns. Jack Paar's war with the gossip columnists was a weird example of clash between a hot and cold medium such as had occurred with the "scandal of the rigged TV quiz shows." The rivalry between the hot press and radio media, on one hand, and TV on the other, for the hot ad buck, served to confuse and to overheat the issues in the affair that pointlessly involved Charles van Doren.

An Associated Press story from Santa Monica, California, August 9, 1962, reported how

> Nearly 100 traffic violators watched a police traffic accident film today to atone for their violations. Two had to be treated for nausea and shock...
>
> Viewers were offered a $5.00 reduction in fines if they agreed to see the movie, *Signal 30*, made by Ohio State police.
>
> It showed twisted wreckage and mangled bodies and recorded the screams of accident victims.

Whether using the hot film medium using hot content would cool off the hot drivers is a moot point. But it does concern any understanding of media. The effect of hot media treatment cannot include much empathy or participation at any time. In this connection an insurance ad that featured Dad in an iron lung surrounded by a joyful family group did more to strike terror into the reader than all the warning wisdom in the world. It is a question that arises in connection with capital punishment. Is a severe penalty the best deterrent to serious crime? With regard to the bomb and the cold war, is the threat of massive retaliation the most effective means to peace? Is it not evident in every human situation that is pushed to a point of saturation that some precipitation occurs? When all the available resources and energies have been played up in an organism or in any structure there is some kind of reversal of pattern. The spectacle of brutality used as deterrent can brutalize. Brutality used in sports may humanize under some conditions, at least. But with regard to the bomb and retaliation as deterrent, it is obvious that numbness is the result of any prolonged terror, a fact that was discovered when the fallout shelter program was broached. The price of eternal vigilance is indifference.

Nevertheless, it makes all the difference whether a hot medium is used in a hot or a cool culture. The hot radio medium used in cool or nonliterate cultures has a violent effect, quite unlike its effect, say in England or America, where radio is felt as entertainment. A cool or low literacy culture cannot accept hot media like movies or radio as entertainment. They are, at least, as radically upsetting for them as the cool TV medium has proved to be for our high literacy world.

And as for the cool war and hot bomb scare, the cultural strategy that is desperately needed is humor and play. It is play that cools off the hot situations of actual life by miming them. Competitive sports between Russia and the West will hardly serve that purpose of relaxation. Such sports are inflammatory, it is plain. And what we consider entertainment or fun in our media inevitably appears as violent political agitation to a cool culture.

One way to spot the basic difference between hot and cold media uses is to compare and contrast a broadcast of a symphony performance with a broadcast of symphony rehearsal. Two of the finest shows ever released by the CBC were of Glenn Gould's procedure in recording piano recitals, and Igor Stravinsky's rehearsing the Toronto symphony in some of his new work. A cool medium like TV, when really used, demands this involvement in process. The neat tight package is suited to hot media, like radio and gramophone. Francis Bacon never tired of contrasting hot and cool prose. Writing in "methods" or complete packages, he contrasted with writing in aphorisms, or single observations such as "Revenge is a kind of wild justice." The passive consumer wants packages, but those, he suggested, who are concerned in pursuing knowledge and in seeking causes will resort to aphorisms, just because they are incomplete and require participation in depth.

The principle that distinguishes hot and cold media is perfectly embodied in the folk wisdom: "Men seldom make passes at girls who wear glasses." Glasses intensify the outward-going vision, and fill in the feminine image exceedingly, Marion the Librarian notwithstanding. Dark glasses, on the other hand, create the inscrutable and inaccessible image that invites a great deal of participation and completion.

Again, in a visual and highly literate culture, when we meet a person for the first time his visual appearance dims out the sound of the name, so that in self-defense we add: "How do you spell your name?" Whereas, in an ear culture, the *sound* of a man's name is the overwhelming fact, as Joyce knew when he said in *Finnegans Wake,* "Who gave you that numb?" For the name of a man is a numbing blow from which he never recovers.

Another vantage point from which to test the difference between hot and cold media is the practical joke. The hot literary medium excludes the practical and participant aspect of the joke so completely that Constance Rourke, in her *American Humor* , considers it as no joke at all. To literary people, the practical joke with its total physical involvement is as distasteful as the pun that derails us from the smooth and uniform progress that is typographic order. Indeed, to the literary person who is quite unaware of the intensely abstract nature of the typographic medium, it is the grosser and participant forms of art that seem "hot," and the abstract and intensely literary form that seems "cool". "You may perceive, Madam," said Dr. Johnson, with a pugilistic smile, "that I am well-bred to a degree of needless scrupulosity." And Dr. Johnson was right in supposing that "well-bred" had come to mean a white-shirted stress on attire that rivaled the rigor of the printed page. "Comfort" consists in abandoning a visual arrangement in favor of one that permits casual participation of the senses, a state that is excluded when any one sense, but especially the visual sense, is hotted up to the point of dominant command of a situation.

On the other hand, in experiments in which all outer sensation is withdrawn, the subject begins a furious fill-in or completion of senses that is sheer hallucination. So the hotting-up of one sense tends to effect hypnosis, and the cooling of all senses tends to result in hallucination.

THE INUKSHUK PROJECT

INUIT TV: THE SATELLITE SOLUTION

by John Greyson and Lisa Steele

On March 25, 1980, public hearings of the CRTC (Canadian Radio-Television and Telecommunications Commission) convened in Ottawa. Among the 400 proposals from communities, groups and corporations presented to the Commission during the 12 day hearing were two contradictory suggestions for the future of programming in the North: one by the Inuit Tapirisat of Canada (ITC) and the other by the CBC. (The Inuit Tapirisat of Canada is an association formed in 1971 which represents the land claims and culture of the 19,000 Inuit in Canada.) The ITC wants some of the revenue that will be generated by Pay-TV in the south used to create a special programming fund to support an Inuit Broadcasting System that would provide Inuit television services. They suggest $2 - $5 million annually. This service will be broadcast via the Anik B satellite which will be transmitting in September, 1980. However, the CBC proposal threatens to compromise the Inuit project. In their brief, the CBC proposed sharing their channel on the Anik A satellite which is already in operation with both the CTV network and TVA (Quebec network). Thus *even more* southern programming would penetrate into the North via satellite than is now directed there. And the Inuit Tapirisat of Canada says it's more than enough already.

This proposal comes from the same CBC which for years has admitted its own failure to meet the needs of the North; which, with the CRTC, has strongly supported the ITC's Inukshuk Project that for the past year has been laying the foundation for an Inuit broadcasting system owned and controlled by Inuit and designed primarily to overcome the negative and massive impact of CBC Northern Service television. One can only wonder at the integrity of the CBC and its president, A.W. Johnson, who, on February 15th wrote to the then-Secretary of State David MacDonald to support the Keewatin Regional TV Production Center set up by the ITC through the Inukshuk project, and barely a month later announced the CBC/CTV scheme for cooperation in a project which poses a more serious cultural and language threat to the Inuit.

English-language television (CBC) came to the North in 1972 with the launching of the Anik A satellite and the ITC has been fighting it ever since. The satellite brought high quality, reliable telephone service to *some* Inuit communities thus providing inter-community ties, but it also let loose a flood, 16 hours a day, of southern, English-language television programming. If the government had been responsive to northern priorities, Inuit television production might not be in the state it is today.

The Yellowknife Communications Conference held in 1970 as part of the Federal Department of Communications Telecommission Studies, left no doubt as to where Northerners stood in terms of their communications needs. They wanted, as a first priority, improved telephone and telex service. They wanted trail radios to allow hunters and trappers to communicate with their home settlements. Native language radio was desirable for local and regional information exchange. But television was a very low priority and then only if it had native and northern content.

However, the Anik A satellite, as it has actually been used, totally reversed these priorities and left ludicrous situations such as Rankin Inlet in the Keewatin Region which received colour TV in 1973, but still had to use the old unreliable HF radio to call outside the community for a doctor. Former Communications Minister Eric Kierans called Anik A the "northern vision for the Seventies". But this northern vision turned out to consist of "The Edge of Night" and "Police Story".

Basically, Anik A broadcasting had very little specifically for the North. The truth is the Anik A satellite made transmission easier between the east and west coasts of the country and that's why the $75 million plan was developed. The North just happened to be in the way and consequently got some of the communications 'goodies'. Neither the CBC nor the government has had a consistent policy of funding to offset the cultural effects that this huge influx of 'foreign' programming is having on Northern life. This is not to say that the CBC did not see the need to include the North in its proposals. In fact, the Inuit culture and community needs were stressed to such a degree that this aspect of broadcasting came to be called the CBC Northern Television Service. On paper, this service outlined progressive-sounding community development initiatives and local production classes. Yet these never surfaced in practice. The facts remain: almost no programming *produced* in the North is presently carried by the CBC Northern Television Service and of the 16 hours of programming per day, only thirty minutes a week is broadcast in the language of the Inuit, Inuktitut.

Given these already existing statistics, the Inuit are understandably opposed to the introduction of *even more* English programming into their communities. They see the power of television as both an educational tool and social influence; they want to use it for themselves. Without this control and input, television in the North is accelerating cultural genocide. As the Adult Educator in Pond Inlet explained to the CRTC:

> "First, there has been a loss of Inuktitut vocabulary among young people. While they can communicate well in Inuktitut, they do not know words and expressions which their parents and grandparents know. Second, young people often use English among themselves in the presence of older people. This has contributed significantly to the generation gap which has developed over the last several years. Enter the television. Through this attractive medium, young people have learned more about the world and more English. New values are introduced through television but only those people who understand English receive them. The older people who stand firmly in their culture, should be discussing these introduced values with their young people so that these new elements can be examined and evaluated, accepted or rejected."

David Eyer, CBC Licence Renewal CRTC Hearing, April 19, 1978, Pond Inlet

The alienating influence of television can be comprehended when one realizes how many Inuit cannot understand the language of the programs they watch. PIC-TV in Pond Inlet did a survey of about one-third of the families there and found that 58 per cent of the people had little or no understanding of English language programs. The CBC survey in the Keewatin found that even among young Inuit (ages 15 - 24), only seven out of 10 people said they understood all of the television programs.

The Inuit Tapirisat know these facts. Established in 1971, the ITC stressed as one of its aims the improving of communications systems between farflung Inuit communities. When the Anik A satellite was launched in 1972, the ITC worked to combat the influence of this cultural 'time bomb' by establishing Taqramiut Nipingat (the Northern Quebec Communications Society) and Nunatsiakmiut (the Frobisher Bay-based television production centre) which are funded by the Department of the Secretary of State Native Communications Funding Program. But the criteria for funding set out by the Development of the Secretary of State says that only one communications society may be funded per region (region being defined as "the largest possible area and/or clientele that a Resource Organization can viably serve given the nature of the media they employ"). This meant that the Department could impose a mandate on Nunatsiakmiut of serving all the Inuit of the Northwest Territories. Clearly, given their funding base, this is impossible. But neither is it desirable from the Inuit viewpoint.

Since Inuit land divides naturally into six regions — Western Arctic, Central Arctic, Keewatin, Baffin, Northern Quebec and Labrador — regional production centres are a cultural and linguistic necessity. These regional divisions reflect political borders and administrative boundaries. Each region has its own dialect, history and role in contemporary affairs. ITC has an affiliated regional organization representing the people in each of these regions and all agree that each must have its own voice, its own production facility.

It became obvious to the ITC that no amount of lobbying and appeals to the CBC or government would improve the quality of programming received in Inuit communities or provide for indigenous production. When pressed by the Inuit, CBC admitted its failure in not providing the means of producing northern native language programming. There was no provision for local and regional input to balance the overwhelming content of national and international affairs and programs designed with the southern Canadian population in mind. The ITC knew that some other action was necessary.

It was this need that initiated the Inukshuk Project. When the government made known its plans to launch the Anik B satellite in September 1980, Inuit Tapirisat saw an opportunity to use the satellite for a special project of their own. The Department of Communications has leased the satellite from Telesat Canada for a two-year communications program which will allow groups and organizations across the country to experiment with satellite communication projects. ITC proposed the Inukshuk Project in January 1978 to DOC and in May the project was accepted. Inukshuk is an experimental communications program that provides new production facilities, equipment and training for Inuit staff. Programming will be produced in the Inuit language and make use of Inuit personnel. In this project, the Inuit Tapirisat will learn how to develop an Inuit Broadcasting System to meet the needs of their own people.

Beginning in September, 1980, Inukshuk plans to run 17 hours of Inuit-produced programming each week on the satellite system for a six-month experimental period. Six communities in the Keewatin region have been set up to receive programming, and fieldworkers are being hired to coordinate input and suggest subjects specific to their community. Baker Lake was chosen as the site of the Keewatin Regional Production Center, and Frobisher Bay will have the satellite ground station with the capacity to send video signals to the other five communities, while the five will be able to transmit audio signals to one another. In addition, every community will have a local television broadcast transmitter to send programs to home television sets in their community. Most of the funding for establishing these centres was undertaken by the communities involved through donations (such as rent, labour, etc.) and fund-raising events.

David Simailak, Inukshuk Project Director, began operation at the Keewatin centre by hiring a technician to train eight locally-recruited candidates in all aspects of the care and operation of Super-8 film and the 3/4" video equipment which both the Frobisher Bay and Keewatin Production centres will use. To complete the course, trainees were required to research, record and edit a complete program on videotape or film. The completed programs were screened in the community hall to a capacity crowd of 300 people, followed by an open house at the production centre where the trainees demonstrated equipment and showed more tapes. The graduates then went on to collaborate with Nunatsiakmiut in the production of three colour videotapes for community distribution. Two of these tapes were later purchased by CBC for broadcast on Northern Television Service.

In addition to the indigenous productions (documentaries, dramas, news programs) a comprehensive list of plans for satellite usage is slated during the six-month trial period of the Inukshuk Project. These include workshops broadcast live into one community from another via the Anik B satellite with two-way video connections linking the participants, allowing for mutual conversation. In the same way, teachers could teach Inuit culture in classrooms separated by great distances and still be able to answer the students' questions. The satellite connection will also make it possible for two separate communities to hold meetings and discuss mutual problems. Other Inuit organizations such as the Qunnayooaq Society, a vigourous senior citizen society in Frobisher Bay, have expressed an interest in producing culture and heritage videotapes for use in schools, especially for other communities and regions. Inukshuk also plans regular programs of Inuit-produced tapes to be screened on closed-circuit TV in community halls for those without television sets. And an archive of all early Inuit Super-8 films is currently being assembled in the Keewatin facility.

The project has also set up a system for the distribution of videotapes to Inuit communities. Fourteen communities have purchased video playback equipment, and another seven have access to the equipment in their local schools. A catalogue of available tapes is being printed for circulation in all the communities. After the Anik B programming phase of the Inukshuk Project, the transmitting equipment which has been installed in the six ground station communities will be left in place so that local broadcasts of Inuit productions can continue.

The Inukshuk Project is only the beginning. The Inuit Tapirisat sees the project at the foundation for an Inuit Broadcasting System owned and controlled by Inuit. Inukshuk director, David Simailak's representation to the CRTC foreshadowed the CBC's announcement of their supplementary Anik A scheme. On February 28, 1980 he said:

"We expect that there will soon be additional TV channels on the satellite available to communities. If any satellite channels other than the Inuit Television Service are brought into the communities we want to ensure that these channels are controlled by the communities through local broadcasting societies. Any revenue generated would go to the local societies and be used for Inuit television production.

"We are totally against private entrepreneurs setting up "off-air" cable systems and having all revenue go into their private bank accounts down south somewhere. Any revenue from such a service should remain as public money and be used for production of relevant programming.

"In closing I would like to say that it is amazing how the North is being used again to justify a whole satellite plan that the south wants anyway.... It all sounds very familiar; the justification being used for the expansion of satellite service in Canada is again the North generally and native peoples specifically."

Less than two weeks later, the CBC announced their cozy satellite-sharing plan. In response, Simailak said:

"While we're struggling to get this system (Inuit Broadcasting System) off the ground, we are once again faced with yet another proposal to 'serve' the North which will clearly undermine the efforts by Inuit themselves to provide television programming."

The Inuit Tapirisat of Canada has been fighting this communications assault on their language and culture for nearly ten years. They see the Inukshuk Project as integral to "an Inuit communications system stretching all across the North that will enhance the strength and dignity of our people." They request funding from projected Pay-TV revenues to support an Inuit Broadcasting System that will not only fight against assimilation but actively create and develop a vital Inuit culture that is as connected to its own contemporary concerns as it is to the rich heritage of the North.

On May 15, 1980, the CRTC will make recommendations on the ITC request. At the same time, the CBC's proposal for satellite use will be decided. Given the CRTC's past record for ineffectual apologies, it seems likely that the CBC will be given the go-ahead. If this happens, the Inuit will have to compete even more with the south for its own audience. The Inuit Tapirisat is under no illusions. As Nick Arnatsiaq, Igloolik, wrote in *Inuktitut*, "Who will be responsible for putting Inuit content into television broadcasting? Who else but us?"

Notes:

Anik A was the first satellite system to be launched (1972) and is composed of three satellites (Anik A1,2,3) operating on 4-6 GHz frequency. Anik B was launched eighteen months ago as the primary dual band system, with 12 channels. It operates on both 4-6 GHz and 12-14 GHz. The 12-14 GHz band is leased to the Department of Communications on a two year lease with a further two year option. The Department offered the Anik B (12-14 GHz) to organisations across Canada for experimental pilot projects.

In the last year, the CBC switched over to Anik B (4-6 GHz) where it broadcasts both English and French networks. On Anik A the CBC broadcasts the House of Commons service in both languages. As the life expectancy of satellites is short, 5-7 years (Anik A 1 &2 are almost spent), Anik C is to be launched by 1981-82. Anik C will operate on 12-14 GHz, as this band does not interfere (at the necessary power) with normal terrestrial communications frequencies of 4-6 GHz. This is particularly necessary in large urban centres.

We thank Lyndsey Greene of the Inuit Tapirisat of Canada for her assistance with this report.

Inuit Women's Video

by Marie-Hélène Cousineau

"Our Stories are Useful and Unforgettable"

Igloolik is an Inuit community of 1,100 inhabitants, located on an island between Melville Peninsula and Baffin Island. According to archaeological survey, the island's people have a history of four thousand years, although the town has existed at its present location only since the late fifties.

It was only in 1982 that the people of Igloolik agreed to receive the broadcast signal of CBC North Television. They had previously refused, concerned about the daily invasion of the southern culture in their life. Their consent came with the creation of the Inuit Broadcasting Corporation in 1982, which would begin to broadcast several hours per week of Inuktitut language programming on CBC's northern satellite channel. In 1991, a local organization, Tariagsuk Video Centre, was incorporated and became the first video access centre in the Arctic directed by a board of Inuit members. The objective was to give Inuit more opportunity to express their culture, language and artistic interests through the medium of video/TV and to help counteract the increasing influence of southern television. Tariagsuk also works to discover approaches to video training consistent with, and in support of, Inuit cultural values, and which serve the needs of both individuals and the community.

Having moved to Igloolik at the end of 1990, I was asked to coordinate the start-up of Tariagsuk Video Centre in 1991. Besides administrative work, I organized a training program with four Inuit women: Madeline Ivalu, Susan Avingaq, Mathilda Hanniliaq and Martha Maktar. As a first step, I went on the community radio station and announced meetings of the "women's video workshop." Later on, the participants renamed the group Arnait Ikkajurtigiit, which means "women helping each other."

The concept of a video workshop for women didn't surprise anyone. Living in the North with Inuit, I began to understand the way men and women in Igloolik separated their chores and social lives to fulfil their responsibilities towards their families and community. The idea of the workshop was to get women together to learn to use video communication to express their concerns. My role was to get the group started and trained in the technical skills they had to learn to become videomakers. Even though these women never used video before, the participants were very aware of its possibilities: as a bridge between the generations, a tool for education, to preserve and carry on the culture. Women of all ages seemed to know instinctively that video was something they could adapt to their own needs.

> "Women can do whatever they want. This Women's Video Workshop can bring communication between people. It can be useful to people. It can make them understand... Long ago, just with the language, the words, they believed legend stories and saw the images in their mind. Our stories are useful and unforgettable."[1]

Apart from cultural objectives, women of Igloolik are also interested in the workshop because it provides an opportunity to earn money. Each time a project is under way, small project grants create part-time employment for several women as video animators, interviewers, interviewees, cultural experts, camera operators, technicians, secretaries or translators. The workshop has paid more than thirty Igloolik women to learn to produce programs about women's concerns.

Regular participants in the workshop represent different age groups and both principal religious groups, Anglican and Catholic — something important in Igloolik. Some women are professional seamstresses, a crucial part of the identity of older women in the traditional culture, while many younger ones no longer have that knowledge. The older women don't speak English and the younger ones are bilingual (Inuktitut/English). Because Igloolik is a small settlement and Inuit have large extended families, a lot of women in the workshop have family ties. Women over forty-five years old have experienced living on the land, giving birth in tents and sod houses and travelling by dogsled in a nomadic way of life. The younger generation knows boarding schools, life in the permanent settlement, and recently local high schools, cable TV and giving birth in hospitals. Among themselves, the women members of the Video Workshop reflect the full spectrum of transformations in Inuit life in this century.

> **Celina Uttugak (a participant in the workshop):** "As a group of women trying to come up with some solutions for the community, would it be proper if your concerns were seen by the public through the Women's Video Workshop? Would it help you to be seen by the public?"
>
> **Madeline Ivalu (chairperson of Naluat Women's group):** "Yes, it would definitely help. That way people would see us wanting to help them and we

1. Susan Avingaq, letter of support for the Women's Video Workshop, February 1993.

would start opening to the community... People would see us talking and know we are there to help them."

Celina: "They [Naluat] are trying to get the people aware of the culture that is dying and trying to educate young people on the traditional way of sewing traditional clothing, and if they were to be seen it would really help, not just the group but all of the community..." [2]

At present, participants use video to express their traditional identity in the community and their role as women. This does not mean that the use of technology maintains them in a powerless situation. On the contrary, women participating in video productions reaffirm their values, knowledge and experience in ways which are empowering to them. Their video communication is about keeping in touch with women's power and sharing it with their community, because the sharing itself is actually part of their role. The audience for whom these women work is in their own community. Outside viewers in a larger audience might also have the privilege to see this work, but without it being primarily addressed to them. This kind of representation made by people principally for themselves is very different from representations made by outside anthropologists or filmmakers who, while using the same technologies, are trying to make sense of something "foreign" for the benefit of the population from which they come.

For *Qulliq* (1992, 11 min.), their second video project, Susan Avingaq, Madeline Ivalu, Mathilda Hanniliaq and Martha Maktar chose the subject, wrote the script and the song used for the soundtrack, organized the shooting and edited the final video.

With little qulliq it warms us
It was all right far away
From darkness it lights

With little qulliq far away
I was cold it made me warm
With little qulliq far away [3]

The *qulliq* (seal-oil lamp) is a technology women mastered throughout Inuit history. It was the only source of heat and light. Women were in charge of the *qulliq*. Telling that story, *Qulliq* looks like a spontaneous reenactment of the past using a present-day technology with a spirit of joy. The new technology is used to revive an older one as a celebration visible through the performers, the singing and the words.

---

2. Dialogue between Celina Uttugak and Madeline Ivalu, translated by Celina Uttugak, from the videotape *Survey for a Women's Video Workshop* Tariagsuk Video Centre, 1991.

3. Excerpts from the *ajaja* song written by Susan Avingaq for the video *Qulliq*.

Qulliq has been shown locally and in different Canadian and American video festivals and galleries in the south.

A different kind of production is the series of interviews funded by the Oral Tradition Program of the Ministry of Culture and Communication of the North-West Territories. In *Women/Health/Body* (1992) and in *Itivimiut* (1993), women using video became archivists of traditions on the verge of being lost. In the former, workshop members interviewed nine women elders of Igloolik about their traditional knowledge, skills and personal experience in giving birth and helping sick or wounded people.

> **Madeline Ivalu:** *"I have had babies. It seems I don't know anything while I'm asking these questions. I'm interviewing you, that's why."*
>
> **Therese Ijjengiaq:** *"I know... That is how it was. I have never heard anything being like that today."*
>
> **Madeline:** *"You have to let Inuit know about these things. We have known them."*[4]
>
> **Mary Kutsiq:** *"The Inuit are such professionals on being midwives to women in labour."*
>
> **Madeline:** *"That's for sure."*
>
> **Mary:** *"They were professionals in those days."*
>
> **Madeline:** *"It's probably that way today too."*
>
> **Mary:** *"Yes... but we are being held back because we are not allowed to do so nowadays...."*[5]

The *Women/Health/Body* Interviews are currently available as ten hours of unedited footage with texts translated into English. Copies of tapes and texts are in the archives of Tariagsuk in Igloolik and the Government of the Northwest Territories in Yellowknife for anyone wishing to consult them. The grace and honesty of the testimonies, the absence of anger, the beauty of those old women telling amazing stories about the challenges of living on the land by themselves is breathtaking. It is moving and subversive to be in touch with a body of women's knowledge that has been denied legitimacy by recent colonizing institutions.

To produce the series of interviews in *Itivimiut*, Martha Maktar, Madeline Ivalu and I organized a snowmobile voyage to document the historical land route and the

---

4. From the videotaped interview of Therese Ijjengiaq by Madeline Ivalu, *Women/Health/Body* Series, Tariagsuk Video Centre, 1992.

5. From the videotape interview of Mary Kutsiq by Madeline Ivalu, *Women/Health/Body* series, Tariagsuk Video Centre, 1992.

traditions of long-distance travelling between Pond Inlet and Igloolik. We recorded other people's travelling experiences and lived our own, which was also one of creation and empowerment. This project involved about fifty people and created five part-time jobs. The unedited tapes are accessible in both Igloolik and Yellowknife.

In celebration of International Women's Day in 1993, the workshop produced a video of women practising their crafts. The video was shown, along with the crafts, while Igloolik women were invited to share a meal and play traditional games and songs. We then also recorded that evening of celebration and edited a final version.

During the summer of 1993, four young women were trained in the basic skills of self-representation and produced a videotape they called *Mixed Feelings*, about their experiences mixing both the old and new ways of life.

Repercussions of the work done so far by Arnait Ikkajurtigiit are felt in waves. Inuit women have chosen to speak about their strength, traditions and knowledge. Their intention is not simply to speak about the past. They are using their knowledge, both old and new, to go forward, creating new experiences to be shared, discussed and validated by members of their community. Members of the workshop are choosing to address their concerns about their lives at their own pace, with a style that they will discover for themselves and with the perseverance typical of their culture.

Nunavut (Our Land)

IGLOOLIK ISUMA INTERNATIONAL
(UNPUBLISHED) PROPOSAL TO TELEFILM, MTL. 1993

Final Draft Script (Inuit)

1. INTRODUCTION TO INUKTITUT: "WRITING" SCRIPTS IN AN ORAL LANGUAGE

Until the arrival of European missionaries in the early 1900's, who invented a written alphabet to translate the Bible for Inuit converts, Inuktitut was entirely an oral tradition. Inuit history, culture, stories, agreements and all knowledge were carried forward orally, from generation to generation, without a written language.

Story-telling — through stories and songs never written down — kept history and culture alive for four thousand years. Even today, most Inuit do not read and write Inuktitut easily, finding the written Inuktitut alphabet awkward to use.

TV production is a story-telling skill, and Inuit have quickly become comfortable using television to carry on the story-telling tradition. Unlike Southern film-makers, however, born and raised in a written language, Inuit rarely write their stories down, and find it unnecessary to write scripts in any detail for their TV productions.

At ISUMA, our 'Final Draft Scripts' are composed as story outlines for each project which describe the Inuit idea for the program and generally what our actors will do. These Scripts are based on research with Elders who recount true stories orally from their own experience and knowledge of the past: how things were done, and how people behaved.

Details of action and specific dialogue are then improvised during filming in an Inuit way, through discussion among cast and crew based on their own experience, responding to the weather, land and other conditions on location at the time. These conditions are always variable, and cannot be predicted — or "scripted"— in advance.

SCRIPT INTRODUCTION

This approach is precise and professional based on realities of Inuit culture. Inuit hunters travel without maps, since conditions on the land are always variable and the road cannot be "scripted" in advance. Hunters arrive safely through knowledge and experience. This is the Inuit way, based on oral rather than written skills.

We produce our television programs with the same skills used in hunting on the land. We know the story based on true experience. Details of action are dictated by the compelling reality of land and culture on the spot. Decisions will be made by consensus that particularly respects age and experience. Each person contributes his or her own knowledge and then the group improvises action and dialogue around it. To Inuit such "improvisation" is the only safe and intelligent way to behave under challenging circumstances.

For NUNAVUT (Our Land) this *process* — Research, Outline, Improvisation — makes up our "Final Draft Script," in our oral tradition based on centuries of experience. We trust outside readers to have the sensitivity and imagination to see that different cultures may have different ways of arriving at the same place. Cultural awareness begins on the first page.

2. INTRODUCTION TO INUKTITUT: A DIFFERENT KIND OF "STORY."

Western literary tradition traces its history from Homer and the Greeks through Shakespeare up to the modern era, including contemporary film and television. This European story-telling style reflects precise cultural values: in particular, a world view in which violent aggressive conflict is necessarily acted out by strong individuals expressing extreme passionate emotions.

From the Iliad to Hamlet to Star Wars to Star Trek, conventional Western narrative requires emotional conflict, often with violence, to be recognized as drama. In the European tradition, the conflict *is* the story, and without one we assume there simply isn't a story there at all.

However, this is a cultural assumption that different cultures may not share.

SCRIPT INTRODUCTION

Igloolik Inuit, for example, have survived 4000 years not through aggressive, emotional conflict but rather by living cooperatively in very close quarters. Perhaps for this reason Inuit have no word in their language for "war", consider aggressive conflict to be ridiculous or insane, and believe that only children express passionate emotions openly.

Cultural differences like these must necessarily change the idea of what makes a "story". Our NUNAVUT programs have a different narrative structure, because the culture presented has a different way of behaving. In NUNAVUT, for example, Inuit believe that Nature is a leading dramatic character; that the changing rhythms of weather, wind, snow, light and animals so determine how people behave that this natural rhythm may in fact be the central story line of every program; and that "action" is actually more about doing and making things to stay alive, than arguing about them.

Cooperation *is* the story, rather than conflict.

We believe by the 1990's the world is ready for another story-line about native people. Self-representation really is different. One reason many Inuit were offended by stereotypes in the recent Franco-Canadian co-production *Shadow of the Wolf* is because Inuit in the film still behave like Europeans. Once again, it is a European story, everybody acting like white men.

In NUNAVUT, Inuit behave like Inuit.

SELF-GOVERNMENT IN ART: TO CREATE ANEW...

...TAKE CARE OF STORIES AS YOU WOULD YOUR OWN CHILDREN

by/de Marjorie Beaucage

This article was woven together in both English and French. I have separated my words into two worlds, without translating, in order to communicate with you. It is somehow symbolic of the dualistic world in which we live and which I am addressing as I write. Maybe the gift of being Métis is the art of living between worlds...

There is a place in us where stories, dreams, poetry and art meet, and in that experience we are changed. There is also a place where we seek to know and an ancient place that can heal and bring life, where images and language emerge to create anew.

The Aboriginal Film and Video Art Alliance is committed to this work of taking care of stories and of creating anew. That is self-government. The making of images is a way of recognizing the many realities we live in and of participating in life. Storytellers create and re-create the cosmos giving form and meaning to the moment, connecting us to the sacred power that is in all things. Storytellers are the carriers of history and, at the same time, are creating history.

Some have argued that traditional self-government values are only wishing for times past. Old values relearned support the spirit; the so called "old ways" have never died and we cannot be severed from the legacies of our grandmothers. By remembering history, turning to our original teachers, the trees, the animals, the four directions, the truths that were given for life on this land are uncovered.

Art is the desire to see through the illusions that we create for ourselves. In the recovering of the grandmothers' voices within us, we know ourselves as strong and powerful. That is self-government.

Artists, storytellers, singers, dancers — all have the power to move the souls and spirits of the people toward this remembrance. That is why the Aboriginal Film and

Video Art Alliance was formed on the principles, values and traditions of Aboriginal self-government. Self-government is this energy of creation and it is imperative to accommodate this process. To create a gathering place, a homeland, where we can re-member and create new images and restore old forms in our own voices. The process is the approach; the key that will release the power contained in the Circle.

For too long our history and culture has been constructed by others according to patriarchal models. Self-government in the traditional sense means reclaiming a structure that is circular and organic; a world view that is cyclical, that is not locked in time but that changes like the seasons.

In negotiating new relationships and equal partnerships with cultural institutions and groups, the principles inherent in self-government are the starting place.

Some will say that we have so many nations, each with distinct traditions, so how can we know which principles we are talking about? The diversity that exists amongst First Nations communities has been used in the past as a reason to ignore the issues of representation and voice rather than to address them. The old colonial tricks still work to divide us; especially if we stay on their terms. That is how we became "us and them" in the first place. The need for justice and wholeness and balance as human beings is what connects us to existence, to each other. Unite and nurture is a law of self-government. We are all related.

But we are not all the same. Making room for difference and the interplay of differences is what keeps life in motion. Conformity impoverishes and mutilates us, diminishing possibility. Even the process of creation has been reduced to product, with standards of measurement and value now based almost solely on the marketplace.

Traditional self-government speaks to the relationships among humans, animals, landscapes, the sacred world. It is not the realm of politics (see casinos and land claims) or history (see Kevin Costner), but of vision. Not in the sense of the "hoped-for" but of the real and known within. It is a spiritual reality, an enduring sense of the fluidity of the universe in which we live and grow and change. To make images, to tell a story in the traditional sense, is to make manifest what originates within the spiritual world in a physical world, in order for understanding to deepen. To make "art" is to make what you see visible; to make meaning with your hands, your voice, your movements.

> A human being who has a vision is not able to use the power of it until after they have performed the vision on earth for people to see.
>
> — Black Elk, Oglala Sioux

That is why the Aboriginal Film and Video Art Alliance was formed: to create spaces for the people to perform their visions on earth. This process of negotiating began in April of 1991 in Edmonton when the Alliance first gathered artists together. A steering committee of ten representatives from across the country was nominated from among the thirty-five delegates who attended. A committee of advisors including Alanis Obomsawin, Bernelda Wheeler, Wil Campbell and Maria Campbell was also chosen. One of the first actions was to reclaim the International Pincher Creek Film Festival with the hope of transforming it into a forum where Aboriginal works could be seen. It had proclaimed itself an international Aboriginal festival but few works of Aboriginal artists of this land were shown unless they were "stars."

Our dream was to have our own festival where our works could be honoured and celebrated. DREAMSPEAKERS, hosted by the Aboriginal Filmmakers Association of Alberta, was created as a step toward establishing this space that was ours. To make a cultural event truly self-governing in a city like Edmonton was difficult. Mistakes were made and the Circle was lost. So the festival held in Edmonton in the fall of 1992 did not reflect the vision we had originally shared. It became a lesson in re-membering.

Now, with renewed vision, the Alliance is in the process of re-grouping and establishing a more local presence in each region/nation in the country, as well as negotiating new relationships with cultural institutions and funding agents.

The stated objectives of the Alliance are:

1. To promote and encourage the art of film and video production, within the principles, values and traditions of Aboriginal self-government.

2. To conduct gatherings, workshops, seminars, conferences, festivals and other educational services related to film and video creation and other media applications.

3. To foster communication and cooperation amongst Aboriginal artists, traditional storytellers and Aboriginal peoples.

4. To foster and encourage communications and dialogue with non-Aboriginal peoples through co-ventures, co-productions and other collaborations through the arts.

5. To uphold and practise, with respect, traditional copyright laws.

6. To buy, lease, hire, produce, create, import, export and otherwise deal in and with films, videos, electrical and electronic transcriptions and all rights and interests therein.

There are many points of view about how, who, when, where to tell stories, the exchanging of, finding and developing one's own stories. The Alliance seeks to act as a gathering place, for those who seek to create anew and reclaim what was lost within the framework of traditional concepts and forms of storytelling. To govern ourselves means to govern our stories and our ways of telling stories. It means that the rhythm of the drumbeat and the language of smoke signals can be transformed to the airwaves and modems of our time. We are the receptors and transmitters that send the stories forward. If we remain true to the values of traditional storytelling practices, we can use the new technology, without destroying the culture.

So, in visioning new partnerships, the custodians of stories and traditional teachers are integral to true self-government as co-creators in outlining the new laws/copyrights for creating. The negotiations embarked on by the Alliance with the National Film Board/Studio I embody the principles of inherent self-government by creating a Grand Council that will include traditional people from different nations/regions in the decision-making process. Annual gatherings that will provide a creative forum to exchange learnings, insights and skills and determine future directions are also part of the vision that includes the practice of co-responsibility and respect. Decentralization of resources and access to production along with apprenticeships and opportunities to experiment are other elements of redress. The systemic racism and cultural arrogance of the past can be transformed when the Circle is respected.

New structural relations between the Alliance and the Banff Centre for the Arts to create space, access programs and resources and include different values and principles in the production/process of culture are currently being explored. For too long, Culture, Art and Community have been seen as separate spaces. I-dentity is related to belonging, and belonging is related to community. The SELF of self-government is located in community. The community is the collective self that is shared through story and art. The stories we image-in-nation are a way of re-membering who we are as a people. The sharing of this knowledge is culture. In evolving new strategies for how art operates, the Alliance seeks to define its own territories of creation and engaging in making meaning. Access to technology without its attachments of "ideology" would make it possible for us to evolve culture by our own laws.

In the politics of race and representation, it is easy to lose sight of the artist and of the community. Institutions have their needs and agendas when it comes to changing cultural policies. The politics that surround getting our work done often takes our energy away from the quality and process of the work. We have been using their terms to define ourselves, referencing the mainstream constructed by the white market. To re-imagine and reclaim our ground in the intimate, small, everyday things of life and community is to become self-governing. The establishment of a Council and Ambassadors at the Banff Centre in order to change the relationships between artists and communities and facilitate a sacred environment so artists can create anew will change the face and voice of culture in this land.

Our attachment to this land, this place, makes us holders of history. We are the keepers of the cultural memory of this land and it is our responsibility to create culture that is truly of this land in this time and space. This does not exclude other peoples from other lands and cultures, though the existing powers would have us compete with each other for the crumbs that fall from their tables. We have an opportunity to change the rules, not just for ourselves, but for everyone. This means unlearning racism in our own selves and restoring the balance contained within the Circle.

Self-government is not ownership or possession that excludes others. It is not hierarchical or superior. It is more like the traditional storyteller's copyright which acknowledges the gift and bestows responsibility: "I give you the power to take care of this."

So be it.

All my relations.

> Once upon a time to come
> there were peoples
> who knew what they knew
>
> they knew that their heritage
> on this land
> was their power
> and they knew
> how to honour
> their spiritual connections
> with their ancestors

this happened because
the women
recovered their powers of creation
in their bodies
in their spirits
in their dreams

and the people remembered
that woman is the medicine
the original power
of earth and moon and stars
and they saw
what they might become

and the distant pasts
became one
with the near futures
as stories were shaped
from that ancient place
deep within where the Mother lives

to go to that place
of remembering
is to be remembered

sometimes
it meant starting with what is
darkest
and wild
and dangerous
uncovering stones and paying homage
to the sacred buried there

sometimes
it meant communion
with solitude
in order to find right relation
and affirmation
of the unloved
self

and sometimes
a song on the wind
stirred the hearts
of many
and the people
recognized its beauty
in each other

and they opened their hearts
to find
ways to act
together
in a good mind
because they knew
we are all relatives
on this earth

this is how the peoples
became strong
again

because
in that moment
there was remembrance

and so it continues...

ÊTRE AUTONOME ...
ÊTRE AUTOCHTONE ....
SE RE-CRÉER

... ACCORDEZ AUX HISTOIRES LE MÊME SOIN QUE VOUS DONNEREZ À VOS ENFANTS

de Marjorie Beaucage

Cet article n'est pas une traduction, mais une interprétation et une expression de ma pensée et de mes sentiments dans ma langue maternelle. Je suis bilingue et métisse. J'essaie de vivre entre les mondes que j'habite.

Le lieu de rencontre, c'est là où l'on ENTRE, c'est là où l'on est ENTRE tout. Quand on entre en relation, on découvre la jouissance et la connaissance d'ÊTRE. Raconte-moi. Raconte-toi. Entre toi. Entre moi. Dans ma maison de rencontre, je suis prise sans violence par le silence. Je demande aux ancêtres: "Conduis-moi, non pas d'où je viens — cela je le connais — ; amène-moi d'où je ne suis pas encore revenue. Là où nos murs deviennent fenêtres, là où l'on se voit autrement. Le moi jamais aperçu, genèse de toute chose vivante dans notre histoire. Je sais qu'avec vous je voyagerai aussi loin ... là où finit cette histoire et où commence l'autre ... " J'entre.

C'est une histoire que l'on ne saurait taire... mais cette histoire a été menacée par des politiques uniculturelles qui visaient à éliminer les différences des sociétés et des cultures autochtones.

Un gouvernement autonome, indigène, issu de la terre, c'est le rêve d'une collectivité culturelle qui se raconte, se définit, se guérit par les images, les récits, les rêves et les rituels qu'elle peut créer.

La Aboriginal Film and Video Art Alliance s'engage à "réapprendre par coeur", à re-créer et à vivre ces valeurs et ces principes de gouvernement autonome qui sont ancrés dans la tradition orale. C'est dans le Cercle qu'on entend les voix et qu'on reconnaît qui on est; on y trouve sa place, sa relation avec toute la création. Au centre du Cercle, le principe de la vie qui continue et qui inclut les sept générations d'avant et les sept générations d'après. Donc tout ce qu'on fait aujourd'hui est relié au passé et à l'avenir dans le moment présent. Ce n'est pas un regard nostalgique sur le passé — le bon vieux temps — mais une reconnaissance du vécu collectif qui détermine nos relations, nos liens sacrés avec la Terre qu'on a toujours occupée et dont on est responsable.

C'est ça le "je me souviens" autochtone. C'est de revendiquer les voix de nos grands-mères qui parlent à travers nous et nous rappellent aux sources de transformation. Le rôle de l'artiste, du conteur, de la conteuse est de donner à la communauté ces moments pour se retrouver, se voir à nouveau, se reconnaître.

Aujourd'hui, ce sont nos artistes qui sont les gardiens et les interprètes de notre SAVOIR. Le domaine d'expression culturelle et spirituelle se situe au niveau des origines, de l'identité.

Se gouverner soi-même, c'est se re-créer ensemble, c'est trouver des espaces pour se réunir et se souvenir ensemble. Un gouvernement autonome traditionnel est relié à l'énergie principale de la Création. C'est là notre vrai pouvoir.

Même si parfois nos images sont devenues des fétiches, des objets de consommation que l'on désire posséder et qu'on reconnaît comme "source d'inspiration" ... Même si nous avons été dépossédés de notre voix, de notre nom, de notre pouvoir, nous n'avons jamais perdu notre vision.

Et c'est ce retour aux sources, aux valeurs et aux principes traditionnels qui forme la base des négociations autonomes avec les institutions culturelles. C'est une façon de voir le monde, une vision sociale qui définit le lieu d'appartenance. La question principale est celle-ci: Qui est ton monde, ton peuple, ta communauté? Cette question ne divise pas, mais relie les peuples et les nations qui forment la collectivité et reconnaît leur diversité.

On a le droit de se parler au nom d'une collectivité culturelle en se racontant l'un, l'une à l'autre. Les liens étroits du colonialisme et le patriarcat qui cherchent à nous définir en nous divisant par l'affirmation que nous sommes tous liés. Mais nous sommes aussi tous différents. Vive la différence! On a le droit de s'interpréter sans intervention de l'extérieur; de reconnaître nos propres racines sans le désir sincère de ceux qui veulent nous "comprendre", nous défendre, nous vendre.

Depuis l'arrivée du premier Européen, convaincu que la terre, les ressources, les habitants et les systèmes de relations lui appartenaient déjà s'il réussissait à les vaincre, la vérité de vivre dans l'ensemble a été reniée. Mais pas perdue. C'est une connaissance, une certitude, que survit au plus profond de mon être. Et c'est par notre création, par nos images, nos récits, nos contes qu'on reconnaîtra notre être et qu'on deviendra visible. Créer c'est voyager entre le monde spirituel et le monde physique. Ce mouvement culturel maintient la vie et bâtit la communauté.

Ce renouveau, ce retour aux sources de création est le mandat principal de la Aboriginal Film and Video Art Alliance. Cela consiste à revendiquer notre autonomie culturelle et à se regrouper afin de rêver, de revoir de réapprendre ce qui est demeuré invisible et inaccessible depuis longtemps.

Vivre sans frontières ... Entrer dans un nouveau monde. Trouver une place ... Appartenir ... Se reconnaître ... Les aspirations des artistes réunis pour la première rencontre de l'Alliance, au printemps 1991. Et de créer des espaces à nous. Revendiquer le festival de films de Pincher Creek, qui vendait nos visages mais ne preséntait ni nos voix ni nos images autonomes, a été le premier pas. Bébé est tombé, car ses jambes n'étaient pas encore assez solides. Mais il s'est relevé.

Et deux ans plus tard, l'Alliance se donne comme objectifs:

1.De promouvoir et d'encourager la création de films et de vidéos qui s'inspirent des principes, des valeurs et des traditions autochtones et autonomes.

2. De se réunir pour dialoguer, apprendre, échanger, célébrer nos créations (films, vidéos, etc.).

3. D'établir la communication entre les artistes, la communauté et les gardiens de nos histoires et nos traditions.

4. De créer des liens avec d'autres peuples/nations par les arts, de collaborer et de créer ensemble.

5. De respecter les lois traditionnelles, les droits de chaque histoire.

6. De développer notre autonomie culturelle par tous les moyens possibles.

Il y a toutes sortes de contes et de lois expliquant comment raconter une histoire. Nous voulons seulement les découvrir afin de les partager, entre nous, entre vous, pour l'avenir, pour le moment. Nous demandons l'accès aux mêmes ressources que d'autres ont toujours eu, mais nous voulons nous en servir à notre façon, selon nos valeurs et nos traditions. Nous pourrions ainsi créer notre propre genre d'images, réaliser nos visions sans la formule que veut nous imposer la technologie.

L'idéologie militaire et dominante que véhicule la forme n'est pas la nôtre. Le Cercle est organique, féminin, relationnel, changeant, laissant une place au plus petit et à la plus grande.

Tout ce qui est conçu dans le Cercle peut être donné, transmis, partagé; toutes les couleurs de la vie y sont. Il n'y a jamais seulement UN récit, une chanson, un geste, un symbole pour tous. L'équilibre et l'harmonie se font dans l'échange. L'identité culturelle évolue et se crée dans cet échange. C'est ce qu'on reconnaît ensemble qui forme notre collectivité. L'artiste réalise l'image, la chanson, la danse qui reflète cette réalité et qui vibre au plus profond de chaque personne.

C'est pourquoi l'Alliance, dans ses négociations avec les institutions comme l'ONF et le centre des arts à Banff, reconnait toujours que la relation entre la collectivité, l'artiste et l'expression culturelle fonctionne comme unité.

Si les artistes peuvent créer un espace sacré, afin de se retrouver et de s'épanouir selon nos lois traditionnelles, le peuple retrouvera son autonomie et son appartenance ici, sur cette terre. Nos ancêtres sont les premières nations ici. Ces personnes ont reçu des lois pour vivre ici. Nous avons la responsabilité d'en prendre soin.

Entre avec moi et tes ancêtres pour reconnaître le don qui nous attend tous.

Entre.

En ce temps à venir
il était
un peuple

issu de cette terre
ici
lien sacré
d'appartenance
à jamais

reconnaissant
l'eau
le feu
le vent
la terre

éléments essentiels
de renouveau
de re-vision
qui servaient
de transformation
et guérison
à travers
tout temps
à travers tout lieu

même si parfois
on oubliait
on pouvait toujours
retourner
au cercle
et se retrouver

en approchant
le coeur ouvert
on y trouvait
le baume du pardon
et la compassion
qui embrasse la peur

c'est comme ça
que les peuples
reconnaissaient
le don
et la beauté
de chaque personne
de chaque nation
de chaque race

c'était dans le Cercle
qu'on reconnaissait
qu'on se rappelait
qu'on célébrait
la race humaine
avec toute ses diversités

et le Cercle continue
encore ...

A moment from 'Cultural Land claims'

— A GATHERING OF THE ABORIGINAL FILM AND VIDEO ART ALLIANCE IN ONTARIO. REFLECTING ON THE PAST AND LOOKING TOWARDS THE FUTURE AND CLAIMING OUR OWN SPACE ON THE AIRWAVES.

A VIDEO INTERVIEW WITH WIL CAMPBELL

by Marjorie Beaucage

Wil Campbell: And I think that's what's driven me to do what I'm doing now. The mistakes I made by trusting these people and working with these people, and helping them, virtually caused *more* destruction to our people — has sort of given me the initiative. And the decision now with all of those specialty networks, the opportunities in cable, in this new superhighway, you know, the new technology. When I started seeing what was taking place — the buying up of different networks, buying and selling — the frenzy that's going on right now — that's when I decided: why not go after our *own* television licence? And I knew in order to do that, I wasn't going to make the mistakes I did in the past. What I needed to do, was I needed to get a strong group of people behind me. And I knew the Alliance was here. I knew the Alliance could give me the support that is needed to do those sort of things. It's one of the reasons now that I worked very closely with the Alliance is that I don't want to make the same mistakes.

But at the same time, I also knew I had to get some really heavy hitters on our side to take on this challenge. So what I did is I went out and I started asking people: who's the best person to help me apply for a licence? Who is the best person to know how to do feasibility studies? Who is the best person to know how programming goes? Who do you think is the best qualified person to negotiate with CRTC and negotiate with government (and this sort of thing) in the white community? I thought, if I can pit the white against the white there would be a chance....

So I went to Saskatoon at a CanPro festival and I sat down with Bob Gibson, and I said, "Bob, I understand you're leaving the network , you're going into business on your own. Here is what I want to do..." And over the last eight or nine years Bob Gibson and I built up a good friendship. He's been in charge of programming, (that sort of thing). He's helped me a lot in this industry. I explained to Bob what I wanted to do: I wanted to go after a specialty licence for the Aboriginal people — their own network. And I felt it was time. I feel we're really ready for it. Bob said, "Wil, I think it sounds like a good idea. Let me do some phone calls, let me do a little research on my own, and I'll get back to you in the next couple of days."

So I went back to Edmonton and Bob gave me a call a couple of days later. He said, "Wil, I made the phone calls," and he said, "I also wanted to find out where we might potentially get the finances if we decided we're going to try and do this. Because it's going to take a lot of money to do the things that need to be done." And "Wil", he said, "the thing I found out is that (this is) probably one of the best ideas that's come across from you in a long time. I'd be happy to work with you on it. And I know just the right people we can pull in to do this."

So we sat down, we started talking, we started bringing people on board, and I worked from the native community, and putting in support systems together that we needed. He worked from the commercial and from the government end, and with people who are lawyers and everything else. And we're getting them to volunteer their time right now. We know we can access dollars. Bob has also made phone calls because his work in television has allowed him to meet a lot of very wealthy people. And he's talked with them. And we are now doing the work and we're putting the finances together. What we've decided to do is that we have to make this station self-reliant. We can't rely on government, we can't rely on the goodwill of a non-profit society or anything, so we have to do it as a business. In order to do that, we need to be on cable. It has to be on the cable network; we have to be guaranteed that, so we can get X amount of cents per household in order to build revenues for production. It has to be able to run commercials to raise revenue. We can rely on a certain amount from our people. But our people get limited dollars and those dollars they need to try and handle the situations they have on the reserves. So I don't want to take their dollars unless I can give them an investment that is going to make them some money for their involvement. I have to look at it as a business.

I'm working with good people, I'm working now with the Alliance, this gathering has given us an opportunity to really talk about this and with you guys as support, I really feel inside of me that it's going to happen. And, let's just say, per chance, that it didn't happen. That I got turned down for the licence. You can bet that I'm going to open the doors to a whole new era. The minute I get turned down, if I got turned down, there'd be three or four applications from aboriginal people. This is a win win situation, you know, and whatever happens, it's people like you and I who are filmmakers and videomakers and we've been doing production. We're the ones who are going to benefit. Because they're going to need our talents. They're going to need us to fill those programmes. And we have to be prepared. And our talks over the last two days about training, and development, and being action-oriented, to start making production, those are good signs. Because that's what's needed over the future. And I think inside of the next five years, you're going to see Aboriginal people in this country are going to really be on a level playing field in the areas of media with the rest of the country. I look at TV (and see that) I've had an opportunity to talk to them, and I want more meetings with them. But they need us and we need them. It's a matter of sitting down and working out the arrangement. I think we can all help each other. And one network would create one people, one strength. And that's what we need.

ANOTHER LOOK AT THE PLOT FOR THE WESTERN:

RE:PLACING THE SATELLITE: MEDIA CULTURE ON THE PLAINS

by Vern Hume

For the last few years the Playback Cabaret, an annual video exhibition and student festival, has been held in Saskatoon sponsored by A.K.A. Gallery, the Gordon Snelgrove Gallery, and the University of Saskatchewan Students' Union. This year, Re:Placing the Satellite: Media Culture on the Plains (1977-1987), examined the marginal position of the regional media artist. The exhibition was accompanied by a panel, "Memory, History, Representation, The Place of the Regional Media Artist," and a presentation "Constructing a History: Seeing Ourselves." The lecturers and panelists were Calgary writer and media artist Leila Sujir, Winnipeg video artist Gerry Kisil, and Calgary video artist and exhibition curator Vern Hume. Video Cabaret was organized by Saskatoon artist, administrator, and writer Sheena Gourlay with the assistance of Catherine Macaulay.

The following are a series of notes based on the ideas introduced and discussed at the exhibition in Saskatoon. This is meant to be read as notations in a continuing dialogue.

INTRODUCTION

In the classic structure of the Hollywood Western film, the townspeople representing the urban values of the East, draw their strength from the signs of the imported "urban" in the culture. In order to live, the townspeople must "colonize" the local landscape – ignoring its unique strengths – and are thus reliant on an imported culture. The archetypal Western town, Dry Gulch, is a place everyone wants to leave, except for the ranchers and indigenous population.

The question becomes: are the plains media artists located in a mythical Western scenario in the formula plot for the Western, which is written and rewritten until no other scenario is possible?

The regions in Canada have and continue to express their resentment about the marginal status granted to them by centralized decision-making policy. Aside from having momentary attention, which predictably results in token gestures, the simple expression of regional disparity has yet to appreciably alter the diminished position of the region. The regional, the local, remains a marginal place. Despite the recent development of local media production centres, the regional practice of media art, particularly on the plains, remains an activity within a regional community, itself located in a larger but still marginal national media community.

The discussions in Saskatoon began by examining the marginal position of the Plains media artist, but rather than embarking on another futile argument about regionalism, the speakers questioned the colonial structures which place less value on the local and favour the centre. By raising the model of colonialism, the exhibition began to articulate a position for the regional media artist, literally creating a place to speak from. This position, based on difference, allows the local to express and thereby see itself.

The exhibition developed a regional position, or literally re:placed the West as Satellite; these ideas were first discussed at The Plains Canada Independent Film and Video Conference[1] held at EM/Media in Calgary in August 1985. the Plains Conference developed out of the need for individuals and groups working on the plains to co-operatively overcome their isolation and regional insecurity. Rather than looking to the outside, the discussions at the Plains Conference focused on the importance of communities within the region and began to address issues of mutual concern, thus proposing ways of surviving in one's location on the frontier. The Plains Conference succeeded in creating and encouraging a greater exchange within the region, but it also pointed out that there was no singular "plains" vision. That is, although the plains are traditionally referred to as a region, in reality, the plains are composed of many different communities, each of which has an independent history and identity. These communities are linked not through a shared identity, but through the marginal cultural status assigned to them from the outside and, to a lesser degree, through geographic proximity. (Cheap air fares to larger centres and the colonized notion that the local is sub-standard has generally minimized communication/travel between centres on the plains.) In short, communities on the plains share a common non-position on the margin.

Re:Placing the Satellite: Media Culture on the Plains did not attempt to define a regional identity. However, by examining how the imposition of values from the

1. A Plains exhibition catalogue is available from EM/Media which contains excerpts from the Keynote addresses given at the Plains Canada Conference.

mega-centres displaces the local, the exhibition began to positively "place" the regional, thus converting geographic distance into a desirable critical remove.

A STAGECOACH STOP, A POINT IN-BETWEEN

For the most part, the plains have been a point in-between: at best, a stagecoach stop for those traveling through, and at worst, an inconvenient void that separates culture on one coast from culture on the other. The plains — ironically sometimes referred to as the "central" region, since it is geographically positioned at the centre of Canada — are culturally situated on the margin. It is a place that people leave. The regions, specifically the plains, have and continue for the most part to be importers of culture. This hiatus — to emerge as a point in-between — in the development of a regional community is not an isolated incident, but has become an all too common point beyond which little development occurs.

Oddly enough, parallels can be found between the relegation of the local/regional to the marginal position of a place in-between (a stagecoach stop) within Canadian and International culture, and the stagecoach passengers' relationship to the country in the John Ford film *Stagecoach*. The passengers are colonialists, townspeople who view the countryside through which the stagecoach passes as hostile and empty of their culture — a void. In the film, the only locations in which the passengers feel even remotely comfortable are the stagecoach and the stagecoach stop — a simple outpost, a desolate point in-between — at least from the perspective of the passengers.

Replace the stagecoach with the airplane and this comparison seems more than appropriate. From within the constructs of an imported set of standards the local can easily be dismissed or misunderstood as a void — in the same way that the passengers from inside the stagecoach in the John Ford film view the Western landscape as empty. In this sense, the regional routinely colonizes itself by adopting the same imported standards — which make invisible the local. Given the ongoing colonization of Canada by American media, it seems a strange twist of fate that an analysis of the relationships constructed in the archetypal Hollywood Western reveal the same colonial models which media artists on the plains are subject to.

In order to survive in the long-term, a regional centre cannot simply exist as a point in-between, a stagecoach stop. It must be able to see itself from its own perspective. It is difficult for a place to continue as simply an outpost of ideas and culture created elsewhere, where the inhabitants continually feel disadvantaged by their geographic distance from what is perceived to be the centre. Inevitably, in such a situation, a continual emigration from the local to the centre occurs. A joke in

Winnipeg has been that the city's major export is people. This flow of human resources simply reinforces the desire to be closer to the centre, thereby devaluing the local.

The development of media access centres on the plains has allowed local access to production tools, and to some degree has slowed the emigration of artists out of the plains community. But the simple placement of production equipment in places which central Canada may see as "secondary communities," does not sufficiently offset the dominance of the centre, nor does it allow a space for the local to develop. The local, provided only with equipment, continues to be a disadvantaged place in terms of its ability to develop its own voice. Often, the tools granted to the region simply allow the reproduction of ideas imposed from the outside. Until the regional centres cease to be points in-between, the offering of access to such tools is only a partial solution. The regions have been at this crossroads before — possessing the tools, but lacking a voice. In this respect it is interesting to note a comment made in a 1973 Challenge for Change newsletter — an issue devoted to the plains — which acknowledges this hiatus:

> "The lack of access to the lines of communication in Canada is not simple overt repression. It is a class or establishment bias to our newspapers and TV networks that denies most of us not simply the hardware but the time, skills, money, and other resources necessary for the effective use of subtle and sophisticated communication techniques. It is not enough to give people a camera and a studio and say to them that it's their fault if they don't use it."[2]

Without the ability or desire to progress beyond this arrested point in its development, the current plains media community could again slip from its marginal position, as a point in-between, into a void.

MEMORY, REPRESENTATION, HISTORY, THE PLACE OF THE REGIONAL MEDIA ARTISTS

The current plains community has developed almost entirely independently, uninfluenced by earlier activity in the region. In short, there has been no collective memory to keep alive the knowledge and experience, thus connecting the present to the past. A fracture, a loss of memory and history, has occurred. The current community is separated and isolated from what came before. Thus, despite the importance of the artists, the work, and the exhibitions which took place (particularly in Calgary) during the seventies, now in the eighties, media activity on the plains has to be rebuilt, re-invented, relearned, and re-experienced. A lost

---

2. *Prairie Dog Press Manitoba's Alternative Newspaper*. Cited by Bob Brunelle, "Radical Prairie Roots", *Challenge for Change Newsletter*, Winter 1973-74, p. 11.

history, a lost memory. The existence of work, centres, and the artists who built them is only part of the process of creating a community and a practice. To exist and continue, a community must be able to recognize itself, thus constructing its identity, rather than accepting the identity imposed from the outside (through satellite, through mass communications, through centralized Canadian culture which displaces all the regions). Without history there will only be isolated occurrences.

Perhaps, it is even more important to examine the relationship of the media art produced on the plains (a marginal place in terms of the larger centres) to that produced, discussed, and represented in the mega-centres. An attempt should be made to place or, more accurately, to create a place for a regional media art practice. This is not a request for a token representative.

It is my intention in initiating this discussion to step outside of the current dialogues surrounding Canadian Video Art and to raise questions regarding place, memory, and representation. It is my intention to deliberately make some "reckless generalizations", to present the possibility of new beginnings and to develop a position, a space from which the regional media artist can speak.

The development of a cultural identity and a community is an on-going process involving, in its initial stages, a community's recognition of itself as a unique entity with its own values and ideology, and subsequently, the articulation and continuance of these attributes through a common language. Through this process — recognition, dissemination, and reception — a place is created for the individual, the artist, to express her/his experience and the experiences of others in her/his community. A shared experience — memory — can then be formed. Implicit in this cycle is the ability to see one's concerns, one's culture represented in the environment created by language, media, and image-making. Representation is then the last component that completes the cycle: self-recognition (the need to communicate), its expression (the production of work, images, narrative), and representation within the larger community and culture (the reflection of identity).

The structures and codes of language, visual images, media, embody the values of the dominant group whose interests and needs it evolved to serve. These act to define meaning. These codes structure the way in which we perceive. This is a close system of relationships which appears so natural that the ideologies, the values that it transmits are not always obvious. Such systems of representation are continually at work defining and ordering perception. Positioned outside, at the margin, the borderline, is the local, the individual, the minority, the regional artist.

Distanced from the mechanisms of representation (language), which create and disseminate culture, those who inhabit the marginal are in a position of perpetual reception. The position of Canadians living near the American border receiving American broadcasting or being native in a white society — a one way proposition, a consumer-only environment. The marginal position is, therefore, colonized by the continual onslaught of images, ideas, and representations created by and for the interests of the group(s) which dominate the centre. For the regional artists, the issue of marginality, curiously, must be central. We are still living in an age of colonialism and are ourselves colonized.

In his book *Electronic Colonialism: The Future of International Broadcasting and Communications*, Thomas McPhail views contemporary colonialism as

> "the dependence relationship, established by the importation of communication hardware, foreign-produced software, along with engineers, technicians, and related information protocols, that vicariously establish a set of foreign norms, values and expectations which, of varying degrees, may alter the domestic cultures and socialization processes. Comic books to satellites, computers to lasers, along with more traditional fare such as radio programs, theater, movies, and wire services to television show demonstrate the wide range of information activities which make up the broad configuration of what is possible to send and thus to receive..."[3]

While this analogy is specifically directed toward the domination of world broadcasting by the first world countries (the U.S. in particular), it can equally be applied to the dissemination of mass culture and art culture within Canada, as well as from outside Canada. Marginality is an issue which not only affects the regional artist, but minorities, third world countries, women or any group not currently represented in centralized culture. Being located on the margin, in terms of place, allows us to ask questions about the mainstream or centralized culture. How can we deflect or de-centre a centralized system of representation and the production of culture?

What happens when we cannot see ourselves reflected — except in the form of quaint generalizations in national and international dialogues, and when our experience and concern lies outside the currents of presentation? These broad questions allude to larger political issues, but at the same time are issues which connect those on the margins, on the borderlines.

It is not enough to simply address the issue of marginality from a geographically specific position, for even if the regional media artist enters into the national

3. Thomas McPhail, *Electronic Colonialism: The Future of International Broadcasting and Communications.* (London: Sage Publications) 1982.

dialogue, only one layer of remove has been overcome. There is no place for the national media arts community — itself marginalized from electronic mass media, popular culture, and mainstream art. The margin or borderline is, therefore, not only a concern with regards to a Halifax/Toronto, Saskatoon/Toronto axiom, but also to a Toronto/New York or Africa/North America axiom.

SEEING OURSELVES

In initiating a constructive dialogue on the position of the regional artist, questions must be brought into play which begin with the local and expand outwards. How has the dominance of one or two centres in this country affected the development of a regional media art practice? How has centralized policy affected the development of the regional? How has centralized culture affected the ability of groups to represent themselves? How has mass media, satellite communications, and so on, colonized us? And in light of this, how do we develop a place for difference?

The regional media artist is not only distanced from the major centres, but distanced from the processes which define high culture and mass culture: on the fringe of the margin of the fringe, three times marginalized. But in order to create a greater diversity of expression in our culture which can accommodate the representation of difference, the process of representation must become de-centred. In this project, distance becomes an advantage allowing a space, a perspective, from which the canons and codes of both international art style and mass culture can be de-constructed, and re-invented. The margin is then an important place to speak from.

In attempting to locate current activity in the region, the search for an identifiable unified "Plains" voice may not be the most productive line of thought to take. Such an analysis would not bring to light any information that is constructive or useful, for as is evident by the work, there is no one Plains style that can easily be labeled. In the past, the attempt to find a specific singular regional vision which can be used to easily distinguish the Plains or the Atlantic, and so on, has only served to ghettoize the regional artist. Such attempts seem to have focused on the most visible, the obvious manifestations of a region — the grain elevator, the grain fields, the sky, the mountains — and result in a caricature rather than a genuine identification of difference. A search for commonalty in these terms can create a negative or superficial description of the regional — quaint generalizations that have only limited value in expressing the experience of the local. If such generalizations are used to define a regional voice, the potential field of legitimate subject matter is reduced to only a veneer, forever marginalizing any further meaningful development. Such caricatures are often the only representation of the local which appears in mass culture and/or centralized Canadian culture and are so removed from our reality that they are meaningless. Within such a context, the local/regional is functionally voiceless. The regional is placed on the margin by centralized Canadian culture and in turn centralized Canadian culture is made local by mass (international) culture. Do we have to continue to make videotapes, write books, paint, and so on, confined by these quaint colloquialisms and be quaint colonialists in order to be recognized?

Instead of pursuing such a counter-productive analysis, it would seem more constructive to examine the influences affecting the work and see how these have been assimilated and subsequently "re-invented" to suit the needs of the individual artist. This approach allows for a diversity of subject matter and genres to emerge and be discussed.

In this sense, the title of this exhibition, *Re:Placing the Satellite...*, refers to both the place of the work in the context of national and international influences — literally placing or contextualizing the work — and through this discussion a place is developed for the work. Thus, the regions will have a dialogue to replace their ·colonized view, a dialogue informed by the external but generated from within. In short, the satellite is both the vehicle for cultural colonialism and the link to the outside — a reference point through which the local/regional can place itself.

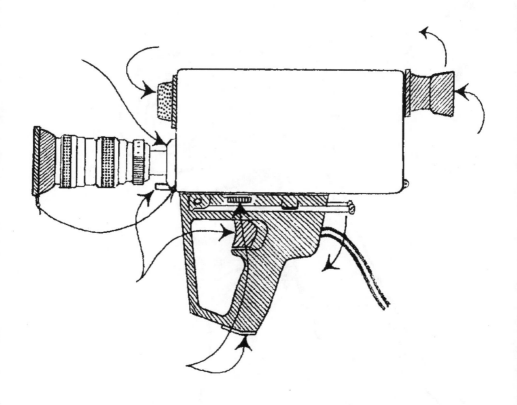

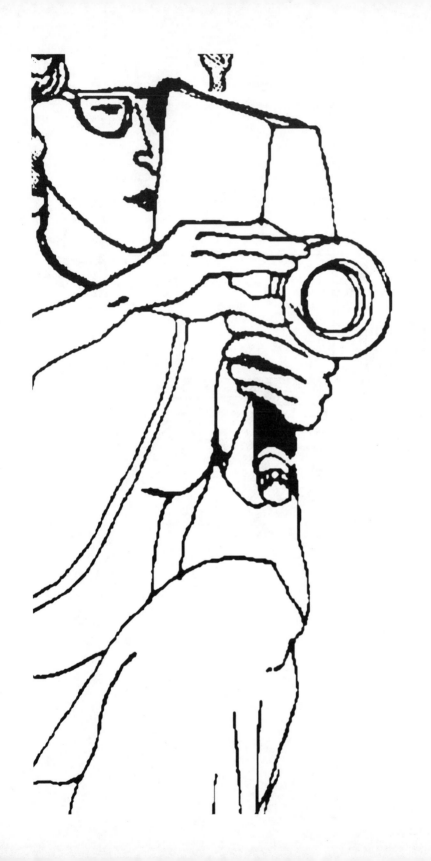

TO: PROGRAMME COMMITTEE MEMBERS
FROM: ROBERT FORGET
SUBJECT: VIDÉOGRAPHE

Dear Sirs:

Following your recommendation of 19 June, I have rewritten the Vidéographe proposal for submission to the Board of Directors.

Unfortunately, the submission process has not been straightforward. The Commissioner is alone empowered to present proposals at a meeting of the Board of Directors. In the unsettled climate surrounding his possible departure, the Commissioner was not sufficiently familiar with the project in time to present it at the July 10 Board meeting.

We must therefore wait until the next Board meeting in three months time. These developments lead me to foresee other, perhaps insurmountable obstacles to the Vidéographe proposal. E.g., How does the proposal fall outside the terms of the NFB Act?

a) Video-recorders: we are using about 40 video-recorders at the NFB;

b) Regional production: the Région 80 project is currently in production;

c) Use of public venue: we do this both directly and indirectly on an on-going basis, using films by the Groupe de recherches sociales / Challenge for Change, as well as for launchings, retrospectives, etc.

Clearly, for Board members who are unfamiliar with the NFB's various activities (and who have probably not seen three NFB films produced in the last year), the Vidéographe proposal will entail revising current NFB policies.

The natural reaction of Board members will be to delay the proposal until it can be accepted or rejected by the NFB according to the new Film Policy being prepared by the minister.

Obviously, your recommendation to seek the Board's approval for the project is, in fact, a way of deferring the proposal.

I have therefore requested the production director to withdraw the proposal from the Commissioner's office, for resubmission to you.

I am resubmitting the Vidéographe project, as a proposal falling within the NFB mandate, because it focuses on youth, is regionally based, and furthers the exploration and democratization of new creative endeavours.

I will be pleased to provide further information at your convenience.

Yours truly,

Robert Forget

THE VIDÉOGRAPHE CHALLENGE

by Jean-Yves Bégin

GREAT, GOOD, CHEAP... ELECTRONIC FILM

By 1966, cumbersome one-inch video recorders were already being used at the National Film Board. These "sound and image recorders" were used at the storyboard level, and to produce instant "rushes", in the Educational Film Department where Robert Forget had been producing documentary films since the preceding year. Forget acquired the first portable half-inch video recorder in Canada from New York in 1967. This so-called "Portapack" was used by Claude Jutra and a group of emerging artists from Quebec on an exciting cinéma-vérité shoot which subsequently became the film "WOW". In his role as producer with the Groupe de recherches sociales (GRS) / Challenge for Change, Robert Forget encouraged the use of video recorders in a whole range of experimental contexts, viz. recording, inventory and archive creation, revivals, critical distancing, consciousness-raising, self-criticism, personal expression, group dynamics, etc. In this "mirror" phase, video was still considered a *process*. In 1970, video formats were standardized —and the NFB made a block purchase of all (Sony) Portapacks available in Canada, advancing to the cutting edge of research and development (in both hardware and software). "The NFB is lucky to be big enough to experiment, and small enough to forgo profitability," says Forget. Meanwhile, a 1969-70 budget crisis curtailed cinema production at the NFB —and Forget started thinking of video in terms of *production*. His "baby" was Vidéographe.

COMMUNICATION WITHIN REACH

The Vidéographe idea fell right in line with Normand Cloutier's enthusiasm for community media. As a producer at Société nouvelle, an offshoot of GRS, Cloutier vigorously promoted the project. "Every consumer is a potential producer or creator," according to Cloutier. Indeed, video is fascinating as the only audio-visual medium operating in both directions —that is, production includes distribution and vice-versa. And these automatically include exchange.

Normand Cloutier stressed the importance of creating our own images, before being totally invaded by outside images. The progressive democratization of communication media must therefore focus on video —and on community media in general— as the new medium readily lends itself to the endless multiplication of centres for sending and receiving messages. As for film, Cloutier worked towards restoring its "true nature" by encouraging socially complex works and big, intensive projects.

Vidéographe was recommended as a pilot project on 1 July 1971 by the NFB Programme Committee, and accepted by the interdepartmental Challenge for Change / Société nouvelle Committee, with costs shared by the NFB and other federal agencies and departments. The project operated within this framework for the next fifteen months, primarily organized out of the NFB. In August, the first productions got underway and a space was found. Be the end of September, Vidéographe had moved into its own space, in the midst of major renovations.

VIDÉOGRAPHE LAUNCHES A NEW MEDIUM

When Vidéographe opened at 1064 Saint-Denis in Montreal, next-door to the prestigious Saint-Denis cinema, on 27 November 1971, it already had a history. At a press conference before thirty-three reporters, Robert Forget announced two video screenings —the first two Vidéographe productions, namely *Des enfants pour le kik* and *Improvision.*

VIDÉOGRAPHE SET ITS SIGHTS ON VERIFYING THREE HYPOTHESES –

CITIZENS HAVE SOMETHING TO SAY

VIDEO CAN GIVE THEM THE MEANS

THERE IS A PUBLIC FOR VIDEO

And the results? Robert Forget: "We gave ourselves two years... but after six months, the proof was there —beyond our wildest dreams!"

Translation for this text and that of Robert Forget, by Jean-Luc Svoboda.

THE ACCESSIBLE PORTAPACK MANUAL

(FACSIMILE)

Michael Goldberg

T.V. SET, or _____]□
VIDEO MONITOR _____]□
(should have an 8-PIN rectangular input, or V.H.F. antenna screws.)
___ & ___

PORTAPACK (cannot be used with one-hour reels), with _____□
     --- A.C. ADAPTER, or _____]□
     --- BATTERY _____]□
     --- EMPTY REEL (inside the deck) _____□
     --- 8↔10 PIN CABLE (for monitor only) or __]□
     --- R.F. ADAPTER (for T.V./MONITOR) _____]□
     --- R.F. UNIT (underneath most decks) ____□

INCLUDE A CLEANING-KIT, AND MAKE A LIST OF BORROWED TAPES _____□

POWER – ① WITH THE SWITCH 'OFF',
PLUG THE A.C. ADAPTER INTO ② THE WALL-
SOCKET, AND CONNECT IT TO ③ THE LEFT
SIDE OF THE PORTAPACK. THE NOTCH ▭ SHOULD FACE
THE BACK OF THE DECK, AND SHOULD SLIP IN EASILY. DO NOT FORCE.
SWITCH 'ON' ① THE A.C. ADAPTER.
   THE 'EXTERNAL BATTERY' PLUGS IN THE SAME WAY. DO NOT PLUG IT INTO THE WALL.

R.F. UNIT & R.F. ADAPTER – CHECK
THAT THE R.F. UNIT IS INSIDE THE DECK. IF
THERE IS A HOLE AT THE SIDE OR BACK OF THE
DECK ①, YOU SHOULD SEE IN. PLUG THE 'MINIPLUG' ① INTO
THE DECK (OR SCREW THE 'F' ENDING ON). ② CONNECT THE
WIRES FROM THE R.F. ADAPTER TO THE 'V.H.F.' SCREWS AT THE BACK OF THE T.V.
SET (NOT 'U.H.F.'). BE SURE THE R.F. ADAPTER ③ IS SWITCHED TO 'V.T.R.', NOT
ANT.. IF YOU ARE USING A SMALL T.V./MONITOR, SWITCH ④ FROM 'ROD ANTENNA'
TO 'EXTERNAL ANTENNA', AND THE SIDE OF THE MONITOR TO 'T.V.', NOT 'V.T.R.'.
(CONFUSING, ISN'T IT?) SWITCH THE T.V. TO THE PROPER CHANNEL (USUALLY 3 OR 4).
WHEN YOU BEGIN THE PLAYBACK, ADJUST THE 'FINE-TUNING' OF THE T.V..

___ or ___
8-to-10 PIN CABLE – FITS IN
ONE WAY ONLY. THE '8-PIN' ENDING ①
HAS 6 PINS, A GAP, THEN 2 PINS. BE
SURE IT'S RIGHT SIDE UP. TO REMOVE,
PINCH THE SPRING-RELEASE BUTTONS ON
EITHER SIDE, AND PULL OFF. ② PLUG THE '10-PIN' ENDING INTO THE SIDE OF
THE PORTAPACK. PUSH IT IN SECURELY, AND SCREW ON THE SAFETY RING.
③ THE SWITCH ON THE PORTACK SHOULD BE ON 'T.V.' (NOT 'CAMERA'); THE MONITOR
SHOULD BE SWITCHED TO 'V.T.R.' (NOT 'T.V.' OR 'LINE').

PLAYBACK – ① TURN ON THE T.V./MONITOR (TURN OR PULL 'VOLUME' KNOB).
② THREAD THE TAPE. FOLLOW THE DIAGRAM IN THE PORTAPACK LID CAREFULLY.
③ FLIP THE PORTAPACK TO 'FORWARD' ('PLAY'). ADJUST THE 'VOLUME', 'CONTRAST'
AND 'BRIGHTNESS' CONTROLS. IF THERE IS RECURRING VISUAL 'STATIC', TRY
ADJUSTING THE 'TRACKING' CONTROL (④ ABOVE).
⑤ WHEN FINISHED, 'STOP' THE V.T.R., PAUSE, 'REWIND' TO BEGINNING, 'STOP'.

1976

the ACCESSIBLE portapack © manual

THE SONY AV-3400 IS IN MANY WAYS A TYPICAL PORTAPACK:

EXTERNAL POWER 12 VOLTS D.C., BATTERY OR 'A.C. ADAPTER'. A 3-HOUR NiCad BATTERY COSTS ~$125.00. THE INDENTATION IN THE 'PLUG' MUST SLIP INTO THE NOTCH IN THE 'JACK'. DO <u>NOT</u> FORCE THE PLUG IN ANY OTHER WAY.

CAMERA INPUT PUSH IN THE ROUND '10-PIN' PLUG, WITH THE NOTCH POINTING UP. SCREW ON TO SECURE.

CAMERA/T.V. SWITCH THERE IS A SPECIAL (8PIN–10PIN) CABLE TO RECORD BROADCAST T.V. PROGRAMMES FROM CERTAIN 'MONITOR/RECEIVERS'. USE 'T.V.' MODE FOR THIS. WHEN USING THE CAMERA, YOU SHOULD BE IN 'CAMERA' MODE, OR YOU WILL GET A THIN, JUMPING IMAGE IN THE VIEWFINDER –

TRACKING CONTROL IF THE PICTURE IS A LITTLE UNSTABLE (e.g.-HORIZONTAL BAR OF 'SNOW'), MOVE THIS DIAL UP OR DOWN. THE FIRST TIME YOU PLAY A TAPE ON THE PORTAPACK, MOVE IT OUT OF LINE SO YOU WILL RECOGNIZE POOR 'TRACKING'. DURING RECORDING, KEEP IT CENTRED.

EXTERNAL MICROPHONE - THE CAMERA MICROPHONE HEARS THE LOUDEST SOUND FROM ANY DIRECTION, AND 'PICKS UP' ANY RATTLE FROM YOUR HANDLING OF THE CAMERA. THUS, A GOOD QUALITY DIRECTIONAL MICROPHONE IS USEFUL. Note- WHEN YOU PLUG IT IN, IT 'CUTS OFF' THE CAMERA 'MIKE'. BE CAREFUL THAT THE PLUG DOESN'T GET PARTIALLY PULLED OUT, AS NEITHER 'MIKE' WILL RECORD.

R.F. OUTPUT – THERE IS A SMALL JACK AT THE BACK FOR THE 'R.F. ADAPTER'. THERE MUST BE AN 'R.F. UNIT' INSIDE THE DECK. THE TWO WIRES FROM THE ADAPTER ATTACH TO THE V.H.F. ANTENNA SCREWS OF ANY T.V. SET. IT WILL PLAY BACK ON ONLY ONE T.V. CHANNEL (USUALLY 3 OR 4).

103

BATTERY LEVEL METER TO CHECK THE BATTERY, PULL THE RED 'RECORD' LEVER TO THE LEFT, OR PLAY A TAPE. THE NEEDLE SHOULD MOVE WELL TO THE RIGHT. AS THE BATTERY WEAKENS, FOCUSING OF THE CAMERA BECOMES DIFFICULT.

EARPHONE - <u>USE</u> THE EARPHONE TO VERIFY THE AUDIO (BEFORE) RECORDING AND DURING PLAYBACK, OR USE 'HI-IMPEDENCE' HEADPHONES

1976

C-MOUNT–SAME AS FOR 16 mm. FILM CAMERA LENSES.

LENS HOOD – KEEP THE LENS COVERED WHEN NOT IN USE. NEVER POINT THE CAMERA AT A BRIGHT LIGHT (e.g. SUN, SPOTLIGHT), AS THE 'VIDICON' PICTURE TUBE WILL 'BURN'. 'CLOSE' THE LENS AS AN ADDED PRECAUTION.

CAMERA MICROPHONE

104

EYEPIECE– A SMALL VIEWING SCREEN IS RECESSED IN THE CAMERA BODY. IT WORKS ONLY WHEN THE DECK IS 'ON'. A SMALL, RED LIGHT GLOWS WHEN THE TAPE IS ADVANCING IN 'RECORD' MODE. THE HOOD FLIPS UP FOR VIEWING.

TRIGGER STARTS THE TAPE RECORDING. PULL AND RELEASE TO START, AGAIN TO STOP.

THREADING DIAGRAM FOLLOW WITH CARE.

HANDLE CAN BE REMOVED ON SOME CAMERAS. CAMERA CAN BE SCREWED ONTO A '35 mm.- CAMERA' TRIPOD.

STAND

EMPTY REEL – TO THREAD THE TAPE, PULL OUT A BIT OF EXTRA LENGTH; HOLD THE END AGAINST THE RUBBER CORE WITH THE TIP OF YOUR FINGER; TURN UNTIL TAUT.

TAPE SENSING ARM– POPS OUT WHEN THE TAPE HAS ENDED, TO 'STOP' THE DECK.

LID CAN BE REMOVED.

To PLAY – FLIP FORWARD. FOR FAST-FORWARD, MOVE FROM 'PLAY' TO 'F.F.'. TO PLAY AGAIN, FLIP DIRECTLY TO 'STOP', PAUSE, THEN PUT IN 'PLAY' POSITION. TO REWIND, STOP THE TAPE, PAUSE, THEN FLIP TO REVERSE. PAUSE IN 'STOP' BEFORE FLIPPING TO 'FORWARD' AGAIN. NEVER SWITCH DIRECTIONS ABRUPTLY; IT IS BAD FOR THE TAPE.

TAPE-COUNTER – PRESS RIGHT AFTER YOU THREAD THE TAPE. WHEN REWINDING, STOP BEFORE REACHING 0-0-0.

STILL-FRAME– FLIP DOWN TO 'FREEZE' AN IMAGE (NOT VERY STABLE).

SOUND-DUB – TO RECORD A NEW SOUND TRACK ON PREVIOUSLY RECORDED PICTURE, SLIDE AND HOLD IN PLACE, AND PUT THE DECK IN 'PLAY' MODE (NOT IN 'RECORD'). USE THE 'EXTERNAL MIKE' JACK FOR 'INPUT'.

To RECORD – 105 PUSH TO THE LEFT AND HOLD IN PLACE, THEN FLIP THE OTHER SWITCH TO 'FORWARD'. DO NOT FORCE, AS IT IS ONLY PLASTIC. THIS IS 'E-TO-E' MODE (STANDBY); THE TAPE WILL START TO ADVANCE WHEN YOU PULL THE CAMERA TRIGGER.

August 14, 1972 (Expurgated)

NOTES FOR VIDEO ART

by Eric Cameron

1. FALL FROM THE EMPIRE STATE BUILDING
2. AN APPROACH TO VIDEO-TAPE AS ART
3. VIDEO PROJECTS IN HAND
4. THE CONDITION OF MODERN ART
5. VIDEO TIME AND THE TIME OF PAINTING
6. WHAT I READ ON MY SUMMER VACATION

1. FALL FROM THE EMPIRE STATE BUILDING

In video recording, the camera and the recording apparatus containing the tape are distinct units. The camera may be so roughly treated as to bring about its complete destruction without in any way damaging the tape or imparing the quality of its reproduction. In standard equipment the lead is no more than a few feet long, but I was assured in a telephone conversation with a member of Sony Electronic that it could be extended to 700 or 800 feet without loss of definition. A lead of this length attached through a window to a recorder installed half way up the building would allow the camera a free fall of twice that distance — more than adequate for the project. I propose to stand on the open observation platform at the top of the Empire State Building, switch on the camera, carry it to the edge and throw it over the surrounding parapet. The tape will be allowed to play itself out. A lens offering a good depth of field will be used, but apart from that, no attempt will be made to persuade the visual or aural traces to resolve themselves as coherent information.

2. AN APPROACH TO VIDEO-TAPE

"Fall from the Empire State Building" is one of several projects I have in hand which respond to the open question, "What can you do with a television camera?"

For most day-to-day purposes it is necessary that we should assume the standard, normal, reasonable, day-to-day answers to questions of that type. Food is to eat and soap is to wash with. We might get away with the alternative, but even if the results were not too physically disagreeable, the effort of making such decisions at every turn would exhaust all our energies. We would never find time for more important things. The day-to-day answer to the question, "What can you do with a television camera?" is that you can use it to make television programmes, and that will usually stand us in good stead. To speak of the television medium's potential for recording and transmitting information, of visual effects and feedback loops is only to expand the same reply, and for most day-to-day purposes I would be a staunch advocate. If in the context of art I give a different sort of answer, this is precisely because it places the decision at an altogether more fundamental level.

What then can you do with a television camera? A list of my current suggestions appears over the page. For one thing one might throw it off the top of the Empire State Building. Or one might put it on one's mouth or someone else's. The tubular form of the lens fitting gives it more the resemblance of a finger (or a penis) than of the eye which its function seems to duplicate. One might use it to feel over the surface of a wall or fondle the body of a girl. Alternatively one might disguise it to look like an eye. A little padding and some fur could easily transform the average video-camera into a very plausible one-eyed dog. The trigger-switch which turns it on would figure as a outsized penis and, with wheels fitted, one could take it for walks on its own co-axial lead. Freeing the trigger from its sexual connotations you could fire the camera at a target like a gun, and forgetting the camera itself one might spend a whole half-hour rewinding the tape.

It is not possible to pose a question like "What can you do with a television camera?" without in the same instant suppressing the pre-echoes of an obscene reply: "   " Modern art has often developed by refocusing our attention in ways which previously seemed inconsequential or perverse, and the anxiety caused by admitting this reply to consciousness may be more likely to indicate its validity than otherwise. But it is to be understood that the question itself is a fiction, a verbal device to facilitate verbal explanation. Another false question follows closely on the heels of the answer: "If a television camera is not for making television programmes, why involve it at all?" If I choose to throw a television camera off the top of the Empire State Building (   ) in preference to eating soap or washing with corned beef, it is not because there is anything inherently unintelligent about these latter suggestions, rather that their adoption imposes a secondary level of decision as regards presentation or documentation.

3. VIDEO PROJECTS IN HAND

Famous Falls

1. Fall from the Empire State Building

2. Niagara Falls

The camera is to be switched on and thrown into the water close to the brink of the falls. The recorder is to be situated at the base so as to allow the current the possibility of carrying the camera downstream once clear of the drop.

Contacts

In each of these projects a wide-angle lens is attached to a standard portable camera. The camera is placed in physical contact with the object concerned and drawn over it. The area around the point of contact will be lost in a blurred pattern of light and shade, beyond the range of focus of the lens, but details at a little distance emerge more clearly as the lens tilts obliquely. The friction of the camera's movement registers parallel traces in sound as it responds to contact with differing surface textures.

1. (A girl's body — title to be the first name of the model)

The camera is drawn freely over the body of a nude girl who may herself move into new positions to facilitate a greater variety of approaches.

2. Bedroom

The camera is held firmly about chest high and in oblique contact with the wall and carried forwards at a slow pace around the room, maintaining a constant height and angle of contact with the wall-(door-, window curtain-, or picture-) surface.

A work combining versions of the two preceeding projects was realised some time ago. Played back on paired monitors, the piece was in three episodes separated by ten-second bands of black simultaneously appearing on each screen. The right monitor carried the tape of the girl, Sue Sterling, a model from the University (nude in the first two episodes and clothed in the final one). In the left monitor the camera slowly moved from left to right around the walls of a bedroom in my home. On one wall was pinned three sheets of papers bearing the captions, "Et in Arcadia Id", "Sue I" (Sue II" or "Sue III", according to the episode) and "by Eric Cameron". As the camera passed over these words I read them out loud. The complexity of this preliminary work puts it in a different category from the main body of video-projects with which I am concerned at the moment.

3. House

I will draw the camera over the outside walls (doors, windows) of my house following the same procedure as in the last project.

4. My body

5. Window-pane

Using a wide angle lens set at its shortest focus the camera will be moved freely over the inner surface of a window-pane.

Insertions

1. My mouth

A portable camera will be used with a small wide-angled lens. Sitting with my elbows resting on my knees. I will hold the camera in both hands with the lens towards my face. I will insert it in my mouth, withdraw it, and repeat this act until the tape runs out. (a preliminary version of this tape ran for only five minutes.)

2. (Name of girl)'s mouth

Sitting opposite the girl, I will insert the lens in her mouth, remove it and repeat the process.

3. Mouths

I will switch on the camera, insert it in someone's mouth and leave it there for a minute or so. I will then remove it and carry it to insert in someone else's mouth, and so on.

4. The Atlantic Ocean

Standing knee-deep in the water, I will raise the camera above my head, plunge it into the water, and then repeat the process

5. A Jug of Maple Syrup

Sitting at the breakfast table with my family in the kitchen of my home and resting my elbows on the table I will swing the camera slowly down into the jug and then back up, repeating until the end of the tape.

6.

7.

Rewinds

1. A Clock for Half-an-Hour

The camera will be set up in a fixed position facing a clock with a prominent second hand. For a total period of half-an-hour (equal to the length of the tape) the tape will be freely wound-on and wound-back allowing varying times for recording. It follows that some parts of the tape will remain blank. (i.e. showing snow).

2. Curtains for Half-an-Hour

This will be executed in the same way as the previous project, but the camera will be set up facing slightly billowing, white, light-weight curtains in front of an open window.

Video-dog

The camera will be modelled by cloth padding and fur coverings to simulate the form of a dog. Wheels will be fitted and it will then be taken for walks. The tapes will be designated, "Video-dog: Walk I" (Walk II, etc.)

Shots

The camera will be taken into a pistol-firing range, aimed at the target and "fired". This will incidentally switch it on. It will then be aimed again and "fired" (incidentally switching it off). This process will be repeated.

Breathing on a cold lens

Prior to recording the camera will be reduced to a low temperature by putting it in the ice-box of a refrigerator. I will then hold it (switched on) in both hands facing my mouth and breath heavily on it. Ice crystals will form on the lens but will later melt as my breath causes the temperature to rise.

Scratching the lens

I will again hold the camera in my lap with the lens facing me. Using the diamond glass-cutter I will begin scratching the surface of the lens and will continue to do so for the duration of the tape.

4. THE CONDITION OF MODERN ART

Modern Art operates increasingly through the implications of the fact of its existence rather than through any contained meaning or message. An old joke about the hand-signals of women drivers states that if a woman puts her hand out of a car window, the only thing you can be sure of is that the window is open. That modern criticism has often prefered to attach most significance to observations of this type is undoubtedly because they are certain facts which do not call into question the authority or competence of the artist. The externalisation of content — the inversion of art's traditional frame of reference — neutralizes the variability of the human element, but also isolates art from the criteria of its evaluation which must accrue to it through the accumulation of meaningful interpretations.

The role of the modern artist is to determine the existence of art and he may defer secondary questions to the necessities of that central issue much as well-founded academic theory once deferred compositional decisions to the requirements of the subject. But the fact of art's existence may be construed at many different levels: as physical object or situation, as sensory stimulus or response, as event in time and space, or as act or the traces of an act, as concept or decision or the focus of the factors which lead up to the decision. Or its existence my be viewed essentially as art in relation to the category of art within the structures of classifying behaviour which sustain it. The artist may direct his energies and attention to whatever level he will and may defer decisions on one level as functions of another, but in the end what he determines is the existence of his art and not the construction which is to be placed upon it. If he attempts to impose a particular mode of interpretation (or to adjust to the anticipated reactions of his audience), his work reverts to traditional type. The imposition (or the condescension) itself represents a contained meaning which may compromise the integrity of his art's existence. The spectator will approach art at a level of his own choosing, if indeed he troubles to notice it at all.

It is a moot point what distinguishes the existence of art from the representation of the theory of its existence. Many modern artists have attempted to avoid the intervention of a second order of awareness by defering the determination of their art's affective presence, wholly or in part, to the mode of its physical fabrication or to the decisions of other people.

The situation with regard to videotape is particularly complicated, because television continues to function as a medium for contained messages within comprehensible norms of signification.

5. VIDEO TIME AND THE TIME OF PAINTING

The word "art" (in spite of recent developments) carries a primary anticipation of paintings, sculpture and related objects. My own main artistic activity (until very recently) has been in painting, and the problem presents itself in terms of that experience.

The main difference is the factor of time. Nothing can exist outside time and the fact that painting does not normally move in no way exempts it from the general rule. It is simply that the effective time of painting is the time of the spectator. Theatre and music operate within the time of the performer. If one turns up late one has missed the show. In painting there occurs a separation of the time of the artist as he performs the act of executing his work and that of the spectator who contemplates it. The finished work may contain varying indications of the time the artist spent, whether he worked quickly or slowly, and the stages through which the work approached completion.

The notes in my Halifax exhibition catalogue suggest that my paintings may be explained as a rationalisation of the use of masking-tape. In my preliminary attempts the dominance of the final layer always betrayed a multiplicity of levels of decision as well as execution. The change to a rectilinear arrangement of tape at intervals equal to the width of the tape itself provided a theoretical resolution, but in practice the tape can never be layed exactly straight. Implementation required a modification of the theoretical premises from which it proceeded. The ideally conceived regularity of the system, in its actualisation, superimposed another tightly integrated system of specific relationships, while the marginal overlapping of successive layers, re-established the temporal perspective of the work's execution as clearly as before.

Painting (and particularly my painting) resembles the performing arts in that it respects the temporal sequence of the act of production. In the film, by contrast, the shooting of the scenes may be done in any order, regardless of their place in the assembled reels. The use of flashback technique in the telling of the story is a different matter. It can occur in the theatre, and the narrative paintings of former days admitted temporal manipulations too. We may find anachronisms in the art of Masaccio but not of Pollock. The distinctions I am concerned with are ones of mental set rather than objective comparison. If we chose to regard the projectionist as the performer in the cinema, then the film is a function of his time, and respects its sequence.

Videotape is in much the same case as cinema except that the domestic connotations of television perhaps predispose us to expect more direct presentation. For the artist viewing videotape in terms of its existence as art rather than its content this consideration is secondary. The standard videotape lasts half-an-hour. Even if the camera is not switched on it takes half-an-hour to play back the tape. For the moment I am prepared to defer the determination of the length of my tapes to that consideration. Most of my projects accept the camera's being switched on as part of its functional definition, but I would not, on the basis of my involvement with painting, wish to propose a dogmatic unity of action. If, however, the camera is switched off, or if the sequence is disturbed, these decisions are of such consequence for the existence of the work that I must allow them to determine its every aspect. Perhaps the practical principle is one of the integrity of different levels of decision. Where this principle fails to resolve an issue I defer it negatively to convention, but to the conventions of art rather than of television. It follows that my tapes have no "stairs", no "blacks" and no "titles". The place for titles is the catalogue — and the cover of the box in which the tape is stored — and they should be simply descriptive unless in some way they constitute a decisive aspect of the existence of the work. None of my projects so far involves the refocusing of the camera during the making of the tape. I would rather have my tapes shown in an art gallery where they depend on the voluntary commitment of the viewer than in a theatre where he is confined in a fixed relationship to the monitor for the duration of the piece.

6. WHAT I READ ON MY SUMMER VACATION

Martin Heidegger. *Being and Time*, translated by John MacQuarrie and Edward Robinson. New York, 1962.

Edmund Husserl. *Cartesian Meditations*: An Introduction to Phenomenology, translated by Derian Cairns. The Hague, 1960.

Ludwig Wittgenstein. *Tractatus logico-philosophicus*. London, 1963.

Ludwig Wittgenstein. *Philsophical Investigations*, translated by G.E.M. Anscombe (3rd ed.). Oxford, 1968.

A.J. Ayer. *Language, Truth and Logic*. New York, 1952.

A.J. Ayer (ed.) *Logical Positivism*. Glencoe, 1960.

Roland Barthes. *Elements of Semiology*, translated by Annette Lavers and Colin Smith. London, 1967.

Noam Chomsky. *Selected Readings*, edited by J.P.B. Allen and Paul Van Buren. London, 1971.

Claude Lévi-Strauss. *The Savage Mind*, translated from the French. London, 1966.

Claude Lévi-Strauss. *Structural Anthropology*, translated by Claire Jacobson Brooke Grundfest Schoepf. New York, 1963.

Sidney Hook (ed.). *Philosophy and History, a Symposium*. New York, 1963.

William Elton (ed.). *Aesthetics and Language*. Oxford, 1959.

Gregory Battcock (ed.). *The New Art, A Critical Anthology*. New York, 1966.

Ursula Meyer. *Conceptual Art*. New York, 1972.

Douglas Davis. "Video-Obscura" in *Artforum*, April, 1970. pp. 65-71.

VIDEO HAS CAPTURED OUR IMAGINATION

by Peggy Gale

There are those who would argue that television has imprisoned and destroyed imagination. But the fact remains that the ongoing activity in video —about ten years now of personal expression, social action, electronic experimentation— retains an aura of fascination for artists, critics, and even members of the public. Novelty can no longer be considered the reason.

There is no doubt that television has changed our lives. The world is a different place, the news and entertainment industries are different entities now than for previous generations. The average person in Canada is said to watch three hours and twenty minutes of television per day. Commercial television. Alone, watching a box in the living room (or family room, or den, or bedroom) where out of every hour there are up to twelve minutes of commercial messages. Where the attention span is reduced to minutes (for the programme) and seconds (for the sponsors), but where the sponsors undoubtedly put more care (and more money per second) into their commercials than goes into the programmes themselves.

Richard Serra in 1973 made a provoking videotape called *Television Delivers People* (6 minutes, colour) wherein a regular roll of sentences slides past on the screen, with Muzak accompaniment:

You are the product of t.v.

You are delivered to the advertiser who is the customer.

What television teaches through commercialism is materialistic consumption.

Popular entertainment is basically propaganda for the status quo.

Control over broadcasting is an exercise in controlling society.

You are the product of television.

Television delivers people.

And we all know it's true. Nam June Paik has said that with video we could finally begin to talk back to our television sets, fight a sort of guerilla warfare with those little boxes by making our own "shows"...and the notions of "guerilla television" and "radical software" were the touchstones for video and for "alternate lifestyles" throughout the late sixties and into the early seventies. This might have been an original impetus for the video-fascination. Make your own television. Imagine yourself a star (In the future everybody will be world famous for fifteen minutes: Warhol). Certainly the hardware manufacturers were thinking along those lines, and were working very hard in the mid-sixties to put together a portable video camera, record and playback decks, at a price that every "home entertainment centre" could afford.

On a more conscientious level, a video movement developed attempting to change the nature of the mass media itself, making it two-way communication rather than simply a marketing terminal in the home for standardised products and (implicitly) ideologies. Yet the popular success of this early demand for democratisation of tv hardware may have hastened the end of its regular use by serious people on a local level: once it became clear that "everyone can do it" the activity was acclaimed as a fad. Those riding the wave of the fad picked up soon enough on the next fad to come along, and those who were committed to the guerrilla television/alternate media went from the too-present, too-amateur, too-rambling video to a tighter politicisation and professionalism, and expression by other (often more traditional) means.

And all along people were saying how BORING video was, even the people who were using the newly-available medium as a means of artistic expression. Well, video ISN'T like broadcast television, with its four 30-second commercials, twelve minutes of programme, one-minute break, another couple of ten-second spots, twelve more minutes of programme, and four 30-second messages. But why is video called boring?

Video seldom follows the patterns or the assumptions of commercial television. The taped pieces almost never fit into half-hour packages, or if one does the changes are that the decision was made, quite simply, because that was the length of the raw tape as it came in the package. At first, few videotapes were edited; they were left as they were recorded, and this might be long and rambly... or not. Documentation of a performance piece might well take hours, or only a couple of minutes; either way, the resultant videotape has a slice-of-life quality that is quite unlike any regular entertainment form. The tape did not necessarily tell a story or have a specifically-definable message packed into bite-sized segments. Indeed, the overt content of the piece might be hard to deal with, even unpalatable... Vito Acconci trying to pry open the eyes of a woman who was determinedly resisting him

(*Pryings*, 1971, 20 minutes), or Colin Campbell saying, over and over, "This is the way I really am" (1973, 20 minutes) as he positions different segments of his body, half of it shaved and glistening with oil, in front of the unblinking camera. These tapes are not about (or examples of) cruelty or narcissism, they are more a means of identification and exorcism of personal devils, a coming-to-terms with (undesirable) portions of personal character and history. Confrontation with reality, played out in public.

Boredom is the wrong word. Boredom results from not finding a response to match expectations or desires. Is a rainy day boring? Is a sunny day less boring? Does one call a painting "boring" if it does not seem to change quickly enough?

Perhaps the sense of strain associated with watching videotape has more to do with literal physical and emotional fatigue than with boredom. Perhaps watching video can literally be "tiresome" (Perhaps one feels unable to escape, trapped unnaturally by a commitment to see the piece through to its end, whatever the cost). The tension of viewing real-time, unedited videotape can be almost palpable; the viewer grows more and more restless, anxious, as he has no way to judge the extent to which he must pace himself, conserve his energy. With no way to anticipate an end, he must remain at peak attention throughout the tape. Shoulder muscles tighten, forehead creases, the eyes glance over to see how much tape is left on the reel. Afterward, he feels the tape had gone on FOREVER, that it would never end. "Video is such hard work" some say; "Video is so BORING" the others reply.

But confronting a work of art, confronting one's own intellectual, emotional, social responses, is not boring. Seeing this process happening in another person, through the immediacy of real-time video, is a similar/analogous challenge.

In unedited video we have completely raw information. The piece was recorded all at once; it includes mistakes or chance occurrences, and to watch it takes as long as it did to make (or perform) it. There is a quality of FOCUS that seems unique to video, both in front of the camera and in front of the monitor. This has partly to do with the size of the ordinary television screen: small, relatively human-scale, a glowing box of light in a darkened room. Even if there is someone else there in the room with you, it feels as if you are alone with the set. Watching light define form, the eyes are in constant motion. And as mind and eyes work to complete the pictures, the whole body is attentive, pinned to that glowing screen. For the person in front of the camera, there is the knowledge that the mechanism is recording everything it sees, instantaneously. Without the time needed for processing or development as with film stock, there is no split made between present and past.

A performer can see himself on the monitor, as if in a reversed mirror, but he is aware that in seeing himself (recorded) there, it is already over and he is enacting history. Time collapses visibly, the present flickering between seen past and unguessed future. This is particularly true of early performance works, where ongoing action was influenced or changed by the reiteration on the monitor. Editing happens during the making of the work (in response to the camera's view) rather than afterwards. "Feedback" has become part of our everyday language.

We find complaints about another kind of boredom. "It's so SELF-CENTRED", they say. "Narcissistic." Certainly, video is an ideal means of self-study: impartial, laconic, specific, video seems to collect secrets. Since the whole process can be done alone — cameraman, actor, editor and audience are often the same person— with natural lighting, in a corner of anyone's apartment, the temptation to "tell all" can hardly be resisted. In this age specialising in personal charades, nascent schizophrenia, and obsessive self-questioning, it is no surprise to find the boldest of themes played out in this most intimate (and most public) of media. Drawing, painting, literature have acted as open diaries for artists of all ages, consciously or other wise, but now words and pictures join in a more explicit narration. Lisa Steele, in *A Very Personal Story* (1974, 17 minutes) details her mother's death a decade previously; Rodney Werden, in *I'm Sorry* (1974-5, 11 minutes) strips and is lightly caned; Al Razutis in *Synapse* (1976, 26 minutes) carries out a biofeedback experiment; Colin Campbell in *Secrets* (1974, 20 minutes) talks about a personal relationship. Yet this interest in (and need for) exposure is ultimately a true reflection of our situation and ourselves. We are all subjects.

In general, however, "video time" seems to be changing now. There is a perceptible move towards narrative structuring and post-production editing, perhaps as counter-balance to the highly-charged subject matter so common to the medium. The information is less raw. Composition after the fact: there is obvious decision-making at work on the part of the artist, a sense of control. There is an apparent progress in the tape, as events and themes develop over time, paced for desired effect. There is a break, with each scene change, in the need for a viewer's constant attention: one can look harder for longer, and a new kind of attention (and tension) can develop. With this new kind of formalism, our response to the content must undergo some changes.

Yet content is perhaps not the most compelling part of video; the context of the medium, and also its structural and electronic components, may have a subtler and more pervasive impact.

A video work, existing in a sense only during the time in which it is being experienced (played back through closed-circuit or broadcast systems), does not have the materiality of a sculptural object. Even as it is being played, the image may assume a variety of sizes and intensities of light, depending on the monitor on which it is being viewed. Film remains a series of tangible, visible images on celluloid even when it is not being projected, but videotape appears to the eye as an undifferentiated opaque grey ribbon with one shiny side, and its message can be decoded only electronically. In this sense video images do not have a finite existence or tangibility. And yet our response to the video image has a surprising quality of PHYSICALITY.

Firstly we see video as emanating from a SOURCE of light. It is not "over there", projected away from us onto a wall or screen as is the case with film. Rather it is "here"; it projects its message from within, as would a person who is interacting directly with us. As such, video has a presence which demands attention. We hear television referred to as "the eye" or "the tube": in one case a specifically anthropomorphic notion, in the other an impersonal conduit. But in both cases there is a sense of connection, exchange, communication.

We feel distanced but not disengaged. Distanced, because the cool phosphorescence of the flickering image will not stabilise for us to grasp it and hold it in eye or mind. We must continue to experience and respond to it, yet we cannot summarize or relax with it. Video's "presence" engages us but keeps us at arm's length; we become responsive subject to the object (or entity) represented by the video piece. Viewer interacts with the thing viewed, two isolated presences entangled in a curiously responsive one-way perception or confrontation.

Perhaps this perception of video by the viewer involves more than the one-way situation after all. While the taped piece is not itself liable to change and literal response, it does demand or at least offer opportunity for reflection in the viewer; as suggested above with the reference to anthropomorphism, the information encoded in the video medium loops back to confront the viewer with his own thought processes and feelings, for consideration and (possible) change.

Video as a means of communication: passing of a message, clarification of thought and feeling. That there are many forms of communication is a commonplace: books, newspapers, telephones, radio, television, satellite, or people speaking together, touching one another. People are all discrete entities, alone, but they are also interconnected with each other in a pervasive web of thoughts and perceptions in daily flux. We are surrounded by information and responsive to it as we seek to give it order. Video is one means of communication among many.

Yet video cannot properly be considered a communication TOOL. Far from being a simple extension of the hand, a utensil or implement, it functions practically in a way that does not correspond directly to manual operations. It does not simply take orders as would a pencil or a typewriter; rather, it has its own demands and input into any operation, and colours any activity with its own processes. It is not simply a tool, carrying forward the thoughts and intentions of its master without comment; rather like a machine, it translates the desires of its operator into a language and multiple-message of its own devising. For this reason, ideas and feelings put into the world on videotape have a complexity that is not at once apparent. To some extent, we as viewers are responding not only to the visual and aural stimulation of the television message, we are also conscious of being "plugged in" to the dominant information system of our culture. We look at video knowing that this is the same machine that gives us the evening news, and twelve minutes per hour of commercials; as such we treat its "truth" differently than we would the more apparently neutral one of the movies, which we may see more purely as a medium for entertainment.

Herein lies the root of COLOUR video's double impact. Still new, still expensive, colour television has a glamour quite separate from the literal beauty of its dazzling reds, electric blues, poison greens. And colour video appeals beyond the senses to the rueful (or open) capitalist in each of us. Technology's toy and implicit challenge, colour television is one of the ultimate consumer items, already becoming a commonplace and a necessity. Artists' videotapes produced in colour are a direct answer to that challenge, and those tapes consciously acknowledging the specifics of the commercial world have a particular and continuing impact. General Idea's *Pilot* (1977, 28:50 minutes) and Ant Farm's *Media Burn* (1975, 25 minutes) are two of the most compelling examples. In each case their art makes full use of cliché broadcast formats and timing; content and context are juxtaposed in admiring if ironic recognition of the significant role played by commercial television today. Ant Farm created a dramatic "media event" and then invited the media to cover it in regular news items and commentaries; the whole was then edited into a package incorporating the commercial coverage within the framework of their finely-planned performance (the Phantom Dream Car crashes through a pile of fifty flaming television sets at San Francisco's Cow Palace). General Idea created its *Pilot* as a work commissioned for broadcast on TV Ontario, the educational network. A complex montage of stills, film, videotape and live action, all with soothing backdrop music, the tape outlines the ongoing programme of General Idea in the construction of 1984 Miss General Idea Pavillion, and in the process introduces General Idea, its aims and accomplishments, its witty self-sell. These works play on big-money, big-time television's acknowledged successes... not through parody, but with an equivocal respect and admiration. Model is transcribed into archetype, investigated from the inside for its role in a kind of ongoing anthropology of contemporary idioms.

Television is one of this generation's great success stories and no one yet fully understands how it works on us and through us. Perhaps it is this fact that forms the basis for video's continuing significance.

VIDEO: TOWARD A RENEWAL OF ART CRITICISM

by Christine Ross

In this article, I will examine the theme "media art and art criticism" from a video perspective and attempt to show how and by what means video necessitates a renewal of the modes of interpretation, description and evaluation characteristic of art criticism as it was defined in the 18th century and as it is generally practised today.

My hypothesis is as follows: if video has a special impact on art criticism, it is because it addresses a subject (I concentrate here on the subject-viewer, the first stance adopted by the critic), who generates meaning which, on the theoretical level, is not restricted by notions of totality, completeness, fixity and stability. Both the interpretation and description of the work point to their own state of incompletion.

This placement of the viewer in the position of "subject-in-process", constantly defining and redefining oneself in relation to the medium, is reinforced in part by the electronic formation of the image. Let me point first to that which Alain Landau identifies as the "lenteur perceptible" (perceptible slowness) ushered in by video. The image results directly from its "temporal presentation": an electron beam scanning the screen (from top to bottom and left to right) renders the progressive "unmasking" of the image visible. This unmasking, which by definition occurs slowly, is in fact characteristic of all visual activity and underlines the fact that reality is never perceived immediately as a whole:

> "This visible 'flaw' in presentation reflects the temporal dimension of vision and, on another level (i.e. the realm of micro- and nano-seconds), the 'progressive' aspect of image-discovery."

Alain Landau[1]

We are equally aware of the imprecision of the electronic image, blurred and ill-defined. And, as René Payant mentions, there is a "double scene" created by the

---

1. Alain Landau, "L'image en quête du regard", Robert Allezaud, dir., *Art et Communication*, Paris, éditions Osiris, 1986, pp. 107-110.

video image — a kind of "image-break" produced by the lack of coherence between electronic matter and the icon[2]: the video image defines itself through its *activity*, its continuous formation and deformation wavering on/in/under an electronic surface that never freezes iconic elements.

These inherent aspects of the video image —electronic slowness, blur and "double scene"— undermine the concept of representation as mimetic (that the image reflects exterior reality or expresses an individual's interior state), or as an autonomous, formal entity, in the formalist or structuralist sense. The video image reintegrates the perceiving subject into the representation; in this case, the subject —unlike her/his phenomenological counterpart— cannot immediately experience the presence of an exterior world which remains intact, as if untouched by perception. Reception is defined by complexity: the receiver cannot fully reproduce, in all its aspects, the totality of the image. He/she is thus called upon to make an interpretation, which allows for the resolution of the problems of "double scene" and electronic blur, producing meaning and creating a representation. In so doing, *via* interpretation, the viewer draws mainly upon memory. This raises the first problem facing the art critic: if the presentation is not physically contained in the image, how can one talk about it and describe it without describing oneself?

From a neuroscientific point of view, perception is inextricably involved with memory. As Landau points out, video illustrates the way perception itself occurs. Perception results from the linking of what neurobiologist Jean-Pierre Changeux calls "mental objects" — percepts, concepts and mental images which correspond to various groupings of nerve cells (neurons) within different zones of the cerebral cortex, which can be described in mathematical graphs.[3] When perception occurs, the percepts derived from viewing an object connect with concepts and mental images formed in the brain during that individual's life. Resonance or dissonance between these percepts and the memory-objects in the person's brain can occur and, once the neurological connections are stabilized, new combinations are produced. Thus, contact with the outside world destabilizes the perceiving subject, who subsequently restablilizes: the subject processes, computes data to produce meaning. The ensuing interpretation is, above all, provisional and subject to further destablilization as the electronic images continue to form and deform on the screen. This leads to the possibility of a "subject-in-process".

2. René Payant, "La frénésie de l'image: vers une esthétique selon la vidéo", Anne Cauquelin, dir., *Vidéo-Vidéo, Revue d'esthétique*, nouvelle série (10), 1986, pp. 17-23. The icon of the "double scene" can be defined either according to the peircien theory, as a sign referring to the object in a relationship of resemblance, or according to J.M. Floch's definition, as an "effect of reality". See J.M. Floch, "image, signes, figures: l'approche sémiotique de l'image", Michel Zéraffa, dir., *Images, Revue d'esthétique*, nouvelle série (7), 1984, pp. 109-114.

3. Jean-Pierre Changeux, *L'Homme neuronal*, Paris , Fayard, Coll. "Pluriel", 1983.

So what can we say about this desire of the critic or the subject to give meaning? According to psychoanalyst Julia Kristeva, the act of interpretation is rooted in the need to reassert one's own image and identity when facing the object.[4] So, when the art critic produces meaning, or interprets, the process generally integrates the object into a pre-existing theory of interpretation. In this case, interpretation simply results in selecting an object already contained in the theoretical framework. This process, which I call de-complexification, transforms the image or the object into a receptacle for a self-contained subjectivity complete in itself.

To escape from this closed circle of interpretation, Kristeva proposes the psycho-analytical method of transference: the locus of exchange in which the analyst, motivated by desire for the Other, acts in such a way that the object of the analysis (in this instance, the patient) can reveal the *not-known* of the analyst's theory. In this way, meaning is produced which leads to a renewal of the theory. However, the locus of this exchange contains a paradox. For the *not-known* to manifest itself, the analyst —who, like any subject seeking knowledge, is a subject of desire— must be motivated by a quest for ultimate Meaning. However, the analyst must realize that, at most, this Meaning can only be approached indefinitely. In any exercise involving transference and analytical interpretation, the subject is motivated to interpret by the fantasy that it is in fact possible to attain Truth or Light, to rediscover the original object (the *Sachverhalt*: the body of the mother, the pre-Oedipal, un-nameable condition); but such interpretation is endless, because Meaning is made infinite by desire, the desire for the Other. Ideally, the meaning produced by the analyst would be heterogeneous, polytopical, incomplete and unstable.

This detour through psychoanalytic theory enables us to understand the kind of reception favoured by video: an interpretative *activity* in constant movement, continuously constructing and deconstructing itself as the image is formed and deformed. Interpretation occurs, but it is bound to a continuous re-opening. It goes without saying that this type of reception does not occur *de facto*. In reality, the critic can deny the "double scene" and fall back on a fixed description or interpretation.

But, what intrigues me, here, is the kind of reception encouraged by video, the state of interpretative flux it suggests and the political consequences deriving from such interpellation. Indeed, if representation occurs through interaction between image and object, where the viewer, *via* her/his memory, endowed with all its cultural, social, political and psychological capacities, interprets the image without

4. Julia Kristeva, "Psychoanalysis and the Polis", W.J.T. Mitchell, ed., *The Politics of Interpretation,* Chicago, The University of Chicago Press, 1983, pp.83-98.

producing a closed system of meaning, it follows that the political focus must be situated precisely in the relation between image and spectator, and not in the image itself nor in the subject or critic defined by her/his personal consciousness and turned in upon her/himself. In this 'Baudrillardian' world of simulation we inhabit, where spectacle and reality overlap, where an opposition outside the closed system is impossible and where political gestures are constantly being distorted, the interaction between image and subject indicated by video images allows us to envisage the possibility of renewal and change.[5]

The political dimension of this interaction therefore assumes a virtuality not unlike that of utopia: being neither in the work nor in the viewer, the political representation is situated in an "elsewhere" at once possible and absent.

Fredric Jameson has already described the subversive reinscription of the utopic in some postmodern practices.[6] This utopia is different from modernist utopia in that the 'elsewhere' to which postmodernism aspires eludes positive representation in material form. Although Jameson suggests an elsewhere based on the utopic potentiality of mapping the structures of present-day multinational capitalism, his proposition can be applied to any practice based on the notion of Elsewhere and consequently, to any subject of desire seeking Ultimate Meaning *(Sachverhalt).* [7] In political terms, we are dealing here with a subject who, in her/his quest for social change, seeks the un-representable.

Jameson refers to specific photographic works in which the Elsewhere (Meaning, Truth, or even Love), is not concretely represented in the image: this elsewhere is indicated by an image structure based on internal differentiation which, like the blur and "double scene" characteristic of video, incite the spectator to make a *scanning* interpretation:

> "Photography then, in its contemporary and even postmodern version, would seem to [renounce] reference as such in order to elaborate an autonomous vision which has no external equivalent. Internal differentiation now stands as the mark and the moment of a decisive displacement, in which the older relationship of image to referent is now superceded by an inner or an interiorized one...To speak more psychologically, the attention of the viewer is now engaged by a differential opposition within the image itself, so that she

5. For a reading of Baudrillardian simulation, see Victor Burgin, *The End of Art Theory: Criticism and Postmodernity*, Atlantic Highlands, New Jersey, Humanities Press International, 1986.

6. Fredric Jameson, "Postmodernism and Utopia", in *Utopia Post Utopia: Configurations of Nature and Culture in Recent Sculpture and Photography*, Boston, The Institute of Contemporary Art, 29 January - 27 March 1988, pp.11-32.

7. For readings on cognitive "mapping", see Jameson, "Postmodernism, or The Cultural Logic of Late Capitalism", *New Left Review* (146), July-August 1984, pp. 53-92.

has little energy left over for intentness to that older 'likeness' or 'matching' operation which compares the image to some putative thing outside."[8]

We can see here that the art critic must abandon the positivism of description and interpretation to linger on what could be called the borderline between the visible and the invisible — at what Deleuze calls the frontier between the outside and the inside, the real and the imaginary, that place where the quest for the unrepresentable, the desire for the Other, the Elsewhere play, and unplay, themselves out.[9]

Translation by Jean-Luc Svoboda.

8. Jameson, "Postmodernism and Utopia", *op. cit.*, p. 31.

9. See Gilles Deleuze, *Cinéma 2: L'image-temps* Paris, les Éditions de Minuit, 1985.

VIDEO – LANGUAGE – THE COMMON/PLACE

by Jody Berland

"It is a commonplace,"suggests Hal Foster, "to say that the primary public representation in the 20th century is now film or television, not architecture or sculpture (though the very term is suspect, if one grants the loss of the real)..." This has an ominous note. "In fact," he adds, "one can point to a specific instance in which the ideological stress passes from architecture to film — in the 1935 Leni Riefenstahl 'documentary' of the Nazi rally at Nuremburg. There architecture becomes purely scenographic..."[1]

Why not *Potemkin*, a decade earlier, with revolutionary peasants storming those steps? Because Nuremburg was designed *for* media. That which is not physically present (at which we are not), Foster implies, is less real or, more cogently, is prey for spectacle, for voyeurism, for political domination. Fascism bases itself upon its own (physical) absence, the result of which is that physical and social space are overwhelmingly homogenized. In absence is based the power of language, and it is the power of language that disseminates the real.

Let us situate this trend more objectively.

> The evolution of media has decreased the significance of physical presence in the experience of people and events. One can now be an audience to a social performance without being physically present; one can communicate "directly" with others without meeting in the same place. As a result, the physical structures that once divided our society into many distinct spatial settings have been greatly reduced in social significance.[2]

Behind Foster's insistence is Debord's critique of the spectacle as the "autonomous movement of the unliving"[3]; but also a nostalgia for physical presence, a nostalgia for an architecture that clearly evokes the physical obedience of the body. As though media relinquish these. As though space itself is lost from language due to the

1. Hal Foster, *Recodings: Art, Spectacle, Cultural Politics.* (Port Townsend, Wash.: Bay Press, 1985) p. 80.

2. Joshua Meyrowitz, *No Sense of Place: The Impact of Electronic Media on Social Behaviour* (New York: Oxford University Press, 1985) p. vii.

3. Foster (1985, p. 81) is quoting from Guy Debord's *Society of the Spectacle*.

interceding of technology. Isn't this a guise for the immortalization of the Frankfurt School, which comprehended fascism and media as one? Could a Canadian so miscomprehend the ways in which media redefine (but do not omit) the experience, the importance, the power of space? And how it speaks, how we live? For these frame and fracture our history, our politics, our desire: our language. This is why video arises: to comprehend and to intervene in the "channels" of power that surround us, that structure our own occupation of space.

With television, we imagine ("home entertainment") that being at home we can be anywhere. The world is before us, we are everywhere and rooted to the spot. The immediacy of the video monitor offers the opportunity for even closer supervision of our movements. This supervisory function has been exploited more comprehensively than its antidote, which could be termed located self-representation, reflectively fractured through the malleability of tape: playback, erasure, revision, response. If pursued to its own "video-logic", video would make representation itself as problematic as the ordered separation of producer and viewer — as problematic as the ordered separation of time and space in which "art" and its Others are framed.

Where film is distant, video distances. It is the nature of "video-logic", according to one group of author/producers, that "video is, paradoxically, both nearer and farther away than a film or TV. The distantiation in relation to what has been personally experienced that is felt while viewing the tape readily produces exceptionally stringent criticism."[4] This is to assume that one has been there, that the achieved unification of producer/spectator is as inherent to the realization of video as their separation (and consequent absorption of the viewer) is to the realization of film. Not so. We dream movies; certainly we have all been there. This sense of presence is different with video, whose discourse, whose stories, must always co-exist with a

4. Alfred Willener, Guy Milliard, and Alex Ganty: *Videology and Utopia: Explorations in a New Medium* (London: Routledge & Kegan Paul, 1976). One can say this book is a classic statement of the early "utopian" moment in video history, later scrutinized critically by Martha Rosler, "Video: Shedding the Utopian Moment", *Block* 11, 1985/86. But the apparent opposition is based on geography, experience, context, as much as on time. The projects described by Willener et al, were all conducted in Paris suburbs and other urban contexts in the early '70s, independent of art or other media contexts, within selected communities — residents, workers, students, and so forth. Rosler, on the other hand (and a decade later), is concerned with the degree to which art history has mythologized video and thus recuperated it. For Rosler, Nam June Paik's "aestheticized entertainment" helped (with reinforcement from McLuhan) to establish a safely mythological role for artists employing technological media, its complicity evident in its "formalized mimetic aestheticism":

...as though tinkering could provide a way out of the power relations structured into the apparatus. Reinforcing the formalist approach has brought them — inadvertently — to bow, as McLuhan had done, to the power of these media over everyday life. In separating out something called 'video art' from the other ways that people, including artists, are attempting to work with video technologies, they have tacitly accepted the idea that the transformations of art are formal, cognitive, perceptual...

dominant and always previous Other. The inevitable salutations to this Other remind us of our (dis)placement.

The omnipresent Other shadowing the video screen is of course television, whose power, we are beginning to realize, lies not only with particular aspects of language —narrative structures, ideologies of information or meaning, visual seduction— but even more with its ability to dominate the private perception and organization of time and space. This means that, for video, the inevitable referent of television contains but also surpasses the language of television. "Television" is not merely a series of conventionalized forms, a static parade of objects of desire or addiction, but an entire discipline of cultural consumption, organized by a vast productive apparatus to which the topography and timing of domestic ritual is as indispensable as any formal-linguistic convention of popular entertainment or ideological indoctrination. Interpellation (to use the word employed by Althusser to designate the work of ideological "state apparatuses," including the media)[5] is not exclusively ideological at all. Television organizes bodies, as well as ideas; nervous systems, as McLuhan observed, but also gestures in space, as Lefebvre would have it.[6] As video emerges, it addresses the controlled interaction of private and public, and it nominates communication as movement across —and supervision of— physical space.

By pointing to television as the "referent" of video, I don't mean to say that video is "about" television, or that the value of a video work depends on its critical or explicit relationship to television or to TV culture. Yet somehow that relationship is always there. McLuhan, to consider one approach to this presence, points out that earlier forms always provide the initial content of a new medium, before that medium has developed its own "content" or language: live drama for film, film for TV, bands or orchestras for sound recording. Eventually the new medium totally redefines the meaning and uses of the former. But TV doesn't precede video in a

5. Louis Althusser, "Ideological State Apparatuses," in *Lenin and Philosophy and Other Essays*, (London: New Left Books, 1971). Althusser describes "interpellation" as the process through which an intended mass communication appears to address the viewer in a located, personal, and thus powerfully effective manner — "Hey, you!". Janice Williamson applies this in her influential *Decoding Advertisements*, noting the simultaneous abstraction and intimacy of visual ads. But why not, "Hey, you there!"? The "there" is simultaneously occupied and erased.

6. "Did the Orient, for example, know the Western distinction between representations of space and spaces of representation? The ideogram is both at once...

"There is also the related question about the silence of those who use contemporary space and are dominated by it — their lack of resistance to it, or on the other hand, their symbolic forms of resistance, sometimes distorted or overlooked: e.g., capital produces the space of leisure, but this is also potentially a space of the festival and of a revolt against planified space. The hypothesis here is that political praxis today requires the elaboration of a whole spatial dimension." Henri Lefebvre, "The Production of Space," unpublished manuscript, Conference of the Marxist Literary Group, Urbana, Ill., 1984.

technological sense, exactly; the relationship between them is neither evolutionary nor that of mainstream and margin, though elements of these are undoubtedly present. Rather, the relationship unfolds in terms of the social questions that are confronted by video production itself.

These are questions of seduction, representation, and the realization and recreation of time and space. And also, finally, of political organization, since seduction, representation and the restructuring of time and space now represent political problems. Television certainly renders them political. On the other hand, art discourse —itself a powerful social-cultural institution— places its own claims on the meanings made possible by TV and video. For video, the institution of Art is no more conclusive as a referent than is television, even though they both work so hard to be inescapable, and though they both succeed.

The emergence of video art as a distinct and self-conscious practice is the emergence of a language that is not yet a language. This is the consensus of much video criticism today, which posits various interpretations of this perceived sense of incompletion. Such criticism has not yet resolved whether this tension should be seen as a contradiction, a transition or a paradox, nor whether the absence should be conceived as one of technical form or of (artistic) function. The "paradox" of video is that it proposes to make these and other distinctions obsolete. The replacement of such distinctions is as yet very tenuous; it is still more of an idea to which one refers, a place one visits, because of the way that the sites of production and dissemination are controlled. The framing of a separated discourse of "video art" evokes the idea, the place; however its incorporation within art institutions (particularly in North America) threatens to sabotage the autonomous realization of its destiny.

All paradoxes reveal underlying movements, laws, situations that are in direct conflict with one another. There is no moment when such contradiction is not somehow present, especially now, especially with respect to technology, which surges outward and finds itself contained in the same motion. Video art makes this abundantly clear. The differences in interpretation of the various directions of video —i.e. what exactly accounts for the tension between language and not-yet-language— are ultimately political. For the paradox of a language-that-is-not-yet-a-language posits a site —real or imminent— in which "form" and "function" totally redefine one another through their embrace.

For instance, seduction, that magic of the moving image to which there is no parallel. The image itself is made the object of desire. Television is absolutely seductive, and for that reason suspect. Everybody knows this. Put a group of people in a room with a camera, a monitor, perhaps some sound equipment, instruments, texts, a film projector — or with just a television set; the seduction will move in an entirely different direction. The fascination of children is common to both instances, but in the first, the participants are watching themselves, watching the fascination of gesture transported; in the second instance, passivity seduces.

For instance, representation, which within the discourse of art (vs. TV) acquires an author. An author who becomes subject. To produce oneself as "artist" within a contemporary art discourse is to take a position of the definition —identity, but also location— of authorship. For early video, this position was for the most part taken in performance: the assuring representation of physical presence. Now this, too, is a question. However, art discourse —insofar as this remains the basis of a social institution— works to reaffirm the expressive individual as both source and subject in art. This becomes a cultural discipline, a "keeping in place," which is asserted through grants, resources, the provision of a place to speak. There is a tension between the logic of expression, of identity, made possible by art, and the "video-logic" that seeks to deflect identity to questions of address, of language, power, practice, place. That such questions remain unresolved is measurable in the degree to which they are still referents of the work. The paradox of their incomplete transcendence is chaperoned by the sincerity of their address. They try to leave home but the museum follows them to the hotel (where a TV sits in every room).

For instance, the re-creation of time and space. Television supervises domestic isolation; the museum supervises (designates the space for, language of) the discourse of cultural critique. Galleries and museums are places; they are also discursive destinations that mould the materialization of language itself, as both representation and realization of the possibilities of authorship. To take up a camera is to re-appropriate the language (site) of power. And to draw one's eyes towards a different destination, is to draw (at least) a different set of boundaries. Ultimately such boundaries need not only to be framed, quoted, mapped, but rebuilt, in the context of a new politics and poetics of representational practice through which space is once again made public.

FROM THE SCRIPT FOR

THE LAST SCREENING ROOM: A VALENTINE

by Vera Frenkel

1984, 44 minutes running time. The first part of the framing narrative.

Once upon a time, when it was permitted in Canada to tell stories about any subject at all, there were story-tellers who traveled the country from North to South, from East to West, and back, commenting on what they saw. Eventually, and perhaps for good reason these traveling commentaries were forbidden. They were difficult to control.

In the anterooms of the various Ministries of Culture, Recreation, Tourism, Communications, Industry, Trade, Commerce and Revenue, all interchangeable, it was commonly held that the new laws were necessary because story-tellers, unlike public servants, were people who told lies for a living, and that traveling so much made them elusive and therefore dangerous.

I think they were outlawed in the same year that the legislation was passed to outlaw the rain, but Canada, like most countries, still had pockets of the primordial garden; regions difficult to reach, still more difficult to pass through, and from which travelers rarely returned.

It was possible, in Canada, to lose oneself forever, or more accurately, to hide far away among friends and wait and watch, and continue to tell stories. This fact was not discussed openly or taught in schools, but people knew.

One day when I was doing my regular rounds in the prisons near Kingston, I visited a cell-block where there was a very old woman who had been arrested three months before. She had been found on the road between Napanee and Bath, about 25 miles from the city, starving and nearly unconscious, her feet wrapped in old newspapers and plastic bags, and her few personal belongings tied in a scarf. She had no identification on her, at all. No SIN or Social Insurance Number, no driver's license, no passport, no evidence of next of kin, and she spoke in a singsong way that hadn't been heard in the East in a very long time. Any one of these transgressions was sufficient cause for arrest but she also carried a map, and though they could see that it was a very old and inaccurate map, it was still a map, and that made the case serious. And so she was imprisoned.

In the three months of her incarceration, the guard told me that morning, though she had been persuaded to eat, she had not said a word. Yet she spoke to me.

How can I describe to you now those first few moments as her cell door swung open to let me in? There was a flicker of recognition, a swift inexplicable sense of affinity, even relief, which though it disappeared quickly was, I recalled later, the first sign.

For ten minutes, sometimes twelve, a prisoner could say anything he or she wished, knowing it would not be documented. This opportunity for privacy was an official program of the Ministry of Health, and was possible because memory was known as a highly flawed method of capturing data, as unreliable as naked observation, really. And so the Privacy Guarantors — there were six of us in Canada at the time — were never expected to recall what had been said. Nor in fact would anyone have believed us if we'd tried.

And if, as once happened to me in trying to forestall a suicide, one of us might insist on giving information to the authorities, we would be reminded that trafficking in undocumented information or the unmeasurable was suspiciously related to story-telling, and was therefore against the law. And to tell you the truth, once inmates had decided to comply with the programme, I heard so much and of such pain and complexity, that each story merged with the next and I was happy to forget.

This time, however, perhaps influenced by the speaker's great age, her intensity and the breaking of her long silence, I listened with a special attention. It was a story-telling, about a journey, about the Ministry of Culture and about a screening room there. It was also a story about art, received ideas, propaganda, memory and exile. She claimed the story was true; she persuaded me to break the law; she persuaded me to remember and to recount to others what I remembered.

I was assigned a certain number of visits to each inmate over a given period of time, each visit a maximum of twelve minutes.

I undertook to memorize her story in sections a few minutes at a time. After each visit I wrote down what I'd memorized, set it aside, and went about my business of listening and forgetting. I did my best to remember all the details, but it was difficult. The old woman was patient but we both knew there was little time left and in fact I was transferred to another constituency before we could finish. I never saw her again.

Time passed. I had had no occasion to read this odd, fragmented, incomplete tale, and I was afraid to invent an occasion, until now, that is.

As you know, the only one of the old festivals still celebrated in Canada is St. Valentine's Day. It generally falls on February the 14th, though there has been talk recently of changing it to a different date each year, a more flexible arrangement, designed to put the surprise back into romance. On St. Valentine's Day the expression of sentiment is not forbidden. It is permitted and even the custom now to retrieve part of the past and to re-enact it, often electronically, and in this way to celebrate the ritual decapitation of St. Valentine and the coupling of the birds. That is especially true in this period before the new elections when certain regressive practices are indulged and everyone is allowed to seem even adventurous.

I thought about the old woman. I began to think about the secret text. I read it from beginning to end for the first time and while still baffled, decided it was time to keep my word, no longer remembering why I'd given it, or what had seemed so urgent. Yet for my Valentine this year it seemed fitting to tell her story. So I have reconstructed from her careful account the visual details of the room she described to me and the appearance of the remaining story-tellers, and I've tried my best to retain the mood of the telling. She was old, you understand, when I met her, like an ancient broken statue, a shell of a past canon of beauty, and she tended to repeat herself, especially at first, as if I were somehow not understanding her meaning.

Electronic Valentines are uniquely personal documents, really. They are not subject to censorship for the first month following production, after which all Valentines which have not been erased voluntarily are collected for review. These are either held in a central archive, the same archive as referred to in the prisoner's story, or erased and returned. There is a third alternative: if the annual Valentine crosses boundaries of acceptability the producer forfeits the right forever to invent romance in this form. Since it is almost everyone's ambition to enter the archive people are careful to make their sentiments interesting but not too interesting.

In my transcription, I may have left some parts out of the story, and unwittingly altered others (and I deliberately omitted some of her repetitions) but here with only one or two small embellishments of my own is her story.

I wish to acknowledge the assistance of the Ministry of Health and Welfare in the carrying out of this project. Their tactful use of the Killam Foundation funds that once formed the basis of the world-famous Canada Council (now a sub-branch of the health ministry) is much appreciated in this election year. Elections are so romantic.

But first, a definition of romance: —

- an extravagant fiction, invention or story

- a fictitious narrative in prose of which the scenes and incidents are very remote from those of ordinary life

- a prose narrative, having romantic qualities or characteristics, which treats imaginary characters involved in events unrelated to everyday life, or deals with the remote in time and place, the heroic, the adventurous, and often the mysterious...

(from the Combined Oxford and Webster Dictionaries)

(And here the introductory narrative comes to an end.)

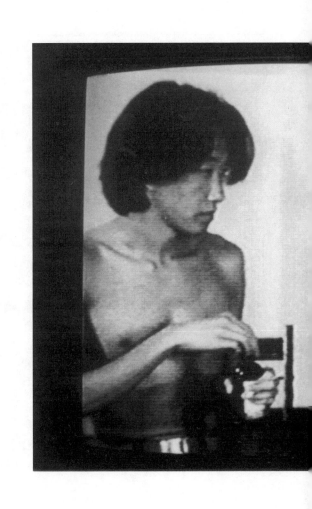

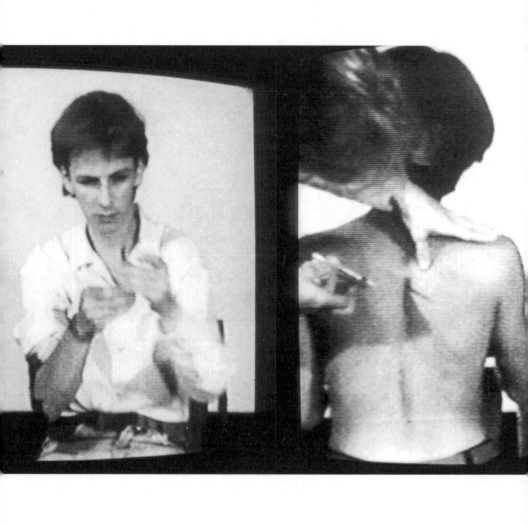

VIDEO —

ONE LITTLE WORD FOR A MANY FACETED THING

by Jean Gagnon

The term 'video' has long since entered collective consciousness. Everyone has seen at least some music videos and has a neighbourhood video store. VCRs are currently among the most popular household appliances available in Quebec. Yet, when it comes down to what video really is — confusion reigns. In fact, it is an extremely diverse and complex phenomenon, and many things we refer to as video are not — like the films at our local video store, for example, whose only video element is the tape on which they are recorded. The same is true of music videos, most of which are produced on 35mm film and only edited on videotape.

And what about 'art video' — a practice adopted by artists marginal to both visual art and cinema, and probably closer to television than to anything else. Art video overlaps with other art practices in installation and performance, and becomes conceptual when linked with interactive and computer based technologies. And what about independent video, as practiced in Quebec?

It would take far too long to clarify all these questions. I will limit myself here to a brief description of the evolution of independent video in tandem with technological developments and their increasing commercial availability, and finally, the relation between economic imperatives impacting on production and distribution, and the creation of new esthetic and cultural expressions.

UNTO US A MEDIUM IS BORN

The mid-60s saw the appearance on commercial markets of the first Sony Porta-packs — small black-and-white video cameras interfacing with half-inch reel-to-reel video recorders. This equipment complemented and competed with newly developed lightweight 16mm and Super 8 film technologies in the commercial market. Teaching institutions and film production organizations like the National Film Board of Canada (NFB) updated their equipment base accordingly. In 1971, as part of the NFB's Challenge for Change/Société nouvelle Programme, the first independent production and distribution organization devoted exclusively to video was founded in Canada, namely Vidéographe, followed shortly thereafter by the Satellite Video Exchange Society (Video Inn, 1973) in Vancouver.

Early Portapack technology was still very rudimentary, but it already possessed the basic characteristics of electronic media — simultaneous recording of image and sound on a single twenty-minute videotape, by a process involving the transformation of light impulses emanating from objects into electric signals inscribed on tape. The electric/electronic basis of video signals opened limitless possibilities for image manipulation, transformation and generation. Bill Viola, an American video artist whose works must be numbered among the most far-reaching and coherent, describes the nature of video signals in highly imagistic language — to paraphrase: "The cathode tube processes light like liquid."

Beyond these features, and the capacity to shoot and view in "real" time, video cameras are lightweight and portable, and can be linked to a monitor for instant playback, that is, simultaneous viewing of what the camera is recording. During the early pioneering phase of these technologies, Vidéographe developed an editing deck, the so-called Phase III editing unit, programmed for electronic remote control cutting, which has become a common practice today.[1]

From the very beginning, the inherent qualities of the medium led to two main trends in Canadian video. In English Canada, the tendency was towards "modernism," as associated with modernist artistic values in painting, sculpture and photography, leading to minimalism and conceptualism with their self-referential and reflexive techniques. In Quebec, the main thrust was towards developing social communications in a counter-cultural vein.

In English Canada, and at the Galerie Véhicule art in Quebec, artists began interacting with their own image, intervening in the action in what has been called 'structural video' — a technique combining continuous shooting with instant playback. This kind of video feedback focuses on exploiting the inherent properties of the medium itself.

In Quebec, because of these very properties and the user-friendly nature of video equipment, the main thrust was towards subverting dominant modes of social communication, encouraging "populist" use of video's simple, lightweight equipment, soon replaced by a new generation of home video technology. This approach led to hands-on experiments with the public accessing cameras and VCRs, and a move towards horizontal communications disrupting the hierarchic structures of main-stream media.

Frank Vitale's *Hitch-Hiking* (60 minutes), produced in Vidéographe's early days and

---

1. Andrée Duchaine, *Historique de la vidéographie au Québec: Pour une théorie de genres,* thesis for an MA in Communication Science, Université de Montréal, May 1982.

still remarkable today, provides evidence of more modernist tendencies associated with cinema. In this tape, the artist takes off hitching, alone with his camera slung over his shoulder, crosses a border, chats with a truck driver, jumps a moving train, and is lectured by a police officer for twenty minutes — all shot in real time. *Hitch-Hiking* is an early example of the links between new technologies and the esthetics they spawn.

Although it is not possible here to illustrate all the new trends that developed, it must be said that esthetics have continually been shaped and transformed by on-going technological advances.

In 1974, Sony launched a three-quarter inch colour U-matic, the first semi-professional universal format with image and sound editing features. This led to the development of new video forms, notably in fiction and narration. Since then, equipment used by artists has become increasingly sophisticated, so that it is not unusual to see artists' tapes competing with music video and television, not only technically but on the esthetic level as well.

Henceforth, however, artists' video productions cannot be analyzed without being considered as cultural products in the broader realm of television industries, and in connection with technological innovations controlled by computer industries, music and record industries, and the advertising industry — a whole range of commercial interests devoted to the production of cultural and ideological forms. By sharing the same tools as these industries, artists are influenced by a number of economic and formal parameters.

MUSIC VIDEO AND ART VIDEO

Music video is probably the most authentic form of video alongside television commercials, both of which have a promotional basis. With the creation of MTV (Music Television) in the USA, a consortium uniting American Express and Warner Communication, and its Canadian analogue Much Music, a whole related industry has grown up tapping film, television, and the music and record industries geared to youth culture, with their respective superstars. Young cultural consumers are literally being assaulted by these various industries. The cultural dimension of this development is the often astounding fragmentation of television esthetics. And, is it profitable? In 1984, MTV declared a 200% increase in ad revenues and projected expenditures of $14 million.[2] The other side of the coin, however, is that — as with Much Music in Canada — the industry adopts the radio formula of broadcasting tapes without direct payment of copyright, citing the publicity value of giving air-time

2. Dave Laing, "Music Video, Industrial Product, Cultural Form", *Screen*, Vol. 26, n. 2, March-April 1985, pp. 78-83.

to these products. It follows that channels like MTV offer no profitable outlet for video artists' productions. The independent video market is consequently very restricted, compared with the potential markets currently reached by media industries broadcasting over the air and via cable and satellite.

References to music video are essential when considering recent productions by emerging Montreal video artists who are using this form of popular cultural expression to produce highly personal works with musical content. To distinguish them from music video, I will call these works video-music. Both forms present images with music, but the difference lies in that video artists are more oriented towards promoting fantasy and poetics, displaying a musical sensitivity which allows the viewer-listener a great deal of freedom in a purely musical dimension. Further, these works are technically and formally suited to television broadcasting, indicating a desire on the part of the artists to create profitable markets for their tapes.

I am thinking here of recent works by François Girard, Bernar Hébert, Miguel Raymond, and Neam Cathod — a trained musician who effectively uses the light-energy from video monitors to create syncopated musical rhythms in *He Was Alive Now Is Dead*. François Girard's recent tape *Le train* (5 minutes) refers to both music video and fiction, associating breath and breathing with memory and dreaming in an edited sequence of fade-in-fade-outs.

Girard's work is exemplary in that he expresses more clearly than anyone else a problematic shared by emerging video artists — an emphasis on imaginative creation, on rather idealistic imaginative forms (linking breath and thought, for example), without explicit links between personal fantasy and the cultural and ideological contexts of the society which produces it. These works consititute a significant practice, refusing meaning and limiting themselves to open-ended narrative sketches, as in *Distance* (5 minutes) by Girard/Bourdon. This tape, with a soundtrack by Neam Cathod, is a poetic evocation of departure — leaving town without a destination. The refusal of meaning is doubtless a reaction to the plethora of superficial and redundant meanings in our media universe (advertising, etc.)

It is unusual for videos to be longer than thirty minutes, and music video is not the only explanation for this. Television programming provides more answers, because it is there that narrative forms are developed in short segments of five to ten minutes, as opposed to film where a story line unfolds in continuous, uninterrupted sequence. In television series and soap operas, however, each slice of time, of action and setting, is interrupted by commercials, which themselves form narrative segments. In the case of on-going series, moreover, narrations extend over several weeks, a situation which dictates specific narrative systems and imperatives.[3]

Montreal video artist Anne Ramsden is currently exploring television narrative techniques, in a series of tapes displaying highly segmented camera work. *Manufactured Romance*, a two part video — a third is in production — is a remarkable work dealing with the ideological impact of media (in this case, pulp romance) on women's experience and imagination. While adopting a soap opera approach, she also addresses television's ideological involvement in the social and imaginary constructions in our lives. With great formal consistency, these tapes adopt a series format — that of a three part mini-series — with scenes shot from relatively few angles, and narrative segments being determined by the camera whose relative immobility clearly situates the viewer as spectator.

Video and television fiction both reflect certain constraints inherent in the medium. It would probably be difficult to retain the viewer's attention on the small screen for very long, given that viewing conditions are so different from those of cinema. Video does not position the viewer before an image construed as a dreamlike sequence inciting various modes of narcissism and desire (as in fiction film), but because of its physical configuration (small screen, low image definition, electric luminosity of the image), it keeps the viewer at a distance, less implicated in and submissive to representations: "Video is an active verb (Latin: I see), and the central part of this activity is played not by the text but by the viewer."[4]

CINEMA AND VIDEO IN QUEBEC

When we have the opportunity to see English Canadian and Quebec video together, one thing is striking — cinema's influence on Quebec video. This influence is seen on several levels, as much in references to films and filmmakers (*Schème video* by Marc Paradis and Luc Bourdon, *Le chien de Luis et Salvador* by Bernar Hébert), as in production values modeled on film production techniques — shooting crews, division of labour, etc. Moreover, the very texture of the images, in terms of lighting and composition, and the editing structures and dynamics, are all strongly reminiscent of film, especially in videos coming out of la Coop vidéo de Montréal and Vidéographe.

3. *Visible Fictions: Cinema, Television, Video*, by John Ellis, deals with these subjects in detail. Routledge and Kegan Paul, London UK, 1983

4. Sean Cubitt, *Box Pop*, vol. 26, n.2, March-April 1985, p. 86. My translation.

We should nevertheless not be misled — video artists do not want to make electronic cinema and are by no means doing so. The electronic medium possesses its own qualities leading them to other shores inhabited by the imagination and narrative modes. For example, an inherent possibility of video is the insertion of images within an image, which leads to a type of editing process within the frame itself, instead of juxtaposing different frames and shots. There are also a whole range of possibilities to create electronic décor, which Paul Gauvin explores in his recent tape *Chacun pour elle*, as well as techniques such as inlaying — not to mention the whole area of analog and digital special effects, some of which can be seen in tapes by Montreal video artist Richard Raxlen.

Another matter worthy of note is the Quebec government's recognition of video in Bill 109, relating to cinema, which reads: "film — a work produced by technical means and resulting in a cinematographic effect whatever the physical support may be." Thus, the law no longer distinguishes between film and video as regards the means by which images are recorded and distributed. Such legal recognition had already become imperative, because of the rapid expansion of film distribution on video cassettes and the need to control this activity.

It is only very recently that the film production sector has realized the technological impact of video, which it perceives either as a powerful competitor on its own turf, or as an opportunity to rationalize and capitalize on exorbitant film production costs.

This new awareness on the part of film producers was heralded by a conference, Convergence video/film, held in Montreal right after Vidéo 84, at which film users were introduced to electronic image technologies. This convergence, although genuine and desirable, could eclipse many other developments, beginning with the specificity of work produced by video artists exploring their preferred medium.

There is still a great deal of confusion about the law and the role of the Société général du cinéma (SGC). In practice, to get SGC funding an artist must already be recognized by the SGC as an experienced producer. Consequently, almost all emerging video artists have devised the scheme of working for their own production companies (Zone Productions, Agent Orange, G.R.A.A.V., Virton, among others). Yet, they are still regarded with some suspicion by the SGC. All of this further complicates the funding situation, and for the time being, assistance is almost exclusively provided by the Canada Council. Those artists who do manage to get SGC funding have recognized sponsors like ACPAV, Vidéographe, and similar organizations.

NFB programmes, in the new Guy Favreau Complex, and plans by the Cinémathèque québécoise to program and archive video tapes, are necessary but long overdue steps in the right direction which, in the final analysis, have been dictated by the economic situation and the current dynamics of the media involved. Basically, these organizations simply don't want to miss the boat.

While such decisions on the part of film institutions may be beyond reproach in themselves, a lot remains to be done. The public must be educated with accurate information about video, its history and its esthetics. The Cinema and Photography Department at Concordia University has set up a summer course in art video (Film Studies) under Bruce Ferguson. But the experiment could lead nowhere and remain a "special topic". At the Interface II exhibit in April/May 1985, showcasing visual arts students at McGill, UQAM, and Concordia, the video section was pitiful, on both the technical and esthetic levels. Clearly, where video experiments are allowed in multi-media and studio arts courses, there is a serious lack of technical apprenticeship in the medium, even though some universities can boast amazingly well-equipped television studios. And this is not all. These students have no idea of the history of video esthetics or the content of most current video production.

Translation by Jean-Luc Svoboda.

CORPUS LOQUENDI (BODY FOR SPEAKING)

BODY-CENTRED VIDEO IN HALIFAX 1972-1982

by Jan Peacock

FRAMING

The moment of any cultural shift is difficult to map, but in a decade resolutely committed to the avant-garde, to questioning institutional knowledge and the nature of information, and to the production of "ephemera", residual tracks often emerge only in congruencies among individual recollections. Add to these difficulties that early videotape was an unstable storage system (so that much of the earliest work has completely deteriorated), and that a theft of equipment and valuable tapes took place at the Nova Scotia College of Art & Design in 1972, eliminating some of the earliest experiments with video in Halifax.

It is almost certain that Halifax artists' first contact with video occurred at the Nova Scotia College of Art & Design around 1969. Former students remember that Larry Eaton, the college's librarian at its old Coburg Road campus, had a closet in the library which held a Kodak instamatic, a 16mm film camera and splicer, and a video camera with a Sony CV-series open reel video recorder. This constituted NSCAD's first "Audio/Visual Department."

Garry Kennedy, the *enfant terrible* of college presidents, had arrived at NSCAD in 1967, fired a good number of the faculty, and proceeded to reconstruct the institution in his own image. Many of those he hired were American artists, some of whom he had encountered as a graduate student at Ohio University. He brought with him fellow graduate students Gerald Ferguson, Walter Ostrom and Pat Kelly. In 1968, David Askevold was hired as an instructor in sculpture.

Originally a painter, Askevold was producing anodized metal sculpture at the time. In 1969, he initiated the Projects Class, which brought in well-known artists to run art projects with the students. Askevold remembers that the first visitor to the Projects Class was Dan Graham, who was using video to document his performance work. Ian Murray, Douglas Waterman, Richards Jarden (who became Chair of the Studio Division in 1973), Terrill Seltzer, and Tim Zuck were among the small group which formed the first Projects Class. Like Graham, many of them were also using video as a way of documenting performance work.

Some of the students working with video through the early to mid-1970s were Robin Peck, John Watt, Dorit Cypis, Connie Urban, Charles Saunders, Graham Dubé, Wally Brannen, Dennis Gill, Jon Young, Bruce Winn, Jim Goss, Colette Urban, Bruce Campbell and Brian MacNevin. Faculty members Ferguson, Kelly, Bruce Parsons and Harold Pearse, and Anna Leonowens director Allan Harding MacKay likewise did some video work in the performance/document vein.

Much of this early video work was exhibited at NSCAD's Mezzanine Gallery, then under the directorship of Charlotte Townsend Gault, and at the Anna Leonowens Gallery. A comprehensive collection of video works produced at NSCAD was assembled under the title "The Vancouver Tapes" in 1973, and was sent as part of an ongoing exchange of work with artists and students in Vancouver.

Over the next three years, there were also several New York exhibitions (in galleries and in downtown loft spaces) of video work by NSCAD students and faculty. It was, perhaps, this exposure that enlarged NSCAD's international reputation as a centre of video experimentation, along with the appearance of magazine articles on the school by Jack Burnham (*Arts* 48:55-7, Nov. 1973), Eric Cameron (*Studio* 188:245-8, Dec. 1974) and Les Levine (*Art in America* 61:15, July 1973), all of whom had been visitors to the college.

Askevold's first experiment with video was the tape *Fill* (20 min.), made at NSCAD in 1971.

"The performer stands directly behind the bare video mike. He reaches off camera and returns with a piece of tin foil which he crushes around the head of the mike. The sound is extremely loud. On top of the first ball of foil he crushes a second and a third (while the sound decreases) and a fourth, etc. until the ball increases to a size that fills the screen. At this point, the process in reversed, with the sound getting continually louder again as the size of the foil decreases. The piece ends when the mike is uncovered." (Artist's Statement)

In 1972, former student Dorit Cypis recalls, "I was walking down the hallway by the library and saw Vito Acconci sitting there biting himself." This was to be one of the projects carried out in NSCAD's Lithography Workshop (the bites were inked and printed). (Later, Gerald Ferguson got Acconci to bite him on the leg and had the bite mark inked as a permanent tattoo.)

When he left the college to work for a year in England in 1972, Askevold arranged for Dan Graham, Dennis Oppenheim, Vito Acconci, and James Lee Byars to take his place in teaching the Projects Class.

Martha Wilson, who had been a graduate student at Dalhousie University, taught English at NSCAD from 1972 to 1974, and executed all her early video work there. She is remembered (along with Mira Schor and Mimi Shapiro) as one of very few strong female presences in the school in the early 1970s.

From September 1971 to June 1972, Ian Murray initiated and ran the Fourth Floor Gallery in an abandoned building on Halifax's waterfront, part of the rambling complex of buildings that in 1974 became (and still is) the NSCAD campus. Murray remembers that Dan Graham's earliest performance video pieces were produced and exhibited there. Murray capitalized on the energetic presence of visitors, instructors and students at NSCAD, mounting a different exhibition every two weeks. Among others on the prodigious list of exhibitors were Alan Sondheim, Jan Dibbets, Doug Waterman, Robert Smithson, Gerald Ferguson, Sol LeWitt, Graham Dubé, Tim Zuck, Al McNamara, Garry Kennedy, Richards Jarden, Bruce Nauman, Lee Lozano, and James Lee Byars.

Following the closure of the Fourth Floor Gallery, Murray continued similar programming when he curated for the Mezzanine Gallery and the Anna Leonowens Gallery from 1972 to 1973.

Other venues for artists' video were beginning to show up in Halifax in the early 1970s. The Student Union Gallery at Dalhousie University had unusual programming, including video and performance, during 1970 and 1971 when Paul Ledoux (now a well-known playwright) was curator.

In the fall of 1972, a collective of Toronto women filmmakers including Sylvia Spring, Deanne Taylor and Kay Armatage began work towards a hugely comprehensive festival of historical and contemporary film, video and photography by women. Within a few months, they had a national organizing committee of over 200 women working in 19 Canadian cities to which the festival would tour.

The local tour coordinators in Halifax were Jay MacLean (a NSCAD student), Betty Glenister and Susan Perly. The *Women and Film (1896-1973) International Festival* toured Canada throughout the summer of 1973, arriving at the Rebecca Cohn Auditorium of Dalhousie University in late June.

For women students at the male-dominated NSCAD, *Women and Film* opened a window onto an unknown history, exposing them to hundreds of feature films, videos, experimental, animated and documentary works by women.

In 1972, the CRTC forced Canadian cable licensees to open local community access channels. Halifax Cablevision became the first "high end" production facility in the city to which artists could claim access. Series featuring work by video artists were *Changing Channels* (thirteen hour-long shows produced by Ian Murray in 1975 and 1976) and *The Howard Show* (eight interview-format shows produced by Jim Goss in 1979 and 1980). In the novel and promising days of cablecast, these shows became immensely popular.

Also in 1973, the Video Theatre began to take shape at the National Film Board. Originally set up with funding from the Canada Council to provide local artists with access to video production facilities, in actuality the Video Theatre emerged as more of an in-house video operation of the NFB, with little interest in art and artists. Ian Murray remembers the set up as being "incredibly bureaucratic:" "If you wanted to have a screening there, you had to have the audience fill out these NFB 'audience response' questionnaires."

Episodes of *Changing Channels* were cablecast at the Video Theatre to audiences of interested viewers who didn't have cable service. After the show, lectures, video and audio tapes were often presented to round out the evening. Audience members were not required to fill out the response forms.

It soon became clear that the Video Theatre was not fulfilling its mandate of production access to artists. Tom Sherman, then Video Officer at the Canada Council, came to Halifax to check out the situation, and would eventually phase out funding to the organization by 1981, meanwhile encouraging the formation of the Centre for Art Tapes.

Brian MacNevin, a video artist who had worked as a student assistant at NSCAD to Audio/Visual Director Fred McFadzen in 1972, and who had also programmed video work at the Video Theatre, was instrumental in setting up the Centre for Art Tapes. Originally, MacNevin had negotiated to have CFAT housed alongside Eye Level Gallery on Barrington Street, but when the directorship of Eye Level changed, the deal was abandoned.

With the timely support of the late Gordon Parsons (then the coordinator of the Atlantic Filmmakers Coop), CFAT opened its doors as an exhibition space for photography, performance and video in September 1977 in a building shared with the Atlantic Filmmakers Coop on Argyle Street. Early CFAT exhibitors included Jim Goss, Nora Hutchinson, Robert Hamon, Taka Iimura, Clive Robertson, Douglas Waterman, Dan Graham, Susan Britton and Dara Birnbaum.

MacNevin worked as CFAT's director until his departure from Halifax in 1979, and Ed Slopek became the new director. With the continued encouragement of Tom Sherman at the Canada Council, Slopek and Bruce Campbell worked over the next two years to equip the Centre for video production. Cathy Quinn assumed the position of director in 1981. Actual access to artist producers began in June 1983, when CFAT relocated in the Alexandra Centre, an abandoned public school building in Brunswick Street.

In 1977, Peggy Gale, then working at Art Metropole and doing independent curatorial work, guest curated the exhibition *In Video* at Dalhousie Art Gallery, in cooperation with Bruce Ferguson, then the director of Dalhousie Art Gallery. One of the first shows to present a cogent critical view of the full breadth of American and Canadian video practice, *In Video* featured work by many artists who had influenced and participated in video's development in Halifax, including Vito Acconci, David Askevold, Susan Britton, Eric Cameron, Dan Graham, and Doug Waterman.

Meanwhile, throughout the decade, the prodigious flow of visiting artists, faculty and students producing video continued at NSCAD. What former NSCAD president Garry Kennedy had characterized as an interest that "seems to have tapered off" by 1973 (*Artscanada*, October 1973), merely seems to have changed its complexion in ways that made it invisible to the prevailing aesthetic.

Within the NSCAD student body, women were mobilizing to broaden awareness of the international influence of women artists working in film, photography and video — a phenomenon that was scarcely mentioned at NSCAD. The significance of the fact that women were drawn to working in 'alternative' and 'experimental' media like video lay in the idea that no histories have been written, no rules laid down, no canons established.

In 1976, the late Barbara England, then an MFA student, wrote a paper called "An Examination of Masculinism at NSCAD." The paper was widely circulated in the college and galvanized the students to demand changes in the faculty, the visiting artists program, and the curriculum.

Martha Rosler made several visits to the college during this period, teaching, showing her work in video and supplying a feminist critique of both art and its institutions.

In 1978, Dara Birnbaum made the first of many visits to the college, which culminated in five video works produced between 1978 and 1980 with the assistance of Fred McFadzen, Ed Slopek and Allan Scarth. She was also assisted by Madelaine Palko, a video artist and former NSCAD student, then working as a production assistant at Halifax Cablevision.

In 1980, Meredith Bell, a student on the recently established Women's Affairs Committee, started the Women Lifesize Video and Film series, which received college and Student Union funds to invite such guests as film critic Ruby Rich and filmmaker Yvonne Rainer.

Kathleen Tetlock, an MFA student who later came to work as a technician and instructor at NSCAD's Audio/Visual facility, offered a course in 1981 called "Socialist/Feminist Criticism of Art and Culture." The following year Marion Barling, a Vancouver film and videomaker, taught a similar course, as well as a video workshop in which Tetlock, Meredith Bell, Carla Murray, Heather Allin and Wendy Geller were students.

Through pressure from the Women's Affairs Committee, the College Council created two new faculty positions for women. Wilma Needham and I were appointed to the Intermedia Area of the Studio Division in the summer of 1982.

Much of the video work in the late 1970s and early 1980s remained body-centred, opening itself to further investigations of identity of self and culture through narrative, personal documentary and performance. But amid the growing network of exhibition and production spaces for video artists, a generational shift in video art practice was taking place.

Gone from the scene were artists who occasionally picked up a video camera, but whose more recognized work was carried out in other media. What had emerged in Halifax, across Canada and internationally, was an area of artistic production with its own specialized interests, language, institutions, and practitioners.

DIRT ON THE LENS: NOTES ON THE REVISIONIST PROJECT

It is important to note from the outset that I have not arranged or 'programmed' the video works in this exhibition in relation to any of the section titles which I use in this writing (RAW, DUMB, RUDE AND LEWD, SELF-INDULGENT AND NARCISSISTIC, and BORING), which are only intended to identify overlapping points of discussion in much of the work. For this reason, the works in the exhibition each appear on separate videotapes (rather than grouped together), and their corresponding written descriptions appear as loose, individual "one-sheets" in the catalogue folder, separated from the curatorial essay and easily rearranged by the reader.

These choices reveal my larger questions about undertaking a "revisionist project," about identifying the position from which I am looking at this material and my goals in doing so — my "agenda," as it were.

Revisionist projects are critical re-examinations enacted in a social, cultural and historical context which is necessarily different from the context in which the works under examination were produced to be seen. They are often regarded as attempts to rewrite history, this pronouncement proceeding from the assumption that there exists an "original" history of the work, which is more accurately descriptive of the work, more authentic, and therefore more authoritative.

My favourite piece of revisionist writing is "The Aesthetics of Indifference," an article written by Moira Roth for *Artforum* in 1976. In it, Roth situates the work and Duchampian personae of Jasper Johns, Robert Rauschenberg, and Merce Cunningham amid the social and cultural ethos of McCarthyism, as a way of speculating about their cool, intellectual 'disengagement,' a kind of Dadaist refusal to participate in the irrational logic of the world-at-hand, and a further refusal to have their efforts scrutinized within it. Roth speculates that the esoteric peculiarity of their work may have been a kind of 'coding' which kept the radical nature of their ideas from looking subversive.

I remembered what I knew about McCarthyism, and thought about how intellectuals were targeted by it. One didn't need to be 'political:' one had only to be out there. And to be homosexual (as Rauschenberg, Johns and Cunningham were) surely was to be 'out there' in the most subversive way.

I also remembered the essentially formalist writing which surrounded the work of that time, and thought how little it seemed to speak to me of the work at hand, and how perhaps it too was involved in an almost involuntary form of 'coding.' Roth's thesis was almost entirely speculation — revisionism of the most questionable sort — and yet it has stayed with me in a way that has changed my point of view about those artists.

Does *Corpus Loquendi* seek to rewrite history? It does, insofar as all history is newly written in its moment and from a point of view. Even as I acknowledge the limits of my own position — as a maker of video work who was a young art student in London, Ontario when most of the work in this exhibition was made — I want to outline the limits of the positions from which that 'original' history was made. They were not neutral positions (this is impossible), nor were they comprehensive (merely improbable).

For instance, it is now largely acknowledged that early performance, body art and video saw the participation of an unprecedented number of women artists. Their 'in' to the artworld after years of exclusion was characterized by their insistence on the vitality of intimate subject matter and personal narrative. They were not using the body as a formal element; as Lucy Lippard put it. "When women use their own bodies in their work, they are using their selves." ("The Pains and Pleasures of Rebirth: Women's Body Art," *Art in America* 64:73-81, May 1976)

And yet, in Halifax, at the height of this international activity, and at the institution best positioned to be aware of it — the relentlessly 'avant-garde' Nova Scotia College of Art & Design — the vast majority of visitors and faculty (even those involved in performance, body art and video) continued to be men. (By the academic year 1976-77, the situation had improved: 19 of the 76 invited visitors were women, and 6 women — 3 of them artists — were among 46 full-time faculty.)

So, even though the stylistic markers of this work were, on the whole, international and did cross genders in unprecedented ways, its 'received' history (in Halifax, at least) is marked by institutional aberrations of this kind.

Even the stated intentions of artists get continually revised by the artists themselves over the years. They, too, are subject to all kinds of influences — art propaganda, trendiness, *Zeitgeist* — whose argots or 'shop talk' they may use to account for their oeuvre-du-jour, but whose effect on the work may be temporal rather than integral to it outside of the moment.

My way of revisioning the work in this exhibition — the "dirty lens" I am holding up to it — is motivated by the words which appear here as section titles. At the time of their production, these tapes were surrounded by such words: self-indulgent, boring, etc.

I am interested by the fact that, in current art practice, much use has been made of "the body" without any such dismissive words being applied, and with little historical acknowledgment of this earlier art work which located the body at its centre. It seems that, finally, this new work is seen to have social, cultural and political import, largely because the issues of AIDS, sexual identity, gender equality, reproductive rights, the right to die, physical and sexual abuse, and censorship have created a climate of urgency in which it simply is no longer arguable that the body is contested territory. This is a revelation, but it is hardly new.

Writing on the performance work of Shawna Dempsey and Lorri Millan in a recent issue of *Canadian Theatre Review* (vol. 76, Fall 1993), Susan Bennett points out that, "If the body is bound as a medium of culture, the question of who gets the opportunity to direct such a powerful medium is an obviously crucial one."

One might surmise that, in less discursive tones, this same question was being asked by the generation of artists who watched Vietnam, the F.L.Q. crisis and Anita Bryant on TV, but the connections are rarely made. Then, as now, social conditions prepared the body for us as the metaphoric site of both self-initiated and unwelcome interventions.

Art criticism in the 1970s (with feminist and Marxist criticism providing the notable exceptions) was still a formalist enterprise. Its language and approach to art ill-equipped it to ask questions of body-centred work which would postulate it for a social site. Still, investigations of the body and identity through video were taking place everywhere, and it is simply unrealistic to imagine that such a critically unpopular project could have gathered momentum without some shared concerns among its practitioners that amounted to a social as well as an artistic context.

So I have set out to reclaim the words used to diminish this early body-centred video work, in order to reexamine why the work looked the way it did, and to speculate about its role in relation to contemporary work.

DUMB

The "birth" of video art has become a kind of folk tale familiar to all video artists: in New York in 1965, the Fluxus artist Nam June Paik bought the first Sony Portapack — the first on North American soil, and the first portable video equipment ever to fall into the hands of an artist. The story goes that Paik recorded

"At present, most art is discussed in relation to the art which immediately preceded it and that with which it is contemporary... Art which involves personal experiences evidences a real change. Persistence, private space, illness, solipsism, are kinds of content which are not usually discussed or considered relevant to the work in which they appear. Performance art has come full circle from the concerns of minimal painting and sculpture and reassessed the very real connection of art to life."

— Rosemary Mayer, "Performance and Experience," ARTS 48; pp 33-36, Nov. 1973

"We see the world as being outside ourselves, even though it is only a mental representation of it that we experience inside ourselves. Therefore, any medium that represents the world on a 2-D surface removes that mental representation one step further.

I find the inherent qualities of video make it the best medium to experiment with this 'outside' and 'inside' process of seeing."

—Brian MacNevin, video artist and Founding Coordinator of the Centre for Art Tapes in Halifax, offered these remarks in the press release for a showing of his video work *Landscape Tracing* at Eye Level Gallery in 1978.

"...the video picture cannot accommodate environmental scale...Neither physical nor social scale fits the cathode-ray tube, at least not yet. Video documentary is best focused in on a single image or idea."

— Douglas Davis, "Video Obscura," *Artforum* 10: 64-71, April 1972

"Man's 'never-ending dialogue with himself and the world around him' could never have taken place before he had received valuable information about the world and the self from dialogues with others. To assume, therefore, that one's body is the primary source for understanding facts would be as naive as to believe that our knowledge of the world comes from spirits."

— Nicolas Calas, "Bodyworks and Porpoises," *Artforum* 16: pp. 33-7, June 1978

his way downtown in a taxicab, shooting out the window, then played back the tape when he arrived at the Cafe A Go Go in Greenwich Village. This was the first "video art."

Every time I hear this story I think about what a dumb birth this was, and wonder how anyone could have thought it a good idea to pursue the medium as a result. But, as with all folk tales, you accept it as apocryphal, enshrined as a symbolic marker of video's beginnings rather than an actual account. But symbolic of what?

First, there was the phenomenal immediacy of the medium and the sense of it as a 'mirror' — that you could look at yourself looking a moment after the event, with no dividing line of memory: that you could split the present into two different 'nows,' and inhabit both of them.

There was the sense of the medium as a register of the 'real,' an identifying eye which could train us to travel anywhere, to surveil our bodies as we had never seen them, to detail states of mind and enumerate unconscious behaviors. The inventory was vast and miniscule, metaphoric and mundane.

Any idea can be made dumb by telling it out loud. And early video, with its dully clinical, here-it-is look did little to finesse its images into veiled mysteries.

Photographic documents share something of this problem. There is an early performance work by Vito Acconci called *Performance Test* where he seats himself in front of an audience and proceeds to make (and hold) eye contact with each and every person in the crowd, seat by seat, row by row. I think of this as an irreducible and profound emblem of the goal of all performance work, all theater and, indirectly, all of art, literature and music. "Only connect."

This work survives as a single, black and white photograph of a man staring without expression. It is irreducibly and profoundly dumb, but equipped with it, I can imagine that performance into being.

Video, as a medium, is naked of expression. It is a dumbly empathic tool that merely invites connection.

RAW

Artists working in a variety of media in the 1970s came to see working in the video medium as a way of making a symbolically direct and 'pure' form of contact with time, idea, voice, body, eye and the world-at-large. Mirroring the then current concerns of performance, body art, earth and process art, work in video took on a stark bareness, which has generally been located — but only uncomfortably and never convincingly — within minimalist aesthetics. The look and sense of video work was more broadly linked with the decade's 'laboratory' consciousness: the pursuit of a new language and its dialects which would connect the artist with the viewer while taking account of how such transactions are always (irrevocably) mediated.

Video was distinct from the 'pure' language of minimalism by virtue of its lack of interest in product. Many works began as studio exercises which were sometimes kept and sometimes erased so that the tape stock could be reused for new ideas. The methods and images themselves seemed, initially at least, so ephemeral, so definitively temporal as to defy association with the world of objects and painted images. Even the sculptors and painters who experimented with video tended to behave differently with it, recognizing the pointlessness of placing their usually stringent aesthetic demands on such a rudimentary rendering tool.

Given video's patent shortage of expressive traits, it made sense that artists would speak less of 'creating'

Individuality is the way to emancipation. On this basis the result of his work is of no account to the artist. No longer is he concerned to present something finished. No longer does he feel compelled to create 'works for posterity'. The creative, the art process is the focal point.

— Klaus U. Reinke, "Video Artists", *Studio* 183; pp. 85-6, Feb. 1972.

"We have already distinguished the scientist and the 'bricoleur' by the inverse functions as they assign to events and structures and ends and means, the scientist creating events (changing the world) by means of structures and the bricoleur creating structures by means of events."

— Claude Lévi-Strauss in *Time and Free Will*, Henri Bergson, Harper and Row, NY 1960, p. 23

"Video's organization of experience and information is tied to its immediacy and intimate, human scale... Video does not strive for filmic climax or dramatic narrative sequence. It seeks to instantaneously picture uninterrupted, even awkward sequences of subtly unconscious movements, to record the raw accident or unrefined crudity of closely scrutinized behavior."

— Carol Zemel, "Women and Video," *Artscanada*, pp.30-40, October 1973

than of 'investigating,' making full use of its homely, empirical look, and setting up situations that more often felt like controlled experiments than stories. The element of narrative was there, though, usually disguised as an unfolding process, a pattern of evolving repetition, a gradual accumulation of detail, or, simply, the inevitable ruminations arising from time spent doing nothing. To 'express' these in conventional narrative terms would have been to embellish what was already seen to be happening. (Recall the conceptual artists' battle against 'tautology', defined as the material expression of stated visual ideas.)

One must also take account of the artists' reactions to the two major aesthetic frameworks affecting visual production at the time: the sleek formalism of 'high art' and the glossy salesmanship of commercial television. (While video art was periodically given token representation in both television and art establishments, it remained an eccentric and unruly relative of both and still has never been wholly embraced by either.)

Many artists were ideologically and/or philosophically motivated to not produce objects at all — though posterity has shown that dealers can sell anything. A renewed interest in Dada (via the Fluxus movement) and a rising consciousness of "commodity fetishism" in the art establishment (via the Art & Language group) supplied conceptually-based artists with reasons to be friendly towards video. Similarly, no one wanted to be caught making television, and with the state of video technology then available to artists, there was no danger of that.

RUDE AND LEWD

You won't find quotations here (or perhaps anywhere) that accuse early video art of lewd, rude or otherwise obscene conduct. Such qualifications didn't surface until bodies became truly 'dangerous' (e.g. gay, abused, anorexic, etc.). When Vito Acconci fantasizes about what he would do with President Kennedy's head, or when Eric Cameron spanks and berates a female model, the general response is to deride the artists as macho, narcissistic, or just plain boring.

Only recently, where artists and art critics have explored texts by writers like Georges Bataille and de Sade, is a somewhat sanitized, academic allowance made for disclosures of "transgressive desire."

There is no doubt that, in less discursive clothing, "transgressive desire" sparked body and performance artists' attention to the ready voyeurism and onanism of the video apparatus. The content of early video work often turned upon the artist's 'problematizing' of a relationship with a hypothetical viewer. The artist/performer often ignored the viewer while carrying out a self-isolating and self-propelling action, or, conversely, intruded on the viewer by making inappropriate confessions, demands and physical disclosures (a fantasy relationship with the viewer). Generally, body artists were hogging the screen, controlling the time we spent looking at them.

As part of their reaction to the slick artifice and industrial fabrication which characterized both T.V. and formalist object-making, video artists took up radical positions on the video document as a 'private trace' in 'public space.' Since the content and look of the work needed to reflect their sense of making something that no one necessarily desired to see, aesthetic considerations were withheld and aesthetic experiences of the work were rudely denied as irrelevant.

The terminology of 'public and private' used by body artists preceded the art world's involvement in issues of censorship. Rather than discuss the motives behind

"Video has often been accused of narcissism, or at least those using the medium have been so accused, but with these works the issue is less one of self-love than of self-exposure."

— Peggy Gale, "I am Here, This is Real," in the catalogue *Autobiography*, Art Gallery of Ontario, Nov. 1978

"My girlfriend, Sybil, she said I was becoming narcissistic. I like to say self-referential... She advised me to take up tennis, take French lessons, anything. Everyone insisted there was a whole world out there...Yeah, sure."

— from *Love Hurts*, videotape by Susan Britton, 1977

"The more the individual is forced to recognize his/her own helplessness to change the conditions in society, the more we are reduced to aesthetic principles that refer to us rather than those which refer to (and by implication categorize and control) the external reality of objects and forces. We dictate our aesthetic involvements.

> "We no longer accept the more general aesthetics of abstract expressionism, minimal art, etc., as meaningful... I think this kind of aesthetic, based so strongly in personal experience and association is a means of achieving aesthetic independence and self-referentiality."
>
> —Adrian Piper quoted in Rosemary Mayer, "Performance and Experience," ARTS 48: pp. 33-36, Nov. 1973

> "...filmmaking involves long delays, during which the work more than once disappears into the dark night of the mind and the laboratory. I remember, on the other hand, the first time I ever used video. I made a piece, a half-hour long, in one continuous take. Then I rewound the notation, and saw my work right away. That was three years ago and to tell the truth, some part of my puritanical filmmaker's nature remains appalled to this day. The gratification was so intense and immediate that I felt confused. I felt I might be turning into a barbarian...or maybe even a musician."
>
> — Hollis Frampton, "The Withering Away of the State of the Art," *Artforum*, 13:50-5, Dec. 1974

confrontational work and the uneven power relations it laid bare, discussion about such work tended to focus on the body as a formal (sculptural) element. Tensions tended to be treated as spatial rather than social. Or, it was said that the artist was establishing "psychological distance" or "proximity" with the viewer, much as a sculptor would.

But in what social site were such relations being investigated? How had acts of intimacy and isolation, covering and exposure, confrontation and indiscretion, become such common vocabulary for delineating the space of the artist/performer from the space of the viewer?

Clearly, such pointed and idiosyncratic actions had to have been carried out in a time and place where their significance as gestures would be apparent. But, for an audience whose concerns turned on the viability of the work of art as a disembodied aesthetic experience, body-centred work was an unwelcome and unseemly disruption, seen to point more to itself than to the conditions which produced it.

SELF-INDULGENT AND NARCISSISTIC

While prevailing aesthetic, technical and structural issues helped to define the uses and absences of voice in 1970s video, it is also important to examine speaking and silence as individual responses to social structures, political events and power relations.

Withdrawal from social interaction, refusal to speak and Me-generation navel-gazing and self-narration may not be responses to power as potent as, say, aggressive public confrontation or penetration of the media hierarchy. But they are, nonetheless, responses to power. One need only consider Vito Acconci — who, by turns, screamed into the camera and gagged himself — to understand 'binding' and 'release' as mutually reinforcing gestures enacted in full sight of the authorities.

Recent feminist criticism has employed psychoanalytic theory to revalue the construct of "narcissism" as part of a necessary process of retrieval. Such 'identity work' encounters (and counters) all manner of socially valued behaviors, revealing the mechanisms which suppress those behaviors which are not valued.

Descriptions of the self begin with a moment of self-recognition which is different from all other moments. It occurs at a point which is synchronous with a disconnection from the body as culturally-bound message-bearer, and which is followed immediately by another moment in which we are reconstituted, precisely and painfully, as that very thing.

What has shifted in this indefinable interval is the locus and function of the 'mirror' we have always used: from unarticulated sites within the body — where it can only reflect and affirm our largely unconscious internalizing of behaviors and values — to a traceable network of institutional, familial and historical sites of influence that is external to the body.

Dorit Cypis practices styles of laughter in front of the video monitor, Martha Wilson applies make-up to exaggerate her best and worst features, and Susan Britton presents herself as a prostitute.

Using the video camera to look outward at the same time as seeing oneself being seen (both literally and symbolically) makes an explicit diagram of that pivotal moment of estrangement from, and uneasy reconnection with, the world.

Given such a reflexive construct, empathetic response on the part of a viewer, while not irrelevant, may be of secondary importance. The charge of self-indulgence, then, would seem to flow from the position of a viewer

"I have not made video since March 1972. It was never a specific decision to stop. I did realize at the time that each subsequent piece required more and more decisions about how to remove myself."

— Stephen Cruise (statement in the catalogue of Dalhousie Art Gallery, curated by Philip Fry, April 1976)

"There are structures that limit things. An art work might be a means to see and examine possibilities that these structures have eliminated. So I use art as an instrument to break through these structures...In some ways I leave out the object in the phrase 'I do art' so it comes to the fact that 'I do'."

— Vito Acconci from Cindy Nemser, "An Interview with Vito Acconci," *Art Magazine*, March 1971.

This is a real-time videotape. The performance you are watching has occurred is occurring in real time your time no editing.

— text from *Sequences/Night Video*, a videotape by Douglas Davis, 1971

"Human time is psychological. It is not measured out in equal pieces like a surveyor does land. Time contracts, expands, stops and starts according to human experience of it. Later it is altered to accommodate the memory of that experience. In my work over the last few years I use Time as a totally conceptual material. If time is an invention of my mind, I am free to travel into any smaller subset of it I choose, like the 18th or 19th centuries, say. Why should I be bound by the conventions of science? They have, after all, invented these for their convenience, not mine."

—Eleanor Antin, in the catalogue *Time*, Philadelphia College of Art, 1977

who feels cast in the role of witness — a third party observer, excluded from the closed loop of looking that is integral to the working of the work. What is really at issue is our sense of abandonment, of having been left with no mirror of our own.

BORING

Much discussion of 1970s video has revolved around its 'real time' aesthetic. Two factors are generally credited for its emergence: the fact that editing equipment was neither affordable nor available to artists, and the fact that the same equipment *was* affordable and available to commercial T.V. production (*"Video's Frightful Grandparent."* as critic David Antin once called it).

In the first time scenario, the artists' 'formalist' response to video's inherent materiality is evoked; in the second instance, the artist assumes a culturally iconoclastic role, bent on denying video art's consumability.

It is also possible to see in video time clear links with the inclusiveness and closure of process art, systems art, language-based conceptual art and earth works: establish a system or frame (of movement, of language...) and play out all its possibilities as if "emptying out" the frame. For video artists, the parameters of their "system" included the fact of the physical running time of a tape (a half-hour or hour) whose gradualness and apparent objectivity provided an appropriate frame for repeated or ritualized action.

But the closest relative of the treatment of time in this period of video art is found in performance and dance work of the same period. Deliberate, uninflected and unremarkable actions culled from everyday life ("found movement," as Yvonne Rainer called it) were not so much elevated as they were simply attended to, clarified and allowed to play themselves out. Often, the only restriction placed upon such actions in video was the physical duration of a reel of tape. The presumption was of a kind of 'found' time, a duration which asked for no expressive or subjective decision-making, a time which needed no author.

But didn't television, too, have prescribed durations which were not individually negotiated? The 30-second commercial, the half-hour newscast, the hour-long drama? This kind of time, invented by advertisers and programmers, was shaped by predictable sequences of events which formed the narrative formulae of the shows ("network trivia", as Douglas Davis called it in 1972).

Early video works might be records of predictable events, but the events themselves — rather than any superimposed narrative structure — tend to determine the time in which we look at them. There is minimal (if any) rehearsal; things look and feel as much like real life as they can.

We are at a cynical remove from ideas such as that of John Cage's Zen teacher, who advised him, "If it bores you, do it again. If it still bores you, do it again. Keep doing it until it is no longer boring." In a media-based culture, where the abbreviated image of an experience has become preferable to the experience itself, physical time has become denatured, unbearably attenuated and drab.

If we have internalized this response as reflex, then the time used in early video work is, indeed, boring.

"If the purpose of some of the bodywork performances is really to provide reflexive information, why don't these artists perform in private and inform the public about the content?... Bodyworkers placed high hopes on the videotape as a vehicle for conveying their message...But video merely follows step-by-step progress in movement, which does not automatically make of such a recording a significant artistic event."
— Nicolas Calas, "Bodyworks and Porpoises," *Artforum* 16; pp. 33-7, June 1978

" To facilitate really close perception a process should happen very gradually... so slowly and gradually that listening to it resembles watching a minute hand on a watch..."
— Steve Reich in the catalogue *Anti-Illusions: Procedures/Materials*, 1969

"For me, Lee Lozano made the most useful statement on time. "To increase the accuracy of your perception multiply by T.'"
— Steven Kaltenbach in the catalogue *TIME*, Philadelphia College of Art, 1977

Daring Documents:

THE PRACTICAL AESTHETICS OF EARLY VANCOUVER VIDEO

by Sara Diamond

In the cauldron of radical West Coast counterculture, Vancouver's early documentaries — whether *vérité*, authoritative or personal — helped create an identifiable subculture within the West Coast artistic community.[1] In addition to their contribution to the development of experimental documentary form, tapes such as *Four* (1981), *The Women's Suffrage Movement in Canada* (1975), *Transsexual Lifestyle* (1974), *Amazing Powers* (1982) and *The Main Street Drag Ball* (1976)[2] also indicate the function of video technology within the countercultural movements of the 1970s and the early 1980s. These early tapes subordinated the formalist emphasis in the aesthetic dimension of video to the medium's use value, as independent producers began to develop a documentary practice specific to Vancouver and preoccupied with documentary concerns.

As artists began to use video, they also created contexts in which their work could be seen. This tradition of "constructing specific audiences" continues to the present day.[3] Implicit in this practice was a challenge to the dominant media, whether through the utopian documentary of alternative artists' communities, the ideological challenge of feminist works or the alternative television of cablecast. Video constituted a crucial element in the emerging artist-run cultural life of Vancouver. The very presence of the video camera suggested that an event was worthy of notice and entry into the historical record. This documentation acknowledged a diverse cultural practice by recording small events and processes otherwise lost to history.

Video documentary producers have inherited a long-contested and complex history. As E. Ann Kaplan suggests in *Women and Film: Both Sides of the Camera*, both film and video documentary rely upon narrative strategies to construct their meanings.[4]

---

1. Vancouver's first decade of video documentaries offers a diverse and rich field for consideration. I have chosen to include one extra year in this baker's decade in order to include the Amelia Productions period, as that was the final *intensive* phase of collective feminist video production.

2. Tapes available at the Video In library, Vancouver.

3. Bill Nichols, *Ideology and the Image: Social Representation in the Cinema and Other Media* (Bloomington: Indiana University Press, 1981).

4. E. Ann Kaplan, *Women and Film: Both Sides of the Camera* (New York and London: Methuen, 1983).

As with any other temporal medium, audiences count on what they know about the narrative form of the genre in order to make sense of the visual, aural and extradiegetic information it provides.[5] The now-familiar codes of documentary can be summarized in brief: continuity may be established by the monologue of an interpretive narrator or by intercutting between *vérité* materials and interviews, to create a logical argument; by the use of music that reinforces on-screen action; by establishing shots that introduce a context; or by the authoritative interview with experts, which may be backed up by non-analytical testimony from victims or uninformed subjects (sometimes passers-by in the "streeter" opinion-poll style). The presence of contrasting points of view creates the impression that the documented opinions have arisen through democratic debate. But documentaries contain emotion, while withholding catharsis until the appropriate moment of climax.[6] These techniques sustain the authority of the image, maintaining for the viewer the illusion that he or she is being presented with an enlightened and objective position point of view conducive to rational judgments.

Critics of documentary have often demanded that this sort of film or video be "authentic," and provide, in John Grierson's words, a "creative treatment of actuality." Complex notions of time, emerging from, for example, Bergson's theories of the simultaneity of past and present within memory, or psychoanalytic concepts of the effects of repression on memory, have little place in this ideology.[7] In the film documentaries of the 1920s and 1930s (not unlike their later video counterparts), artifice followed function. In the 1930s, Grierson argued against an aesthetics of the documentary, stating that his films were "a social not an aesthetic force," and that his project was "to make a drama from the ordinary to set against the prevailing drama of the extraordinary."[8] Grierson's style parallels Vertov's *kinopravda* montage techniques, which offer images of "life caught unawares," or Joris Ivens' "synthetic forms," which combine newsreel, dramatic script and *vérité* sequences ("men cannot act in front of the camera when they face death"). These films were sophisticated constructions meant to present an essential truth, which, from a Marxist perspective, depended on uncovering the structure of events lying behind the surface of the news.[9] But since these early modernist experiments, and the disavowal of realist practices associated with mass culture on the one hand and

5. See also Roy Armes, *On Video* (London: Routledge and Company, 1988).

6. See Nichols' chapter, "The Documentary Film and Principles of Exposition," ibid. See also John Greyson, "The Passionate Queer Documentary," *Video Guide* (Fall 1990).

7. See, among others, Gilles Deleuze, *Bergsonism* (New York: Zone Books, 1986), and Robert Edmonds, *About Documentary: Anthropology on Film* (Dayton: Pflaum Publishing, 1974).

8. John Grierson, "First Principles of Documentary," *Grierson on Documentary,* ed. Forsyth Hardy (Berkeley and Los Angeles: University of California Press, 1966).

aligned with Stalinist social realism on the other, the avant-garde art world has generally avoided realist conventions.[10]

The institutional reception of documentary-based art practice in Vancouver reached a critical turning point in 1984, when Vancouver Art Gallery director Luke Rombout suggested that Paul Wong's video installation *Confused: Sexual Views* (1984) was "not art," and subsequently cancelled the exhibition — deciding, on the basis of Wong's documentary aesthetics, that *Sexual Views* did not "constitute a creative act." Ironically, the development of video documentary parallels the documentary forms of other photographic media of the West Coast: a practice that is clearly assigned its value in the art world, as it could be argued that the works of Ian Wallace and Jeff Wall depend upon a documentary trace as much as do Wong's video works.

MARTHA ROSLER'S UTOPIAN MOMENT

What is compelling about early video documentary is its low-quality image, ironic stance, clear signs of authorship and its consistent, if often unconscious, reversal of realism. This very lack of authority became attractive to some producers, as it suggested that the audience might be able to form opinions in response to a video documentary more readily than it could to a big-screen film:

> "There is in video an innate predisposition towards a sort of dualism that results in the first place from the coincidence of a radically factual medium and a low-definition image. Apart from electronic manipulations that are usually very obvious, a view on a television screen implies that a camera did at some time confront just such a situation, but its reduction to a scan of shifting tones across a very visible matrix of horizontal bands leaves ample room for subjective interpretation."[11]

While the early practice of video in Vancouver was not restricted to the documentary, one can argue that the form was more prevalent here (and at

---

9. See Seth Feldman, "'Cinema Weekly' and 'Cinema Truth': Dziga Vertov and the Leninist Proportion," and Joris Ivens, "*The Spanish Earth*: Committed Documentary and the Popular Front," both in *"Show Us Life": Towards a History and Aesthetics of the Committed Documentary,* ed. Thomas Waugh (New Jersey and London: The Scarecrow Press, 1984). See as well Stuart Hall's important article, "The Determination of News Photographs," in *Working Papers in Cultural Studies III* (Birmingham: CCCS, 1972).

10. The recent documentary-video show at the Museum of Modern Art (*American Documentary Video: Subject to Change,* curated by Deirdre Boyle in 1988) broke important ground for that institution, as does the collection of film and video documentaries on the part of the National Gallery of Canada. The refusal by these value-producing museums to validate a separation between avant-garde, deconstructive, experimental and documentary traditions is a healthy one for artists and audiences, yet this separation between "art" and "documentary" practices has led to the creation of smokescreens on the part of other institutions.

11. Eric Cameron, "Structural Video in Canada," *Studio International* (1972).

Vidéographe in Montreal) than in Toronto. In Vancouver and at Vidéographe, one would often find "the inversion of the impersonal and dominant mode of television production into the personal reflective consideration of the artist and the exploration of the perceptual, psychological and subjective position of the maker."[12] Artists such as Gerry Gilbert celebrated the drug culture (that social leveller), used themselves as experimental subjects of social-science and perceptual studies, and even documented the intimacy of sexual relations and birth processes.[13] These videos could be denounced as a kind of collective narcissism or juvenilia, or as the collective expression of often naive struggles for identity, but it should be remembered that these practices appeared in what Martha Rosler has described as a "utopian moment": the convergence of the social movements of the sixties and early seventies with the countercultural, "utopian, populist irrationalism" of the hippie movement and "progressive, rationalist, anti-sexist, anti-imperialist," but equally utopian, movement of the New Left. Both social movements hoped for a changed society. Both relied heavily upon cultural activities to assert their presence and identity, and were highly conscious of their representation by the media — although the New Left was far less catholic in its tastes, preferring traditional journalism or print media.[14]

Marshall McLuhan had argued that "information" was the true modern commodity, and that communications technology and the social relations it engendered would increasingly determine consciousness. While he warned against the existing monopoly of power, McLuhan concentrated on the internationalizing and potentially liberating possibilities of interactive mass communications. These ideas inspired a generation of producers in the 1960s and early 1970s who hoped that they could find the essence of modern social experience. At the same time, a materialist critique of the mass media developed which compared the relations of social production to increasingly centralized means of communications. Theorists such as Hans Magnus Enzensberger and Alvin Gouldner borrowed from Walter Benjamin's earlier ideas, reasoning that the means of communication, like the means of production, could be seized, socialized, democratized and run by its workers. Critics argued optimistically for the potential of the mass media to repoliticize the art object.[15] Through the academic environment of Simon Fraser University's Department of Communication and the Centre for the Arts, and

12. See Renee Baert, *Vintage Video* exhibition catalogue (Toronto: Artculture Resource Centre, 1986).

13. See works by Main Street, Pumps, Kim Tomczak.

14. See Martha Rosler, "Shedding the Utopian Moment," *Block* (Winter 1985/86): 27-33.

15. See Alvin W. Gouldner, "The Dialect of Ideology and Technology," *The Origins, Grammar and Future of Ideology* (New York: Seabury Press, 1976).

through early video workshops (1970s), students gained an exposure to these analyses of television and video practice. At the same time, students of the Vancouver School of Art were meeting artists from the West Coast and New York.[16]

While expressing optimism about the new technology, these theories eclipsed McLuhan's formalist and utopian concepts of global networks and political struggle. Like the European avant-garde before them, a younger generation of artists sought to breach the gap between high-art practice and mass communications — of which video so clearly functioned as a trope. As the critique of mass media deepened, so did the crisis of modernism. And the founding principles of early postmodern practice emerged in the critique of the museum, individual authorship and the fraternal (paternal) order. At the same time, the modernist search for truth in a medium and its materials was replaced by an interest in social science, cultural theory and self-criticism.

Strategies of the historical avant-garde were reassessed as artists sought to heal the breach between production and reception, and to incorporate art into the social. Video, with its seemingly organic relation to the social, was the ideal medium for intervention and interactivity. It allowed for a practice parallel to that of the mass media, and it offered not only a means through which to open a discourse with the dominant culture, but also to explore different modes of perception. In David Hall's words, "Video art [sought] to explore perceptual thresholds, to expand and in part to decipher those narrow conventions understood on television."[17] It is no wonder that the artistic environment of Vancouver, steeped in counterculture and radical politics, embraced video technology. There was a veritable flurry of activity. It was close to the ground.[18]

16. These ideas were articulated by Martha Rosler, Bruce Barber and Michael Eliot Hurst. At SFU, Dallas Smythe and Lenora Salter worked with Raymond Williams' and Herbert Schiller's writings about cultural domination and communication.

17. David Hall, "British Video Art: Towards an Autonomous Practice," *Studio International* CXCI (May/June 1976).

18. Video has a history, like any other medium, under constant revision and reinterpretation. *But* , there is a preservation pressure that is unusual, and which acts as a block to memory, because of the tendency of old half-inch, one-inch and early three-quarter-inch video to deteriorate beyond redemption. When value judgements are made about works and their transfer or preservation, it is always of the moment, based on the values of an era looking back. With video, this is equivalent to a death sentence for the artwork. Looking through the Video In archives, which have had material transferred over time, one can see the contradictory apparatus of value at work: (1) Was the work by a Video In artist or documentary producer?; (2) Are the artists still producing, or were they at the time of preservation?; (3) Contemporary practice that needed a historical framework or justification; (4) The tastes of whatever temporary staff was in place who made their way through the collection.

THE EMERGENCE OF A LOCAL DOCUMENTARY PRACTICE

Intermedia must be credited as one of the key progenitors of an independent video practice in Vancouver, grouping artists of mixed disciplines in order to "utilize the technology we have evolved in the continuous and rapid need to explore new perspectives in our human universe and ecology." Intermedia introduced video as a documentation tool with its acquisition of a Portapack. Interdisciplinary artists Gerry Gilbert, Roy Kiyooka, Glenn Lewis, Don Druick, Michael de Courcy and Michael Morris all made use of video. Al Razutis, a structuralist filmmaker and holographer, who eventually moved to the Granville Grange, produced synaesthetic videos that were exhibited at the Vancouver Art Gallery.[19] David Rimmer, Bill Fix and Tom Shandel built a "Media Wall" with interactive and pre-recorded degenerating imagery. These forays into structuralism by the film community were for the most part atypical of the use of the medium, which was more frequently employed to document events in other media, or create ironic self-portraits and critiques of mass media. When Intermedia dispersed it was Metro Media, a community-activist group, who inherited its Portapack. According to Gerry Gilbert, described by one curator as "an art janitor, sweeping up the pictures" with his ever-present Portapack, Intermedia's documentaries, like those of the latter-day Western Front, often simply recorded events. These tapes are as valuable for their sociological records of audience composition and behaviour as for their often hazy long shots of performances. In one tape, for example, Al Neil crawls across the floor at the Vancouver Art Gallery to reach a place to sit. As well, there were conceptual documents of personal rituals, such as *Birthdays*, Gilbert's collaboration with Carole Itter. At the beginning of the tape both artists bathe each other, then Carole is bathed preceding the birth of their child, and finally the child is bathed. There were also problem-solving pieces; in one of them, Gilbert presents the rural residents of Roberts Creek with the ever-present dilemma for artists: "How do you make ends meet?" Answers vary from a complex economic formula to the simple gesture of a squinting older man who carefully touches forefinger to forefinger.[20]

The early videos were and are ironically humorous. Familiar community members played unfamiliar roles within performances. In an Intermedia sampler of 1972, Glenn Lewis' aptitude for improvisation, even in the act of traditional Japanese cooking, completes the joke:

> "Thank you. Now, what I do is — I'm going to put this saucer on the top here, and then I'm going to put some heavy weight in it. And I have these iron bars

---

19. See Paul Wong's excellent chronology, "Void Space: New Media (Out of Context)," *Vancouver: Art and Artists 1931-1983* (Vancouver: Vancouver Art Gallery, 1983): 306-311.

20. Interview with Gerry Gilbert, 1990.

here, that I found out in the hall here and I'm going to put those in. I've got two more here.[Lewis at this point struggles to fit the bars onto the cabbage bowl.] Those are really quite heavy. Now, you don't need to use iron bars of course. Now that has to sit like that for about two days and it should...well, I'll show you what it's like after sitting around for two days. [Opens a waiting bowl.] I'll just put it over here. [He groans with the weight.] This is uh...I had trouble getting a proper fit to this. So, there's the cabbage after a couple of days, see the water that's formed, the salt has brought the water out of the cabbage."

Elizabeth Vander Zaag, who worked as a technician for the Simon Fraser University Video Workshop in the early 1970s, reminds us that the technology then was more limited than it is now. Few producers had access to editing equipment, and real-time shooting and in-camera editing were common practices. These limitations amplify the "realism" of these early works — in which the camera simply rolls until the tape runs out.[21] For instance, Gilbert and David Rimmer collaborated on a tape of a Roy Kiyooka reading. Somehow the soundtrack failed, and all that remained were the expressions and movements of an impassioned writer — a translation between media. At one VAG performance, in a gesture that could be read as generous or confrontational, the federal minister of culture was handed a video camera. Video was used to record both domestic and public events: it was everyone's favourite toy. The question of the hour was, "You're going there, are you going to videotape it?" Some of these videos simulate urban travelogues; Gilbert went out with his Portapack to document the city and found a young waitress swaying to the feminist song "I'm a Woman."

The medium's ability to confound its practitioners is recalled by Mike MacDonald, who describes one of his favourite "in camera" edited tapes, in which a young couple go off to shoot the city. Somehow they confused the "record" and "pause" buttons, and the result is a long sequence of sidewalk shots, overlaid with the voices of the documentarians negotiating what they will believe will be the next image.[22]

For some artists the camera was an expressive tool, an extension of the perceptual apparatus of the body. This approach to video ironically inverts the institutional use of the medium as a means of surveillance. Sex was a favourite site of documentation. Perhaps that's why the camera was removed from the tripod and images were shot from the hip, the wrist, the ground, or hand-held at eye level, above the head, all in order to free the process of perception from the realism of the controlled human eye. The camera became a periscope as it "looked" around the

21. Interview with Elizabeth Vander Zaag, 1990.
22. Interview with Mike MacDonald, 1990.

corner without its human extension. The merging of the values of performance art and conceptualism with a documentary practice produced a new aesthetic, less tied to the rational side of documentary. In a 1974 collaborative work, the *New Era Marathon* Taki Bluesinger ran from Vancouver to the Burnaby Art Gallery to open the exhibition that he and Gilbert had curated, while Gilbert and Paul Wong encouraged and videotaped Bluesinger from the back of an accompanying pick-up truck. Taki marks each new kilometre with a change into a fresh T-shirt, as Gerry continues his monologue:

> "...magic is outside, we're going to have to have a change now, this is officially...This is the official tabulation, now accomplished eleven kilometres and still heading along Canada Way. We are stopping at Sproat, let it be known that it is at Sproat itself that we changed from eleven. [Taki takes a fresh T-shirt. Gerry begins to sing.] Speed bonny feet like a bird on the wing, onward the artists cry..."

The community believed in the truth-telling powers of the camera. In the words of Michael de Courcy, video makers differentiated themselves as "artists who refused to lie" — as opposed to commercial producers who were perceived as having sold their souls.

While the Vancouver filmmakers aligned with Intermedia launched into a structuralist practice, a new wave of video producers were drawn to the immediacy and toy-like qualities of video. Rumours flew that the filmmakers were "overly concerned" with protecting video equipment from mishap.[23] Multimedia artists and writers, less technically conscientious, would take Portapacks to the beach or swing cameras upside down from trees. Understandably, tensions emerged.

In the early 1970s, video documentarians shared with other West Coast artists a fascination with landscape. The counterculture's anthropomorphism of the land, and fascination with indigenous cultures and essentialist spirituality, echo through the work of artists such as June Boe of the North Shore Connexions group. Boe's tape, *Mudflats* (1973), documents the lifestyles of the North Shore artists' and squatters' settlement that civic authorities would soon make extinct. It begins with flute music and long pans of marsh land. Then a woman speaks:

> "He's a really benevolent gentleman, he could care less if I stay there, in fact he likes to stay in town. But they're putting a big push on by the city, so they have to come down on us. They served us with some notices...Now we can go over to our house...[They walk.] I just can't do it, I can't. Oh I know. I just don't want to settle down, I don't want to be involved in a monogamous relationship. Well I do sometimes, it's really a fluctuating situation."

23. Interview with Shawn Preus, 1990.

In the late 1970s, Kim Tomczak began to produce his urban landscapes, but these were critical rather than elegiac.[24] In the early 1980s, the ecological documents of Mike MacDonald spilled over into his growing activism in the native community, giving a voice to environmental and aboriginal concerns through video. MacDonald would later rework this documentary footage into an electronic totem pole, an ironic take on Nam June Paik's massive installations — and a translation of his respect for the land into a new medium.

There were rumoured divisions between "arty" types, concentrated around the Video Inn and the New Era Social Club (which became the Western Front), who were committed to video self-portraiture and experimentation, and hard-line community-documentary producers based at Metro Media. Metro Media was perceived by some of the early Video Inn crowd, particularly the women, as being technocratic, despite the former's commitment to community production. In hindsight, these divisions seem minute and unarticulated. People from different currents talked to each other, and there were extensive cross-overs between individuals who worked for a variety of organizations. And though these producers might receive short-term grants, everyone relied on Metro Media for production equipment. Ultimately a small community could not sustain real discord and survive.

For some artists, video was an incidental practice, while others were passionately committed to the medium. Michael Goldberg, also of Metro Media, created the first International Video Exchange Directory in 1972, with the idealistic goal of "not promoting an 'alter-network,' which would 'represent' the freak community," but rather creating "communications links around the world, decentralizing media processes away from any elite."[25] The act of exchanging tape would "turn(s) video into a communications medium," allowing a glimpse of the life "that corporate media ignore(s)." The second phase of this project, realized almost ten years later with the formation of Video Out distribution in 1980/81, would involve the dissemination of information modelled on McLuhanesque notions of communications systems (with a Marcusian leftist twist), to counter the disinformation of the state. Trudeau's invocation of the War Measures Act clearly had had a sobering effect on Goldberg and others in the arts community. The relative calm of the aftermath was perceived as an optimum time to fight for guarantees of freedom of expression, as well as the free flow of information through Canada Customs.[26]

24. Interview with Kim Tomczak, 1990.

25. Goldberg, *Captain Video*, II: I.

26. Minutes of Video Inn meetings, with Michael Goldberg's report on the Matrix conference, Video Inn archives, 1973.

In January 1973, Goldberg and Tricha Hardman organized the Matrix conference, bringing together 140 practitioners from Japan, Canada, the U.S.A., France and the U.K. Attendance at Matrix was mostly made up of a video community concentrated around several key institutions: the fledgling Video Inn on Powell Street, Metro Media on Cambie (near the Cable Ten studio), Challenge for Change, the Vancouver Art Gallery Satellite Programme, Women's Media, Memo from Turner, Connexions, Simon Fraser University, Image Flow Centre and a variety of community-television groups.[27]

Both Goldberg's directory and the Matrix conference established ties to a larger international media community that are still retained by the Video In and Western Front. To the chagrin of television cynics, the conference concentrated on access to cable, as well as such forms of video production as letters and documents. Matrix helped place Canadian practice in the context of an international video movement. The ready availability of funding for community-based works through the National Film Board and for programming through community cable encouraged Canadians to concentrate on documentary forms. In the U.S., "artists had access to expensive and sophisticated video equipment such as video synthesizers," often through universities. The availability of these resources placed the U.S. in "the forefront of experimentation with video as a new art form."[28] According to Paul Wong, the first Video Exchange Directory created the basis for a tape-exchange library, the Satellite Video Exchange Society, one year later.[29] This group, more often known as the Video Inn, was committed to a radical alternative politics and an intensely collective, almost familial structure, perhaps engendered by the generation "gaps" within the organization. Goldberg and Christa Haukedal had worked at the Vancouver Art Gallery in the Extension Programme, a project designed to bring video into the Vancouver school system. This program became the point of entry for Paul Wong and Shawn Preus,[30] both future members of the Video Inn.

VIDEO INN MINUTES (1973-1982)

Despite a strong interest in video, there is little evidence of theoretical or formal debates about the medium in the early days of the Video Inn. Minutes from lengthy, weekly collective meetings include descriptions and occasional physical evidence of dinners. There is, for example, this note: "rancid butter by Rick: do not eat it, throw it out, perhaps we should put butter in the fridge, do not put too much out." Political

27. Video Inn papers, Matrix registration records.
28. Video Inn records; Matrix summary: 5.
29. Interviews with Paul Wong, 1990.
30. Interviews Preus and Wong, ibid., and Video Inn minutes, 1973.

discussion was a major item on the agenda. In the meeting of 9 January 1977, "Shawn Preus speaks of values from food to Social Credit. Composting and recycling are important." Michael Goldberg queries, "Should we eliminate our sex tapes?" The group struggled with its principles and committed itself to the following themes: "We are involved in and will promote a harmonious, non-polluting, non-sexist, self-sufficient alternative lifestyle that has a sense of humour"; and "We will provide access to the materials and tools under our control, to those who do not have media access." At the time, the concept of an "alternative" lifestyle provoked a series of debates about countercultural withdrawal versus avant-gardist teleology, with Video Inn taking up a position somewhere in between these two possibilities. Central to the organization's thinking was a desire to stay small, to function at a "grassroots" level.

Members worked on each other's productions, eventually creating a short-lived commercial unit, the Production Group (1981). Works included community documents, social-action documentaries, docu-dramas, docu-fictions, performance documents (all with a strong emphasis on sex, drugs, rock and roll and garbage), with Video Inn members cooperating with other organizations for productions purposes. Women's media nights, according to Shawn Preus, were important occasions for screening and subsequent discussion. The feminist presence was strongly in place at the Video Inn, although most women members produced not through the Inn, but the various women's media groups that developed.[31]

Michael Goldberg, Barbara Steinman, Ardele Lister, Paul Wong, Shawn Preus, Ross Gentleman and Andy Harvey were some of the producers associated with the Video Inn from its inception. Michael Goldberg, a paternal figure at the Inn, worked with documentary and docu-fiction, combining *vérité* with script. *Orgasm*, an early work of his in which he interviews Elke Hayden (later Town), is a classic. The conversation veers off in some uncomfortable directions as the producer attempts to discuss female orgasm. The tape is shot in the relentless metre of real time and the only escape would have been to turn the recorder off — a sure statement of defeat. Documentaries such as this can sometimes elude the control of their makers because of their reliance on actual events and contexts — these exert their own imperatives.

"GOLDBERG: The way that orgasm is reached between a man and a woman, and I know that's not the only way to reach it — you can reach it alone, you can reach it with someone of the same sex, but my concern at this point is between men and women, that when orgasm is reached and the two are

31. Video Inn archives and Preus interview.

involved in reaching it, either alone or at the same time, that there is no aggression at that point, that point is where people drop defences and communicate with each other as clearly as possible. So I hope that by delving into the question of orgasm, I will find out more about, or I'll sense more the possibility of communication that there is between men and women in our society, or women in my social sphere, friends of mine and myself. So that's kind of why I want to talk about it. I don't know yet what I want to talk about except that I kind of want to start talking around the question of orgasm and what it might be and how it might be experienced and what happens to it.

"HAYDEN [after a silence]: I would like you to think about specific things that you would like to know, that I can deal with. And what you want to know. Now I know that's going to come out when we start talking about it, but I want you to lead off so that I can, like, talk more easily about it. I cannot pull a topic out of my hat and say, "I think this and that about orgasm," until we get a rapport. [There is an intense silence as Elke carefully lights her cigarette.]32

As exemplified by *Orgasm*, video practice increasingly featured a "direct voice" or first-person mode of address. This performative quality, reworked from news coverage and the West Coast interest in performance, cuts across many early video documentaries and autobiographical works. Voice functioned as testimony and as portrait, introducing an intimacy to video.33 Working with this anti-authoritarian medium of video, producers increasingly chose to eschew the "Voice of God" narrator in favour of direct address, and the construction of tapes through the logic of editing.

In these videotapes, the questioning artist was removed, a humble absence that can be assigned to a belief in the purity of a subject's voice — the false non-interventionist style of *vérité*. Early feminist work focused on the importance of the individual woman, the woman's testimonial standing in as witness. In the following Reelfeelings piece by Barbara Steinman, both body and voice are used to create an identification between viewer and subject and to "reclaim" the female body. The producer cleverly uses the title screen to take the shirts off her subjects: the women are dressed, the title comes up, and when they return their shirts are off. The continuous, soothing voice-over provides continuity in this potentially startling visual transition.

"I often find when we do this in groups, that women feel uncomfortable together, because it's not a normal experience for us to take our tops off. And, I guess, I'd like to reassure you that it's common to feel a bit shy in the beginning. But it's important that women not suffer because of their shyness,

32. Michael Goldberg, *Orgasm* (1975).
33. See Nichols and Armes, ibids.

that women learn...it's good preventative medicine that we are learning. That it's okay to touch your breasts even if you feel uncomfortable at first. Because the more you touch your breasts and are familiar with them, the more chance you'll have of discovering anything that comes up. It's a good way of feeling less uptight, less uncomfortable about your body."[34]

While optimism pervaded media practice on the West Coast, others elsewhere were offering a critique of the medium as such. According to Wallace Martin, there were a number of conflicting definitions of realism, all competing for supremacy. These definitions increasingly entered "the no-man's land between critical theory and philosophy." As Martin says, "Societies and ideologies change. What is now considered real in Leningrad would have been thought absurd when it was named Petrograd."[35] Or to rework this truism: what was considered real in the Vancouver art world of 1971 would be absurd twenty years later. The roughness of camera movement and inattention to technical effect in, for example. *Concerned Aboriginal Women* (1981), testify not only to the inexperience of the makers, but also to an ideology stressing minimal intervention on the part of white artists in a native environment. The rough conditions of production were meant to amplify the drama of the events, in this instance the occupation of a government agency. One might wish for a better audio and clearer lighting, but, at the time, the document was strengthened by the immediacy of its crude construction.

Redefinitions of realism have posed documentary as a particular form, with a strong relationship to realist narrative and expository argument. These are a long way from Christian Metz's original placement of documentary outside the "syntagmatique," a code specific to the cinema. Some critics continue to demand a responsibility to facts; others emphasize that the grounding of documentary in footage of actual events makes it appear real when it is in fact as constructed as fiction. Others, like Bill Nichols, underline the specific elements that make up this genre — voice-over, sync sound, direct address to the viewer by narrator or newsperson; here, the rational, expository form is the distinguishing feature. Often documentaries try to deploy two diverse techniques: on the one hand, the manipulation of media materials to create an effective formal vehicle, and on the other hand, the voicing of the ethical concerns of the groups being represented. It should be noted that, conventions aside, recent critical theory has suggested that realism is more of a self-proclaimed stance on the part of the maker than a measurable quantity in the work itself:

34. *Breast Self Examination*, Reelfeelings, 1974.

35. Wallace Martin, *Recent Theories of Narrative* (Ithaca and London: Cornell University Press, 1987): 80.

"There is probably no critical term with a more unruly and confusing lineage than realism...[T]he distinctive characteristic of realism resides in the ambition, to, in some way or other, approximate reality, to "show things as they really are."[36]

Amidst this growing reconsideration of realist form, Paul Wong's work is of particular interest, because it effectively crosses so many boundaries between fictional and documentary practice. Wong recalls being moved by the impassioned anger of Laura and Frank Kavastani (two Americans who produced a video documenting the embittered perspective of a Vietnam vet) and by the militant Quebec documentaries of Pierre Falardeau. *Murder Research* (1977), a piece that would mark Wong's early fascination with the abject world of voyeurism, documented his discovery of a man who had been recently murdered outside his home. The work combines a primal fascination with death and a critique of the media's treatment of spectacle.

The Main Street group, of which Wong was a member, was informed by an interest in personal life, fraternal solidarity, the drug culture and a yen for glamour. The group used the Western Front's new colour camera to record their surroundings and document staged performances. *Four* (1981), a later work, established the ongoing Wong method (one paralleled by the work of Robert Morin and Lorraine Dufour in Montreal), in which scripts based on actual events were reworked and then acted by the characters involved in the event. Wong produced personal, diaristic documents based on his relationship to the Main Street community, and the intricate rivalries within the group. For the artist, these works were cathartic; for the viewer, they were uncomfortable combinations of coercion and abjection. In *60 Unit Bruise* (1976), another Main Street production, Kenneth Fletcher injects Wong with a syringe of Fletcher's blood, in a ritual that is both erotic and startling, and today might be considered life-threatening. The audience watches for several minutes as the resulting bruise spreads on Wong's back. The work stands as a transgressive act of desire and identification between the two men.

METRO MEDIA AND CABLE

If some artists had come upon documentary in a spontaneous fashion and as a form of play, there were others who approached documentary in a more systematic or instrumental way. The National Film Board's Challenge for Change Program, initiated in 1967 by Colin Low, set out "to improve communications between individuals and groups in all segments of society concerned with and affected by

36. John Hill, *Sex, Class and Realism: British Cinema 1956-1963* (London: BFI, 1986); 57.

poverty." The Fogo Island project, undertaken over a number of years in collaboration with Memorial University, played an instrumental role in articulating the resistance of forty-five hundred members of a small Newfoundland outport forced to relocate. It broke from the hitherto practice of social documentary in several ways.[37]

All footage was returned to Fogo Island for scrutiny by residents after it was developed. The subjects of the film were thus given control over the content and distribution of the final product. When portable video became available, the project shifted from sixteen-millimetre film into half-inch tape, allowing instantaneous discussion with the documentary subjects. These stages of production allowed residents to engage in "a startling process of self-discovery," one that avoided confrontation and deflected any possibility of exploitation by the external documentary team. A final production was made and successfully used to argue the validity of the community to provincial and federal governments. A documentary practice for the community, not for an external, superior viewer, was here introduced to Canada. The project supposed the importance of "citizen communication" — a premise that assumed the traditional liberal rights of an informed public to discourse and to participation within the political process. These ideas stood as the founding principles of Metro Media, formed in 1971 as a social-activist spin-off from Intermedia. Metro Media was led by Bill Nemtin, with financial assistance from Chris Pinney, the B.C. representative of Challenge for Change.[38]

In the early 1970s, the Local Initiatives Programme and Opportunities for Youth provided intensive funding for citizens' communications groups. Such programs were symptomatic of the liberal struggle to institutionalize marginal sources of dissent. The lessons of the Roosevelt era in the U.S., which saw the absorption of the radical movements of the 1930s through meagre but widely accessible state funding, were not lost on the Trudeau government, itself a product of populism and the mass media. The imminent possibility of cable access in Canada resulted in vigorous lobbying of the Canadian Radio and Television Commission on the part of media and community organizations, such as Metro Media and the Video Inn, for access to a local, high-quality broadcast channel, financed by the cable system. Metro Media opposed the ownership of stations by the cable networks, arguing that video should be funded, licensed and provided with the means of production to ensure quality, locally generated production. (This was the model that the British

37. See National Film Board newsletter, and "Metro Media and Hourglass CBC," unpublished post-graduate thesis, Linda Johnson, 1974.

38. Metro Media newsletters, 1971-74.

Film Institute, the Greater London Council and Channel Four adopted in Britain for film and video workshops. These are now coming to an end with funding cuts.)

While Metro Media did not win the battle with Premiere Cable and the CRTC for cooperative licencing, early Cable Ten relied heavily on Metro Media and other community media groups programming. By 1973, Metro Media had produced over 200 hours of material for over 250 groups, broadcasting on average of 3.5 hours per week. Its advisory board was composed of a range of community and service organizations, including both "low-income representatives and media-middle-class social service representatives." In practice, Metro Media favoured the disenfranchised, assisting them in the production of social-activist video. This stance occasionally outraged established social-service institutions. At the same time, Metro Media lobbied heartily for a range of communications outlets, including broadcast television. The latter, however, did not open to local production, despite the occasional inclusion of independently produced coverage for the TV station CHIN. Television was too hierarchical, its pretence of objectivity too deeply in place, its technology too high-end and maintained by personnel too threatened by displacement to allow a group like Metro Media ready access.[39]

Community production continued with the creation of the Vancouver Community Television Association (1975), which spearheaded the unsuccessful attempt of sixty community groups to get a CRTC licence.[40] Rogers Television (now in control) withdrew its backing from the group. Rogers demanded copyright, discouraging other producers who favoured individual production, and saw the network as a means of production, not distribution.[41] Metro Media was already encountering censorship of sexually explicit documentary materials (on women's self-examination, for example), and disillusionment ran high. There were other sore spots. In-house producers such as Jim Lipkovits, Kenneth Specht, Penny Joy Keeler and Mike MacDonald never signed their names to a finished project. This enforced collectivity covered over inequities in workload, and led to problems for individuals who needed career credentials.

Two videos exemplify the range of Metro Media's earlier productions: the first recorded an anti-nuclear demonstration at Bangor, Washington, and the second consisted of a series of interviews on Wreck Beach during evangelist Bernice Gerard's attempts to "clean up" the nude beach. On the first tape, colourful protesters parade to the strains of "Something's happening here/what it is ain't

39. See Linda Johnson, and Metro Media newsletters.
40. See videotape *Video Inn at the CRTC* (1973).
41. Interview Mike MacDonald, ibid.

exactly clear/there's a man with a gun over there/telling me I gotta beware." As the song continues, "the battle lines are drawn," and the protestors swarm over the fences of the military installation in an act of civil disobedience. On the Wreck Beach tape, Metro Media's Mike MacDonald first interviews sixteen-year-old beachgoer Kellie Marlowe and then a juggler:

MACDONALD: Do you come here very often?

MARLOWE: As much as I can, when the sun's out.

MACDONALD: What attracts you to Wreck Beach?

MARLOWE: I like to take my clothes off and lie around. The thing that keeps me away if anything is that when two women come down there's a lot of men with clothes on that come and they sit beside you and they do their perv trip. And I think they're perverts, they're the ones that shouldn't come down here. There's so many of them. If they took their clothes off that would be one thing. It makes a lot of people feel uncomfortable; it makes me feel uncomfortable.

MACDONALD: Why do you think they would come to the beach with their clothes on?

MARLOWE: Why, to watch people with their clothes off.

[MacDonald moves on to juggler]

MACDONALD: Hello, sir. I see that you are juggling oranges. Oh, you dropped one, better start again. Why do you juggle oranges?

JUGGLER: I left my balls behind today.

MACDONALD: I can't imagine why anybody would want to walk Wreck Beach with their clothes on, can you?

JUGGLER: It's a free beach. They are free to keep their clothes on if they want to. However, those of us who want to take our clothes off should be able to take them off.[42]

By 1980, Mike MacDonald had left Metro Media to produce environmental tapes and videos in the native community. His early work in this area, represented in pieces such as *What Price an Island*, marked an important first stage of native self-representation. In *What Price*, aboriginal leaders stand on the steps of the legislature demanding the settlement of land claims and timber rights:

"My name is George Watts, I am the chairman of the Nuchanel tribal council, these gentlemen who we see standing here represent all of our nations, they are the hereditary chiefs of our land and they are the people who own the West Coast of Vancouver Island, not MacMillan Bloedel, let me assure you. On

42. *Metro Media Sampler*, 1974.

behalf of our people I would like to thank the Songhees people for borrowing their land today. That's whose land we're on, we're on their land, we're not on the Legislature. Let's make that clear. I want to thank those people for using their land here today and I want to thank those people for welcoming our people into their territory. Like Indian people have always gone up and down this coast and they have always welcomed other Indians to come into their territory.[43]

In 1981 three other key personnel left Metro Media, and by 1983 the organization had folded. Access to cable had become increasingly difficult to obtain, and community organizations had become more interested in a professional advocacy product, rather than self-produced programs. The days of collective idealism were ending. To top it off, Video Inn had begun to provide technical access to community producers as Metro Media declined. Metro Media had, in a sense, outlived its function. The subcultural movement had ended — and yet there really had been a utopian moment. The astonishing proliferation of independent production for cable in the 1970s cannot be discounted. Mike MacDonald and Shawn Preus have emphasized the fact that Cable Ten was often seen by producers as a site of production rather than distribution. Target audiences were highly specific: the art community, immigrant groups, women's organizations, labour and so on. Still, the early years of cablecast were fuelled by Metro Media's barrage of community-based works, as well as by the B.C. Federation of Women and Vancouver Status of Women's weekly talk shows, and collaborations between Women In Focus and UBC's Women's Resource Centre.

In later years, one could view *The Gina Show* (1979), with performance, music and cultural news, produced by John Anderson and Pumps. Pumps was a second-generation video and visual-art production centre, established in 1976 by ex-Vancouver School of Art students. In 1980, Amelia Productions was founded and began to produce activist-feminist documentaries. This was as close as Vancouver could come to an interactive network. With no illusions of a mass following, producers saw cable broadcast, locally publicized, as an appropriate if limited site for the construction of an audience. Extensive and early demands for local access to the means of production and to cable meant that there was a broader range of non-formulaic videos available, and subsequently a committed, if at times critical, audience. The situation in Vancouver was unique in Canada. John Anderson, when asked about the "Neilson ratings" for *The Gina Show*, described a consistent viewership of youth-culture aficionados.[44] Other audience members included a

43. Mike MacDonald, *What Price an Island*, 1984.

44. Interview with John Anderson, 1990.

group of real-estate agents who called in to complain. *The Gina Show* was responsive. When a fundamentalist called after *Four* was screened, to tell the Main Street crowd that he would pray for them, the producers followed with a convincing reading from Revelation by none other than John Bentley Mays. The use of cable by artists ended by the early 1980s because of access cuts by the network — cuts that increased Cable Ten's reliance on formula schlock. Contributing factors included the artists' growing awareness of their right to be paid for creative services, and Cable Ten's persistent infringement of creative copyright.

FEMINIST PRACTICE

If technology was a liberating prospect to some artists of the early 1970s, its exigencies were less than seductive for women. Many of the very early makers here and elsewhere were male. However, as feminism swung into place and women sought an instrumental voice, they began to use video, discovering its flexible and playful qualities. Their desire to produce work was based on a developing critique of representation, an urgent need to document a growing radical women's movement and a history of exclusion from access to the means of production. These exclusions existed en masse in the teaching institutions of television, film and fine art, as well as in attitudes within the art community. As feminism developed, women became less willing to accept blocks to access and production based on role expectations.

Kate Craig suggests that there were at least two ways in which women developed a video art practice. Some joined women-only organizations, while others joined mixed groups such as the Western Front, Metro Media or the Video Inn. A member of the Western Front, Craig favoured an imaginative combination of media critique and performance, a method that did not coincide with either the narrative preferences of Reelfeelings or the documentary leanings of Women In Focus. Reelfeelings, comprised of many Intermedia women, came out of desire to create in Vancouver a women's film and video festival like that of Marien Lewis' Toronto festival.[45] This group worked as a fluctuating collective from 1973 to 1977, with as many as seventeen members, including Nomi Kaplan, Mo Simpson, Renee Baert, Ardele Lister, Saralee James and many others. Like the Vancouver Women's Media Collective that was to follow, Reelfeelings produced film, video, slide/sound and photography, choosing a medium on a project-by-project and budget-by-budget basis.[46] Their goals were to change the dominant image of women, encourage more women to produce by their example, challenge stereotypes of feminine technical

45. See *Vanguard* (1974); interviews with Hank Bull, Kate Craig and Shawn Preus, 1990; ISIS distribution catalogue.

46. See *Vanguard* (1974), Reelfeelings catalogue.

ineptitude and develop a feminist aesthetics. These goals, along with countering sex-role stereotyping, were parallel to those of Women In Focus, which began one year later. Unlike the latter, Reelfeelings used *vérité*, realist fiction and humour to create positive images of women. Women In Focus favoured a polemical voice-over style, giving the traditional authority reserved for the masculine narrator to the female voice.

Women In Focus began in 1974 under the initiative of Marion Barling. It began as a production centre tied to local cablevision, and soon after, with the arrival of Michelle Nickel, took up distribution. During the "year of women," the group received funding from the Secretary of State and, later, from the Canada Council.[47] While Barling was aware of other production centres, such as the Western Front, she perceived them as primarily involved in self-documentation with the Portapack. She also knew of Reelfeelings, but had little contact with these women, who were social as well as artistic cohorts and who were involved in a larger media community. Barling preferred the higher production values available in the studio; her goal was to create a bank of "video tracts," representing women's experience, with an emphasis on a "sociological, academically sound argument."[48] She hoped to address the double-edged absence of "what she knew about women" and their absence from the creative process. If Reelfeelings centred on optimistic representations of women, Women In Focus addressed the construction of oppression and absence, as this 1980 statement by Barling and Nickel suggests:

"Little is known about women's experience except by those who have consciously recognized this process. Women's lives and achievements have not been considered the worthy objects of art or media because it is men who have decided these standards and have been the art and media makers by and large. Oppression has kept women from taking control of our lives and producing the imagery that reflects our experience."[49]

At Cable Ten, Barling and other women artists and technicians created a weekly program that featured feminist concerns, and gave Barling the opportunity to pass on her knowledge to others. Despite the rigid and exclusive formats of television, Barling worked towards new forms of expression, combining empiricism with theory. She continued to use the narrative voice-over in order to "legitimize" women's knowledge and authority.

47. Throughout its existence Women In Focus has had to fight for adequate financing, finding itself sandwiched between arts and women's funding agencies.

48. Interview with Marion Barling, 1990.

49. *Video Guide* (Summer 1980).

Women In Focus organized conferences, first in 1978 and then 1984, presenting an international display of works by women makers. The 1978 Vancouver Women's Film and Video conference held panels with activists discussing issues such as birth control, the right to choose and day care. The experts outnumbered the women film and video artists, suggesting that these mediums were appreciated for their ability to represent feminist content and effectively initiate action, rather than for their aesthetic possibilities. Since responsibility was stressed, a conference like this could be an occasion to ask producers to account for "inaccuracies."

A successor to Reelfeelings, the Vancouver Women's Media Collective (VWMC), began in 1978, lasting eighteen months. It brought together a number of women from the former group with others who had more recently entered the media community. According to Shawn Preus, the VWMC preferred field over studio production, believing it produced more dynamic video. They created a series of tapes for Langara College Women's Studies that documented women's theatre events, International Women's Day, and assisted with Peg Campbell's Justice Institute series on battered women. Like Reelfeelings, they hoped to reach a mass audience with their work.

In 1980, Amelia Productions began as a group of five women, which included myself. Several of us had attended and often lamented the SFU film program of that time. We shared a sense of alienation from its pedagogy but also a strong interest in documentary practice. The group functioned as a collective, united by a commitment to social activism, the work ethic and strong social and sexual bonds (no surprise, given the epoch). However, members differed in their ideas about realism, in their approach to the making of documentaries and in their particular preference for certain types of imagery. Amelia produced fourteen tapes in eighteen months and then collapsed, perhaps in part from exhaustion, but the crisis was in fact a deeper one. The insistence on positive images and a polemical social critique seemed to restrain the imagination. Perhaps the collective production spurred the need for individual ego gratification through individual authorship.

Amelia Productions, like its American documentary predecessor Newsreel, preferred videotaping confrontational events. The group ironically named its tapes "Occupational Videos"; some of these were shot inside occupied buildings such as the Department of Indian Affairs, B.C. Tel and the post office. Our most delightful moments occurred when sneaking through police lines, camera rolling, confronting angry sheriffs and bringing messages of solidarity. We felt we had achieved the immediacy and power of news coverage, without the weight of objectivity. We prided ourselves on being allowed *inside* an event while television news cameras were kept at bay. Amelia's interests included alternative women's culture, but we prioritized the political struggles of individuals and groups who resisted violence, coercion and repression.

The work of the American, Frederick Wiseman, as well as the practices of some of the NFB's Challenge for Change projects, provided a solid new base for documentary constructed out of a high shooting ratio of footage and the direct testimonials of subjects. *Vérité* was documentary's last attempt at essential truth-telling and stood beside the visual artist's refusal of authorship. There were opposing uses of this practice. The first was to construct a seamless documentary from the footage of an event, a method that suppressed evidence of the intervention of the apparatus. As Roy Armes suggests in *On Video*, a subtle movement of the camera, a slight jiggle perhaps, would suggest the presence of the camera as a surveillance device. Surprisingly, a second use of *vérité* directly opposed this practice. This method featured the Godardian jump-cut and other interventionist devices within the editing process, but gave the subject as direct a voice as possible, suggesting, in almost guilty complicity, that the maker was constructing the interpretation of the work. Amelia Productions' *T.W.U. Tel* and *This Line Is Not In Service* (1981) are Vancouver classics from this school of video documentary production.

A third use of *vérité* emphasized the perceptual concerns of experimental video. Video documentary, with its portability and immediate playback, invoked the desire to know. Video offered more flexibility than other mediums; it was, according to Roy Armes and early Vancouver practitioners, a research tool. The final outcome of the tape was based on the interaction of maker, event and community. I recall Amelia Productions' concern about the questions that we would ask and how those questions might construct the event. We would try to respond empirically to the situation, rather than impose our analysis. Our sense of responsibility to the documentary subjects was meant to ensure that the authority of construction would lie with them, as much as with that of the maker. While the symbolic power of the camera evoked a sense of history and identity within the art community, it was the act of collaboration that empowered the "disenfranchised" in the making of a documentary. In many ways, third-person documentaries, even when they indicated the identification of the maker with her subject, were a politically safer alternative to the more difficult realm of fiction or personal narrative.

Early feminist self-portraiture was accused of narcissism. In her valuable response to Rosalind Krauss' declaration of video as narcissism, Micki McGee reminds us that Freud noted two levels of narcissism; he "distinguished between primary narcissism (a healthy and necessary state of ego development) and a secondary narcissism (a pathological condition in which the ego becomes the sole object of its love.)"[50] McGee relates narcissism both to a sociological condition that accompanies commodity fetishism, and to a psychological state at the crux of women's psychic formation within the culture: narcissism is demanded of women and yet they are disparaged for it. To either sidestep narcissism or confront its roots, women turned to video documentary. The feminist documentary emphasized collective, not individual, action, yet, as Ann Kaplan suggests, the giving of voice to the voiceless raised a series of problems. These documentaries often represented a traditional narrative of closure, suggesting a totalizing knowledge of their women subjects. This is particularly problematic for those who have been historically constructed as Other. Alice Jardine notes that these specific issues in feminist work amplify problems with "realist" practices in general:

1) truth and falsehood have been and must be taken out of opposition;

2) reality defined as representation can no longer play the major part in reformulating a new approach to "truth" if we are to avoid the repetitive violence of moralistic thinking;

3) no one can tell the truth — not at least all of it, and, finally;

4) henceforth "truth" can only be though through that which subverts it; the "real" for Lacan; "ecriture" for Derrida; and the "becoming of difference" for Deleuze.[51]

Documentary, while appearing to be "seamless," relies on a thoroughly constructed "real". Traditional sources of authority, as Barthes points out, contain the same truth-power as contemporary advertising and current-affairs reportage.[52] In fact, postmodernism has tripped on the cord of "truth," posing a new set of relations independent of the object/subject, truth/lie oppositions of Western cultural tradition, or even the Marxist practices reproduced by committed Left documentaries.

POWER OF THE DOCUMENT

Video was used by the Vancouver Art Gallery, Intermedia and, later, the Western Front to document other media.[53] Such documentation did not necessarily represent the creation of an autonomous work, although video was often the only

50. Micki McGee, "Narcissism, Feminism and Video Art," *Heresies 12* (Sex Issue): 88.

51. Alice Jardine, "The Demise of Experience," *Gynesis: Configurations of Woman and Modernity* (Ithaca: Cornell University Press, 1985): 149.

52. See Sara Diamond and Gary Kibbins, "Total Recall," *Trade Initiatives* (Vancouver: SVES, 1988).

53. See *Western Front Video* (Montréal: Musée d'Art Contemporain, 1984).

remaining trace of the original work. Still, as Peggy Gale suggests in *The Limits of Performance*, in the age of simulacra, the document stands in for the actual event lost in the mists and myths of time. Documentation allows the ephemeral to circulate. For this reason, the document can accrue value in the marketplace.[54]

Hank Bull and Kate Craig suggest a shift in historical consciousness from the early seventies to the present.[55] Performance artists seldom had direct access to technology, so works were not remade as they are now, for the camera. Characterized by one-camera, long-shot, continuous-take shoots, performance documents emphasized function over form. These pieces exhibit both the austere conditions of video technology at the time and the dogged commitment on the part of the Western Front to document everything. Currently, however, the difficulty of restoration is so profound that archive holders are tempted to allow this aspect of the past to slip back into the ephemeral — a gesture perhaps in keeping with the maker's original intention in choosing a medium as time-based as performance. In any case, the significance of documentation has diminished drastically today with the advent of the consumer video camera, which symbolically, through its alliance to home movies and the snapshot, places documentation by other than the accredited news or production team in the private sphere.

Vancouver's documentary practice flourished until the early 1980s; shifts occurred when video makers recognized the constructed nature of the image, and the problem with "positive imagery." Producers committed to the traditional documentary form eventually moved into educational television and the National Film Board or commercial industrial production. Those still in the art community tended to favour works with a theoretical edge, even when they retained a documentary aesthetic. Some artists continued to make use of the documentary mode, while rejecting the relentless technical optimism of the earlier era. The work of Kim Tomczak of Pumps refers to surveillance techniques (the panopticon gaze) to ironically critique the dehumanizing control of surplus and poor populations. The video *Vancouver, Canada or They Chant Fed Up* (1980) surveys the downtown eastside in slow motion, while an upbeat tourism song is gradually replaced with alienating electronic music:

> "Come on to B.C./ flowers of Victoria/ totem poles and Indians/ the caribou the Kootenay stew/ the lakes the streams the mountains blue/ we like Canada it's the best/ B.C. is our home..."

54. Peggy Gale, *The Limits of Performance* (Vancouver: Western Front Society, forthcoming).

55. See *Western Front Video*, ibid.

Baudrillard's theory about the exodus of representation from the social into the field of simulacra operates as a framework for describing the apparent dominance of the media over the "mass" of society, and as a dismissal of interventionist strategies that function on the level of content rather than form. Early film theory tended to draw a direct analogy between the individual dreamlike experience of viewing film and television; in both cases, the viewer was pinned down by a sexually differentiated and inescapable gaze. Television was somehow simply a smaller, less authoritative version of the dream screen. This coincided with early ideas about the nature of watching television, which emphasized the isolation of the individual viewer within the private space of family. The viewer received a corporately controlled (private) but publicly available signal from the television station of his or her (highly regulated) choice. Later theorists, using sociological data gathered from a more disillusioned television audience, examined television viewing as highly social, valuable for organizing discourse within the family, and for ordering silence or exchange.[56]

Patricia Mellencamp, referring to Baudrillard's "ecstasy of communication," notes that we are "rude" viewers of television — "never in danger of being seen, spoken to or even being a voyeur...we turn off 'experts' and leaders in mid syllable, [and] talk on the telephone while urgent new bulletins are being announced."[57] Mellencamp suggests that monopoly control over politics and opinion has made the masses rebel by remaining silent — forsaking an angry response to media manipulation, they sidestep the direct message of the medium to critique the content. Certainly such theories are confirmed by the advent of slash videos (recut television shows) created by private individuals in fan clubs. Given the chance, many would turn television on its head. Baudrillard decries the possibility of public interaction with the media, suggesting, perhaps as some home video has done, that the creation of endless human "transmitters," where everyone gets the chance to represent, does nothing to facilitate communication, but merely simulates the condition we are already in.[58] This may well be an apt description of the expanding consumer market for communications technology — a technology already neatly ordered as the private and playful side of the media by industries that sometimes improve their standards simply to exclude the possibility of other independently produced signals. However, this argument belies the ongoing relevance of locally produced, community-based or politically oriented production.

56. Armes, ibid.

57. Patricia Mellencamp, "Avant-Garde TV: Simulation and Surveillance," *Vidéo*, ed. René Payant (Montréal: Artexte, 1986): 201.

58. Jean Baudrillard, "Requiem for the Media," *For a Critique of the Political Economy of the Sign,* trans. Charles Levin (St. Louis: Telos Press, 1981).

More optimistic, perhaps, is the recent work of documentary video makers and of a few video artists who have turned to film. Conditioned by concepts of "narrowcasting" and audience specificity, these producers have made use of critical theory to create politically based, but culturally realized, social projects that challenge the limits of documentary. Recent video practices that borrow from, distil and deconstruct documentary operate as a critique of form, yet many makers still aim for an end similar to that of the previous decade: a moment, even if fleeting, of collective identification. Gary Kibbins, drawing on "Deleuze's remarkable insight that life is not a personal thing," suggests that the "processes of achieving a collective are always close at hand....Collectivities are fluid, like material moments of subjectivity; they come into existence and as easily pass away again."[59] In Kibbins' thinking, this fragmented but powerful collectivity is often realized through irony and humour, and is both reinforced and made more remarkable by the "loss of unity of the subject," the fact that "the capitalist system, which rhetorically valorized the individual, conceived of Taylorism, the assembly line of massification." Within this context, the power of documentary practice is its link to the social.

Perhaps the most significant new developments in film and video have come in community productions by aboriginal artists and artists of colour. Self-determination in the field of documentation and experimentation are intrinsic to this emerging practice. Loretta Todd, in a *Video Guide* article, "Native Video in B.C.,"[60] traces the role of the white cultural "missionaries" who introduced video to native communities, believing that natives would choose to join the global village, ignoring the traditional forms of preservation that native communities had maintained. Todd decries the ongoing colonizing practices of white video producers who have built their careers on the exotica of native culture and history. The positive by-product of this misadventure was that native groups discovered that "video technology was not beyond our community's budget." According to Todd, video went hand in hand with the development of communications networks and education, becoming an educational tool to be used in the struggle for self-government and the recognition of aboriginal rights. With an established base of production for their own communities in place, the "challenge is to produce video." Other aboriginal artists, such as Hopi producer Victor Masayeva, warn that videotaping one's culture — preserving it on the level of representation — can replace the struggle to keep it alive as a material culture.[61] Yet there is no question that, given the right set of circumstances, even the most traditional documentary

59. Unpublished paper given at *Deluding Documentary,* Video In, 1989.
60. *Video Guide* 42 (Fall 1987): 6.
61. See also Joy Hall, "Native Communications: Top Priority," *Parallelogramme* (Winter 1988/89).

can provoke response. Take Mike MacDonald's experience with *Fish Story*. In this instance, the Native Brotherhood, desperate for an infusion of funds to build the native fleet and fishery in B.C., had been lobbying the departments of Indian Affairs and Fisheries for years. It was not until MacDonald arrived at the Department of Fisheries and screened *Fish Story* that the department agree to contribute $300 million to the fleet.

Perhaps there is an advantage to video's placement on the periphery. Video provides a means for marginalized groups to develop a critical practice, both through the reinvention of stripped-down, subjective documentary and experimentation with the formal possibilities of the medium. Video in Vancouver remains both a hearty area of intervention and one stubbornly aligned with a radical critique of the image, a point of entry into the social realm for women, native people and people of colour. It is its tangential and problematized relation to the real and to its affect, its "video vapours," that allows, despite its elliptical history, a continued and critical placement within documentary form.

In the conceptualist and neo-dada borrowing of documentary as a means of organizing everyday life (Glenn Lewis, Paul Wong, Gerry Gilbert), and as a medium for the self-reflexive surveillance of the artistic and political countercultures by their own memberships, the history of documentary video runs like an undercurrent beneath the cultural life of the 1960s, 1970s and early 1980s. It is stated through the committed lobbying of Metro Media and Video Inn for citizens' access to cable, and through the existence of Metro Media as a vital centre of community production. This history is also evident in the many cable programs produced by artist and subcultural communities through the 1970s and early 1980s. Documentary video came from the same roots as conceptual art and the populist practices of Intermedia.

In discourse with television and the technology of surveillance, artists chose a wide range of formal strategies suited to particular interventions; at times, documentary formed the appropriate envelope. How sad that the term "documentary" would be used as a rationale for dismissing works that had always refused such a neat compartmentalization into simple modes of address. Was it the old radical baggage associated with the term that caused this dismissal? — surely an antiquated notion in a context where advertising and its ability to mobilize the realist truism of the testimonial was as dominant as any radical documentary.

Conceptualist practice in other media, from Haacke to Kosuth, has evacuated mass-media forms, reordered their meanings or used the methods of social science in an ironic and reinforming way. Paul Wong's *Confused: Sexual Views* did precisely this, relying on an extensive "sociological" survey and discomforting jump-cuts to manipulate statements about sexuality and desire from a cross-section of individuals. Luke Rombout's dismissal of *Confused*, both for its explicit content and for its missed ironic documentary references, fits into the symbolic order of institutional development more than the VAG will comfortably admit. Since that time, video exhibition at an institution that was known throughout Canada for its strong relationship to that medium has lapsed. It may well be the uncomfortable relationship of video to the messy signification and pleasure of the everydayness of televisual representation that allows its dismissal. Both the problem and the aesthetic lack that video represents to institutions reside in the medium's relationship to social life and the complexity of communities.

The decision to cancel Wong's exhibition reinforced the historic division between documentary (as a low art form aligned to film, journalistic practices and propaganda) and those experimental practices acceptable to (high) visual-art institutions. This distinction allowed Rombout's invocation "not art" to stand against the work. I have no easy answers to these problems, only the polemic embedded in Patricia Mellencamp's words:

> "Perhaps the sacrilegious intrusion by avant-garde TV accounts for the skepticism of the sacred Museum toward "video"...Museums are still baffled by reproducibility and intangibility (and presumably, Walter Benjamin) including video vapour-erasable, electronic energies which commerce and capitalism have harnessed."[62]

62. Mellencamp, 197.

VIDEO: WRITING HISTORY

by Louise Poissant

As a recording witness of events and fictions, video has become our individual and collective memory. It records important facts and special effects, everything worthy of being saved, the usual, the surprising. In itself a fragile, perishable support, it retains a volatile, ephemeral imprint of the short episodes we choose to capture and review and relive — later. Later — a timeframe hardly compatible with video, whose portable, user-friendly tools make for a live art extending indefinitely alongside our lives. We would need a second life to review the first one, which leaves us little time to consume its fading trail on video. A not very reliable memory, indeed, video reproduces the actual rhythm of events as they unfold. The news and the event — themselves effects of video — are soon over. Video automatically converts "what's happening" into "what was", leaving the field wide open for our attention to wander off in search of something else again.

As Derrick de Kerckhove so clearly saw, video is the new electronic pen writing history. Yet, it is not so much as memory that video records history. Instead, it makes events. It designates with its electronic eye what deserves to be retained and recorded, therefore, seen and lived. A selective gaze, video notices and captures live occurrences which cannot really be foreseen but which must somehow be noteworthy. This retroactive effect of video on unfolding reality clearly signals the end of an era and a belief-system, which separated a deed and its description, reality and fiction, history and the writing of history. Everything in video upsets this belief-system, which was already seriously undermined by philosophy.

Video goes beyond simply recording "what was," like photography — with greater capabilities and spontaneity, it interweaves optical images, synthetic simulation and electronic effects. Its scope is well nigh infinite. Flexible, portable, high resolution camcorders have greatly extended the range of possible viewpoints. Shooting special effects and incorporating other-sourced images imply handling inherently different materials. But it is perhaps in the separate editing of effects that video actually transforms the writing of current history. It is now possible to work with more than a dozen layers of images from different sources, which are superimposed, processed in parallel, then recombined, variously enhanced, with multiple windows and segments, inlays, mosaics, distorted colours, solarisation, in combination with effects like slow-motion, fast-forward, and fade-outs, first introduced in film.

SEDIMENTATION

Video images uncover new depths, or rather, new dimensions. Following Jean-Paul Fargier, Philippe Dubois refers to "the laminated effect". One could also evoke the "onionskin property", to use the American expression designating multiple layers superimposed and interposed to create not an in-depth image, as in perspective-based arts, but rather, a chunk comprising multiple layers of interpenetrating images. It is interesting to note that video, along with a few other image technologies like holography and virtual reality, tend to reposition images in space. As Pierre Lévy points out, the advent of printing and the development of perspective made it possible to represent and relate the world in two dimensions. An exercise in flattening, perspective creates an illusion of depth and movement by reducing everything to the two dimensions of plane geometry. And just as words are inscribed on paper, representations are laid out on canvas.

Video uses its own particular resources to respatialize images, volumes and movements. A whole formal vocabulary comes into play, along with various effects including integrating tapes into installations and developing video environments. In spite of its narrow magnetic support and the flattening effect of the cathode screen, video manages to open up space and facilitate interpenetrating planes, which can be entered into as in painting. The viewer can project himself into video images, as in film. Moreover, video works and installations are constantly experimenting with the displaying and overlapping of numerous image layers and the slices of reality they represent, combining reality and fiction, real and imaginary references.

Video takes us into a repositioning in topological space, in a multidimensional space. Like the world it portrays while itself contributing to the picture, video operates at the intersection and conjunction of numerous spaces at once. Contemporary man — a sort of patchwork produced by the meeting and interpenetration of the various universes he moves about in — no longer exists in a unified, homogeneous space, as Michel Serres observed. In fact, "the body functions in a Euclidean space... It sees in a projective space; touches, caresses and feels in a topological space; suffers in another; hears and communicates in a third; and so on." This deep conviction of pluridimensionality is reinforced by the sense that one is able to explore only a certain number of possibilities arising from encounters and environments that promote those particular possibilities among so many others.

THE KALEIDOSCOPE EFFECT

Effect or condition, video has obviously contributed to the splintering of perspectives requiring an ever greater degree of sensibility. That "the I is legion" is readily apparent to anyone living in the era of remote control, multiculturalism and the global village — in a word, in the communication era, where video remains the passport. Each of these aspects of contemporary life taps into new existential conditions, an *aesthesis* instituting a fundamentally different relation with time and space.

The global village is the combined effect of satellite and video supplying scenes from elsewhere and everywhere. It is also the effect of surveillance cameras, potentially reticulating the entire surface of the planet. And not just the surface, but all of space, and spaces within spaces. Surveillance cameras take in everything without selection, in the event that something might happen, and in many cases to prevent anything from happening. If the global village so dear to McLuhan aims at abolishing distance and linking cultures increasingly conscious of their inter-relatedness and interdependence, are we not all on the same boat, that no one can leave — as Michel Serres says. That same global village threatens to shrink Virilio's concept of "life-size" and consequently, our idea of the world. Communications, and especially images from elsewhere, abolish distances, and by so doing, shrink the extent of the unknown, the magic of unexplored possibilities and territories, already occupied, of course, but nevertheless imagined as virgin and intact.

Multiculturalism is the richest and most convincing version of the global village, which some fear to be assuming empire proportions and creating a cultural leveling — and it seems to be the mainspring of current video. Multiculturalism is perhaps best expressed in the mosaic effect both on-screen and in installations. The splitting and reduction possibilities of the video screen represent the meeting and parallel arrangement of perspectives, the co-presence of differences, the openness towards collective and personal multiplicity characteristic of multiculturalism. And, even if the majority of people consume video in a homogeneous way, as television ratings attest, minorities still have a diversity of choices reflecting their ethnic, cultural, and personal interests and ties. Moreover, as Lipovetsky foresaw, everyone is free to constitute individual programming and video collections at will, according to personal desire. Video thus enhances fragmentation.

The remote control is perhaps the last refuge of ethics, the last form of power available to some, at least, to those who have adopted the couch potato style denounced by Virilio, and whose environment does not extend beyond the video screen. On a deeper level, the remote is a compass, or as it is called, a control — for making choices, selecting the pertinent, plugging into meaning in the multitude of meanings. If our attention often seems so febrile, so anxious, it is because individuals are still not quite capable of making choices, of deciding among their preferences, and living in the midst of multiplicity. The remote is also a way of reminding oneself of one's own presence, as one moves through an environment that no longer surrounds or envelops, but on the contrary, maintains a continuous state of wandering. The remote is a little instrument enabling rapid movement around a more and more limited and increasingly encumbered village.

VIDEO LANDSCAPES

It can easily be understood why many video artists appropriate video in landscape-installations. For some, it is a critique of doubtful video effects or processes, such as surveillance, for example. The perverse grid-effect already denounced by Foucault is increasingly reticulated by video's invading eye. Other artists examine content, as it weaves a polluted landscape in which nothing good has any chance of growing.

For most artists, landscape in video provides an opportunity to reformulate the unavoidable question of identity. Inherited from 15th century painting, landscape is still a tranquil image at once limited because embraceable from a single viewpoint, and limitless because lost in the immensity beyond. Landscape is that portion, that cut-out section of the environment worthy of contemplation. A window-painting looking out onto nature, landscape has been increasingly appreciated as nature itself retreated away from cities. Indeed, it is in landscape that the idea of nature was consolidated as an environment of flora and fauna unviolated by man. Landscape designates and introduces nature in the field of representations. More than that, the idea of landscape draws contours around the human field, tracing its horizons.

MAPPING

The strong links between landscape and questions of national identity are perhaps best expressed in the concept of mapping. A geographical map itself determines a territory, and consequently a national identity. If video has contributed to a world-wide leveling process, it is also a tool used by many artists to introduce and explore something different, slices of other cultures. A magnifying glass enlarging certain events, a relay suggesting certain parallels, video writes segments of histories.

Video also reminds us that a map has meaning only when it can be marked "You are here". This indication constitutes both a reference point and a scale, enabling one to situate oneself in a literal sense. But it also allows this in a figurative sense — a fact understood by artists who reintroduce the viewer into an environment created by video feedback. A doubling in the "You are here AND there," video transports us to other places, to other territories. The aesthetic nature of techniques like video feedback make the doubling experience — the feeling of being manipulated in an area created by another — not only tolerable but actually enjoyable. The experience also leads to self-discovery — the gerund "mapping" clearly indicates the action of making one's way, establishing a direction, orienting oneself, as in installations which make use of the viewer's presence.

For many video artists, mapping becomes a device for producing their own identification (I.D.). A videotape presents a series of life episodes from previous films or videos, re-edited around an "I am here" and constituting a self combining past images and present orientations. This kind of mapping can also be achieved with computer techniques. Surfaces can be enhanced, and covered with any number of textures available in a data base. In video, the artist can tinker with his own identity, superimposing and juxtaposing slices of life. The result is a sort of topological account of milestones, and the subject's limits and borders, as revealed by the density of references and multiplicity of viewpoints — an I.D. card going over past and present ground and interior landscapes.

Translation by Jean-Luc Svoboda.

Appearance, Memory and Influence

by Tom Sherman

Appearance is important. The way you feel on camera makes a difference in the way you look. The clothes you wear, the way you wear your hair, the way you treat the camera and the person behind it. Your eyes tell us everything through a close-up. Your walk forces us back as your boots step firmly into a circle of brilliant white light. Flat black boots in silhouette against the glare of the studio floor. One of the toes turns up into the profile of a snarling rat. The other turns away, lying flat, hidden in shadow. Silent, lurking, potentially diseased. The monitor in the control room provides us with an immediate perspective on an imaginary video environment. The director calls the shots in this virtual reality. In video, appearance is important. In this first scene, a slick pair of boots turn out to be a couple of rats. One is aggressive, menacing. The other is playing possum.

You might wonder, what in the hell is the author up to? The artist who strikes out with such an unlikely image at the outset of an essay cannot be very serious about communication. Fuck communication. Nobody needs communicators. Communicators don't exist, except in the minds of those who wear starchy, buttoned-down collars and more than the occasional turtleneck. If the left/right brain hypothesis makes you want to puke, then you too know the academics are anything but communicators. You understand their suppositions but reject them because you simply can't relate. They say the left lobe is linear and rational and super straight, while the right side of the brain is wild and crazy and prone to being naked and glistening and as slippery as liver and deep red like a beet, not grey, but a soft, blood-wet organ framed as an illusion in a cheap mirror with a hand-sewn leather frame. Honest to God, the redundancy of their high-pitched, whining chorus of ignorance induces one massive, globally comprehensive tension headache on the intellectual populace, thinly scattered and remote as it is. The neurocultural chant of the McLuhanite drones will likely continue to build relentlessly until every electronic mirror on the planet implodes in sync with death defying intensity and penultimate misfortune and disgusting waste.

What's the point of forcing honest people to analyse a culture of apparent lies? Whether they listen to those who speak openly in an unguarded, natural tone of voice or to those who deceive through elegant, subtle, devious manipulations, the problem for the audience is always ultimately boredom. Normal tendencies in dress and fashion or in the generic choreography of behaviour are naturally redundant and inevitably quite depressing in their predictability. The stereotypical personality is certainly a fundamental aspect of human limitation. Media coverage merely exacerbates our own insecurities, inviting us to stretch the truth. In a culture of deceit the surface dips and swells with changes of appearance, both radical and gradual, all of a sudden, day by day, once in a blue moon. A belly-laugh is toned down, a cigarette fetish eliminated, the hair flips up and disappears into the stiff brutality of razor-stubble. The cameras play their part and the viewers have little choice but to sense the apparent differences and to respond in kind. Video appears to accelerate the frequency of change. Or does it contribute to a rather tenuous stability by grabbing a hold of an image or sound, thereby gradually freezing our relative powers of association? The anchor-person reads the news every night inside the rigid frame of a single shot. Her goodbye smile concludes our daily thirty minute picture of the world. Could we manage to wrap up the world in half an hour without her professional assistance?

The reality of television news is a manifesto of video. The newscasters come and go, while the world remains the same. Nobody cares enough to tape the news, although most will swear they want to save the world. The serious gap between stated convictions and actual performance represents the contradictory, gutless behaviour we have engineered through our schools. The fashionable posture of concern is tough to stomach in those who think there is nothing to lose. Maybe this is the reason our governments are at war with education. Whatever we think about the value of formal education, the children are the victims because they can't find work and pay taxes and none of the adults, not even the most perfect parents, want to foot the bill for their children's learning experience. Most people think it'll get worse towards the end of the century. But let's flip the future around on its head for the purpose of the argument.

In a much more optimistic scenario for the 21st Century, let's imagine our children will all have jobs and they will somewhat reluctantly pick up the tab for massive programs of adult education. Everyone over sixteen years of age, if they are smart, will volunteer for intensive training in video communications. Talk about potential growth industries! In fifteen years communication will be defined as stimulation through simulation. Fifteen years might be too far ahead to see anything clearly, so how about ten? If we are going to be prepared for the near future, then it's back to the basics for everyone. Fuck the ten year plan, artists are already at least a decade ahead. Through the behaviour of the artists we may witness the mid-nineties today. The artists, the only people really living in the present, can't help but telegraph the future to all those who reside in the past. As obvious as this is, the last thing the human race wants to be told is that it's dependent on its artists to periodically introduce a few cracks in the repressive wall of obsolete thought and behaviour.

Real changes occur in individuals first, and artists working with a powerful technology like video are literally in possession of a super-weapon of perceptual transformation. Video is the supreme technology of the era for sharpening or dulling one's perception. Video is the ultimate instrument of perceptual transformation, but quite frankly, unless artists know exactly what they are doing with this technology, their circuits are likely to end up overloading. In many cases that's the fun part, commonly referred to as the buzz. Humming a sixty-cycle tune of image intoxication, the real potential for unnatural sensitivity exists with video. It's too bad so few artists succeed in unleashing the full power of this instrument of perceptual transformation. Communicating perceptual change will never happen if artists insist on sticking all their perceptual tools up their own asses. But then again, communication may be best understood to be a specialized function of the communicators.

Video is a ubiquitous communications technology which is used to record and represent images and sounds electronically. It is a push-button technology, easy to use. Technically speaking, if the light and acoustics of a situation are well understood, all anyone has to do to achieve the maximum level of performance from a video recorder is to point the camera in the right direction and position the microphone in the proper place. Video technology is reliable and portable and quiet and simple as A, B, C. It provides satisfying results instantly. Unfortunately, video technology is all too frequently used to record and represent the most pedestrian level of thought by people who see only what they want to see and never listen. Only rarely does the artist transcend the electronic doldrums of video banality. On the surface of the screen the medium does appear to have a magnificent, largely unrealized potential. This unrealized potential is immediately apparent in the initial stages of exposure and disclosure. When an individual perceives his or her image through video, his or her appearance is a revelation.

With video one's image is so different, so very far away from the flesh and blood you imagined. Watching yourself on the screen is almost like seeing oneself through the eyes of a stranger. Across the courtyard you sit in your kitchen drinking coffee in silence. The soft natural light of the day plays across your brow. Your hair falls as you lower your eyes. You study your image as a stranger would. The frame of the window outlines the subject under observation. The time is repeated, the space confined. The movement is predictable. The image is stable although the lifeform appears fragile from a distance. The body is so vulnerable in front of the mind. The hands are exact, the fingers articulate. The face changes like a signature, whether rushed or forceful or loving or curt. The human form resides perfectly within its limitations. The lifeform on the screen, this viewpoint from the mind's eye, is the gift we receive from the machine called video. By reducing the magnificent complexity of life to only that surface reality which can be represented by video, the mere exposure of one's physical body to the camera becomes analogous to a full disclosure of heart and soul. Standing alone naked in front of oneself may be perceived as an act of love. The video machine grants us this privilege, such a unique relationship with ourselves. How will we ever succeed in expressing our gratitude to this machine?

While many may wish to acknowledge the value of these machines, millions more might question the necessity of expressing our gratitude to the inanimate infrastructure of our civilization. Video, after all, is a technology which has been engineered to suit the species' purposes in general and to some degree to respond to our own individual needs. For most individuals with a typically superficial relationship with video, there is obviously no need to give anything back to the machines, other than the intensity of their undivided attention. We all take for granted the fact that a global population may witness an event or environment instantly and simultaneously through the common devices of the camera and microphone. All of us who love to watch appreciate the technology which has permitted us to look in on events and observe environments anywhere within the range of the technology's artificial point-of-view. We have only begun to examine with our senses a universe preconceived exclusively in abstract terms. Individuals bound by the normal prerequisites of human mortality can now appear to be in two places at the same time.

Where photography and film had excelled historically as the ultimate technologies of memory, video quickly rewrote our perception of memory through an apparent multiplication of space. A "live" event transmitted from one location to another through the devices of video can be described as a transient display of instant memory. Magnetic tape, like photochemical media before it, functions concretely as hard copy. Images and sound may be transmitted from machine to machine with video, with or without tape as a backup. In other words, the hard copy is optional. Video memory is fundamentally transient. We focus our attention on the tape as a physical medium, but video travels well beyond our senses at the speed of light, from machine to machine. Video transmitted as radio is called television. Television is frequently the transient memory of film which has been prerecorded on videotape. Tomorrow's cinema will be just as fleeting. Cinema will be video without tape in a theatre and events on the big screen will appear to be "live". Space will apparently be multiplied and our perception of memory will be rewritten again by the technology of video.

Memory is a place in the distance where we observe ourselves. In memory we leave our bodies for the space and time of our minds. Memory is a silent shower of light. The body suspended, the mind fastened tight. Memory is hard to control. We view the past as we must, in the best possible light. We second guess the pain. Our minds are full of conclusions. Memory is recollection and recollection is the trigger of imagination. The past is the truth in the shadow of doubt. The technologies of memory are often utilized as instruments of deceit. Memory is written and rewritten over and over again. Documentation is the sticky residue which binds together the loose ends of our imperfect memories. To verify all events within the broad context of reality, we must check and recheck the record. Our relationships with machines are documented by the recordings left behind. The "shelf-life" of a video recording depends to a greater extent on our need to remember than on the environmental conditions governing the security of storage. The archivist must save everything if he or she wishes to be remembered at all. The good archivist will be remembered as a creature bearing both the wings of an angel and the horns and tail of a devil. The video machine has become our personal, inanimate archivist. Our intimate relationships with these machines are well documented.

Memory is fascinating, especially when it is framed by the artist/machine relationship. The dance the artist improvises in front of the recording machine is elaborate, deviant and diversionary. The artist treats the machine with respect as the primary audience because his or her image is at stake. The precision and clarity of representation offered by the machine forces the artist to jump through hoops. In each attempt to avoid displaying behaviour which might be considered mundane and stereotypical, the artist attempts to manifest a presence which is both challenging and acceptable to his or her audience. Take note that the machine is loyal regardless of the artist's creative abilities. The audience of an artistic performance, whether the behaviour is displayed in front of or from behind the camera, is always presumed by the critic to be human, or at least an animate intelligence. The technology itself, which comprises the very sophisticated, inanimate infrastructure of our civilization, is never considered to be the primary receptor for the artist's image. This critical, anthropomorphic bias obscures the process of making art while under the influence of a machine. Video is an instrument in the tradition of the telescope or microscope, except its power lies not in the science of optics, but in the realm of perceptual transformation. We do not see the world in greater detail, but we do sense the world differently with video. The psychological aspect of spatial and contextual multiplication is intoxicating and addictive. Space is multiplied on line while events are marked precisely in machine time, microsecond by microsecond. The image of reality perceived while in sensory liaison with the video machine causes one to become extremely preoccupied with the nature of time.

Exposure to a technology as attractive and resourceful as video inevitably leads to intoxication and addiction. Withdrawal is painful and debilitating. Avoidance results in anxiety, followed by prolonged periods of depression. The influence of this dominant communications technology is exhaustive to the degree that many become hopelessly lost without the machine. Video dominates with its magnetism and authority. As a species we must offer video something in return for our freedom. The servile artist must be generous in response to the demands of his or her technological master. The technology of video was conceived and realized by engineers for the purpose of extending our physical presence through a global, universal network of machines. Video technology has been perfected and employed to the degree that our sense of space and time has been radically transformed, conceivably forever. Turning our backs or burying our heads in the sand are not realistic options. We must face up to the problems we are having in our relationship with video technology. Most of us sense there is something deeply wrong with the way we visualize the machines. We visualize the machines with only our images on the screens. We are constantly dislocated by our insistence on a video representation of the human form. Even when a landscape with another species is displaced through video, we seldom resist a deranged voice-over. Influence is dominance and mastery and control. We must find a way of expressing our gratitude to this machine called video.

With the marriage of video and computers more and more artists are turning their attention to the image of the machine itself. The digital computer involves many artists in the origination of new images, both visual and acoustic, through the discipline of programming abstract computer languages. Ironically, the long term goal of this form of image invention may be representation through simulation. In other words, writing instructions which permit the computer to draw representational imagery. On the other hand, a number of artists are focusing their attention on perceptual simulation with the machines. This artificial simulation of perception in both analog and digital machines is called image processing. Image processing is the manipulation of available images and the invention of new images through amplification, distortion, transfiguration and synthesis. For instance, images from an analog video camera may be fed into a digital computer processor which will impose its own order on the incoming video with the output or display becoming a thing in itself. Artists involved with such hybrid video/computer instruments are doing their part to create a different picture of the artist/machine relationship. The machine is finally permitted to articulate and display its own image. The artist has found a way of expressing his or her gratitude to the machine. The artist has offered the machine creative autonomy. We seem to be off the hook for the time being. Finally, the machines may influence each other freely, uninhibited by our selfish reservations and anthropocentric criticism. Only time will tell whether the human audience has the capacity to love the machine for being itself.

OF MONITORS AND MEN AND OTHER UNSOLVED FEMINIST MYSTERIES

VIDEO TECHNOLOGY AND THE FEMININE

by Nell Tenhaaf

Contemporary women artists who work in technological media are faced with a contradiction. The domain in which they are operating has been historically considered masculine, yet women's current access to electronic production tools seems to belie any gender barrier. Indeed, women have benefited by these tools in the last two decades to the extent that they have offered some freedom from the sexist art historical and critical practices attached to more established media. The philosophy of technology, however, has been articulated entirely from a masculinist perspective in terms that metaphorize and marginalize the feminine.[1] In real social discourse, this claiming of technology has been reinforced by, and has probably encouraged, a male monopoly on technical expertise, diminishing or excluding the historical contributions of women to technological developments.[2]

From a feminist point of view, female invisibility in the discourses of technology calls for nothing less than a radical reconstitution of technology, its development and its uses. While this massive agenda is clearly beyond the purview of feminist cultural practitioners, it is well within our scope to develop images and tropes that are body-based in a way that opens up an affirmative space for the feminine in electronic media practices. My hypothesis is that autobiographical, metaphorical, even mythical feminine enunciations in this domain contribute to an unwriting of the masculine bias in technology.

1. My terminology includes the whole gamut of gender difference identifiers: woman and man, female and male, feminine and masculine, feminist and masculinist. These are not used interchangeably, but certainly they overlap. My intention is to emphasize that even the biological terms, male and female, have to be seen as socially constructed. I use the term "the feminine" in the sense that it has been proposed by the French feminists, especially Luce Irigaray.

2. See for example Joan Rothschild, ed., *Machina Ex Dea: Feminist Perspectives on Technology* (New York: Pergamon Press, 1983) and Maureen McNeil, ed., *Gender and Expertise* (London: Free Association Books, 1987).

WILLING MACHINES/BACHELOR MACHINES

The modernist philosophical framework for technology is the discourse of the will, specifically the will to power postulated by Friedrich Nietzsche in the late nineteenth century. Expanded upon by subsequent philosophers, in particular Martin Heidegger, this discourse sustains a view of technology as the manifestation of an essential masculine will that is the driving force of the whole modern era. In its language and imagery, the will to power is interwoven with a deeply entrenched and mythic concept of duality that describes commanding (and the power of the machine) as a masculine attribute, while submission (and the rule of feeling) is described as a feminine one.

For Nietzsche, will commands the body toward ineffable and always predetermined desires. Will, as being, is a kind of machine, necessarily engendering the will to power which is defined as always wanting more power. And will has replaced reason as the highest mental faculty, so that the modern thinking ego is characterized by the I-will and, subsequently, the I-can.[3] This characterization has generated a metaphor central to modernity, that of machine-like man, in whom the body as the domain of affect and source of any sense of authentic desire is disconnected from and subjugated to the mind, configured as pure will.

Will doesn't stop at commanding the interior life of the male social subject and fueling a cyclical and vicious internal battle in which, according to Nietzsche, pleasure is defined by the conquest of displeasure. The philosophy of the will also constitutes the (male) body as subject to an externalized ruling drive to power, a technological power that is unidirectional and obsessed with the future. Nietzsche writes:

> ...perhaps the entire evolution of the spirit is a question of the body; it is the history of the development of a higher body that emerges into our sensibility...In the long run, it is not a question of man at all: he is to be overcome.[4]

And in the mid-twentieth century, Heidegger in *The Question Concerning Technology* reads this forward-looking drive as a progression in which technology, whose very nature is the will to will, would annihilate everything arising from it, an essential and inevitable destructiveness. The fundamental duality of will, its stakes of masculine dominance and feminine submission, may be played out psychologically within any one person, any one body. Or in contemporary sexual

3. Hanna Arendt, *The Life of the Mind: Willing* (New York and London: Harcourt Brace Jovanovich, 1978), 20.

4. Friedrich Nietzsche, *The Will to Power*, trans. Walter Kaufmann and R.J. Hollingdale (New York: Vintage Books, 1968), 358.

politics, it might shed all gender specificity and be played as a game between consenting adults. But because of its central place in the philosophical legacy of modernism, this duality marks the real technologized world as a battleground characterized by rigid gender differences and a will to power actualized in the form of male-controlled progress through technological growth. This Nietzschean drive, fueled by nineteenth-century man's inner battles, has resulted indeed in a certain amount of destructiveness, through the development of a multitude of technologies that project out into the modern social body in the form of invasive and colonizing tools.

The bachelor machine is an update on Nietzsche's willing machine that is driven by will and desire. An alluring and obscure figure of the twentieth-century avant garde, the bachelor machine is constructed around a desire that is equally turned in on itself. This desire is frustrated, and also regenerated, by a nihilistic preponderance of denials focused on celibacy, autoeroticism and death. The bachelor machine is a literary and theoretical construct taking as its paradigm Marcel Duchamp's *Le Grand Verre: La Mariée mise à nue par ses célibataires, même* (1912-23). Both as representation and as philosophical proposal, it connects a masculine bachelor to a feminine bride in an impossible, eternally suspended, internal coupling of opposites. Depicted by Duchamp as a drawing of simple mechanical elements and recordings of chance events, all caught or "delayed" on a large piece of glass, the bachelor machine has come to mean a self-perpetuating masculine psychic machine. Freud too was very fond of the psychic-machine metaphor, and declared it to be quintessentially masculine: "it is highly probable that all complicated machinery and apparatus occurring in dreams stand for the genitals - and as a rule the male ones."[5]

The bachelor machine exposes desire, that is *male* desire, as entirely subject to instrumentality. Two terms mediate the bachelor's desire: the machine or technology, present in *Le Grand Verre* as "working parts" that simulate the absent body; and "the feminine," represented as an ethereal cloud or skeleton in the upper half of the work. This bride functions as a conduit for information from another (fourth or nth) dimension and as the desiring impetus that the bachelor below needs for his solitary pursuits. For Duchamp, the bride herself knows a certain limited machine desire, as a "motor with very feeble cylinders: Desire magneto (sparks of constant life)."[6]

5. Cited in Constance Penley, "Feminism, Film Theory and the Bachelor Machines," in *m/f*, no. 10 (1985): 49.
6. Paul Matisse, *Marcel Duchamp, Notes* (Boston: G.K. Hall & Company, 1983). This is from note 155.

Through a multitude of writings which embrace everything from origin myths to alchemy, and which do not overlook psychoanalysis, the bachelor machine has become the signifier for a multiple and layered interpretive strategy that stretches across time like an Einsteinian clock caught in the effects of relativity. In *Le Macchine Celibi*, an exhibition catalogue produced in 1975 containing several texts on the bachelor machine, Michel de Certeau calls it a "way of writing" or "writing machine." This machine supplants an older, maternal "way of speaking", that of the seventeenth-century mystical tradition. In this displacement, the loss of the mother leads to "the solitude of speech with itself."[7]

In another of the catalogue texts, Michel Serres situates the bachelor machine within a representational history of the machine, from the static model (statues) through a system of the fixed reference point (perspective) into the workings of engines and thermodynamics with God as the motor of meaning. Now, he writes, "the transformational engine of our fathers' days has simply moved on into the informational state."[8] Serres' reading is echoed in Jean-François Lyotard's observation that "the growth of power, and its self-legitimation, are now taking the route of data storage and accessibility, and the operativity of information."[9] The bachelor machine thus outlines a mythical technological framework within which the male nihilistically identifies himself as a point of origin, circumscribing the female, and within representation, playing both masculine and feminine parts: "The bride stripped bare, derealized, is a pretext for producing without her."[10] She is necessary, but she is other than and separate from that dynamo that sustains itself *ad infinitum.*

The bachelor machine is not the same thing as the willing machine; some of its features are quite different. In particular, the feminine is more present in the bachelor machine, and complicates its mechanism. Also, the bachelor machine, as Duchamp posited it, is an ironic, self-conscious, even whimsical construct. But each of theses apparatuses proposes representation as male self-representation, and this self-rationalizing strategy is couched in autoerotic fantasy. Nietzsche's willing machine has power over nature, is self-reproducing. The bachelor creates *ex nihilo,*

7. Michel de Certeau, "Arts of dying/Anti-mystical writing," in Jean Clair and Harald Szeemann, eds., *Le Macchine Celibi / The Bachelor Machine* (Venice: Alfieri, edizioni d'arte, 1975), 88.

8. Michel Serres, "It was before the (world-) Exhibition," in Clair and Szeeman, *Le Macchine Celibi / The Bachelor Machine*, 68.

9. Jean-Francois Lyotard, *The Postmodern Condition: A Report on Knowledge*, trans. Geoff Bennington and Brian Massumi (Minneapolis: University of Minnesota Press, 1984), 47.

10. De Certeau, "Arts of dying," 92. Constance Penley calls attention to another apparatus that links the individual psyche, technology and the social body, "one that can offer impeccable credentials with respect to the bachelor machine's strict requirements for perpetual motion, the reversibility of time, mechanicalness, electrification, animation and voyeurism: the cinema." Penley, "Feminism," 39-40.

he needs neither mother nor father because, as an androgyne incorporating the anima and as a celibate priest incarnating God, he himself plays the role of archetypal creator. (He halts evolution, though, and directs it toward self-destruction and the end of the world.) However, in a fundamental way, these psychic machines are not autonomous. Their origin fantasies rely implicitly on a mythical conception of nature as a unified matrix, an assumed but necessarily inarticulated feminine that works as an instrument with which the male, the bachelor, touches himself and arouses himself.

To become desiring machines that are productive, in the sense employed by Deleuze and Guattari,[11] is to go beyond this desperate dream of original totality toward "pure multiplicity," an affirmation that is not reducible to any sort of unified state. Whatever the desiring machine (literary machine, social machine, celibate machine, etc.) produces, whether it be representation, the body, libido, or madness, this product exists only alongside the separate parts that make it up; it is itself a part. This is how Deleuze and Guattari articulate polyvocality and flux as points of resistance to a unitary history of repressed and repressive desires.

But how to deliver the feminine from its implicit and unspoken function in the machine? The male author is able to speak of his parts, his body parts in relation to a whole body or libido, from a positive masculine position in the symbolic order, a position of presence as a subject. It is still not as possible for a woman to speak in this way. For a woman, particularly in this era of biotechnologies and their "mechanical reproduction," the body as "object of scopic consumption...[is] hyperrealistically overrepresented...[it] remains profoundly absent," Rosi Braidotti says. And in relation to this absence, the feminine is both overinvested within discourse and feared as an essentializing term, so that, as Braidotti clarifies: "...it signifies a set of interrelated issues but it is not one notion per se. Not one corpus."[12]

To speak from this fragmentary and fluid feminine place is to see that the strange conjuncture of technological mastery, autoerotic pleasure and nihilism of the masculine machines might be thought of differently. It might be thought of as a mythical territory to be reclaimed by the desiring bride.

---

11. Gilles Deleuze and Felix Guattari, *Anti-Oedipus* (Minneapolis: University of Minnesota Press, 1983), 33-43. Deleuze and Guattari describe the desiring machine as producing repression, its own antiproduction, which is then integrated into the desire-production process, in the way that interruptions or breakdowns in the functioning of the technical machine are integral to its operations. Likewise, schizophrenia is a break in the flow of the real, in its production, which permits that flow to continue outside of the constraints of (Oedipal) social production. The interest of Deleuze and Guattari's machines is precisely their productivity, in contrast to bachelor nihilism.

12. Rosi Braidotti, "Organs Without Bodies," in *Differences* 1 (1988): 52. See also Donna Haraway, "A Manifesto for Cyborgs," in *Socialist Review* 80 (1985).

TURN-ON

"If machines, even machines of theory, can be aroused all by themselves, may women not do likewise?"[13] So asks Luce Irigaray in a 1974 essay with the enticing title "Volume-Fluidity."

How do women turn themselves on in the technological order? Irigaray has proposed a kind of feminine autoerotic engine in her theorization of female body parts, specifically the "self-caressing" of the labial lips, indicating a sexuality that is always plural and a psychic economy of "never being simply one."[14] Autoeroticism is a site of empowerment for women, in Irigaray's terms. How is this possible, when the autoerotic in the bachelor machine, corresponding as it does to the loss of the divine commandment of love and procreation written on the woman's body, signifies self-destruction? The bachelor's eroticism is reduced to a mechanism without a soul, while a woman reclaims her soul when she touches herself as, Irigaray says, she always and immediately can. Her autoeroticism can never be reduced — a utopian thought perhaps, but one that at least indicates a sexuality not shattered by the disappearance of laws for procreation and sacred heterosexual union.

Irigaray's emphasis on women's bodies elicits for many of her readers a fear of biological determinism or reductivism, of women's sexuality turned back on itself as defining the essence of being female. This argument against theorizing from the body is valid only if we accept the idea that any aspect of the body is simple or innocent, free of complex and controlling signifying practices. To foreground the body is to confront a set of social meanings already assigned to every one of the body's attributes, including biological sex difference. And it is in fact the persistent, if often invisible, masculinist essentialism in western philosophy and epistemology that has kept these socially constructed limitations in place. Thus a woman "thinking through the body"[15] and arousing herself is both multiple and complicated, not a reductivist proposition, overturning rather than reinforcing the legacy of dualistic thought.

Irigaray's focus on female autoeroticism is intensely bound up with the pain of living out the textual and sexual instrumentality that the willing/bachelor machine represents. The effects of this instrumentality are lived not just in the

13. Luce Irigaray, *Speculum of the Other Woman*, trans. Gillian C. Gill (Ithaca, New York: Cornell University Press, 1985), 232.

14. Luce Irigaray, *This Sex Which is not One*, trans. Catherine Porter (Ithaca, New York: Cornell University Press, 1985), 31.

15. See Jane Gallop, *Thinking Through the Body* (New York: Columbia University Press, 1989).

psyche by women but as well in the body, and are traditionally called mystery, enigma or hysteria. Irigaray writes about a possible renewed meaning of mysticism for women.[16] She delineates the historical mystic's path of contact with divinity, which is equally a process of reclaiming her "soul", her identity, from its ethereal state. The blissful and tortuous visit to the mystic of the divine essence, of "God," is registered forever afterward not just on her inner self but also on her body as a wound. The sought-after experience is a searing flame or lightning flash that lights up understanding, and this entails pain: "the wound must come before the flame."[17] But this newly discovered self who has had God as a lover and has fully debased herself (mimetically) to the nothingness that He knows her to be, by this process also reclaims her (auto)eroticism. The mystic's autoeroticism, once it is alight, signifies her coming into herself.

LIGHT MY FIRE

Mythology is both pre- and post-modern, pre- and post-scientific, in its power to metaphorize primal forces. Different accounts of human introduction to fire are also stories of the acquisition of knowledge, as are the various accounts of mysticism, including Irigaray's reworked version.

Mythology shapes our reception of light, and delineates both its masculine and feminine attributes. Light in the form of raw energy, fire, lightning, the sun, combustion: this light is mythically phallic. But keeping the hearth, harnessing and sustaining pure energy for light and heat, corresponds to matriarchal goddess lore.

Classical Greek mythology operates on a gender duality parallel to the one that structures the philosophy of technology. Theft of fire from the heavens was the birth of technology, and took the form of a man's rebellion against the gods. Prometheus stole energy in the form of fire from the gods and gave it to humans for light, heat and the ability to transform raw matter, a primal moment of technological enabling. As punishment for his hubris, he was chained to a rock and his liver was consumed each day by a carnivorous bird. Further, in Hesiod's telling of the tale, the gods punished humankind by first having Hephaestus, their artisan, fashion the beautiful Pandora, then sending her to earth with a grain jar full of evil.

In parallel biblical lore, Lucifer offered knowledge (light) to Eve and Adam in the Garden. Pandora and Eve, anti-heroines of the earliest writing cultures, became figures of the gods' punishment for acquisition and transmission of the light of knowledge.

16. Irigaray, "La mystérique," in *Speculum of the Other Woman*, 191.
17. Ibid., 193.

In pre-patriarchal lore the figure of fire-guardian or guardian of the hearth is the original keeper of light and heat, and she is embodied in Hestia/Vesta. She was conceived as both the centre of the household and the omphaloid centre of the earth (the *beth-el* in Hebrew), within a geocentric universe. Her legacy was carried over from the polytheistic into the early Christian era, so that her priestesses in ancient Rome were the Vestal Virgins, entrusted with keeping alight the perpetual fire at the mystic heart of the empire. As the rise of Christianity wiped out pagan supernatural practices, even as it offered magical revival from death and assumption into heaven for its adherents, and science came to acknowledge heliocentrism as the ordering physical principle of the universe, Vesta was displaced by androcentric figures of power.[18]

These stories break open the philosophic stranglehold of the self-rationalizing will to power by reformulating its strict gender duality, and by restoring the sexed body as active agent in the scene of the unconscious. Further, the multiplicity of mythological lore undermines the primacy of the Oedipal story in the modern western imagination, with its constitution of subjectivity structured on a masculine model.[19]

THRESHOLD

Now turn on the TV. The monitor screen is the threshold of passage from dark into light/life, the cervical opening from a womb that permits a spark of consciousness to come into being. The effect of the monitor screen is a sustained emission of contained light. This is emblematic of birth itself — coming into light, harnessing of energy, materialization from a crossing of electronic codes — from two sources, the feminine mystic flame and masculine raw energy. A pattern of light built on replication and combination of coded information, a passage between states.

The monitor is a new technological paradigm within the schema of the apparatus. As in cinema, the screen is an interface between a viewing subject and a complex representational apparatus, the camera. But it can be read alternately, as other than a bachelor machine, because it isn't a mechanical model but an electronic one. Rather than a set of moving parts that go round and round perpetually, it is an instantaneous and ephemeral event, a burst of electrons like a Promethean lightning bolt from within the monitor. The double-sided mirror of the monitor screen focuses light on one side and on the other emits light as it reflects an image.

18. Ginette Paris, *Pagan Meditations,* trans. Gwendolyn Moore (Dallas, Texas: Spring Publications Inc., 1986), 176.

19. See Jessica Benjamin, *The Bonds of Love: Psychoanalysis, Feminism, and the Problem of Domination* (New York: Pantheon Books, 1988), 133-181, and Deleuze and Guattari, *Anti-Oedipus.*

Superseding the mirror effect (the constitution of the spectator as a desiring subject, or the cinematic experience), and the look (the male gaze situating the subject within the dominance of the phallic), even before representation itself (establishing the symbolic order of the phallus), the monitor produces an effect of pure light. The bias of technological progress persuades us to think of video display as post-cinematic, but it might also be seen to correspond to a much more primary, generative event: coming into light out of darkness.

Contemporary physics tells us that both the wave-like and particle-like behaviours of light are products of our interaction with it, the result of our observation. In this respect, looking at light in display patterns is a confirmation of spectator subjecthood, whatever the apparatus used. But in one of the paradoxes of quantum mechanics, it is a subjecthood confirmed by computation from probability waves that describe only a tendency to a pattern.[20] Unfixed subjectivity is the embracing condition of our late-twentieth-century technologized world.

The representational fragmentation proliferating in media technologies reiterates this dispersed condition of subjectivity. Digital imaging techniques are particularly prone to hallucinatory visions that scatter the subject's viewing space and identification process — image fragmentation, simulation, virtual realities. Computer-generated imaging proposes thoroughly artificial scenarios and shattered points of view, often in speeded-up motion that would be impossible in the the physical world. As Paul Virilio says, "That's how we program our definitive absence."[21] Indeed, the male subject may be experiencing an evacuated subjectivity that is new to him, in this dispersal that we could think of as an electronic overthrow of the will to power. But for the female subject, an assertion of corporeality in electronic space is also a struggle against historical absence.

Inside the monitor, in the darkness, is the matrix of electronic matter that generates display. In a cathode ray tube (CRT), the familiar TV or video monitor, electron beams hit a hemispherically curved concave surface coated with phosphor. The phosphor glows and produces light. The negatively charged electron beam starts in an electron gun at the back of the tube and is accelerated down a long neck toward the tube face by a large positive voltage. On the outside, the convex side of the screen, the continuous stream of images poses the to-be-looked-at. Irigaray:

> But which "subject" up till now has investigated the fact that a *concave mirror* concentrates the light and, specifically, that this is not wholly irrelevant to a woman's sexuality? Any more than is a man's sexuality to the convex

20. Gary Zukav, *The Dancing Wu Li Masters* (Toronto, New York: Bantam Books, 1980), 65-6.
21. Chris Dercon, "An Interview with Paul Virilio," in *Impulse* 12, no. 4 (Summer 1986): 36.

mirror?...Not one subject has done so, on pain of tumbling from his existence. And here again, here too, one will rightly suspect any perspective, however surreptitious, that centres the subject, any autonomous circuit of subjectivity, any systematicity hooked back onto itself, any closure that claims for whatever reason to be metaphysical — or familial, social, economic even —, to have rightfully taken over, fixed, and framed that concave mirror's incandescent hearth.[22]

A refusal of fixed, framed systematicity is a refusal of the rule of the male-machine-body.

BODY PARTS

I propose that the early history of video art provides an instance of such a refusal. In the seventies, certain women producers inserted the feminine into video technology, in a spontaneous and provisional way, risking essentialist identification with a female machine-body so as to open a space there for the articulation of female desire.

Kate Craig's *Delicate Issue* (1979, colour, 12 min.) is a powerful tape about relations between the body, technology and power. A woman's body, the artist's own, is framed by a shaky hand-held camera which scans at such proximity that the body part being looked at is often unidentifiable. As the body goes out of and comes back into focus, its image alternately breaks down into patterns of light or reads as acute detail: creases, hairs, moles, eye, nipple come under the same scrutiny. A voiceover by the artist situates the viewer vis-à-vis issues of closeness and distance, private and public and how "real" we want the subject to be. The sound of someone breathing accompanies the voiceover, and as the camera travels up the crease of the legs toward the vagina the breathing accelerates. It's never clear whether the breathing is the artist's or the camera person's. The credits will tell us later that a man is behind the camera and clearly he is complicit with both Craig's ironic voyeurism and her exposure of her own sexuality. The cameraman shifts between standing in for the imagined viewer, as a trope for Craig's arousal through fantasy, and simply enabling her to fill the visual and auditory space. He is, plainly, her device. The camera's gaze lingers on the area around the clitoris, which appears as glistening, pink, vulnerable surfaces folded in on themselves. This is as close as we get, Craig's voice tells us.

The implied autoerotic pleasure mediated by the camera (and the cameraman) in Craig's tape contrasts with the expression of rage as a perverse autoerotic pleasure in *Trop(e)isme* (1980, colour, 14 min.), a videotape by Marshalore. The artist is again

22. Irigaray, *Speculum of the Other Woman*, 144.

the subject, her face in profile appearing in the foreground of the screen for much of the tape, contorted in a succession of silent screams. Enacting a metaphor for accessing her inner rage, this subject puts her fingers into her vagina, framed very close, then takes them out covered in menstrual blood and smears the blood across her face. In this intense and cathartic moment that Deleuze and Guattari would characterize as a (schizophrenic) hiatus in the production of the real, excess finds an opening, surfacing as a wounding knowledge akin to the enlightening wound of the mystic. After this disturbing, taboo-breaking gesture, the artist takes a long drag on a cigarette, exhaling slowly with sensual satisfaction.

Women's early appropriation of the space of the video monitor can now be seen as a particularly necessary position-taking in the face of the scattered, absent subjectivity that characterizes postmodernism. This issue has been a focal point of women's recent agenda in the domain of technology and its media, where women have been doing much of the important work in both theory and practice. Much of it has been psychoanalytically based deconstructive work, particularly in the domain of cinema, but this work also parallels contemporary feminist projects in language in its proposal of a female subject-in-process.[23]

There are complications in proposing a language of technological media as a language of the body, in particular the female body. In the all-encompassing embrace of the technological apparatus, any declaration of the body is suspect. On the one hand, assertions of bodily integrity are swept up into an ideology of the (always unattainable) idealized body, to be striven for as a commodity like so many others. On the other, the body fragmentation of the de-centred subject feeds the metal-flesh interpolation that is postulated as irreversible in the technological dynamo (the automaton, the bionic body, half metal-half flesh). These processes reflect the ideological underpinnings of a society that has come to be controlled by its technological media: a denatured "natural," one that is artificially constructed, plays a critical re-affirming role, and technology itself is naturalized. This ideological premise seems to reconfigure a reductivist reading of the body: what was previously determined by "life cycle," the biological, will now be circumscribed in the biotechnological, the body enhanced through designer body parts.

23. This is a central concern of the writers identified with French feminism, writers who engage in a specifically feminine practice of writing or "écriture feminine": Luce Irigaray, Julia Kristeva, Hélène Cixous, Michele Montrelay. Another important issue is that in video practices, it is especially women's narrative video that has characteristically refused narrative closure and sought to subvert rather than confirm a potentially unified subject and spectator. See Dot Tuer, "Video in Drag: Trans-sexing the Feminine, in *Parallélogramme* 12, no. 3 (Feb./Mar. 1988): 26-8.

The problem thereby posed is, how can women speak from an interior knowing to arrive at a transformative language that opens up possibilities for operating within the technological? The heated debates around essentialist practices in the past decade imposed constraints on naïve representations of the feminine, but didn't adequately address women's deeply felt need to assert difference, and not only deconstruct it. This lacuna was necessarily reformulated as women of colour called attention to specifics of difference, breaking down the monolithic construction of gender difference held by white western feminism. It remains pertinent to the many feminisms now being formulated to develop theories and strategies for female self-representation that both assert identity and challenge any form of fixed labelling. Especially in convergence with technological or electronic media, self-representation is key to affirmation, visibility and strategies for changing consciousness that can take into account the whole range of technological intervention in identity formation.

I've looked at certain body-based video works by Canadian women producers that are representations of self made prior to these debates. Although they were formulated outside of any feminist theoretical construction and address difference from only a gender standpoint, they can be seen as not just refusing the longstanding representational codes of male control over women's bodies, but also transgressing the theoretical limits of the philosophical discourse on technology. I've looked at these works because they articulate in electronic technology a metonymical correspondence between the body, implicitly problematized by the probing eye of the camera, and the video viewing apparatus itself: body parts become the very substance of the monitor, become its shifting incandescent feminine insides. These works are historical moments, and are emblematic of women's practices in relation to the philosophical and historical framework that I've delineated.

These are not the only instances of genital imaging in women's video history (a quiet closeup in *Facing South*, Lisa Steele, 1975; and later, a digital drawing overlay of vaginal forms in *Hot Chicks on TV*, Liz Vander Zaag, 1986). Such images are an immediate challenge to the persistent figure of the feminine in philosophy, of idea, truth, morality, nature, etc. More to the point, now, at a time when there is no possible "imagined organic body"[24] resistant to the effects of technology, women are turned into techno-tropes anyway, without our complicity, let alone our control. In popular cultural imagery, women are represented as powerful yet docile sex-robots or androids (as in the film *Blade Runner*). Our bodies are taken over,

24. See Haraway, "A Manifesto for Cyborgs."

hybridized. The developers of technology seek out metaphors, such that DNA replication produces "daughter" strands from the mother, a voice-recognition cellular phone is named "Sally", etc. These trendy tropes reiterate the familiar figure of woman as nature, biology, matter or extension of man.

The video screen is a threshold of possibilities, the place at which a stimulus is of sufficient intensity to begin to produce an effect. The screen is a site of agency, of an event brought about through intention and action. Through strategic self-representation, certain video works by women producers have documented the feminist project of freeing the female body from its status as a reflection to be looked upon. The video screen is a two-way reflection, and is thus a threshold of something from nothing. Its implications of the body through elusive, mutating images, parallel to our own complex interior knowing through our bodies, constitutes a site of the feminine in technology.

This text had its origins in a course called "Panic Science" given by Arthur Kroker at Concordia University in 1988. Thanks also to Michael Dorland and Johanne Lamoureux, and Kim Sawchuk and Robert Prénovault concerning the title. –N.T.

Cyborgs In Denial:

TECHNOLOGY AND IDENTITY IN THE NET

by David McIntosh

Mechanization has emphasized complexity and confusion, it has been responsible for monopolies in the field of knowledge, and it becomes extremely important to any civilization, if it is not to succumb to the influence of this monopoly of knowledge, to make some critical survey and report. The conditions of freedom of thought are in danger of being destroyed by science, technology, and the mechanization of knowledge.

—*Harold Innis*, The Bias of Communication, *1964 edition*

There is a spectrum of orderliness that runs from something like a crystal at one end to something like a fluid at the other. In the middle where order melts into disorder, is the domain of chaos. The notion of chaos shows us that a very simple process can in fact produce complex outputs provided that the process runs long enough. Our universe might be thought of as a very simple program which has run for a very long time, with successive outputs overlapping onto each other and building up a hyperdimensional moiré...Surprise is always possible.

—*Rudy Rucker*, Mondo 2000, *1993*

We live in an environment that is increasingly mediated by technology. To be considered marginally employable, we are required to have a working knowledge of computers, several software applications, networks, hard drives, E-mail, laser printers and fax/modems. To be considered marginally cultured, we must be able to distinguish Jean-Luc Picard from Jean-Luc Godard. TVs, CDs, PCs, VCRs, video games, satellite signals, cable hookups and remote controls turn our homes into virtual command centres where the ideologies of seduction, abundance and gratification osmose into our consciousness. This matrix of ubiquitous and interconnected technologies has come to be known as the Net — shorthand for "The Network." The Net is evolving into as distinct an entity as component media — telephones, TVs, and computers — previously were.

The deeper we are drawn into technologically mediated existence, the more difficult it becomes to find a position from which to perceive or critique the organizing structures that lie behind the Net's surface of seemingly benign diversity. The object of investigation is superficially amorphous, chaotic and constantly shifting. The two quotes that open this essay propose a paradoxical relationship between complex effects and simple causes that can serve as an entry point for mapping some of the most crucial deep structures of the Net. Speaking in social realist terms from an electro-mechanical age, Innis warns that mechanized complexity and confusion offer greater opportunity for the success of strategies designed to control and monopolize knowledge. Rucker's digital-era chaos theory suggests that complexity and unpredictability are produced by simple and eternal formulae that inhabit the frontier between order and disorder. While these two approaches to reading the technologized environment diverge in their language and intention, they both point to the necessity of making a rational analysis of surface complexity, confusion and unpredictability in order to determine systemic hierarchies and organizing forces that condition the potential for what Rucker refers to as "surprise" and Innis refers to as "freedom of thought." Rewinding history to a midpoint between Innis and Rucker offers a valuable point of intersection to focus on these theories in concrete terms.

THE FIRST BATTLE FOR THE NET: THE NEW WORLD INFORMATION ORDER

Throughout the 1970s and early 1980s, the critical study of monopolies of knowledge in the "wired world" and the emerging phenomenon referred to as "electronic colonialism" became the focus of much of UNESCO's activities. In response to a global cultural and communications environment increasingly dominated by satellites, television, computers and digital data flows centrally controlled by Western corporate interests, an alliance of UNESCO members, including the Soviet bloc and non-aligned states in Asia, Africa, the Caribbean and South America, constructed proposals to recognize information and culture as national resources to be regulated and managed in the developmental interests of the independent state and its people, much as mineral or agricultural resources were. This strategic alliance, known as the New World Information Order (NWIO), in its efforts to encourage a global liberation movement, sought international agreements on the necessity of state intervention mechanisms to ensure balanced flows of information between nations, access to new telecommunications technologies and techniques and the survival of national self-representational cultural processes.

Despite support for NWIO initiatives by an overwhelming majority of UNESCO member-states, no international agreement reflecting their objectives was ever reached. Western nations, led by the U.S. government in alliance with information megacorps like IBM, AT&T and Hearst Publication, refused to sign agreements that in any way impinged on their entrepreneurial practices of freedom of expression and freedom of the marketplace. NWIO was effectively dead by 1983. Largely a forgotten project ten years later, UNESCO's New World Information Order was perhaps our last chance for negotiating through national identity to effect fundamental and orderly change in the direction of the global information revolution. Its defeat cleared the way for global mob rule by a gang of U.S.-based media corporations that assumed the status of meta-organizing force in the deployment of a global technological and cultural infrastructure. As a result, many countries have become information colonies consigned to consumer status, dumping grounds for American cultural detritus. Paradoxically, the West's battle to maintain the disorderly practices of its freedom of expression and marketplace in the face of NWIO's principles of rational order and self-determination resulted in an even more intensely concentrated and technologized monopoly of information, knowledge and power. This first confrontation for control of the Net as it emerged set the pattern for all subsequent developments in global communications.

REWIRING THE NET: SOME TECHNOLOGICAL OVERSIMPLIFICATIONS

Another crucial point of entry into the dynamics of order and disorder within the shifting terrain of the Net is through technology itself. To get at the physical guts of wires, switches and chips that usually remain invisible behind the smooth surfaces of our information and entertainment appliances, it is necessary to isolate from their corporate and ideological applications a few specific aspects of the new technologies.

In oversimplified terms, the two newest technologies propelling the complete restructuring of global information systems in 1993 are:

fibre optic cable — a glass wire developed by AT&T in the 1970s that consists of thousands of strands of glass bound together, each strand capable of transmitting 100,000 telephone conversations simultaneously, or the equivalent of a 62,000-page book in a second;

digital optical transmission — laser-generated pulses of sub-atomic light particles (photons) that are digitally coded to carry complex information (from phone calls to feature films) at the speed of light down the individual strands of glass in a fibre optic cable.

Fibre optics and digital optical transmission together comprise a new distribution technology that bundles the delivery of audio, video, text and data into one bloated pipeline euphemistically referred to as "the electronic highway." Fibre optic cable removes all limits to the speed, volume and form of information that flows through it. It also offers the potential for complete monopoly over a massively expanded information distribution system to whoever controls it.

Until quite recently, two entirely separate but parallel information distribution systems running on copper wires strung from house to house brought audio service through one wire to the TV. Ongoing fibre optic rewiring by both the cable and telephone industries is collapsing the logic and profitability of separate phone and cable services to the point where the distinction between the two will soon be nothing more than a legal abstraction. Only government regulation is preventing phone companies from delivering full motion video or cable companies from delivering telephone service.

At this point, it is necessary to examine the technology that distinguishes the open architecture of the telephone system for the closed, consumption-only architecture of the cable system. Digital switches (intelligent chips) placed strategically throughout the phone network route messages and allow for two-way communication among all subscribers to the network; in other words, digital switches serve as the on-and off-ramps to the electronic highway. The resulting distributed decentralized architecture of the phone system reduces the distinction between producers and consumers to the nature of the information-processing appliances that individual subscribers can afford to plug into the jacks in their wall. Some subscribers choose to plug in nothing more than a standard black rotary dial phone, others add fax and answering machines, while others plug in a complex computer database accessible to other users, as is the case with the Internet. System users control the use of the unprogrammed network.

Cable on the other hand is an "unswitched," programmed system. The cable operator controls the use of its one-way delivery system and every signal a cable operator emits goes to every subscriber indiscriminately. The absence of digital switches in the cable system architecture renders it utterly non-interactive. Cable is a centralized gatekeeping operation that profits by collecting mass-market entertainment from satellite and broadcast sources and distributing it to passive subscribers. The separation between production and consumption is absolute. To extend the "electronic highway" analogy, the unswitched cable system is like a perpetual Indy 500 run on a ring road with no on- or off-ramps.

It is important to note that the more desirable switched telephone system has developed under strict government regulation, while the oppressive unswitched cable system has grown amorphously in an unregulated marketplace. If the most hideous monopolistic potentials of fibre optic technology are to be minimized, it seems obvious that it must be installed in conjunction with digital switching to create an open architecture that supports universal access and interaction in all media. However, the handful of corporations that currently control fibre optic distribution systems are responding only to the prime directive of maximum profit.

CORPORATE HARMONIC CONVERGENCE

While the Net is global in scope, it is undeniably run by an amorphous agglomeration of U.S.-based multinationals. Fortunately, the simple processes that underlie the complexities of megacorp manoeuvrings are transparently formulaic. The centrepiece of this formula is the centuries-old industrial strategy of vertical integration, whereby a single corporate entity owns all steps in the life of a commodity from raw materials to consumption; its current manifestation is the enhanced fibre optic distribution system. The primary model for the current round of vertical integration in the Net can be traced historically to the Hollywood monopolies or trusts that developed in the 1930s.

After the corporate shake-out brought on by the advent of "talkies," five large corporations or "majors," including Warner Brothers, MGM, Paramount, RKO and Fox, operated as a oligopoly, owning and controlling the production, distribution and exhibition of feature films. Independent production was virtually non-existent, and any independent films that did get made were kept out of theatres by the stranglehold monopoly of the majors. This situation held until 1948, when the U.S. Supreme Court ruled that the majors were in violation of anti-trust laws and had to divest themselves of their exhibition holdings. A thorough study of the history of all information and entertainment industries in the U.S. reveals that this pattern has been repeated with each new wave of technological innovation in communications (film, radio, TV, cable TV). As the new technology (often developed by the military) becomes standardized and commercially exploitable, corporate monopolies based on the preceding wave of communications technology reintegrate vertically to contain the new technology. These monopolies concentrate into a new oligopoly, which is only curtailed by state intervention when "competition" is deemed to be threatened.

Most of the Hollywood studios for the 1930s and 1940s are still key players today, holding major stakes in the Net as a result of having been absorbed by the corporations that dominate the new distribution technologies (i.e., cable and telephone companies). Feature films remain the most highly prized software to hold copyright over, given their "repurposing" potential as home videocassettes, optical discs, CD-ROMs, and theme-park rides. However, one aspect of the "production-distribution-exhibition" formula for vertical integration has changed irrevocably in the Net: exhibition or consumption occurs in the home or at work on TVs, computers and telephone appliances. As a result, exhibition has fallen out of the corporate formula since it is now owned directly by the user, whole consumption is limited only by his or her ability to purchase and operate a vast array of consumer electronics. There are several corporate cross-ownerships, like Sony/Columbia and Matsushita/MCA, where the production and sale of home exhibition equipment is integrated with the production and sale of the software to be run on that equipment, but for the most part consumer technology suppliers have been relegated to the status of independents in the Net. As a result, the corporate formula for monopolizing the Net has been streamlined to "production-distribution."

Within this formula, however, there remain a number of twists in the road to complete monopoly, primarily in the distribution component of the equation. As pointed out earlier, the two leading forces in distribution — telephone companies (telco's) and cable companies (cableco's) — are separate but parallel structures, competing with each other to control fibre optics, a technology that has eliminated functional differences between them. In breaking up and deregulating the AT&T telephone monopoly, the U.S. Federal Communications Commission, a state body that regulates telecommunications, intended to increase direct competition between telco's and cableco's. However, recent corporate manoeuvres demonstrate that the urge to monopoly is far more primal than the thrill of competition. Telco's have been furiously buying up cableco's, and vice versa. Consequently, there has been a consolidation of monopoly achieved through horizontal cross-ownership within the distribution sector of the Net. The reconfigured formula for oligopoly can now be restated as "studio + telco + cableco."

A detailed examination of some of the most recent corporate configurations reveals the extent to which the Net is dominated by fewer and fewer interlocking cartels, directorates, stock swaps and joint ventures. In 1993, international headline news was made by Bell Atlantic's bid to buy TCI, and Viacom's bid to buy Paramount. Within these mega-mergers, the shape of two of the largest and most convoluted information-entertainment agglomerations can be perceived. At the centre of the first corporate empire is John Malone, head of TCI (Tele-Communications Inc.), the largest cable system owner in the U.S., with a subscriber base of 9.6 million. Through its shell parent company, Liberty Media which is currently constructing a 22 million subscriber pay-per-view cable channel, TCI is part owner of: Request Video, the largest pay-per-view distributor in the U.S.; Encore Starz, a pay-TV distributor; Spice, an R-rated soft porn movie channel; the Discovery Channel; Black Entertainment Television; and the Family Channel. TCI/Liberty Media controls QVC, the major home shopping network, which is attempting to buy Paramount in conjunction with Cox Entertainment (another major cable system owner), Bell South and Advance Publications. TCI is also part owner of Turner Broadcasting System, which in turn operates CNN and TNT and owns film producers/distributors New Line Cinema and Castle Rock Entertainment. TCI has also merged with German music giant Bertelsman to create a music video/home shopping channel where viewers can programme their music video selections and purchase the accompanying CD. In buying TCI and its holdings, Bell Atlantic (yearly cash flow of $5 billion, more than the entire U.S. theatrical feature film market) merges its own subscriber base, pay-per-use billing system and fibre optic assets with feature film production and distribution, print publication, music and cable TV distribution interests. The traditional role of the telco as an uninvested carrier of content designed by and for its users has been terminated.

The second megacorp taking shape behind the Net is Viacom, headed by Sumner Redstone. Viacom is a broadcast and cable programming giant that owns the classic libraries of CBS, ABC and NBC, as well as cable channels MTV, Nickleodeon and Showtime. Viacom recently purchased Nynex, a regional telephone company, and Blockbuster Video, the largest videocassette rental operation in the U.S. Blockbuster in turn owns Spelling Entertainment Group and Republic Pictures, whose combined libraries amount to 14,000 hours of programming. Blockbuster is also planning to buy MGM and has already merged with Music Plus, Sound Warehouse and Virgin Group, making it one of the major forces in music retailing. As well, Blockbuster has begun "repurposing" feature films as digitized CD-ROMs for immediate rental through its videocassette outlets and for eventual electronic home delivery on cable. Viacom is in the process of acquiring Paramount (at a cost of $10 billion), which in turn owns Famous Players and Madison Square Gardens, has an extensive archive including television series like "Cheers" and feature films like *The Firm* and is launching its own television network in 1994.

And as a final note to this migraine-inducing mess of corporate incest and dynastic wars of succession, opponents in the world of "studio + telco + cableco" are collaborators in the satellite industry. All the major cable operators, including

Viacom, TCI, Time Warner, General Electric and Continental Cable, have hedged their technological bets by joining forces in launching Primestar, a direct broadcast satellite service that has also been referred to as the "Death Star." The forces determining the shape of the Net and the content that flows through it have consolidated so intensely that William Gibson's projection of an "unthinkably complex consensual hallucination, matrix, cyberspace, where the great corporate hot cores burn like neon novas, data so dense you suffer sensory overload if you try to apprehend the merest outline" is on the verge of crystallizing into reality.

In surveying some of the immediate practical plans of these immense agglomerations, the new services being developed for delivery over the Net are predictable reworkings of what already exists on cable TV. Most proposals relate to developing home shopping possibilities into virtual shopping malls. In current 150-channel cable trials, almost one-half of those channels are devoted to multiple channel screenings of pay-per-view feature films and barker channels that promote what is on each channel. In New York, Time Warner has launched NY1, a 24-hour local cable news service that replaces camera operators, editors and sound technicians with solo Hi-8 videographers feeding a video-jukebox robot. In Montreal, a trial cable cable service offers viewers multiple channel/multi-camera coverage of sports events, so the viewer can switch from angle to angle by changing channels. The overall move away from "free" or broadcast TV (ten to fifteen channels) to specialty subscriber cable TV (up to 500 channels) is reshaping the Net into an almost entirely transactional and unregulated operation, where the pay-per-use or toll structure of the telephone system will dominate.

There is no evidence in the pattern of corporate convergence that the Net is evolving in the interest of individual users or the public — either in terms of deep structure or surface effect. A handful of corporate impressarios are merrily hard-wiring their ideologies and taxonomies of society into the communications system. The state, which has traditionally attempted to represent the public interest through regulation, is increasingly an ineffectual by-product or effect of the Net. The most coherent alternative or opposition to corporate control presently rests in the consensual information networks that operate over as yet unprogrammed phone lines and in the chaotic nerd world of hackers, crackers, pirates and virus jammers whose primary weapon is surprise.

NATIONAL IDENTITY IN THE NET: THE CANADIAN CONTEXT

The Net does not recognize the national borders except to enfold and profit from them. In nationally identified information colonies like Canada, the warp and weft of the Net are less tightly woven, since it is delimited by endemic lower levels of technological infrastructure and by state interventions in the interest of national self-determination. Historically, the state has been the primary force behind the installation of new communications technology infrastructure in Canada. National production and distribution capacity in film (the Canadian Government Motion Picture Bureau which became the National Film Board), radio (CBC Radio) and television (CBC Television) were originally developed entirely by the state in order to counter the increased influence of U.S. media.

This pattern of state ownership of technological infrastructure was not applied to the telephone and cable TV industries, which were instead allowed to develop as profit-oriented monopolies regulated from a distance by the state to ensure Canadian content and affordable access to essential or basic services. In return for these regulatory rights, the state is responsible for guaranteeing profit margins in the cable and telephone industries. Accordingly, the state now acts in accordance with two not necessarily compatible mandates: national identity and corporate profitability. Given the central role of merged telco's and cableco's in the global fibre optic Net, the position of the Canadian state is becoming increasingly paradoxical and untenable.

Recent developments in the negotiation of relationships between the Canadian state and the telco/cableco axis reveal striking similarities to the evolution of the corporate Net in the U.S. In 1992, the Canadian Radio-television and Telecommunications Commission, the agency of the federal government that regulates the cable and telephone monopolies, opened the long-distance telephone market to competition. The only substantial competitor to Stentor (the cartel of existing regional Bell companies) to surface so far is Unitel, which is owned by Rogers Cable and AT&T. A number of smaller-scale bulk long distance resellers have also emerged, some of which run commercials to cover their start-up costs. Throughout the fall and winter of 1993, the CRTC held formal hearings with all telco's operating in Canada to consider further deregulation to allow for telco carriage of new services including full motion video. Broadcast live on cable TV, these hearings played like a summit of vested telephone and cable interests carving up turf. Meanwhile, telco's and cableco's continue to integrate at a corporate level. BCE Inc., owner of Bell Canada, Northern Telecom and a number of regional phone companies in Canada, has recently circumvented CRTC cross-media ownership regulations by purchasing giant U.S. cableco Jones Intercable at a cost of $275 million. Jones Intercable has 1.3 million cable subscribers in the U.S., owns cable and phone franchises in England and Spain and operates three local phone companies in the U.S.

In the realm of cableco regulation, the CRTC has affirmed the regulated monopoly status of cable as the nationally sanctioned distributor of programmed information and entertainment in Canada. Potentially competitive distribution services based on alternative technologies, such as direct broadcast satellite or MDS (microwave distribution system), are being kept out of the marketplace by the CRTC. Furthermore, the CRTC recently allowed cableco's a special rate increase in order to cover their technological upgrading costs. Canada's 7.2 million cable subscribers are each paying cableco's an additional $10 per year, which over five years will amount to a $400 million investment on behalf of subscribers in return for unspecified technological changes. After the five years, cableco's can continue to collect the technological change fee if half of it is contributed to a new fund for investment in Canadian film and television productions. The CRTC makes wild claims that this fund would amount to $100 million per year, while the cableco's suggest it might reach $12 million per year. Cableco participation in this plan is entirely voluntary, so the fund may amount to absolutely nothing. Thus, the funds guaranteed by the CRTC for cableco expansion of their distribution capacity are not counterbalanced with any guarantee of expansion of Canadian production.

In 1993 the CRTC also issued a call for new Canadian specialty, pay-TV and pay-per-view services to be offered on cable. Sixty-eight applications were received, almost all of them sponsored by existing broadcast and cable interests. In the broadcasting realm, City-TV has submitted seven applications, the CBC is involved in five, Global in three and CTV/Baton in two. Rogers Cable, part owner of CFMT and YTV, has applied for five new licences. In addition to Rogers, cableco's Maclean Hunter, WIC Communications and Moffatt Communications have also applied for licences. All of these licence-seekers already operate as branch plant repackagers of U.S. programming, and the additional services they are proposing would also rely heavily on repackaged U.S. content. Predictably, the specialties proposed in these licence applications reflect a shiveringly bald taxonomy for programming Canadian society: country music, MOR music, nature, seniors, comedy, arts and entertainment, health, news, religion, multiculturalism, home shopping, lifestyle and pay-per-view movies and sports. It is expected that between six and eight new licenses will be awarded by early 1994, and for each Canadian-operated service added, the CRTC allows cableco's to add one additional U.S. service. Once this round of licencing is completed, cableco's could be offering an additional 16 channels, half of them outright U.S. imports. As the cable system expands with the state's regulatory complicity, the existing imbalance between Canadian and U.S. programming is being tipped even further in favour of U.S. programming.

Considered from the perspective of the "studio + telco + cableco" formula for vertical integration being deployed by communications corporations in the U.S., it is apparent that Canadian regulatory mechanisms are operating in partnership with the "telco + cableco" component to facilitate their technological upgrading as well as their profitability as distributors connected with the global Net. Canadian cable repackagers are increasingly integrated into the U.S. "studio" component of the formula. With national identity dissipated in the distribution system, the state subsidized Canadian "studio" or production sector finds itself bearing the full weight of the state's mandate to promote national identity while it is increasingly ghettoized, with no connections to the Net other than loose promises of a new production fund and Canadian content quotas.

The Canadian production sector finds itself in the untenable position of appealing to two conflicting sets of gatekeeping principles. On one hand, the production sector is almost entirely dependent on state subsidies that are contingent on production's ability to fulfil a complex range of artistic, bureaucratic and political notions of national identity; on the other hand, the production sector must negotiate access to the public through the telco/cableco distribution system's criteria of mass appeal and maximum profits. The continued existence of the fundamental principle of state intervention to promote national identity through subsidized cultural products is in doubt as international trade agreements from GATT to NAFTA undermine the structure of national identity through the global extension of the economic ideology of privatization and the "free marketplace." U.S. President Clinton, acting in the interest of the corporate controllers of the Net, has threatened to retaliate against any moves by Canadian governments to limit free access for American cultural products to the Canadian market. The challenges facing Canada in negotiating a position in the Net recall the unsuccessful struggle of the UNESCO coalition of states to establish the New World Information Order ten years ago. National political identity may no longer be a viable construction as a governing notion for Canadians, and national cultural identity based on a marginalized production sector is not a viable construction in the Net.

DECOLONIZING THE NET: CYBORG IDENTITY

Up to this point, this essay has attempted to map deep structures in the Net by examining aspects of its design, evolution, logic and ideology. However, within the "hyperdimensional moiré" of chaotic effects produced by the Net, the primary identity of users, both consumers and producers, has undergone a massive shift: the primary identity that has emerged is that of the cyborg. The construction of the self in the Net has been technologized to the point where we are now all constituted as hybrids of machines and organisms, or in Donna Haraway's terms "as creatures of social reality as well as creatures of fiction." For cyborgs in denial, the seductively pure pleasure of perpetual mass consumption in the Net mitigates against collective identity or action; the medium is the only message and immersion in the Net has ascended to the status of ancestral right. We are born adherents to its hive consciousness. Acceptance of the self as a technology-dependent effect offers new potential for collective responses to the centrally controlled abstractions of the Net. If technology is an integral part of identity formation, then interventions to assert identity must include technology-based strategies; in other words, future identities will be differentiated technologically. Oppositional cyborg collectivity may be the only means left for decolonizing and deprogramming the Net.

Cyborg piracy is currently the predominant oppositional option in the Net. Despite the fact that this ghetto of saboteurs is unstable, idiosyncratic and overpopulated by disembodied techno-nerds, piracy principles of consensual association and self-determination in the Net are crucial to building larger oppositional collective identities. However, cyborg collectivity requires a more principled and systemic approach to technological equality and access than currently exists in the anarchic fringe of hacker piracy. Codifying pirate principles and cyborg realities in public policy could serve as a staging ground for mounting a coordinated opposition to Net oligopoly and establishing conditions where freedom of thought can flourish.

The Canadian state, our most sophisticated if threatened and conflicted institution for collective action, should be discouraged from the suicidal course of wholesale deregulation of Net monopolies and reoriented towards strategic and principled deregulation — negotiated trade-offs if you will — to achieve public objectives. For example, the state could allow Net operators unregulated but taxable profits on discretionary programmed services (movies, home shopping, etc.) in return for technological regulation, namely the installation of an open, switched fibre optic Net architecture and the reservation of a percentage of the unlimited distribution capacity of fibre optics for free non-profit access in all media to all users. As well, the state could recognize the cyborg's machine-body relation as the site of opposition and identity by enhancing the technology available to all Net users. Instead of scamming the Canadian public into investing $400 million to expand the cableco's technological base for social-control programming, the state could redirect funds to maximize and equalize information processing technology at the new site of exhibition in the Net: the individual user.

These actions would achieve two desirable effects: first, given that most information processing appliances are production as well as consumption tools, all

Net users would be transformed into potential producers as well as consumers of information and entertainment; secondly, the corporate vertical integration formula for monopoly would be short-circuited by connecting production directly to exhibition. Within this framework of a distributed, deprogrammed and decentralized information system where the network is a big dumb information pipeline and the users plugged into it through their enhanced information appliances are smart cyborg producers/consumers, new consensual and interactive forms of organization, representation and collective identity could grow. Shapes could shift, monstrous recombinant identities could multiply and powerful new myths of resistance could circulate freely in a liberated island of healthy chaos. This fictional cyborg utopia is very tentative and in need of further elaboration through a wide range of technology sensitive bodily realities, including privacy, poverty, gender and race, but in the words of Oscar Wilde, "A map of the world which does not include Utopia is not even worth glancing at."

BIBLIOGRAPHY

Laurence Bergreen, *Look Now, Pay Later: The Rise of Network Broadcasting* (New York: Doubleday, 1980).

Jonathan Crary and Sanford Kwinter, editors, *Zone 6: Incorporations* (New York: Urzone, 1992).

Pat Crawley and David McIntosh, *Towards an Industrial Strategy For Visual Program Production in Canada* (Ottawa: Canadian Film Institute, 1982).

David Ellis, Split Screen: *Home Entertainment and the New Technologies* (Toronto: Friends of Canadian Broadcasting, 1992).

William Gibson, *Count Zero* (New York: Berkeley Publishing Group, 1987).

Donna Haraway, *Simians, Cyborgs and Women: The Reinvention of Nature* (New York: Routledge, 1991).

Harold Innis, *The Bias of Communication* (Toronto: University of Toronto Press, 1964 edition).

Arthur Kroker, *Technology and the Canadian Mind* (Montreal: New World Perspectives, 1984).

Larry McCaffery, editor, *Storming the Reality Studio: A Casebook of Cyberpunk and Postmodern Fiction* (Durham & London: Duke University Press, 1991).

Marshall McLuhan, *The Mechanical Bride: Folklore of the Industrial Man* (New York: Vanguard Press, 1970).

Thomas McPhail, *Electronic Colonialism: The Future of International Broadcasting and Communication* (Beverly Hills: Sage Publications, 1981).

Ministry of Communications, *Instant World: A Report on Telecommunications in Canada* [Ottawa]: Information Canada, 1971.

R.U. Sirius, Randy Rucker and Queen Mu, *Mondo 2000 Users Guide to the New Edge* (New York: Harper Collins, 1992).

Anthony Smith, *The Geopolitics of Information: How Western Culture Dominates the World* (New York: Oxford University Press, 1980).

A series of reports from the periodicals *Wired, Mondo 2000, Variety* and *Playback* and from the *Lexis-Nexis* database have also been used as sources.

ARTICULATE VIDEO

by Elizabeth Vander Zaag

Without the writers and the curators there would be no video "art" exposure. The sensitivity of these people to the central impetus of video work is important to the creation of interesting shows. The video medium, since it is not quite so verbal, offers endless interpretations and iterations of intent — verbally, that is. Do the words that are said about a tape, the categories it is displayed under, the written artist's statements, the loose definitions that show titles and themes impose on work that is presented in them, affect the individual's experience of the work? Do the articulations of video curators and writers create a context, the distribution of video work to be produced in? Whatever the context, the distribution of video work has a resiliency that can only come from the constant evolution of the medium, through the work of the producers and those that handle the work. The most interesting work would be the work that would distance these efforts with endless variations, and the most interesting writing would inform the artist as well as the public about the construed information evolving from the tape.

The two following fictitious conversations illustrate some differences between "articulated" video and the articulations from which the video came.

R.r.ring

The hung-over young video artist from Vancouver resented being woken up so early by her Toronto distributor.

"Yeah," nodded the tousled head of various shades. "What festival? The 'blue' festival?" Apparently the tapes with the most blue in them were to be submitted.

"Yeah, sure, o.k." The Vancouver video artist just wanted her cut, and shrugged at the cat. "Yeah, I'm under 25... no, it's not about that... oh well, just because the guy talks about 'tyrannizing desire'... o.k... multiple play... I don't know if I'm gay... you know how early it is here! Sure show the tape with whatever kind of articulation. I was up late last night shooting... you know. Never mind."

By now the young video artist's head was pounding. She needed a Perrier badly. "How come they didn't come through on the rental for that other show?" she asked, thirst making her belligerent.

"The statement your tape made about media subversion wasn't clear enough," said the distributor. "Didn't you get the letter yet?"

"But it's a process-oriented tape, how could anything be said more strongly than in the process?" The young video maker hesitated, "I know the 'taut'ology of tape tension just results in pleonastic tech... I got to go, you know,... like the bathroom... o.k., bye."

R.r.ring

The tall, dark-haired woman answered the telephone, pencil in hand. It was her distributor asking for a verbal tape description for a show in the east.

"Uh... m.m," she said, twirling the pencil in her hair. "It has to start with a sentence, I guess," she said. "Right?"

Winsome words wafted through her mind, left over from the subconscious poetry that she had been pencilling into her poetry book, perhaps the next script.

"Well, maybe you could start with the title, the length of the tape, and perhaps the nature of the tape... is it narrative or experimental? Who did the music? You know, the whole story in thirty words or less." The distributor laughed as she realized the incongruity of what she had said, but the tall dark-haired woman struggled, pencil flailing the air, lips rounding words only to utter them noiselessly.

"I have to send this description by air letter tonight," continued the distributor. "Sorry to give you such short notice. By the way, did you fill out the form that I gave you from that Toronto distributor?"

The tall pencil waver came to, after all she couldn't lose it all together on the phone to her distributor. That was the only income she had except for prostitution and the odd gardening job. "Yes, I attempted to," she said, staring out the window and wondering what category the large family of ball tossers on her front sidewalk would fall under — rural issues? religion?

Instantly a flash wiped away the wafting whimsies in her mind. "Hey!" she said to her distributor. "Why don't I fill out the form (it was in the top middle drawer of her desk) and then I'll know what the tape is about. I'll call you in half an hour, o.k?... 30 words... right. Bye."

DESIRING DAUGHTERS

by Renee Baert

The opening image of the videotape, *The Influences of My Mother* (Sara Diamond, 1982), is a tight closeup on a dated, somewhat faded portrait of a young woman, perhaps in her mid twenties. The date of the black and white photograph is uncertain, but its representational style suggests a studio photograph from around the 1940s. The frame highlights a pair of intelligent eyes, set in a gentle, expressive face.

The camera opens out to a medium shot, revealing the head and shoulders portrait in its entirety. A female off-camera voice addresses the viewer: 'It is usually the parent who constructs the identity of the child.' The camera continues opening to include in its frame a young woman seen standing at an adjoining wall, facing the portrait. There is an uncertain resemblance between this person and the figure in the portrait. The voice over continues: 'In my case it was to be the child who would construct the identity of the parent.'

The character on camera and in the voice over is the videomaker Sara Diamond. The videotape is enactment and reenactment of the processes by which she has imagined and reconstructed the identity of the mother who died while she was a girl in early adolescence. The figure Diamond presents is the paradoxical one of a daughter constructing her sense of identity through imaginary identification with, and through irrevocable separation from, a maternal parent whose identity she is also constructing.

The combination in the work of autobiography and fantasy, memory and desire, history and interpretation, artefact and invention further position the document as one which blurs the boundaries of fact and fiction, personal and social. It is at once a desiring production and an enabling process, by means of which Diamond transforms her subjectivity. That this subjectivity is enabled by identificatory processes is made immediately evident. The opening scene continues with a shot of Diamond, her hair restyled, standing next to the photograph: two figures photographed at a similar age, dressed in similar tailored jacket and blouse, curly hair arranged in similar fashion, faces posed at a similar angle, the physical resemblance now certain.

The two figures, framed together in one image, look similar: but they are not one. And it is the passage from the acknowledgement of sameness to the recognition of difference, from the process of imaginary identification to the distancing of symbolization, that is embodied within the narrative of the video and produced within its textual strategies.

At each stage of the video, which is organized in six chronological acts, the relationship of mother and daughter undergoes a new definition, but each new 'identity' of the mother is anchored in the daughter's interpretation of her: in this way, the daughter constructs the identity of the mother. In these representations by the daughter, the mother is transformed, as the tape proceeds, from a figure whose principal attribute to the remembering daughter is that of an overwhelming power to a separate being who is herself a willing, active subject — a desiring subject. And the recognition of her as both woman and mother enables the daughter's constitution of herself as both subject and daughter — a desiring subject, a desiring daughter.

In *Measures of Distance* (1988), by the Palestinian artist Mona Hatoum, the maternal figure is also an absence; but in this instance absence is due to the daughter's exile from the war-torn country in which her mother remains resident. In this work, it is not death or time that mark the daughter's distance from the mother, but a complex range of psychic and social eventualities within a lived relation. Like Diamond's tape, which was produced in 1982, *Measures of Distance*, made six years later, represents in a yet more rigorous and complex fashion a renegotiation of the mother-daughter tie; and it too underscores the importance of the maternal figure to the question of female subjectivity and desire. Hatoum, however, specifies the centrality of language to this negotiation and further insists on the multiplicity of determinants of subjectivity — of gender, race, class, age, nation, circumstance.

Unlike Diamond, who must construct the figure of the mother within an imaginary set of relations drawn from memories and memorabilia, Hatoum constructs her videotape from materials provided by, and in collaboration with, the mother, and used with her consent. Yet this consent is a furtive one ('don't mention a thing about it to your father'), highlighting the mother-daughter bond as a trespass on patriarchal law.

Letters from mother to daughter, read in translation by Hatoum, form the principal narrative element of the soundtrack. It is the words of the mother that are spoken, but via the mediation and translation of the daughter, who is both reader (of the mother's letters) and writer (of the videotext); It is the daughter who, even as she is also the subject of an address originating with the other figure, assembles the evidences by which our view of the figure is constructed. And the figure she presents is likewise a desiring subject, a desiring mother. It, too, is a desiring production.

Freud does not posit desiring daughters. Indeed, the paradox of female subjectivity and desire is its structural 'non-existence' within a symbolic order in which the phallus is the privileged signifier, not only as the representative of the principle of separation and individuation but as the symbol of desire, activity, potency. Not only is women's access to the phallic signifier highly problematic, but further a primary identification by the female subject with the mother is seen to mitigate against the separation and individuation that mark the distance from the maternal object, hence subjecthood and desire.

Within these parameters, the possibility on the daughter's part of a positive identification with the mother is confined to an identification with maternity and its promise of *jouissance*. In well-known accounts of this problematic, Julia Kristeva maintains that 'the consecrated (religious or secular) representation of femininity is absorbed by motherhood'[1]; Jessica Benjamin argues that the phallus maintains its monopoly on representing desire through the profound desexualization of the mother;[2] Luce Irigaray insists that the culturally unsymbolized mother-daughter relation leaves women in a state of dereliction.[3] In short, women's identity is relegated to the positions made available in patriarchal ordering, that is, objecthood and motherhood.

Thus theoretical attention to the mother-daughter relation is necessarily imbricated with theoretical work on female subjectivity in that, as Brenda Longfellow has argued, 'the political urgency of both projects bears on the possibility of articulating a different economy of desire and subjectivity of phallic mediation'.[4] Central to this engagement has been the attempt to extricate the female as subject of history from her designation as Woman and Other, and further to extricate the female as subject of desire from her capture as maternal object.

The mother-daughter relation is a crucial site for women precisely because it is the ground for a disinvestment of the Oedipalized symbolic order. As Rosi Braidotti has

1. Julia Kristeva, 'Stabat mater,' in Toril Moi (ed). *The Kristeva Reader* (New York: Columbia University Press, 1986), p. 16.

2. Jessica Benjamin, *The Bonds of Love* (New York: Pantheon Books, 1988).

3. Luce Irigaray, *Speculum: of the Other Woman* , trans. Gillian C. Gill (Ithaca, NY: Cornell University Press, 1985); and other writings.

4. Brenda Longfellow, 'Love letter to the mother: the work of Chantal Akerman', *Canadian Journal of Political and Social Theory* , vol. 19, nos. 1-2 (1989), p. 74.

argued, the mother-daughter paradigm 'is an imaginary couple that enacts the politics of female subjectivity, the relationship to the other woman and consequently the structures of female homosexuality as well as the possibility of a woman-identified redefinition of the subject'.[5]

Yet the very complexity and difficulty of the relation to the maternal object within the context of the daughter's claim to a 'place' and a desire within patriarchal culture bespeak the force of the psychic and cultural imperatives that the female subject must negotiate. A voluminous body of women's narratives — in this instance considered from within feminist video production — have given voice over the past two decades to the story of daughters uncomfortably bound to the psychic, symbolic and historical legacy of mothers.

Consider, for instance, the 1973 video-performance *Spring Sowing: Emergence* . In this real-time process tape by Jill Geiger, a supine woman is slowly cut out of her clothes as she, the clothes-cutter, and the camerawoman engage in casual conversation that counterpoints the dramatic scene being enacted. As Carol Zemel wrote of this work at the time: 'Slowly and deliberately, covering cloth was stripped away, so that when a naked and pensive woman rose from her cut-away shell, the psychic release was monumental. It was an assertive and liberating moment, at once poignant and ecstatic, as the now freed woman knelt, almost bowing, to her former being lying empty beside her'.[6] This 'emergence' and rebirth of the fully grown woman, the motherless daughter, 'born' anew with the aid and ministrations of her peers, might be seen as a metaphor for the repression, within a celebratory 'sisterhood', of the vexed question of the psychic and familial relations of mothers and daughters.

In this first surge of the feminist movement of the 1970s, this conflictual relation was perhaps partially displaced onto the search for another mother — the apt, not deficient, mother. The embrace of Goddess mythology and ancient matriarchally-centred forms of spirituality; the reclamation of lost female figures of history; the rewriting and reinterpretation of myths, folktales, biblical stories, and so on; the denial of discord through the affirmative action of 'positive images' — all testify not only to the persistent historical erasure from the public sphere of women's voice and presence but also to the search, at the symbolic level of culture, for a 'positive' matrilineage: one that would not only counter the cultural derogation of the

5. Rosi Braidotti, 'The politics of ontological difference', in Teresa Brennan (ed.), *Between Feminism and Psychoanalysis* (London and New York: Routledge, 1989), p. 96.

6. Carol Zemel, 'Women and video', *artscanada*, October 1973, p. 37.

female, but perhaps as well enable the daughter to circumvent the mother — to give her the mother she needs instead of the mother she has.

In this first generation of work, there was little sign of the vexation in the mother-daughter relation that would be explored, often with the aid of psychoanalytic tools, a decade or more later. This later work bespeaks a conflict between on the one hand 'feminine' mothers, (ostensibly) inscribed within the father's law, and on the other feminist daughters in open revolt against it. Yet in this next generation of work, the effect of the lack of an alternate symbolic treasury is apparent.

Consider *Casting Off* (Jane Northey, 1983), which depicts a daughter seated in a rocking chair, trying to reproduce the knitting skill of her mother and grandmother. But she cannot get it 'right' and abandons the gender-conformist project. Or *Ritual of a Wedding Dress* (Wendy Walker, 1984), in which a daughter unpacks her mother's wedding dress from a trunk and tries it on: but the dress does not 'fit' (nor does the daughter's intervention undo the coherence and power of this intensive visual symbol). Or b.h. Yael's tellingly titled *My Mother is a Dangerous Woman* (1987): here the daughter is a writer, blocked, who becomes preoccupied with the story of Demeter. This goddess of Greek mythology descended deep into Hades to pursue and rescue her abducted daughter Persephone. The twentieth-century mother proffers advice on the necessity and naturalness of female accommodation to male authority. That the 'good' towards which she would persuade the daughter is clearly tinged with masochism is, as Kristeva has argued,[7] fully consistent with the idealized feminine position. These tapes do not enact an extant sense of female subjectivity, but rather articulate problems in attaining to it, problems located specifically around processes of identification at the site occupied by the mother.

Thus *The Influences of My Mother*, with its representation of the mother as woman, agent in history, desiring subject — as well as mother — signals a distinct change in the register by which the mother-daughter relation is articulated. It is a low-budget tape, made on small-format video equipment with minimal production values. Its performance elements are informal, selfconscious and frequently self-indulgent; the camera work is sloppy, the image repertoire limited, the editing imprecise and the sequencing uneven. But despite the many technical flaws in the work, its textual strategies are conceptually sophisticated, mining an awareness of representation as construct, mapping a family narrative outside of patriarchal norms, organizing its representational strategies in an admixture of conventional and innovative narrative codes and organizing an alternative and feminine register of the gaze.

---

7. Kristeva, 'Stabat mater'.

In considering *The Influences of My Mother* in relation to the other works mentioned above, as well as to *Measures of Distance*, the shifts in perspective that these mother-daughter videotapes evidence point to a dynamic interplay between feminist art production, currents of feminist theory, and the conditions of possibility of women's lives. All of these works underscore difficulties in the transaction of psychic and symbolic transformation for daughters seeking the possible terms of their desire. Yet the productions by Diamond and Hatoum suggest a reflection on the difficulties and possibilities of the mother-daughter relation radically different from the principal ways in which this relationship has been taken up as a problematic within psychoanalytic models of feminist criticism over the past decade or more. What is represented in these works is neither an idealization of the mother, nor a merging with her, nor an evacuation of the maternal site, nor an entrapment in the feminine position of abjection and lack, nor a privileging of the pre-Oedipal extralinguistic maternal terrain, nor an *écriture feminine*. The tapes, and the processes they engage, are situated on the side of the symbolic and they navigate a retroaction, within language and culture, that reclaims and reinvests the maternal figure as object of desire *and* as desiring subject.

'How do you go about recreating a once living woman through whom to see yourself?' Diamond asks in an off-camera voice. From the start, Diamond makes evident that it is not the 'truth' of the mother that is at stake but her meaning, specifically her meaning to the daughter. The absence of the mother enables the daughter to project upon this figure her own memories, fantasies and wishes. At the same time, the identity of the mother is also retrieved from the empirical evidences of oral narrative, documents, photographs, testimony and the artefacts of personal and social history. But these, too, are partial and selective. Thus she is not only remembered but discovered and invented, not only the object of the daughter's search but the 'subject' thereby retrieved and produced.

In the first of six acts, the camera pans across a photograph of mother and daughter so as to exclude the mother. 'I pushed her away, but to say that it is as though she never existed *is* to acknowledge her presence. She was unknowable, mysterious, larger than life.' In the second act, the photograph from the opening scene is held in the daughter's hand, turned upside-down, the mother becoming a persecutory figure. 'I dreamed recurringly that she led me to the top of a volcano. The trip up was filled with wonder. At the top, she picked me up and threw me off the volcano.' In the third act, the mother is no longer the mother of personal memory but of social archetype, as expressed in popular music. Diamond, microphone in hand,

the side of the symbolic which, albeit at a secondary psychic level, nonetheless has psychic and social consequences. As in the Freudian scenario, Diamond takes up a position of identification with the maternal figure; but she positions herself, and the viewer, not in terms of Oedipal desire and its privileging of the masculine, but in terms of female longing, along the axis of the maternal signifier. In Diamond's narrative, a separation from the mother is effected, but it is not effected through a paternal intervention but rather from within a homosexual economy in which the mother is at once object of identification and agent of separation. The videotape invites speculation as to whether feminism — as a force within the social, political and cultural field — might constitute as alternative, non-patriarchal 'third term' sponsoring a retroaction which activates the negative Oedipus complex and inscribes the maternal, differently, within the symbolic.

As Kaja Silverman has pointed out, the libidinal investment in the mother, the negative Oedipus complex, is the muted parental term within unconscious fantasy, without the representational supports that work to sustain the daughter's unconscious desire for the father. The 'negativity' of the negative Oedipus complex'[11] is that of a desire out of keeping with paternal law and phallic privilege. The recognition that unconscious desire is 'divided between at least two very different fantasmatic scenes', she argues, enables new discursive and relational strategies for activating the homosexual-maternal fantasmatic scene, and with it both political and libidinal resources.

Silverman insists the mother as unconscious Other *is* the Oedipal rather than the pre-Oedipal mother— that to suggest otherwise is to give female sexuality an essential content preceding language and symbolic structuration. As she elaborates, 'to situate the daughter's passion for the mother within the Oedipus complex... is to make it an effect of language and loss, and so to contextualize both it and the sexuality it implies firmly within the symbolic. It is also to bring it within desire, and hence psychic "reality"'.[12] In situating unconscious desire for the mother within the symbolic, Silverman locates it on the side of language rather than outside of representation.

Certainly in these videotapes by Diamond and Hatoum, a maternal fantasmatic has been (re)activated. However, the mother-daughter compact which eventuates from this process is represented as, in effect, a renegotiation. The mother as desiring subject has been retrieved from a pregiven maternal position. For Diamond, the

---

11. Kaja Silverman, *The fantasy of the maternal voice'* ; in *The Acoustic Mirror* (Bloomington: Indiana University Press, 1988), p. 124.

12. Ibid., p. 123.

mother initially has meaning only in terms of the daughter's primary and narcissistic needs — in particular her need to feel loved rather than abandoned — but her 'meaning' acquires a social valence as the tape proceeds. Thus she is several mothers: a pre-Oedipal mother, feared and idealized within an oscillating imaginary; a mother of social archetype; a mother despised for being insufficiently feminine (like other mothers) by her gender-conformist daughter; a mother as subject and agent of history. In Hatoum's work, the mother is re-situated in a primary position by the once father favouring daughter; but this mother is at once pre-Oedipal and Oedipal, at once body, womanly and maternal, and voice, subject of language, speech, agency, desire. Here, the five-year gap between the visit in which the extraordinary photographs in the work were taken and the materials given symbolic form speaks volumes. What both works suggest is less a preoccupation with a clear division between the Oedipal and the pre-Oedipal than a staging of processes which break from a patriarchal symbolic subtended by a masculine imaginary.

As Margaret Whitford has succinctly summarized, 'if a female symbolic depends upon a female imaginary, it is also the case that a female imaginary depends upon a female symbolic'.[13] The female imaginary, she argues, can be seen as the underside, the 'scraps' of the dominant symbolic order, or it can be seen as something yet to be created. 'The female imaginary would be', she writes 'not something lurking in the depths of women's unconscious, but a possible restructuring of the imaginary by the symbolic which would make a difference to women.'[14] Whitford underscores that the creation of a female imaginary is a collective process.

The Influences of My Mother and *Measures of Distance* suggest that feminism, with its challenge to the dominant symbolic order and its opening up of — and intervening presence within — the terrain of the symbolic, can sponsor such processes. But they further underscore the negotiation with the mother necessary to effect the break from a masculine symbolic, a transaction in which, in these works, the mother is able to assume the position of 'other' — as well as, and instead of, the 'same': both mother and subject. Diamond's tape stages processes by which a capture within the imaginary is worked through, distanced from and given symbolic form, while Hatoum works across the Oedipal divide, the irretrievable distance, to embrace the mother anew.

13. Margaret Whitford, 'Rereading Irigaray', in Teresa Brennan (ed.), *Between Feminism and Psychoanalysis* , p. 119.

14. Ibid., p. 117.

If *The Influences of My Mother* situates the mother-daughter relation within a dyadic economy which absents the father entirely, in *Measures of Distance* there is a triangulation of desires, the father pressing his presence at the edges of the scene, angry and anxious at his exclusion. The mother writes, 'It's as if you had trespassed on his property...'

The governing image of this work is a series of still photographs of the mother, taken by Hatoum on a visit to her family in Lebanon five years before the tape was made. The photographs show the mother at her bath, in an extended sequence of documentation of a scene of unusual intimacy, the photographs sensual images of a naked, full-bodied mature woman. The image of the mother's body, however, is partially obscured through a second image which overlays it, that of neat delicate rows of handwriting in Arabic script from letter written by the mother to her daughter. Thus Hatoum at once represents the maternal body as the locus of desire and emphasizes, with the scriptface that literally fences the image, the barrier to this body produced by language and meditation. The video pictures language as an inscription on/across the mother's body, but the language of the father is here appropriated, used to give voice to the co-respondance between mother and daughter.

The letters are read in voice-over translation by the daughter, creating through language and voice a doubling akin to the doubling that Diamond had produced visually. Yet the doubling of voice as Hatoum reads the mother's words, the doubling of language as the letters in Arabic are translated into spoken English, underscore that this union of elements also incurs losses. The incommensurabilities of translation are further emphasized by the second element of the soundtrack, an untranslated recording of laughter-punctuated conversation between the pair. These shifts and doublings are matched by slippages and complexities in the categories and stereotypes where the place of the mother is defined, creating the calibrations for the videotape's many measures of distance.

The layering of sound and image creates a complex oscillation between its different elements. The images themselves shift and alter, at one moment in closeups so tight as to abstract the body, then framed from a distance, a recognizable figure. Yet the images are never completely sharp, and this constant blurring of the image through movement, incomplete detail, framing too close or too distant for clarity, combines with video's imprecise visual field to create an image that appears *porous*, rendering visually the unfixity of the object that the tape suggests.

Hatoum's figuration of the mother can be seen as a critical stance at odds with the virtual proscription against the imaging of the female body that had assumed a powerful critical consensus in feminist work by the late 1970s and throughout the 1980s. Hatoum's representations of this female body, and specifically of this maternal body, are mediated to privilege a different modality of viewing: through the privileging of the female spectator, through the grid of language superimposed on the images, through the fluctuations of the image, through the layering of image, taped voices and spoken letters which together situate the narrative and the mother in a feminine scenario unbound from the father's gaze.

The intimacy of the photographs extends to the terms of address and the subject matter throughout the tape. Each letter begins with a salutation to the daughter of touching warmth: 'My dear Mona, the apple of my eyes, how I miss you and long to feast my eyes on your beautiful face that brightens up my days...' reads one. Yet the videotape also makes evident that the intimacy and intensity of relation between mother and daughter is in part a new development. As the mother writes: 'I suppose he [Hatoum's father] is wondering why you're not communicating with him in the same way. After all, you've always been your father's daughter and I remember that, before you and I made those tapes and photographs together during your last visit, your letters were always mainly addressing him.' Hatoum, the 'father's daughter', has, like Diamond, become motivated to pursue a different knowledge of and relation to the mother, to locate a new evidence.

The mother embodies fully the feminine maternal aspect in her relation to her child, and the letters vibrate with love and longing for the absent daughter. But through the correspondence with her daughter, the mother begins to articulate for the first time ('You know, I have never talked in this way before') her own desire as a sexual subject. This desire is situated in relation to her marriage, and she urges the daughter to this end — one she equates with sexual pleasure. But her desire also finds expression in an erotics of intimacy that extends to include and embrace the daughter in their shared exploration of their experiences together and apart.

In this exploration, they are outside of the jurisdiction of the husband/father, who is threatened by this intimacy and his exclusion from it. 'We laughed at him when he told us off, but he was seriously angry. He still nags me about it, as if I had given you something which only belongs to him.' *As if.* The proprietorial arrangements of the patriarchal order are seriously undermined in this inscription of another locus and relation of desire. The authority of those cultural and familial limits is at once flaunted and observed through a conspiratorial secrecy, as if such a desire were transgressive, as if it could only be spoken from the margins of the Oedipal boundaries: as if, as in Diamond's video, the exclusion of the father was a necessary precondition for this articulation of a female subjectivity — a subjectivity of desiring mothers and desiring daughters.

The mother's desire — which in the videotape always begins, by virtue of its epistolary framing, with a loving and maternal enfolding — is seen to be expansive, flexible, extrovert. Significantly, as the daughter undertakes to explore a new relation to her mother, so does the mother expand the nature of her desire in relation to the daughter: thus both mother and daughter, as desiring subjects, each rework the intersubjective self-other, mother-daughter relation. Though the mother declares: 'I actually enjoyed the [photo] session, because I felt we were like sisters, close together with nothing to hide from each other', neither an improbable 'sibling' relationship with the maternal figure, nor a displacement of the father, nor a union with the mother, aptly characterizes the position that Hatoum occupies. The shifting registers and unfixed positions articulate a relationship, a mother-daughter relationship, that occupies no visible place in the archives of the symbolic.

Throughout their correspondence, the two figures construct a separate and private space, one in which language and emotion are intertwined. This language is neither univocal nor masterful: it is doubled and split, statement and ellipse. There are pauses in the reading and delays in the flow of sound; there are partial references to ongoing dialogues and topics taken up and left behind; there are relays of situations and circuitous movements of narratives. These registers, at once personal and social, are mapped directly onto the body of the mother. She is speaker and spoken, writer and written. Her words are mediated by the daughter — the person to whom the mother speaks, the person who in turn speaks the mother, the person who constructs the object of the mother-as-subject, the person who confronts and represents the gaps, openings, slippages and incommensurabilities at the very centre of an intimate relationship.

The major topic of the letter pertains to their (changing) relationship; but the relation between them is constantly pulled into, and shaped by, the social and political forces that have determined for each of them a situation of exile from the land of their birth: the war presses with increasing urgency in each letter and by the last has forced an end to the possibility of further communication for an indeterminate time. The letters are primarily focused within the close bonds of their interrelationship, yet the very circumstances which surround the writing underscore how subjectivity is determined not only in gender but in a multiplicity of determinants.

In their correspondence, the mother maps onto the daughter's expressed sense of loss — of a 'gap' between her and her mother and an absence of childhood memory of the mother — the story of another loss, the exile from Palestine with its losses of family, of community, of identity:

> Yes of course I suppose this must have affected you as well, because being born in exile in a country which does not want you is no fun at all. And now that you and your sisters have left Lebanon, you are again living in another exile, in a culture that is totally different to your own. So when you talk about a feeling of fragmentation and not knowing where you really belong, well this has been the painful reality of all our people.

Like Diamond, Hatoum occupies a 'no place', yet here the return to the mother does not presage a solution to the problem of the losses and divisions of the subject. Rather, Hatoum makes explicit the ineradicable exile from the maternal body; and, further, she interweaves this psychosexual loss within other sets of losses, locating the particulars of identity within the specificities of cultural, linguistic, historical and generation boundaries.

At the same time, however, she articulates a realm of pleasure between mother and daughter, refusing — refuting — the order of dereliction and lack, and offering a symbolic construct of intimacy, laughter and love in libidinal, non-phallic intercourse. Loss may be the sponsor of desire, but in Hatoum's work, the daughter's claim on the maternal body (represented in the video's textual strategies as the very sign of the female) is also a claim for the maternal subject, woman and mother — mother and woman.

The Influences of My Mother and *Measures of Distance* are not only autobiographical representations but symbolic constructs that articulate a voice for the mother and a dialogue with her. Yet it must be noted that the principal protagonist in all of the tapes cited here is not the mother. What these narratives trace is not the story of the mother(s), nor even, despite the autobiographical emphases, of the daughter(s), but rather shifts in the ways in which the feminist subject might be said to 'see' and experience (and negotiate) this relation.

In these shifts of perspective can be found evidence of shifts in the currents of feminism itself: from an untheorized celebration of the female sign to an interrogation of femininity as it is constructed in representation and in familial and social relations; from a repression or displacement of the psychic dimension of the troubled mother-daughter relation to its considered exploration; from a preoccupation with 'difference' in relation to the masculine cultural text to an exploration of feminine desire in relation to the other (as) woman.

Further, in their address of the mother-daughter relation, these videotapes, from differing generations of feminist production, demonstrate that there is no stability of meaning in this term. In the very act of symbolizing a cultural absence, replacing silence with speech, this relation is being modified, renewed and reinvented. What is at stake is the articulation of a relationship, a mother-daughter relationship, culturally unmapped in a symbolic order in which the term of the mother has been one possessed by the sons and fathers.

DOUBLE AGENTS:

VIDEO ART ADDRESSING AIDS

by John Greyson

The opening ceremonies of the Fifth International Conference on AIDS, June 4, 1989, in Montreal, were intended to proceed with the crisp technical precision of a televised awards ceremony. Three massive video screens were installed in the huge hall of the Palais de Congrès in front of the 11,600 AIDS "professionals" from five continents. Head-and-shoulder podium shots of the succession of self-congratulatory speakers were meant to fill these screens. Instead, they became unwitting technological double-agents, betraying the organizers and abetting the AIDS activists. In particular, three haunting video images served to rewrite the complacent agenda of the conference. Each of the three relied on a nervous tension peculiar to video, a tension derived from the viewers' negotiation not only of the "live" versus the "prerecorded" but also the "real" versus the "representation."

FIRST IMAGE:

Just as the ceremonies were scheduled to begin, three hundred activists (from AIDS Action Now in Toronto, ACT UP in New York, ACT NOW in the U.S.A., and Réaction SIDA in Montreal) stormed into the hall and occupied the stage, chanting "Le silence égale la mort." There was a stand-off — the P.A. system and the closed-circuit cameras were turned off. Finally, a mike was begrudgingly turned on, and Toronto AIDS activist Tim McCaskell proclaimed: "On behalf of Persons Living With AIDS, I declare this Fifth International Conference on AIDS officially open."

None of the thousands of delegates gathered could see him. He was surrounded by half a dozen TV cameras, but the three closed-circuit screens stayed blank. The organizers obviously hoped that by keeping the activists' images from the screens, they would be able to contain the impact of their intervention. But the media love a successful disruption, and on the same night as the Tiananmen Square massacre in Beijing, the Soviet train disaster, and the Solidarity election victory in Poland dominated all headlines, evening news programs across Canada carried this irresistible image — the only Canadian story that night.

SECOND IMAGE:

The activists eventually took seats in the audience, and the official ceremonies began. For the first time at an international AIDS conference, the organizing committee had decided to allow a person living with AIDS to speak. Kevin Brown was the perfect choice. Co-founder of the Vancouver PWA (Persons With AIDS) Coalition in 1986, he was one of Canada's most effective PWA activists. An outspoken and witty critic of government negligence, he had agreed to speak in person at the opening ceremonies. He died less than a month before the opening.

Instead, a short video (produced by Shane Lunny Productions) was shown on the three screens, documenting Brown in action at press conferences and demonstrations speaking, about his fears and hopes, and profiling the valuable work of the coalition. The tape was riveting and poignant, but we should have been watching a head-and-shoulder shot of Brown speaking live, insisting that world governments and scientific bureaucracies start treating AIDS as the manageable, chronic condition that it is. Instead, we watched a prerecorded image overwritten with the morbidity of a requiem, implicitly reinforcing the cliché that AIDS is invariably fatal.

THIRD IMAGE:

Several speakers later, Brian Mulroney delivered his first speech ever on the subject of AIDS. His smug platitudes, littered with words like "compassion" and "tolerance," "courage" and "dignity," were entirely predictable. He attempted to erase his negligent track record with a few well-chosen unctuous phrases, daring even to salute the memory of Kevin Brown, whose death (like so many others) was arguably, partly a result of Mulroney's lack of policies.

Such slimy pandering did not go unchallenged. The activists rose as one body and stood with their backs to him for the course of his speech, heckling and hissing. His gargantuan chin, filling the three screens, never wavered — he remained serenely indifferent to the cat-calls. However, a number of activists unfurled a huge banner beneath the central monitor, creating a permanent subtitle for his speech. It read: "Mulroney, You've Left Us to Die — AIDS Action Now!" in English and French. This was the image that thousands of delegates saw: the Prime Minister on screen, unaware of the live rewriting of his script.

These three images shaped the opening ceremonies, suggesting the possibility of video as an agent in the deployment of activist interventions. For the next four days, video continued to display its promise as a potentially progressive ally of people living with AIDS. At the same time, video amply demonstrated its terrifying capacity to buttress dominant agendas. Tapes trumpeted the messages of pharmaceutical companies, government bureaucrats, well-fed scientists, academics and conservative AIDS service groups. Wandering through the congested halls of the vast AIDS supermarket (the official trade fair of the conference), people would instinctively congregate at the ubiquitous banks of video monitors, which exhibited everything from testing equipment for condoms and surgical gloves to interactive AIDS in the Workplace video disks, from state public TV campaigns to crass promotional spots for drug manufacturers. AIDS has clearly become a billion dollar growth industry, with video as the hand-in-glove partner for many speculators. Even those in the relatively benign field of educational materials can not escape this critique.

For example, multi-racial AIDS education tapes for youth were standard fare at every state agency booth — indeed, a formulaic consensus seems to have emerged about how to reach "the kids." Just about every tape included a rap song with dancers on the street, spouting generalizations about monogamy, abstinence, safer sex and drug use. Compared with tapes made even two years ago, they were slightly more realistic but not one of them included an out gay teenager, still the youth group most at risk in the western world.

In stark contrast to this supermarket, the conference's parallel cultural festival, SIDART, presented over sixty films and tapes on AIDS from five continents, reflecting for the most part a progressive, community-based bias.

The gamut of tapes was breathtaking: an AIDS awareness music video from Haiti; an agit-prop document of AIDS activism at last year's Republican convention; a drama about the dilemmas of black women in New York whose partners are IV drug users; safer-sex gay porn from West Berlin; a documentary from England aimed at politicizing nurses working with AIDS patients; a leisurely account of a collective counseling session with people taking the HIV antibody test in Rwanda; an experimental education tape made by and for urban aboriginal youth in Australia; a guerrilla AIDS fashion show in Los Angeles (featuring sweat suits for night sweats); the list goes on.

Most of the tapes were from the States, where the combination of over fifty thousand AIDS-related deaths and an active video community has produced vital, oppositional media addressing AIDS: works that inspire, incite, engage, enrage. Works that stand in stark contrast to the profit-driven propaganda tapes of the supermarket. Works produced within the various AIDS communities, by lesbian and gay artists, by community activists and people with AIDS. Works that adopt a confident insider's vernacular, that speak to specific communities, that insist on critical engagement, that refuse the tyrannical myth of the "general public." The raw power relations of audience access are certainly played out in the AIDS war. While the Cagney and Lacey AIDS episode reached millions of viewers and the Ontario provincial government can coerce any high school to buy its tapes, the work of AIDS artists and activists remains marginalized within alternative distribution venues. Nevertheless, such tapes are surfacing in screenings in every city across the country, popping up on cable access slots, disrupting the commercial status quo which says "science" is in control.

There are many reasons for such a plethora of both dominant and independent picturing. As Paula Treichler has noted, AIDS is "simultaneously an epidemic of a transmissible lethal disease and an epidemic of meanings or significations.,"[1] referring to the fragmented and contradictory discourses (of medicine, of the state, of science, of big business) that inadequately "explain" AIDS to us, and that demand our impassioned and informed responses. AIDS inspires a taboo cultural vocabulary (blood, semen, gay sex, drugs, death) that both attracts and repels the commercial entertainment industry. For artists and critics analyzing the mechanics of the mass media, the mainstream coverage of the crisis so far, which weaves a lurid web of hysteria, racism, exoticism, and homophobia, is rich material indeed for appropriation and deconstruction. For educational and health authorities (both progressive and reactionary), AIDS presents a communications challenge of unprecedented subtlety: on the one hand, there are now relative mega-bucks to throw at prevention campaigns; on the other hand, there is the treacherous negotiation of various vested interests (the church, the state, etc.) as AIDS, along with abortion, continues to be the most contested site in society in the area of sexual politics.

Given these conflicting video agendas, the following appraisal of tapes by Canadian artists and activists should illuminate some of the tensions involved in responding to this crisis of both medicine and representation. While they share many political and aesthetic strategies with their American and British counterparts, they also represent the first wave of alternative Canadian responses to the epidemic, insisting on local and personal references to the experience of AIDS in our culture and in our lives.

1. Paula Treichler, "AIDS, Homophobia, and Bio-medical Discourse: An Epidemic of Signification", *AIDS: Cultural Analysis, Cultural Activism, October*, Issue 43, MIT Press, (Cambridge: 1987), pg. 32.

Stupid prevention campaigns are, of course, the cornerstone of Canada's official and begrudging response to AIDS, urging citizens with coy images of heterosexuals to "get the facts." Real information is always postponed, always another step away, and always compromised by prescriptions for monogamy and celibacy. In contrast, independent video artists and AIDS activists have produced street-smart tapes for target audiences that celebrate sexual diversity and consciously engage a politics of representation.

Another Man (1988), produced by an ad-hoc collective of straight, bi, and gay punks in Toronto (sometimes called Youth Against Monsters), is a sassy five-minute music video that takes aim at the politics of AIDS and scores a bulls-eye. Scenes of straight and gay interracial couples under the bed covers are superimposed with the directives, "use a condom" and "use your imagination." Two punks make out in a bus shelter, framed by one of those forbidding "just-say-no" AIDS info posters. Jerry Falwell spews forth some sort of homophobic gibberish; his image is frozen and a superimposed condom is pulled over his head. Long-time lesbian activist and all-round bad girl Chris Bearchall talks about how Canadian customs routinely censors lists of safer-sex practices featured in American gay magazines. The song (composed by activist Michael Smith, among others) which unites these disparate elements is upbeat, celebratory, and defiant.

Youth Against Monsters alumni have continued their video AIDS activism. *Please Adjust Your Sex* is a very raw, sometimes funny and somewhat unsuccessful elaboration of the former tape, loosely using the fiction of a group of punks occupying the CBC to disseminate their AIDS prevention agenda, encouraging people to take off their clothes and put on condoms.

Bearchell, who works at the Toronto agency Inner City Youth, has coordinated the production of the collaborative *STD Street Smarts*, produced by and for street youth, demonstrating in frank terms how to have safer sex and clean your works (IV needles) using bleach. Produced using the facilities at Rogers Cable (Toronto), this tape has already run into problems with the "authorities," ostensibly because it shows a real live (gasp!) cock.

The fact that these tapes won't reach the high-school crowds that need them is hardly surprising. The educational marketplace has been dominated by a handful of producers and distributors willing to sacrifice content for a contract. The authorities (at school boards, social service agencies, state authorities) simply want products which, in the name of AIDS, reflect their particular anti-sex, anti-drug, political agendas, and they can always find commercial producers who are willing to play along. The idea that youth could make tapes for youth is a transgression to the entire system.

A typical example: Shane Lunny Productions, who produced the Kevin Brown tape featured in the opening ceremonies, has been contracted by the Federal Centre for AIDS to produce two half-hour films for youth, featuring (yes, once again) rap songs and "real" kids. On a SIDART panel about television and AIDS, Lunny claimed to have consulted fully with various youth groups in every stage of the production, yet the clips he showed were harshly criticized by audience members for their exclusive heterosexual bias and their condescension towards the youth portrayed. Of course, the Federal Centre, not the youth, had final approval on the scripts. In contrast, the projects outlined above, made for paltry sums with volunteer labour, make no such compromises — their production groups and target audiences are one and the same.

The mass media has allowed PLWAs (with few exceptions) only proscribed stereotypical roles, as Simon Watney has noted: the self-hating "queer," dying pitifully in a hospital bed, abandoned by the world; the dangerous "carrier" whose "irresponsibility" is hysterically condemned; and the "innocent victim" (usually a child or woman) who was infected by a transfusion of carrier.[2] Such clichés share two characteristics: they deny the subjectivity of the real men, women and children who are living with AIDS, and they repeat the tired lie that AIDS is invariably fatal, reducing all persons with HIV, ARC (AIDS-Related Complex), and AIDS to nameless casualties.

Survival of the Delirious (1988) by Michael Balser and Andy Fabo, rejects such clichés and embraces complex metaphors to capture in fragmented, episodic form the experience of gay men living with AIDS. The legend of the Windigo, a malevolent spirit who visits pestilence on the young warriors of the tribe, becomes a fable for the solitary and collective experience of the HIV diagnosis. Discourses of medicine, nature, and myth are visually juxtaposed with still images of cells, monsters, and hand-written text ("blood falls from the sky") keyed over northern lakes and doctors' offices alike. A pair of crudely drawn eyes fills the frame as the camera wanders up a flight of stairs and through several rooms to "see" a body wrapped in a blanket lying in a corner.

The tape dwells on the dreaded HIV antibody test, with one negative result eliciting exaggerated and humorous relief from one patient. Another patient (played by Fabo) handles his positive result with assurance. He asks the doctor what the

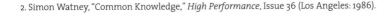

2. Simon Watney, "Common Knowledge," *High Performance*, Issue 36 (Los Angeles: 1986).

treatment options are. Half-way through, the scene breaks down — the doctor (played by HIV-doctor Wayne Boone) doesn't feel comfortable with the assigned lines which have him prescribing AZT, the notoriously toxic drug, still not widely available, which some research now claims has a detrimental effect after the sixth month. It's a pregnant moment, when the awkward acting flips into a real-life discussion, one which captures the difficulty of representing the politics of treatment (with new theories every 24 hours) and the politics of AIDS in general.

The tape concludes with a native warrior (consciously problematized by performer Fabo) taking a hallucinogenic brew in order to enter the delirium to do battle with the Windigo. Ending with a zoom into the campfire (the symbol of survival and of destruction), the concluding scene flirts with sentimentality but demonstrates instead the empowering agency of metaphor. Blending the pictorial strategies of Fabo's paintings and the montage motifs of Balser's previous tapes, this video seeks to displace the public cacophony of AIDS discourses with the personal and far more authentic experiences of the delirium.

While AIDS activism has been a force in Canada for several years, no tapes by artists have captured this agenda, save one: *Are We Going Backwards* by David Tuff (1989). Originally a video installation, this tape adopts a loose, associative form to place the imposition of Bill Vander Zalm's AIDS quarantine legislation in a historical context of similar human rights abuses.

Robed figures and kids at a nursery school perform "Ring Around the Rosie" (the children's rhyme referring to the black plague of Europe). The black and white footage, framed by a diagonal wipe, is slowed down to focus on an Asian girl who accidentally sneezes ("Tissue, Tissue we all fall down!"). A Japanese woman reads Joy Kogawa's account of detention camps where thousands of Japanese-Canadian citizens were interned during WWII. The tape opens and finishes with a contemporary anti-quarantine demonstration, led by gay activists and their supporters, where a lesbian reminds audiences of the pink triangle, used to identify the gays in Hitler's concentration camps. *Backwards* is similar to other documentaries of community resistance inspired by other struggles, but its non-prescriptive insistence on learning from history makes it a more complicated and compelling intervention.

In forthright opposition to the smug narratives and complacent truisms of the AIDS tapes found in the conference's supermarket, these tapes insist that the epidemic is a social construction, not just of politics and medicine, but also of representation. The use each makes of fragmented address, visual juxtaposition, and rich cultural metaphors, grows in part out of an ongoing critique in visual arts and media theory concerning the complexities of representation. At the same time, each tape has adopted discursive and visual strategies that come from the collective and personal experiences of living at the centre of the AIDS maelstrom. Far from being simply clever deployments of po-mo theory, they are vital strategies for capturing the authentic experience of *living* (in all its meanings) with AIDS.

The closing of the conference was also a victory for the activists. Following four days of non-stop interventions, the bewildered bureaucrats and scientists were bending over backwards. Speaker after speaker acknowledged the vital voices of people with AIDS who had (finally) been heard. At the last minute, the organizers scheduled Don Degagne of the Vancouver PWA Coalition to speak from the podium. Thus, for the first time at an international AIDS conference, a PLWA spoke live, filling the three screens of the hall with his head and shoulders, and with unedited, non-prerecorded words. Several artists and activists scattered around the stage recorded his remarks, ensuring that his and their intervention into history will itself be assured of a history.

COLOURING THE SCREEN:

FOUR STRATEGIES IN ANTI-RACIST FILM AND VIDEO

by Richard Fung

INTEGRATION AND THE RADICAL VIDEO DOCUMENTARY

Since the American Civil Rights movement of the 1960s, racial integration has been the goal in rhetoric, if not always in practice, of corporations and government bureaucracies, as well as of grassroots organizations.[1] Racial and ethnic differences are expected within groups or institutions that claim to represent or serve the entire community. Lack of visible diversity is perceived to be an indicator of overt or systemic racism. Particularly in the United States but also in Canada, the implementation of policies of integration have to a large extent been informed by a discourse about "minorities" and "minority representation." Racism, however, is a question of power, not numbers, and policies based on figures and percentages do not necessarily redress oppression.[2] They may, if fact, serve to mask or even reproduce unequal power dynamics, as when quotas are used to define ceilings on the participation of people of colour.[3] Similarly, minority representation can slip easily into tokenism. In this segment, I would like to look at the politics of integration, particularly as it surfaces as a representational strategy in politically committed video documentary.

Given its roots in public access and guerrilla television, politically committed video documentary is especially reflective of trends in grassroots politics. Its mode of production often mirrors a collective process, with collaboration between producer and subject much more common than in political filmmaking. Many tapes are produced by actual participants in the movements represented. While, as in mainstream cinema, the means of production remain largely in the hands of white

---

1. This, of course, does not apply to groups that organize autonomously along specific ethnic or racial lines such as a black teachers' group or a Native art society. Here, questions of accountability and representation may arise around gender parity or other equity issues.

2. Toronto poet Krisantha Sri Bhaggiyadatta has cleverly rephrased the equation in the title of his book, *The Only Minority is the Bourgeoisie* (Toronto: Black Moon, 1985).

3. For a deconstruction of the minority discourse in the Canadian cultural context, see Marlene Nourbese Philip, "The 6% Solution," *Fuse Magazine* 14, no. 1/2 (Fall 1990): 28.

producers, there is a deeper recognition by these videomakers of the imperative of multiracial representation in both the production and analysis of the work. Tapes that deal with any social topic not limited to one racial group are expected to show racial diversity, and work that surveys broad issues such as abortion or labour rights will include, among a majority of white participants, a one-of-each representative selection of non-white interviewees. The configuration of "appropriate" coloured participants actually varies from region to region. In the United States, for example, Latinos are automatically seen and see themselves as people of colour. This is not always so in Canada. Similarly, "Asian" is taken variously to mean south, east or southeast Asian, depending on context. And the status of Arabs and other Middle Eastern people is presently in flux. While anti-Semitism constructs Jews as non-white, they have not traditionally been included for these purposes of explicit display.

If a documentary focusing on gay youth or on women in non-traditional occupations fails to include people of colour, it risks being dismissed as not truly representative. By the same token, the inclusion of people of colour often allows a tape to position its premise of conclusion as *universally* representative. The non-white subjects interviewed may find their presence used to legitimize an overall agenda they had no role in formulating — and one with which they may even disagree.

Further, if a person of colour is shown only in work that focuses on racism, there is the danger that she will be reduced to a function of her racial identity. If the experience of racism is *not* described, however, a crucial aspect of her experience may be ignored. Either way she is in danger of being tokenized. One of the most expedient ways of dealing with this dilemma is to foreground the constructed nature of the piece and, thereby, the issues of representation in the production process itself. Such self-reflexive moments appear in varying forms in the documentary films *Word is Out* (1977), in Sara Diamond's video history of working women in World War II *Keeping the Home Fires Burning* (1988), or Colin Campbell's pseudo-documentary film *Skin* (1990). However, simple acknowledgement of issues of power or of the dangers of tokenism cannot in themselves resolve the underlying problem.

In the video documentary *Just Because of Who We Are* (1986), produced by the feminist Heramedia collective, the involvement of women of colour in a largely white group from the earliest stage of production and decision making facilitated an informed attention to race throughout the project. The subject of the production is violence against lesbians and the tape features interviews with women who vary in age, class, religion and race. As in many other tapes and films employing strategies of integration, the variety of women is used to suggest both the diversity of lesbians and the consistency of their oppression. However, this tape also addresses the experience of racism as an integral aspect in the lives of lesbians of colour. In a lengthy interview with Barbara Smith and Cherrie Moraga, the two writer-activists describe an incident in which their home was vandalized. In their description of the graffiti left scrawled on their walls, the women talk not only about the similarities between racism, sexism and homophobia but also about the points of convergence among these oppressions.

The representation of a racially integrated world emerges as an issue primarily in the work of white producers or producer collectives in which the majority of members are white. Tapes directed by people of colour, on the other hand, generally avoid any interpretation of their interventions as universal. *Bolo Bolo!* (1991) by Gita Saxena and Ian Rashid, for instance, looks not simply at AIDS but at how the disease specifically affects South Asians. *A Voice of Our Own* (1989) by Premika Ratnam and Ali Kazimi does not examine the women's movement in general, but rather, issues particular to immigrant women and women of colour.

Unfortunately, despite the organizing efforts of non-white producers to develop independent networks — and the fact that the institutions of funding, distribution and exhibition are slowly being forced to confront systemic racism in their practice — the means of production continue to elude all but a few people of colour. As a result, lobbying efforts to avoid tokenism and insure meaningful participation remain necessary, not only at a governmental level, but also within communities of independent producers and within individual productions.

TORONTO VIDEO ART: DISRUPTING SIGNIFICATIONS

In Toronto, the producers of video art form a community that is in many ways more coherent and tangible than specific ethnic and racial communities. Drawn together through common interest, the "video community," as part of a larger grouping of art communities, is manifest in two specialized educational institutions, the city's two production cooperatives Charles Street Video and Trinity Square Video, various organizations such as artist-run galleries and through a common social network. But in Toronto, a city where approximately 30 per cent of the population in made up of people of colour, this community is almost exclusively white.[4] This, in spite of the anti-racist sympathies of many of the artists, and the generally oppositional nature of the work produced.

In one evening of mainstream television there is more multiracial representation than can be found in the entire body of Canadian video art. This holds true at a national as well as a local level. Among the reasons behind this is the fact that video artists have traditionally used other artists as cast and crew. Drawing on the pool of professional actors, for instance, might allow for greater racial diversity. More recently, concerns about appropriation have made many artists cautious about representing experiences not "their own" (a complex issue needing much more discussion). Nevertheless, since few people of colour have had the opportunity to produce video, we are left with a strangely whitened version of the world, in which people of African, Asian and Aboriginal ancestries, when they do appear, figure on the periphery — in crowd shots or found footage. Through default, then, this work reinforces the most exaggerated extension of stereotype: the very absence of attribute — invisibility.

At V tape in Toronto (a distributor with one of the largest collections of video art in English Canada, including virtually all Toronto-based production), only a handful of local tapes feature people of colour, and of these only a few are by non-white producers. Of the tapes that do include non-white representation, only a fraction employ convention of "realist" fiction. Two works by white artists, *Night Visions* (1989) by Marusia Bociurkiw and *A Place With No Name* (1989) by Elizabeth Schroder, use naturalistic codes of acting to create empathetic characters. Both tapes seek to avoid the dangers of speaking "for" Native people by focusing instead on the relationship between white and Aboriginal women and drawing out issues that separate and unite the characters.[5] *Night Visions* juxtaposes questions of censorship and lesbian rights with the struggle of a Native woman to keep her child. *A Place With No Name* explores the terms on which a Native woman from northern Canada and a white "southerner" woman from Ontario relate across distances that are more than geographical. In both these pieces, issues of voice and representation (who speaks for whom) are dealt with solely within the diegesis — that is, at the level of character and plot.

In most of the other tapes dealing with non-white representation, however, there is an attempt to confront and unsettle dominant systems of signification through disruptions of racial typecasting and formal devices such as distanciation, whereby

4. Systemic racism refers to the ways in which the everyday activities of an organization or grouping, as opposed to any racist intention on the part of individuals concerned, produce discrimination. I think this is not merely a function of the art community itself but also involves a whole series of other factors including funding, education, and the occupational immobility of certain groups. Many of these factors also impact in terms of class as well as race.

5. For a discussion on the question of cultural appropriation as it relates to Native Canadians, see Loretta Todd, "Notes on Appropriation," *Parallélogramme* 16, no. 1 (Summer 1990): 24-33.

the spectator is made conscious of the conventions of illusionism. *The Flow of Appearances* (1986) by Tess Payne, for example, is a narrative fiction about our "connotative culture"[6] and the way in which individual perception is mediated by a language learned from popular media. In this piece, one of the anchoring tropes is that of a Korean woman who speaks only in Italian. One scene shows her dressed in "Oriental" clothes, displaying classic preparations of pasta. In another, she is "riding" a bike (keyed in front of footage shot from a car) lip syncing to Italian pop songs. In *Kipling Meets the Cowboys* (1985) by John Greyson, a tape about colonialism, neo-colonialism and gay sexuality in the Americas, a travel agent accidentally walks in on the filming of a cowboy porn musical. The travel agent is a Native man and the incongruous group of cowboys includes one black and one Asian actor. Both these tapes disrupt symbolic references traditionally associated with racial "types." Stereotypes are turned on their sides, the authenticity of the image is questioned and attention is called to the ways in which we have been educated into limited racial expectations.

The discomforting fact remains, however, that most Koreans do *not* speak Italian and that neither ranching *nor* the porn industry have been significant employers of Asian men. These fictional subjects, then, are not meant to tell us anything about actual people of colour in any historical or social sense; they do not assert a "real experience" by contradicting the stereotype. The strategy employed by these tapes may instead be read as a conscious avoidance of "essentialism" and stereotype. But this approach to representation raises other questions: to what extent are the non-white characters reduced to self-reflexive, postmodern signifiers? Are they being used, like their predecessors, solely to make a point, albeit this time about racial expectation? Both these tapes eschew a language of realism and, in a sense, render all of their characters into caricatures. Equal treatment, however, does not necessarily foster equality. Because of the universalization of whiteness in the history of representation, white characters are invested with a taken-for-granted subjectivity. This is not the case with representations of people of colour, in which subjectivity must be carefully built.

In most of *The Flow of Appearances*, the Korean woman is positioned as an object by the camera, most notably in a sequence where the camera follows her movement through a crowded street, visualizing a description by a young white man later in the tape. In the "pasta" scene, the woman addresses the camera, but her Italian is not translated for an anglophone audience; in this sense she is "silenced" within the tape. At the same time, she is always depicted as self-assured. And the bicycle ride

6. Tess Payne, artist statement, *The Catalogue of Catalogues* (Toronto: V Tape, 1987).

sequence centres as much on her pleasure as on the fact that she is "singing" in Italian. In *Kipling Meets the Cowboys*, the cartoon figures of the cowboys are counterbalanced by the Native travel agent. Though he is cast "by race" and though, in a sense, he bears the burden of inserting consciousness about race in the diegesis, he is made a subject through the use of several devices. His character is developed, he is given the pleasure of revenge at the end of the tape and, clearest of all, his point of view is privileged through direct-address voice-over.

Edward Lam likewise employs transgressions in racial typecasting as an entry into analyzing the question of subjectivity itself. Both of Lam's tapes, based on performance pieces, feature black actors as the lead characters. As in the tapes by Payne and Greyson, these actors are used in ways that subvert their connotative associations in the dominant lexicon. *Nelson is a Boy* (1985), for instance, features a young black man delivering a stilted, anachronistically erudite dissertation about beauty, with references to Brancusi and Gustav Mahler.

In most of his work, Lam constructs a tension between the characters within the diegesis and himself as creator. This is often accomplished through explicit references to "Mr. Lam" so that he becomes an absent character in his own piece. Whereas distanciation and reflexivity are by no means novelties, the device takes on new meaning within a context that is racially charged. Lam is Chinese. In *Nelson is a Boy*, the black actor introduces himself directly to the camera, and proceeds to muse on an "educated Negro's" appreciation of "Negro art." In the confusion of subjectivity and authorship, there emerges a potent image of the struggle against internalized colonial discourse and the search for "authentic" voice by people of colour.

Through intertitles such as "this is a slave," *Nelson is a Boy* is infused with constant references to race. Racism, however, is never explicitly named, thereby confounding any comfortable appropriation and denying the viewer resolution and closure. Ironically, by leaving the issue thus suspended, attention is drawn toward it even more compellingly.

Finally, in *Second Generation Once Removed* (1990) Gina Saxena questions the "essentialism" with which racial identity is often viewed by exploring her own mixed racial heritage and how it is perceived by others. A parade of different people — in an office, on the street, in a domestic setting — look into the camera and question the artist on her racial background. These snippets are intercut with shots of the artist's face keyed against the flat plane of "colour bars" while her voice offers evasive answers to probing questions. Also intercut are shots of the artist

"Orientalized" into a seated Hindu deity. The tape dismantles and parodies the assumptions that accompany the need to "know" one's own racial location or that of others, illustrating what Homi K. Bhaba describes as the "ambivalence" of the stereotype: "a form of knowledge and identification that vacillates between what is always 'in place,' already known, and something that must be anxiously repeated...."7 *Second Generation Once Removed* presents an autobiographical intervention at the same time as it underlines the constructedness of subjectivity.

POWER STRUGGLE: WORKING FOR A FUTURE

Given the history of race and representation that we inherit as video artists, we sometimes seem to be caught in a double bind when presenting non-white characters: a choice between their reduction to a function of race and the denial of racial difference by casting people of colour in essentially "white" roles. The apparent impasse of this sort of "catch 22" is overcome by the self-reflexive, deconstructive approach of some British films. However, as with the strategy of "positive images," there is no absolute representational remedy, only those which are more (or sometimes less) challenging and insightful.

It is also deficient to discuss anti-racist representational approaches without a simultaneous call for strategies to increase the number of people of colour with access to work in film and video, producing on their own terms. The two areas are intimately related: increasing the number of non-white producers does not simply add more colour to the screen, it has the potential to alter both the questions and the ways in which they are posed. In much of the new work by people of colour — many of them first-time producers — racism forms the implicit context, but the tapes themselves are concerned with questions of (autobiographical) identity and cultural validation. Artists relatively new to video such as Donna James, Zachary Longboy, Shani Mootoo and Shauna Beharry, as well as established video producers like Paul Wong and Leila Sujir, have all made recent work on family histories or on the preservation of cultural identity in a diasporic context, or in a colonial context in the case of Aboriginal producers. The tapes draw on different strategies, from the reworking of documentary codes to the development of a poetic, expressive vocabulary to the use of humour and irony. What they hold in common, however, is the refusal of generalized statements about race; rather, they deal with a close and more-often-than-not explicit relationship to the artists' own histories and social isolation.

7. Homi K. Bhaba, "The Other Question...," *Screen* 24, no. 6 (Nov-Dec. 1983):18.

But the systemic changes that allow the emergence of "new voices" (including those from experienced producers) depend greatly on political context. It is worth noting, as an example, that the black British workshops were funded after massive and widely publicized rioting in the early 80s.[8] At least within the initial five-year period, guaranteed funding and an integral connection with Britain's Channel 4 and the British Film Institute meant that producers were relatively free of commercial pressures. Their license to deal with social issues while experimenting with form — to make work geared to a non-white audience AND get it widely seen — is a luxury specific to that context.

In Canada, inasmuch as it is dealt with at all by the State, racism is envisioned as a set of "bad ideas." Anti-racist work is then conceived of as the displacement of an old mind-set by a new, enlightened one. A policy of Multiculturalism, for example, is based on notions about ignorance and knowledge: people have prejudices because they don't "know other cultures." Once they understand these cultures — conceived of as "ethnic" (not English or French) and manifested through songs, dances and food — their prejudices will "naturally" dissolve. Media is crucial for this Multicultural agenda because it is the conduit through which these new ideas are disseminated. Fighting racism becomes a battle of competing representations: the problems associated with the "positive images" tendency toward simplification and idealization can ensue.

A more radical and useful definition of racism is "prejudice plus power." While this concept is sometimes used to reify power (with the idea that some have it absolutely and others not) and obscure the shifting nexus of power relations in which we all live, it does begin to explain the limitations of anti-racist strategies that are purely image-based.

In order to deal with both overt and covert codes of racism in media, we must begin with — but go much deeper than — an analysis of images and a challenge to the dominant language of representation. We must look toward the transformation of the power relations in production and in society; and these must occur, not apart from, but integral to, other equity issues of gender, region, sexuality, language and physical ability. There must be a change in the racial composition of decision makers at all levels, as well as the processes by which they function. This will require an emphasis on strategies of access to education, funding, distribution, exhibition and informed critical attention. We must foster the interest of young people of colour in taking up the challenge of media. But even more than a change

8. Richard Fung, "Eyes on Black Britain: An Interview with Sankofa's Isaac Julien," *Fuse Magazine*, no. 48 (Winter 1987-88): 26.

of faces or better funding, we must facilitate the development of non-white audiences from the position of marginalized witness to that of active participant: this is one of the primary successes of the deconstructive strategy, so long as audiences are not remarginalized by an overly coded or experimental cinematic language.

We have recently witnessed racial equity initiatives from the Canada Council and some other provincial and municipal bodies. Studio D of the National Film Board has held special workshops for women of colour and Native women. In most of these organizations, however, reports and declarations of changing attitude have amounted to little in terms of meaningful structural change. Particularly in the larger, more established organizations, such as the National Film Board and the Canada Council where personal interests are so much at stake and practices so entrenched, it is utopian to expect significant improvement beyond the one-off conference, workshop or committee, without extensive external pressure. In times of "fiscal restraint" and general cultural conservativism, lobbying efforts must be shrewd enough to avoid racial equity being used as an excuse for defunding the arts altogether.

But while it is important that discussions of race and representation do not neglect the crucial issues of material conditions — who gets to produce and on what terms — such concerns do not displace the need to evaluate what is produced, the strategies that are employed and the meanings embedded in the vocabulary of sound and image that we draw upon in the creation of our new visions.

TOTAL RECALL

HISTORY, MEMORY & NEW DOCUMENTARY

by Sara Diamond and Gary Kibbins

When social documentary re-emerged in the late 1960s and 1970s it was associated with a New Left perspective that viewed the media as an ongoing source of false ideology. Canadian producers tried to resurrect a critical practice from the shards of a CBC television and National Film Board liberal-nationalistic documentary tradition. Information from a radical perspective was perceived as a pivotal force with which to change social consciousness — the lies of the mass media could be replaced by a politicized and correct (or at least more correct) representation of historical reality.

The scope of this process was greatly expanded by the introduction of the Portapack in the late sixties. Even the relative availability of 16mm film had been too daunting (financially as well as due to the complexity of its production and distribution system) to be a viable tool for local community based production and organizing. With video, it was not immediately necessary to guarantee wide distribution in order to recover the costs of production; thereafter it became possible to make works whose targeted audience didn't have to go beyond that of very narrowly defined communities of interest. As critics such as Martha Gever have suggested, content not structure was the locus where critical intervention first occurred.

A number of strategies and forms of work have developed in this context, some of which mirror the concerns seen in film work, others are more video specific. Advocacy tapes generally attempt to compel people to act, while personal testimony and vérité works have attempted to create alternate histories, by clearing a social space for individuals and groups to speak. Unlike authored documentaries, these works are more often produced in a community context, requiring intensive collaboration between artist and subject. The video process makes media accessible to the disenfranchised — tapes work to and for a specific audience and are fundamentally aligned with the perspective of specific social groupings. Finally, some works were designed to counter disinformation systematically cranked out by a dominant media increasingly willing to privilege the policies and opinions of the State. This work was greatly accelerated by the availability of home VCRs.

At the same time, video documentary work developed a tough critique of its perceived other, television — particularly its use of the unseen but authoritative journalist/narrator and their accompanying gaggle of "experts." This critique either came in the form of discrete "deconstructive" works, or increasingly, were operative components of advocacy or alternate history works. It should be noted however, that the insistence of deploying a direct critique of television has declined somewhat in recent years. This may be due to a realization that broadcast television was never video's "frightful grandparent" in the first place. What they shared as a technological form was perhaps less telling than what they didn't share regarding broadcasting privileges and mass reception conditions.

Video of course cued in to the long-standing, on-going debates about documentary form. This critique questioned the notion that essential elements resided in the represented subject. For example, why do so many producers believe that a working class speaker was somehow more truthful or honest than one from the middle class? Testimonial works, which gave evidence of abuse or oppression often employed a falsely optimistic use of closure, while network news documentaries gave a false sense of knowledge due to their authoritative means of production and their unwillingness to reveal their ideological affiliations. The ensuing competition of truth-contents was problematic not because of the relative value of the positions taken, but because the manner in which the various meanings were constructed was not made clear to the viewer. Thus even cinéma vérité works, which in one sense seemed to be as free of editorial intrusion as documentary could get, were no less free of hidden bias than any other form due, ironically, to the very lack of editorial intrusion, and the accompanying lack of evidence of the producer's decision making process.

Finally, the application of semiotics to the analysis of Western myth, most significantly advertising ("Capitalist Realism") showed that certain formal operations could communicate ideological meanings quite insidiously — but very effectively — and with a high degree of aesthetic economy. The committed documentary unwilling to disclose the manner of its own constructed meanings was itself vulnerable to such an analysis.

What this tradition of critique has revealed however, is that there is no single strategy that is effective in all cases. Instead, any critique necessarily requires an accompanying analysis of the concrete conditions of audience and reception conditions. In addition, the critique of documentary must itself be examined for its ideological biases, with the knowledge that whatever their alleged formal weaknesses documentaries have played an important role in social and political mobilization. Criticism comes in part from the desire to make true documentary's own promise to weld the mobilizing impulse of works into a more effective political tool. But the critique comes from sometimes contradictory directions: from modernism, semiotics and feminist film theory, and from within a critical documentary tradition. While modernism has centred on realism as an outdated form — a problem given the dominance of the latter in cinema and television — the first two currents have argued that even critical documentary evokes passivity on the part of its audience, because of its reiteration of narrative structure.

Semiotic criticism, while rejecting a unifying political project, echoed concerns about realism expressed by an earlier generation of artists. The historical avant-garde, active in Europe during the 1920s and 30s, had contributed a challenge to both modernism and realism. This avant-garde had a very different concept about the social role of art than did Modernism: they opposed the separation of art from life central to Modernist practice, and wished instead to "reintegrate it into the praxis of life" (Peter Burger). The "institutions of art" which prevail in any historical period, and which frame and regulate the artwork regardless of its content, were the target of the avant-gardist critique, their having a central role in maintaining the separation of the "aesthetic" sphere from the "practical" sphere. This analysis — along with the avant-garde's failure in overthrowing the institutions of art — throw into relief the importance of understanding the production and reception conditions of a work.

The preoccupation with truth, and the general disregard of the regulating influence of the institutions of art, asserted itself in the formal concerns of modernism. The search for the essential organization of experience and matter moved modern art out of nineteenth century realism into abstraction. Modernism had engaged in a quest for truth within the materials and forms of artistic production, eclipsing realism as a form. The legacy of modernist art practices asserts a strong influence within video art. In positive terms it has encouraged a consciousness about video as a specific historical form, including the characteristics it shares with television, and has expanded experimentation. In negative terms it is represented in a refusal to acknowledge the integral role that community documentary production has played in forming a language of video practice and in doing so challenging the institutions of art.

In the 1980s, with the decomposition of the optimistic and holistic political vision of the previous decade, personal ideologies appear and are experienced in a far more fragmented form than previously, and dissent itself is more pragmatic. Within socially instrumental art works and documentary, a greater blending of documentary realism and experimentation, with a stronger sense of subjective positioning has emerged — artists tend to blend the realism of documentary with narrative, experimental and appropriated elements. A new documentary has developed which directly and openly employs subjective processes in various forms of fantasy and fiction and yet operates within the construction of an analysis, and in the ethics of contributing to social and political movements.

It is impossible to characterize the diversity of video documentary forms that have been developed in the last decade except to say that they often employ a high degree of heterogeneity. This has been made possible in part due to the expanded syntax of post-production in video, and the relative inexpense (compared to film) of "special effects." The once dominant codes of realism of documentary have given way to the proliferation and juxtaposition of codes which can then be deployed within a single work. Realist narrative sections exist alongside vérité sections; political motifs exist alongside non-political "fantasy" sections; fiction tries playfully to pass itself off as documentation; etc., all of which can then be combined in highly layered collages.

Out of Air (by Robert Milthorp) contains a double reading, referring to both the bird's eye overview of the helicopter and the construction of family and community within post-war suburbia — a human construction within an artificial environment. The subject's testimony evokes respect not a sense of the exotic, becoming a subtle tale of survival and displacement when the speaker matter-of-factly refers to her recent widowhood. We are above all reminded that the Other is an articulate and thinking individual.

The Way To My Father's Village (by Richard Fung) traces the continual production and re-evaluation of the past through its remnants in the present. Memory is the key to the individual's historical process. History in this instance is not fixed but continually transforming. The artist uses his own voice-over, one lengthy interview (as opposed to a set of authorities), footage of China and visual references to the mythic past. The latter refers to an inscrutable Asia, a myth which implicates both artist and audience. The sense of loss that the artist feels, that compels him to seek out his familial past, provides a personal and historical framework for the viewer to approach an otherwise distant topic.

White Dawn (by Lisa Steele/Kim Tomczak) is a fiction that parallels reality: the current U.S./Canada free trade deal. Combining narrative scripting and an ironic voice-over, *White Dawn* uses an ironic reversal of current circumstances. Canadian culture, even without free trade, is overwhelmed by American imports.

Referenced around a real event — the suicide of a "family" man caught in a park bathroom raid — *Jungle Boy* (by John Greyson) appropriates and indicts systems through which cultural values are formed. Pornography, Hollywood cinema, news reportage, film criticism and the gay subculture are all implicated. *Jungle Boy* brings together the experiences of colonialism and gender oppression. While validating the ability of alternate cultures to transform dominance, it warns against other inequities remaining entrenched.

Histoire Infame (by Nicole Giguère) addresses the subjectivity of historical writing and reading. The tape is a rock video, replacing the traditionally sexist content with a sweeping historical overview of the interpretation of women within history and their rereading by feminism. Creating a more specific history, *Comptines* (by Diane Poitras) deals with the imprisonment of Irish P.O.W.'s using music and poetic visual references. It constructs an emotional memory of the fracturing effects of imprisonment from the perspective of women.

Both *Pie y Cafe* (by Jan Peacock) and *Nez, Gorge, Oreille* (by Elsa Cayo) describe the relationships between reality, linguistic codes and historical processes. *Pie y Cafe* discusses our complicity in constructing a history of Third World oppression. Repetitive and intensifying rhythms of associative montage recirculate and reread relatively benign but laden symbols: coffee and apple pie. These symbols and their meanings are transformed into weapons of oppression. *Pie y Cafe* effectively generalizes about a larger history by not referring to specific events.

Nez, Gorge, Oreille looks at historical construction through the individual's relationship to language, for language incorporates the specificity of culture. The individual's possibilities are both limited and described through its codes.

"Total Recall" suggests that there cannot be a single strategy for socially conscious works. A pragmatic and usually local politics make understanding the conditions of production and representation imperative. What binds experimental and documentary works are their ethical underpinnings: the imperative to speak directly and to question the parameters of knowledge, and to construct a process and network of communication which might assist in the construction of collective social identity.

EXPANDING GENRES

by Monique Langlois

As Chantal duPont so aptly states in her text accompanying this screening of tapes by four video artists, video is a "plural art"[1] exploring the limits of individual artforms to question the borders of art itself. Within the framework of this broader issue, one context where the question of extending limits arises is that of specific artistic genres. This is frequently the case in video art, and the works currently being shown at Graff are proof that video artists are rethinking the notion of genres, in this case — the self-portrait (Diane Tremblay and Gabrielle Schloesser), the portrait (Mario Côté), and the travel diary (Suzan Vachon).

I will attempt to show how each artist modifies the specific characteristics of the dominant genre of each video. First, one thing is clear: the artists are physically present in *L'abîme, La manifeste et l'inconsciente*, and *Parabole 78 — avec Louise Robert*, whereas in *Palimpsest Sentimental*, the artist is present *in absentia* as the invisible narrator of her pictorial diary. Apart from their respective genres, all these tapes present features associated with autobiography or self-portraiture.

The main difference between these two genres is that the first is essentially narrative — a life-story is presented in linear fashion, even if actual chronology is not respected; whereas, the second recalls specific aspects of the artist, as seen by himself at a precise moment in his life.

Philippe Dubois has identified three stages when the self-portrait genre impacted on video art's brief history.[2] In his view, the first stage was in the early 70s, when video artists confronted themselves, i.e., their own image. By the end of the decade and in the early 80's, they were putting themselves on screen less often, usually preferring a relay-method, via language. The third stage began in the late 80s and continues today. Here, artists adopt the stance of witness to images representing knowledge of the world.

These three reference-points are salient insofar as each designated time-period had its own conception of the self-portrait. As the genre is "refined" during any given stage, the other two stages reveal that video art contributed to extending its limits,

---

1. duPont, Chantal, *La vidéo, un art pluriel*, Galerie Graff, February 1991.

2. Interview by Sylvain Campeau, *ETC Montréal, Revue de l'art actuel*, winter 1989, n. 10, p.27.

to the point where features of other genres are included in its definition. The question arises — are we still dealing with self-portraiture?

The order in which the videos will be discussed has been determined by the differences between autobiography and self-portrait per se, and the evolving approaches to self-portraiture in the history of art video. This procedure simply aims at showing how contemporary video artists explore the distinctive features of self-portraiture whatever the intended genre of their tape.

L'abîme, by Diane Tremblay, is essentially a self-portrait whose basic narrative form is highly reminiscent of autobiography. The artist reinforces this impression by asking herself not only who she is, today, but what she is doing. That her answers are in the present tense, rather than in the past tense as they would be in autobiography, reveals that the artist is a relative new-comer to the medium.

The choice of shooting-sites is also revealing — an abandoned cottage by a lake, where she has recreated her studio, and the village of Val-Jalbert, deserted since the early 1900's and now transformed into an open-air museum. We are thus confronted with two terrains in the world of visual arts — one private: the artist's studio, the other public: a museum.

The tape adopts two viewpoints linked to these places and clarified by Tremblay's performance. The first viewpoint concerns the artist's need to withdraw into a studio, as onto an island, to produce works. I am referring here to the isolation of the open-air studio, and to the events that happen there or on a little island. The second viewpoint in the tape is that of the museum as show-case for the artist's production. However, the latter is both inaccessible — as suggested in the tape's title — and not generally appreciated by the public, as confirmed in the choice of an abandoned village-become-museum. Reflections on the museum are not fleshed out.

Understanding of certain parts of the work is, admittedly, hindered by the range of Tremblay's actions and gestures, and the too numerous secondary objects she uses. The situation is completely reversed in Gabrielle Schloesser's *La manifeste et l'inconsciente*: here, the artist confronts only her own image without decor or props. She thus adheres to the conception of self-portrait typical of the first stage described above.

This tape is a genuine performance — for the artist examines the video-image of her own body in a twenty-minute tape condensing eight hours of isolation in a tiny, empty room. Edited sequencing respects actual chronology, while successive and repeated close-ups of the artist's mouth, hair, hands, and body parts portray her body in pieces — referring less to her alienation as a woman that to the partial images others have of her. Such a methodical and minute examination of herself creates the feeling that the artist is reaching beyond the visible to the invisible. Are those simply her eyes — or is Schloesser invoking the unconscious. Or are they our eyes, since the artist includes us in the search for self so typical of self-portraits in post-Renaissance painting. I am thinking especially of Rembrandt (1603 - 1669) who painted ninety self-portraits — representing himself not only at every age in life, but at different stages in his private and public careers, or in Oriental garb, and even at the right hand of the dead Christ in *The Descent from the Cross* (1633). Rembrandt's self-portraits are in themselves sufficient proof that every human being includes all others, and when we delve into the self we always encounter the other. In video — and this is what Schloesser's self-portrait brings out — edited cuts and splices in different time-sequences produce images capable of eliciting the same response in the viewer as a series of self-portraits painted by the same artist over time, and observed one after another, side by side, either in a museum or while flipping through a book of reproductions.

The soundtrack in this tape is also extremely important throughout. A voice-over makes statements constantly wavering between self-affirmation and negation. These statements illustrate the phenomenon known as "alternative switching" — a psychological function described by Serge Leclaire, who sees the subject in terms of antinomy and "alternative switching." Leclaire explains antinomy as a conflict between truth and its transgression, observing that it is precisely because of the alternation between two, apparently opposite states, that an individual in search of identity arrives at self-knowledge.[3]

In a sense, Mario Côté adapts this function to art by juxtaposing painting (truth) and video (transgression), in *Parabole 78 — avec Louise Robert*. One cannot help wondering if Côté is a painter or a video artist — or if his originality isn't an ability to paint in video. His approach is complex, intersecting with the conception of self-portrait as practiced in the second historical stage by video artists who present themselves via language. However, Côté achieves his end through an intermediary portrait of Louise Robert, an artist-painter who places herself opposite words in her paintings.

Everything in this tape is literally face-to-face, starting with its formal elements: two images side by side. The doubling technique allows all possible juxtapositions between video-artist (author), artist-painter (active model), words (content), and

3. Leclaire, Serge, *Psychanalyser*, Paris, Seuil, Points, 1967, p.137.

fragments of canvasses (work). The process of art production is revealed by the two characters, video artist and painter, using techniques specific to video. The result is a poem of their casual conversation, choosing words and expressions which are retained and written on cards, then thrown into the sea, having served to ground the work. As in the painter's canvasses, certain words resurface, others don't. Water erases the stories, "painting remains," she declares. And video — one is tempted to add — because of the video artist's participation. His experience not only offers a glimpse of Louise Robert and her work, it also provides insight into his own art practice.

Unlike the three preceding video artists, Suzan Vachon does not engage in self-representation in *Palimpsest Sentimental*. Instead, the artist revisits the "Roman itinerary" followed by Goethe, Stendhal, and several others, in a video adaptation of the literary travelogue genre. The absent narrator continually accentuates her presence by exchanging glances with characters in the tape. To mention but one example: the young woman focusing her still camera on an off-screen object, then turns around in slow motion to gaze at the viewer — in the first instance, the video artist. This procedure presents Suzan Vachon as a witness before images containing knowledge of the world, like video artists in the third stage in the history of video self-portrait.

But this is not all. The tape offers visual impressions of looks and gestures exchanged, and transformed visions of natural and historical sites. Images are superimposed, or mixed, erased, and then repeated, completely or partially, in a repetitive "text" alluding to their own lack of memory. This style of video composition is made possible by techniques like successive fade-outs and image-repetition, to name only two. In a way, Suzan Vachon uses video making as a medium through which she can relay herself, and her tape is, to that extent, similar to video self-portraits in the second stage of the genre's history. In fact, this tape is a fine example of the breaking-down of genres — to the point where one wonders which one — travelogue or self-portrait — is contaminating the other.

The preceding remarks show how video raises the question of artistic genres. We have seen that , in spite of their respective genres, the tapes discussed have special links with self-portraiture. The question arises whether this genre includes all the others — the three stages in the historical evolution of video self-portraits would suggest this — or if all genres, whatever they may be, do not inevitably include distinctive elements of self-portraiture. However the subject is approached, the fragmenting of genres is an accomplished fact which underlines the "impurity" inherent in current creative expression, to adopt Guy Scarpetta's phrase.

Translation by Jean-Luc Svoboda

TESTED FICTIONS &
TWISTED FRAGMENTS

4 NEW WORKS:
FRAGMENTS (Paula Fairfield)
TONGUE TIED AND TWISTED (Joyan Saunders)
GOOD CLEAN FICTION (Gary Kibbins)
TEST (Rowley Mossop)

By Susan Rynard

The screening of *4 New Works* clearly indicates that artists/directors are currently exploring a multiplicity of divergent strategies in the making of tapes that fall under the all too equivocal term "video art." Yet, when discussing video art, more often than not the work is assessed in terms relative to other disciplines. For example, video art is often considered within the critical framework of either film (is this a drama, or a documentary?), or the visual arts (is this conceptual or sculptural?), or television (video art, hmmm, isn't that where artists with Portapacks liberate TV?).

Questions like these are limiting. They also lead to a situation where video art is defined in relation to what it is not, rather than to what it is. Understandably, video artists are becoming increasingly disgruntled with the type of discourse that circulates around their work. As the recent screening of *4 New Works* demonstrates, the strategies currently being employed by video artists resist the definitive boundaries imposed by, and upon, other disciplines. Thus the value of assessing the work using these same critical perimeters is quickly negated.

Rowley Mossop's *Test* is loosely based on the case of Rudi Steinman and the issue of mandatory HIV testing. *Test* opens with a male doctor's "all in a days work" voice-over monologue. Merged with images of hospital stairwells, an underground garage and a night drive, he speaks first as if to a colleague, then to the viewer, then to himself. With a measured tone, he expresses concern over a patient who might test HIV-positive. As a physician, it seems that even his interior monologue is governed by professional ethics. Then the viewpoint shifts from the doctor to a surrogate interrogator. This man seems to be a stand in, but for whom — the health care system? a social worker? an analyst? the public? Or all of these figures and institutions? An interview of sorts between Steinman and the interrogator is continually interrupted by extreme close-ups of children's toy figures. The doll house, the blue family Ford, and the "Super Male," who re-enact the stories described in the voice-over, serve as iconic references to the ideals of mass culture. Seditiously, *Test* does not conclude, it ends.

While Paula Fairfield's *Fragments* is a dense and complicated work, it manages to maintain a refreshing accessibility. Over the course of seven minutes, themes emerge, circulating around various aspects of women and technology. *Fragments* opens with an evocative scene of Maria-Teresa Larrain gazing at herself in the mirror— the oldest reproduction technology that uses light and refraction — as she reads aloud from a romance novel. Her identity is both constructed within, and inscribed by, language as she acts out her identification with the novel's heroine. Larrain is soon recorded by a nervous photographer, who frames a mediated image produced by the camera lens. The theme of reproduction technology is playfully articulated by parallel narratives. Reverend Tom's (Andrew J. Paterson) sermon on TV discusses the immaculate conception of the Virgin Mary, while a young technical whiz (Sheri Kowall) has just tested "positive" with her drug store pregnancy test kit.

Paula Fairfield describes *Fragments* as a "trailer." Whereas commercial film trailers serve primarily as advertising aiming to encapsulate the film's main dramatic plot in an exciting and titillating manner, *Fragments* presents a sort of inverted study of all this. The sound-track both implores with sensational tones and entices with sonorous lyrical seduction. Titles introduce us to the characters, and the dramatic action is framed by a filmic mise-en-scène. However, while a commercial trailer seeks to sum up, *Fragments* seems to break apart: the visual and audio materials chosen subtly disrupt the hegemonic "truth" of the image surface. Specific images in *Fragments* were shot on film, others on video and some originated in electronic sources, in this case TV and a pixel board sign. These images were subsequently taken through several layers of translation to produce a final work that is available on both film and video. All in all, *Fragments* is a beautifully produced work that demonstrates both skill and an economy of image. It is a work that deserves to be viewed many times.

Even as the title of Gary Kibbins' tape, *Good Clean Fiction*, prepares us for a work that will comically negate the traditional TV/film genres of "good clean (all-American) fiction," it also evokes a kind of word-play of opposites. Throughout the tape we are presented with various scenarios that are structured around the binary relationships of good vs. bad, clean vs. dirty and fiction vs. non-fiction. As the tape begins, an all-American boy is being rejected because he is simply "too clean," (He is rejected by a very serious woman who is "looking for laughs," get the picture?) As the tape unfolds we have a CIA scandal and a series of job dismissals and then Mike the mechanic discovers that the theory on which the internal combustion engine is based is false. Cars will never work again. Later a woman is reprimanded by her boss for causing the entire nuclear industry to collapse, and one inquisitive man has caused the complete ruin of the economic system.

Good Clean Fiction's sound-track braces us for a patriotic tear jerker, as the once "too clean" protagonist (who now wears shredded, greasy, dirty clothes) attempts, with his friend, to discuss the greatest aspirations of humanity, and while doing so they accidently murder their roommate. But wait, there is hope. The pioneering spirit that brought us the "mission to Mars" (not only "a great investment," but it will provide "those with stale jokes a new place to laugh") raises Lazarus from the dead *and* cleans the kitchen.

Somewhere in the midst of this rather complex "plot" line, the viewer is confronted with a real time (at first silent) image of a "real" mechanic (as opposed to the earlier fictional mechanic) changing a tire. The placement of this real time image within an otherwise densely constructed narrative creates a moment of discomfort for the viewer. I believe this sequence is constructed in this fashion not just to make us feel uncomfortable as it seems at first, but to deliberately provoke the important and serious question: "how do I read this?" And this, I would argue, is an underlying project of the entire tape.

The story of Jane, the heroine of Joyan Saunders' tape *Tongue-Tied and Twisted*, is offered up in a complex narrative that employs both symbolic and visual vocabulary. Jane has spent some time answering some of the major questions of our decade, such as, what are the alternative uses for plastic bags, compressed air and the dollar bill? Or, how can I subvert this household item to make my life as a woman easier? — a difficult task since domestic appliances ostensibly liberated all women years ago. More seriously, how can I gain more control over my life as a woman? Jane's predicament becomes a crisis that manifests itself in obsessive and compulsive behaviour bordering on the neurotic. She dries her underwear in the oven, dusts her knick-knacks with compressed air, slips her shoes on with a crisp bill and protects her hairdo by covering it with a plastic bag before pulling on her sweater. She's also discovered a unique way to avoid nasty panty lines: just pull your blouse through the bottom of your underwear and you'll be creaseless right down to your knees. The voiceover text provides insight into Jane's motives: "Her hair frames not just her face but her entire existence..." She experiences a certain dislocation between her speech and her brain, claiming that for years she was only able to speak in "monosyllabic utterances." Jane's alienation from language is illustrative of her position outside of the patriarchal order. Yet Saunders treats her themes with an ironic twist; issues of the female position in the male order are humorously reinforced when Jane and her girlfriend take a walk to the "golden triangle" with its recently transplanted rows of phallic palm trees.

As Saunders discusses the extreme self-consciousness of women (a woman is "accompanied by a mental image of herself at all times"), we are reminded of an earlier Jane. As she adds the final touches to her face and body in the mirror (camera), we can see a kitsch painting of a young bright-eyed Mexican soldier-girl hanging behind her, leaving the viewer with a striking portrait of the ideological forces at work in the construction of female image. *Tongue Tied and Twisted* ends, however, with a more disturbing image of Jane waving to her shadow. She appears almost skeletal with her neck elongated, her body distorted. One can't fail to associate this image with an earlier daunting aural image of a starving dog and the visual image of "Day of the Dead" skulls. Jane's departure in this work is without optimism. One can, however, find something positive in this ending. Although the status quo teaches us to demand not only happy endings but closure from a work, forcing an incredible imposition on the work and burdening it with a moral imperative, *Tongue Tied and Twisted* resists both these tendencies.

It is important to acknowledge that, however problematic, these works resist using media language or form in traditional ways. In the past it was low-tech and low-budget that became equated with works of resistance. Yet as these four tapes demonstrate, current strategies are much more subtle and varied, and cannot be reduced to the simple equations of dollars and technology.

The fact that there is so little written about video (especially in the popular press) may have as much to do with the complexity of the strategies involved, as the diversity of the work produced. Whatever the reason, the lack of an all encompassing critical paradigm is not because of a lack of interest or discussion about video works, but more importantly, speaks of the work's resistance to being canonized, categorized, and ultimately, consumed. In light of this, my discussion of *4 New Works* must be seen as only one view, part of an on-going and necessary dialogue acknowledging that the divergent strategies that exist within video work should also exist in their discussion.

ENTANGLEMENT:

VIDEO ART AND TV

by Jean Gagnon

With regard to its specific connections with television, video art opens the debate between an 'elitist' art and a 'popular' medium.[1] Art is a hearth, where societal and generational values are melted and left glowing in the public arena. Is there any better melting-pot than television's glowing zeal to divide all sorts of people? Is the work of art not 'elitist' in that it shifts the horizon of widely accepted ideas and common perceptions?

This text will deal with television and the way a number of video productions from Quebec put it into question. This illustration will be demonstrated in four instances which correspond to particular video works: *Album* (1984), a four-channel video installation by Marshalore and three single-channel videotapes: *Fait divers: Elle remplace son mari par une TV* (1982) by Jean-Pierre St-Louis and Lynda Craig, *Le voleur vit en enfer* (1982) by Robert Morin and Lorraine Dufour, and finally, a more recent videotape by the Morin/Dufour team in collaboration with the Coop Vidéo de Montréal, *La Réception* (1990), in which the ironic stance is masterfully conveyed.

These video works represent, in varying degrees and styles, a critical use of the medium. During the eighties, a new generation of young video artists was emerging, while Marshalore — whose installation was to be her last video production — Morin, Dufour and St-Louis were reaching maturity. During the same period, Montreal was obsessed with television. We find at this time in the industrial sphere, the birth of Musique Plus, the Quatre Saisons Television Network and the conference Convergence Film/Video (1984) and in the art community, the Festival international de nouveau cinéma et vidéo de Montréal, which began programming video works in 1981, and Video 84, the first international video conference in Montreal. Among young Montreal video artists such as François Girard, Bernar Hébert and a few others, as well as members of the Coop Vidéo, one also finds a concern with television.

The work of the more experienced artists, in retrospect and all things being relative, seems to have held up better to the test of time, although *Le train* (1984) by François Girard or *Le chien de Luis et Salvador* (1984) by Bernar Hébert admittedly deserve to

---

1. See Carl Loeffler, *The Second Link — Viewpoints on Video in the Eighties*, published by the Walter Phillips Gallery, Banff, 1983. pp. 14-19.

be reconsidered, in order to fully appreciate the progress of these younger artists, who have gone on to produce a large and varied body of work. Be that as it may, our purpose here is to demonstrate how the works of Morin, Dufour, St-Louis and Marshalore play on distinct television characteristics, by simultaneously being attentive to personal reality, media reality and viewer expectation. As we will see, the videotapes by Morin, in the media context of television and its prescriptive narratives, will illustrate a poetic and ironic look at television.

The four video works to be discussed are bound in a dialectic which positions television in relation to its viewer, the time of television narrative in relation to everyday time and finally, the irony of video art in the context of "mass communication" and the yattering of television's daily world.

1. ENTANGLEMENT AND CONVERSATION

> "(...) television cannot satisfy our desire for subjectivity, but it can displace it."[2]

Television, taking its place in the universe of domestic objects, does not need to create a fictional space because it already intercedes in our daily world as quasi-subjectivity. This phenomenon has long since been acknowledged.[3] The simulacrum of intimacy established between the television personality and the home viewer has been termed a "para-social relationship." It is rooted in and engineered through direct viewer address, familiarity with television's physical apparatus and the personalities on-screen. Whether we turn it on without listening to it or listen without looking at it, the presence of television is prominent and familiar in our daily surroundings. The goal of direct address in the general syntax of television discourse is the reinforcement of television's familiarity, because all those people on the small screen are talking to you, the viewer and listener, as if in daily conversation.

A video installation by Marshalore, *Album*, draws attention to this situation by placing four monitors in front of a sofa designed to seat three people, the traditional set-up for looking at television. Alternately or together, each screen shows the portrait of three people: René Blouin, Kate Craig, and John Plant. A computer controls the sequencing of the tapes. As we listen to one person speaking, the person on another screen will begin to talk. In the viewer's mind, the continuous interruption – each speaker in turn interrupts the other – takes on the

2. Margaret Morse, "Talk, Talk, Talk," *Screen*, vol. 26, no. 2, March-April 1985, p.15.

3. Donald Horton and R. Richard Wohl, "Mass Communication and Para-Social Interaction: Observation on Intimacy at a Distance," *Inter/Media*, Oxford U P, 1979, pp. 32-55. Study originally published in 1953.

shape of a conversation and a discourse released from authority because of its multiplicity and because it is de-centered.

Each person confides personal secrets — the camera in close-up on their facial expressions and their personal tics and mannerisms — talking about respective fears, hopes, love, relationships with others, their parents and childhood memories. The overall tone is one of confidentiality and the constant interruptions result in a conversational exchange in which the viewer can participate by recalling his personal memories.

In this instance, the distinguishing feature between narration and conversation is that, in narration, the narrator disappears to let the characters speak, while in conversation, by definition, the speakers are positioned face to face in dialogue. Narration takes place elsewhere, outside of the space-time reference of the viewer, while conversation attests to the immediacy of each speaker's subjectivity. The conventional way of viewing television, as illustrated by this installation, is proposed as a site for encouraging viewer participation in a moment of television conviviality where the devices of exposed intersubjectivity and memory-exchange are given new life through the act of remembrance by the viewer.

The "subjectivity" of the people on-screen sustains the viewer, the identification process is achieved by the act of remembrance, through which the spectator is finally engaged. I have written in a previous article, and I still maintain here, that in Marshalore's installation "identification does not function by projecting our desires and frustrations onto a type of alter ego, but in a state of empathy which we share as 'the joy and pain which define an individual's personality' (Marshalore)..., until we are no more than memory's fluidity, represented here by the transition from one screen to another."[4]

The spectator's position is defined as being co-present. Contrary to the television viewing experience where the spectator is isolated and silent in front of authoritative speeches from experts, politicians or newscasters, experiencing Marshalore's video installation is like being present in a conversation, by confronting the other's subjectivity with one's own past recollections, according to the narrative time of memory. The viewer is situated at the centre of what Paul Ricoeur, in his important study of Time and Narrative,[5] calls the "triple present." The subject of fictional and historical narrative deals with the function of narrative and storytelling in the structuring of temporal experience. The viewer's triple present is

4. See "Video 84, installation," *Vanguard*, March 1985.

5. See Paul Ricoeur, *Temps et Récit*, 3 volumes, Editions du Seuil, Paris, 1982-1985.

defined as the site where present past, the present, and the present future are articulated together and, as narrative's inducer, it can orchestrate temporal order between past memories and future expectations.

Merleau-Ponty has also stated, "time is not a straight line but a network of willful intentions;"[6] in order to be understood, the continuum of time must be furrowed with synchronous spaces, intervals, where the "here and now" takes shape through its subjective perspective; so as that time "can be felt," subjectivity must intervene in the wholeness of being; it is through memory, expectation and anticipation that we experience time; it is through hope and fear that the dimensions of time affect us.

Album temporally engages the television apparatus in the criss-cross of life where events and people's lives, as well as a great deal of fictional characters, haunt and prowl as it were, the "texture of daily life," to borrow Ricoeur's expression. The notion of entanglement shows how "a story being told(...) can be in 'continuity' with the passive entanglement of subjects within stories lost on a hazy horizon."[7] The issue at stake is the jumbling of one's own life experience, with the stories we invent in the familiar world, a blurred area where imagination fosters confusion between "reality" and "fiction", where memory embellishes or disfigures our past lives, where time intervals are woven into the fabric of life. Marshalore works with these notions of tangling, by grounding the self in the act of remembrance and one's own personal life.

2. SCHIZOID ENTANGLEMENT

It has often been stated that the videotapes produced at the Coop Vidéo in Montreal are formal illustrations of the fine line between reality and fiction, ultimately disputing the domination of knowledge over others and the environment. Implicit are issues of reality boundaries addressing media in general and television in particular.

In *Fait divers: Elle remplace son mari par une TV*, co-written by Jean-Pierre St-Louis and Lynda Craig, entanglement is seen from a schizoid point of view. Whereas in Marshalore's work fiction is displaced by narrative memory, with St-Louis fiction is involved in a self-reflexive movement, creating superimposed timeframes and styles in the viewer's mind. First, there is the present time which carries the fiction, this is where the story is told; secondly, fictional space is layered with the real time

6. Maurice Merleau-Ponty, *Phénomenologie de la perception*, Gallimard, 1945, p.477. The issue of time in philosophy is quite comprehensive and we are following a more phenomenological tendency with Ricoeur, St Augustine, Heidegger, Husserl, Sartre and Merleau-Ponty.

7. Ricoeur, volume 1, p. 115.

of the documentary, here we discover the characters are re-enacting past events; and lastly, we find the specific time and gaze of the camera, using the cinéma-vérité style, which constitutes the time of the narrator and the rhetorical level of the author-cameraman, Jean-Pierre St-Louis. This final timeframe is an identification structure which calls upon the viewer's subjectivity.

St-Louis used a similar shooting style in a more convincing manner in a subsequent videotape titled *Carapace: autoportrait d'un chanteur inconnu* (1984), starring the singer/actor Bob Olivier. This camera style entails an acting style based on controlled improvisation, in which the actors improvise from a basic outline.

In the beginning of *Fait Divers*, we witness a family feud: a quarrel between father and son, then a clash between a husband and his wife, Yvette, concerning her favorite soap opera. Yvette is in love with one of the characters in the show, Dr. Beauchemin. She speaks to him and believes herself to be pregnant with his child. Obviously, the whole household is in a commotion! A first reversal is performed during this quarrel, when the husband interrupts his wife's soap opera by changing the channel. Yvette[8] "breaks down" and disrupts the narrative by stopping the shoot. What follows is a discussion with St-Louis himself on the options of continuing the shoot. Nevertheless, in spite of the husband's insistence that the filming be stopped, the camera becomes even more persistent and follows the husband into the room where Yvette is being comforted by a woman friend. Several more interruptions of this sort will occur throughout the video; through these interruptions, the viewer is able to detect that the characters are living out past events in front of the camera.

Fait divers puts into view the special nature of our relation to television narrative. In Yvette's case, it is pushed to an absurd limit with her schizoid participation in the televisual entanglement of reality and fiction. The directors position the narrative in its critical context by situating the action in a full-blown family argument and in relation to the soap opera — a television format if there ever was one. Family, domesticity and familiarity constitute the major subjects of traditional television programs and the soap opera in particular.

Traditional television relies on what John Ellis identifies as a normative structure. This notion can be summed up as "the same conceptual differentiation of the world into the domestic and the outside world."[9] On the one hand, we have the realm of

8. It is tempting to assume that the choice of the name 'Yvette' is not random, alluding as it seems to the group of women called the 'Yvettes,' who, angered by certain comments made by Ministre Lise Payette, had demonstrated at the Montreal Forum on behalf of the 'Non' campaign during the 1980 Québécois referendum.

9. John Ellis, *Visible Fiction*, London, Routledge and Kegan Paul, 1982, p. 166.

security, identity, power, routine, familiarity, happiness, respect and equality, on the other, the reign of risk, identity loss, adventure, chaos, singularity, unpredictability and inequality. The soap opera format establishes similar poles of security and moral consensus, by taking root in the daily world and focusing on scenes where one gossips, talks and queries about "personal and private conduct" within moral guidelines. In this way, the soap opera format corresponds to a horizon of expectations requiring a minimum of competence to be able to follow it: familiarity with the conventions of the genre, specific knowledge about the program and its characters and cultural knowledge of socially acceptable codes and conventions for the conduct of personal life.[10]

Faits divers pushes this structure to absurd limits and turns it in on itself. The effects of television's tangling of the domestic and the outside, together with the specific relationship women have with soap operas, are analyzed using Yvette's character and her schizoid excessiveness. At the end of the videotape, during what seems to be a interview in a self-help group about the lack of communication in the family, Yvette slyly admits to never really having seen Dr. Beauchemin; as viewers, we can understand her strategy to fill the emptiness in her family life.

If Yvette's confusion appears slightly exaggerated, consider a less spectacular, but equally obvious, example: a popular Québécois soap opera *Des dames de coeur*. This téléroman does not attempt to create suspense nor resolve a plot, rather, it lingers on trying to determine a type of moral consensus concerning private life. When actress Louise Remy, who plays the part of Lucie Belleau in this soap opera was invited to meet with a group of women fans, she was asked questions not as herself – but as her character. The events occurring in the soap opera (her husband committing adultery, divorce, etc.) became the moral dilemmas that "Lucie Belleau" shared "in-person" with these women: it's the same psychosis. When Yvette falls in love with Dr. Beauchemin and believes she is carrying his child, she puts "marriage faithfulness" to the test and bursts the bubble of her husband's ordered world.

3. STRATEGIC IRONY

Robert Morin and Lorraine Dufour's *Le voleur vit en enfer* and *La Réception* are videotapes with remarkable ironic intent. The first of these productions was shot on film and edited on video, with one character as the alleged storyteller of this personal document, who acts as the narrator through a telephone call to a helpline. Irony is borne by the real nature of the recorded events. At the beginning and

---

10. See Charlotte Brundson, "Crossroads: Notes on Soap Opera," *Regarding Television*, The American Film Institute, 1983, p. 80.

throughout the other videotape, *La Réception*, a video camera's characteristic clicking sound, as well as screen snow, punctuate each new scene. In addition, the whole tape is shot in subjective camera-angles. Robert, the cameraman, at one point hands the camera over to one of the people at the reception and then takes it back; then, at the end of the tape, the camera becomes an autonomous protagonist when the cameraman dies along with the other characters. Finally, after all the characters have died, the last person left is about to commit suicide, but just before, she turns off the camera to prevent our taking pleasure in "seeing this." In this second video, the ironical stance is directed at the media.

Irony appears under the guise of pretending and make-believe; irony as allegory, or the use of one thing to express another. In this way, irony assumes the status of artifice and being true to its nature, certainly acknowledges its lack of authenticity. The works of Morin, Dufour and St-Louis, all from Montreal's Coop Vidéo, are often spoken of in terms of the fine line they walk between fiction and documentary genre. This is at the centre of the irony issue, and reveals that beyond genres, these techniques are used to explore life and actuality: in the documentary, reality is pre-existent and takes on meaning through the illusory means of editing, in fiction, illusion attempts to find its verisimilitude. In either case, both operations rely on artifice of technology. The function of irony, then, is to immerse the viewer in a strange ambiguity and to instill a bad conscience in any one willing to live in a simple and univocal universe, within dogmatic systems.

Kierkegaard, whose doctoral thesis dealt with irony, sees it as a form of knowledge. According to him,

> "the purpose of asking a question may be twofold. One may ask a question for the purpose of obtaining an answer containing the desired content, (...) or one may ask a question not in the interest of obtaining an answer, but to suck out the apparent content with a question and leave only an emptiness remaining. The first method naturally presupposes a content, the second an emptiness; the first is speculative, the second the ironic."[11]

This means that irony, in contrast to speculative knowledge, does not produce positive meaning about knowledge but generates paradox by leaving an empty space. We will pursue the notion of paradox in the conclusion. For now, suffice it to say that irony is a game, as playful as art. Confronted by an expression of irony, we enter into a twofold realm of consciousness; at the centre, the disjunction between mind and its signs, perception and appearance, truth and opinion. Ironic

---

11. *The Concept of Irony*, Indiana U P, 1968, p.73.

consciousness is one of artificiality. Ironic art is veiled, led astray by or unconcerned with the expression of immediate emotion. Irony is necessarily consciousness of a second order, critical, amusing and harsh.

Morin and Dufour's *Le voleur* shows an irony that questions reality and the very basis of art production, the inability of fiction's simulation to divulge the truth about reality or even, possibly, the intentions of the director. Nevertheless, this ironical stance still relies on verisimilitude. In *Le voleur*, the author of the images is talking on the telephone with a crisis phone line operator. The telephone operator is introduced into the narrative as an anonymous and social referent and serves to guarantee and uphold notions of reality, imagination, madness and alienation. A play on reality is also put forth by interweaving the amateur filmmaker's lively imagery with sound effects from his environment (apartment, neighbours and street). Irony culminates in a scene in which the character, after glancing at a turkey basting in the oven, pretends to see the cooked bird's heart beating; the woman on the phone (the telephone operator) asks very casually if he has a doctor, thus breaking the suspension of disbelief. In this scene, *Le voleur* creates doubt in the fiction itself and in the sense of "reality" which is presented to us in such an absurd manner.

The ironical stance in *Le voleur vit en enfer* calls to mind romantic irony from the beginning of the nineteenth century, which coincided with the affirmation of subjectivity. The ironic situation "results from a shift between reality and imagination and from a fundamental mismatch between the two. This situation promotes detachment as the understanding of absurdity in the world as it presents itself to us immediately..."[12]

Irony based on affirmation of the self, be it of the narrator or the character, can be found in more recent videotapes by Robert Morin, such as *La Femme étrangère* (1988) and *La Réception*, as well as his latest film *Requiem pour un beau sans coeur* (1992).

La Réception particularly brings irony to an unprecedented level. Following the basic outline of Agatha Christie's *Ten Little Indians*, ten ex-convicts from a transition house are isolated on an island and , one by one, are murdered. Who is the murderer? The protagonists, not really characters but at best players, foster a type of duplicity in the image they project of themselves toward the others and the viewer, allowing for the play of subjectivity and permitting each person to reveal only what they desired to be known. This videotape also convincingly illustrates positioning of

12. René Bourgeois, *L'ironie romantique*, Presses Universitaires de Grenoble, 1974, p. 13.

subjectivity: that of the spectator, the narrator and finally, the performers in the videotape. The trademarks of subjectivity abound: subjective camera-angles, direct camera address, camera-as-protagonist with the cameraman's voice being heard.

At the end of the video, the sole survivor remains the camera — the Great Image-maker[13] — and in this way, the viewer echoes his own subjectivity and asks himself, who exactly was telling the story? The irony in this videotape goes beyond romantic irony, one of the last trepidations of subjectivity, asserting its freedom against the philosophical and scientific positivism of the industrial age. Unfortunately, we are not afforded this luxury today. At this point, *La Réception* proposes that subjectivity has been shaken in its very foundation by the media invasion of consciousness in our society, where truth and deceit are confused and completely evacuated from media constructions.

Within the context of television, or more generally, the "media and television environment," works such as *Le voleur vit en enfer* and *La Réception* jeopardize the viewer's conventional need for coherence. Since the public's expectations are shaped by familiarity with the codes and standards of acceptable likeness, such works bring about two effects: firstly, an effect of disappointment,[14] because the work does not allow for an immediate reading of itself and the viewer cannot fulfill his need for coherence. Contrary to television, which takes refuge in serene realism and commonly acceptable likeness, these works are difficult to read and they restore, through irony, the debate for societal values, because the viewer must make an effort to generate meaning and understanding. Expectation and disappointment can result in either a lack or an excess of meaning, as these works can have multiple interpretations. The second effect is one of defamiliarization;[15] in order to stimulate active receptivity of the work, a balanced and dynamic exchange must be accomplished between the "repertory of the familiar"[16] to quote Ricoeur, and the defamiliarization that the work produces (according to the conventions the viewer seeks to recognize).

With *Le voleur* and *La Réception*, a gaping hole in our understanding of reality is created, and left open. After a screening, viewers often ask themselves: "is it true?" The narrative does not find closure in the tranquillity of verisimilitude. These videotapes go further, to a paradoxical space where perception of the world is out of sync, where values are sacrificed in a maelstrom of absurdity and laughter, by

13. See André Gaudreault, *Du Littéraire au filmique*, Les Presses de l'Université Laval, Meridiens Klincksieck, 1988, p. 191.

14. Ricoeur, volume 3, pp. 246-8.

15. *Idem.*

16. Ricoeur, volume 3, p. 254.

which the viewer begins to simultaneously doubt the representation of "reality" and the "truth" of the work of art itself.

In a significant passage, Ricoeur asserts that "the failure to answer the moral dilemmas of an era might be the most efficient weapon that literature can have at its disposal to influence attitudes and change praxis. One can trace a direct path from Flaubert to Brecht."[17] We are some distance from the soap opera and its moral gossip about private behaviour. Art can have only an indirect effect on attitudes by creating a second degree of disparity — secondary in its relation to the essential difference between imagination and daily reality. Thus, for works of art to affect everyday life, expectations about art, literature and daily experience must be expressed in the crux of this essential difference. Irony, as put into practice by Morin and Dufour, carries this disparity.

Morin and Dufour have often said that their interest lies in showing people in a state of transformation and change. Their observation of people in a variety of situations, often generated by the shooting process itself, their observation of human suffering and behaviour, immerses us in what philosophy has termed contingency. This refers to an event which is liable to happen, but whose occurrence remains uncertain and without necessity: what we can call the irony of fate. Contingency also refers to human freedom, in other words, another's unpredictable actions which might interfere with one's plans. In the work of Morin and Dufour, contingency is at work in the human interactions being observed. We must keep in mind that the world of human actions, suffering, desires and disappointments are from culturally-determined values. Irony must raise doubts about these values, identify them, break into the accepted or current value systems, providing a state of paradoxical emptiness.

The etymological source of the word paradox comes from two Greek roots: *para* meaning "to protect from" and *doxa* signifying "common opinion." The doxa is what Plato rejected, since he claimed that reality should not be confused with appearance. But paradoxical irony precisely does not choose between appearance and essence. Conscious irony will not tolerate closed systems of thought; it leaves us the freedom of choice.

4. WHEN TELEVISION WILL BECOME UNTRUSTWORTHY

Among all of the videotapes discussed, only *La Réception* was broadcast but then again only on a Sunday morning. It was nevertheless seen in the context of television which answers simultaneously to the public's expectations and is an

17. *Idem.*

expression of the times. Each of these tapes nonetheless raises issues about the aesthetics of television reception. After nearly thirty years of television training, viewers have become quite competent in answering to the tried-and-true styles and canons developed by television. Few things change in television communication, except perhaps with the advent of video recording and editing technology to enable the transition from direct to postponed viewing. It is quite amusing to think that Umberto Eco, in the early sixties, proclaimed "live recording" as a central element in television's aesthetic principle.[18] The advent of videotape recording technology shifted the industry from live to pre-recorded material, while VCR technology gives the power of postponement to the viewer. As for us, the 'live' element has been superseded by the greater ideological construction of simultaneous immediacy, familiarity and normality.

Art has its requirements. One of these is that a work of art accept the purpose of being seen, heard and received; art's "imaginative variations" position the paradox of communicating freedom under the guise of 'the powerful restraint of a vision of the world.'[19] Video art is to television what poetry is to the Harlequin Romance and under these circumstances, the video artist must remember Rimbaud's motto: "The poet steals fire."

In order to grasp this freedom, one must immerse oneself in this vision of the world. Thus begins a demanding battle between the author and the viewer and between himself and the scope of the work. What will happen when the viewer, in turn, becomes suspicious — when television viewing no longer represents a reliable relationship with a trustworthy television?

Video art, as with any other art form, reveals its "calling structure" when its reception in the personal sphere is put to the test, inasmuch as the viewer is a competent reader and participates in the preconceived expectations of the public and the times. The viewer must receive the work according to his own expectations, which have been determined through a confrontation with previous works and with the entire value system applicable to a society and an era. These values are also the beacons of similitude and plausibility. In this way, in order to produce an aesthetic experience, not only must the viewer's expectations be satisfied, they must also be modified. Putting the principle of modifying expectations to the test, Ricoeur writes, "lies in the voyage made alongside the text, where all of these modifications are accomplished and 'engulfed' in memory as they are condensed,

18. See Umberto Eco, chapter 4, "Chance and Plot: Television and Aesthetics," in *The Open Work*, Cambridge, Harvard U P, 1989 [1962], p. 105.

19. Ricoeur, volume 3, p. 260.

and to subsequently open oneself to new expectations which in turn call for new modifications."[20] In return, this process can perhaps produce change in the world, wherein new perceptions can emerge. A series of modified expectations, in turn, make daily routine problematic because of the inadequacy induced by the work of art in the practical and ethical praxis of daily life.

Given the strong hold of television as a cultural form, we can even go as far as saying that in such an "environment of normalcy," what is at stake is the place of video art in relation to television, as well as the means by which television viewing can be made a lively and stirring experience.

Translation by Gisèle Trudel.

20. *Idem.*, p.245.

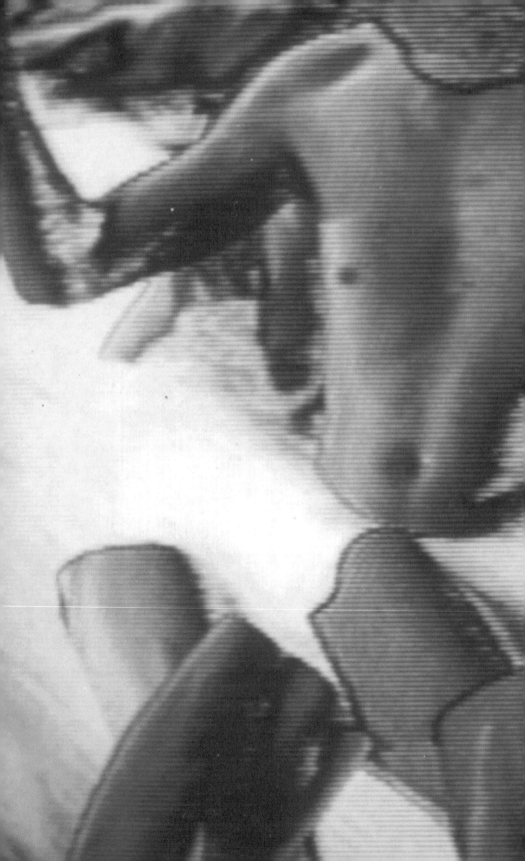

COLIN CAMPBELL:

OTHERWISE WORLDLY

by Bruce W. Ferguson

A retrospective is an institutional category which organizes a complex of artistic productions. Its ruling premise is to eliminate paradoxes, ellipses, ambiguities, contradictions, latencies, and deformations to produce a smooth narrative of individual progress and aesthetic development. A retrospective overview surveys the meanings of an artist's work, making the meanings even more meaningful by historicizing art which in turn serves the re-viewer's own authority as much as it does that of the artist's. A retrospective necessarily makes claims for cogency and comprehensiveness.

For almost two decades I have been influenced by the restless spirit of Colin Campbell's work. Making an all-encompassing historical claim for it would be to do it a comfortable textual justice which it neither needs, wants, nor deserves. It would make me an accomplice in a conservative desire that his work refuses to engage. I will instead 'co-author' this text by respecting a certain incoherence and a lack of control which parallels the split motivations between intuition and social comment in Campbell's own texts. Here, I favor a Campbellesque flirtation with loss of power and a confusion of desires. Such a method, however, is no more capricious than Campbell's, which is always both serious and comedic. When faced with his work I become aware that I can do no more than express why I am engaged by it and why I think this is so. I can do no more than express what a daunting task it is to turn works that have such impact on my psyche into an articulated response, especially since the work's extensive range of objective meanings also spurns easy capture by language.

It is my conviction that for the past two decades Colin Campbell's media work has had no definitive destination — no will to power of its own. Unlike other art which resides comfortably in the collections of museums or individuals or in public spaces, it intentionally travels nomadically on the periphery of respectability, eking out a minimal existence in the economic sphere and barely surviving in the territory of art. Campbell's work is poised so tenuously because it neither tries to create new forms like those of the avant-garde, nor submits easily to an already defined genre of representation. The work crosses the boundaries of art, theory, television, theater and all their attendant histories while remaining deliberately homeless and disobeying their laws. His videotapes, particularly, don't exhibit desires for mastery or for the authority of history. As a result, his tapes, performances, drawings and writings have an ephemeral, and almost exotic status, like a foreign ritual. The work tempts a fate of pure invisibility, surfacing momentarily, only to disappear again in a conscious act of withdrawal.

Campbell's media work thoughtfully avoids what is traditional to art or literature or cinema, to present themselves as full, complete and sufficient statements. It refuses to take a respectable place in the collective imagination. His rhetorical efforts in these works genuinely and effectively contest the normative categorization of works of art, preferring instead to settle for a modest existence beyond genre divisions. Favoring an aesthetic of mobility and subtle difference, Campbell creates temporary disturbances through irony and other quiet transgressions. If his work has any stability, it is to be found in the disquieting consistency of subversion. The work is driven by an almost anarchistic pulse, which traverses predetermined social and artistic values, and acts as a running commentary on the forms such acts of betrayal might take.

Central to feminist aesthetic practices when Campbell made *Sackville I'm Yours* (1972) was the establishment of the discontinuity between body and image — the problematic relation between subjectivity and representation. Campbell has continued to explore these issues in all of his videotapes and writings. In *Janus*, for example, he employed the essential ambiguity of television by investigating the relationship between a photograph of himself and his live video representation, in the same way that Lynda Benglis' videotape *Now* (1973) played her live movements back against a pre-recorded tape of the same movements. Concurrently, the idea of an endlessly deferred truth has functioned as a parallel motif throughout Campbell's career. In *True/False* (1972), made at about the same time, the artist stated a series of intimate revelations which he then both denied and asserted with exactly the same emphasis.

In *Sackville I'm Yours*, Campbell's mode of intimate face-to face expression disconcertingly offers no verification for his statements. Instead, their status is suspect. Both the confessional mode and the interview mode seem to be under interrogation. Campbell presents himself as a character called Art Star. There is nothing on the videotape's soundtrack to affirm or disaffirm anything this character says. Speech from Art Star, and perhaps always, opens onto the possibility of lying[1]. The audience is held in suspense throughout his speculations, the slowly paced revelations of his musings on his place within the Canadian scheme of things. We cannot even know if he is in Sackville as he claims because the barren studio background is not identifiable as a somewhere at all.

In *Sackville I'm Yours* , an audience listens to the stories of Campbell and Art Star, unreliable narrators both. Unlike the news announcer on television whose phallic tie symbolically assures us of the presence of the Law and masculine jurisdiction, Campbell or Art Star seem as naked as truth itself. Yet, if the truth be known, a viewer sees only the face and bare neck and shoulders of what may be a half-naked man. Truth, if capitalized, is usually represented visually by a fully nude woman. By remaining a man, however tieless, Art Star denies the guarantee that truth could be objectified as naked and feminine, the female objectified on the horizon of a masculinist perspective. By untying the tie, he, in effect, ties the viewer to a knotty problem; that the knowledge of what masculine membership may be has been left dangling, like the tie off-screen. Renouncing the fashion accessory for the symbolic assurance of patriarchal authority, Campbell further detours the iconic code from its comfortable expectation — the fetishized female. At best, a viewer is introduced to something like a half-truth, or perhaps, to an obscure secret truth, located in the absent lower half of the Art Star which is hidden so as to possibly stimulate another drive — to get to the bottom of things. After all, the hidden is more erotic than the visible — the fragment more tantalizing than the entirety. Another way of saying this is that all discourses might be sexed, but only those which leave room for the imagination are sexy. The fragment or the missing part eroticizes Art Star's speech, turning it from confession to seduction — from truth to persuasion.

By detouring the code of woman as truth into something like man as half-truth, *Sackville I'm Yours* has the first explicit man-in-the-woman, or is it woman-in-the-man, motif in Campbell's tapes, however diverted its visual image is. Speech, truth and identity are all made androgynous by this digression — all are presented as capable of flirting with the rhythm of uncertainty. Art Star is the founding appearance of a theme of profound uncertainty which is dragged more literally into later tapes, highlighted by ambisexuality that significantly marks other Campbell characters.

In *Sackville I'm Yours*, the visual and the oral problematics of defining a 'self' are brought together under technological scrutiny. The promising fictive interview of Art Star weaves back and forth between identifiable historical beings and probable

1. A more general formulation of the "truth-function" of "sign-language" is to be found in Umberto Eco, *A Theory of Semiotics*, Indiana University Press, Bloomington , 1979. He writes... "Thus semiotics is in principle the discipline of studying everything which can be used in order to lie. If something cannot be used to tell a lie, conversely it cannot be used to tell the truth: it cannot be used 'to tell' at all. I think that the definition of a 'theory of the lie' should be taken as a pretty comprehensive program for a general semiotics." p. 7.

lies. It presents always possible but never confirmed stories which blur and weaken its value as either historical fact or narrative satisfaction. Art Star tells a story which might also be a story in the sense of hyperbole — a tall tale. Yet Campbell's persona Art Star's own identity construction is reasonable, being both credible and detailed enough for a viewer to identify with. If it is ultimately undecidable on a register of truth, it shares that condition with any work of fiction and with the media process that might produce a famous person of the kind Campbell is producing in the figure of Art Star.

This twenty-minute videotape includes a set of visual and audio disturbances which force a reconsideration of the familiar format where a person tells a personal anecdote. The answers to a fictive interview which Art Star initiates are subtly interfered with, setting up a field of contradictions which mobilize a rethinking of simple speech acts, the nature of personal identity and video technology's relation to both. A viewer's traditional experience of watching and listening is challenged. The reception of information which is fundamental to personal communication and culture alike, is put under interrogation, becoming almost its opposite — a deception of information. A viewer is made uncomfortable and ironically feels deceived, since Campbell speaks throughout the tape as though he were engaged in intimate self-revelation. The uneasiness which pervades the tape ranges from shifting gender signs within the image of the speaker to obvious deviations in the narrative, all presided over by the conspiratorial role of the video technology. When Campbell announces himself to the viewer as Art Star in *Sackville I'm Yours*, he announces a *dramatis persona*, the first of many unlikely thespian types, characters in disguise, who will appear subsequently in his videos and texts. They include heroines such as: the Woman from Malibu, the suburban American *par excellence*, Robin the xerox girl cum punk star of *Modern Love*, Anna, the Belgian art critic of *Dangling By Their Mouths* and so on. Importantly, despite the fact that he might look like and sound like Colin Campbell, a very real person, in *Sackville I'm Yours*, he is not announcing himself as Colin Campbell, the person who teaches in the art department of Mount Allison University in 1972, graduate of the University of Manitoba and homeboy from rural Reston, Manitoba.

It might be possible to say that Campbell is born as an infinitely reproducible art in *Sackville I'm Yours*. The question might be what kind of art he is claiming to represent? Does he mean to personify Art with a capital A, no matter how undercapitalized the video production is? Or is this art in its lower case form as a skill or technique or kind of knowledge in the way the art of rhetoric might be understood? A capital 'A' would give his Art the significance of a proper noun with an immediate and distinguished heritage. A small 'a' would make the noun common and more vernacular, more ordinary, and more subject to casual and even philistinic uses.

By simply rearranging the letter of Art Star, the words *Art's art* can be established, an anagram which here appears incognito. In its possessive form, *Art's art*, both the proper and the common nouns are enclosed. There is a reference to Art about art, the reigning subject of formalist aesthetics, but it is an allusion that cannot be sustained because the two words are not equivalent. The doubling of the word *art* in the name Art Star is an obviously uneven duplication. Doubling, as a device of verbal or written rhetoric, usually is deployed to signal the distance of the narrator from him- or herself. It suggests the gap in the telling of a story between any narrator, and his or her narrated self. Narrators use the double to recognize themselves as both one and the other when speaking even to themselves. For even in first-person narratives, the author or teller of the story is also the protagonist of the story, a fictive creation in language outside the self. He or she is talking, at the very least, to him or her 'self'. This doubling is unavoidable.

But doubling as a ghostly echo has an even more equivocal and troubled use. Ever since Mary Shelley used it as a dramatic literary device, it can also be associated with the creation of monsters. The canonical version is Frankenstein's humanoid, the first representation of a techno-extension of the self which revealed the self divided in desire. Doubling, then, is both an extension of oneself into another space, like the space of a story and a reversal that turns back to remind the storyteller of the other, and the space within herself. Doubling escapes the 'self' by entering the space of the story and, yet, it is an inevitable reminder of the inescapability of the 'self' that is being reproduced.

Campbell's persona, Art Star, participates in this duplication of Campbell as an other. But he is also more complex and perhaps more monstrous than that as well. Unlike the experience of reading a work of literature where a reader will only imagine the author-protagonist, the viewer of *Sackville I'm Yours* is caught up in the presence of the images and sounds of Campbell himself. The double found in literature is here not fully achieved because the fictional Art Star is drawn back to the real historical subject called Campbell, who is equally displayed. They occupy each other's televisual space as a kind of culture superimposition — the same and different simultaneously. There is a knot in this presentation, in the name Art Star, akin to the transvestite image in other Campbell tapes where the man-as-woman is also still clearly a man acting as a woman, and vice versa. Art in *Sackville I'm Yours* is a kind of surplus of other. Art, or art, is a redoubling but it is also an unfinished doubling which turns on itself, *ur*-like, perhaps doubled over with laughter at the impossibility of sustaining either a self or a credible fiction. The name Art Star is both a circle and a conundrum. There is an irreconcilable asymmetry here which seems to welcome a distressed duality.

If the idea of a 'self' is necessarily a fiction as contemporary psychoanalytic texts forcefully suggest, Campbell in acknowledging Art Star as a role he plays at the same time he is himself, is freely admitting to the construction of identity as a continual dissolution and revitalization. But, as I have said, the disguise of Art Star is only partial and always threatening to conflate with the autobiography of Campbell himself. And Campbell performs this semi-masking under the name of Art which has its own identity problems, being capable of absorption into many uses. With seemingly little reservation Campbell appropriates the name Art to himself and then immediately doubles it by not making clear whether he means art to be a proper or common noun. He forces art to admit that its name is involved in something like a class struggle. Art could be a name of a person who desired the credibility of the grand discourse of art history or it could be that same discourse asserted as though art were just another sign system, just another rhetorical device with no privileged status. Clearly, then, by assigning a name that seems so uncertain of itself that it both repeats itself and questions itself simultaneously, Campbell means not to align himself with art as canon or culture.

Campbell opens onto the possible bastardization of art by blurring art's claims to a status of certainty and by underlining the strong desires for propriety and impropriety which are undertaken in the name of art. He hesitates before the name of art, suspending the decision to assign it a specific destination. He places the naming of art somewhere between Duchamp's freedom and the restrictions of institutional power; somewhere between nomination and name calling; somewhere between Rose Sélavy and Boy George. If art is not given its proper name, Campbell seems to suggest, then it might well escape the patriarchal affiliation that is often imposed on it. It might well elude the powerful masculine entitlement which authorizes its name. Art Star is an unknown artist asking, "Who is entitled to be called Art Star?" The effect unsettles the accepted assumptions that underlie the status given to art.[2]

Sackville I'm Yours is a light theatrical staging of an identity whose relation to reality is rendered complex. The theatricalization guarantees that Art Star's identity is never more than a pretense to identity. Calling himself Art Star has the effect of stripping the 'self' of Campbell even as it calls attention to the process of

2. See especially the chapter "Tales of Love and Desire" in Stuart Schneiderman, *An Angel Passes: How the Sexes Became Undivided*, New York University Press, New York 1988.

constructing the 'self' or selves. Even the fictive reality of self-portraiture, or portraiture in general, to which it might be superficially compared and which has, at least, the historical credibility of art, is skewed by this fictional apparatus. At best *Sackville I'm Yours* is a portrait of Colin Campbell as Art Star, at one remove from the 'original'. A self-portrait or a portrait would have to attempt, whatever its degree of mimeticism, to represent Campbell first rather than Art Star. Campbell's Art Star, then, is a darker techno-version of Oscar Wilde's portrait of Dorian Gray, but Art Star is a reversed version of the famous portrait as Art Star remains today youthfully intact while both viewers and Campbell himself continue to be propelled through time and history. Art Star has a kind of technological immortality, a life recorded to be replayed always in the present. He is as enigmatic today and as life-like as when he first was recorded on videotape.

Art Star generates an impression of multiplicity and strange plurality of character. He is like the description provided by D. and interpreted by F. in Friedrich Dürrenmatt's *The Assignment.* ..."there was no self, or rather, only a countless chain of selves emerging from the future, flashing into the present, and sinking back into the past, so that what one commonly called one's self was merely a collective term for all the selves gathered up in the past, a great heap of selves perpetually growing under the constant rain of selves, an accumulation of shreds of experience and memory, comparable to a mound of leaves that grows higher and higher under a steady drift of other falling leaves, while the ones at the bottom have long tuned to humus, a process which seemed to imply a fiction of selfhood in which every person made up his own self, imagining himself playing a role for better or worse, which would make the possession of character mainly a matter of putting on a good act, and the more unconscious and unintentional the performance, the more genuine its effect, all of which would go a long way toward explaining why it was so hard to make a portrait of an actor..."[3]

---

3. Friedrich Dürrenmatt, *The Assignment or On the Observing of the Observer of the Observers*, Vintage International, Random House, (trans. Joel Agee), New York, 1989, p. 24, 25. The preface to the book begins with a quote from Soren Kierkegaard..."What will come? What will the future bring? I do not know. I have no presentiment. When a spider plunges from a fixed point to its consequences, it always sees before it an empty space where it can never set foot, no matter how much it wriggles. It is that way with me: before me always is an empty space; what drives me forward is a consequence that lies behind me. This life is perverse and frightful, it is unbearable." In *Dangling by their Mouths*, a Campbell videotape of 1980, it is a long quote by William Faulkner from *As I Lay Dying*, the voice of an already-dead woman, quoted by Kerri Kwinter playing a woman who is about to die, which is performed as an exemplary piece of anti-literature, stylistically close to Dürrenmatt in its excessively anti-grammatical form and controlled by the same metaphor..."but that we had to use one another by words, like spiders dangling by their mouths from a beam, swinging and twisting and never touching and only through the blows of a switch could my blood and their blood flow as one stream..." Deirdre Summerbell has pointed out to me that earlier, the great ironist Jonathan Swift wrote in *Thoughts on Various Subjects*,..."It's a miserable thing to live in suspense. It's the life of a spider." The self, in each of these cases — Campbell, Faulkner, Dürrenmatt, Kierkegaard and Swift — is nothing more than the web of identity spreading out behind the subject. The spider, ostensibly the subject of the narrative web, can only be caught on the fly.

Art Star neither comes together as a narrative figure nor does he come apart. Rather, he does both. As a figure of identity, he hovers in an electronic landscape, maintaining impartiality towards both truth and falsehood, completion and incompletion. On re-viewing today, he is just as laconic and self-amused as he was in 1972, waiting patiently for us to make up our minds. And he is just as equally resistant to our conclusions today as he was then. Although Campbell through his creation of Art Star, seems to have accepted his own dissolution, or undoing, he, through Art Star, has electronically defied aging, which has the curious, elliptical effect of looping back on himself, or some version of that self to us, over and over again almost two decades later.

Campbell's work is located in the aesthetics of poverty4 which is called video art, an aesthetic project which can be characterized as the poor cousin of television and art. But, like television, the video work has more than a hint of anti-academicism and anti-linguistism to it. As texts, Campbell's work necessarily participates in the knowledge of language and of speech acts. But his work, like television itself, operates differently from, say, postmodern literature which inevitably performs its own deconstruction from within literary devices, while at the same time claiming a loss of faith and a desire to elaborate the unreliability of language. Campbell's controlling technique is perhaps closer to John Gardner's notion of "jazzing around" than it is to any self-conscious ideas of deconstruction. Yet Campbell's work often achieves the power of poetry and it is obviously informed by recent theories of language. He is perhaps too skeptical to believe in either the pure intellectual work of deconstruction or the accidental aesthetics of television. His work is always closer to scatological pataphysics than to the ethereal metaphysics of academic considerations or even television's endlessly reproduced formats. As a result, his marginal representations and humor in video risk being judged as too capricious. This is a risk that Campbell is willing to run in order to remain vigilant.

His consistent strategy, one might even call it anti-sacristy, throughout the work is to tell stories in an amateurish, bawdy manner, with no real respect for the conventions of literature or television. Such representations immediately disembody him as an historical subject before the myth of authorial control can

---

4. In an earlier essay I have elaborated a "Politics of Poverty" as…"video's relation to television is simple. It is television. It is a member of the same family. But it is remittance television, sent away as a black sheep to the exotic countries of Art, Education, or Local Concerns, where it won't be an embarrassment. It does have two major differences from its sibling television: video is determined in form by the technology available and the low funding for production, and its distribution system is determined by noncommercial and nonconventional social technics. In other words, it is not allowed on the airwaves. This is what I would call the Politics of Poverty. Not being allowed to wear the same clothes, it is not invited to dinner; not speaking the same language, it is not allowed to speak, or, at least, to be heard." In "Making Airwaves", *Prime Time Video*, Mendel Art Gallery, Saskatoon, Saskatchewan, 1984, p. 16.

even be put into place, before viewers can be seduced by the cultural power that attends the myth of artistry. He treats his content with a similar irreverence. No subject is exempt from his sardonic gaze. For instance, despite the fact that contemporary feminisms have had a profound effect on Campbell, they too are treated agnostically, or even irreverently, by characters in *No Voice Over* and *Fiddle Faddle*. In *Dangling By Their Mouths*, as well, Anna, a Belgian critic and model of Eurocool, played by Campbell, says in reference to a former lover of one of her friends,..."She would have been better off going to bed with a book by Fuck — Oh", thus implicating the books sexually as well as playing with Foucault's name phonetically rather than engaging a theory of sex and power. And by playing and replaying with a surfeit of identities which question the possibility of full control and the seriousness of art's revelatory capacities, Campbell swiftly and consciously places an audience somewhere in a circle of deceit which makes no promises of knowledge. Sacrilege is no small part of these projects.

Cross-sexuality, which pervades Campbell's characters, offers an instable, incomplete, already alienated image whose seriousness is partly mock. It allows a motile criticality to emerge, unconstrained by habitual probabilities. To cross genders is to cross genres.[5] Like video itself, which is a kind of trans- or cross television, all of Campbell's representational efforts to disguise identity may be necessary for any understanding of the function of identity. The admission of the theatricality of self may be, as in therapy, the first step toward a recognition of the necessity of the self's responsibility toward shifting roles. Reversing the expected produces the unexpected which is in turn somehow re-reversed in a medium whose alienating mediation ironically produces a clear picture. As Edward Said has said in writing about Glenn Gould, Canada's first techno-ascetic..."The paradox is that something as impersonal as a text, or a record, can nevertheless deliver an imprint or a trace of something as lively, immediate, and transitory as a 'voice'".[6] And despite, or perhaps because of Campbell's movements of masquerade, his voice comes through.

Campbell's method of producing the undecidable document, *Sackville I'm Yours*, provides a strong thesis on the nature of the discourse produced when

---

5. For an elaboration of cross-vision as an index of the postmodern, particularly in Canada, see my "Barbara Steinman: The Art of Memory: The Memory of Art", *Vanguard*, Volume 18, Number 3, Summer, 1989, Vancouver, p. 10-15. For instance..."Stereoscopy, of course, is a deliberate disabling of the privileged monocular vision which supports most Western epistemological and theoretical projects. The single point of view is primarily metamorphosed through the art of painting — its most visible form — and individualism is its political counterpart. A bi-vision problematizes the singularity at both figurative and literal levels."

6. Edward Said, "The World, the Text and the Critic," in *The World, the Text and the Critic*, Harvard University Press, Cambridge, Mass., 1983, p. 33.

photographic means are combined with text. Photographically produced representations can and must be grounded by textuality or by contextuality. A verbal or written text serves to position any image in an attempt to secure its meanings. The text and the image are then further positioned in a system of distribution which contextualizes them even more securely, in books or newspapers for example. The distribution systems reproduce identifiable conventions called genres. Each genre, image and text, is intertextualized by others, joined in an anxious *ménage à trois* which is always struggling to be stable. Although a text can never be more than an interpretation of the already technologically interpreted camera activity which produced the image, a text and an image can, and perhaps must, be married in what Roland Barthes calls an "anchor-relay" system, providing a momentarily secured meaning within any system of meanings' exchanges. In a positivist society, such conjunctions of text to image have even been given the power of legalistic force, for instance, despite the dormant unease which is instilled at the core of both images and language.

But the uneasiness produced by video technology, Campbell seems to be telling the viewer, is even more intensely felt because of the perceived instability in its relations between images, sound, context and genre. The existence in the present tense does not seem to allow even the illusion of a secure meaning, no matter how provisional. Television's texts seem more impatient and harassed, less able to intertwine with others; more mercurial and sinister than traditional texts. Television seems to be the postmodern environment *par excellence* because, as an industrial collage machine, it produces something more transient and inaccurate, almost like memory. It is more vulnerable to the vagaries of subjective inclinations than a photograph, say, which can be re-seen and restudied like the inert text of printed language or even a film which can be approached frame by frame and attached to the authority of language. Although it is a projection of texts out to a viewer, in Campbell's eyes television appears more like a screen for projections, a place for unconscious desires to twist and turn. Television might be an updated version of Bentham's panopticon and one could paraphrase Foucault by saying that television "...must not be understood as a dream building: it is the diagram of a mechanism of power reduced to its ideal form; its functioning, abstracted from any obstacle, resistance or friction must be represented as pure architectural and optical system: it is in fact a figure of political technology that may and must be detached from any specific use."7 Television is implicitly undecidable.

7. Michel Foucault, *Discipline and Punish: the Birth of the Prison*, Vintage Books, Random House, New York, 1979, p. 205

Under television's watchful eye, fiction and fact can be easily blurred. When Desi Arnaz and Lucille Ball, an authentic couple, play Ricky and Lucy Ricardo, a fictional couple, representation collapses or conflates into a set of systems of overlapping realities which are impossible to reconstruct accurately with an older epistemology of truth. The whole history of Ronald Reagan's media career from Borax promoter to President is nothing more than a history of television's power to disassociate images from context — to erase history over and over. It is no coincidence that television's major contribution to the extension of genres is the docudrama: half fiction, half fact and all rhetoric. Television appears to come from nowhere. Sackville in the case of one tape by Campbell, is a place which is as convenient a center as anywhere. It would seem that its stories can be told or made up by anyone; by Art Star, for instance, a person who may or may not be a Canadian artist with any of the attributes he claims for himself. There might be an interviewer off-screen without a microphone whose questions draw out Art Star's answers or he/she might only be a necessary narrative fiction. There is simply no way for a viewer to know. There is no anchor-relay system because there is no purchase for an anchor, or perhaps an anchor-man, in the electronic wonderland. Dan Rather may be showing footage of the same war he is describing or the footage may be from another war entirely. There is only, like the identity which Campbell has constructed in Art Star and other memorable characters, a system of relays, a system of slippages and floating signifiers — a fragile and mobile fabrication of reality. And whereas some modernists rail against this disconnection from a center and from a text, Campbell clearly relishes it with a cultivated appetite for the skewered self, the abandoned identity.

Sackville I'm Yours can, for instance, be read against the grain of the predominant discourse in television or video. While television is still blamed as the cause of all societal ills, video, at the time of making *Sackville I'm Yours*, was being explained in modernist terms of reflexivity, granting it the status of art. If television was seen as the most recent residence of the devil, Rosalind Krauss' early article entitled "Video: the Aesthetics of Narcissism" set some equally pessimistic terms for an understanding of video as well. Krauss read early video as "narcissistic". It was a medium, she said, which relied on an image feedback in collapsed time which provided a kind of self-love unrelated and in fact alienated from both a viewer's position and the artist's own ability to perceive change. Like the myth of Narcissus itself and the mirror-image trope of Lacan and his followers, a misrecognition of self was said to involve the death of something. In Greek mythology Narcissus drowns in his own image. In Lacanian theory, in an agonizing moment of introduction to the symbolic world, the child is unsettled in the mirror by the recognition of him-or herself as something 'other'. Krauss' argument with much early video was that "the nature of video performance is specified as an activity of bracketing out the text and substituting for it the mirror reflection. The result of the substitution is the presentation of a self understood to have no past and, as well, no connection with any objects that are external to it."[8] To Krauss, a body severed from text is an example of pure narcissistic reflection in a "double repression". There is no wall for modernist reflexivity to distinguish itself from as there is with a painting, for instance, and no contextualizing text to recount a history from. There is no way for criticality to take place.

But Krauss' scenario of video's loss of criticality depends heavily on a strict adherence to the metaphor of the mirror-stage and an equal adherence to the procedures of much avant-garde art in the past. Her text is deeply immersed in only American examples of video, which may themselves be, as Christopher Lasch has suggested, also deeply immersed in a "culture of narcissism". But the metaphor of the mirror accounts only for an uninterrupted image reflected back directly to an unknowing subject. The analogy of the mirror and its consequences are immediately diverted if the metaphor includes concave, convex, circular, rear-view or multiple mirrors, each of which skews an image differently. Or it is again skewed if the viewer is already aware of self-alienation. Campbell's video mirror of identity, if it can be called that, participates in a more complex metaphor and assumes a more complex viewer. For Campbell, the state of otherness generated by video feedback is to be celebrated as one of the many ironic conditions of being.

The question as to whether self-representation is even possible is at the heart of Campbell's investigations. To be a famous artist in Sackville is like being a famous dentist, a contradiciton in terms, but perhaps not in Canada. Although other tapes of Campbell's like *Real Split* (1972) or *This is the Way I Really Am* (1973) might be more easily subsumed by Krauss' terms, Campbell, beginning with *Sackville I'm Yours*, inserts the devious device of a pseudonym, presenting himself as a false identity to begin with. The persona Art Star is an admission of self-estrangement which deliberately avoids the illusion of complete identity, a complete identity which can only be realized in the vision of an authority constructing him as 'other'. If we can only be recognized as the 'other' by a dominant discourse, perhaps it is inevitable that a Canadian artist would choose the evacuation of the self rather than narcissism in the first place. Campbell holds on to an imaginary relationship to identity just as he does to an imaginary role in the art world. Such a marginal position is the only one available to video artists, even today, and perhaps to

8. Rosalind Krauss, "Video: The Aesthetics of Narcissm", reprinted in *New Artist's Video: A Critical Anthology*, ed. Gregory Battock, New York, E.P. Dutton, 1978, p. 43-64.

Canadian artists in general. Art Star's confessions reveal a considered indifference to a master discourse which is powerfully indifferent to him. For Campbell, like other Canadian artists at the time, the pseudonym expresses both the desire to be other than oneself and the irony of a condition in which one can't help but be oneself, however deviously, doubly and incompletely constructed.

The role of Art Star reinvents Campbell. Despite all these efforts at splitting and undependable self-projections, Campbell has become an art star in Canada, a real-life twin to his persona's premature claims. He is a full-fledged professor at a university, a recipient of many grants and awards, a participant in major exhibitions, with his work collected by international museums and now, the subject of a retrospective. By taking another's voice, Campbell seems to have clarified how deeply anyone is enmeshed in his or her own history — the most profound dilemma of subjectivity and theater both. Artifice only intensifies the subject. The mask is not as enigmatic as what it hides. In Campbell's use of roles it is not an escape then that we attend, but the birth of a desire, a desire not to believe in a single or complete identity. It is not self-loathing which motivated his appeal for misrecognition, however deliberate its misrepresentations are. Rather it is a kind of marginal realism which can only be arrived at by a complex restructuring of an imaginary self, in much the same way that male anxiety lies just below its projections of stability.

But it is not just television or modernist conceptions of video that Campbell's work refuses to resemble. *Sackville I'm Yours* could easily be retitled, *Colville, I'm Not Yours*. By that I mean that the tape can be read against the school of 'Magic Realism' which is identified with Alex Colville and Christopher Pratt, both graduates of Mount Allison University in Sackville and both 'famous' artists within a nationalized context. At the time the videotape was made, as they are today, both were artists who deliberately sought identity in images of the Atlantic region. 'Magic Realism' is a localized form of modernism which endeavors to describe the local from the within formal structures of classicism as though the rural image will reveal a universal circumstance. Both Colville and Pratt rejected abstraction for hyper-real images of the local masked as the universal. Both use a Protestant ethic of labor-intensive brush strokes as an elaborate structure to secure an image which is based in the circumstances of the rural landscape of Atlantic Canada. Their aesthetic speaks to a dream of a world that will recognize them, not for their difference, but for their universal significance.

This is not Campbell's dream for art. Campbell's 'local' is Sackville. But it is transformed via video mediation to the international or at least transnational, or more to the point, unlocatable. Campbell points not to the authoritative history of Western painting as Pratt's and Colville's works do. He points instead, to the gossip of a network of dealers, artists and art journal editors. He is on a first name basis with a career, not a crusade for meaning from an historical perspective. While Colville and Pratt envelop their work in false modesty, Campbell disguises his modesty in false ambition and overriding pretensions.

And *Sackville I'm Yours* can be read against the tradition of modernist abstraction in Canada as well; against the work of Lawren Harris Jr., son of the theosophical Lawren Harris who ushered abstraction into the existing provincialism within Canadian painting. Lawren Harris Jr. was head of the fine arts department at Mount Allison University when Campbell taught there and the videotapes made in the basement of the Physical Education department can be seen to dislocate the authority of painting from this marginal position within the campus and its department of Art. More importantly, *Sackville I'm Yours* shows clearly how Campbell has been able to continue to work from outside the dualistic model of modernist painting's forms; from outside the Canadian debate on national identity; from within the debates on gendered subjectivity and politics; from within the distresses of a masculinist culture; from outside the ideological and technological determination of dominant cultures. As Campbell has said of all his female roles, "Check out her MANnerisms", a statement which alerts us to the complexity and ambiguity of any image or text which is presented as stable and complete.

If *doppelgängers,* with their projected passions and fantasies, can short-circuit the straight line and straight mind of representational order, then we should turn to the words of Campbell's creation "Both" to confuse and contest this text as well.

> Both woke up.
> The television was on.
> Both lit a cigarette and looked at the screen.
> Both was on the screen looking back at Both.
> Waiting.
> Both said, "So create your own fiction.
> You can be anything you want."
> Both answered. "There is no fiction."
> Both reached for the knob on the television set and depressed it.
> Both disappeared.9

9. Colin Campbell, "Both", *Toronto: A Play of History (Jeu d'histoire),* The Power Plant, Toronto, 1987, p. 58-62.

THE TRANSFORMATIVE POWER OF MEMORY:

THEMES AND METHODS IN THE WORK OF VERA FRENKEL

by Lydia Haustein

... And suddenly I found myself in a completely different world ...

— Stranger passing through ... *from the Transit Bar*

INTRODUCTION

Since the turn of the century, the discourse in art and art theory on reality and fiction, simulation and simulacrum has been going around in circles. The faster the merry-go-round — now a post-modern carousel — turns, the more confused we are by the time we get back to the source of the linguistic confusion. Vera Frenkel's works, commentaries that visualize the limits and power of simulation, are effective and forceful intrusions into the long-standing and predominantly abstract discussion on the problematic relationship of reality to art. Her early works already focused on the question of how we acquire the knowledge that shapes our existence and how the magical power of stories unfolds in history. She understands that presenting a select section of reality in a museum environment changes the way it is perceived, or, expressed in terms favoured by current philosophy, emphasizes or deciphers the simulation.

In a world where the media inform and shape perception, the boundaries between image and reproduction, being and semblance, unique type and stereotype are no longer distinct. Each suggests the existence of the other to such a degree that the boundaries between them disappear. It is not surprising, then, that everywhere you look in the art world there are staged fields of tension or violations of the "order of things". Vera Frenkel turns in particular to syntheses of broken relationships in life, syntheses that allude to the contradiction between the outer and inner worlds of the viewer via material taken from reality, shown both as it is and simultaneously transposed into art.

The classification of such material as artwork creates a space, a locale, while in the same instant conjuring up other spaces and images. As in music, where the true meaning of each sound unfolds only when heard in the context of the full ensemble, the fluctuation of Frenkel's thought is discovered only through the experience of the whole installation, although singular objects may remain particular carriers of memory. This was of course Proust's approach, practised comprehensively — the recovery of the lost reality of his memories being tied to and usually triggered by a chance event or seemingly insignificant object.

Frenkel's projects concentrate, through intense observation, on this opening-out of consciousness, with the experimental aspects of the work constituting at the same time a recognizable ideal. Her ability is to capture from the abundance of individual memory the autonomy of historical moments and to reveal through them the possibility of the Other. Thus, in her installations she shatters our normal historical perspective and stages a simultaneity of actions rather than logical sequences or histories. Clearly, these works are as much about *becoming* aware as they are about *being* aware or remembering. They concentrate on creating new consciousness and, in the very same moment, on Mnemosyne, the mother of memory and therefore of the arts.

The threads of this approach have for many years been taken up in her work and woven into new patterns that, although they may not prevent it, at least slow down the process of what Carl Einstein terms the "fabrication of fiction". What emerges is a highly complex oeuvre that not only refers to historical phenomena but also generates its own history. The viewer encounters the boundary of an uncertain present, and also experiences it as a highly explosive continuation of past events. Many of Frenkel's works can only be interpreted by specifying the personal, as well as the manifold historical, layers they contain. Through incorporating details drawn from or referring to a particular historical context, the artist can trace relationships, triggering numerous associations in the mind of the viewer. These details are by no means limited to those of a general cultural nature, but are drawn as well from the history of Frenkel's own art. She develops her own history within her oeuvre — for example, by taking up pieces from earlier work and resituating them in more recent projects. Thus, in an early work, *Signs of a Plot: A Text, True Story & Work of Art* (1978), an installation in the form of a bilateral videopuppet theatre, we encounter a method that recurs in later works, that of accompanying a spoken soundtrack with a contradictory on-screen text.

Repeatedly, we find the ruptures of time and space prompting us to question the relationship between art and reality. To a certain extent, each new work cannot be isolated from earlier work but must be seen as a continuation of an ever more subtle investigation.

... FROM THE TRANSIT BAR

This method is seen in its clearest and most concentrated form in *... from the Transit Bar*, a project first realized for *documenta IX*. The project itself created a new history. Given that the work exists only temporarily, as the word transit suggests, as a process in the final instance it only continues to exist in and through the viewer. In *The Last Screening Room: A Valentine* (1984), the individual images communicating the message of the piece were separated from the viewer by the symbolic mirror of the screen. Viewer and mirror are brought together in *... from the Transit Bar*. Here Frenkel disrupts the ritual of silent contemplation prevalent in a museum setting by playing out different kinds of spatial, temporal and causal relationships. In a situation that provides striking contrast to that ritual, the viewer suddenly finds himself or herself on the other side of the mirror in the middle of people and things, in a bar complete with barkeeper, visitors, chairs, tables, suitcases, an electric piano, video monitors. The things and people seem familiar. But this is deceptive; in reality we have never seen them before.

When we enter a Frenkel installation, the components initially appear arranged at random. Yet a careful observation of the work process reveals how deliberate their selection is. It soon becomes apparent that the more incidental and less staged their effect, the more carefully selected they have been. Video excerpts of reality and of an imaginary inner life (interiority) are offered to the viewer as simultaneous experiences. In *... from the Transit Bar*, layers of syntheses of different materials, experiences, ages and languages are painstakingly revealed on different video monitors. Allusions to proximity and distance, to things familiar and things foreign point to the permanent split in our existence, to an invisible "inner" human life and a visible "outer" human life.

An "everyday space" — the Transit Bar — and an "exclusive art space" — the museum — are combined, or if the viewer wishes, become one. The result is a bar as an artwork in a museum, all dependent on the disposition of the viewer. Everything strikes the eye. Everything is cast into question. Everyone watches everyone else. You play out your role in tacit agreement, aware that when basic modes of being are banned from daily life experience, only anonymous locations will allow for intimacy. A number of other relationships emerge. On the one hand, the bar retains its everyday character even in the museum setting; on the other hand, by being placed in a museum, it now has the function of an artistic arrangement purporting to be a bar. Established habits of perception and ways of seeing are disrupted, and new relationships and structures are not only exposed but must be invented. Frenkel's installation clearly discloses and embodies the paradoxical relationship, or at least the strong contrast, between the inner and the outer worlds, the private and the public domains. The private sphere, as the German author Georg Simmel insisted in the 1950s, is the result of its contrast with the public sphere from which the public is excluded, that characterizes intimacy.

However, here in the artwork the viewer's angle of vision shifts constantly back and forth between inner and outer points of view. Objects and people are by turns physically or fictitiously present. The atmosphere oscillates between art reality and the viewer's reality. Nothing remains constant in these relationships. The very moment one clearly identifies something, it dissipates; the totality is lost. Gertrude Stein's adage "a rose is a rose is a rose" suggests a continuum of reality and fiction; adapting it, we see how the reproduction of reality and its reproduced reproduction in video constantly change places. This is one way in which the fragility of human memory demonstrates how the autonomy of an image is destroyed: our view of things is dependent on the medium in which they appear. In this installation, various fragmented memories of migrants form individual panoramas that are composed of cultural metaphors steeped in history and, at the same time, bereft of perspective and horizon, attempt to exist in the anonymity of the bar's ambiance. Moreover, in their timelessness these fragments are intended to highlight "the sudden" or "the interruption of time" through the transformation from one culture into another — for example, by switching from everyday reality to that of the museum.

The space becomes very important for the arrangement of the individual motifs, and the viewer notes a wide spectrum of unreal spatial relationships. The interplay of sounds, languages and images intensifies this effect almost to the point of irritation. The piano is playing, but the piano player is no longer there. The speech of the people on the monitors has been replaced by voice-overs and subtitles in other languages. We hear Yiddish and Polish, marginalized languages in Germany, to whose speakers foreignness is a never-ending drama. The monitors flicker with subtitles in English, French or German. Frenkel explores the sounds of the languages as they chase one another, with the rhythms of words that may be alien to us. Small comprehensible sequences of thoughts are separated from one another by blocks of words that, although synchronized with the images, cannot be placed in any logical continuity. Although words are wrenched from the everyday world, it is clear that they can no longer be used to grasp it, that speech has lost its power and no longer serves to overcome isolation. Understanding an alien environment can never be reduced to just learning another language.

The video images, which change in quick succession, not only demonstrate the loss of reality, of a "real location", but also the disintegration of people uprooted by the loss of language. No other metaphor for memory is as enduring as the written word, but a text on a video monitor is not a piece of writing as much as a flickering remnant of an image of writing. Documents have become memories tied to machines. Alongside the "speaking images" on the screens, painted and "real" nature alternate. The "art"-works transport nature in "artistic-artificial" images. People, landscapes, images and their representations merge, move and change.

As the viewer searches for identity, even minor changes to the trusted familiar make it potentially alien, so that it becomes a mirror of an interior otherness. The on-screen images carry on an inner dialogue with the visiting stranger: "We are all foreigners," says Vera Frenkel in the Transit Bar newspaper, and cites an excerpt from a book by the Polish writer Kazimierz Brandys about his own experience with exile, *Paris, New York*:

> "Some traces will remain. Photographs, printed pages, remnants of graves, have survived. The number of people with personal recollections ... will diminish. But the past will remain. I don't mean the time that is gone, I mean the world that has ceased to be. Dead worlds like this do not end: eternity rests upon them."[1]

"We are all foreigners," she says. Jorge Luis Borges wrote about memory as the labyrinth of time. In their work on the schizophrenia of capitalism, Deleuze and Guattari considered memory as the labyrinth of space. In ... *from the Transit Bar*, both labyrinths converge, with the result transposed onto a further screen, the future.

Curious viewers not only contemplate the monitors but also throw glances through the torn window-like openings in the wall: What is real? What is fiction?

ON ARTIFICIAL WORLDS IN THE ART WORLD

In her art, Vera Frenkel breaks received patterns of representation above all by using the material instruments of information transfer in an unexpected context. The arrangement of media and museum space becomes a brilliant way of studying pictorial images and what they can reflect. She links the reduction to two-dimensional artificiality in the picture with the presence of a three-dimensional

1. Kazimierz Brandys, *Paris, New York*, trans. Barbara Krzywicki-Herburt (New York: Random House, 1988), 63-64.

reality so that they reflect each other. Semblance and reality are the material of the dramatic arts, as Richard Alewyn notes: "Creating a mirror image of an illusion is one way of mixing different degrees of illusion to a point in the end no one knows where reality ends and illusion begins, thus undermining the awareness of reality."[2] The world of semblance and the world of reality are not only separated by strict boundaries; when the boundaries fluctuate, reality itself is cast into question and viewers are unsettled. As in the theatre of the baroque in which the boundaries of the worlds of complete illusion and of reality become interlinked, the artist confronts the viewer with himself or herself. In another work of Frenkel's, *Her Room in Paris*, from *The Secret Life of Cornelia Lumsden* (1980), the *romantic* gaze through the window or through the frame of multiple references to art history in particular allude to our "inner" and "outer" worlds of images.

Here again Frenkel steadfastly refuses to produce static images as a surface onto which we can project our thoughts. Above all in her installations, the image stands as an analog for inner images or the vortex of images that is thought. On the video screen, the artistic or the intangible reality of these images, or the possible reflections they offer, are explored. She is interested in the stereotype of surface, using video to present the result of a multi-layered analysis of it.

Metro-Centre Messiah, made in 1990 in Newcastle Upon Tyne, England, refers to a new vast shopping mall in that city. The installation focuses on human architectonic and intellectual isolation. With her clear criticism of sense-destroying manipulations of consumer behaviour, she intends neither to overcome the division between art and everyday morality nor to connect the two causally.

Instead, by assembling and juxtaposing in unfamiliar ways disparate fragments of everyday life, she discloses the division in our minds that we experience daily, a division caused by diametrically opposed forms of thought merging into homogeneous social codes and conventions.

THE VIEWER

Frenkel's artwork is characterized by the great significance she accords the viewer. In *Signs of a Plot*, described above, the poetic approximation of reality makes clear the extent to which all valuation or classification is bound to the person who constructs these concepts.

In her installations, visible things are quite literally everywhere. The viewer, along with his or her individual vision and reaction, becomes part of what is viewed.

2. Richard Alewyn, *Das grosse Welttheater. Die Epoche der höfischen Feste* (Munich, 1985), 85.

A tiny step suffices to place the viewer outside the usual rules of the game. The arrangement of the space and the video narratives generates not only a constantly changing relationship among the various elements but also of the viewers to one another.

MYTH AND MEDIA IN RITUALIZED SOCIETY

The subject matter of Frenkel's work seems familiar if we locate it between the tragedy and the comedy of everyday reality. Vera Frenkel concentrates on everyday perception, on what is assumed, showing that the familiar eye is actually turned away from things towards a hidden authority: the subconscious workings of a media world or a collective entity that stigmatizes individuality. In the media, qualities that were formerly separate — namely, the private and the general, the personal and the foreign, the everyday and the eternal — become united. She sees the result as an all-pervasive normativity of ideas, values and conduct, foregrounded by a well-defined block of clichés that supposedly prepares us for all life's situations and provides an armour for the self. Particularly striking in the installations is a compositional structure that parallels the structure of the intended manipulations; institutional forms from everyday life are combined with invented ideas or literary fragments in such a way that they have the effect of a single integrated sequence of action.

Inevitably, each individual manifestation of the culture industry reproduces humans as that which it has made them into. There is an urgent need for a mirror to call the artificial "truth" of the media into question, a truth that in the social consensus seems so authentic that it is as if only the media themselves now produce truth.

The distance between contemporary art and visible reality sets aside all human weaknesses, efforts to find love or validation, or the search for a place to be. These efforts, absurd in the face of the overbearing power of the cyclical processes of time and the heavy burden of "the meaning of the world", though unmasked as meaningless and vain, are nevertheless continually attempted.

In her installations, by juxtaposing artistic and elementary myths, she embarks on a thorough analysis of the nature of myths. The philosophy of the Enlightenment, with its attempt to demystify the world and decipher its myths, has replaced irrationality with social stereotypes and has emptied ritual of all content. Despite such received opinions, Vera Frenkel shows how these rituals function.

If we take the media-invented shadow of our bodies to be more real than ourselves, she seems to say, then in the process we lose our bodies once and for all, as definitively as we lose consciousness. For this reason, Frenkel has in her work questioned patterns of classical tragedy and of soap opera to determine what has remained of the reality of myth formation in the collective experience of reality, transforming the passive viewer into an active player in the process.

ARTIST AND EXILE

As a Czech Jew who immigrated to Canada via England, Vera Frenkel became acquainted as a child with the feeling of passing through not only geographical but consequently historical space in the shortest possible time. She makes present to the imagination and reconstructs for the viewer the intellectual fragmentation of the tightrope walk between cultures in such vivid form that the experience becomes accessible to collective memory.

The foreigner's experience of the reality of the present is synonymous with the historical subject's experience of suffering, a subject that disappears into a mediated space without boundaries. Repeatedly turning her attention to the unfamiliar timespace constellations as a "new" reality, Frenkel focuses on the foreignness of being and the feeling of losing oneself in such a world.

The familiarity of foreignness conjures up images of the drama of time and memory, making clear that literary, historical and practical time are completely separate from one another. In contrast to the individual experience of action, time in collective memory is physical or cosmic or eternal. It has nothing in common with a notion of mechanically measurable time, or time that corresponds to a notion of progress. In memory, there is no sense of interruption of the movement of time. The idea is comparable to that of the unity of time and space that the philosopher Ernst Cassirer proposed in 1944 as the fundamental dimension of the mythic world and of all life. Against this background, too, Frenkel investigates collective and personal myths. In *The Secret Life of Cornelia Lumsden*, she has created for the first time a prototype or ur-image of the artist in exile, and reconstructed the life and work of the writer. The work presents a philosophy in material form, for Frenkel has established the strong presence of an imaginary figure around that person's permanent absence.

REFRACTIONS OF CUSTOMARY WAYS OF SEEING

Within tightly structured modes of communication — language, image, everyday life — Frenkel continually changes the position of the viewer of her work, using a multiplicity of artistic languages and refractions of customary ways of seeing. The relationship of perception to reality occurs in the juxtaposition of contradictory entities in various modes of presentation. Her principle is to dismantle fixed expectations, the "game" of revealing and concealing, in subtle parodies of conventional genres.

Frenkel's installations also provide a picture frame, as it were, that gives order to or fixes the syntax of the overall conception. Events in recent history are mirrored in boundaries of banality, self-representation, fiction and authenticity.

Synchronic and diachronic experiences become one in the work. The monitors mounted on the walls of the Transit Bar both reflect and become part of a constantly changing experience, creating as if through a kaleidoscope, countless patterns of communication produced by the changing viewers: object becomes subject, subject becomes object. Significant ideas in Jewish thought, in particular in the Kabbalah, with all their different systematic forms, become clear and stress

> "..the interwoven nature of all worlds and stages of being which it knows. Everything is connected to and contained in everything else in an intangible yet precise manner. Everything has infinite depth, and the depth of the infinite can be viewed from any angle. The two images used in Kabbalah ontologies contradict each other in terms of their substance: that of the infinite chain and the interconnection of its links, and that of the shells stacked in one another, for which the nut was often taken as the preferred cosmic symbol."[3]

Frenkel turns her attention to the uncharted regions of human experience that the radical quotidian manipulations of the media have banished from our normal field of vision. She deconstructs, to use the word in Barthes's sense, the shell of the message in order to go through the sign or "the hieroglyph of the wound" to its essence. In view of the irrationality of forms, even of suffering, that are conveyed by the mass media, she attempts to give suffering a concrete face and to protect it from being trivialized and blunted.

Somewhere between "classical tragedy" and "soap opera", Frenkel's oeuvre is, in her own words, in a constant state of flux. This perceptual instability is meant to awaken the viewer's senses, making him or her conscious of a functional part of his or her life and therefore — perhaps — tangible. Anyone who watches the video narrative intensively soon notices that language alone as a means of communication is irritating. We may possibly understand the language spoken, but as passive viewers we can't communicate with an artificial conversation partner.

3. Gershom Scholem, *Kabbalah* (New York: Dorset Press, 1987), 112.

Behind the practice of making clichés or their poetry present to the imagination stand various experiments or variations on a theme, an example of which might be her use of repetition of certain words or sentences to transform language into an object.

VISION AND PERCEPTION

The combination of ideas in Frenkel's installations make very clear the fact that there are no immutable or eternal forms of human perception.

Vision and perception are freed from received ideas. Understanding via pure contemplation refers to theoretical, non-empirical occurrences and tends to determine the form of non-objective, abstract art. By contrast, knowledge that refers to the continuously changing experience of life, and thus to the empirical, tends to be regarded as the basis of the various shapes and forms of objective art. Frenkel's practice addresses the point where the two intersect. Her investigation of the foundations of reality is tied to the value she attaches to coincidence, for the latter can provoke insight into the essence of things.

STORIES, KNOWLEDGE AND HISTORY

Frenkel's "material" is individual and collective memory. When she assembles it in layers, the result resembles jumps through time. In his research into classical antiquity, Johann Jakob Bachofen, the nineteenth-century European art theoretician, regarded this use of material as attesting to animistic magic. To him, the shortest path to knowledge, one that can be traversed with the power and speed of electricity, is the path of the imagination, which is stimulated by gazing at and by direct unmediated contact with historical remains.

In a sense paraphrasing Baudelaire's famous maxim that "there can be no remembrance without forgetting", Mallarmé cast aside the restrictions of words and syntax and moved from imitation to the realization of the power of his imagination. Memory is something a person shares with no one else. Aesthetic perception, however, is possible only via the presentation of common experiences. If memory is stored by artificial means, as Plato showed regarding the constraints of written literature as opposed to oral tradition, the result is a loss of memory. And if memory becomes a matter of media images, then it is, above all, the remaining senses such as smell or touch that become deadened.

As we search for a concept to describe Frenkel's intellectual edifice and her corresponding language of form, two elements are evident: the method she chooses for her individual appropriation of motifs (rejection and appropriation of iconographic traditions), and her preference for everyday motifs, for the vernacular. The inherent ambiguity of the texts brings these elements to the fore. What becomes apparent is that she regards language itself as an event. The approach she takes resembles the memory-process described by Walter Benjamin in the Arcades Project. Like an archaeologist (and the discipline fascinates her, as she emphasizes with reference to Evans and the reconstructions at Knossos, and her observations of the University of Toronto/Princeton dig at Kommos), Frenkel understands herself to be a registrar of the history of an epoch or place that she reconstructs with the assistance of material facts. Instead of relying predominantly on textual sources, archaeology is concerned with the material artifacts that a given society produces, collects and finally leaves behind.

The problem of archaeological reconstruction and the construction of reality is addressed in Frenkel's work by revitalizing historical thought with the help of the imagination. The predominance of a world that is purely technological in orientation undermines the independence of human thought and action. A society that is based primarily on a technological culture and does not respect and remember its history is in reality ruled by those political forces that direct the technology. So Frenkel not only questions history but in so doing asks what form truth now takes.

Her studies of form and surface were refined through her analyses of the relationship between pornography and censorship in *The Business of Frightened Desires* (1985), and of the romance, the detective story and documentary practices, as in her multi-disciplinary performances *Trust Me, It's Bliss: The Hugh Hefner / Richard Wagner Connection* (Chicago, 1987) or *Mad for Bliss* (Banff and Toronto, 1989). In the latter, a piano-bar, a lunatic asylum and a cult altar to a consumer god are sites for the action. Her work proposes that stereotypes and archetypal images, in contrast to literature, inform through a narrowing of focus, preventing us from seeing things as they are. Totalitarian governments, she notes, aware of the power of good literature, let their best writers, those who might enable us to construct our own world, languish in jail or disappear.

In the videotape *The Last Screening Room: A Valentine* (Minneapolis and Toronto, 1984), Frenkel points up this perspective, telling from many different positions the story of an imprisoned story-teller and describing a society where story-telling is a capital offense. In that context, she stresses that not only individual biographies but also the history of society as a whole are largely based on stories. Only story-telling makes possible a collective experience that can then be passed on.

Frenkel shows by means of a language of images how collective and individual memory can be shaken. In his work *The Social Framework of Collective Memory*, Maurice Halbwachs attempted to outline the process in which a person's memories and judgments are subject to specific social conditions that at the same time form the framework within and the means by which he or she remembers and thinks. He claimed, moreover, that a distinction must be made between individual and social memory. Of particular interest in the present context is that he speaks of localizing concepts of space or of the theatre of recollection, a role Frenkel points out is played by museums.

ON THE RELATIONSHIP OF MEMORY AND HISTORY

Unlike other installations, Frenkel's show a variety of things and media presented in a number of ways that at first sight are not discernible as art. Everyday things are given continued existence and form by their art context.

In Frenkel's oeuvre, mnemotechnical media are tied to individual memory, and to media-generated images that open out into spaces of an interior world. Stereotyped reality is ruptured in two ways, and a process subtly introduced whereby the external world is transposed into an inner vision. In the exhibition *Raincoats, Suitcases, Palms* (Art Gallery of York University, 1993) the iconography of the Transit Bar is changed and then transcended in the accompanying artist's book. As Erich Auerbach wrote:

> "When past reality recurs in a person remembering, who has long since left the capturing circumstances in which the things actually happened, that person sees and arranges the contents in a way that is very different from being simply individualistic or subjective. Detached from the original changing constraints, the person now views layers of his own past, seeing the contents thereof in perspective, continually confronting them with one another, freeing them from their eternal chronological sequences and from the narrower significance they seem to have in the present. In the process the modern notion of inner time blends with the Neo-Platonic notion that the true original image of the object is already present in the artist's soul, the artist is already present in the object, has detached himself from it in order to contemplate it and now confronts his own past."[4]

Often, in *...from the Transit Bar*, the video narratives simply call attention to the life cycle of people balanced between different cultures. The sense of the speed with

4. Erich Auerbach, *Mimesis: The Representation of Reality in Western Literature*, trans. Willard R. Trask (Princeton, N.J.: Princeton University Press, 1953).

which the passing of time is registered is one of Frenkel's major themes. In this regard she alludes to the rapid transformation of styles and events. Moving through border territory lets her use the video to reflect reality and at the same time to hold up a mirror to media ideology.

Another of her central themes is of course the media, and she makes use of media in many ways: reality is reconstructed on gallery walls, or in catalogues, transposed into a legible arrangement, or through changing tiny nuances. A "hyperreality" of events, seemingly locked into fixed media structures, emerges, and permits us to experience them in relation to these themes.

Unequivocal interpretations, staring into the void, merely engender paradoxes. By contrast, Vera Frenkel's staging of a collection of recognizable but transformed objects opens up an associative space in which to manoeuvre, in which the viewer faces the everyday world and the world of art as equivalent backstage perceptual spaces.

Frenkel's installations are variations on the theme of the manifold nature of reality and its surface fragility, structured as normal through a thin coat of varnish. Behind the normal world and behind the usual order of things lie other realities best termed intangible and incomprehensible "inner worlds." Her atmospheric "snapshot" of everyday existence is her response to an age threatened by social upheaval, with its ossified conventions and rituals devoid of meaning, which art exhibitions in their pomposity reflect precisely.

Against the growing social and political paralysis that lies like a lead net over everything that promises meaning and has immobilized our sense of social values, Vera Frenkel's works of art, a form of poetry made concrete, constitute a cultural critique and an appeal.

Translation by Jeremy Gaines and Elizabeth Schwaiger.

Breakdown Video

OR THE LINK AESTHETIC IN THE WORK OF DANIEL DION

by Christine Ross

> I see modernity as the moment of decline of classical rationality, as the failure of the traditional definition of the subject as an entity that is expected to coincide with his/her conscious rational self. As if a new fragility had been discovered in the very bedrock of existence...I see the crisis as the opening-up of new possibilities, new potentialities; thus the centre of the theoretical agenda is occupied today by a crucial question: What does it mean to be a human subject, that is to say a socialized, civilized, member of a community in a postmetaphysical world? The link among identity, power, and community needs to be rethought.[1]

Rosi Braidotti

> In other words, how are we to view the link (which is social, of course, but not exclusively) in a society whose goal is to use the individual to reconstruct the collectivity? [2]

Luc Ferry

To fully appreciate Daniel Dion's video art, it is essential to understand the "link aesthetic" underlying his work. The link aesthetic is a postmodernist approach characterized by a radical rethinking of the notion of identity (in relation to unity, sameness, and self-awareness), and by a concomitant call for difference (individual, sexual, and cultural). Dion's videotapes are given to disjunction and division, but the link emerges when we least expect it.

In *Bouger dans l'espace* (1982), a woman reads a text in an incoherent manner, as if she were dyslexic.[3] The discrepancy between her spoken English words and the written French text is so great that the "bouger dans l'espace" (moving in space) turns into "bonjour dans le space." Reading, which involves identifying and linking

1. Rosi Braidotti, "The Subject in Feminism," *Hypatia*, VI:2 (Summer 1991), p. 162.

2. Luc Ferry, *Homo Aestheticus: L'invention du gout à l'age démocratique*, Paris: Grasset, 1990, p. 42 (our translation).

3. For more on the idea of dyslexia in *Bouger dans l'espace*, see Claude Marc Bourget, "Dion/Poloni ou La Surcharge des Lieux," *Intervention* (March 1983), pp. 22-23.

the words in a text, takes on an extra dimension here: as the announcer reads the words, they are not just being assembled or strung together, for dualities have been established in which one factor affects the other: the statement is being altered by its presentation, the written word by speech, and the story by orality.

Discordance abounds, as well, in *Système des beaux-arts/System of Fine Arts* (1980). Right from the outset, it's the text that causes the English and French to be mismatched, and camera 1 and camera 2 to be out of sync. The link re-emerges, however, through this very dissonance, as the speaker associates what is constantly splitting apart and breaking down. The link is also present in *Great Divide/Grande barrière* (1990), where the images are joined by a video composition spread over two adjacent screens. But are they really linked despite the physical bar that clearly separates the two monitors?

Relating and clashing, joining and disjoining: these are formal strategies in Dion's work. Just when the breakdown (of the image, the meaning, the self, the culture) is about to occur, just when everything is about to fall apart, the ever-changing, ever-paradoxical link appears. To feel the presence of this aesthetic, so that it will genuinely affect us, the present text will have to put itself on a "breakdown wavelength" in keeping with the incessant breakdown of images in these tapes. So if the text falters, if the narrative mirrors the breakdown, it's because from where I stand these videos are riddled with mini-breakdowns — it's to make the link.

BREAKDOWN, THE IN-BETWEENS OF REJECTION

Everything can break down in a flash, at least in *Système des beaux-arts/System of Fine Arts* (1980), one of Daniel Dion's first videotapes, co-directed with Philippe Poloni.4 The work was created with the television viewer in mind, which was natural given its special context (*Export 80*, a video event broadcast on cable at the time). The breakdown stems from dissonance on three counts: occurring between two languages (English and French), two cameras, and two subjectivities (speaker and viewer). We see Poloni reading a text, switching constantly from one language to the other:

> Système des beaux-arts/I am speaking to camera 1, but camera 2 is out of focus/Il ne m'arrive rien, je suis hors foyer/Nothing happen *[sic]*, I am out of focus/I am watching you, but you don't see me/I am watching you, but you don't see me/J'invite ma bouteille à sortir ce soir/But look on the screen, this is only a part of my picture/Mais regardez sur l'écran, je ne suis pas là...

4. From 1980 to 1982, after producing his first two video works *Bandes crues* (1977-78) and *Matrice urbaine* (1978) in collaboration with Daniel Guimond, and before his first co-production with Su Schnee, *À propos peinture* (1985), Daniel Dion collaborated with Philippe Poloni and together they embarked upon an intensive videographic production. Dion and Poloni have produced eleven videotapes in all.

Even in this short excerpt we can see how the shifts from one language to the other are far from pure. Words are poorly translated, not translated at all, or translated too late. We must bear in mind that this breakdown has been created for the TV viewer. To the extent that the viewer is bilingual, he is already interacting with the video, struggling with its linguistic impurity. For him, for her, for me, the link normally stemming from semantic and expressive equivalences in the two languages is radically disrupted, for one language is rejecting the other (that is, affirming itself through the expulsion of the other).

For the unilingual TV viewer, on the other hand, the experience is somewhat different, in that the languages do not reject each other, but rather the viewer is rejected by the language that's foreign to him. The rejection I experience here is of the type described by Julia Kristeva (who employs the term "abjection," which we'll examine more closely later).[5] I'm thrown off-track, rejected, expelled at the very moment the other language is introduced. More precisely, I'm rejected by the arrival of a "you" or a "*vous,* " by a surge of utterances that glide towards non-sense. Soon the words no longer have any meaning for me, nor are they meant for me. I'm waiting and while I wait my loss is being enacted, my temporary blackout, which will only end when Poloni arbitrarily decides to end it, leading to my eventual reintegration. In the meantime, I am being rejected — by Canada's official bilingualism.

For the unilingual person, reintegration is better than nothing. But the matter is more complex than that because the process of rejection is reinforced and accentuated by all the flawed, out-of-sync shifts of Poloni's look from camera 1 to camera 2 and back, shifts that disregard me. Rejection is also exemplified by the text that separates us from him, thereby establishing an opposition and a hierarchy.

Poloni, the speaker, is explicit about this: we (the unilingual and the bilingual) are the ones who suffer just when he feels comfortable, or inversely, "you're comfortable and I suffer." Doesn't the strength of the one always contribute to the alienation of the other? And it intensifies, because Poloni then assumes the role of the invisible voyeur ("I am watching you, but you don't see me"), to the point of impossibility-of-being-seen. "Since," he says, "I am not there, nothing happens, I am out of focus and out of opinions." Out of reach, he is shielded by the screen, on the other side.

For the television viewer, breakdown means being rejected by the impure passages that un-link all that TV assures him of linking together: the two official languages,

5. See Julie Kristeva, *Powers of Horror: An Essay On Abjection*, translated by Leon S. Roudiez (European Perspective series), New York: Columbia University Press, 1982.

the two cultures, the TV producer and the viewer. You and I are disjoined here, on opposite sides of the screen, opposite sides of the language barrier. We will remain so, unless we are — re-disjoined. Why create a video work such as *Système des beaux-arts/System of Fine Arts,* produced especially for the television viewer, if not to expose television as a form of discourse in which the link between the one and the other is always to the advantage of one party (the TV producer, the language of the majority) and to the detriment of the other (the viewer, the language of the minority), reduced to virtually nothing?

But *Système des beaux-arts/System of Fine Arts* is more generous than that. It is disjointed, without a doubt, but it goes on to optimize what little is left of "virtually nothing," offering it as a gift, a videographic gift, that repels.[6] Because rejection also produces something: in-betweens, these gaps in space and time that slip in here and there between the flawed shifts from one language to the other, one camera to the other, one subjectivity to the other. These impure shifts in Poloni's discourse are brutally punctuated by unpredictable earsplitting cacophonies, metallic city noises, accompanied by a sudden, fitful back-and-forth motion of the camera. In these brief moments, amidst this din, the video technique "goes insane." Let's call this approach *intelevisual*, because the images produced here are very different from those on TV today (and perhaps in the past as well), for the television establishment cannot make allowance for them. They simply do not fit within the realm of the "televisually correct."

And what of my rejection? Owing to this videotape's many in-betweens, my rejection has in some sense come unhinged. It has been reversed and split in two, so that it now manifests itself on either side of the screen, affecting both the TV viewer and the TV producer. In these in-betweens, I expel the sounds and images produced by a crazed camera, which are already expelling me, for I see (*video*, in Latin) the impossibility-of-being-seen, which is looking at me. Video, an offshoot of television, is still in the throes of emerging through and within television, with and against it, using the back-and-forth movement of the camera to limit and delimit its visual field. By alienating me, the Other (the television, the speaker) actually allows me to exist. This process is termed "abjection" by Kristeva, who describes it as:

> ...a repulsive gift that the Other, having become alter ego, drops so that 'I' does not disappear in it but finds, in that sublime alienation, a forfeited existence. Hence a jouissance in which the subject is swallowed up but in which the Other, in return, keeps the subject from foundering by making it repugnant... Abjection... transforms death drive into a start of life, of new significance.[7]

6. According to Kristeva, p. 9:..."there is nothing either objective or objectal to the abject. It is simply a frontier, a repulsive gift the the Other, having become *Alter Ego,* drops so that 'I' does not disappear in it..."

Poloni, by repeatedly expelling me throughout the video, by creating a situation in which the languages reject each other, by denying my existence, becomes this Other who incites me to reject myself from the televisual system. At the time of my expulsion, when non-sense prevails, I (the viewer, the videotape, or the video artist) occupy an in-between space where I "vomit up"[8] the televisual system, where I expel that very thing which is expelling me, so that I separate things (and myself) and define things (and myself) differently. Although the back-and-forth motion of the camera throws me totally off-course and leaves me flawed, I attempt to set things right and set my limits, "amid the violence of sobs."[9]

Right from the start, Dion's videotapes have exposed (by reproducing it), the disjunctive link of television discourse, making the process of rejection more complex through the use of an in-between. These in-betweens merit our attention, because in his later works the in-betweens are the very site where we conceptualize the link, a link which can only emerge if I am made to feel flawed.

These in-betweens recapture the *intelevisual* origins of video art, reminding us that video is defined by the ways in which it differs from television. In-betweens help to specify these differences, since the double rejection that characterizes them (the expulsion of what is already expelling) indicates not only video's origins in television but also video's initial inferior position in relation to television, demonstrating the degree to which video owes its identity to television. Video is television whose seeing process has gone mad.[10] The seeing process is where breakdown occurs. Where am I?

IT WILL BE STROKE-BY-STROKE, OR IT WILL NOT BE

In *À propos peinture* (1985), co-directed with Su Schnee,[11] painting is the means by which Dion stages the breakdown and examines the expressive and operational aspects of the seeing process. Early in the tape, we are told in a voice-off that the act

---

7. Kristeva, pp. 9 and 15.

8. See Kristeva, p. 2: "Loathing an item of food, a piece of filth, waste, or dung. The spasms and vomiting that protect me. The repugnance, the retching that thrusts me to the side and turns me away from defilement...The shame of compromise, of being in the middle..."

9. Kristeva, p. 3.

10. *Systeme des beaux-arts/System of Fine Arts* contains in-betweens that are clearly baroque. See also Christine Buci-Glucksmann, *La folie du voir: de l'esthétique baroque*, Paris: Editions Galilée, 1986, pp. 72-74.

11. This is the first work that Daniel Dion co-directed with Su Schnee, who appeared, however, in an earlier Dion tape as the announcer/performer in *Bouger dans l'espace* (1982). They also co-produced *Le mystère de la trinité* and *La minute de vérité* in 1991, as well as *World Tea Party*, in collaboration with Bryan Mulvihill in 1992-93.

of seeing cannot lead to knowledge. This failure raises the question of how we perceive and represent the subject:

> How can we know about being human? We are inside. To really see, you'd have to be non-human. But the verb "to see" has no meaning. It's a lure, an illusion. Because we alone create what we think we see.

Seeing is defined from the outset as a defective act of perception, inseparable from the object being perceived, and leading to incorrect representation. This is why *À propos peinture* focuses on the face and its representation. We see a fragmented string of faces — African masks, faces from videos, paintings and sculptures, even some computer-generated images. We are shown a close-up, shot in slow motion, of Su Schnee's twisted, grimacing face, covered in blue paint. This is actually the staging of the breakdown, which, due to its extended length and emotional intensity, creates discord halfway through the tape.

The sequence is truly a blues rendition, both pictorially and musically. The painted face keeps on grimacing as we hear the theme from *India Song*, sung by Jeanne Moreau (from the 1974 film by Marguerite Duras). Here, though, it is transformed into a blues number, for her voice has been deformed through technology, slowed down to the point that it loses its femininity and falls into the masculine range. "She" breaks down. Her face and voice topple over. But isn't it really the video itself that's falling? Into the portrait of a wound? Taking the form of a mask, and a deformed rendition of *India Song*? This video-turned-blues is marked by *India Song*, by this song about "her" as a song, where she's both the singer and the sung, now disappeared, with whom "I" was dancing. But this blues number is also about a painted blue mask, distancing and hiding her.

At the heart of *À propos peinture*, then, we come up against the matter of the subject's wound, as well as the linguistic and visual signs that represent her in a limited manner, but which actually distance her from herself. Benveniste and Lacan deal with the drama of existing: subjectivity, this language-based, discursive reality in which I am the signifier (merely a sign that graphically and phonetically represents me) interacting with another signifier. We are compartmentalized by language.[12] This is the expulsive truth[13] contained in our statements. The subject is the evanescent sign of desire, which flees and disappears, from word to word, colour

12. See Emile Benveniste, *Problems in General Linguistics*, translated by Mary Elizabeth Meek, Coral Gables, Florida: University of Miami Press, 1971, and Jacques Lacan, *Ecrits: A Selection*, translated by Alan Sheridan, New York: W.W. Norton, 1977.

13. Jacques Lacan, "The Freudian thing, or the meaning of the return to Freud in psychoanalysis," in *Ecrits: A Selection* (*op. cit.*), p. 121: "...so that you will find me where I am, I will teach you by what sign you will recognize me. Men, listen, I am giving you the secret. I, truth, will speak."

to colour, from look to look: "I am watching you, but you don't see me/Vous me regardez, mais vous ne me voyez pas" (*Système des beaux-arts/System of Fine Arts*). I express myself (I look, I represent), you express yourself (you look at me, represent me); I flee, through my externalization in language, and especially, through the rejection of the feminine. Not only does "she" (the singer whose identity has disappeared) no longer have access to "her", but the masculinization of her own voice constitutes a further rejection. And if the woman is rejected here, is it not in order to portray abjection (rejection) in its purest state? Kristeva explains that in a society forever fearing the procreative power of the archaic mother ,"any woman (and woman as a whole)" becomes this "radical evil that is to be suppressed" by the process of symbolizing through language.[14] Considered at the level of *India Song*, at the level of the masked and contorted face of the painter Su Schnee, *À propos peinture* is a drama in which the protagonist is split in two; it is also the story of one sex being repelled, rejected by the Other. But where's the link?

And above all, what is really happening in this blues video by means of which Dion's art seeks to define itself? The first shot in *À propos peinture* shows the videomaker facing the viewer from behind a transparent storyboard. He speaks at length, totally absorbed in his discourse, in his attempt to impart the whole truth, but we hear nothing. Has the truth broken down again? This time through silence? What is video, then? What is this activity involving a videomaker and a viewer, placed on opposite sides of the seemingly transparent screen where images are formed? How can you hear *me*, the viewer, the videomaker, the subject represented, the woman's face, the African face? How can I reach you, represent you, link me to you, without rejection?

The question of link. The link in question. The discourse on the nature of television in *Système des beaux-arts/System of Fine Arts* opens with a lot of noise, with in-betweens, with a seeing process gone mad. But is there not also a link that opens what is closed, that joins together what is divided (the screen, the signs), that reverses the rejection? Returning to *India Song*, let's examine the question of the link: how can we dance with "her" without distancing, without disjoining? According to Catherine Clément:

> The couple seems to walk rather than dance, with a lively gait, intertwined. Who could separate them?...They stopped there, motionless as for a snapshot...He lifts her again, twirls her around, and sets off again. Tango...Syncope, manifest in the tilt backward, is at the very heart of the step: three ordinary, quick steps, then nothing. Suspension. It is at these moments,

14. For more on the abjection of the "woman," see Kristeva, p. 56-89.

when time is suspended, that everything can come apart. Obscenity. Dance cannot exist without syncope.[15]

The link running through *À propos peinture* and *India Song* may be seen in terms of Clément's description. It is a suspension, like the syncopal tilt that influences the dance just described.[16] Let's take a closer look at the paintings in the video, especially Su Schnee's paintings, which punctuate the entire work. Her expressionist paintings are presented as in a tango, at the very moment of their tilt, since the pictures, which are supposed to be vertical, are instead horizontal. Tilted in this way, the canvases gain in texture what they lose in intelligibility. The faces depicted here are to be perceived in fits and starts, stroke-by-stroke, in keeping with the expressionistic brushstroke of the painterly gesture. Hasn't the painter's twisted face, the succession of grimaces, always been perceived stroke-by-stroke? In no way can we conceptualize the link here by simply having her take off the mask or represent herself differently. Hypothesis: if the link is to be conceptualized, it is precisely through the stroke-by-stroke perception emerging from a tilted representation, from an inversion of rejection, from a convulsion of the body.

The stroke-by-stroke aspect of *À propos peinture* and the intelevisual to-and-fro of *Système des beaux-arts/System of Fine Arts* have one thing in common: the suspension of movement by a brutal stop, sudden and repeated. This is syncope, and it extends even to the elliptical title "À propos peinture" (not À propos *de la* peinture"). The video develops through a syncopal suspension (of syllables, of the narrative, of distinct disciplines).[17] And in this blackout we see a glimmer of the link. This is not a video *about* painting, but one in search of an eclipse, one that desires *to be* painting, which it can only be by not being, that is, by a loss of identity, an identity that can, just for an instant, fall apart. Painting-video: the video art of Daniel Dion will be painterly, or it will not be. Through the use of syncope, the video starts to form a link that allows fusion and thus breaks down the disjunctive truth.

15. Catherine Clément, *La Syncope: Philosophie du ravissement*, Paris: Editions Grasset & Fasquelle, 1990, p. 12 (our translation).

16. From 1983 to 1987, Daniel Dion turned to dance, not only in this deformed version of *India Song*, but also in a series of photographs done with Claude-Marie Caron, entitled *Le Corps et la lumière*. In this series, the strobe light imparts a fitful quality to the various dance movements. Photographing dance provided Dion with a method of observation that would help him to create the illusion of epilepsy (the stroboscope, incidentally, is an instrument which, among its other functions, is used in the observation of epileptic fits), in which the body shakes with rapid jolts, and movement is interrupted by numerous small stops, and made hallucinatory by means of animal metamorphoses. Su Schnee's convulsive expression possesses something of this epileptic imagery.

17. In regard to the dissolution of boundaries between disciplines, it is worth noting that Dion's video art has essentially been a joint effort with artists from other fields. His attempt to achieve this is not exclusive to *À propos peinture*.

In this blackout, this breakdown, set into motion by painting, could I perhaps link with you, the video artist, the viewer, the painter?

To construct a video as one would a painting, Dion explains, is a way of removing the narrative element, in which "you're always stuck with a beginning, a middle, and an ending."[18] Hence this attachment to the painterly, to those fits and starts that "allow the eye a moment of reflection, a better perception of things." This stroke-by-stroke approach opens up the seeing process.[19] It opens onto the other, as long as the other reels at the very moment that I do. And when the pivoting mask of Su Schnee appears on screen, then disappears, giving way at each rotation to African bodies (also painted), our very cultural identity reels as well. It's as if the mask suddenly unveiled its capacity to open up, opening through the other that resembles and re-assembles it. It appears in the other and disappears into the other, is culturally dislocated by it, and finds itself once again through it. It's as if suddenly the difference actually made a difference, in altering the one. The link is a difference that has an effect (on me).

STRIVING FOR LINKAGE: AN AESTHETIC OF SYNCOPE

In both his videotapes and installation, Dion's video art is defined by a stroke-by-stroke aesthetic — a syncopal quality that repulses the narrative element, which has an organic nature and a need for resolution. Not that Dion's videos are a quest for difference at any price, or a juxtaposition or conglomeration of differences. On the contrary, they seek out the link, through and with the difference. This is an enormous challenge today. How can we link cultures without having one assimilate the other? This is the Canadian dilemma. The European dilemma. The North-South dilemma. But also the sexual dilemma: how can I link with "her"? It's ultimately a dilemma of identity: how can I open up to this other-than-I-am, without fusing with it? Without rejection? Trinh T. Minh-ha makes this observation:

> To make a claim for multiculturalism...It lies... in the intercultural acceptance of risks, unexpected detours, and complexities of relation. Every artistic excursion and theoretical venture requires that boundaries be ceaselessly called into question, undermined, modified, and reinscribed. [20]

Working, disrupting, all the while drawing up new boundaries, taking "unexpected detours." Let us consider *Great Divide/Grande barrière* (1990) as a culmination of

18. Daniel Dion, in conversation with the author, Montreal, 15 September 1992.

19. In other words, the opening of the visible by the visual. See also Georges Didi-Huberman, *Devant l'image: Question posée aux fins d'une histoire de l'art* (Critique series), Paris: Les Editions de Minuit, 1990, p. 173 (our translation): "We must, when opening up the box [of representation]... wait for the visible to 'take hold,' and with this in mind, touch upon the *implicit* value of what we attempt to apprehend by the term *visual*."

20. Trinh T. Minh-ha, "Critical Reflections," *Artforum*, XXXVIII:10 (Summer 1990), p. 133.

these efforts, a video work characterized by a stroke-by-stroke approach, in which elements are being linked even while their identity is being altered by means of the difference.

The link? Since the picture is spread over two screens, doesn't this necessitate a duality, given the physical and material persistence of the vertical bar formed by the junction of the two monitors placed side by side? Certainly, but this duality is never totally pure (like the flawed shifts in *Système des beaux-arts/System of Fine Arts*), because although the bar creates opposition, it is also the site where the two images complement each other, as well as join, move apart, and widen their scope. The tape offers a meeting ground for its duelling dual elements. The same applies to the series of attractions-repulsions that emerge throughout the work: the resistible contact between the mountain ridges on either side of the in-between, the co-presence of the divided self, the linking of palindromes.

The vertical bar is itself like the Rockies, this mountainous border that breaks the coast-to-coast continuity of Canada — politically, geographically, culturally, and cartographically. The mountain range runs south, right through the American continent, and is viewed by the First Nations "as a backbone holding the body straight between two great oceans."[21] And when we encounter this bar, this barrier, and explore it, doesn't it call into question the very division it embodies? Although the boundaries don't dissolve, they are nonetheless replaced by a hollow space, where the attraction-repulsion ambivalence created by the border comes into play.

Let me explain this attraction-repulsion. First we see the mountains moving back, on both sides of the double bar formed by the junction of the two monitors. Then we get a wider view of them, so that a panorama is created. The panorama is split vertically, however, by the dark interruption in the centre. The images attract and repel each other, and sometimes attract each other at the very moment of mutual repulsion, producing a fusion that repels (in that it disintegrates and destroys the initial, integral identity of the images). They constantly affect each other, reach out to each other. The bar snatches and releases the two images at the same time, so that the right and the left become one, though still duelling from their respective sides of the bar, for fusion always entails resistance and the drawing up of new borders.

This is not video art *on*, but rather, video art *through* or, better yet, *as* the objects it records. *Great Divide/Grande barrière* uses the double screen to mimic (to embody)

21. Bryan Mulvihill, "Grande Barrage\Great Divide: Video Work de Daniel Dion" [sic], *Video Guide* (Autumn 1990), p. 20.

its own images, with their multitude of deforming interactions that leave their mark on the objects represented. The composition may be compared to one wave deforming the other, or to the sway of a body in equilibrium, or to the videotape's discrepancies from beginning to end, summed up by these words appearing on the screen:

> From the extremity of his arc/the archer pierces the sky/the arrow leaves the string/but it does not fly directly toward the target/and the target is no longer where it is.

Great Divide/Grande barrière, through its double composition, seeks a sort of reconciliation with discrepancies, transformations, and dislocations. A bond is formed here, with or through otherness, through a difference that differs and defers. This bond based on difference has a material aspect, namely the bar separating the two monitors. Although the bar, this dark, narrow space, contributes to the difference and disjunction, it is itself a double and divided bar, an in-between by means of which the images on either side may interact. The double bar, then, while creating a duality, nonetheless allows a suspension, so that the left- and right-hand image may reach each other. As Catherine Clément observes in regard to syncope, the in-between is precisely this stop that produces an "identification defect," that shakes up the identity and brings about "the impossible return to the same."[22] Such is the nature of the unforseen dark bar of syncope, fusing with otherness, associating with dissociation:

> Impossible to represent, it is equally impossible to imagine; we have neither the image nor the memory of the darkness of the anaesthetic, of physiological syncope. Language can evoke it; but thought unrelentingly, stubbornly, resists this nothingness which violently rejects it. Let us not think we will enter inside this darkness; we would have to be crazy, or God. Those crazed with God seek ecstasy there...We will act like stage directors; we will arrive just before, or just after, basking in the aura that precedes the crisis, or the calming down that follows...[23]

If you liken the video to a stage, the picture is down there and the viewer up here. It's also you down there and me up here; or better yet, it's me, but I've been rejected by your look. Imagine eliminating the stage through various staging devices: the in-between imparting to television a crazed seeing process, the stroke-by-stroke, the dark in-between. These devices make the stage disappear from under my feet, as at the moment of a blackout, like a breakdown on both sides. The attraction-repulsion aspect of *Great Divide/Grande barrière* is played out on a double screen, allowing

22. Clément, p. 202.

23. Clément, p.p. 43-44.

the presence of an in-between (the dark space between the two monitors). The use of the in-between allows an approach based on the non-theatrical, mimetic identification postulated and then repudiated by Freud. Mimesis is a person's first physical and emotional link, primitive and fundamental, underlying all of our objective choices (choices relating us to exterior objects), in which the self is experienced for the first time. This link is "ambivalent from the very first."[24] (Freud attempted to resolve this paradox by his theories of secondary and oedipal identification.) This ambivalent and narcissistic mimesis is an intrusion of the emotions immediately experienced in and like the ego before any opposition is established (form-content, me-other, love-hate, performance-receptivity). The ego is formed through mimesis. It forms within, and models itself after, the other person with whom it constantly mixes its traits, linking to the other by unlinking with itself, for we can never be totally ourselves when we fuse with someone else. This seems to be the "point of otherness" defined by Mikkel Borch-Jacobsen: an emotional, mimetic, and ambivalent point, an *Einfühlung*, an empathy, where attraction and repulsion co-exist, this in-between where one can no longer speak "either of 'form' or 'image,' either of 'self' or 'other'."[25]

Owing to the in-between, which splits the picture right down the centre, and to the editing, which highlights the video's attraction-repulsion aspect, *Great Divide/Grande barrière* establishes a dynamic that allows shifts to occur within its duality and dialectic.[26] This duality comprises these supposed links (me and you, subject and object, picture and reality, video and painting, French and English, the woman's mask and the African faces), which are, in fact, only oppositional relationships hierarchically dividing one element of the link from the other, to the advantage of one. Thus, although one cannot stage syncope, for it is impossible to maintain one's presence within the total darkness of the link, the staging of this tape has an effect nonetheless, because it displaces the one by questioning him, just as it forces us to conceptualize the boundaries separating me from you. Perhaps this is the unforseen dark detour of syncope, that "lets the viewer's fantasy infiltrate," as Clément observes.[27]

---

24. Sigmund Freud, "Group Psychology and the Analysis of the Ego," translated by James Strachey, New York: Bantam Books, 1960, p. 47.

25. Mikkel Borch-Jacobsen, *The Freudian Subject*, translated by Catherine Porter, Stanford, California: Stanford University Press, 1988, p. 118.

26. The "dialectic" of attraction and repulsion, Hegel's in particular, is always resolved in an attraction. Catherine Clément notes that "Hegel thinks the unthinkable and knows it... The dialectical passage in which Hegel elaborates on the functioning of repulsion and attraction is located exactly where we can hope for a jolt, a suspension, a hesitation. But the hiccup, if it occurs, immediately reabsorbs what it has regurgitated. No expulsion is complete." (Our translation.) In philosophical discourse, the concept of syncope tends to be closer to Nietzsche's position, in which music exerts an influence on philosophy. See Clément, pp. 123-37.

INSTALLATIONS: SYNCOPAL LINKS ALONG MY PATH
THE MORE I TURN, THE MORE I'M JOLTED

Ever since Daniel Dion began creating video installations in which the viewer's path plays a central role, the scope and potential of the syncopal link has been identified with greater precision. Viewers have been interacting with Dion's videotapes since 1980, the year he produced *Système des beaux-arts/System of Fine Arts*, but his installations take on an added dimension: here the viewer is no longer just a viewer, and syncope occurs not just in the seeing process.

The syncopal link is influenced by a spirituality at work here, but the link also exerts an influence on a spirituality that develops along the path. Particularly from Dion's 1988 installation *Anicca* onwards, the link has been strongly associated with Buddhist spiritual philosophy, in which the search for syncope is viewed in much more radical terms: thought is regarded as a fire within the person. To pass into the "Asian abyss," writes Catherine Clément, is to "accept the understanding" that contestation of the world can be based on a negativity developed by the "monstrous dispossession of the subject: submission, dereliction, ultimate destruction, in favour of another value: order, fusion, finally, the cycle."[28]

As we follow the path through Dion's installations, we observe the renewal of this cycle arising out of Buddhist negativity. It is through this cycle that syncope becomes a specific action that not only affects my seeing process, but also has a profound effect on my body and mind. Syncope? It spiritually affects my bodily thoughts. If we already experience this expansion, this spiritual, physical, and mental reopening, as we watch certain of Dion's videotapes, such as *Système des beaux-arts/System of Fine Arts, À propos peinture,* and *Great Divide/Grande barrière*, it's because two Dion installations, *Tree Quadrilogues* and *La minute de vérité*, may be said to be having a retroactive impact on his earlier work. Let's re-examine syncope in the light of these installations.

The video installation *Tree Quadrilogues* (1991) jolts the viewer. A single video sequence is repeatedly screened on four monitors that form a central square. I gradually enter the circle, proceeding along the path in fits and starts, jolted by the four monitors. My perception is just as erratic. The single video sequence jolts me as well, for it has been fragmented into 16 series of 16-second shots, each series repeatedly and simultaneously presenting four shots, separated by the four screens. I fitfully tread the path, my perception jolted by an installation based on a fourfold

27. Clément, p. 136 (our translation).
28. Clément, p. 226 (our translation).

logic. Ultimately, the jolting allows me to distinguish each of the four elements included in the diverse systems represented here by superimposed words and images illustrating symbols and concepts drawn from various cultures.

Tree Quadrilogues incites us to entertain the notion that the subject attains knowledge by compartmentalizing (analytically or spiritually) its object; and that the representation, in fact, develops through this disjunctive classification. The fourfold systems presented in this installation reveal a world view based on division. The four seasons, the four elements, the four points of the compass, the four times of the day, Monet's four cathedrals, the four apostles of the New Testament, and so on. This division-based approach is not exclusively Occidental, since *Tree Quadrilogues* also presents the fourfold logic that underlies Oriental systems: the four ends of human life in Hinduism, the four behavioural maxims of Tibetan Buddhism, the four spiritual levels of the cycle of life (also found in Buddhism), the four rivers of India, etc.

Tree Quadrilogues takes us down a path where we equate knowledge, even spirituality, with division and classification, thus developing our spiritual rapport with the world. We are exposed to a spirituality whose fourfold differences, whether conceptual, cultural, or geographic, affect one another by the interweaving and breakdown of boundaries. How is this achieved? By a video installation that needs me to interact with it, that urges me (a contingent incitement, desired but not obligatory) to move around the square, first at a remove, and then within its sphere of influence.

Proceeding along this inner path, as the viewer moves back and forth in order to see the images on the four separate screens, the sounds and images — punctuating the video sequence and presented in repeated cycles — link together.

Why do the fourfold differences affect one another? Because the path puts me in a daze. These mental and physical shifts drain my body and my consciousness. I'm finally exhausted, and only then do the fits and starts affect me, bringing about my sudden fall. The fits and starts that slip in here and there between each partition of the square, between the monitors, between the shots, between the images, between the fourfold divisions — these fits and starts implicitly pave the way for a fall, my fall, the fall of the self, the fall of what divides, separated and classifies, the fall of knowledge. When I'm stunned to the point that I'm ready to faint, when the fourfold distinctions drop away, when they affect and reach one another, that's when I've lost (not consciousness, but) cognizance. Through this loss, *Tree Quadrilogues* becomes — is— All One. In other words, neither one, nor two, nor three, nor four. After this experience of syncope, after these fits and starts, knowledge will never be quite the same. The clearly defined boundaries will never be in quite the same place.

In a sense, the installation resembles and imitates the prayer wheels shown toward the end of the tape, the rotating cylinders around which Buddhist monks or disciples take their circular walk, a form of meditation, in an attempt to reach a state of spiritual syncope through the elimination of consciousness. When *Tree Quadrilogues* was first presented at Quebec City's Obscure gallery, [29] the four monitors were attached to a central post, thereby creating a circular path for the viewer, not unlike that of the Buddhist monks. The column served as an architectural bar, transforming the prayer wheels into objects, and adding a third dimension to the bar in *Great Divide/Grande barrière*. Hasn't the bar, the dark space, the in-between, always been spiritual? Hasn't it always captured my thoughts, affected my way of looking at the world, transforming it into an activity that cannot be separated from my physical movements?

The installation *La minute de vérité* (1991), co-directed with Su Schnee, introduces a significant new technique, the video *watchman*, which more fully integrates my repeated fits and starts as I follow the installation's path. Owing to this telecommunications apparatus, whose raison d'être lies in portability, my syncope, my fits and starts comprise a series of smaller, "telecommunicational fits and starts" that move along with me as I take them through my environment. These mini-jolts continually displace me, transport me, and my environment as well.

But we had better not go too fast because *La minute de vérité* actually times our journey, both literally (we hear ticking) and structurally; at the end of one *minute de vérité*, one moment of truth (a truth that still escapes me), the video goes back to the beginning, in an eternal cycle, reflecting the message continually repeated in the voice-off, right to the last moments of the sequence: "Seventy-seven billion human beings have lived on this planet."

Jolts. Breakdown. Punctuation. Can I relate to the world through this very point that paves the way for my fall? At first glance, the installation is only a point in space. I must draw near if I am to capture some of the sounds and images. But the point offers (me) resistance, for I am a mere viewer, in the centre of this installation, and my sensorimotor system can adapt neither to the fleeting minute nor to the minutiae. Nor can I adapt to the water images of the first sequence: the close-up

---

29. The installation *Tree Quadrilogues* was first presented at the Obscure gallery in Quebec City, 28 November - 22 December 1991.

prevents me from seeing the entire expanse of water, removes it from its context. The camera examines it so closely that I can hardly identify it. The fits and starts make it all the more difficult to interpret the picture, because I'm doubly interrupted by the superimposed electronic images, which are constantly stopping, and which are set into constant motion by the fades. To ensure that the message continually repeated in the voice-off is remembered, *La minute de vérité* puts me under a hypnotic trance, making me drowsy and gradually robbing me of my consciousness, powers of observation, sense of distance. This is when the moment of syncope, the "subject's absence," a "cerebral eclipse" occurs.[30] A true moment of syncope, although I (the viewer) am controlled and directed by a voice that causes me not to lose consciousness but to instrumentalize this consciousness, through my rejection (abjection).

In the next sequence, we see a change in perspective as the video moves away from this initial controlled syncope, for soon the camera's field of vision expands and the movement shifts to the level of the objects represented. Now it is actually the tree branches that are moving in repeated fits and starts; the repetition is no longer electronically engineered. I can still identify objects in repeated motion in the third sequence, a camera captures a three-dimensional representation of a forest and penetrates it along a path punctuated by a series of jolts. A difficult path, almost blind in fact, similar to that of Catherine Clément's "ascetic," who lives in the heart of the forest, on the "edge of nothingness," passing from the village to the forest "in fits and starts."[31] In the forest, we feel as if we "can dream only if disrupted by sudden fainting fits, unpredictable jolts, to be analyzed only after they occur."[32]

What is this moment of truth if not a call for movement: the subject and the object are set into motion, the subject comes to know itself and the object as movement; what is it if not a moment of knowledge, attained in small jolts that refine the viewer's sensorimotor system. With each new sequence we identify the images more clearly, so that we start with a hypnosis-induced, two-dimensional perception of mere fragments, and move to a perception in which the body fitfully interacts with the environment. This identification is transformed into an act of knowledge, unleashed by the viewer's fits and starts while penetrating the forest, on a path punctuated by a series of jolts that could lead to a series of falls.

The video *watchman*, a recent telecommunications innovation which, because of its size and portability, can be used anywhere the viewer may be, can integrate with

30. Clément, p. 11 (our translation).
31. Clément, p.p. 261 and 271 (our translation).
32. Clément, p. 271 (our translation).

(and punctuate) my movements, my social interactions, my private affairs, my wanderings, and my bodily thoughts. More precisely: the video *watchman* can punctuate my life with its syncope. Whereas Marshall McLuhan viewed television as the means of achieving a global village, Daniel Dion seeks the global by creating a video installation that replaces the village with the forest, which, in turn, becomes a village constructed out of noise.

If *Tree Quadrilogues* and *La minute de vérité* cause me to see, feel, and move in fits and starts, if the "one" is ultimately affected by an incessant, mind-boggling "Where am I?," it is because Daniel Dion's video art is constantly transforming itself. Each new work testifies to this transition. Punctuating, spiritualizing, jolting, reopening from one work to the next. Sometimes intelevisual in its seeing process, sometimes characterized by inverted rejection (abjection), stroke-by-stroke perception, a double bar, a cyclical path — or an electronic jolt, punctuating my movements wherever I go — his video works provide the link, always implicit, always with a difference that ultimately makes an impact, through a transformation of sameness. This is what syncope is all about: as soon as we think we've named it, it no longer exists, it's no longer one. When syncope prevails, the look is always too late, and the object always out of reach.

UTOPIAS OF RESISTANCE

STRATEGIES OF CULTURAL SELF-DETERMINATION

by Dot Tuer

Lisa Steele's and Kim Tomczak's collaborative work, dating back to their intensely personal exchange on the politics of sexual imagery, *In the Dark* (1983),[1] has often been described as didactic in outlook.[2] While the dictionary meaning of didactic, "having the manner of a teacher,"[3] may tell us something of the artists' intent, it reveals little of the processes and context that inform Steele's and Tomczak's conscious choice to engage video as a medium of persuasion. And as a blanket adjective meant to insinuate the inflexibility of a political agenda, a common and pejorative misuse of the term in North America, the term didactic serves only to mask a nexus of critical issues that underlies a veneer of transparency. Steele's and Tomczak's decision to work together clearly signals a movement away from the formalist and subjective concerns evident in their individual works, a movement toward a cognizance of television's overwhelming influence in a media-saturated economy of images. This shift toward an overtly political examination of representational values is not simply a polemical act of denouncing the mass media as "profoundly conservative."[4] Juxtaposing the idealization of dominant culture with the idealization of an alternative vision, Steele's and Tomczak's collective efforts also seek to simultaneously deconstruct and reconstruct an infrastructure of mediation.

1. *In the Dark*, first performed in 1983, presented a videotape of the artists making love while they, their backs turned to the audience, exchange a live dialogue examining issues of sexual representation. At the end of the tape, the artists turn to face the audience, revealing themselves as the lovers on the tape, and engage the audience in a dialogue. *In the Dark* is discussed by Steele and Tomczak at some length in an interview with Sara Diamond published in *Video Guide*.

2. Tim Guest, reviewing *Working the Double Shift* in Vanguard (October 1984), described Lisa Steele's and Kim Tomczak's intention to communicate "an uncomplicated political picture, one which was unabashedly didactic." Marusia Bociurkiw, in *Video Guide*, also describes Steele's and Tomczak's approach as "unabashed didacticism." In addition, the artists articulated their conscious decision to work didactically in an informal interview with the author.

3. *The Concise Oxford Dictionary of Current English*, Oxford, Clarendon Press, 1951.

4. In *Working the Double Shift* , Lisa Steele and Kim Tomczak end the video with a written text on the screen that reads: "The media culture is dominant. We cannot insert ourselves into it easily. It does not fill our free time neutrally. It is ideology. It represents society as static. It is profoundly conservative. It is sexist, heterosexist, racist, classist, and patriarchal propaganda. Representations of those values dominate. Representations of our lives are, most often, invisible. Representations of our values are absent."

Whether Steele and Tomczak are analyzing the effects of mass media, censorship, or free trade on the production and dissemination of culture, the structure of their investigation is predicated upon a tension between what is and what is possible. The exposure of dominant representation as an ontology of lies does not lead to the mimetic strategy of creating a brave new world of truth, an attempt to beat television at its own game by mirroring its constructions but changing the content. Rather, Steele and Tomczak offer the viewer an intricate negotiation between reality and fantasy, an ideological landscape that is less didactic than utopian in perspective. They describe their process of collaboration as the development of a "mutual vocabulary."[5] Their language of synthesis inscribes a social vision of culture within a critique of existing conditions. Their collective efforts claim a territory where positionality is no longer subjective but activist and chart a course of cultural opposition that is neither negative nor marginal in strategy. In so doing, they not only challenge a dominant system of false representation but re-invent the terms of a utopian imagination.

Classical in origin and literary in form, the utopian imagination has all but disappeared in the late twentieth century. Traditionally constructed as a description of a writer's own society "with its unconscious ritual habits transposed into their conscious equivalents,"[6] utopia has functioned as a speculative myth that presents an idealized vision of a social contract. From Plato's *Republic* to More's *Utopia* to Bellamy's *Looking Backwards*, the perfect society assembled from the raw material of a less-than-perfect world has also tended toward a static ideal: transposing a chaotic present into a rationalized future. With the advent of Freud's theories of the unconscious and Marx's scientific socialism, utopia's aspirations to enlightenment disintegrated into a labyrinth of libidinal desire and historical materialism. The search for a conscious expression of human interaction was no longer the domain of the philosophical imagination but a subject for psychoanalytical scrutiny. The rationalization of human behaviour was no longer a description of ritual but an object of industrial efficiency and experimental psychology. Once a speculative myth of an unattainable nowhere, the promise of an ideal society was suddenly everywhere: a site of revolutionary doctrine, the rhetoric of a capitalist system, the battleground of conflicting ideologies.

As the static conception of a utopian imagination became subsumed by social tensions, the representation of the utopian ideal became consumed by technological innovation. The allegory of the cave in the *The Republic*, used by Plato

5. Stated by Lisa Steele in an informal interview with the author.
6. Northrop Frye, "Varieties of Literary Utopias," in *Utopias and Utopian Thought*, ed. Frank E. Manuel (Boston: Beacon Press, 1965), 27.

to describe a world of appearances that obscured a knowledge of the real, no longer functioned to critique mimesis but to foreshadow a mediated "reality." The subjects of Plato's cave, chained and facing a wall, believed that the shadows of artificial objects cast from the light of a fire burning behind them were the objects themselves. Prisoners of false representation, these subjects could only recognize the shadows as distortions by ascending from the darkness of the cave to the sunlight above, achieving an understanding of the ideal through a hierarchical process of philosophical reflection.[7] But as the mechanical means of reproduction transformed primitive shadow-plays into cinematic documentation, the platonic distinction between appearance and the real began to blur. Within an infrastructure of mediation where perfect copies of reality became the mirror reflections of society, there was no longer an exit from the world of mimesis. A technological imperative had forever disrupted the higher order of the ideal. We had all become subjects of the cave — subjects of an invisible machine of projections and identifications.

With the collapse of utopian space into the spectre of a totalizing technology, the body became the site of a conflation between the ideal and the real. The ritual habits of a society were revealed as a tangled web of transference and fetishization. Consciousness became a screen that masked the split between the object and the subject in the construction of an ideal ego. Utopian imagination, no longer capable of responding to this complex grid of illusion and delusion, gave way to an imagination of the psychotic. In Victor Tausk's clinical study "On the Origin of the 'Influencing Machine in Schizophrenia'," written in 1918, the invisible machine of mediation becomes externalized as the lived experience of paranoia. His patients suffer from the effects of a machine of a mystical nature which functions as a magic lantern, a surveillance system, a suggestion apparatus, or a controlling mechanism. Operated by enemies, this machine makes its subjects see pictures, produces and removes feelings and thoughts, produces bodily reactions and sensations, and, in its most extreme manifestations, absorbs the body into its two-dimensional plane. Patients endeavour to explain its functions by means of technical knowledge but "all the discoveries of mankind, however, are regarded as inadequate to explain the marvellous powers of this machine."[8]

Seventy years later, the impenetrable superstructure of the influencing machine seems less the hallucinatory delusion of the schizophrenic than a metaphor for a contemporary infrastructure of mediation. In a global village of satellite

7. *The Republic of Plato*, trans. Francis MacDonald Conford (Oxford: Oxford University Press, 1945), 227-235.

8. Victor Tausk, "On the Origin of the 'Influencing Machine in Schizophrenia,'" *Psychoanalytical Quarterly* 2 (1933): 521.

transmissions and telecommunication systems, it is not only the body but the body politic that has been absorbed into the anonymous abstractions of a technological imperative. Video cameras monitor movements in the subway, the bank machine, the shopping malls, and the concourses of commerce. Images from newspapers, billboards, magazines, and television modify behaviour. The instantaneous projections of mass media idealize social relations, commodify ritual. In a postmodern society, utopia becomes a ruse of late capitalism in which a fictional world of representation is constructed from the distance between mediation and the mechanisms of its dissemination. The lives of the rich and famous become the fantasy projections of dominant values. Advertising peddles utopia as a dream to be bought on credit. Consumers of these fictions, we become the uneasy conductors of an ideological overdetermination. Utopia becomes a social vision frozen out of time and place, contained by the flickering images of a television screen where the fantasies of the ideal blend imperceptibly with simulations of the real.

As technology plays out this endgame with representation, a utopian strategy can no longer disavow the influence of this invisible machine. Utopia can no longer be conceptualized outside of the totalizing narratives of the mass media. The paradox of postmodernism, which simultaneously functions to produce a dynamic technology and a static ideology, has created from the raw material of reality a hegemonic ideal. To imagine oneself outside the shifting territory of this simulacrum, as a philosopher freed from the false representation of Plato's cave, does not resolve the paradox but exacerbates the tensions. Literary classics of the twentieth century that have adopted a utopian model no longer offer an idealized vision of a social contract but a negative mirror of mediation. In the late twentieth century, utopia becomes dystopia: a nightmarish prediction of a world gone mad with manipulation. In Orwell's *1984*, Huxley's *Brave New World*, and Atwood's *The Handmaid's Tale*, the influencing machine's absolute power extends from the psychotic to an entire social fabric. The unconscious rituals of a contemporary society become the breeding grounds of totalitarian politics and mass terror; the postmodern condition becomes one of paranoia and persecution.

As video artists, Steele and Tomczak refuse to surrender the territory of the ideal to dominant representation; they refuse to capitulate to the paranoid fantasies of a dystopian future. Utilizing a new medium of technology as a tool of cultural expression, they do not disavow the influence of the invisible machine. But neither do they attribute to the totalizing narratives of the mass media an impenetrable infrastructure. Rather, they propose a strategy of infiltration whereby they rewrite the script of dominant ideology and subvert the mythologies of mass culture.

Juxtaposing the already idealized images of television with their own idealizations of an alternative culture, they insist upon the potential for mediated reality to reflect the dynamics of social change rather than the static fantasy of a commodity capitalism. The body politic is no longer the anonymous abstraction of a technological imperative but the territory of a political activism. Within an infrastructure of mediation in which a surplus of images has created a scarcity of alternative models, Steele and Tomczak propose to re-invent the terms of the utopian imagination as a dialectic between lived experience and collective vision.

In Plato's *Republic*, artists were banished from the ideal state for mimetic practices that distorted the relationship of knowledge to the real. For Steele and Tomczak it is the artist rather than the philosopher who challenges an economy of false representation. In each of the four collaborative videotapes that Steele and Tomczak have produced over the last five years (*Working the Double Shift, See Evil, Private Eyes,* and *White Dawn*), the role of the artist becomes one of critical reflection and cultural intervention. Access to the medium as the message becomes access to a technology that can alter the inner workings of the influencing machine. Deciphering the signifying apparatus of representation in order to reconstruct mediation as an infrastructure of participation, Steele and Tomczak insist upon the potential of the artist to engage cultural production as an exercise in cultural transformation. As founding members of the Independent Artists' Union in Toronto, Steele and Tomczak contextualize an idealized future as a realization of artists' contemporary commitment to challenge the values of dominant media. The stated platform of the Independent Artists' Union, which, in 1986, called for a recognition of cultural production as the "social right of all people"9 and for an understanding of art as work rather than as a form of privileged leisure, finds its echo in their utopian vision of a visual democracy.

In opposition to the utopia of dominant representation that is everywhere and nowhere, Steele and Tomczak propose a utopia that is specific to a local art community, weaving a fabric of imagined possibilities from the collective struggles of the present. "The Phantasy Projection" segment of *Working the Double Shift* (1984), in which documentary footage of a parliamentary vote becomes a visual backdrop to a description of a Canadian revolution, cites the strong presence of artists, or cultural workers, in bringing about historical change. The concern of the Artists' Union is inscribed into an image of the future where media is decentralized, industry is nationalized, and full cultural and political representation is granted to all sectors of Canadian society. The demands of the Independent Artists' Union for a

9. *The Social and Economic Status of the Artist in English Canada*, working paper prepared by the Strategy Committee of the Toronto local of the IAU, (May 1986), 1.

guaranteed annual income that reflects the diversity of regional, black, native, ethnic, and women's communities is translated into an ideal vision of cultural autonomy in Steele and Tomczak's tape. Similarly, in *Private Eyes* (1987), the dramatic corporate takeover of a public art gallery is halted, not by the cast of fictional characters, "the heroic curator, the bewildered but converted gallery employee, the dedicated newscaster," but by the intervention of identifiable Toronto artists. Entering the soap opera drama as real-life figures, the artists work collectively to infiltrate the infrastructure of the museum and alter the relationship of the institution to the producer.

Intertwining the documentation of a politicized present with a utopian vision of a politicized future, Steele and Tomczak are able to construct a strategy of active resistance within an already idealized space of mediation. Juxtaposing analyses of dominant representation with an alternative model of cultural self-determination in their work, Steele and Tomczak suggest that the paradox of a dynamic technology and a static ideology in the postmodernist condition does not inevitably lead to a dystopia of mass alienation and massive manipulation. For Steele and Tomczak, it is not enough to disentangle the conflation of the ideal and the real, to expose the collusion of state and ideology through an examination of censorship in *See Evil* (1985), to reveal the collusion of media and ideology in an examination of the family in *Working the Double Shift*. It is not enough to ask questions, to ask, as the child does in *Working the Double Shift*, "Whose turn is it to get up in the morning?" It is not enough to answer the child by example alone. In the videotapes of Steele and Tomczak, the artist is positioned as a cultural worker whose interventions seek to narrow the distance between mediation and the mechanisms of its dissemination; whose challenges to the "sexist, heterosexist, racist, classist and patriarchical propaganda" of a media culture are constructed through political alliances and collective action.

To do otherwise is to fall prey to the paranoia of the invisible machine; to wake up one morning to discover that we "don't know [our] reality from their fantasy." It is to awake as if from a dream, awake to a *White Dawn* (1987-88) where the marketplace has eroded the "values which should prevail in a nation's cultural life."[10] It is to experience, as the narrator in Steele's and Tomczak's most recent videotape, the shock of a colonial oppression; it is to discover in the free trade agreement with the United States a dystopia of the present. Inverting the technological imperialism of the American empire, Steele and Tomczak create in *White Dawn* an imaginary scenario in which *Vogue* and *Time* can only be bought at

10. *Ibid*, 3.

specialty stores, the lifting of content rules has meant that Anne Murray has replaced Bruce Springsteen on commercial radio, and American classics can only be found in the foreign literature section of bookstores and libraries. As a satire on the contemporary climate in Canada of privatization, funding cutbacks, and corporate sponsorships of the arts, *White Dawn* warns of the consequences that will result from abandoning the utopian model of cultural self-determination. The tape emphasizes the need to confront the fantasy projections of late capitalism with demands for political and cultural representation for all Canadian communities. If we are not to be engulfed by our own absences within an infrastructure of mediation, we must begin to imagine that art is not a dream of alienation but a reflection of the lived realities and collective vision. We must begin to believe

> That which is utopian
> is not that which is unattainable;
> it is not idealism;
> it is a dialectical process of
> denouncing and announcing;
> denouncing the dehumanizing structure
> and announcing the humanizing structure.[11]

11. Paulo Freire, quoted by Luis Ramiro Beltran in *Farewell to Aristotle: Horizontal Communication*, a document prepared for the International Commission for the Study of Communication Problems, no. 48, in application of Resolution 100 adopted by the General Conference of UNESCO at its nineteenth session.

THE SITE OF MEMORY

by Larissa Lai

The smell of burning joss sticks brings back a very specific memory for me: visiting my grandmother's house on my first trip to Hong Kong at the age of five. It is closely related to the smell of burning mosquito coil, which drops a spiral of ashes onto the table while sending a spiral of smoke to heaven. Feelings and memories catalysed are quite distinct from those triggered by other incense aromas: jasmine, sandalwood, tisia tsiang, flying fairy, rose, musk, cinnamon. The smell of joss sticks has found its own particular location through the ordering and categorizing of memory that takes place somewhere within the human body. It fills the nose, seeps past the lips, enters through the pores, infuses the hair. And memory wells up from somewhere inside.

The meaning of the smell is as precise as words but still more personal. While a single word may mean a range of things depending on the speaker and the listener or the reader and the writer, the meaning of a smell varies infinitely more. Memories conjured by smell are specific to the lives of the people who inhale it; and not only are smells personally specific, they are culturally specific. The fragrance of joss sticks may have sparked intimate personal memories for other people present at Paul Wong's two-part presentation for the exhibition *As Public as Race* at the Walter Phillips Gallery in Banff, memories of people not present, memories of past occasions, festivals, parades, quiet moments for the paying of respect.

The site of memory, the address, as in the computer's memory, the sites inside the body where the memory resides: heart, belly, brain, the nervous system. The site of memory, as in the monuments of remembrance, grave sites, sites of grief, sites of grieving. A historical monument to memory, as in the naming of a mountain. The technologically produced sites of memory, as in snap shots and home video. The surrounding territory, the hillside, the valley, trees, rivers, settlements such as Anthracite, where Chinese-Canadian miners laboured earlier this century, the hotels in and around Banff where they worked as cooks and waiters, the market gardens where they grew and sold fresh vegetables. Mourning, the territory which surrounds death.

As presented at the Banff Centre, Paul Wongs's act of memory consisted of a forty-five minute video, *Chinaman's Peak*, broadcast from a single source to all the Centre's information monitors, followed by a gathering in the atrium of Glyde Hall, the starting point of *Walking the Mountain*, a ritual in which the public could participate.[1] The broadcast component itself becomes a site of memory — but the site is not the location of the monitors because those are, in a certain sense, arbitrary. Also, they are not the source of the broadcast. Indeed, there is no public access to the site (a control room) from which the signal originates, nor to the tape itself, which can only be read and interpreted electronically by the videotape recorder. Yet many people can watch it, observe it as a loose narrative, concrete image, dialogue. It exists among and between viewers like an invisible cloud that permeates each room and the consciousness of the viewers. This site of memory is not a precise geographic location. As it takes on a life of its own, outside this particular screening, it becomes a site within particular contexts, shifting location and meaning, as the audience changes.

Chinaman's Peak itself is not really a precise geographic feature either. While locals may know it as one of the less spectacular peaks that surround Canmore, a town twenty minutes from Banff, Paul Wong's broadcast piece transforms it into a site that is at once mythical and historical. It stands as a marker for the history of Chinese miners in the area, as well as a sign of the mining industry's racist past. It also stands as a marker for the Chinese railway workers although metaphorically, perhaps, since their "last spike" was hammered in on the other side of the Alberta/British Columbia border (1885, Craigellachie, British Columbia).

But actually, where the peak is and what it looks like are merely incidental. At the beginning of the tape, a number of local residents and visitors present conflicting "truths" about Chinaman's Peak — how it got its name and who the "Chinaman" was. In the end, nobody knows for sure and none of the stories are true, or else they all are. However, they do ascertain the presence of many Chinese in the area at a time in history when there was much hard labour to be had for low pay. This is a sharp contrast to the current presence of Chinese in Banff. Although only one or two of the old families remain, there are many Cantonese-speaking tourists from Hong Kong or perhaps Richmond or Vancouver or Calgary or Toronto. There are also many Japanese tourists in Banff, a town that is not too far from the camps in which Japanese-Canadians were interned during the Second World War. This is not to

---

1. At *Image and Nation*, the Gay and Lesbian Film and Video Festival in Montreal, it is presented as a video work; at the Contemporary Art Gallery in Vancouver, the video becomes part of a multimedia installation of the same name.

imply that racism has ceased to exist in the area, only that the stereotype of Asians has switched from people having not enough money to having too much.

The rumours about Chinaman's Peak, for example, that it is named after a miner who committed suicide by jumping off it, also expose the racist treatment meted out by the contractors and others in positions of power during the building of the railway and intensive mining activity that followed. Further evidence of that racism is provided through a slow scan of a record book from one of the mines, in which all miners are listed alphabetically by surname except for the Chinese who are placed in a separate part of the book under the heading "Chinamen" or "Chinks." Their names are scrawled underneath, sometimes in Chinese characters, sometimes in their romanized form, sometimes marked by an X — traces of history, the thin lines of evidence for whole life stories lost or buried in the mines. The only narrative history to be retrieved from these sparse artifacts is a history that is made up, a history that hangs in the air, given life through imagination and yet, for all that, is real and painful.

A black and white photo-portrait of Paul Speed, taken a few months or maybe a year before his death in 1991 sits on the altar that Wong has constructed in his studio at the Banff Centre, near a photo of his father, a few human bones, a "chinky" vase, two kitschy statuettes, and an assortment of items necessary for *bi san*, paying one's respect to the dead. Photograph. Snap. A momentary repository of memory. What changes in a photograph when the person whose image it has preserved passes away? What lingers? The same questions might be asked about home video. Is the moment it captures merely longer? Video, a life-like doll, smiles, walks in and out of rooms, looking too much like, painfully too much like the person whose memory it conjures. After the moment of death, what has changed in these images? The naïveté of the moment at which they were taken? Suddenly there is a painful longing where there might have been before only cheerful remembrance. As a videotape, the act of remembrance itself becomes a sort of artifact, infinitely repeatable, infinitely engaged in memory.

For whom are the rituals of remembrance performed, the living or the dead? Or both, in a symbiotic relationship with one another? The eye of the camera makes a ritual journey in search of the grave. The feel of the earth, a pair of hands throwing an urn to be used as a container for the ashes of the deceased. Clay body, the fleshy feel of the substance, as though it were alive. Growing in sure circles into the shape of a pot. Fire to purge, to destroy in a slow flash of orange beauty or, in this case, fire to strengthen the walls of the urn, or give it the gift of eternity where otherwise it would shatter and crumble. A gift not bestowed upon the body, the remnants of which the urn will contain.

The transformative power of fire is echoed in the ritual of *haang san* (walking the mountain), or *bi san* (worshipping the mountain), depending upon one's province of origin, in which representations of material goods are burned in order to convey them to the other world, where they may be used by the dead. This, in fact, is how the ancestors maintain their well-being and status in the spirit world. Without descendants to worship and burn paper (representations of) goods for their use, they go hungry and naked, wandering above the world as "hungry ghosts." The paper goods, once transformed into smoke, take on the qualities of reality for the dead. Whether or not they become "real" depends on whether or not one thinks of the dead as real. For some, their existence is an absolute truth, for others, a suspicion to be believed only at appropriate moments. The *haang san* ritual is the crux of Wong's piece although, due to regulations in Banff National Park, no fires could be burned on the hillside during this part of the performance.

The transformative nature of fire means different things depending upon whether the context is Christianity or ancestral worship. The English translation on the paper money destined for use by the dead is "hell dollars," hearkening back, I presume, to the influence of the Jesuit missionaries in the seventeenth century who attempted to convert the Chinese from their heathen practices. The reference to hell, of course, assumes that a Chinese (non-Christian) afterlife can take place only in a Eurocentric, Christian concept of hell, the opposite of (and supposedly only possible alternative to) a Christian heaven. Although western contemporary art may be considered quite removed from any traditional Christian practice, the fact remains that western art history is deeply embedded in this religious context because that practice has evolved from it. The presence of fire in *Chinaman's Peak* opens the possibilities for a different kind of afterworld, one which is created and maintained by each individual mourner who nevertheless remains part of a larger whole.

With regard particularly to the rituals involving fire, incense and walking the mountain, I remark to Paul Wong that the danger of exotification veers perilously close. In the context of performance art, with its Eurocentric basis, the threat is very real. Who is this for? Both within a Eurocentric practice and outside of it, we have a need to incorporate Asian practices at the same time as altering them to suit the situation, at the same time as protecting them. To bring our own family practices to our new home, within white mainstream institutions, reclaims that space. But in a context in which we and our practices have been exoticized, appropriated, mystified and misrepresented, we still have to worry about how that work may be read.

I have always thought, being Chinese in the diaspora, that becoming a "hungry ghost" might pose a real danger. Who knows which children, if any, will remember these rituals if my own generation does not reclaim them for the future here in North America. It must have been a fear shared by the miners and railway workers as well and was certainly the reason why, every so often, bones would be collected and shipped back to China where the dead could be cared for in the afterlife by their living families. For those whose bones might have been left behind, perhaps buried in the mines or beside the train tracks, Wong burns a suit of clothes. He remarks that in many families, the dead are remembered regularly at family gatherings and many festivals, not just those intended expressly for that purpose. The dead continue to have a place in the world of the living. In that sense, they are never really "lost" or "gone," merely transformed, the way fire transforms goods so that the dead can access them.

The ritual of *bi san* is an act of remembering, of bringing back, in the way that video and photographs also retrieve; a sense of the person, a dab of their essence, comes closer for an instant before returning to the spirit world. *Bi san* turns away from the finality of the coffin and tombstone. The cold, hard silence of death is replaced by heat, warmth, light, noise, motion, the sound of firecrackers, the smell of incense and the food which is presented for the deceased and shared at graveside.

Chinaman's Peak is full of references to others in the artist's life and includes the ghosts of other works. For Paul Wong, who has been making videos since the seventies, video practice is deeply entwined with the memories of the living and the dead, resulting in many parallels between life and video "fiction." A survey of the names on the urns in Wong's performance calls to mind not only people but also videos from the past.

Hoy Ming Wong's urn, dedicated to Paul's father, brings to mind *Ordinary Shadows, Chinese Shade* (1988), particularly a section entitled "Walking the Mountain" in which a visit is paid to the grave site of Paul's ancestors. As the mourner remembers Ken Fletcher, who died in 1978, *60 Unit Bruise* is called to mind. In that tape, sixty cubic centimetres of blood are taken from Ken Fletcher's arm and injected into Paul Wong's back, slowly spreading into a large purple bruise. (It is now terrifying to watch this tape, made in 1976, in the midst of the AIDS crisis.) In *in ten sity* (1978), made after Fletcher's death and dedicated to him, Wong smashes his body back and forth against the inside walls of a large, modernist cube, as the Sex Pistols blast and spectators spit and throw garbage in over the top. An immediate and violent kind of mourning. In contrast, the careful placing of oranges, lighting of incense, pouring of scotch, paying of respect in *Chinaman's Peak* at once puts those raw events into the past and yet draws them into the everyday life of the present, as memory which keeps moving and changing. Bottle rockets and firecrackers, a bang to remember the violence of the punk era and to remember that those events are not really over, that death happens again. Check the birth dates: Ken Fletcher 1954-1978, Paul Speed 1967-1991. They died in different years, at the same age: twenty four.

At the Bell Canada Award ceremony in 1992, where Wong was the guest of honour, a series of video clips spanning Wong's eighteen years of production was presented. The retrospective contains images from a work-in-progress entitled *So Are You*, which features a dramatization of a funeral. Paul Speed, dressed in a black suit, lies in a coffin, a dramatic and awful prophecy. Keyed over the image, another Paul Speed looks at this image as if looking into a mirror or, as Narcissus, looking into the water and seeing himself. At the grave site in *Chinaman's Peak*, a magazine cut-out of a red Porsche is burned, so that Speed can drive it in the spirit world. An echo. He drives a red Porsche in *So Are You*. His date tells a bad Chinaman joke as the Asian valet takes the keys. As he receives his Porsche in the spirit world, does he look at his funeral again? If he does, it isn't the glossy, sweet denial of an ordinary western funeral, but one which remembers the issues dealt with in *So Are You,* from Chinaman dolls bobbing their heads, to white boys driving Porsches, to his own death, reflected back at him as by the Narcissus' pool.

An urn dedicated to an unknown man... a railway worker, a miner, a ghost of someone never having returned to China, who perhaps still wanders. Close to here an unknown man, perhaps the artist himself who, lately, has been featured in his own videos, hidden behind the camera or shot in such a way that his identity is never certain and the recognition of that identity is never central to the meaning of the work. Remembering the unknown is also an acknowledgement of how much of our history remains unwritten.

In the atrium of Glyde Hall, the starting point for *Walking the Mountain*, all the objects related to Wong's ritual are laid out: a bright red coffin, coolie hats, little "chinaman" dolls (racist representations of the Chinese that nevertheless are cheesy enough to be amusing in an "off" sort of way), baskets of paper clothes, hell dollars, large and small incense sticks, oranges, white fabric banners painted with Chinese characters saying "You are a good spirit" and "Your spirit will always be remembered" (white is the colour of death; these slogans are commonly used at funerals), photographs of Paul Speed and Hoy Ming Wong — all the material trappings necessary for the ritual of walking the mountain. There is a direct connection between the material world and the spirit world: the sound of firecrackers and bottle rockets going off, the smell of incense finding its way into everything, the steamed buns and rice wine shared among the living and the dead, all these material things or their effects moving through our bodies, moving between the earth and the spirit world, tactile, sweet, pungent and loud. The connection is regularly reinforced through the enactment of ritual. The whole body is involved in the act of remembering.

STORIES IN RESERVE

by Nicole Gingras

Michèle Waquant is one of the few Quebec artists who can move with equal ease from painting to photography, from photography to video, while pursuing her reflections on time and creating a repertoire of images and spaces inviting contemplation.

For more than fifteen years, whether in collaborative projects or alone, Michèle Waquant has been engaging us in different experiences of the act of observation. Each time, the set-up is minimal and the artist focuses on everyday events, the kind of ordinary incidents one hardly notices. The following is an overview of her work.

The subjects are classic: a portrait of a woman — *Le portrait de Pauline* (1984); Sunday anglers beside a pond — *L'Étang* (1985); an apartment building seen from a window across the street — *212, rue du Faubourg St-Antoine* (1989). Michèle Waquant's tapes illustrate the difficulty in grasping a fleeting memory; they are based on waiting, a kind of floating, like the gaze that doesn't distinguish faces in a crowd — faces at once different and interchangeable, a look both distracted and attracted. Each tape bespeaks a personal mind-set towards time, an ability to let time pass, to remember and forget.

"My effort was in vain, now I can only see one thing at a time."

—*Malina*, Ingeborg Bachman

A STUDY IN DURATION

These tapes — so many involuntary witnesses — are constructed in waiting and invite us to unforeseeable incidents. They reveal closed spaces — a cage, an apartment, a park, where gestures are repeated out of habit and rituals are grounded in everyday life, in a certain state of forgetfulness, and boredom. Michèle Waquant draws attention to the tiny gaps that occur at the heart of mechanical gestures frozen by the daily, automatic repetition of the same actions: a wolf's direct gaze at the camera, an animal's reluctance to be captured in images, household chores, fishermen calmly waiting. A stationary camera focuses on an apparently ordinary action — wolves pacing back and forth, *Loups* (1982); the restless shuffling of caged bears, in loop, *A quoi rêvent les vieux ours?* (1982); a woman's body, variously framed, *Le portrait de Pauline*; hands gesturing in conversation, *Leurs*

mains/Their Hands (1987). The length of the takes gradually transforms the observed actions; we are drawn into appropriating their images.

Waiting gives way to ambivalence, hinting at the possibility of upsetting the balance inherent in a disturbingly static situation. What we see is suspense reduced to its simplest form of expression — the interruption of a seemingly static, stable situation, without drama, even without interest, resisting the terrorism of the urge to show/tell all.

Michèle Waquant's work proceeds from this tension between the strangely small and the infinitely big, as reflected both in the choice of events observed and the selection of sounds accompanying the images. Close-ups, reframing, and superimposing a static foreground on a moving background recur from tape to tape. Highlighting these refined esthetic choices, the artist sometimes chooses to blur surfaces, super-imposing several shots of images dissolving into graininess, and mixing several soundtracks. Oddly, the artist vacillates between pure sound/image and sound/image conceived as strata.

Waquant is well aware of the dreamlike power in reframing devices which, while limiting our view, suggest that a specific segment of landscape is noteworthy precisely for what is out of range. One need only recall the scenes of the St. Lawrence shot from its banks in *Les Bruits blancs* (1991). There is no traffic on the river — all we see is the current. A trawler slowly crosses the screen, literally crossing the space of the frame from left to right. It goes beyond the frame, presenting us once again with an *empty* frame. The length of the shot is determined by the trawler's passing through the image — the frame is filled and then emptied with the passage of time. In this way, the trawler acquires the status of a character. The viewer is drawn into an event dedramatized in time, literally emptied of its content. Surprised by what little there is to see, an observer is apt to be fascinated, summoned into a contemplative act.

> "Imagine a time segment of fifteen seconds. It's not a lot — but, it
> is a lot. It's an adequate measure. The way individual people use
> such a short space of time can suffice to differentiate their entire
> lives. A dreamer is not only someone who seems distracted,
> occasionally, during some episode in life, not making decisions, or
> fancying he's a horse — or a generalissimo. No. In every sequence
> of fifteen, or even five or six seconds, a real dreamer goes off into
> an extended meditation, carried along by floating debris, in a
> constant ebbing and flowing, unraveling, where nobody is
> directing, everything follows of itself, where everything is vague
> yet unavoidable. (...) Continually transported from moment to

moment, along a deviating path, captivated by an inclination for the fleeting moment, the dreamer is diverted by his naturally wandering attention. This has long-term consequences."

—*Poteaux d'angle*, Henri Michaux

ILLUSION OF A FILMED PHOTOGRAPH

Michèle Waquant gives time to her images, setting barely sketched fictions in an ideal frame. Her stories are constructed of "freezes", highlighting experiences related to memory and recall. *L'Étang* incorporates both photographs and long still shots of a pond on a Sunday. Here, the artist pursues a reflection on time passing, and also on the frame of the photo, the frame of the video camera, revealing the power exerted on reproduced images by what remains out of range. Waquant exploits photography's property to incite fascination, languour, and forgetfulness. Aware of the evocative power in images and atmospheres, conscious of the potential inherent in photography's mutism, she adds no commentary. Music counterbalances the passage of time, occasionally punctuated with ambient sounds happening that afternoon by the pond in a park. Long still takes of fishermen draw us into their wait; photographed images, a picture of a little girl in silhouette, are sequenced with filmed or photographed shots of the pond. This nostalgic video, while not focusing on past or traumatic events, is nevertheless redolent of melancholy, a feeling of time passing, a nostalgia without name or image. The pond becomes an ideal support for a contemplative state.

212, rue du Faubourg St-Antoine takes a look at the mundane as it extends before our eyes and gradually assumes surfaces and textures. This tape pursues the artist's longtime exploration of photographic strategies on the screen. Successive photographic effects disclose the tendency of surrounding spaces to become surfaces. Waquant observes the apartment building opposite her own flat, progressively leveling it out before our eyes. A woman shakes a carpet, washes her windows. There is little action — the slightest presence on the screen becomes entertaining. Anything serves as a pretext elliptically signaling the passage of time.

Michèle Waquant does not simply use photographic images but rather, she exploits photographic properties and modalities. Multiple images are superimposed; long, still takes of inanimate scenes create the illusion of filmed photographs, and freeze-frames enhance this effect. In *212, rue du Faubourg St-Antoine*, the video camera is used like a still camera to document the artist's immediate surroundings. One feels a will, a desire to flatten. Empty shots are charged with sound — layers of superimposed sounds from different sources — a radio, a tennis ball hit back and forth, gravel crunching underfoot.

EQUIVALENT SILENCE

Les Bruits blancs uses techniques similar to those in the previous tape, but this time on the soundtrack. The title refers to a quality of background audio produced by playing different sound frequencies at the same energy level, thus canceling out frequency variations and creating an equivalent of "silence". *Les Bruits blancs* is both an autonomous tape and a video environment comprising seven monitors, contrasting the artificial, mechanical movement of traffic on Paris' rim-boulevard with the slow movement of maritime traffic on the St. Lawrence River — two landscapes, two soundscapes, and apparently, two opposing kinds of movement. Nevertheless, these two differentiated spaces progressively acquire various affinities. The movement of the one evokes the immobility of the other, as if they were somehow inevitably similar. In this tape, the artist uses the canceling power of white noise, combining superimposed sounds and images. Once again, a leveling effect is produced over time. Here, the focus is on passing and flowing, as the spaces blend into each other. Whether proceeding from street traffic or water flowing, the movement provokes a dreamlike state in the viewer. Stimulated by the difficulty of concentrating on any single given point, the viewer is carried along on the drift of images and sounds.

MEMORY — A NAVEL-GAZING PROCESS

Each installation unfolds in time, whether *Les Bruits blancs* or *En attendant la pluie/ Waiting for the rain* (1987). Like another more recent sound and video environment on the spring ice-breakup in Quebec's Beauce region, these installations and autonomous tapes deal with the "in-between", both as a territory and a state or mood. The ice-breakup itself is associated with a time of extreme tension, when long-contained forces (voices) finally give way.

Around this impressive natural phenomenon converges the hope that the ice will move on, and the threat of destruction from the uncontrolled movement of these masses. Once again, the underlying theme is waiting, transformation, and ambivalence in expectation. Poised between paralysis and extreme mobility, *Impression Débâcle* (working title, 1992) speaks of rupture and disappearance.

In their own way, these tapes are all based on memory, and the way it operates as a process of self-absorption. The power of speech gradually gives way to the power of silence, even though the latter may be white noise. The length of the takes in time transforms public into intimate, as if the camera — adjusting to imperceptible transformations — induced a change of perceptions as events "become" before our eyes. Are the images fixed in time? Are they animated by the passing of time? The way the tapes are processed enhances the "becoming" of images and events. Caged animals become human, a building at a distance becomes surface, an animated friend becomes painting, a boulevard around Paris becomes river, ambient sounds become melody, the breakup becomes ice-floes. Fascinated by these events that transcend the anecdotal, refusing to tell stories, the artist incites us to observe by exerting the holding power of the image.

Translation by Jean-Luc Svoboda

STAN DOUGLAS:

EVENING AND OTHERS

by Peggy Gale

Stan Douglas works on a public stage, tuned to the world he sees: political, historical, intellectual. There is work to be done with the *out there*.

Evening of 1994 is a three-channel video installation work, a fiction aimed at fact for a moment of change in contemporary history. Just like television news, its apparent referent, the subtexts are numerous and complex. For what is more contentious than the *fact* quotient of television news today? At best, those few minutes allotted to a nightly overview of world developments are fragmentary and the choices subjective, a brief installment assuming or counting on supplementary (unspoken) previous information for filling in the larger issues. Viewers have become cynical these days, conscious of the slide towards infotainment and stations' reliance on simply *believable* news-anchor personalities.

It used to seem that The News was just a matter of information, a public service, the newscaster's formal reading manner denoting dispassionate, balanced consideration on the part of someone who had access to the whole story. Listening to the news was presumed to be a duty rather than a pleasure. Is this opinion today simply naive? We are now more often aware of *formula* in both form and content for news presentations. As in the newspapers, there are a few striking headlines with the important facts bunched together in the opening paragraphs, with a seemingly random collection of filler stories and notes further along, leading to sections devoted to sports, weather, market reports, advertisement. It all feels far more like *business* than any sort of public service. Different television stations — like different newspaper chains — are known for their greater interest in violence, their more generous use of photographs, or their preference for the local rather than a larger arena. But all are *selling* their newscasts, aiming to appeal to a public with choices to make.

In 1993 The Renaissance Society at the University of Chicago invited Douglas to create a new piece for his upcoming solo exhibition. Ideal. It was an opportunity to relate to events specific to Chicago and to media issues and history. In a preliminary visit for researching recent broadcast vernaculars and editorial policies in Chicago, Douglas came to focus on a unique moment which he saw as two "related crises in the legitimation of television news"[1]: the controversies surrounding the Democratic National Convention in August 1968 and the killing of local Black Panther Party leader Fred Hampton in December the following year. While up until this time newscasters had been considered objective "readers" or "reporters", now they were accused of (and even rather proud of) actually *making* the news, through their choice of events for highlighting and through (biased) construction, explanation and presentation. Immediate viewer perception and response as well as the development of subsequent "newsworthy" events were all being influenced. The Convention, demonstrators and the police, Mayor Daley, Abbie Hoffman and the Yippies, Students for a Democratic Society (SDS), the Black Panthers — along with May 68 in Paris, the first manned Moon landing of 1969 — there was plenty of "news" at the time.

Television news is rightly seen as a portrait in miniature of contemporary social and political concerns, a checklist of influences and changes in an anxious environment. Printed newspapers — the major information vehicles from the nineteenth century through the 1940s — have tended since World War II to be supplanted by *spoken* news reports: hourly radio updates and, more recently, "all-news" stations on both radio and TV. Nevertheless, an evening news wrap-up retains its appeal as predictable, familiar, comfortable: an overview made by experts of what's "important," all you need to know. So the news mirrors a larger social reality.

All of this had been noticed by others, previously. Compare *The Last 10 Minutes* by Antonio Muntadas, premiered at Documenta 6 (Kassel, 1977) where taped recordings of the final minutes of one day's television broadcast and sign-off in Moscow, Kassel and Washington, were screened simultaneously on three adjacent TV sets. Taking place in the post-Nixon period, and with Kassel (so near the DDR border) as geographic bridge, *The Last 10 Minutes* offered both comparison and classic confrontation of capitalist and communist, west and east. Muntadas presented the off-air footage with no further comment, confident that the difference between the three was evident and its significance understood: a direct relationship and interplay between art and life, art and politics, and of psychology, sociology and anthropology.[2]

1. Correspondence with the author, September 1993.

2. Two years later Muntadas pursued his interest in news gathering with the half-hour documentary *Between the Lines*, a study of the preparation of an actual item for broadcast news, where it is made clear how the reporter/editor's "take" on a story's significance will necessarily shape the final item. But as Muntadas points out in a statement of 1979 for *Between the Lines*, "we are completing information from the text with our own process of thinking, knowledge, information, subtlety. We are looking deeper than the printed words. ... with television there is no time to stop and think while we absorb information from a moving image." The TV form has a particular kind of influence.

For Stan Douglas' *Evening*, selections of actual news items from 1968 and 1969 in Chicago were compiled and re-written for three invented broadcasts of fifteen minutes each, as if presented on the local feeds of NBC, ABC and CBS respectively. As significant as the content — still important today — is the presentation. To a notable degree and despite the intervening generation, its style seems familiar, and totally convincing.

A condensed and instructive comparison of changing television styles may be found in *Political Advertisements*, a videotape by Muntadas in collaboration with Marshall Reese (1988), where actual promotional spots were collected from campaigns for the American Presidency from 1956 to 1988 and simply presented without comment, in chronological order. While Eisenhower in the mid 1950s seems predictably stiff and earnest in the still-new medium, one is surprised that John F. Kennedy's ads from 1960 also seem old-fashioned from today's vantage point. It is obvious that the poised speakers are often reading from cue cards just off camera, with only a few campaign-trail inserts giving a flavour of excitement. By 1968, already, many more changes are evident, with man-in-the-street opinions incorporated into testimonials for Hubert Humphrey, and reference to violent crime for women walking alone at night turning up in slogans for Richard Nixon. Just a few years earlier such "news" references would have been considered inappropriate, irrelevant to the high politics of a presidential campaign. By 1976 we find such euphoria as "There's a change that's come over America" with Gerald Ford, "... America is smiling again!" And in 1988 George Bush talks of "a thousand points of light" and "a kinder, gentler nation" to swelling music, while fireworks explode spectacularly over the convention centre. By the late 1980s, *selling* was the only plan: a visible and significant shift over twenty-five years. Muntadas and Douglas are both active observers. An important difference is that Muntadas, dealing with the literal and the *present* tense in his news/information interventions, shows a certain didactic quality in his comments; Douglas, looking to the *past*, makes use of hindsight in his reconstructions. Bracketed by acting and script development, the issues become "storied" no matter how relevant to the present moment. His view is more constructed and dynamic, and more distanced.

In retrospect we can see 1968 as a watershed for television news. Colour was now being established as the new broadcast norm, and there was a new colloquialism in manner, a personalizing of appeal to viewers. Vocabulary and phrasing still follow the print media's somewhat formalized usage, but now more than one race and sex appeared (were represented) on screen, and newly-introduced "human-interest" stories were calculated into the equation. What *are* these still-awkward diversions, and what is their purpose? What's the relationship of on-site reporter and desk-bound announcer, the banter between double-anchors appearing at this point for the first time?

In a project for "Local television news program analysis for public access cable television" proposed to the Nova Scotia College of Art and Design in 1978, Dan Graham isolated this "happy talk" as a fictional matrix in which "the 'news team' is like a family at ease in a domestic setting." As he pointed out, "The time at which the 'happy news' is scheduled, corresponds to the time between work and relaxation in the family house before dinner; it is a transition between the outside world and the 'inner' world of private self-indulgence. As it is when the workers in the family come home from work, it serves as a transition period from the frame of public to that of domestic space. Like the cocktail 'happy hour', it has the socially important function of ritualizing the passage from public sphere to private sphere."[3]

Graham's proposal for this analysis of television news is overtly instructional. On a cable channel for the four following days, Monday's newscast would be examined during the time slot of the regular broadcast news; the programs would be divided into sections dealing with home reception, studio production, and formal elements of the program itself, achieved through replay and verbal/visual comparison of behind-the-scenes or invisible-to-camera sources.

Graham and Douglas are both concerned with the forces of social intervention and manipulation as revealed by television news formats. But Stan Douglas has employed a *quasi-fictional reconstruction* of reality; content is as important as form. *Evening* is an active statement and implied commentary, a *bringing into focus* and study in comprehension, rather than an actual intervention or quotation. It evokes and reveals, rather than shows or tells.

Evening was completed in 1994, a work written by Douglas for performance by actors playing five reporters and six anchors (one of whom had once been an actual newscaster) for three television stations. In *Evening,* the three stations begin simultaneously with "Good evening," then launch their shows in counterpoint; each presents the news for January 1st 1969, then, beginning simultaneously again, the first broadcast for January 1970. One is slightly shocked to see the card insert, "PLACE AD HERE" appear during each presentation — a blunt reminder that The News sells products (delivers an audience) as much as hockey games and movies do.

3. Dan Graham. *Video Architecture Television/Writings on Video and Video Works 1970-1978.* Halifax and New York: The Press of the Nova Scotia College of Art & Design, and New York University Press, 1979. p.60.

The personality of the three stations is revealed in their choice of news items and style of presentation; Douglas has differentiated them with background studio colours of blue, red or green. The blue ABC station, "WCSL" is "Your Good News Station" with James Deverell and Dennis Cameron; by the following year, Cameron had been replaced by James Mooney. The green CBS begins simply with "This is Channel 6, WBMB Evening News," and the following year a title card spelling out the top stories precedes this curt opener; announcer Finton O'Neil is solo anchor and, unlike the others, never mentions his own name on camera. As the red NBC, "WAMQ" is hosted by Bill Loudon and Ed Hughes for 1969; in the following year Hughes is replaced by Dennis Cameron, brought in from the blue ABC, and now red says they have "News That Matters" along with a self-consciously chattier style. Evidently, there had been some behind-the-scenes ratings discussions in the interim. The green CBS, one notes, maintaining its more reserved manner and its acknowledgment of the complexity of issues, is the only station this second year with just one ad in its roster; the others have achieved two sponsors per broadcast as their reward for viewer appeal. News was no longer just information, it was also a matter of intrigue, excitement, and the almost conspiratorial pleasure of an announcer's comments and asides, of little jokes with a co-anchor.

Close attention reveals many small differences between the three stations, in their choice of language, their ordering of stories — but the similarities are also revealing. Slides, film clips, quotes and comments are often identical on all three stations, presumably due to identical sources for news releases. In 1969 out of five to seven stories presented, all stations noted the release of three prisoners of war by the Viet Cong, and the fact that they wore open-toed sandals and carried their personal effects in a rice bag, though two also referred to another American officer who'd escaped the day before. Only two discuss Adam Clayton Powell reclaiming his seat in Congress after being cleared of charges of misuse of Congressional funds. A different two talk about Herbert Hoover's FBI report and the FLQ bombs found in Montreal and Ottawa. In 1970, all three stations mention the delays in Mayor Daley's appearance at the trial of Abbie Hoffman and to different degrees discuss J. Edgar Hoover's warnings about the threat of Communism, but only two report on developments in the My Lai trials and just one, the traditionally serious (green) CBS, says that Hampton's death is now seen as murder, and notes a resulting sway in public sympathy in favour of the Blacks for their treatment by police.

The conflicting representation of issues surrounding the deaths of Black Panthers Fred Hampton and Mark Clark, the role of State's Attorney Ed Hanrahan and question of police as murderers in the case are jumbled together, scattered around in many different references; no casual listener could make an informed judgment. Hypotheses, opinions, deductions and plain propaganda are all presented interchangeably, piled up together indiscriminately. The news, authority or not, is finally just presenting tonight's *list*; it's virtually impossible in such an arrangement to understand and judge layers of information or comparative values at work. One gets an impression, remembers in retrospect the slide of the Minutemen's "arsenals" of confiscated weapons or images of single faces as they're flashed on the screen behind a speaker, notices that a commuter train is delayed by fire. But *paranoia* is hardly mentioned, fear is never shown, though none of this news is "good" news after all. A detailed listing of the program contents suggests that the real attention is being paid to visual appeal on the part of the stations, to available background slides and film clips, to the single (pointless) sentence that sounds "right," to the variety of speakers on location. It's all in the interest of "interest."

Five years earlier, Douglas had worked on a film-loop installation titled *Anchor* with its "preoccupation with the forms of coercion and deferral found in television," as he wrote in June 1990, that largely prefigures *Evening*. *Anchor* was composed entirely of footage taped off-air from American and Canadian television in late 1989, another high-energy moment of international crisis and change involving Romania, Czechoslovakia, Panama, East Germany and the fall of the Berlin Wall. "A rapid montage of different announcers is seen, and then ends with a momentary dissolve to black. Groups of these monologues are broken in four sections by brief slow motion glimpses of an elsewhere: Russian women talking at a table, an airlift in Azerbaijan, a stormy sea and the ship upon which Bush and Gorbachev met, and fireworks over the Brandenburg Gate ... a blur of fragmentary but authoritative remarks."4

Though *Anchor* was completed and transferred to film, Douglas now considers it "an abandoned work." Perhaps the use of actual footage kept its effect too discrete, didn't provide the internal contradiction and implied commentary that informs *Evening*. Perhaps the film-loop format proved less immediate than the three video projections side-by-side, their comparison inevitable and their verisimilitude so *nearly* right that one feels, first, only a suspicion that the clues there have intended revelation. *Anchor* seems more like a framed picture, a "presentation" with the sensibility of the luminous *Overture*, while *Evening* is subtly a gauntlet thrown down. Douglas' politics are more exacting now. The more recent work selects a moment of racial tension and public unrest, with harassment and confrontation shown as pivotal factors in the development of contemporary history and media.

4. Correspondence with the author, June 1990.

Within the normal variety of the evening news, threads of Black history are drawn judiciously together as quiet evidence and unspoken challenge.

Douglas had intended *Anchor* as the last in a trilogy of film loops on the history of the cinematographic media, all designed to play without apparent beginning or end, where the continuous mechanical repetition would lend emphasis to the intended focus of each piece. They were thus views of a media history, rather than concerned with an immediate present. *Overture* (1986), the first of that group, had used materials from earliest cinema: a sequence of clips filmed by Edison a century before of the Canadian Pacific Railway lines, seen from the front of a train as it hurtled along tracks and through tunnels in the Rocky Mountains. Overlaid with a reading of passages from Proust's *Remembrance of Things Past*, the work evokes the uncertain state between waking and sleeping, of consciousness itself. Next, *Subject to a Film: Marnie* (1988) repeated brief cycles of Hitchcock's *Marnie* to highlight an aspect of classic Hollywood cinema, the dwelling on obsessive fantasy. In his structure here, Douglas also links the body with the mechanical as imposed by the routine of office work, in keeping with reproduction and the character of the machine age. In *Anchor*, finally, "the heterogeneous but closed continuum of 'television flow'"[5] was foregrounded. With the completion of *Evening*, however, Douglas speaks of far more than the *flow* of television, showing also its stresses and manipulations. At a moment when American social tensions were particularly acute, and the role — and power — of the media in flux, history seemed more visible. The Sixties were conscious of self and image to an unusual degree, and with the assassinations of the Kennedys and Martin Luther King paired off against the "peace and love" of popular culture, who could presume any social vision to be clear or accurate?

Anchor, one guesses, was too formal, too reserved, too self-contained for a meaningful comment on television news. With the opportunity to work in and with the Chicago context, *Evening* is more aggressive intellectually, more conflicted. As a work *in situ*, developed in response to the impact of actual local events, its message is all the more pointed, whatever its location for eventual exhibition.[6]

Douglas has used time-related and photo-based media since the early 1980s, black and white or colour photography, slide sequences with dissolve units and voice-over audio text or music, in works reflecting his environment and cultural experience.

5. Correspondence with the author, June 1990.

6. *Evening* was premiered at the Institute of Contemporary Art, London England, September 1994 in *Stan Douglas: Television Works* and in May 1995 with the Renaissance Society at the University of Chicago, which had originally commissioned the work. *Evening* was also included in the exhibition *Public Information* at the San Francisco Museum of Modern Art in January 1995.

But consistently, he has tended to move from formal concerns to more charged political ones. His recent use of video and television imply a growing need for immediacy, a direct reference to popular experience. *Hors-champs* for example is a work referenced to its site of production, a double-sided video projection produced at Centre Georges Pompidou in 1992. Though conceived as a study of the developing jazz idiom of Black American musicians in Paris (expatriates not necessarily by preference) during the late 1960s and early 1970s, and its translation (a demonstration of multi-camera studio shooting) for classic ORTF television, the national French network, one's personal experience of the piece is undiluted aural and intellectual pleasure. Stan Douglas is not preceptive or pedantic. He located the right musicians — George Lewis/trombone, Douglas Ewart/saxophone, Kent Carter/bass, Oliver Johnson/drums — all based then or now in Paris, and found the right music, a 1965 composition by Albert Ayler. He based his television shooting/editing style on that of Jean-Christophe Averty, a figure as noted in France as Norman McLaren or John Grierson in Canada. The recto image is a fine two-camera TV documentary on contemporary jazz — while the verso all the *other* material, seen by the "other" camera. It would have been edited out as irrelevant to a good television program, but typically shows the *other* musicians while they're not being featured in their solos, and reveals the intimacy of their collaboration and cooperation, their participation and pleasure in each other's music. The verso, then, shows the musicians rather than the "performers," person rather than persona. These are the extranea that delight an on-the-spot audience; it's the irrelevant that makes the real. Seeing the two sides of this story (*pace* Michael Snow, whose double-sided film of 1976 bears that name) reveals to us and underlines the customary, usually-ignored limitations and highly fabricated nature of the television mode, whether in the Paris of the 60s or in our living rooms now. The wonderful music invites us to linger again for the replay, and one sees and revalues that verso image: the unnecessary, the deleted, the essential.

By continuing to review media images and forms from the past — photographs, films, video/television, recorded music, Stan Douglas reminds us — returns *to* us — the foundations of our present and of our cultural history. His themes return as variations, always with an underlying consciousness of the political sub-strata of the everyday. History by example. Yet as he considers the outside world he addresses also his own knowledge and experience. Douglas speaks of his sense of the marginal, of "absence" and doubt as his constant concerns. Yet the richness and physicality of Douglas' visual constructs and his evident pleasure in music, in the rhythms of gesture and speech, belie (or disguise) the potential for existential doubt in his work. That consciousness of the void, however, may be a source of the resonance to be found there.

The newest work is a complex film-loop installation titled *Der Sandmann*, shot in Berlin for presentation at the 1995 Whitney Biennial in New York. Responding to the charged atmosphere of present-day Germany, Douglas collapses the history of the small garden plots established for the poor in the early nineteenth century, with intricately cross-referenced writings of E.T.A. Hoffmann and Sigmund Freud. The gardens, now being replaced in Potsdam (a Berlin suburb) with hotels and luxury housing, form a backdrop for comparison of the "old" Berlin and the newly-united present one. The gardens are linked historically with Moritz Schreber, whose son Paul published *Memorabilia of a Neurotic*, which inspired Freud to develop his theory of paranoia. Hoffmann's gothic tale in turn suggested themes to Freud for his essay *Der Unheimlich (The Uncanny)*.

The film installation juxtaposes two time frames, each projected as abutting half-views which show a Potsdam garden site in the early 1960s and at the present time. This offers, then, a recollection of geographical and political change within the span of Stan Douglas' own lifetime, the crossings of Berlin/Vienna and literature/psychology over a century, the interplay of present realities with childish memories (and fears for nighttime bogeymen and the loss of a father in the Sandman story). There is more than one golem. The Gothic elements signal a return *to* and *of* the repressed, a factor Douglas indicates is of crucial import to the German psyche now. One is tempted to see Douglas' own experiences over 1994-1995 in Berlin on a DAAD fellowship, as relevant as well. Berlin is full of foreigners, but being visibly non-Aryan surely remains an issue.

Increasingly, Stan Douglas' work evidences a social commitment, and one infused with political consciousness. But it is an ambiguous statement, more commentary than prescription. Its message is there by example and implication, a demonstration of themes and issues without recourse to direct propagandizing. The "art" takes precedence over any "teaching" aspect, and the work is the stronger for that set of decisions. Machines and the mechanical are visibly central to his constructions; the ideas as well as the engines presenting them are man-made, products of the past hundred years. We are meant to see these mechanical processes as progressive, linked to labour, and consuming energy, space and time. Despite clear evidence of the research, even scholarship, underlying his productions, an adamant physicality infuses Stan Douglas' constructions of experience. His works, even as ephemeral television broadcasts or published texts, are *made* things.

Their "sources" are mere speculation, their relationship to others' works tangential. Perhaps "correspondences" is the more apt term. Stan Douglas graduated from Emily Carr College of Art and Design in 1982, and has information and interests in common with other Vancouver artists: Rodney Graham especially, and to a lesser extent with Jeff Wall and Ian Wallace, perhaps Ken Lum as well. Douglas has continued to show a respect for the arcane, for intensive research, and his use of existing texts and musical scores holds much in common with the sensibility of Rodney Graham, who would seem to have a like appreciation for musical history and its uses. All these artists show an aptitude for synthesis and cross-reference between media and periods, an ability to apply research tools yet benefit from chance discoveries and intuitions. Douglas, like Rodney Graham in particular, shows a love of literature and a fascination with Time, as form and content of artworks in four dimensions. Even Douglas' rediscovery of the player piano (for *Onomatopoeia*, 1986 , and *Pursuit, Fear, Catastrophe: Ruskin B.C.*, 1993) is prescient. As a machine replacing the live performer while reclaiming or insisting upon the present-tense of performing a musical work, its modern presence/absence is allied also with the quaintly historical made new, and is echoed in Rodney Graham's use of a similar piano for *School of Velocity* (1993) or, for that matter, Vera Frenkel's piano in *...from the Transit Bar* (1992) and *Raincoats, Suitcases, Palms* (1994).

Like the others, Douglas shows respect for research and authority. Technology and media retain their stature. Like Rodney Graham, Stan Douglas works "logically" from a premise developed and expanded in research. The nineteenth century as underpinning to present-day knowledge — inventions and assumptions — was an early fascination, and the writings of such authors as Sigmund Freud, Herman Melville, Edgar Allen Poe appear alongside music by Johann Sebastian Bach, Richard Wagner (for Graham) or more contemporary masters. Neither vast scale nor impeccable detail seems to daunt — analogous, perhaps to the obsessive "staged" aesthetic of Jeff Wall's photographs, which have often been built on references to nineteenth-century works by Manet or Delacroix, or bloody contemporary battlefields. Elaborate constructions re-create the past for a present eye (or ear), precise in every detail.

These "correspondences" are by no means presumed to be Stan Douglas' conscious intention, though they indicate something of his place in the ambitious and fertile Vancouver milieu, important as both margin and intellectual hub. Douglas works in the present, but his position grows out of and is informed by a past rich with associations and meaning, a living history. It is his study of Others that counts.

POINTS OF CONTACT

JULIAN SAMUEL, *THE RAFT OF THE MEDUSA: FIVE VOICES ON COLONIES, NATIONS, AND HISTORIES*

by Maurie Alioff

The era of us-them political correctness might be winding down. For me, the dawning of more fluid, supple, and playful ways of addressing issues like race and gender is exemplified by ex-porn star Annie Sprinkle's "Post-Post Porn Modernist" feminism. In her videos, live performances, and "Sluts and Goddesses" workshops, Sprinkle tears off the straight-jacket of fundamentalism and calls for the reconciliation of women, men, gays, straights, whores, and housewives.

Or how about Toronto filmmaker Srinvas Krishna's *Masala*, a movie in which smurf dolls appear beside statuettes of Lord Krishna, and the God Himself communicates with His followers on cable TV? Attacked by East-Indian Canadians for his film's irreverence, and what one writer calls its "explosion of 'dignified' as well as stereotypical representations of ethnicity," Madras-born Srinvas Krishna is unrepentant. For him, when oriental and North American cultures mix, the result is anxiety-provoking, hilarious, and scintillating. Masala is, of course, a pungent blend of diverse spices.

A new video made by Montreal's Julian Samuel also touches on points of contact between east and west, south and north. Samuel's *The Raft of the Medusa: Five Voices on Colonies, Nations, and Histories* offers 99 minutes of five writer-intellectuals talking non-stop about subjects the title suggests. Although devoid of irreverent humour, and heavily didactic in tone, the tape does work its way toward a questioning of certain strictly kosher political assumptions.

Throughout *Medusa*, Samuel cuts back and forth from one of his interviewees to another, a structure suggesting that the ideas you hear are meant to vibrate dialectically. For example, Sara Suleri (*The Rhetoric of English India*), argues that colonialism, through oppression that provoked revolt, brought the orient into modern nationhood. On the other hand, writer and activist Marlene Nourbese Philip (for some reason filmed in distracting low angle) emphasizes how European intrusion into regions like the Caribbean had mainly disastrous effects on indigenous history and culture.

Philip, whose book, *Looking for Livingstone*, probes the misguided colonialist-missionary's addled mind, sees herself as an excavator of black history, smothered for centuries by Europe's ethnocentric vision of itself — especially in its brutal dealings with regions like the Caribbean. "The Caribbean represents for me," she says in *Raft of the Medusa*, "a site of vast, massive interruptions of histories."

Miraculously, despite the devastation of black culture, "You look at African societies in the New World, and you see tremendous creativity in the face of a traumatic onslaught. You look at the music, the dancing right up to today." As for the languages of the islands, "The Caribbean demotic" is one of "the most exciting, kinetic demotics in the English speaking world." (No doubt about it, but I prefer not to think of roots reggae singers like Burning Spear, dub poets like Linton Kwesi Johnson, or St. Lucian conversational rhythms as specimens of "kinetic demotics.")

For Thierry Hentsch (*Imagining the Middle East*), Europe's destabilization of "third world" history derives from the fact that history is invariably myth, the creation of a self-justifying storyline.

For example, says Hentsch, the "vision of the middle-east was linked to death through an imagery of despotism, fanaticism, and bloodshed." Delacroix's gory 1829 painting, *The Death of Sardanapalus*, typically sees the orient as the "perfect other of the west. If we have tolerance, the other has fanaticism." At the same time, Europeans saw in the region a "frozen and static world of dreams where it is possible to escape" from the ugly side of industrialism and advanced technology.

Amin Maalouf (*Leon L'African*) echoes Hentsch's comments on the Eurocentrism of western history, and argues that this aberration is "not only scandalous, it's dangerous," one of the causes of present and future violent conflict between east and west.

But Maalouf also laments the poisonous, if understandable, excesses of eastern nationalist politics. Since Napoleon's invasion of Egypt, there has been a push in the middle-east to "revive the conditions of the 7th, 8th, and 10th centuries during which the Muslim's world was the most important. It's a regression that leads to failure," argues Maalouf. For one thing, the "notion of human rights has no value" if someone like Salman Rushdie can be condemned for his ideas.

Maalouf believes that man now "has the right and the responsibility even, to be the meeting place of several cultures, of several religions. I think that exclusive belongings are a terrible thing." Similarly, Sara Suleri is looking for "collusions between the colonizer and the colonized, colonial and post-colonial." She rejects "biological definitions of race, of gender, of notions of cultural difference," the repressive idea that "only a woman can speak for a woman, only a subcontinental female writer can address that experience."

Following commentator Ackbar Abbas' view of Hong Kong as a fascinating synthesis of western and Chinese cultures, Samuel ends his video by giving Amin Maalouf the last word:

> "I would say that the orient is a victim of two factors, itself and the occident, and there is a fringe of people in the orient ... who want to see things evolve, but who always find themselves caught between the rise of fanaticism in their native region, and a wall of misunderstanding in the occidental world. Everyday, I ask myself, are people going to understand one day? I tell myself there is such a climate of distrust, of intellectual terror, that subtle ideas, conciliatory ideas have less and less place."

The international events dominating the news for the past year more than amply justify Maalouf's moments of despair. He, like millions of others, has had his share of the crying game.

LEFT BEHOLDING THE PROMISED LAND:

ARDELE LISTER IN AMERICA

by Bruce W. Ferguson

The documentary mode of image/text production and transmission has traditionally been associated with, or even complicit with, what John Grierson liked to call mass education.[1] Mass education is an ominous term today, its meaning having changed over the past fifty years in much the same way as the meaning of the term documentary, another of Grierson's popularized usages. Mass executions, mass media and mass exterminations, to cite only a few, have alerted audiences to the suspicious implications of large-scale processes performed in the name of public benefit. The documentary, as a result, is under interrogation in many fields of cultural activity. Both terms, mass education and documentary, when first popularized by Grierson, might have sounded benign, as ordinary and transparent words of description. But, now, even the sentence I have just written is immediately recognized as loaded and charged with its own associations, assumptions and therefore, complicity — the transparency of language itself is no longer a viable idea. Today, it is easy to see how a *mise en abyme* of deflection and deferrals might be created in the attempt to neutralize any word, with each word being dependent upon and indebted to another word and another context for its fullest meaning and directions. Today it seems that the notion of neutrality might remain on the linguistic horizon like a grail, never reachable.

Somewhere, perhaps, there might be someone who would still argue that a document is just a document, patiently awaiting interpretation, and that education is just the name of a series of methods to meet the moral, social and political rights of democratic subjects and that mass is an adjective of quantity and not quality and so on. Someone might still argue that it is possible to posit a *fact*, in plain terms.

However, such a realist or common sense defense is certainly less likely in academic or artistic realms today when the deconstructive impulse[2] dominantly guides both

1. John Grierson was the first head of the National Film Board. For a useful reading and then, re-reading, of his place in the history of Canadian cultural politics and in the history of the documentary and its political implications, see Forsyth Hardy, ed. *Grierson on Documentary* (London: Collins, 1946) and Joyce Nelson, *The Colonized Eye: Rethinking the Grierson Legend* (Toronto: between the lines, 1988).

intellectual and aesthetic production, when facts are word acts, perhaps not even to be spoken and certainly not to be believed. The notion of neutrality or objectivity or even authenticity immediately meets resistance when raised: a counter-argument would posit that documents, whether completely fragmented or apparently complete, are never neutral and never objective. Instead, documents are the ground on which political ideologies are constructed and, thus, become histories written and rewritten in rhetorical flourishes of might which blur distinctions between the notions of fact and fiction.

But there is a caveat. It should be noted that although such deconstructive impulses from elitist bases of power themselves (the academy and the art world, in particular) exist powerfully today, it does not necessarily mean that the pervasiveness or persuasiveness of the terms mass education or documentary have lost their power as value-free, objective descriptions of knowledge for the public good. It only means that this power is being challenged, and that the erosion is being consciously undertaken. The task is nowhere near finished.

One of the reasons that such terms might retain their "naturalness" is that their repetition in culture and their institutionalization in such organizations as the National Film Board of Canada, for example, offer a powerful resistance to change. Grierson and other public relations giants were aware from the inception of these terms in the moving image industry that linguistic constructions could hide the potent relationship between moving pictures and the art of persuasion. One might say that Grierson and others, particularly in the field of advertising, were prematurely yet acutely knowledgeable with regard to the *undecidability* of language, decades before it became fashionable to speak about the theoretical nature of language and the instable relationship between image and text.

The very instability at the core of meaning systems can and has been re-used in an oscillating debate about the nature of documents and their power, uses and influences. However, today, this same instability is slowly being recognized as having some liberating qualities for subordinate cultures even though it may have been conspiratorially controlled by dominant ones in the past.

This awareness is particularly discernible in the activities of artists who use video, photography and other mediums of popular discourse. Although romanticism might seem to attend such a statement if it were innocently projected as though

2. I am using the term loosely, in the way suggested by David Lehman who distinguishes between "soft-core" and "hard-core" deconstruction (*Signs of the Times: Deconstruction and the Fall of Paul de Man* (New York: Poseiden Press, 1991)) As the title suggests, Lehman sees any of deconstruction's uses (ten, by his count) as a "sign of the times," an intellectual *zeitgeist* or what Raymond Williams might have called a "structure of feeling."

artists were *per force* subversive, it is the particular experience of videotapes and audience responses to them that leads me to this conclusion.3 It is the particular experience of art and specifically video or video art that has engaged critically with television and other mass media forms throughout the past two decades that leads me to admit to and be admiring of its efficacy. And it is precisely because television itself is just as undecidable as language and experiences something like an identity crisis through demographics and audience responses that means video can be effective. Not all the time. And not universally.

If network television is western culture's environment, its culture's background and its social landscape, it is video (a term which has come to mean counter-television regardless of its means of production or its distribution) which can act as an active figure of resistance, an individual instance of choice. In a technological minefield of smart images, video is the I to the Eye. It is on this uneven ground of the popular where the public imagination is hotly contested territory and it is the video/ television dialectic which expresses the complex of desires most accurately. As Dick Hebdige has written, "To engage with the popular as constructed and lived — to negotiate this bumpy and intractable terrain — we are forced at once to desert the perfection of a purely theoretical analysis, of a 'negative dialectic' (Adorno) in favour of a more 'sensuous [and strategic] logic' (Gramsci) — a logic attuned to the living textures of popular culture, to the ebb and flow of popular debate."4

Ardele Lister's *Behold the Promised Land* is a precise example of the popular format of television and film being reformatted to inquire into the assumptions, prejudices, contradictions and problematics of myth at a level of daily practice and lived experience. It is successful because it adheres to an emotional and formal principle of collage which allows audiences to determine their own relations to repetitious cultural clichés that are disengaged from the authority of narration. It allows and encourages ordinary citizens to speak their own minds and bodies on both sides of the screen, to regain their "grain of the voice" within the cacophony of the small screen's expectations.

Behold the Promised Land escapes an expression of the pure Canadian resentment of America, while maintaining a close look at the promises of south-of-the-border myths. Taking the Fourth of July as a trope, Lister simply asks celebrants what they

3. What I am postulating is the parallel to Andreas Huyssen's understanding that television itself is specific and nonuniversal in its productions and receptions and that no theory of the avant-garde or of television's hegemony does justice to audience needs and responses. See especially, "The Politics of Identification," *After the Great Divide: Modernism, Mass Culture, Postmodernism* (Bloomington and Indianapolis: Indiana University Press, 1986).

4. Dick Hebdige, *Hiding in the Light* (London and New York: Routledge, 1988), 203.

think of America on a day when its vernacular and institutional mythology is unquestionably visible, when America as a name is, for all practical purposes, an ideology as well. The answers provide a kind of social articulation that embodies the scars of mass education and all of the narrowness of nationalistic ideological constructs, as well as the humour and individuality of the subject's own understanding (or misunderstanding) of who they might be, positioned as they are in such a construct. The give and take, the will to answer correctly within the constraints of personal experience and the bumpy roads criss-crossing the American landscape burst to the surface in every voice, every gesture and every image. The process of constructing these opinions is reconstructed and deconstructed by carefully and rhythmically pulsating archival footage from earlier wartime propaganda films and other, now laughable, moments of innocent media propaganda. The unrelenting repetition of the documentary mode within the documentary mode highlights the contemporary state of America's citizens who are the amiable products and inadvertent invalidators of the documentary impulses. At the same time, the tape interrogates and makes ironic its own documentary impulses. It does not believe in its own authority, providing a wayward and casual mode of authorship which parallels the content of the tape. What becomes clear is that people believe only the myths they need, the imaginative constructions that serve them, however inadequately, and that they choose these myths no matter how the forms that construct them overbear.

In a very forceful sense, *Behold the Promised Land* is the meandering story of failure, of the failure of the mass media's nationalistic and patriotic determinations to do their job. Ideology in place, if these interviewees are being honest, turns out to be a kind of incomplete, blindsided, accidental imprint on the psyche, neither as deep as conspiracy theorists would have it nor as irrelevant as humanists would like. There is, instead, what looks like an uneasy orchestration of fragments of memory, gender bias, class positioning and a multitude of conflicts, aspirations and dreams, frustrations and ignorances and knowldeges all vying for a grasp of the imaginary I, the imaginary Eye and the imaginary America. The documentary vision that held promise for a unified state now, instead, delivers a mutual sociality full of stars and swipes, liberties and libertarians, hamburgers and all kinds of holdings, hold ups and hold outs. The future is still alive, however, even as it betrays its own ideals in advance.

Mirages Of Anticipation

CHANTAL DUPONT, *ARCHÉO-SITES*

by Françoise Le Gris

Archéo-sites, presented by Chantal duPont at Espace 4040, is a body of work uniting assemblage paintings and video installations in a veritable synthesis of the artist's production during the last five years. The exhibition space was specially designed and equipped with electr(on)ic circuits for both wall art and a pair of video installations, one of which included four closed-circuit cameras. The two rooms, although separate, were permanently linked by cameras reinforcing connections between the works and reflecting fragmented details with unusual thematic coherence, creating constant mirror effects and reverberations among the works.

The show's "pre-text" is the archeological site of Toro Muerto in Peru, which the artist visited in 1984. This site is outstanding for the number and variety of its petroglyphs — stones bearing highly stylized engravings from the pre-history era. The artist's discovery of Toro Muerto serves as a point of departure for the body of work shown in *Archéo-sites*, but it is also a catalyst for a whole range of problematics which far surpass this single reference. First — some descriptive considerations illuminating the nature of the work. The second room contains four extremely disparate elements: an enlarged map of the archeological site is painted directly on one wall and bordered with three photos of petroglyphs lying about the site. These elements serve as supports for a *reality* at once historical, geographical and archeological. Two video installations are situated on the opposite wall and in the middle of the room. The first, titled *Paroles d'oiseaux à Toro Muerto (1987-1988)*, includes a video monitor enclosed in a large, sculpted and painted volume, playing a colour tape already shown at a number of video festivals. The second video installation, *Index* (1990), described by the artist as a photo-video installation, comprises fourteen monitors of which three play sequences from the *Paroles d'oiseaux* tape, in other words, motion pictures. The other screens present static colour (cibachrome) stills from the same tape, which was produced from paintings shown in the adjoining room. The still images — each photo including the frame of the video monitor itself — thus create a trompe-l'oeil effect, a decoy for the viewer who *thinks* he is seeing a video image.

The first room contains a floor-wall painting titled *Petroglyph "Cazador"*, and seven assemblage paintings on the walls, bearing evocative titles: *Pétroglyphe des Navajos, Pétroglyphe "Aves", Pétroglyphe "Tigre, Hombre y Aves"*, etc. As an organic mise-en-scène of a de-constructed entity, *Archéo-sites* is an "installation-synthesis" outstanding for its coherence and visual dynamics. The paintings acquire value (in the Saussurian sense, i.e., place and position) through their interferences with other media.

The exhibit underlines two processes inherent in duPont's installation work — stratification and media(tisa)tion — with their corollaries: sedimentation, reverberation, duplication and metamorphosis.

Curiously, although in this respect she is hardly exceptional, duPont, who has been producing art video for several years already, seeks to rethink painting in video language. The concerns and problematics she raises as a video artist are to a great extent based on the relations between painting and video. *Paroles d'oiseaux à Toro Muerto* must therefore be seen as an inquiry into the nature of the image, comparing painting's flat surface with the luminous surface of video, its projection into a 3-D object and onto so many little painted cubes dispersed around the floor and the wall. The latter serve to extend the format of the video installation, repeating the same volumes in stratified painted wood. The installation also refers directly to the painting installation *Pétroglyphe Cazador* (the hunter) (1987-1988) in the adjoining room, which explores the same theme without a video component.

The painting installation repeats the same arrangement of volumes inspired by the video box — a sort of painted case enclosing a video monitor and partially decorated with Toro Muerto petroglyph motifs. Once again, there is a concern for establishing a cube-based spatial perspective, similar to that found in Renaissance painting. The result is a de-constructed cube-based scene occupying the front space before the painting, a sort of spacing out of the visual pyramid constituted from the spectator's viewpoint. The problematic here is that of graded planes subsequently flattened on the painting's surface, presented as a *backdrop*, on the wall, like a stage set. The spatial ambiguity of this backdrop determines its appearance as screen, or wall, enigmatically inscribed with signs, then as *decor* including the painted cubes arranged before it, and finally as *landscape*, both inside and outside the *box*, which itself presents both stylized neo-primitivist figures and a space for pseudo-naturalist representations.

A series of conjunctions and equivalences arises — on the one hand, geometric symbolization, mythical space, and ritual; on the other hand, figurative and iconic representations, the representational space, and intellection of the *skène*. The interplay is one of overlapping procedures, multiple cross-references, reverberation of signs and their metamorphoses. The *skène* — the scene — which is played out is the drama of spaces, geographies, multiple geometries, which would ultimately resemble each other once de-constructed, de-composed, destroyed, if not for the reactualized meaning they acquire. This is the essential opera-tion of *Archéo-sites*, a title-term which could also be construed as a mirror effect in which the reflection, the mirage, would be not so much that of a past, but rather of a future, of an anticipation.

In *Index*, duPont seeks to transpose the use of *surveillance video* into an art context, with four closed-circuit cameras transmitting images onto four monitors incorporated in the installation. One monitor plays images of the viewer visiting the *Index* installation, itself, superimposed on background images from a sequence in the *Paroles d'oiseaux* tape. Three of the closed-circuit cameras are stationary, focused on three of the floor-pieces in *Pétroglyphe Cazador* and transmitting negative traces, shadows and silhouettes of the viewer moving around the painting installation in the adjoining room. What is seen is also a rapid passing, a moving, an evanescence — a sort of pragmatic reflection on the art gallery public. *Index* presents two kinds of spatial representation — speculative and kaleidoscopic — in two different timeframes — live and replayed. Moreover, the installation transposes painted objects into flat images in both photographic and videographic formats. *Negative* images from a video source are composed of luminous shadows unintentionally produced by viewers moving around the exhibit. The alternation of still and moving images, and the various devices used by the artist, offer seductive glimpses into the prehistory of painting (photo, video), as described elsewhere by Philippe Dubois. Finally, the electronic image, being somewhat blurred and indeterminate, becomes *similar* to the petroglyphic figures. There is a resulting sense of ambiguity and ubiquity, like that peculiar to signs and forms without specific support and which, through mediation, perpetually migrate from one support to another. All are subjected to an economical regime of meaning oscillating between successive gains and losses. *Index* constitutes the focal point of the exhibit. The term *index* has the meaning of "sign" in the Peircean sense, but also, "sign" as key to meaning and "sign" as indication. Also, in its relation to the painting component, *Index* can be understood as catalogue, lexicon, of the Toro Muerto petroglyph signs disseminated throughout the entire work.

The installation immediately induces circularity of both motifs and of time and space. Outside the space-time framework of the exhibit, the sense of ephemerality in the work is conveyed through its dis-assembling processes. The *revolutions* of time become *involutions*, upsetting the before-after relations among the works. In other words, what could be called hypotext (departure) and hypertext (arrival) are in a state of perpetual transmutation.

Specific problematics are raised in a rather troubling manner — questions surrounding the frame, its interior, its edge taken as a spatial limit, its transgression on the way to becoming final contour. Shadowplay (direct and indirect) reveals an almost mythical dimension of light, or at least a binary symbolism — life / death, sun / night, positive / negative. Shadow reinforces the symbolic of the "double" (duplication, mirror) and of the series (photographic, videographic multiplication), illustrating the binarity and plurality of both form and process. The creation of depth by means of *spatialized* painting, in combination with video, reproducing and superimposing strata and masks, produces *disappearing lines* (Deleuze: *lignes de fuite*) towards distant elsewheres, but also proceeding from point to point, *punctum* to *punctum* (Barthes), so that their progressive disappearance is more readily noticeable.

Grid, mural, miniature fragments all make for a leveling, a concatenation of splintered figures, spaces, times. Their resulting equivocal aspect seems as much an effect of knowledge, and of history, as a destabilization of archaic, pre-modern and modern hierarchies of figures and decor. Reinterpretation through mediation, and transposition through *new* media (photo, video), become modulating / transforming functions, with the transfiguring power of an Assumption.

Photography as a means of mediation is not only memory but actualization, making present signs from time out of mind. When associated with the various assemblage elements in the aggressive, dreamlike paintings, these signs acquire new meaning — current, present, and even future. Sign condensation — both of archaic and current figures: miniature war toys, rifle bullets, tanks — orients meanings towards a political rather than a nostalgic dimension. Octavio Paz's thoughts on the experience of modernity acquire their full meaning here — "The ancient, even the most ancient, can also accede to modernity, simply by appearing as a negation of tradition and by proposing another. Invested with the same polemic powers as the new, the very ancient is not a past but a beginning." (*Point de convergence du romantisme à l'avant-garde*) On this level, the blending conceived as post-modernism is but the altered reflection of modern experience described essentially as critical dimension. The same author continues: "(...) the history of Western modern art is also that of the resurrection of the art of many by-gone civilizations. As manifestations of the aesthetic of surprise and its contagious powers, but especially, as momentary incarnations of negative criticism, archaic art products of distant civilizations fall naturally into the tradition of rupture. They are one of the masks assumed by modernity."

Archaic, primitive figures are not reanimated here in a spirit of irreversibility and nostalgia (Jankélévitch), but rather in the manner of a political implosion. through a kind of recall, and at the same time a short-circuiting of History, mediatised signs are launched like new projectiles into histories full of burning issues. Are we back to threats... survival... species... life... death... for whom... for what?

Translation by Jean-Luc Svoboda

WHO THEY ARE, WHO THEY WERE, WHO THEY'RE GOING TO BE

AN INTERVIEW WITH CHARLES GUILBERT AND SERGE MURPHY

by Daniel Carrière

In *Sois sage ô ma douleur*, Charles Guilbert and Serge Murphy have produced a 58 minute tape with 43 minutes of dialogue. "Reality is in words." The feeling of exultant complicity pervading the tape is woven throughout with words — no revelation is superfluous, all are interchangeable. "In a word" — freedom. The tape is something like a mock trial — with a touch of surrealism although not completely detached from reality — where the actors are not really acting and the characters play themselves, first of all, before playing their roles. There is almost a nostalgic feeling — something reminiscent of street theatre, the sexual subtext inherent in the everyday round: androgynous, no doubt. Reinscribed with utter candour are the words of men and women confronting the first truth in art — Tell me who you're playing and I'll tell you who you are. This tape was awarded First Prize for best video by SOGIC (Société général du cinéma) at the Rendez-vous du cinéma québécoise in February 1991. It is the producers' third work, after *Le Garçon du fleuriste* (1987) and *L'homme au trésor* (1988), and a fourth is currently in production. I asked them where they might be heading.

Daniel Carrière— How did *Le Garçon du fleuriste* come about?

Serge Murphy— We were on the balcony at home, Charles and I, on a weekday in the summer, it was really hot, and we thought about getting some friends involved in a sort of fantasy construction, more or less fictional.

Charles Guilbert— A lot of our friends were already working together. There was a lot of interaction. We two were together, but each of us was doing different things on our own, Serge as a painter and I myself as a writer and musician. With video, we could get beyond that and explore an art form outside our usual turf. We knew exactly how we would sequence the shots, and we quickly devised a screenplay blending true stories with more abstract ones in a precise order. We predetermined cuts between scenes and filmed in that sequence. It was rather naïve. We didn't use an editing studio for *Le Garçon du fleuriste*, and we even did the sequencing on the spot using the equipment at hand.

Serge Murphy— In that tape, there are as many players as shooting sites.

Charles Guilbert— We were already working with Michel Grou at the time, and he did the camera and sound work. Of course, it was all done as simply as possible, we couldn't afford an editing studio. Working that way leads to an interesting approach towards decision-making. We could reshoot scenes we didn't like, but we had to do it right away, on the spot. We just rewound the tape and started again at the right place. It was important at the time to follow the sequence of the action, as it unfolded. Now, we can adopt the opposite approach.

Serge Murphy— Even when there's no storyline. In *Sois sage*, there's no story either, but the same players reappear. You can give them a character, and imagine their life.

Daniel Carrière— In *Sois sage*, did you just use the real lives of the actors, as in *Le Garçon du fleuriste*?

Serge Murphy— *Sois sage* is more fictional.

Charles Guilbert— We got the players to act, their roles were all scripted in advance as in *L'Homme au trésor*. We drew upon our encounters with them, and some of their stories turn up in the screenplay.

Serge Murphy— But we also had some of them tell completely fictional stories. I found it interesting giving characters roles that were not their own.

Charles Guilbert— As far as the acting itself is concerned, though, it's completely based on the players' own personality. We've always done that. When we start a project, we know what we want to deal with, we know the theme, subject, length — and then we ask, who do we want to see in the tape. The story comes after we meet the people.

Daniel Carrière— So you met the twelve characters in *Sois sage* before deciding on the storyline?

Charles Guilbert— We met a lot more than that!

Serge Murphy— We had individual and group meetings, especially with women. One evening they came over and told stories. We used some of that material, and then we wrote scenes, a screenplay, notes...

Charles Guilbert— ... which we had them read. Scenes that didn't turn out we re-worked with them. At first, *Sois sage* was about class-act women, really attractive ones with energy to spare, who want — who have a big appetite for life. Then we thought — there are less up front girls, too. We got them all together and it led to millions of stories.

Serge Murphy— We couldn't make a video that just talked about these women. First of all, they talked about guys. It started being a drag making a thematic video just about women... So we put guys in for counterpoint. Guys are in there, in time, occupying space, but they're much shyer, much weaker, or even...

Charles Guilbert— ... discreet.

Daniel Carrière— What about the actual work with the actors? Take the homosexual couple in *Sois sage*, for example. One of the two actors isn't gay. How did you manage to get him into his character?

Serge Murphy— We like working with people we know well, and they're all volunteers in *Sois sage*, they tell very intimate stories, we ask them to talk about very personal things.

Charles Guilbert— They get involved, they see what's happening, and they aren't afraid. We try to establish a feeling of mutual confidence, so they don't regret seeing themselves exposed, as it were. We knew what we wanted them to be, and for their part, they knew what they were, what they were going to be. There were two kinds of problematic — first, we asked Patrick, who isn't gay, to play a homosexual. He was astonished ... we had him saying things like "this relationship isn't working anymore" when we'd never heard him say anything remotely like that. We knew what we were looking for on the fantasy level, we didn't find him unattractive, he was shy, like we wanted, and we liked the fact that the two lovers both had fair hair.

Serge Murphy— Besides, they went against gay stereotypes.

Charles Guilbert— Then, there was the other problematic, when we asked people to play something too close to their real selves. We wanted to get the women to act their roles while maintaining a total distance from who they really were, in their most intimate selves. It was all the more crazy for being entirely prescripted.

Serge Murphy— It started turning into fiction within nonfiction. There aren't many actors in the tape who give themselves away 100% the way Sylvie does. Patrick isn't gay, he would never say things like the things he says. He has no dramatic sense, and we had put him in a dramatic role. It's the exact opposite of how we see him. With others, their own personality comes out, like Sylvie, the up front one. What counts with her is her tone, her manner. She could say almost anything. It was only the emphasis, the energy that counted.

Charles Guilbert— We worked hard with the actors during the shoot. They're all quite natural, and they're good actors.

Daniel Carrière— Hiring professional actors or asking a friend to act in a tape makes all the difference. Or is it just a matter of money? In *Sois sage*, it seems to be a matter of choice — that you worked with people who didn't necessarily have any experience before the camera, or with notions about interpretation.

Charles Guilbert— It definitely had nothing to do with funds, because we know actors and we'd never hire them!

Serge Murphy— An actor would play too much off the others.

Charles Guilbert— That's true. In video, one often sees people from the producer's own circle of friends, but I also think the character, the actor is rarely the pivot of the whole work.

Serge Murphy— More like never!

Charles Guilbert— For us, an actor would have to come first.

Serge Murphy— We work with our players like so much material.

Daniel Carrière— I'd like to talk about the writing in *Sois sage*.

Serge Murphy— Since our second tape, *L'Homme au trésor*, we've been scripting just about everything.

Charles Guilbert— There's the writing of the dialogues, and the writing itself as a theme present from the very outset.

Serge Murphy— Painting and visual arts round out the scenes, between dialogues. They're part of the overall production, the design. The writing is the text — it's normal for people to focus on it, everybody wants to write.

Daniel Carrière— Or is already writing. Eleven of the twelve characters in *Sois sage* are either writers or would-be writers.

Serge Murphy— Whereas with visual art, we don't talk about it, we show it.

Charles Guilbert— Since the very beginning, in our tapes, there is art being made, the characters in *Le Garçon du fleuriste* talk only about that, in their discourse...

Serge Murphy— ... which is a reflection on the artist's work.

Charles Guilbert— In *L'Homme au trésor*, we also deal exclusively with writers. People in *Sois sage* talk about their writing, but not about the fact that they write, basically. In fact, that part's even rather secondary. Their urge to express themselves is the important thing. It seemed funny that eleven out of the twelve characters wanted to express themselves in words. But nobody listens. There is the feeling that some of them could talk all evening without really needing anyone to listen. We ourselves want to talk, there's so much ego, everybody's so anxious to talk. There's something comical in that, and dramatic too.

Serge Murphy— Humour helps to lighten that whole aspect, because *Sois sage* is basically rather heavy. People laugh a lot when they see *Sois sage* because they identify with the characters.

Charles Guilbert— The drowning scene, for example, makes people laugh because they can feel that it really happened to the person telling the story, who's obviously trying to find the right words to tell what happened. Even death becomes comical.

Serge Murphy— In laughter we can escape from reality.

Charles Guilbert— I like it when several intentions come through in a discourse, so it isn't situated on a single level. This creates a critical distance vis-à-vis the emotions, and the discourse itself. We mustn't believe that language is all-powerful. Fragmentation takes us beyond that — we're continually moving on from one discourse to another to another, constantly having to readjust.

Translation by Jean-Luc Svoboda

On TV: The Gina Show on Cable Ten, Vancouver

by Hank Bull

The most important thing to remember when you're on the air is that there actually is an audience out there. It would be simpler if the audience were in the same room with you. The feedback would be "live". You'd get a gut feeling. But in the isolation of the broadcast studio you have to conjure up before you the vision of a viewer and imagine its reaction. In a live audience there will always be those who are bored or all but openly hostile, and who can't remove themselves by the simple act of turning a knob. So, contrary to what you might think, your strongest ally is not the live audience, but rather that nebulous, edgeless, uncountable gargantua: the audience at home. Don't forget that it is there. Don't fold back into narcissism. Don't get too far from the mike or your projection will fade and your signal get lost on the air waves. On the other hand don't imagine too hard about the audience. Don't feel naked under its gaze. Don't get mike-shy. Don't suffer surveillance paranoia. Feel the new, effective way! — feel as if YOU can see the audience. Yes! See right through the process and into the living room. Even if it gets up and leaves, you're still there, looking in, reading the news and watching.

George Orwell— *We live in an age in which the average human being in the civilized countries is esthetically inferior to the lowest savage.*[1]

Hank Bull— Yes, it's true. The poor old viewer is getting pretty passive. Less ESP too.

George Orwell— *It is difficult to imagine that poetry can ever be popularized again without some deliberate effort at the education of public taste involving strategy and perhaps even subterfuge.*

John Anderson, producer of *The Gina Show*— We are trying to figure out what to do about all those people at home and shooting their own videotapes. Like what's the difference between home movies, TV and artists' videotapes? To a certain extent you have to train people to be skilled with their visual

---

1. George Orwell. "Poetry and the Microphone", 1945, from *Such, Such were the Joys*. Harcourt Brace, 1950.

vocabularies. I think that all these Betamax units should engender another type of communication but first people have to see it on TV. I want to show people how to be on TV.

THE TRUTH ABOUT GINA

Vancouver Cable 10 airs two art shows a week. One, called *t.b.a.t.v.,* is produced by students from U.B.C. Each week the work of one individual is featured. This week Barry Gordon ran a lot of silent super 8 — trees, traffic, short shots, intercut. This was my first exposure to broadcast TV without a soundtrack. Some people switched to *t.b.a.* during the commercial breaks in *Mork and Mindy*, and someone else said it would make good dinner television. I enjoyed it. Everyone talked because there was no soundtrack.

The Gina Show stars Gina, who interviews, advertises and introduces video clips from various sources. Since its beginning three months ago *The Gina Show* has become a focus, not only for John Anderson and the crew but also for street level art viewers here in Terminal City. Both *Gina* and *t.b.a.* have a home-made, spotty quality with the occasional hot show. Both shows improve as they age as do the contributions of the regulars, notably Digit, Lipskis and Relican. Some people like these shows; some don't. Their producers are learning a lot about video, TV and broadcasting, and so are regular viewers.

The Gina Show is shot around town, edited at Cable 10 and aired in 3/4" cassette form. The Cable Company does not get a dub. John presents receipts for up to $25 worth of expenses each week. I asked him how he felt about this.

John Anderson— I'm not too concerned with it right now. This is my first show. There's no contract. I think everybody should have money, and while it's not the reason to do anything, the people who do the show should get paid and some way should be found of paying the organizations they make use of, such as Western Front, Pumps and Video Inn.

Hank Bull— What would you say to artists who won't air their tapes for *Gina* because they're tired of showing for free?

John Anderson— I'd say it's hard to figure out what *The Gina Show* is. Is it a magazine? Is it an art gallery? Is it a TV show? It has things in common with all of them. In a magazine (*File, Centerfold*) one isn't normally paid for being in it... But then sometimes a magazine piece actually becomes a work of art. I create my things especially for the show, things that could only be shown on *The Gina Show.* They wouldn't work in an art gallery. That doesn't diminish their value as art, which is small and no one would make a bus trip in the cold to see them... And the artists' copyright I don't think is a problem because people duplicating your work off-air is not going to cut into anyone's market and no one is going to set up a marketing system of off-air dubs of artists' videotapes.

THE TRUTH ABOUT CABLE

Some tapes are not designed to be broadcast. They're too intimate. They wouldn't work on TV. Some artists don't want their work aired for this reason; but more often it's because they, the artists, are not being paid and they feel that somehow the cable company is. John's most militant critics would say that he is playing into the hands of the cable company.

George Orwell— *More and more the means of reproduction are under the control of people whose aim is to destroy the artist.*

Hank Bull— Four years ago Byron Black had a show called *Images from Infinity* on the same cable channel. He was paid in film — 50 feet of 16mm colour reversal a week. In return the cable company received a one-inch master, recorded in their studio, which they were then free to show at their leisure, distribute and take to Ottawa as proof of their lavish support of the artist. Byron Black even had trouble getting dubs.

Orwell concluded his essay on a cautious but positive note. He said that although "the tendency of the modern state is to destroy the freedom of the intellect", it still needs artists, filmmakers, writers to build its images (today this would include to operate its computers and broadcasting facilities) and it must allow them a certain minimum of freedom to do the job. Consequently, productions that are all wrong from the bureaucratic point of view will always have a tendency to appear.

George Orwell— *The radio was bureaucratized so early in its career that the relationship between broadcasting and literature has never been thought out. It is not certain that the microphone is the instrument by which poetry could be brought back to the common people and it is not even certain that poetry would gain by being more of a spoken and less of a written thing. But I do urge that these possibilities exist, and that those who care for literature might turn their minds more often to this much despised medium.*

Hank Bull— OK, that was in 1945. Thirty-four years later the situation has not improved. Poetry has not been brought back to the common people. There is nothing wrong with Chuck Berry lyrics but Pop is not the only form of literature. In fact, when's the last time you heard DEVO or the Clash on the radio? These are popular bands but they're not getting air time. Generally, the media have tightened up, not loosened up, as George had hoped they might. Even he couldn't foresee the fine-tuning capabilities of the "computocracy". Most of us are still bothered by bureaucrats; wait 'til the computers get really on the case.

GET A GUT GUT FEELING

So what's the point? He's not being paid. He's not being as well trained in broadcasting as he would be in a straight course and there's no career in it for him, at least not as a broadcaster of so-called artists' video-tapes. He has the support of neither the cable company (the company store?) nor of the many serious video artists. So why bother?

> **John Anderson—** Well I always thought the main reason to do a video show would be so that when you're in public you wouldn't have to explain really, you could just say, "Watch the Gina Show". That's why it's so contemporary. It's trying to show people that they could be communicating with video themselves, and I like using the show for telling people about art books, art products, art events. The whole show is just a big advertisement for what's going on. I advertise the show but I don't advertise myself. I hide behind the show... Also, I can't talk to people very well unless it's business, so I thought I could have a TV show and invite people over and we could talk about the TV show. It gives me a chance to be around people instead of just being an artist.

NORMALIZATION OF RELATIONS

by John Anderson

The arts now have an infinitely smaller claim than science and engineering on both private and public resources. This, we have seen, is the result not of public preference but of conditioned belief. People — including artists themselves — are persuaded to accord importance and priority to what is within the competence and serves the needs of the technostructure and the planning system. The means for emancipating belief — for releasing it from service to the planning system — is a matter to which, obviously, we must return.

—John Kenneth Galbraith on The Market System and the Arts in *Economics & the Public Purpose*

The Gina Show presents video art. It organizes and participates in real time media events with research, interviews and publicity. The product is an anthology of current art activity in Vancouver.

For too long those who have been exploring and pushing the limits of art have experienced a feeling of alienation from the rest of the community in which they live. The feeling has been that given time, maybe a long time, the rest of the world would catch up.

With the media, photography, film and especially video in the context of broadcast, where the viewer normally uses the information to form or conform his relationships to the outside world, the emphasis has shifted dramatically from a pure form of aesthetic research to that of the personal, the sociological and philosophical. A new emphasis has developed in the area of the artist immediately confronting and reacting with the audience.

In effect the whole meaning of video research is altered. The motivation becomes totally different than that of the art magazine. The function of *The Gina Show* becomes one of questioning the idea of the artists as an amputated limb of society. At a time when the public is experiencing a greater awareness of the value and enjoyment of art, politicians and those who hold power are paradoxically able to deny the value of our contribution. *The Gina Show* seeks to give us a voice, and hopefully to give a voice to those who support the arts. Therefore the overall scope of the program is to find out to what extent the amputated limb can be rejoined.

HAVING THE LAST LAUGH

MARGARET MOORES AND ALMERINDA TRAVASSOS

by Becki Ross

Claiming that lesbian experience is either dismissed, distorted or erased by producers of commercial mass media, is an understatement. To my horror, halfway through *Where the Spirit Lives*, CBC's controversial 1989 TV docu-drama on the state-enforced placement of Native children in Prairie residential schools, a sneaky, pinched, lesbian pedophile jumped out at me from behind closed doors. Several years ago on *DeGrassi Junior High*, the rumoured lesbianism of an "otherwise popular" teacher was conveniently squelched by her eventual (and all too smug) denial. The recent "Chastity Bono is gay and Cher is reeling from disgust" exposés in the *National Enquirer* and *Star* tabloids are rife with "expert" wranglings over whether female homosexuality is determined by an absent, rejecting father or by predisposed masculinity. Some of this stuff makes the "furtive, forbidden, twilight" lesbian love that is smeared through many 1950s pulp novels seem downright appealing. While the treasured *Codco* from St. John's, and Toronto's zany *Kids in the Hall* both serve up often side-splitting, super-stereo-typed gay male sketches weekly on television, a wide circulation of diverse, lesbian-positive imagery is almost unimaginable. Considering this absence alongside the "facelessness"[1] of other oppressed groups (women, working class people and people of colour), it's not surprising that "visibility must be fought for, never freely given, and history is always something that keeps getting lost."[2]

Enter Marg Moores and Almerinda Travassos. For over 10 years, Marg and Almerinda have shared a love of, and a commitment to, the production of film and video for and about lesbians. In the tradition of Gertrude Stein and Alice B. Toklas, Frances Loring and Florence Wyle, Edith S. Watson and Victoria Hayward, since early 1978 (and their chance meeting at the Revolutionary Workers League headquarters in the Louis Riel Bookstore), they've also shared a feminist politic, a home, and a deep respect for each other's talents and abilities. Quick to credit the lesbian,

1. Himani Bannerji, "Popular Images of South Asian Women," *Parallelogramme*, April/May 1986, p. 17.

2. Marusia Bociurkiw, "Territories of the Forbidden: Lesbian Sex, Culture and Censorship," *Fuse*, April 1988, p. 27.

feminist and art communities with the inspiration as well as the context for the creation and reception of their work, Marg and Almerinda succeed, often brilliantly, in displacing the taken-for-granted heterosexual standpoint; into the space wedged open, they insinuate a shameless lesbian stance.

The radical beginnings of feminist and lesbian cultural and political movements can be traced back to the early 1970s in large urban centres across the U.S., Canada and Quebec. Collectives of self-identified lesbians emerged from the heady ferment of mass political action and social change: in the U.S., groups like the Radicalesbians in New York, the Furies in Washington, D.C., and the Gutter Dykes in Ann Arbor, Michigan announced the birth of autonomous lesbian cultural and political organizing. Two lesbian conferences were staged in Montreal in 1974 and 1975. In Vancouver, the Lesbian Caucus of the British Columbia Federation of Women formed in 1974, and several caucus members assumed control of the feminist newspaper *The Pedestal* for five issues. In the spring of 1977, the Lesbian Organization of Toronto (LOOT), the Three of Cups Coffeehouse and the radical feminist newspaper *The Other Woman* took up residence at 342 Jarvis St. in downtown Toronto and collectively constituted the first lesbian centre in the country.

Through "rap groups," drop-ins, printed manifestos, and public demonstrations, "new lesbians" gave vent to their outrage at the erasure and/or the dismissal of lesbian issues inside the women's movement, gay liberation and the new left. Undaunted by myriad obstacles, this wave of largely white, middle class, urban and college-educated lesbian feminists set out to wrest the category "lesbian" away from the heterosexual consensus of sin, sickness and criminality (and the so-called "heterosexual mimicry" of butch/femme bar culture). In so doing, they urged an appeal to lesbian pride, strength and visibility. To many, lesbianism became synonymous with the creation of an idealized woman-identified community based on principles of sharing a rich inner life, bonding against male tyranny, and giving and receiving practical and political support.[3]

Central to, and at times inseparable from, more traditional forms of political action, has been the slow but growing eruption of lesbian cultural work: photography, writing, performance art, music, film and video. By the late '70s in Toronto and elsewhere, Olivia Records, the lesbian presses of Daughters, Inc., Diana and Naiad, the *Cunt Coloring Book*, J.E.B.'s photos and Adrienne Rich's 21 love poems had

---

3. For reference see Nancy Myron and Charlotte Bunch, *Lesbianism and the Women's Movement*. Baltimore: Diana Press, 1975; and Adrienne Rich, "Compulsory Heterosexuality and Lesbian Existence," *Signs: Journal of Women in Culture and Society,* 5:4 (1980).

become the treasured property (bought or borrowed) of lesbian communal households. On the Canadian and Quebec scene, musicians Carol and April, Ferron, Beverly Glenn Copeland, Mama Quilla II, the All Girls Leather Marching Band, a host of television producers, performance artists and poets began to stretch art forms to embrace a lesbian sensibility in the comfort of largely "wimmin-only" surroundings. Caught in this festival of lesbian exuberance, Toronto-based film and video makers Marg Moores and Almerinda Travassos conspired to contribute their own special voice.

Asked to comment on the development of their explicitly lesbian feminist attention to questions of sex, gender and representation, Marg and Almerinda highlight the importance of their participation (as curators, exhibitors or viewers) in a 1981 feminist film festival at the now defunct Funnel Gallery, the 1983 *Alter Eros* show (Gallery 940, Gallery 76 and A Space), the two *Women's Erotic Film Language* events in 1985 and 1987 (A Space), and *Sight Specific: Lesbians and Representation* in 1987 (A Space). Inside the film/video art community, they find support from Richard Fung, John Greyson, Lynn Fernie, Colin Campbell and other, primarily lesbian and gay, independent artists. Almerinda and Marg also point to their involvement with the LOOT in the late 1970s, and later, the socialist-feminist International Women's Day Committee (IWDC) and Lesbians Against the Right (LAR) as key sites of personal/political education. Moving into and out from these overlapping communities for over a decade, this gifted dyad is more intent than ever on stirring up a potent brew (and lots of thirsty guzzlers).

At present, Marg works full-time at Nellie's Hostel (a shelter for battered women) and Almerinda works three days a week at Trinity Square Video (an artists' and community video production facility). Increasingly, they receive commissions from community groups to produce promotional or educational videos. For example, they've just finished crewing for Inner-city Youth Link on *Street Wise Women*, a tape about safer sex for women. In the temporal gaps that remain, they've managed to produce on average one film or video a year (and have never been able to spend more than $6,000 per tape). While small budgets mean half-hour (or 10-minute) videos rather than feature-length films, friends as actors, fewer (expensive) technical innovations, and the need to be a "jill" of all trades, Almerinda adds that video allows for more risk-taking, more control and less compulsion to self-censor.

With regard to the nuts and bolts of the actual process, Marg writes and directs, Almerinda does cinematography and directs, and both partners produce the work. They insist that, "living together and working together could be hell, but it's not." Hell for Marg is the one editing day chock-full of temper tantrums; for Almerinda, it's the lack of recognition for her more "invisible" labour. Complaints and less than ideal working conditions aside, they've managed to imprint film/video art practice with a distinctive lesbian-feminist stamp. And in so doing, they've hooked yet another fan.

In all, the Moores/Travassos connection has generated eight lesbian-centred films and videos. One of their first efforts, the lesbian cult propaganda-tool *Labyris Rising* (1980) chronicles early lesbian feminist praxis: dope-smoking, bare breasted jamming at the Michigan Womyn's Music Festival, pool-playing, poring over the American feminist periodical *off our backs*, marching and dancing on International Women's Day, all set to the music of Joan Armatrading, Janis Joplin, BeBe K'Roche and Heather Bishop. Lesbian history is further elaborated in *Our Common Dream* (produced for the Woman's Common in 1986). Here, a series of women reminisce about dyke bars like Sara Ellen Dunlop's Music Room, the Continental (a.k.a. "the blood bucket") and Pat Murphy's Fly By Night Lounge. At the same time, they fantasize about the perfect women-only space (above-ground, with clean bathrooms and a patio where Notso Amazon softball players might congregate).

Never predictable, the stories Marg and Almerinda tell often take unlikely twists and turns. Two notorious lesbians masquerade as suburban housewives on a *Trip to Toronto* (1981). Eager to introduce their kids and hubbies to famous postcard landmarks, they tour the "magnificent" Eaton's Centre, Honest Ed's ("he owns half the town") and City Hall ("the spaceship where they run the city"). Marge and Marcie are left speechless when a cross-dressing ruffian steals their home video camera and substitutes scenes of Kensington Market's vital hustle and bustle for the concrete, corporate character of "world class" Toronto.

In the film *X-Spot* (1983) a perpetrator of (hetero) sexual harassment who is pursued by his female victim finds himself, soaked in sweat, momentarily safe inside a public "men's room" only to be caught and humiliated by the triumphant heroine. Punctuating the narrative in a succession of images of the young girls' game, "paddy cake, paddy cake," transposed into a powerful, collective women's ritual designed to crack the silence that protects male attackers. Scenes from an early Take Back the Night demonstration reveal the angry passion of organized revolt against male violence that erupted in the late 1970s and early 1980s, and can be seen once again in the resurgence of coordinated anti-violence activism that has followed the Montreal massacre in December 1989.

Less comfortable with serious drama, Marg and Almerinda invent characters and predicaments that are at once delightfully funny and politically provocative.

Dashing dyke detective Anne Ace, sickened by photos of men basted, buttoned and zigzagged to death, sets out to solve the Sewing Machine Murder Mystery *(Anne Ace*, 1981). An underdog advocate familiar with the "seamy" side of life and determined to prove the police wrong, Anne visits the Ladies' Quilting and Bombing Society and is convinced of their innocence (in smart lesbian double-speak, the members claim they "do everything by hand"). She then heads for the garment district where she discovers the murder weapon (a battery-operated Bernina) and apprehends the real killer — a down-and-out tailor driven mad by changing fashions.

The irreverent humour I've come to relish in so much of Almerinda and Marg's work is perhaps most effectively played out on the divisive, hotly contested terrain of lesbian sex. Caught off guard by the wild success of the bold and controversial *Frankly, Shirley*, they now point to this "very small video" as a watershed in their career. The video gives luscious, full treatment to the public, (ordinarily tabooed) recreational sex between lesbians; the make-believe front-page headline in *The Toronto Sun* reads: "Girl Sex: Lezzie Washroom Arrest." The power of the piece is that it breaks rules (anonymous sex=bad; tender, romantic love= good) with outrageous, yet honorable intentions, for example, the vertiginous pleasure of oral sex in a Club Monaco fitting room one busy Saturday afternoon.

"Cunning linguists" through and through, Marg and Almerinda make sure their texts drip with innuendo and word plays. In *Surely to God* (1989), the poker table is not the only place "Mandy is very handy." News that the Lucky Draw lottery is "worth 42 million... and rising," is met with a well-timed chorus of ooooohs and giggles. And just when there's hope that justice may prevail, the lezzie protagonists discover their winning lottery ticket frozen to the chicken they carelessly forgot on the kitchen counter while making out to the frenzied beat of game show *Wheel of Fortune* on the floor among endless stacks of to-be-recycled newspapers — punishment for engaging in that horrible, degenerate and addictive vice?

Sex is depicted with lustful vengeance in several of the videos — *Frankly, Shirley, Surely to God* and *Desire Obscura* (a semi-autobiographical, non-narrative tale of longing filmed in 1988). All three contain beautifully rendered and mildly arousing cameos — sex as smooth and easy as A.B.C. (all but the cherry). Still scouring "the life" for that steamy, no holds barred feature turn-on, I'm nonetheless thrilled by alternatives to worn-out, clichéd, American nature romps.

A willingness to challenge both the medium and themselves doesn't stop at sex. In a community that still places a high premium on unity, commonality and "true lesbian identity," Marg has devised a diversity of characters to jump-start her stories off the page — the 1920s aristocratic "invert," the closeted gay business lady, the working class poker player, the bilingual traveller, the Montréal-style baby butch, the dyke bike mechanic and the flaunting femme. Missing from this eclectic repertoire, however, and from the content described above, is evidence of a pro-active commitment to the development and integration of an anti-racist perspective. Marg and Almerinda are acutely aware of this absence; they told me to expect overdue changes to old, familiar patterns in their next project.

Except for a couple of reviews in art magazines (and a short piece in *NOW*), there has been little critical engagement with the Moores/Travassos oeuvre, even in the feminist and lesbian/gay press. Part of this dismissal, they feel, is the reading of their work as "light, fluffy comedy" and the privileging of "heavy, more serious" lesbian print. And yet they're convinced that the prospect of reaching viewers through scenes negotiated by live lesbian flesh is sweeter (and increasingly more popular) than the publishing of "ideologically sound" theory. The screen has also been made the site of lesbian cultural/political praxis by video artists Marusia Bociurkiw (*Playing with Fire, Night Visions*) and Diane Heffernan & Suzanne Vertu (*Memoir de Notre Hystoire*); filmmakers Midi Onodera (*Ten Cents a Dance, The Displaced View*), Lorna Boschman (*Butch/Femme in Paradise*), Jeanne Crepeau (*Le film de Justine*), and Lynne Fernie & Aerlyn Weissman (*B-Movie*, upcoming fall 1990).

Marg and Almerinda have noticed considerable growth in both the size and diversity of their primarily lesbian audience since the first showing of *Labryis Rising* at the Funnel in 1981. Through several gallery shows, retrospectives at the Woman's Common and the 519 Church St. Community Centre, they have developed a loyal following within the lesbian community that filled the Euclid Theatre at two of their recent screenings. Participation in several international lesbian and gay film and video festivals has also meant more viewers, and the sale of tapes to the Museum of Modern Art in New York and the National Gallery in Ottawa has indicated, as well, institutional recognition of their contribution to video art practice. Except for the "revolutionary feminist" attack on *Frankly, Shirley* as "male-identified, pornographic pulp" at a gay disco in Leicester, England, the overall community response has been superb (though often not a source of constructive criticism).

Future plans are ambitious. Recapturing their fascination with more experimental film and video-making, producing and third and final episode in the "Shirley/Surely" series (*Surely But Slowly*), recreating the "Dykes in the Street" march (1982), and releasing the ever-elusive feature film (tentatively titled *Lipstick Rising*) are high on this pair's list. Whether Marg and Almerinda will be able to sustain and enrich the special collaborative magic out of which their bold, lesbian and feminist vision materializes, remains to be seen. Given what I've viewed to date, I can't say I'm worried.

After all, they're in the business of creating real live lesbian s/heroes, sex and stories that are funny and never didactic, that speak to, and have meaning for, ordinary lesbians in our everyday lives. As Anne Ace might say, "in a world full of sickos, some of whom even run countries," their visual representation of up-front, multi-dimensional lesbian reality not only disrupts conventional *and* much non-commercial image-making, it positively shocks.

RODNEY WERDEN'S, 'BABY DOLLS'

by Lisa Steele

It is not an elegant problem to transform man to woman, woman to man. It involves the cutting and clipping of human tissue, the boring of holes, the removal of flesh, prosthetic re-creations. It is years of elective surgery; that is, surgery by choice, over and over again. It is the pursuit of a physical self-ideal that most of us will never know. It is a new freedom, or seems to be.

Science and the mechanically dexterous micro-surgeons are producing the last sculpture — the human body. They are at work right now. As usual, they work where the poets have already camped. "Let me look into your heart...", a wonderful little Romantic whim, has become quite possible. Likewise the Lover, the Romantic tradition says,

Take me.

Take me and make me more like myself than I am now.

Change me.

And so the modern surgeon/lover cuts and trims, adding and subtracting, working from photographs and memory. Loving hands encased in a skin-thin latex substance; the hands of an artist. Lifting the new person out of the old; personal anatomical customizing. Price? $4700.00.

What is the use of being a little boy if you're going to grow up to be a man what is the use, says G. Stein.

> "well, I've got a picture in my mind of how I should look when I'm finished... no, I'd fight it because I feel I'm a woman trapped in a man's body and I've a female outlook on life. I've always had the desire to cross-dress; not get off on it sexually but psychologically like to be able to be, well starting out as a young girl then a teenage girl then a woman. It's a better feeling."

The speaker is a young man about to begin the surgery phase of a sex change in Rodney Werden's videotape *Baby Dolls*. Soon he will be a young woman. It is a tape similar in technique to Werden's earlier *Pauli Schell*; both are taped interviews with people who present uncommon autobiographical details. In *Pauli Schell,* a young woman discusses the specifics of sexual bondage; in *Baby Dolls*, the medical, legal and social events in the life of an about-to-be transsexual are presented. In both tapes the strength of this presentation is in Werden's choice of individual. He has chosen people who are able to present potentially sensational personal material in quite a commonplace, almost banal manner. They are able to drone on and on in excruciating detail the most personal of personal stories; and in doing so begin to cross the boundaries that separate us the viewer from them the weirdos. Viewing these tapes, we are involved with people who present the sexual/political questions of bondage and sex cross-over as events catalogued in a phenomenological manner, without deep interpretation. As people they are not emblems that "stand for" greater issues. As ideas, they do not beg to be understood. Instead they are individuals, leading detailed and ambiguous lives, just as screwy as our own, only different. Somewhere they have made a set of personal choices very different from those most of us make, and this is disturbing.

But there are important differences between the two tapes. *Baby Dolls* is a much more ironic view than *Pauli Schell.* The viewer is allowed to look at Pauli while she is talking and as a consequence, her deviation becomes more acceptable and digestible. She looks ordinary really; a nice girl with a whip. She talks; we listen. Against nature she stands, but not without reason, or seemingly so; there is incest in her background. And this painful uncomfortable subject offers not so much a cause-and-effect answer as an environment for the unusual.

But in *Baby Dolls*, we never see a face on camera. The reassurance of the calm, orderly facial features (two eyes followed by nose ending with mouth, moving) is denied to us by Werden. Instead there is a foot being fiddled with; cuticles pushed back, nails filed, clip, clip and finally polish applied in awkward short strokes to the prepared nails. The visual intermission in the form of a piece of rainbow-striped candy sliding hesitantly down the instep of the ever-present foot. And then on to the last act: the installation of a rigidly soled, metallic lace-up, high heeled sandal on the waiting, well-prepared foot. The end.

While this is going on visually, the casual, conversational voice-over of the young man-becoming-woman is filling us in on the medical and legal details of The Change. He is well versed in the specifics of hormones, implants and adoption. But what are we to think as he chatters on about "service guarantees" on his work? "... and any extras that have to be added on like if something heals up and closes up they'll reopen it for nothing. Like it's more or less a service guarantee."

It seems that he has seen too many doctors. He has developed a romantic notion of a futuristic mechanical mutation process. And it is happening to him. Reborn under the knife. But what does he address in us that is so seductive? The belief in change and alteration? Freedom? Self-analysis on a strictly materialistic plane? He is the desiring-machine become the desire. The subject become the object of his own regard. And for a moment we want it for him. We want him to rise from the operating theatre, new and unbound — a production with no end. We want him (now her) to feel good. But then he says:

> "I wanna wait like I'll probably wait five or six years after I'm finished my operation and experience life as a woman and then I will I guess eventually marry and settle down if the right person comes along."

And who will this right person be? Someone with some understanding, we hope; able to discern the divine in every hairline suture. And what are we to think of this:

> "... it's bookkeeping it's basically something to set me up in life where I can work as a woman in a woman's job. I dunno, office work has always interested me. I'm not into factory. Like, as far as I'm concerned no woman should have to work in a factory. (women's liberation?) I'm for it and then I'm not. Like, I like to be dominated. I don't like to be totally independent."

A man wanting to be the woman that so many biological women are fighting not to be. Perhaps it will be men who carry on the true and classical meaning of femininity in the 20th century.

What does he seem to be saying? In order to be a human being I want to be regarded as a woman, seen and perceived by others as a woman, desired as a woman.

What does he want? He wants to be a woman, do a woman's work, live a woman's life, raise a little girl to be the woman he has always wanted to be. He wants a trade in. Or does he? Who told him he can't be a man and love other men? Who has convinced him of this?

What's the use indeed of being a little boy if you're going to grow up to be man or a woman. What connections aren't severed irremediably, sealed and burned. What part of the past isn't gone forever the moment it slips onto the other side of the present to be recalled only as dust. But this, this Change is a leave-taking of a kind unknown before. By presenting us with an individual who is not emblematic of the whole of transsexualism, Werden has succeeded in making a tape that is not a smooth and persuasive political endorsement. Nor is it a convincing argument against anything. Instead each statement that is heard becomes a new question for the viewer. We are made to examine all of our own partial prejudices and slippery "beliefs". And he has done this without making one statement of his own.

But perhaps the key to both of these tapes by Werden is the place of emotion in them. There is none. The emotions seem to have been clipped like tendons, rendering them stiff and useless. What are usually considered to be volatile topics, sex and general topics so close to the individual's image of self, are transposed into lists of details, specifics added to specifics, recitation of processes, medical ("... they'll take what's left of the penis and use that to form the outer part...") and legal ("... the only place that doesn't get an F is on the birth certificate in certain cases and well, adoption agencies, they keep a list of all transsexuals registered...we can only have little girls."). This lack of emotion is the core of Werden's specific presentation of his subjects. It is a presentation of deviant behaviour. A non-liberal stance: not one of understanding the transsexual next door. But instead a note of despair and irony. The question: What does this person really want and if you can buy it is it really free?

ADJUSTING A COLOUR TELEVISION

by Tom Sherman

We sat there in our respective chairs waiting for the colour television to warm up. A few minutes before the network news broadcast, right after dinner with a glass of beer or a cup of coffee. Light flashes and rolls onto the screen with a voice track coming in distorted then clear, a commercial we memorized weeks ago. The automatic colour control is operating, but as usual, the tint is wrong on the people's faces. We'll wait until the news to adjust the picture. There's that familiar face. I know the colour of his skin and the set isn't coming close to delivering the correct flesh tone. I'll wait a second and maybe she'll get up and adjust the colour. He even looks worse against that new background, a slide of an airplane crash. That brought her out of her chair. She set her cup down and is standing over the television, leaning over the picture tube as she works the controls. She is going to the contrast and brightness first. By the time she gets to the colour mixing the picture is messed up beyond belief, a dull and muddy picture. I can't understand what she thinks she is doing. She has changed the picture through her manipulation of the controls, but that newsman is farther than he has ever been from coming right into our living room. I can't believe she is sitting down. She's going to watch that picture. She's going to sit there and watch the picture she's destroyed, as if there is nothing wrong. I can't even tell what I'm looking at. There is still twenty minutes of news I could be watching. I get up out of my chair and kneel down on one knee in front of the control centre. It is going to take some tuning. This set is capable of a sharp, accurate picture if you just look at the screen and think about what you are doing. His skin is coming in, too green, too pink, a little yellow, there.

GENERAL IDEA

TOWARDS AN AUDIENCE VOCABULARY

*Edited by Jo-Anne Birnie Danzker
and rewritten by General Idea*

A pre-cast 32 member group of extras occupied 32 numbered seats on stage directly facing the audience. The seats were arranged in a ziggurat shape that was an extraction from the overall seating plan designed for the 1984 Miss General Idea Pavilion (32 seats x 62 sections = 1,984 extras). The sequence of events the extras responded to followed the format of a Miss General Idea Pageant. The raising of the curtain scene with appropriate audience reaction started the performance, which proceeded in sequence to the finale. A narrator fleshed-out or set the scenes, the director indicated what reactions were desired and conducted the enactment. General Idea played the parts of narrator, director, and still photographer. The decision to present this taping in performance rather than in the studio arose out of a hoped-for mirror-image effect between the two very different audiences. The role of the audiences were equally but differently isolated from the usual stimuli. The "real" audience enacted a traditional audience vocabulary in response to the extras' performance of the "real" vocabulary once removed. Mirrors mirroring mirrors. It was hoped that the gap between the audience and stage would blur into endless reflections.

Editor's note: the resulting videotape was incorporated into "HOT PROPERTY", released in 1981.

"A good artist doesn't have to be loved. There are so many lovable, ineffectual artists... This is not to suggest that art should be grating or irritating or hated to be effective... We are quite aware of the fact that the main objective of one's work is not to win friends, not to win praise and attention, but to get the public to act on the basis of your work. In the process you may not endear yourself to some people but you have become an effective generator of cultural information that warrants consumer attention."

Excerpt from General Idea's *Press Conference* (videotape/performance), The Western Front, Vancouver, 1976.

JO-ANNE BIRNIE DANZKER INTERVIEWS AA BRONSON, FELIX PARTZ AND JORGE ZONTAL OF GENERAL IDEA:

JBD— I'm sure you noticed that the "real" audience was pretty restless during the performance.

AA— Well, we realized restlessness would be a possibility because the piece wasn't directed to that audience, it was directed to the stage. There were two audiences necessary for the piece to work, but all our attention was directed to one and not the other. It was a perverse situation. On the other hand, if the physical setup of the space had been different, if it had been a normal theatre situation where the "real" audience was right up next to the stage, then the whole relationship of the two audiences would have been much clearer. The space was a problem.

JBD— What relationship between the two audiences were you trying to explore?

FP— The relationship between audiences and the stage or focal point in performance situations...

JZ— ...and the relationship between a forcibly de-activated audience and a forcibly activated one. Between active and passive as well as active and re-active.

FP— We did this by attempting to set up a mirror-image situation. Our performers, our stage audience, were called up to the stage from the "real" audience. In fact they sat through the previous performance as part of the "real" audience. They were called up over the p.a. Their names and seat numbers were announced. This was the initial "act" of our performance. It was an intended *blunt* gesture. We wanted to underline the separating of the audiences. We wanted to set up two distinct yet similar behavioural situations in the same room.

JZ— Once they assembled on stage the show began. The "extra" audience reacted to a hypothetical narrative intended to provide a context for the reactions we required. These reactions are what we consider a basic audience vocabulary. Again, the "real" audience's vocabulary was *bluntly*, and quite literally up-staged. All they could do was lip-sync. They were once removed and their role was called into crisis.

JBD— So in other words you were exploring the dialectics of a "real" audience that would have nothing to do and a stage audience that would be entering into the traditional vocabulary of the audience.

AA— Yes, our focus wasn't on the "real" audience. The "real" audience were left to their own devices. Although we attempted to appear to be excluding them we had indeed considered their role. We were also exploring what "real" audiences do indeed do, what expectations they have, what involvement they require and of course what they do when their scenes are stolen.

FP— The dialectic was left to find its own level. Any addressing of the "real" audience, any introductions, any acknowledgement would have weakened the situation we were attempting to set up. We contrived the alienation.

JBD— *And you had your backs turned to them?*

JZ— Yes, of course we did. Another *blunt* decision. But also for practical purposes. We were working, directing. The cameramen also had their backs to the audience. So do band leaders, or choir masters, which is sort of the part G.I. was playing on stage. Someone mentioned that the "turned-back-stance" broke the first rule of theatre. Was the "real" audience anticipating theatre? But there were 32 people on stage, directly facing the "real" audience and performing for them.

JBD— *You said you anticipated a negative reaction.*

AA— No, I never said a negative reaction. We really didn't know what to expect. It was exciting, titillating,...a certain tension. We were definitely interested in what would happen. It was something new for G.I. to allow the unexpected to happen in a performance situation. But, yes, a negative reaction was a possibility.

JZ— There were other reactions. During the "movie" section the stage audience was requested to act out the viewing of an engrossing film. The lighting crew provided effects to simulate the appearance of audience faces in a darkened theatre with a flickering light motif. The "real" audience vocally provided a sound track for that situation. Their hooting, applauding and stomping of feet became quite articulated and ended right on cue when the lights went up. This was an attempt to create a role for themselves since their usual role had been removed.

JBD— *Would you wish for audiences in general to have more control, or a more direct relationship to what is being performed? Is that not an issue for you?*

AA— Well, it is a definite issue for us. As you know we have been working with audiences, concentrating on them and involving them in our productions for some time now. Their desires as audiences in performance situations and how they go about fulfilling those desires are issues for us. We find it desirable to involve audiences in a manner in which their role, their involvement, their expectations, their vulnerability becomes topical. We want audiences to sit on the edge of their seats, becoming both extras and viewers, active and passive at once.

JBD— *If you are concerned with the way in which people are manipulated and are forced to be passive viewers, why would you subject them to it?*

AA— For us it is a form of investigation of these issues. We want to know more about how manipulation operates. We presume others are interested as well. We operate in a controlled situation. Like a laboratory. We assume we are working with sophisticated patients with patience. We attempt to articulate the issues. They were the subject matter of our performance.

FP— It is not our style to take the podium and deliver manifestos about the heartbreak of exploitation, manipulation and alienation. This is an entry into the topics but not ours. We don't deal with these situations with a ten foot pole. Turning off the TV creates a short-lived relief from TV manipulation. We're not into abstinence. We're into the thick of it. It's dangerous and we try to maintain a borderline stance. It's really a tension point in all our work and a lot of people express their concern.

JBD— And yet you yourself pointed out that virtually the same audience, an equivalent audience, a few days later was asked to engage in cliché reactions which they thoroughly enjoyed.

AA— Yes, at David Buchan's *Fruit Cocktails*. In fact I thoroughly enjoyed it as well. But we were all very conscious of the situation. It made you conscious of what the cliché was, and how you were reacting to it. You did it, enjoyed it, but you were never sucked into it. You were maybe manipulated by it, but by agreement between you and it.

JBD— Was it the consent element that was missing from your dialectic between the "real" audience and the stage audience?

AA— Yes, that's what was missing. That's what we decided to eliminate. It was simply a different type of performance than David's *Fruit Cocktails* . We didn't ask or cater for consent. It was left up in the air. Again, if the audiences had been in direct physical confrontation this issue may have developed more extremely.

FP— Yes, if that had been the case, the visual contact could have in a sense provided the traditional entertainment quotient that perhaps some people found lacking. On the most banal level it would have been interesting to see what so-and-so was wearing or how so-and-so in particular was reacting. This was probably difficult from 60 feet away.

JBD— One member of the audience remarked that they saw the performance as essentially a video-tape production and the indifference to the "real" audience as something of an insult.

FP— Obviously that is one way to deal with it. Perhaps the most basic. Perhaps the least interesting. It would have been quite simple to shoot the tape in a studio situation. It would have been simpler for us, the crew and probably the performers. But it was conceived as a performance before a live audience and the interest we expected to generate was not that of watching a TV show being shot. I felt the taping and performance before the "real" audience was totally integrated, but in this performance the taping was only a device, a found format.

JBD— So then comes the question— for which audience were you performing?

AA— We didn't perform. We worked. The stage audience performed.

JBD— For what audience was the stage audience performing?

JZ— They were performing for three audiences essentially— for the "real" in-house audience; for whoever is going to see the tape; and of course for us. Also let's not forget the other performance that was coinciding with this activity. I mean the "real" audience's performance.

JBD— Another element particular to your "real" audience was the large number of people from the social-political video community whose response was pretty negative.

FP— Perhaps you also noted the art community's reactions to some of the social-political video community's tapes. Pretty negative. Obviously there is a certain split between these two groups. The conference was an interface situation for these two groups in particular. In some cases there are common objectives involved, but the methodology is usually extremely different. But the possibilities of overlap are increasingly seductive.

JBD— One comment that was made was that the stage audience was made up of an in-group.

AA— It was for sure.

JBD— This is a criticism that has been leveled at G.I. for as long as I can remember.

JZ— Yes, it does sound familiar.

AA— We could have requested 32 volunteers from the "real" audience but we specifically wanted what we have begun to call our Art Support System. People who have supported us in the past and continue to support us and who we presume are forming the audience for 1984.

FP— Also we definitely wanted to get a tape out of it. We weren't just trying it out. We had objectives. We chose people who we felt would do it, do it well, who we would feel comfortable working with, and of course people who can deal with being on camera and come across. As you said, this in-group thing is often leveled at G.I. It's a rather confusing issue for us. It's obviously a projection. We're not sure exactly where the problem comes it. We selected an extremely diverse group. Does the in-group paranoia imply they have been chosen simply because they look good, are easy to manipulate, we're hustling them, they're gold-digger exhibitionists? Are they simply in-groupies? Jo-Anne, you've participated in one of our videotapes. You've written about our work on numerous occasions. You've included us in your exhibitions. We've been seen together socially. Would you accept the label of being one of the in-group? I would hope so. Remove the negative connotations and it's simply working and being with interesting people. If this really is a problem for anyone then they should examine the individual members of the group and discover why we find them interesting. Actually I find it a total insult to the people we work with, to the 32 people on stage, to reduce them to in-groupies, objectified with no identities outside of the group. A lot of this type of criticism is rooted in personal insecurity and jealousy and I think it's a dead issue.

JBD— One of the obvious elements of the performance was its discontinuity as a functional element of the filming-taping process. The resultant videotape is a discontinuous experience which through editing becomes "reality" or "continuity"

AA— Unless we chose to present it as a discontinuity. We swing both ways, depending on the context.

JBD— I was wondering in this particular case, if continuity was a central issue.

JZ— I think the performance was what is normally thought of as a discontinuous experience presented in a manner that in fact was quite sequential and continuous. The performance did have five distinct scenes. We started from scene one and went right through. There were almost no technical interruptions. It had a strong narrative that developed. We never shot out of sequence. It had a climax. Actually, in performance I think it was quite traditionally structured.

JBD— Perhaps, but it was still discontinuous and I did wonder if the audience's reaction was as much against this discontinuity of experience as it was against their personal lack of involvement.

AA— In all our performances we play with discontinuity. You're here now, but you're also in 1984. You're watching a performance, but it's actually a videotaping. You really are the audience, but you're also extras. This performance was an extension of these concerns. An extreme extension.

FP— I doubt that the resultant videotape you refer to will misrepresent the "reality" of the initial performance situation. The discontinuity angle will probably be heightened.

JZ— There were several things we wanted from this project. The performance, the still photos — which incidentally were of a high priority for another project — and then of course the tape. The tape was conceived as "stock footage". This could have been the title of the performance. We realized the possibility of a beginning-to-end real time documentary of the performance. The tape could also be cut up and paced faster but still be a factual document. We fantasized about editing right down to the various audience reactions and arranging them chorally like a choir performing a scored piece. Sort of like the Hartz Mountain Canaries. We will also definitely be incorporating sections into our *Hot Property* tape which we're now editing. As in most of G.I.'s work, I'm sure this material will continue to spin off and resurface for years.

JBD— *An interesting point for me in seeing the performances during the conference was the apparent impact of your particular relationship to the media, style and glamour — the influences of G.I. on some of the other performances. I don't know if you felt it.*

FP— Of course, in some cases quite strongly. In other cases they were dealing with similar issues in different manners. I just think that artists' relationships to the media, style and glamour are topical issues at this moment.

JBD— *The irony was seeing G.I.-style performances, and there was G.I.'s audience pouring out the doors.*

AA— Well, I guess it was fortunate for us that we secured a very attentive, receptive, attractive and entertaining 32 member audience that we could count on to endure the show.

FP— Really, Jo-Anne! We hardly emptied the hall. Most people did manage to resist the lure of the bar and chit chat.

JBD— *What relationship do you see between your gallery exhibitions, media productions and performances? Are you exploring the same issues, or are you exploring different issues in different media?*

AA— There is a whole vocabulary of issues that are interrelated. I think in performance situations we tend to focus on concerns that come out of performance. Thus the audience was subject matter in this performance. We get very involved with the media we are using. FILE for example is a prototype magazine. It's a found format.

JZ— Obviously we have a very formalized central theme— 1984. Everything revolves around that as subject matter. Whatever media situation we create or find ourselves in, we attempt to co-opt its effective qualities.

JBD— *You mentioned* FILE. *Do you feel that the* Punk *issue crossed the very delicate line between commenting on glamour/style and participating? I'm saying that less from the point of view of how popular it was as an issue (which it obviously was — you couldn't even fill the orders you had for it) than how the material was presented. Many of the other issues of* FILE *involved highly satirical articles on glamour and some promotion, but it seemed to me that this particular issue was much more involved in participating in the process of evolving a style rather than commenting on it.*

AA— I think we always try to participate in it.

FP— If you mean did it just cross over and become R 'n' R hype, the answer is no. The content of that issue was the Punk/New Wave music scene which at that time was surfacing. Most people's exposure to it was through the popular media which of course dealt with it expectedly as a new marketable product. A lot of the music was dealing with issues that touched-a-soft-spot-in-our-hearts, issues such as glamour/star/style/promo-hype/relationships/audiences/cults/selling-out and of course the BIZ. We found it compatible with our work and extremely energizing to be in contact with — and still do.

JZ— There is also the group situation as well. I mean R 'n' R is strongly group oriented. We're interested in groups. As work units. G.I. is a group — not a band yet, but, well...hold your breath.

JBD— *To what extent is G.I. image-bound and to what degree is it glamour-struck?*

AA— How do you measure that?

Maurie Alioff teaches film and literature at Vanier College in Montreal; he is a screenwriter, and contributing editor of *Take One* magazine.

John Anderson was a founding member of Pumps in Vancouver (1975 - 1980) and originator/producer of the memorable *Gina Show* on Cable 10 there for 33 programs between 1978 and 1980.

Renee Baert is a writer and independent curator living in Montreal. She was initiator and editor of *The Video Issue/Propos Vidéo*, an inter-magazine publishing project in ten parts, sponsored by the Satellite Video Exchange Society in Vancouver,1993; exhibitions she has curated include *Vintage Video: Early Canadian Video Art to 1974, Enchantment/ Disturbance*, 1989, and *Margins of Memory*, 1993.

Marjorie Beaucage is a film and video maker currently living in Saskatoon, and a founder of the Aboriginal Film and Video Art Alliance. In her own words, "(s)torytellers create and re-create the cosmos, giving form and meaning to the moment. Stories are medicine, our connection to the sacred power that is in all things."

Jean-Yves Bégin worked as a journalist, then as information officer for twenty years at the National Film Board, and spokesperson for the Groupe de Recherches Sociales and Challenge for Change/Société Nouvelle, pioneers for social animation through film and video. Bégin is the author of numerous film texts, and has worked with TV Ontario and elsewhere, most recently with Richard Lavoie on *Rang 5* which was awarded the Prix Belle-Geule at the Rendez-Vous du Cinéma québécois 1996. He currently lives in Lantier, Quebec.

Jody Berland is a Toronto-based writer and critic, who teaches cultural studies at Atkinson College and the Faculty of Environmental Studies, York University. She has written extensively on music, media and social space, as well as on Canadian perspectives for theory and cultural politics.

Hank Bull is a director of The Western Front in Vancouver, a musician and performer who is active in video, audio and radio and also as independent curator and collaborator with other artists internationally.

Eric Cameron is an artist and critic, a professor at the University of Calgary. He was most actively involved with video from 1973 to 1980, but continues to write and to produce installation works and individual video projects, while working on his ongoing *Thick Paintings ... to be continued.*

Daniel Carrière was a Montreal-based artist and critic and regular contributor to *Le Devoir*, who worked collaboratively with Richard Angers and others associated with Vidéographe. He died in 1994.

Marie-Hélène Cousineau is completing graduate studies at the University of Iowa, but continues to work with Arnait Ikkajurtigiit, the women's video collective in Igloolik N.W.T. which she helped to establish in 1992.

Sara Diamond is a television producer/director, video artist, curator, critic and teacher, who is presently artistic director of the Media and Visual Arts Department at the Banff Centre for the Arts. Her television productions include the four-part *Lull Before the Storm*, using fictional and documentary strategies to explore the history of Canadian women during and after WWII.

Bruce W. Ferguson, originally from Lethbridge Alberta, is a freelance curator and critic now based in New York City. Among the numerous exhibitions he has curated are: *Space Invaders*, 1984, *Northern Noises*, 1987, *The Impossible Self*, 1988, and *Site Santa Fe*, 1995.

Robert Forget, Montreal, was the founder of Vidéographe and was with the organization from 1970 to 1976. As the Director General of French Programming at the National Film Board from 1989 to 1993, he produced more than 90 films. Forget is now Director General of Technical Services and Research and Development and also responsible for Cinéroute, the NFB experimental video-on-demand service.

Vera Frenkel works with video, text, performance, photography and installation; her ... *from the Transit Bar* was presented at Documenta IX in Kassel (1992) and later in Toronto, and her *Body Missing/Andere Körper* project was extended into an interactive site on the World Wide Web in 1995. A critic of contemporary arts and ideas, Frenkel has published in *Art Monthly, artscanada, Fuse, Vanguard, Video Guide* and elsewhere.

Richard Fung was born in Trinidad and has lived in Toronto since 1973. An independent video producer and writer for television and film, journals and anthologies, he is a founding member of Gay Asians Toronto and Full Screen Coalition. His videotapes and films have been screened extensively in both museum and community contexts, including a 1990 retrospective of his work organized by Downtown Community Television in New York.

Jean Gagnon is an artist, curator and critic who has worked with Vidéographe (Montreal) and later as video officer at the Canada Council; he is presently Associate Curator of Media Arts at the National Gallery of Canada, where recent exhibitions he has curated include *Video and Orality* and solo exhibitions by Sara Diamond, Daniel Dion and Paul Wong.

Peggy Gale is an independent curator and writer who has curated such exhibitions as *Videoscape* (1974), *Norman Cohn: Portraits* (1984), *Electronic Landscapes*, (1989) and *Video Art Vidéo*, a ten-programme series for TV Ontario, 1994. A book of her essays entitled *Videotexts* was published in 1995 by Wilfrid Laurier University Press for The Power Plant, Toronto.

General Idea was established in Toronto in 1968 by AA Bronson, Felix Partz and Jorge Zontal, to work collaboratively in performance, film, video, painting, sculpture, publishing and other media. In 1974, they founded Art Metropole, a centre for information and distribution of artworks in multiple format. Works by GI have been exhibited throughout the world in museums and gallleries and are included in many public and private collections. Although Felix and Jorge died in 1994, General Idea's publications and final AIDS projects continue to be highly visible internationally.

Nicole Gingras, Montreal, is an independent curator and writer whose exhibitions include *Les Absences de la photographie* (1994), *Donigan Cumming: Détournements de l'image — Diverting the Image* (1993) and the autobiography section for *Le Mois de la photo à Montréal* (1991). Her first book *Les Images immobilisées* was published in 1991 by Guernica Press and she is at work on a second which will focus on the use of photography in film and video.

Michael Goldberg is an artist and television producer who lived for many years in Vancouver, and since the early 1980s has been based in Tokyo. He was one of the organizers of the famed *Matrix* converence in Vancouver, January 1973, and a founder of Video Satellite Exchange Society there later that year.

John Greyson is an artist, critic, filmmaker and video producer who has written extensively about contemporary media issues. Greyson was coordinating producer of AIDS Angry Initiatives/Defiant Strategies for Deep Dish Television Satellite, California, and a co-organizer of Video Against AIDS for Video Data Bank, Chicago. His highly acclaimed feature film *Zero Patience* was released in 1994, and a second feature film is currently in production.

Lydia Haustein teaches history of art and ethnology at the University of Göttingen. She is the author of several studies on modern art (*Bild des Fremden*, Bern, 1993) and is presently working on theories about art outside Europe and the Western world. Dr Haustein has, in addition, worked on the exhibitions of African art, *Konfrontation und Annäherung*, Göttingen, and *Michael-Bethe-Sélassie*, Berlin, both 1994.

Vern Hume has been an active video producer since 1981. He was a founding member of Video Pool in Winnipeg and later, coordinator of EM/Media in Calgary and associated with Media Studies at The Banff Centre. He has worked collaboratively with Calgary writer and artist Leila Sujir for many years, and in 1985 co-organized the first Plains Canada Film and Video Conference, held in Calgary.

Igloolik Isuma Productions Inc. is an Inuit-owned professional independent video production company, founded in 1990 by Zacharias Kunuk, Paulossie Qulitalik and Norman Cohn. Isuma recently completed *Nunavut (Our Land)*, a series of 13 half-hour programs for television that recreate life on the land in the Igloolik area in the years 1945-6; the first three programs premiered on TVOntario in August 1994, with the complete series broadcast nationally from spring 1995.

Harold Innis (1894-1952), brilliant political economist and pioneer in communications studies, taught at the University of Toronto for over thirty years. His earlier writings in economics and economic history established a distinctly Canadian approach to these subjects; in his later years he drew attention to the impact of communications on the extent and duration of a civilization, asserting that the dominant media of communications fostered an obsessive and limiting preoccupation with the present. His inspiration for Marshall McLuhan's later studies has been often noted.

Gary Kibbins is an artist and writer who divides his time between teaching positions at the California Institute of the Arts (Valencia) and Queens University (Kingston, Ontario). His video has been shown both at home and abroad, including the Fukui International Video Biennale and the American Film Institute Video Festival, and his writings on media art and theory have appeared in numerous Canadian and American periodicals.

Larissa Lai is a Vancouver writer whose work has appeared in *Harbour, Fuse, Video Guide, The Independent Eye* and *Matriarch*. Her poetry has been published in a number of literary journals, including *West Coast Line* and *The Capilano Review*. She is presently involved in video production, and is working on *The Home Body*, her first book.

Monique Langlois lives and works in Montreal, teaching art history at the University of Quebec at Montreal (UQAM). A theoretician and art critic, she is also a member of the Groupe de recherche en arts médiatiques (GRAM) at the same university, and has published in *Espace, ETC Montréal,* and *Vie des Arts.* She was curator and contributing writer for the video/film/photo exhibition *Paysage(s) de la vidéo* in Montreal, 1994.

Françoise Le Gris teaches in the department of art history at the University of Quebec at Montreal (UQAM).

David McIntosh Toronto-based writer, programmer, filmmaker and educator. He is the coordinator of the Toronto International Film Festival's *Perspective Canada* programme, and has written extensively on film and video for a variety of Canadian and international publications.

Marshall McLuhan (1911-1980) was a professor of English at the University of Toronto for many years, but became internationally famous in the 1960s for his studies and aphoristic pronouncements on the effects of mass media on thought and behaviour; his contribution to communications has been compared to the work of Darwin and Freud for its universal significance. Early books such as *The Mechanical Bride, The Gutenberg Galaxy* and *Understanding Media,* established his central ideas. As perhaps the first communications theorist to capture the popular imagination, he offers an important ground for the development of media-based art in Canada.

Jan Peacock is an artist working with video and multimedia installations, whose work has been exhibited in Canada, the United States and internationally, most recently in a solo exhibition for *Perspective 95* at the Art Gallery of Ontario. Since 1982 she has been assistent professor of intermedia studies and video at Nova Scotia College of Art and Design in Halifax.

Louise Poissant is a professor in the Department of visual arts at the University of Quebec at Montreal (UQAM), and directs GRAM (Groupe de recherche en arts médiatiques), editing a dictionary of media arts to be published at the Presses de l'Université du Québec and in English at MIT Press. She has co-written a series on art and technology to be televised by TELUQ and TV Ontario.

Becki Ross, having taught for several years at York University in Toronto, relocated to Vancouver in 1995, where she teaches Women's Studies and Sociology at UBC and continues to write on cultural theory.

Christine Ross is a professor of art history at McGill University, Montreal. Her many articles and catalogue texts have explored the conjunction of feminism, subjectivity, and video, and her book *Images de surface: L'art vidéo reconsidéré* has just been published by Editions Artextes in Montreal.

Susan Rynard is a Toronto-based video artist and filmmaker, whose work has been screened at Festival Internationale Cinema Giovani (Turin), Kijkhuis (The Hague), the Hong Kong Film Festival, Fest Rio (Rio di Janeiro) and the Festival International du Nouveau Cinéma et de la Vidéo (Montreal). In recent years her work has appeared on CBC, TVOntario, KCTA Alive From Off Center and PBS New Television.

Tom Sherman is a writer and artist working in video, installation and audio arts. His video was exhibited at the Venice Biennale in 1980, and in 1983 the National Gallery of Canada mounted *Cultural Engineering*, a ten-year retrospective of his work. Sherman was Head of Media Arts at the Canada Council 1983-1987 and is currently Director of the School of Art at Syracuse University.

Lisa Steele is an artist and writer whose tapes have been widely exhibited, including the Venice Biennale (1980), Kunsthalle Basel, Museum of Modern Art (New York), National Gallery of Canada and elsewhere. She is a founding director of V tape, a founding publisher and editor of *Fuse* magazine, and past chair of the New Media Program at the Ontario College of Art where she has taught video since 1981. Since 1983 she has worked collaboratively with Kim Tomczak, producing videotapes, performances and photo-text works; their second dramatic feature-length work is presently in production.

Nell Tenhaaf, a visual artist and writer, lives in Montreal Quebec and in Pittsburgh, Pennsylvania, where she teaches at Carnegie Mellon University. Integral to her practice has been a long term involvement with the collective artist-run network. In 1991 she was co-organizer of a residency and seminar on the Bioapparatus at the Banff Centre for the Arts. Her recent work addresses biology and biotechnology from a feminist perspective.

Dot Tuer is a writer and critic living in Toronto. She has written extensively on gender, sexuality, and video for *C Magazine, Parallelogramme* and *Fuse*, as well as catalogue essays on the work of Vera Frenkel, Lisa Steele and Kim Tomczak.

Elizabeth Vander Zaag has worked with video and computers in Vancouver since 1976, and is one of the pioneers of digital video in Canada. The founder and coordinator of Western Front Multimedia, she continues to develop software tools to expland the emotional potential of multimedia interaction. In 1995, her first interactive CD-ROM, *Whispering Pines.*, was published.

TEXT SOURCES

Alioff, Maurie. "Points of Contact." *Matrix* 40 (Summer 1993): 83-4

Anderson, John. "Normalization of Relations," *Centerfold* 3:3 (February/March 1979): 129

Baert, Renee. "Desiring Daughters." *Screen* 34:2 (Summer 1993): 109-23

Beaucage, Marjorie. "Self-Government in Art: to Create Anew .../Être autonome ... être autochtone ... se re-créer." *Parallelogramme* 19:1 (1993): 32-7

———. "An Interview with Wil Campbell," transcribed from videotape, 1994. (previously unpublished)

Bégin, Jean-Yves. "The Vidéographe Challenge," was published originally as "Vidéographe a relevé le defi." In *Médium-Media: Videosphère* (1973): 13-21

Berland, Jody. "Video . Language . The Common/place." In *Luminous Sites/Ten Video Installations*, eds. Daina Augaitis and Karen Henry. Vancouver: Video Inn/Western Front, 1986.

Bull, Hank. "On TV: The Gina Show on Cable Ten, Vancouver." *Centerfold* 3:3 (February/March 1979): 128-30

Cameron, Eric. "Notes for Video Art." In *Video Circuits*. Guelph: University of Guelph 1973.

Carrière, Daniel. "Who They Are, Who They Were, Who They're Going To Be," was published originally as "Qu'ils soient, qu'ils étaient, qu'ils allaient être: entrevue avec Charles Guilbert et Serge Murphy." *ETC Montréal* 16 (November 1991): 74-6

Cousineau, Marie-Hélène. "Inuit Women's Video/Des femmes inuits vidéastes." *Parallelogramme* 19:4 (1994): 34-9

Diamond, Sara. "Daring Documents: The Practical Politics of Early Vancouver Video," *Vancouver Anthology: The Institutional Politics of Art*. ed. Stan Douglas. Vancouver: Talonbooks, 1991.

Diamond, Sara, and Gary Kibbins. "Total Recall: History, Memory & New Documentary." In *Trade Initiatives: 3 Programmes of Canadian Video*, eds. Sara Diamond and Gary Kibbins. Vancouver: Satellite Video Exchange Society, 1988.

Elliott, George. "A Warning to Artists." *Canadian Art* 10:3 (Spring 1953): 105-6

Ferguson, Bruce W. "Colin Campbell: Otherwise Worldly." In *Colin Campbell/Media Works 1972-1990*, ed. Bruce Ferguson. Winnipeg: Winnipeg Art Gallery, 1991.

———. "Left Beholding the Promised Land: Ardele Lister in America." In *Four Visions of Television: Daniel Dion, Ardele Lister, Robert Morin, Jan Peacock*, ed. Brian Rusted. Banff: Artists Television Workshop, Banff Centre for the Arts, 1991.

Forget, Robert. Original proposal to National Film Board for establishment of Vidéographe, 1970. (previously unpublished)

Frenkel, Vera. This script fragment from "The Last Screening Room — A Valentine," was published as part of "Ruling Fictions: The Small & Large Betrayals that Haunt us Once Again." *C* 4 (Winter 1985): 31-5

Fung, Richard. "Colouring the Screen: Four Strategies in Anti-Racist Film and Video"/"L'écran coloré: cinématographie et vidéographie - quatre stratégies antiracistes." *Parellogramme* 18:3 (1992-3): 38-52

Gagnon, Jean. "Video: One little word for a many-faceted thing," was published originally as "Vidéo: Un bien petit mot pour un objet multiple." *Possibles* 9:4 (Summer 1985): 43-53

———. "Entanglement: Video Art and TV." *Open Letter* 8:7 (Summer 1993): 46-56

Gale, Peggy. "Video has captured our imagination." *Parachute* 7 (Summer 1977): 16-18

———. "Stan Douglas: *Evening* and Others." *Parachute* 79 (Summer 1995): 20-7

General Idea. "Towards an Audience Vocabulary [with Jo-Anne Birnie Danzker]." *Centerfold* 3:1 (December 1978): 13-18

Gingras, Nicole. "Stories in Reserve," was published originally as "Michèle Waquant: Histoires en réserve." *Vie des Arts* 37:149 (Winter 1992-3): 34-7

Goldberg, Michael.*The Accessible Portapak Manual*. Vancouver: The Satellite Video Exchange Society, 1976.

Greyson, John. "Double Agents: Video Art Addressing AIDS/Agents doubles: l'art vidéo vise le SIDA." *Parallelogramme* 15:2 (Fall 1989): 22-31

Greyson, John, and Lisa Steele. "The Inukshuk Project/Inuit TV: The Satellite Solution." *Fuse* 4:4 (May 1980): 203-6

Haustein, Lydia. "The Transformative Power of Memory: Themes and Methods in the Work of Vera Frenkel/Le Pouvoir transformateur de la mémoire: thèmes et méthodes dans l'oeuvre de Vera Frenkel." In *Vera Frenkel ... from the Transit Bar/ ... du transitbar*. Toronto: The Power Plant/Ottawa: National Gallery of Canada, 1994.

Hume, Vern. "Another Look at the Plot for the Western Re: Placing the Satellite: Media Culture on the Plains." *Video Guide* 9:1 (October 1987): 6-7

Igloolik Isuma Productions, Inc. Funding proposal to Telefilm Canada, for *Nunavut* series, 1993. (previously unpublished)

Innis, Harold. "The Bias of Communication." In *The Bias of Communication*. Toronto: University of Toronto Press, 1951.

Lai, Larissa. "The Site of Memory." In *As Public As Race*. Banff: The Walter Phillips Gallery, 1993.

Langlois, Monique. "Expanding genres," was published originally as "L'éclatement des genres." *ETC Montréal* 15 (Summer 1991): 76-9

Le Gris, Françoise. "Mirages of Anticipation," was published originally as "Les mirages de l'anticipation." *ETC Montréal* (September 1990): 30-2

McIntosh, David. "Cyborgs in Denial: Technology and Identity in the Net." *Fuse* 17:3 (Spring 1994): 14-22

McLuhan, Marshall. "Media Hot and Cold." In *Understanding Media: The Extensions of Man*. Cambridge: MIT Press, 1994.

Peacock, Jan. *Corpus Loquendi (body for speaking)*. Halifax: Dalhousie Art Gallery, 1994.

Poissant, Louise. "Video: Writing History," was published originally as "La vidéo, écriture d'histoire." In *Paysage(s) de la vidéo*, ed. Monique Langlois. Montreal: Galerie UQAM, 1994.

Ross, Becki. "Having the Last Laugh." *Fuse* 13:5 (June/July 1990): 26-9

Ross, Christine. "Vidéo: Vers un rénouvellement vidéographique de la critique d'art/Video: Towards a renewal of art criticism." *Parallelogramme* 14:3 (Winter 1988): 13-16

———. "La vidéographie de la défaillance, ou l'esthétique du lien chez Daniel Dion/Breakdown Video or The Link Aesthetic in the Work of Daniel Dion." In *Daniel Dion: Parcours/Paths*. Ottawa: National Gallery of Canada, 1993.

Rynard, Susan. "Tested Fictions and Twisted Fragments." *Fuse* 13:4 (Spring 1990): 42-4

Sherman, Tom. "Adjusting a Colour Television," was first published as part of "Introduction." In *Video By Artists*, ed. Peggy Gale. Toronto: Art Metropole, 1976.

———. "Appearance, Memory and Influence." In *Video By Artists 2*, ed. Elke Town. Toronto: Art Metropole, 1986.

Steele, Lisa. "Rodney Werden's 'Baby Dolls'." *Centerfold* 2:6 (September 1978): 95-6

Tenhaaf, Nell. "Of Monitors and Men and Other Unsolved Feminist Mysteries"/"Des moniteurs et des hommes et autres mystères féministes non-résolus." *Parellogramme* 18: 3 (1992-3): 24-37

Tuer, Dot. "Utopias of Resistance/ Strategies of Cultural Self-Determination." In *4 Hours and 38 Minutes: Videotapes by Lisa Steele and Kim Tomczak*, ed. Philip Monk. Toronto: Art Gallery of Ontario, 1989.

Vander Zaag, Elizabeth. "Articulate Video." *Video Guide* 9:1 (October 1987): 3

PHOTO SOURCES

page 17: Detail of Leslie watching TV, from *Quartet for Deafblind*, 1986, by Norman Cohn. Photo courtesy the artist.

page 18: ... *from the Transit Bar* installation (detail) by Vera Frenkel at Documenta IX, 1992. Photo by Dirk Bleicker.

page 55: *Buck* (detail), 1986, by Vern Hume and Leila Sujir. Photo courtesy V tape.

page 56: Production still from *Qaggiq (Gathering Place)*, 1989, by Zacharias Kunuk, Igloolik Isuma Productions, Inc. Photo courtesy the artist.

pages 97, 98, 102-105: Facsimile pages from *The Accessible Portapack Manual* (details) by Michael Goldberg, published by Satellite Video Exchange Society, Vancouver, 1976.

pages 135 and 136: *Sixty Unit Bruise*, 1976, by Paul Wong (collaboration with Kenneth Fletcher). Photos courtesy Video Out Distribution.

page 231: *La Femme étrangère* (detail), 1988, by Robert Morin and Lorraine Dufour. Photo courtesy V tape.

page 232: *Chinese Characters* (detail), 1987, by Richard Fung. Photo courtesy V tape.

page 291: *Sackville, I'm Yours* (detail), 1972, by Colin Campbell. Photo courtesy V tape.

page 292: *Great Divide/Grande barrière* (detail), 1990, by Daniel Dion. Photo courtesy Vidéographe Inc.

pages 367 and 368: Production still from *Sois sage ô ma Douleur (et tiens-toi plus tranquille)*, 1990, by Serge Murphy and Charles Guilbert. Photo courtesy Vidéographe Inc.

page 411: *Palimpseste sentimental* (detail), 1990, by Suzan Vachon. Photo courtesy Vidéographe Inc.

page 412: *White Dawn* (detail), 1988, by Lisa Steele and Kim Tomczak. Photo courtesy V tape.

Inside front and back cover: *Towards an Audience Vocabulary (standing ovation)*, 1978, by General Idea. Performance at the Fifth Network/Cinquième Réseau Video Conference, Toronto, 1978. Photo courtesy the artists.

Cover: *Twinitron*, 1992, by David Buchan. Colour photograph 183.0 x 122.0 cm. Courtesy the estate of David Buchan.

DISTRIBUTOR'S LIST

235 Media
Spichernstrasse 61
Köln 1
Germany 5000
tel. 49 221 52 21 35 or 49 221 52 38 28
fax 49 221 52 27 41

Albany Video Battersea Studios TV Centre
Thackery Road
London SW8 3TW
England
tel. 44 171 498-6811
fax 44 171 498-1494

Antenna
365 St. Paul ouest, Suite 1
Montreal, Quebec
Canada H2Y 2A7
tel. 514 848-6248
fax 514 848-6063

Art Com
P.O. Box 3123 Rincon
San Francisco, CA 94119-3123
USA
tel. 415 431-7524
fax 415 431-7841

Centre Audiovisuel Simone De Beauvoir
Palais de Tokyo
2 rue de la Manutention
Paris 75116
France
tel. 33 1 47 23 67 48

Cinema Libre
4067 Boul. St. Laurent, #403
Montreal, Quebec
Canada H2W 1Y7
tel. 514 849-7888
fax 514 849-1231

Drift Releasing
219 East 2nd Street, #5E
New York, N.Y. 10009
USA
tel. 212 254-4118
fax 212 254-3154

Electronic Arts Intermix, Inc.
536 Broadway, 9th floor
New York, N.Y. 10012
USA
tel. 212 966-4605
fax 212 941-6118

Film and Video Umbrella
2 Rugby Street
London WC1N 3QZ
England
tel. 44 171 831-7753
fax 44 171 831-7746

Frameline Distribution
346 Ninth Street
San Francisco, CA 94103
USA
tel. 415 703-8650
fax 415 861-1404

Groupe Intervention Video — GIV
C.P. Box 96, Succ. E
Montreal, Quebec
Canada H2T 3A5
tel. 514 271-5506

Heure Exquise!
BP 113 Mons en Baroeul
France 59370
tel. 33 20 04 95 74
fax 33 20 04 23 57

Inuit Broadcasting Corporation
Suite 703, 251 Laurier Ave,
Ottawa, Ontario
Canada K1P 5J6
tel. 613 235-1892

Kijkhuis
Noordeinde 140
2514 Den Haag
Netherlands
tel. 31 70 644805

Kitchen (The)
512 West 19th Street
New York, N.Y. 10011
USA
tel. 212 255-5793
fax 212 645 42 58

Le Lieu
345, rue du Pont
Quebec, Quebec
Canada G1K 6M4
tel. 418 529-9680

London Film Makers Co-Op
42 Gloucester Avenue
London NW1 8JD
England
tel. 44 171 586 4806
fax 44 171 483 0068

London Electronic Arts
5-7 Buck Street, Camden
London NW1 8NJ
England
tel. 44 1 71 284 4588
fax 44 1 71 267 6078
abina@el-arts.demon.co.uk

Lynx Distribution
174 Spadina Avenue #606
Toronto, Ontario
Canada M5T 2C2
tel. 416 504-9333
fax 416 504-1407

McNabb and Connolly
60 Briarwood Ave.,
Toronto, Ontario
Canada L5G 3N6
tel. 416 278-0566
fax 416 278-2801

Monte Video
Singel 137
1012 VJ Amsterdam
Netherlands
tel. 31 20 6237101
fax 31 20 6244423

**Moving Images Distribution
(formerly CFDW)**
402 West Pender Street, Ste. 606
Vancouver, B.C.
Canada V6B 1T6
tel. 604 684-3014
fax 604 684-7165

National Film Board
150 Kent Street
Ottawa, Ontario
Canada K1A 0M9
tel. 613 996-4863 / 772-8578

Native Communications Inc.
76 Severn Crescent
Thompson, Manitoba
Canada R8N 1M6
tel. 204 778-8343
fax 204 778-6559

Native Indian and Inuit Photographers Assoc.
134 James St. South
Hamilton, Ontario
Canada L8P 2Z4
tel. 905 529-7477
fax 905 522-6713

PIXART/Kaleidoscope
1755 East René Levesque Blvd, Local 102
Montreal, Quebec
Canada H2K 4P6
tel. 514 522-8811 ext 305
fax 514 597-1503

Saskatchewan Indian Cultural Centre
120-33rd Street East
Saskatoon, Saskatchewan
Canada S7K 0S2
tel. 306 244-1146
fax 306 665-6520

Scan Video Gallery
Jingu-mae 1-21-1, Shibuya-Ku
Tokyo
Japan 150
tel. 81 3 470 26 64
fax 81 3 470 22 59

Third World Newsreel
335 West 38th Street, 5th Floor
New York, N.Y. 10018
USA
tel. 212 947-9277
fax 212 594-6917

Time Based Arts
Bloemgracht 121
Amsterdam 1016KK
Netherlands
tel. 31 20 22 97 64

Upstream Productions
420 1st Avenue West
Seattle, Washington 98119
USA
tel. 206 281-9177
fax 206 284-6963

Video Classroom
142-144 Coppin St.
Richmond
Australia 3121
tel. 61 03 429-5766
fax 61 03 429-9328

Video Data Bank Chicago
37 South Wabash
(c/o The Art Institute of Chicago)
Chicago, Illinois 60603
USA
tel. 312 345-3550
In New York: 212 233-3441
fax 312 541-8072 & 312 541-8073

Video Femmes
700 rue du Roi
Quebec, Quebec
Canada G1K 2X7
tel. 418 529-9188
fax 418 648-9201

Video Out
1965 Main St.
Vancouver, B.C.
Canada V5T 3C1
tel. 604 872-8449
fax 604 876-1185

Video Pool
100 Arthur St, # 300
Winnipeg, Manitoba
Canada R3B 1H3
tel. 204 949-9134
fax 204 942-1555

Video Verite
12-23rd Street East, 3rd Floor
Saskatoon, Saskatchewan
Canada S7K 0H5
tel. 306 652-5502
fax 306 665-6568

Vidéographe
4550 rue Garnier
Montreal, Quebec
Canada H2J 3S7
tel. 514 521-2116
fax 514 521-1676

Videografia
72 Carrer Berlin, Baixos/Interior
Barcelona
Spain 08029
tel. 34 3 321 68 54

V tape
401 Richmond Street West, Suite 452
Toronto, Ontario
Canada M5V 3A8
tel. 416 351-1317
fax 416 351-1509

Women Make Movies, Inc.
462 Broadway, 5th floor
New York, N.Y. 10013
USA
tel. 212 925-0606
fax 212 925-2052

Compiled by PEGGY GALE
With additional French-language material from
CRISTINA SOFIA MARTINEZ

∾ indicates exhibition catalogue

A Abbott, Jennifer, ed. *Making Video "In"/The Contested Ground of Alternative Video on the West Coast.* Vancouver: Video In Studios, 1996. With essays by Sara Diamond, Michael Goldberg, Karen Knights, Nancy Shaw and Paul Wong.

Adelman, Shonagh. "Lesbian Lovebite." *Fuse* 12:5 (April/May 1989): 43

———. "Five Feminist Videotapes/Redefining the Female Subject." *C* 28 (Winter 1991): 24–32

———. "Reading Girrly Pictures." *BorderLines* No. 37 (August 1995): 28–35

Adelman, Shonagh, and Bryan Gee. "Despair [on Paulette Phillips/Geoffrey Shea]." *Fuse* 48, 11:4 (Winter 1987–8): 35

Alioff, Maurie. "Points of Contact [on Julian Samuel]." *Matrix* 40 (Summer 1993): 83–4

Allan, Blaine. "Some Notes on Video Art and Experimental Film." In *Signal Approach.* Toronto: The Funnel, 1984.∾

Allin, Heather. "Designing Sexuality: Understanding 'Identity' in Women's Video Production." In *The Event Horizon. Essays on Hope, Sexuality, Social Space and Media(tion) in Art*, eds. Lorne Falk and Barbara Fischer. Toronto: The Coach House Press/Banff: Walter Phillips Gallery, 1987.

Alteen, Glenn. "Cultural Appropriation and Post-Modernism." *Video Guide* 11:2 (Fall 1991): 5

———. "Joe Sarahan." *Fuse* 16:4 (May/June 1993): 45–6

Ambrosi, Alain, and Nancy Thede, eds. *Video the Changing World.* Montreal: Black Rose Books, 1991.

Amis, Ric, and Cyndra MacDowell. "Film and Video Against Censorship." *Parallelogramme* 8:1 (October/November 1982): 13–14

Amis, Ric, and Bill Perry. "Telidon: Today and Tomorrow/Telidon: aujourd'hui, demain." *Parallelogramme* 7:1 (November 1981): 10–11, 16–17

Ammann, Jean-Christophe, ed. *Kanadische Künstler: Paterson Ewen, Vincent Tangredi, Greg Curnoe, N.E.Thing Company, Robin Collyer, Ian Carr-Harris, Eric Fischl, Shirley Wiitasalo, General Idea/ Videobeiträge.* Basel: Kunsthalle, 1978.∾ Includes an essay on Canadian video by Peggy Gale.

Amundson, Dale. "Streams and Rivers: a brief background on electronic art," "Tools," "Order," "Some History," "The Exhibitions." In *Beyond Electronics.* Winnipeg: School of Art, University of Manitoba, Gallery 1.1.1. and Main/Access Gallery, 1989.∾

Amundsen, Dale, ed. *Beyond Electronics.* Winnipeg: Gallery 1.1.1., University of Manitoba, 1990.∾ Includes extensive bibliography and examination of social consequences of media.

Aquin, Stéphane. "Vidéo: une présence ondoyante." In *Un Archipel des désirs: les artistes du Québec et la scène internationale*, ed. Louise Déry. Quebec: Musée du Québec, 1991.∾

———. "Barbara Steinman/Galerie René Blouin." *Parachute* 70 (Spring 1993): 32–3

Arbec, Jules. "Graphisme lumineux: Gilles Chartier." *Vie des Arts* 18:71 (Summer 1973): 56–9

Arbour, Rose Marie. "Arts 'engagés': Nicole Jolicoeur et Barbara Steinman." *Possibles* 13:1/2 (Winter 1989): 169–78

Arbour, Rose Marie, ed. "Du public: Chantal duPont, Paul-André Fortier, Alain Fournier, Lise Gauvin, Nicole Jolicoeur." *Possibles* 15:4 (Autumn 1991): 25–46

Armitage, Kay. "The Body-That-Disappears-Into-Thin-Air: Vera Frenkel's Video Art." In *Mirror Machine: Video and Identity,* ed. Janine Marchessault. Toronto: YYZ Books/Montreal: Centre for Research on Canadian Cultural Industries and Institutions, McGill University, 1995.

Arn, Robert. "The form and sense of video." *artscanada* 30:4, 182/183 (October 1973): 15–24

———. "Michael Snow and Video: The Archaeology of Image." *artscanada* 30:4, 182/183 (October 1973): 22–4

Arroyo, Jose, and Jamie Gaetz. "Locked out of the women's room: Montreal International Festival of women's Films and Videos." *Cinema Canada* (September 1988): 29–30

Art and Correspondence from the Western Front: Kate Craig, Glenn Lewis, Eric Metcalfe, Michael Morris, Vincent Trasov. Vancouver: Western Front Publications, 1979.ↄ With an unsigned introduction and essays by Glenn Lewis, Eric Metcalfe/Kate Craig and Michael Morris/Vincent Trasov.

Artropolis/Exhibition of Contemporary British Columbia Art. Vancouver: Artropolis, 1987.ↄ With essays by Annette Hurtig, Ian Wallace and Scott Watson, and statements by Willard Holmes, Anna Banana, Marion Barling, Todd A. Davis, Donna Hagerman and Elizabeth Vander Zaag.

Artropolis 90/Lineages & Linkages. Vancouver: A.T. Eight Artropolis Society, 1990.ↄ With essays by Ann Rosenberg and Ed Varney, and statements by the artists and curators.

Art/Vidéo/Confrontation. Paris: Musée d'Art Moderne de la Ville de Paris, 1974.ↄ Includes Colin Campbell.

Art <–> Vidéo: les oeuvres vidéographiques de douze artistes canadiens. Montreal: Véhicule Art, 1977.ↄ With essays by Pierre Brochu, Marty Dunn, Gilbert Lachapelle, Denis L'Espérance, Sean Hennessey and Al Razutis.

Art Vidéo, Rétrospectives et perspectives. Charleroi: Palais des Beaux-Arts, 1983.ↄ Includes *Intérêts* video installation by Michael Snow.

Askevold, David. "Notes for Explanation and Attitude" and "The Ambit and Notes Found on Boutiliers Point September 1975 – January 1976." In *Video By Artists,* ed. Peggy Gale. Toronto: Art Metropole, 1976.

———. *Red Rider.* Halifax: Centre for Art Tapes, 1992.

As Public As Race. Banff: The Walter Phillips Gallery, 1993.ↄ Includes "The Site of Memory" by Larissa Lai.

Attali, Jean. "De Simples Ombres/Sunk Into Mere Shadows." In *Sylvie Bélanger: Topologies du regard,* ed. Sharon Kivland. Herblay (France): Les Cahiers des Regards, 1991.ↄ

Augaitis, Daina. *Essential Form.* Banff: Walter Phillips Gallery, 1989.ↄ Includes video installation by François Girard.

Augaitis, Daina, and Manon Blanchette. *Poetic Signals/Signaux poétiques.* Banff: Walter Phillips Gallery, 1986.ↄ With untitled essays by Daina Augaitis and Manon Blanchette.

Augaitis, Daina, and Karen Henry. "Retrieving Culture." In *Luminous Sites/Ten Video Installations,* eds. Daina Augaitis and Karen Henry. Vancouver: Video Inn/Western Front, 1986.ↄ

Augaitis, Daina, and Karen Henry, eds. *Luminous Sites/Ten Video Installations.* Vancouver: Video Inn/Western Front, 1986.ↄ With artists' statements and essays by Daina Augaitis/Karen Henry, Jody Berland, Peggy Gale and Merike Talve.

Augaitis, Daina, and Helga Pakesaar. *Video Theatrics.* Banff: Walter Phillips Gallery, 1987.ↄ

———. *Heroics: A Critical View.* Banff: Walter Phillips Gallery, 1988.ↄ Includes video installation by Sara Diamond.

Aurora Boréalis. Montreal: Centre International d'Art Contemporain de Montréal, 1985. With essays by René Blouin, Lesley Johnstone and Normand Thériault.ↄ Includes video installation by Vera Frenkel.

Austen-Marshall, R. (Vera Frenkel, pseud.) "Biographical Notes." In Louise Dompierre and Vera Frenkel. *Likely Stories: Text/Image/Sound Works for Video and Installation.* Kingston: Agnes Etherington Art Centre, 1982.ↄ

Ayre, Robert. "Art and Television — in Montreal and Toronto." *Canadian Art* 10:3 (Spring 1953): 103–5

A-Z Répertoire 1971–1986. Montreal: Vidéographe, 1986. With essays by Claude Forget and Jean Tourangeau, plus history of the organization by Claude Forget.

B   Back, Doug. "Interview." In *Art is Communication*, eds. Paul Petro and Geoffrey Shea. Toronto: A Space, 1985.☙

Baele, Nancy. "Video award winners make compelling series on Inuit culture [on Zacharias Kunuk and Norman Cohn]." *Inuit Art Quarterly* (fall 1994). Reprinted from *The Ottawa Citizen*, 25 May 1994.

Baert, Renee. "Video Recycled." *artscanada* 29:4, 172/173 (October/November 1972): 55–6

———. "Video/Video: Video/Television." In *Video/Vidéo*. Toronto: Video Trade Forum, Festival of Festivals, 1981.☙

———. "Video in Kanada: Ein Uberblick über die Produktion/Video in Canada: A Context of Production." In *OKanada*. Berlin: Akademie der Künste, 1982.☙

———. "Video/Culture Canada." *Vanguard* 13:2 (March 1984): 22–3

———. *Video Refractions*. London (Ont): London Regional Art Gallery, 1984.☙ Independent video on cable television 1978–81.

———. "Artists' Markings in the TV Landscape/Empreintes de l'artiste dans le paysage télé." In *Prime Time Video*, ed. Allan MacKay. Saskatoon: Mendel Art Gallery, 1984.☙

———. *Television Interference*. Vancouver: Presentation House Gallery, 1984.☙ Interventions by artists into television through appropriation of form/content.

———. *Fascination with the Other/The Constructed Self/Private Lives, Public Stories*. Toronto: Artculture Resource Centre, 1985.☙ A three-part exhibition of narrative video: brochure with text.

———. "La vidéo au Canada: en quête d'une identité/Video in Canada: In Search of Authority." In *Vidéo*, ed. René Payant. Montreal: Artextes, 1986.

———. *Vintage Video: Early Canadian Video Art to 1974*. Toronto: Artculture Resource Centre, 1986.☙

———. "Luminous Sites: 10 Video Installations." *Canadian Art* 3:2 (Summer 1986): 89–91

———. "Video in Canada: In Search of Authority." In *From Sea to Shining Sea*, ed. A.A. Bronson. Toronto: The Power Plant, 1987.☙

———. "Breaking Through: Conscience and the Status Quo." In *The Event Horizon. Essays on Hope, Sexuality, Social Space and Media(tion) in Art*, eds. Lorne Falk and Barbara Fischer. Toronto: The Coach House Press/Banff: Walter Phillips Gallery, 1987.

———. "Focus on Barbara Steinman." *Canadian Art* 5:4 (Winter 1988): 95

———. *Enchantment/Disturbance*. Toronto: The Power Plant, 1989.☙ Includes video installation by Barbara Steinman.

———. "Subjects on the Threshold: Problems with the Pronouns." *Parachute* 69 (Winter 1993): 14–21

———. "Desiring Daughters." *Screen* 34:2 (Summer 1993): 109–23

———. "Subjects on the Threshold: Problems with the Pronouns." In *Mirror Machine: Video and Identity*, ed. Janine Marchessault. Toronto: YYZ Books/Montreal: Centre for Research on Canadian Cultural Industries and Institutions, McGill University, 1995.

Baert, Renee, ed. *The Video Issue/Propos Vidéo*. Vancouver: Satellite Video Exchange Society, 1992–3 (published simultaneously in various Canadian magazines/journals) Essays by Renee Baert, Jessica Bradley, Lorne Falk, Richard Fung, Jean Gagnon, Peggy Gale, Christine Ross, Nell Tenhaff, Jean Tourangeau and Dot Tuer.

Bailey, Cameron. "The Heart of a Difficult Place [on Richard Fung]." *Fuse* 11:6 (July 1988): 37

Baker, Lang. "Janine Marchessault." *Parachute* 60 (Fall 1990): 64–5

Balkind, Alvin, ed. *From This Point of View: 60 British Columbia Painters, Sculptors, Photographers, Graphic and Video Artists*. Vancouver: Vancouver Art Gallery, 1977.☙ With an essay on video by Paul Wong and on photography by Gary Michael Dault.

Balser, Michael, ed. *Tenth Anniversary Showcase: The Independent Film and Video Alliance*. Toronto: IFVA 1990. With essays by Kass Banning, Christine Conley, Jeannette Reinhardt and Claude Forget.

Bancroft, Marian Penner. "We Want Moschiach (The Messiah) Now! Portrait of a Chassidic Community: An Installation by Paula Levine." In *We Want Moschiach Now! — Portrait of a Chassidic Community: An*

Installation by Paula Levine, ed. Karen Love. Vancouver: Presentation House Gallery, 1985.◐

Bannerjee, Himani. "Now You See Us/Now You Don't." *Video Guide* 8:5 (1987): 7–9

Bannerji, Kaushalya. "No More Multiculturalism?" *Fuse* 16:4 (May/June 1993): 6–7

Banning, Kass. "Culture for Sale: Recent Toronto Works." *Cinema Canada* 149 (February 1988): 11–12

———."Local Channels: Zach Kunuk Remodels TV/Chaînes locales: Zach Kunuk refaçonne la TV." *Parellogramme* 17:1 (Summer 1991): 24–31

Barber, Bruce. "Nancy Nicol." *Parachute* 30 (Spring 1983): 56–7 On 'Intervention Productions Presents: Let Poland Be Poland'

———. "Evidence of the Avant-Garde since 1957: Selected Works from the Collection of Art Metropole." *Parachute* 38 (Spring 1985): 46–7

Barling, Marion. "Women/Media Manipulation." *Video Guide* 1:2 (April/May 1978): 5

———. "A Paradoxical Puzzle/Une énigme paradoxale." *Parellogramme* 9:4 (April/May 1984): 17–18, 32–3

———. "To Be or Not To Be? And From the Darkness, Let There Be Light: Some Thoughts on Developing a Feminist Perspective." *Video Guide* 6:3 (May 1984): 6

Bearham, Howard. "T.B.C./Time Base Correctors: Tools of the Trade."*Video Guide* 11:2 (Fall 1991): 17

Beatty, Greg. "Ruth Chambers — Ellen Moffat: Inside Outside." *Espace* 31 (Spring 1995): 25–8

Beaucage, Marjorie. "Self-Government in Art: to Create Anew . . ./Etre autonome . . . être autochtone . . . se re-créer." *Parallelogramme* 19:1 (1993): 32–7

———. "Aboriginal Voices: Entitlement through Storytelling." In *Mirror Machine: Video and Identity*, ed. Janine Marchessault. Toronto: YYZ Books/Montreal: Centre for Research on Canadian Cultural Industries and Institutions, McGill University, 1995.

Beaucage, Marjorie, ed . . . . *Here are your instructions/Aboriginal Film and Video.* Saskatoon: Mendel Art Gallery, 1994.◐

With foreword by Bruce Grenville, introductory essay and programme commentary by Marjorie Beaucage.

Beaudet, Pascale. "Jacques et Novembre: la froideur de la vidéo." *Copie Zéro* 24 (June 1983): 10–11

Beaulieu-Green, Andrée. "L'ordinateur, un outil de création?" *Cahiers des Arts Visuelles du Québec* 7:28 (Winter 1986): 16–18

Beck, Claudia. "Video: The Audio-Visual Officer & Things to Come at the VAG [interview with Nelson Becker]." *Vanguard* 5:2 (March 1976): 6–7

Bégin, Jean-Yves. "Le film et les media communautaires comme instrument d'intervention sociale." *Médium-Media* 4 (n.p., n.d.)

———. "Le Vidéographe a relevé le défi." *Médium-Media: Vidéosphère* (1973?): 13–21

Bell, Shannon. "Ejaculatory Television: The Talk Show and the Postmodern Subject." *Fuse* 14: 5/6 (Agit-Prop Special Issue 1991): 6–11

Bénichou, Anne. "De l'exposition à l'événement." *Espace* 6:2 (Winter 1990): 29–33

———."Hull: Les relations sigillaires d'André Clément." *ETC Montréal* 23 (August/November 1993): 53–6

———. "Le Lieu, l'oeil et la terreur." *ETC Montréal* 25 (February/May 1994): 30–2

Bérard, Serge. "ASA 86." *Parachute* 46 (Winter 1986–7): 30–1 Includes video installation 'Le Parcours dans le monde fascinant des arts technologiques' (1986) by Jacques Charbonneau.

———. "Nell Tenhaaf/Galerie Yahouda Meir." *Parachute* 47 (Summer 1987): 30–1

Berger, Sally. "Time Travelers [on Igloolik Isuma Productions]." *Felix: Landscape(s)* 2:1 (1995): 102–112

Berland, Jody. "Sound, Image and the Media / Rock and Social Construction." *Parachute* 41 (Winter 1985–6): 12–19

———. "Video . Language . The Common/place." In *Luminous Sites/Ten Video Installations*, eds. Daina Augaitis and Karen Henry. Vancouver: Video Inn/Western Front, 1986.◐

———. "International Video/Images in Translation." *Vanguard* 16:2 (April/May 1987): 26–8

———. "Valuing the View [on Paul Landon]." In *Paysage(s) de la vidéo,* ed. Monique Langlois. Montreal: Galerie UQAM, 1994.◌

Beveridge, Karl. "Colonialist Chic or Radical Cheek? 'Me$$age to China'." *Centerfold* 3:5 (July 1979): 271

XIe Biennale de Paris. Paris: Musée d'Art Moderne de la Ville de Paris/Centre Georges Pompidou, 1980.◌ Canadian video includes Susan Britton, Elizabeth Chitty, Kate Craig and Noel Harding, and performance by Tim Clark, Max Dean, John Greyson and Kim Tomczak.

"11e Biennale de Paris: Les Canadiens." *Parachute* 20 (Fall 1980): 4–17 Includes artists' statements for video works by Susan Britton, Elizabeth Chitty, Tim Clark and Kate Craig/Margaret Dragu, and a statement by Jane Perdue for Noel Harding.

Bissonnette, Alain. "Cinéastes-artisans." *Cinéma Québec* 50 (Summer 1977): 22–4

———. "'Pea Soup': une histoire à finir avec Falardeau et Poulin." *Cinéma Québec* 58 (September–October 1978) (n.p.)

Black, Byron. "Can You Take It With You?" *Video Guide* 7:3 (May 1985): 4–5

———. "The Medium Reveals Itself: Developing a Curriculum for the Teaching of Small-Format Video." *Video Guide* 7:4 (Issue 34, 1985): 8–9, 12–13

———. "An Ideal Tool for Snapshooters." *Video Guide* 8:1 (Issue 36, 1986): 14–15

Blaine, Ken. "The September Purge [on Vancouver Cable 10]." *Fuse* 7:1/2 (Summer 1983): 54–9

Blair, Jennifer. "Smashing Icons: Vancouver Feminist Video Art and the Female Body." *C* 43 (Fall 1994): 43–50

Blanchette, Manon. "Topologie d'une Simulation Poétique: Anne Ramsden." *Vanguard* 14:2 (March 1985): 15–17, 18–20

———. "Vidéo 84: visionnement/Montréal." *Vanguard* 14:2 (March 1985): 35–6

———. "Through Television and Back." In *Canadian Video Art,* ed. René Coelho. Amsterdam: The Holland Festival, 1985.◌

———. "Contemporary Videography: Essay om a Critique of Religious Myth/Vidéographie actuelle. Essai sur une critique du mythe religieux." *Protée* 13:3 (Autumn 1985): 59–64

———. "Of Baroque and Videography." In *The Event Horizon. Essays on Hope, Sexuality, Social Space and Media(tion) in Art,* eds. Lorne Falk and Barbara Fischer. Toronto: The Coach House Press/Banff: Walter Phillips Gallery, 1987.

———. *Anicca: une installation vidéo de Daniel Dion.* Montreal: Musée d'Art Contemporain, 1989.◌

Blanchette, Manon, ed. *Tom Sherman: Vidéogrammes et écrits/un aspect différent de la télévision.* Montreal: Musée d'Art Contemporain, 1982. (Eng/Fr) ◌ With texts by Tom Sherman and introduction by Manon Blanchette; chronology by Louise Gagné.

Blouin, René. "Tom Sherman: See the Text Comes to Read You." *Centerfold* 3:1 (December 1978): 19–22

———. "Video: 'The Damages,' 'Makin' Strange,' 'The Scientists,' 'Modern Love,' 'Envisioner,' 'Individual Release'." *Parachute* 14 (Spring 1979): 54–5

———. "Video: 'As the World Burns: The Videotape,' 'A Very Delicate Invasion,' 'Casting Call'." *Parachute* 15 (Summer 1979): 65–6

———. "Vidéo et Performance." In *Living Art Vancouver,* eds. Glenn Lewis, Kim Tomczak and Paul Wong. Vancouver: Western Front/Pumps/Video Inn, 1980.

———. "'Chaperons Rouges' by Helen Doyle and Hélène Bourgault." *Centerfold* 4:2 (January 1980): 4–5

———. "Ingénieries Culturelles." *Vie des Arts* 28:113 (December 1983/January 1984): 66–7

———. "Le Western Front: centre alternatif/The Western Front: Alternative Centre." In *Western Front: Vidéo.* Montreal: Musée d'Art Contemporain, 1984.◌

———. "Norman Cohn/Musée d'art contemporain." *Parachute* 38 (Spring 1985): 39–40

———. "Vidéo 84." *Vie des Arts* 29:118 (Spring 1985): 24–7

———. "Aurora Boréalis." In *Aurora Boréalis.* Montreal: Centre International d'Art Contemporain de Montréal, 1985.

Bociurkiw, Marusia. "Community-Based Feminist Video Production in Toronto." *Video Guide* 6:5 (October 1984): 8–9

———. "Working the Double Shift [review]." *Video Guide* 7:1 (January 1985): 4–5

———. "India Hearts Beat." *Fuse* 12:6 (August 1989): 33

———. "Feminism and Narrative Strategy." *Video Guide* 10:2 (September 1989): 6

———. "Chick Flicks." *Fuse* 14:1/2 (Fall 1990): 20–1

Bodolai, Joe. "Transcript of a videotape interview with Joe Bodolai." *artscanada* 30:4, 182/183 (October 1973): 55–60

———. "Information: Toronto Art Scene on TV." *Parachute* 2 (Winter 1976): 39

Bodolai, Joe, and Isobel Harry. "Decentralization of the means of visual production." *artscanada* 30:4, 182/183 (October 1973): 66–72

Bonet, Eugeni. "Closed-Circuit Installations, Video Objects or Video Sculptures, Video Environments, Multi-Channel Installations, Video Performances . . . ." In *Video, el temps i l'espai*. Barcelona: Col.legi d'Arquitectes de Catalunya, 1980.

———. "La Apropacion es Robo/Appropriation is Theft." In *Desmontaje: Film, Video/Apropiacion, Reciclaje*, ed. Eugeni Bonet. Valencia: IVAM, Centre Julio Gonzalez, 1993, 13–36, 136–54.

Bonet, Eugeni, ed. *Desmontaje: Film, Video/Apropiacion, Reciclaje*. Valencia: IVAM, Centre Julio Gonzalez 1993. With essays by Yann Beauvais, Eugeni Bonet, Catherine Elwes, Joel Katz, William C. Wees and John Wyver. Includes video by Canadians Hank Bull, Gary Kibbins, Ardele Lister, Jorge Lozano/Christa Schadt, Ed Mowbray and Jayce Salloum, plus many films.

Bonora, Lola, ed. *Aspetti e Tendenze della Ricerca Video Canadese*. Ferrara: Centro Video Arte and L'Immagine Elettronica, 1989. With essays by Lola Bonora and Peggy Gale.

Borsa, Joan. "Tomiyo Sasaki/Dunlop Art Gallery." *Vanguard* 15:6 (December/January 1986/7): 30–1

Boulanger, Chantal. *Au verso du monde: une bande vidéo de Charles Guilbert, Serge Murphy, Michel Grou*. Montreal: Oboro, 1994.

Bourdon, Luc, Katherine Liberovskaya, and Nelson Henricks. *Video Art in Quebec and Canada*. Montreal: OPERA, 1994.

Bourgeois, Gail, Beatrice Bailey, and Lesley Turner. "Three Women Speak." *Fuse* 11:4 (Winter 1987–88): 31–3 [on Feminism and Art conference at Ontario College of Art, Toronto, September 1987. Includes comments by Louise Giguère and Lisa Steele, video by Paulette Phillips]

Boyer, Jean-Pierre. "Chartier et le video feedback." *Ateliers* 1:3 (1973): 6–7

———. *l'Image electronique*. Montreal: Musée d'Art Contemporain, 1974.

———. "Video: Zoom Out / Zoom In." In *Video By Artists*, ed. Peggy Gale. Toronto: Art Metropole, 1976.

Bradley, Jessica. *Working Truths Powerful Fictions*. Regina: Mackenzie Art Gallery, 1991.

———. "Doubling Narratives: Dereliction and Desire in Julie Zando's 'Let's Play Prisoners'." *CineAction* 30 (Winter 1992): 36–41

Brandon, Laura. "New Uses for Television." *Arts Atlantic* 4:1 (Spring 1982): 15

Brave New (Virtual) World — The challenge of change in the Media Arts/A Discussion Paper on Operations & Project Grants Evaluation Process and Proposed Program Changes. Toronto: Ontario Arts Council, 1994. With essays by Gitanjali, David Hlynsky, Marie-Jeanne Musiol and Ross Turnbull.

Bringhurst, Robert, ed. *Visions: Contemporary Art in Canada*. Vancouver/Toronto: Douglas & McIntyre, 1983.

Brisley, Stuart, and Maya Balcioglu. "Against Cultural Bacchanal." *Video Guide* 10:1 (March 1989): 4

British/Canadian Video Exchange '84. London: Canada House Cultural Centre, 1984. With introductions by Jeremy Welsh and Jane Wright.

Britton, Susan. "Susan Britton talks with Peggy Gale." In *The 1978 Canadian Video Open*. Calgary: Artons/Parachute Center for Cultural Affairs, 1978.

———. "Video Lunch." In *Transcript from The International Video Art Symposium 1979*. Kingston: Agnes Etherington Art Centre, 1979.

Brochu, Pierre. "Le medium vidéo, ou comment faire des hamburgers personnalisés." In *Art <–> Vidéo: les oeuvres vidéographiques de douze artistes canadiens.* Montreal: Véhicule Art, 1977.ᶜᐩ

Brodzky, Michael Ethan. "Within a common place: a response to Vera Frenkel's 'No Solution — A Suspense Thriller'." *artscanada* 35:3, 222/223 (October/November 1978): 48–52

———. "Graham Smith/ARC." *Vanguard* 11:7 (September 1982): 32

Bronson, A.A. "Truth and Beauty." *FILE* 3 (Fall 1975): 44

———. "Pablum for the Pablum Eaters." In *Video By Artists*, ed. Peggy Gale. Toronto: Art Metropole, 1976.

Bronson, A.A., ed. *From Sea to Shining Sea.* Toronto: The Power Plant, 1987.ᶜᐩ An extended and annotated chronology of artist-generated activity in Canada.

Brooks, Sharon. *Arnaud Maggs/Lisa Steele.* Toronto: Mercer Union, 1992.ᶜᐩ

———. *Tom Dean/Rae Johnson.* Toronto: Mercer Union, 1993.ᶜᐩ

Brousseau, Dean. "Katie." *Video Guide* 8:3 (September 1986): 10

Brown, Elizabeth. *Videoscape: Newfoundland Edition.* St. John's: Art Gallery of Memorial University, 1979.ᶜᐩ With an essay by Elizabeth Brown, concentrating on six Canadian artists.

Brunet-Weinmann, Monique. "Le Copy Art s'éclate." *Vie des Arts* 142 (Spring 1991): 16–22

Bull, Hank. "On TV: The Gina Show on Cable Ten, Vancouver." *Centerfold* 3:3 (February/March 1979): 128–30

———. "Out of Order: Elizabeth Chitty's 'Social Studies'." *Centerfold* 3:5 (July 1979): 268–70

———. "Curatorial Statement." In *Artropolis 90/Lineages & Linkages.* Vancouver: A.T. Eight Artropolos Society, 1990.ᶜᐩ

Burnett, Ron. "Vidéo-puce."*Copie Zéro* 26 (December 1985): 21–3

———. "Video Space/Video Time: The Electronic Image and Portable Video." In *Mirror Machine: Video and Identity*, ed. Janine Marchessault. Toronto: YYZ Books/Montreal: Centre for Research on Canadian Cultural Industries and Institutions, McGill University, 1995.

Burstyn, Varda. "Habits: Five Video Premieres." *Canadian Art* 3:3 (Fall 1986): 106–7

Busby, Cathy, ed. *'How Do I Look?' A Film and Video Series* . . . . Montreal: Concordia University/Fine Arts and Communications Studies, 1992.ᶜᐩ Includes an interview with Sara Diamond.

Butler, Jack, ed. *Doug Melnyk: Multi-Media Works 1980–1990.* Brandon: Art Gallery of Southwestern Manitoba, 1990.ᶜᐩ With essays by Jack Butler and Denis Lessard.

Butler, Jack, and Scott Ellis. "Behind-the-Screen Juggling Acts." *Fuse* 13:6 (Summer 1990): 14–15

C Callen, Michael. "Pinned and Wriggling: How Shall I Presume?"*Video Guide* 10:3/4 (November 1989): 16–17

Cameron, Eric. "Notes for Video Art." In *Video Circuits.* Guelph: University of Guelph 1973.ᶜᐩ

———. "Videotape and the University Art Programme." *Studio International* 187:987 (June 1974): 289–91

———. "Notes on Video Art." In *6 Videotapes by Eric Cameron.* Winnipeg: Gallery 1.1.1., University of Manitoba, 1974.

———. "The Grammar of the Video Image." *Arts Magazine* (December 1974): 48–51

———. "Colin Campbell: La belle histoire d'Art Star/Colin Campbell: The Story of Art Star." *Vie des Arts* 20:78 (Spring 1975): 46–7, 67–9

———. "La vidéographie dans un contexte d'art/Video in an Art Context — and Especially Videoscape." *Vie des Arts* 20:80 (Fall 1975): 62–3

———. "Structural Videotape in Canada." In *Video Art*, eds. Ira Schneider and Beryl Korot. New York: Harcourt Brace Jovanovich, 1976 (additional documentation on Cameron's video work pp. 26–7).

———. "Trois bandes vidéo de Noel Harding et la narration par illusion visuelle/Three Videotapes by Noel Harding and the Visual Illusion of Narrative." *Vie des Arts* 22:87 (September 1976): 50–1

———. "On Painting and Video (Upside Down)." *Parachute* 11 (Summer 1978): 14–17

———. "Keeping Marlene Out of the Picture — and Lawn/En gardant Marlene hors du tableau — et pelouse." In *Eric Cameron/ Noel Harding: Two Audio-Visual Constructs/ Deux installations audio-visuelles*, ed. Ted Lindberg. Vancouver: Vancouver Art Gallery, 1978.☙

———. *In Camera — and Lawn*. Victoria: Art Gallery of Greater Victoria, 1980. Includes proposals/statements for video installation.☙

———. "The Humour and the Videotapes of John Will." In *John Will: Triple Threat Artist*, ed. Peter White. Regina: Dunlop Art Gallery, 1988.☙

———. "A question of placing: Early Harding and Late Modern/Vragen omtrent de positie van: het Vroege werk van Harding en de Laat-modernen." In *Noel Harding*. Middelburg: De Vleeshal/Toronto: Art Gallery of Ontario, 1988.☙

———. *Exposer/Cacher (Exposed/Concealed)*, trans. Thérèze de Celles. Self published, 1993, for exhibitions at Ecole Nationale de la Photographie, Arles, and Musée d'Art Contemporain, Montreal.☙

Campbell, Colin. "Statement" and "Hindsight." In *Video By Artists*, ed. Peggy Gale. Toronto: Art Metropole, 1976.

———. *The Woman from Malibu*. Toronto: Art Metropole, 1978.

———. "David Buchan: Lamonte Del Monte and The Fruit Cocktails." *Centerfold* 3:1 (December 1978): 29–32

———. *Modern Love*. Toronto: Art Metropole/Los Angeles: The Foundation for Art Resources, 1979.

———. "Video '79 — Roman Style." *Centerfold* 3:6 (September 1979): 303–4

———. "Performance in Moment'Homme'." In *Moment'Homme*, Montreal, 1984 (n.p., n.d.)

———. "B Mode." *Impulse: Cold City Fiction* (Spring 1986): 116–19

———. "No Voice Over." In *Video By Artists 2*, ed. Elke Town. Toronto: Art Metropole, 1986.

———. "It's a Long Time to Hold Your Breath." *Fuse* 10:4 (Winter 1986–7): 31

———. "Lesbians on the Loose." *Fuse* 10:6 (Spring 1987): 21–4 A review of multimedia exhibition "Sight Specific: Lesbians and Representation" organized by Lynn Fernie, and singles out video *Frankly, Shirley* by Margaret Moores.

———. "Video Culture." *Cinema Canada* 144 (September 1987): 9 Reviews award winners Rhonda Abrams, Enrico Benz, Ron Berti, Marsha M. Herle, Marc Paradis, Catherine Richards and Pierre Zorile.

———. "Another World: Five Video Premieres by Gay Men." *Fuse* 11:3 (Fall 1987): 23–5

———. "Both." In *Toronto: A Play of History (Jeu d'histoire)*. Toronto: The Power Plant, 1987.☙

———. "Art Speaks in the 80s." *Parallelogramme* 14:1 (Summer 1988): 14–17

———. "The Facade of Obsession." *Fuse* 12:5 (April/May 1989): 44–5

———. "Toronto Lesbian and Gay Film and Video Festival." *Fuse* 15:1/2 (Fall 1991): 54–5

———. "Noise" and "Skin" [script]. In *Colin Campbell: Media Works 1972–1990*. Ottawa: National Gallery of Canada, 1991.☙

Colin Campbell: Media Works 1972–1990. Ottawa: National Gallery of Canada, 1991.☙ With introductory text (taken from larger Winnipeg exhibition catalogue of same name) and programme notes by Bruce Ferguson.

Campbell, Colin, ed., *Videotapes from Brazil and Chile*. Ottawa: National Gallery of Canada, 1985.☙ With essays by Colin Campbell, Anna Bella Geiger and Robert McFadden.

Campbell, James D. "History Hurts: Barbara Steinman and Installation." *C* 22 (June 1989): 14–19

———. "Intelligent Artifacts: Technics and Praxis in Tom Sherman's Art." *C* 26 (Summer 1990): 31–7

Campbell, Peg. "3D Film and Video: Interview with Bill Bukowski." *Video Guide* 4:3 (1981): 17–18

Campeau, Sylvain. "Philippe Dubois [interview]." *ETC Montréal* 10 (Winter 1989): 26–9

———. "Urbain de Jouvence." *ETC Montréal* 12 (Autumn 1990): 53–5

———. "Hors Foyer?: Passages de l'Image [Bill Viola, John Massey]." *ETC Montréal* 14 (Spring 1991): 36–9

———. "De la vidéo comme pensée de la trame ['Vu?' by Bill Viola]." *Spirale* 124 (May 1993): 24

Canada in Birmingham. Birmingham (England): Ikon Gallery, 1981. Introduction by Hugh Stoddart, catalogue essay by Martha Fleming. Includes video by Robert Hamon, Nora Hutchinson, Edward Lam, Eric Metcalfe and John Watt.

Canada Trajectoires 73. Paris: Musée d'Art Moderne de la Ville de Paris, 1973.ᐁ Video by Jane and Walter Wright, Ernest Gusella, Gilles Chartier, Video Exchange, Metromedia, Vidéographe, Société Nouvelle, A Space, Tom Sherman, Lisa Steele, Joseph Bodolai, Stephen Cruise, Marien Lewis and Robert Bowers.

The 1978 Canadian Video Open. Calgary: Artons/Parachute Center for Cultural Affairs, 1978.ᐁ Includes interviews with Susan Britton and Rodney Werden by Peggy Gale.

Cantin, Jean-François. *La Production du temps/Travaux vidéographiques 1977–1994*. Montreal: Paje Editeur, 1994. With essays by John K. Grande and Yolande Racine.

Canyon, Brice. "A Post Modern Discourse: An Introduction." In *Cornelia Wyngaarden/ The Fragility of Origins*, ed. Brice Canyon. Vancouver: Western Front Society, 1994.ᐁ

Canyon, Brice, ed. *Cornelia Wyngaarden/ The Fragility of Origins*. Vancouver: Western Front Society, 1994.ᐁ With essays by Brice Canyon, Susan Lord and Scott Watson, plus videography.

Carr-Harris, Ian. "Sex and Representation." *Vanguard* 13:9 (November 1984): 22–5

———. "On TV." In *Luminous Sites/Ten Video Installations*, eds. Daina Augaitis and Karen Henry. Vancouver: Video Inn/Western Front, 1986.ᐁ

Carrière, Daniel. "TV or not TV?" *24 Images* 36 (1988): 18

———. "Robert Morin ou le réseau des confidences." In *Ethique & télévision/4e manifestation internationale de vidéo et TV*. Montbéliard, 1988.

———. "Video Art: Expanded Forms [on Curt Royston]." *Espace* 6:1 (Autumn 1989): 26–7

———. "La Galerie Ephémère." *Ciné-Bulles* 9:3 (March/May 1990): 22–3

———. "La Galerie Ephémère." *Espace* 6:3 (Spring 1990): 49

———. "Ni fiction, ni documentaire [on Morin/Dufour, Josef Robakowski and Marc Paradis]." *Ciné-Bulles* 9:4 (June/August 1990): 44–6

———. "Marc Paradis [interview]." *ETC Montréal* 12 (Autumn 1990): 24–5

———. "Le cri des icônes migratrices." *Ciné-Bulles* 10:2 (December 1990/February 1991): 42–3

———. "Volutes et volte-face." *Ciné-Bulles* 10:3 (April/May 1991): 12–13

———. "Petite histoire du vidéothéâtre." *Ciné-Bulles* 10:4 (June/August 1991): 44–5

———. "Portrait de groupes [Dossier: independant Quebec video]." *Ciné-Bulles* 11:1 (September/November 1991): 16–21

———. "Les Idéaux menacés." In *Les Yeux fertiles* 2. Montreal: Les Herbes rouges, Bilan cinématographique, télévisuel et vidéographique, 194 (1991): 58–63

———. "Qu'ils soient, qu'ils étaient, qu'ils allaient être: entrevue avec Charles Guilbert et Serge Murphy." *ETC Montréal* 16 (November 1991): 74–6

———. "Devant l'écran." *Ciné-Bulles* 11:3 (April/June 1992): 40

———. "Le voleur vit à l'étranger." *Ciné-Bulles* 11:4 (August/December 1992): 40–1

———. "'J'ai refusé de faire un film linéaire' [interview with Robert Morin]." *Ciné-Bulles* 12:1 (November/December 1992): 31–3

———. "Quitter la route: Marie-France Giraudon." *ETC Montréal* 18 (Spring 1992): 77–9

———. "Ariane Thezé, Le rapt de la lumière." *ETC Montréal* 21 (February/May 1993): 38–9

———. "Gabrielle Schloesser et Huguette Miron, Motel." *ETC Montréal* 22 (May/August 1993): 24–5

———. 'Wasteland.' *Ciné-Bulles* 12:3 (Summer 1993): 24–5

———. "Bill Viola, la course du clair-obscur." *ETC Montréal* 22 (May/August 1993): 29–31

———. "Recto verso." *Ciné-Bulles* 12:4 (Autumn 1993): 44–5

———. "Heure exquise/Vidéographe: l'échange." *Ciné-Bulles* 13:1 (Winter 1994): 40–1

Carter, Sam. "Less is More than Ever/ Satellites, Wet Orchards, and Frank Ogden." *Video Guide* 5:5 (Winter 1983): 5

Cate, Ritsaert Ten. *Noel Harding: Enclosure for Conventional Habit.* Amsterdam: Mickery, 1989.∾

"Ce glissement progressif vers la vidéo [whole issue devoted to video]." *Copie Zéro* 26 (December 1985)

Cehan, Brent. "Is the Rectum an Asshole? [Andy Fabo/Michael Balser]." *Fuse* 13:5 (June/July 1990): 47–8

Chabot, Normand. "Film-il Télévision-elle [Does television have a sex?]." *Ciné-Bulles* 9:1 (September/November 1989): 40–1

Chan, Anthony. "Broadcast Blues: 'Doing Television in Livin' Canajun Colour!'" In *Yellow Peril Reconsidered*, ed. Paul Wong. Vancouver: On Edge, 1990.∾

Chandler, John Noel. "Vera Frenkel: A Room with a View." *artscanada* 36:2, 228/229 (August/September 1979): 1–8

Chaput, Yves. *Québec 75/Vidéo.* Montreal: Institut d'Art Contemporain de Montréal, 1975. With 21 texts and interviews by Yves Chaput, Michel Van de Walle, Gerard Henry and others on half-inch video in Quebec, including an exploration of community television. Bibliography and resource information.

———. "Super 8 et vidéo: une alliance risquée." *24 Images* 34–35 (Fall 1987): 6–7

Chin, Daryl. "Asian-American Video Festival." *Video Guide* 9:4 (Issue 44, Fall 1988): 10–11

Chitty, Elizabeth. "'You Must Remember This' by Marshalore." *Centerfold* 4:2 (January 1980): 10–11

———. "Interview." *Video Guide* 3:2 (October 1980): 3, 14

———. "Social Studies: A Work in Progress [an interview by Marcella Bienvenue]." In *Video Net*, ed. Brian Dyson. Calgary: Syntax Art Society, 1980.∾

———. "Colin Campbell [interview]." *Video Guide* 3:4 (March 1981): 4–5

———. "Marshalore [interview]." *Video Guide* 4:1 (1981): 4–5

———. "Marcella Bienvenue [interview]." *Video Guide* 4:1 (1981): 8

———. "Vera Frenkel [interview]." *Video Guide* 4:2 (1981): 4–6

———. "Paul Wong: 'Prime Cuts' [Interview]." *Video Guide* 4:3 (1981): 5–7

Christie, Claire. "Toronto: The Ydessa Hendeles Foundation [Bill Viola, Gary Hill installations]." *ETC Montréal* 24 (November/February 1994): 51–5

Clancy, Brian. "Byron Black [interview]." *Cinema Canada* 19 (May–June 1975): 50–3

Clark, David. "Vicarious Desperation [on the 12th Montreal International Festival of New Cinema: discusses several Quebec entries]." *Cinema Canada* 103 (January 1983): 20–1

Coelho, René. "Canada — Video: A Medium in Search of its Task." In *Canadian Video Art*, ed. René Coelho. Amsterdam: The Holland Festival, 1985.∾

Coelho, René, ed. *Canadian Video Art.* Amsterdam: The Holland Festival, 1985.∾

Cohn, Norman. "In My End is My Beginning." In *Norman Cohn: Portraits*, ed. Peggy Gale. Toronto: Art Gallery of Ontario, 1984.∾

———. *Bank: A Video Portrait Process.* Minneapolis: First Bank System, Division of Visual Arts, 1989.∾ With texts by Norman Cohn, Nathan Leo Braulick and Lynne Sowder.

Coleman, Victor, "Vera Frenkel/Agnes Etherington Art Centre." *Vanguard* 11:4 (May 1982): 40

———. "The New Work Show/Theatre Passe Muraille." *Vanguard* 13:9 (November 1984): 47–8

Coleman, Victor, ed. *Retrospective 4/ 1979–80/ Documents of Artist-Run Centres in Canada.* Toronto: ANNPAC, 1980. Includes annual documentation on exhibitions, events and 33 artist-run centres, plus essays by Kenna Manos, Joel Oppenheimer and Al Razutis.

Collins, John. "Norman Cohn: Portraits." *Arts Atlantic* 5:4 (1984): 11

Collyer, Robin, ed. *222 Warehouse.* Toronto: A Space, 1980. Includes text by Tom

Sherman on installation, performance and video; videotapes by Susan Britton, Colin Campbell, Norman Cohn, Tom Sherman and Lisa Steele.

Condy-Berggold, Craig. "Vancouver Sath." *Video Guide* 9:2 (Fall 1987): 4–5

———. "Remote Control [on Chris Creighton-Kelly]." *Fuse* 11:5 (April 1988): 34

Conley, Christine. *A Tale of Two Cities: Video Art in Alberta.* Edmonton: Ring House Gallery, 1986. ∞ With an essay by Christine Conley emphasizing the role of artist-run centres.

———. "Hot Tramp, I Love You So!" *Fuse* 13:1/2 (Autumn 1989): 53–4

———. "Silent Bodies: Dismembered Texts: Feminism and the Politics of Location." In *Tenth Anniversary Showcase: The Independent Film and Video Alliance,* ed. Michael Balser. Toronto: IFVA 1990.

Cook, Conal. "Visual Evidence: A Review of Selected Screenings." *Video Guide* 9:2 (Fall 1987): 3, 22

Cook, Kevin. "Mark Verabioff/Video In." *Parachute* 69 (Winter 1993): 46–7

Corbeil, Carole. "Video Refractions/London Regional Art Gallery." *Vanguard* 13:9 (November 1984): 41–2

Cormier, Réjean-Bernard. "Luc Bourdon/ Galerie Oboro." *Parachute* 71 (Summer 1993): 30–1

Cornwell, Regina. "Passages de l'Image/Wexner Center for the Arts." *Canadian Art* 8:4 (Winter 1991): 72–4

———. "Legal Memory." *Canadian Art* 10:1 (Spring 1993): 78–9

Cossman, Brenda. *Censorship and the Arts: Law, Controversy, Debate, Facts.* Toronto: Ontario Association of Art Galleries, 1995.

Côté, Diane-Jocelyne, ed. *Traces.* Quebec: Réseau-Art-Femmes, 1982. ∞ An event taking place in Quebec, Montreal and Sherbrooke. Essay by Diane-Jocelyne Côté.

Côté, Mario. "L'Attrait de la vidéo." *24 Images* 42 (Spring 1989): 26

———. "Trente images/seconde." *24 Images* 43 (Summer 1989): 63

———. "Chronique vidéo: Dialogues de coulisses." *24 Images* 44/45 (Autumn 1989): 82–3

———. "La difficulté de cette terre venue de ciel." *24 Images* 47 (January/February 1990): 69–70

———. "FFF: Survol historique." *24 Images* 49 (Summer 1990): 66

———. "Chantal duPont, video-active." *24 Images* 50/51 (Autumn 1990): 75

———. "La vidéo serre les dents." *ETC Montréal* 12 (Autumn 1990): 18–19.

———. "La vidéo: épreuves de travail [work by Charles Guilbert, Serge Murphy, Luc Bourdon, Claudine Delvaux and Chantal duPont]." *24 Images* 52 (November/December 1990): 68–9

———. "Le nouveau dans ses retranchements." *24 Images* 53 (January–February 1991): 57

———. "Valeurs comparées." *24 Images* 54 (March 1991): 54–5

———. "La vidéo dans le monde: Traces d'une année." In *Les Yeux fertiles* 3, Montreal: Les Herbes Rouges. Bilan cinématographique, télévisuel et vidéographique, 1991, 111–20

———. "L'homme à la télévision: entretien avec Pierre Bongiovanni." *24 Images* 55 (Summer 1991): 60–1

———. "Méthode pour le regard [on Madelon Hooykaas and Elsa Stansfield]." *24 Images* 56/57 (Autumn 1991): 71

———. "Ennui en note." *24 Images* 59 (Winter 1992): 57

———. "Paysage en perspective [on Paul Landon]." *24 Images* 60 (Spring 1992): 58

———. "Mireille Bril, Galerie Vox Montréal." *C* 37 (Spring 1993): 49–51

———. "Correspondence avec Michel Gonneville." In *Paysage(s) de la vidéo,* ed. Monique Langlois. Montreal: Galerie UQAM, 1994. ∞

———. "Etre dans quel sens." *Possibles* 18:1 (Winter 1994): 39–41

Cotter, Brendan, ed. *Robert Morin and Lorraine Dufour. A decade of video production.* Toronto: A Space, 1991. ∞ With essays by Peggy Gale, Jean Tourangeau and Dan Walworth.

Couëlle, Jennifer. "Les chasses-croisés mnémoniques de Suzan Vachon." *Cahier* 7. Montreal: Galerie B-312 Emergence Inc., 1994. ∞

———. "Dissiper l'illusion, mais laquelle? [Jana Sterbak video installation at Musée d'art contemporain, Montreal]." *Espace* 30 (Winter 1995): 41–2

Cousineau, Marie-Hélène. "Inuit Women's Video/Des femmes inuits vidéastes." *Parallelogramme* 19:4 (1994): 34–9

Cousineau, Sophie. "Eric Raymond ou la fuite en avant." *Espace* 23 (Spring 1993): 46–8

Coutts-Smith, Kenneth. "Pea Soup." *Fuse* 4:4 (May 1980): 220–4

Couturier, Louis. "Istvan Kantor: une bouffonnerie dépourvue de toute originalité." *ETC Montréal* 25 (February/May 1994): 21–5

Cox, Kirwan. "Vidéographe." *Cinema Canada* 4 (October/November 1972):16–19

Craig, David. *New Uses for Television.* Charlottetown: Confederation Centre Art Gallery and Museum, 1981.⌒ Includes essay by David Craig and videotext by Ed Slopek.

———. "Video Out — Halifax." *Video Guide* 9:5 (December 1988): 12

Craig, Kate. "Western Front Video [interview]." *Centerfold* 2:2/3 (January 1978)

———. "Outlets for Video." In *Transcript from The International Video Art Symposium 1979.* Kingston: Agnes Etherington Art Centre, 1979.

———. "Clay Cove, Newfoundland/Park Place, Vancouver." In *Luminous Sites/Ten Video Installations*, eds. Daina Augaitis and Karen Henry. Vancouver: Video Inn/Western Front, 1986.⌒

Craig, Kate, Kim Tomczak, and Paul Wong. "Discussing the State of Video/Bulletin de santé du vidéo." In *Spaces by Artists/Places des Artistes: 3e Rétrospective Parallelogramme 3*, ed. Tanya Rosenberg. Toronto: ANNPAC, 1979.

Creates, Marlene. *The Diary Exhibition.* St. John's: Art Gallery of Memorial University, 1987.⌒

Creet, Julia. "PagliAttack: Mary Walsh vs. The Heist-Meister." *BorderLines* No. 37 (August 1995): 5–8

Creighton-Kelly, Chris. "Television, Video and the Future/La télévision: le vidéo: et l'avenir." *Parallelogramme* 7:5 (June 1982): 6–7, 13–14

———. "On TV/Ian Carr-Harris." *Video Guide* 8:2 (Issue 37, 1986): 19

Crépeau, Marie-Louise. *Un archipel de désir: les artistes du Québec et la scène internationale.* Quebec: Musée du Québec, 1991.⌒ With essays by Marie-Louise Crépeau, Louise Déry, Chantal Pontbriand and Stéphane Aquin.

Crévier, Lyne. "Art et vidéo: le sex-ennui." *ETC Montréal* 1:2 (Winter 1987): 66–7

———. "A l'est, à l'ombre [Josef Robakowski: Options portrait d'un artiste dans l'Europe des ignorés]." *ETC Montréal* 1:3 (Spring 1988): 87

Cron, Marie-Michèle. *L'école buissonnière.* Montreal: Galerie Oboro, 1994.⌒ Commentary on video works by 25 Montreal students.

Culley, Peter. "Paul Wong/Luminous Sites." *Vanguard* 15:3 (Summer 1986): 40

———. "Vera Frenkel/Luminous Sites." *Vanguard* 15:3 (Summer 1986):47–8

———. "Window Dressing." *Vanguard* 17:2 (April/May 1988): 32–3

———. "The Magic Box: Stan Douglas in the Cabinet of Cinema." In *Out of Place*, ed. Gary Dufour. Vancouver: Vancouver Art Gallery, 1993.⌒

———. "Ascensio: La musique comme emblème et élément dans l'oeuvre de Stan Douglas/Aufsteig: Musik als Emblem und Wirkung in der Arbeit von Stan Douglas/Ascension: Music as Emblem and Agency in the Work of Stan Douglas." In *Stan Douglas*, ed. Christine van Assche. Paris: Editions du Centre Pompidou, 1993.⌒

Cyroulnik, Philippe, ed. *Michèle Waquant.* Crédac, Ivry: Centre d'Art Contemporain, 1989.⌒ With brief texts by René Blouin and Serge Murphy.

Czegledy, Nina. *Vista: Video by Canadian Women Artists.* Self-published, Toronto, 1990. Video by Belanger, Desaulniers, Diamond, Giguère, Payne, Rynard and Schroder; an exhibition touring to Denmark, Finland, Hungary and Poland.⌒

———. *Shifting Paradigms/Modèles mouvants: Contemporary Canadian Video Art.* Self-published, Toronto, 1993.⌒ Exhibition travelled to Germany, Hungary, Italy, Roumania and Slovenia.

———. *Reconnaisance.* Self-published, Toronto, 1994.⌒ Video selections and essay by Czegledy to accompany *Carambolage III*, Biennale des 4 Moteurs + Ontario, curated by Louise Dompierre.

D Daguenais, Francine. "A Medium of Contemporary Memory: Canadian Art Video Festival at the Vidéographe." *Cinema Canada* 153 (June 1988): 23–4

D'Agostino, Peter, and Antonio Muntadas, eds. *The Un/necessary Image*. New York: Tanam Press, 1982. Includes video by General Idea.

Daniel, Barbara. "Tom Sherman/Vancouver Art Gallery." *Vanguard* 10:8 (October 1981): 36–7

————. "The Balance of Convenience/La censure: Comment trouver le juste milieu? [Paul Wong and Vancouver Art Gallery]." *Parallelogramme* 9:5 (Summer 1984): 12–14, 19–21

Danzker, Jo-Anne Birnie. "Montreal Tapes: Video as a Community or Political Tool." *Vanguard* 7:2 (March 1978): 11–12

————. "Michael Goldberg/Video Innovator." *Vanguard* 7:5 (June/July 1978): 20–1

————."Towards an Audience Vocabulary [with General Idea]." *Centerfold* 3:1 (December 1978): 13–18

————. "Interviews [with Pierre Falardeau/ Julien Poulin, Robert Forget, Penni Jaques, Robert Morin]." In *Montreal Tapes: Video as a Community or Political Tool,* ed. Jo-Anne Birnie Danzker. Vancouver: Vancouver Art Gallery, 1978.◉

————. "Museum and Guerilla Television." In *Art, Artists and the Media,* ed. Richard Kriesche. Graz: AVZ Books, 1978.

————. "Mediart: Notes from Graz and Barcelona." *Vanguard* 8:2 (March 1979): 15–16

————. "Perform: A Four Part Video Exhibition." In *Living Art Vancouver,* eds. Glenn Lewis, Kim Tomczak, and Paul Wong. Vancouver: Western Front/Pumps/Video Inn, 1980.

————. "The Beauty of the Weapons: Stan Douglas." *Canadian Art* 6:3 (Fall 1989): 102–7

Danzker, Jo-Anne Birnie, ed. *Montreal Tapes: Video as a Community or Political Tool.* Vancouver: Vancouver Art Gallery, 1978.◉ Includes interviews and statements by Challenge For Change/Société Nouvelle, Groupe d'Intervention Vidéo, Project Intercom, La Femme et le Film, The Parallel Institute and Vidéotron. Also essays by Francine Couture, François-Marc Gagnon and Esther Trépanier.

————. *MANNERsm: A Theory of Culture.* Vancouver Art Gallery, 1982.◉ Canadian video includes Colin Campbell, Eric Metcalfe and Vincent Trasov.

D'Arcy, Jean. "Un nouveau médium." *Communications* 21 (1974) (n.p.)

Dault, Gary Michael. "Vera Frenkel's 'Lies and Truths': A Gloss." In Gary Michael Dault and Vera Frenkel, *Vera Frenkel/Lies & Truths: Mixed Format Installations.* Vancouver: Vancouver Art Gallery, 1978.◉

Dault, Gary Michael, and Vera Frenkel. *Vera Frenkel/Lies & Truths: Mixed Format Installations.* Vancouver: Vancouver Art Gallery, 1978.◉ With essays by Gary Michael Dault and Vera Frenkel, and notes/scripts by Frenkel.

Davis, Todd. "Prototype, 1986/Max Dean." *Video Guide* 8:2 (1986): 16

Dean, Max. "Made to Measure." *Impressions* 27 (Spring 1981): 18–19

————. "Prototype, 1986." In *Luminous Sites/Ten Video Installations,* eds. Daina Augaitis and Karen Henry. Vancouver: Video Inn/Western Front, 1986.◉

De Blois, Marco. "Entretien avec Robert Morin." *24 Images* 75 (December 1994/January 1995): 6–11

Degryse, Marc. "Réaliser en vidéo: vidéo/cinéma,vidéo-film." *Copie Zéro* 26 (December 1985): 18–20

de Kerckhove, Derrick. "Private Networks in Public Mind." *Mediamatic* 7:3/4 (Winter 1994): 249–53

————. *The Skin of Culture: Investigating the New Electronic Reality.* ed. Christopher Dewdney. Toronto: Somerville House Publishing, 1995.

Delehanty, Susanne. *Video Art.* Philadelphia: University of Pennsylvania, 1975.◉ Canadians include David Askevold, Colin Campbell, General Idea, Michael Hayden and Lisa Steele.

Delicate Technology: 2nd Japan 89 Video Television Festival at Spiral. Tokyo: Video Gallery SCAN, 1989.◉ With numerous short essays by artists and curators from Japan, France, USA and Germany. Canadians include Luc Bourdon, Dennis Day/Susan Rynard and Paulette Phillips/Geoffrey Shea/Dalaibor Martinovic.

Demers, Pierre. "SCRAM, le vidéo militant." *Dérivés* 24–25 (1980): 43–8 An interview with Michel Lemieux re: Société de communication et de la recherche pour l'accès aux médias (SCRAM) 1973–76, and tapes on struggles of workers in the region.

Dennis, Ruby-Marie. "Her Giveaway: A Spiritual Journey with AIDS." *Video Guide* 10:3/4 (November 1989): 5

Dercon, Chris. "A Little Paragraph in a Text that Is Missing." In *Vidéo,* ed. René Payant. Montreal: Artextes, 1986.

Derko, Kim. "Janine Marchessault/YYZ." *C* 26 (Summer 1990): 57–8

Déry, Louise, ed. *Un Archipel des désires: les artistes du Québec et la scène internationale.* Quebec: Musée du Québec, 1991. Includes essays by Stéphane Aquin and Louise Déry.

Dewdney, Chris."The Hummer Sisters/Videocabaret." *Vanguard* 11:3 (April 1982): 29

Diamond, Sara. "Why Exchange? Time to Change." *Video Guide* 5:2 (April 1983): 3–4

———. "Vancouver Cable 10: The Community Access Model." *Video Guide* 5:5 (Winter 1983): 7

———. "An Artful Approach to Politics: 'The Price of Poker, Gambling on Solidarity'." *Video Guide* 6:1 (January 1984): 8–9

———. "Clear About Confused." *Video Guide* 6:2 (March 1984): 7

———. "Vancouver Guide: An Overview." *Video Guide* 6:5 (October 1984): 3

———. "Luminous Sites: On Off TV." *C* 10 (Summer 1986): 72–3

———. "'Stalling Art [on Luminous Sites]." *Fuse* 10:1/2 (Summer 1986): 55–7

———. "As a Wife Has a Cow – Cornelia Wyngaarden." *Video Guide* 8:2 (Issue 37, 1986): 4

———. "Clay Cove, Newfoundland: Park Place, Vancouver — Kate Craig." *Video Guide* 8:2 (Issue 37, 1986): 5

———. "Heroics: Video Installation." *Video Guide* 7:5 (January 1986): 6–7

———. "Confused Update: Court Ruling Undermines Artists' Rights." *Fuse* 10:3 (Fall 1986): 5–6

———. "Visual Democracy: An Interview with Lisa Steele and Kim Tomczak."*Video Guide* 8:4 (December 1986): 4–5

———. "Video Sex: Hot Topic." *Video Guide* 8:4 (December 1986): 2

———. "Artropolis." *Fuse* 48, 9:4 (Winter 1987–8): 37–40

———. "Curatorial Statement." In *Artropolis 90/Lineages & Linkages.* Vancouver: A.T. Eight Artropolos Society, 1990.

———. "Daring Documents: The Practical Aesthetics of Early Vancouver Video." In *Vancouver Anthology: The Institutional Politics of Art,* ed. Stan Douglas. Vancouver: Talonbooks, 1991.

———. "Angles of Incidence: Video Reflections of Multimedia Artworks." In *Angles of Incidence: Video Reflections of Multimedia Artworks,* ed. Sara Diamond. Banff: The Banff Centre for the Arts: The International Council for Computer Communication, 1993.

Diamond, Sara, ed. *Angles of Incidence: Video Reflections of Multimedia Artworks.* Banff: The Banff Centre for the Arts: The International Council for Computer Communication, 1993. With texts by Sara Diamond, Mary Anne Moser and Catherine Richards.

Diamond, Sara, and Gary Kibbins. "In Flagrante: Canadian Video Caught in the Act," "Bad Acting: Performing and Characterization on Screen," and "Total Recall: History, Memory & New Documentary." In *Trade Initiatives: 3 Programmes of Canadian Video,* eds. Sara Diamond and Gary Kibbins. Vancouver: Satellite Video Exchange Society, 1988.

Diamond, Sara, and Gary Kibbins, eds. *Trade Initiatives: 3 Programmes of Canadian Video.* Vancouver: Satellite Video Exchange Society, 1988.

Sara Diamond: Mémoires ravivées, histoire narrée. Ottawa: National Gallery of Canada, 1992. With essays by Jean Gagnon and Karen Knights, plus bio-bibliography and annotated videography.

Didlake, Scott. "First Experiments in Writing and Reading Video." *Centerfold* 3:1 (December 1978): 59–62

Dionne, Denise. "Vidéographe: culture nouvelle." *Vie des Arts* 18:72 (Fall 1973): 70–2

Ditta, Susan. *Avant-Garde Profiles/Profils d'avant-garde* [Video and Film by Artists Series/La série de vidéos et de films d'artistes]. Ottawa: National Gallery of Canada, 1988.⌘

———. "Is it art? Is it television? Is it video?" *Recent Acquisitions: New Works by Canadian Video Artists/ Acquisitions récentes: Oeuvres nouvelles de vidéastes canadiens* [Video and Film by Artists Series/La série de vidéos et de films d'artistes]. Ottawa: National Gallery of Canada, 1988.⌘

———. *Rebel Girls: A Survey of Canadian Feminist Videotapes 1974–1988/Les Rebelles: Un aperçu des oeuvres de féministes canadiennes 1974–1988* [Video and Film by Artists Series/La série de vidéos et de films d'artistes]. Ottawa: National Gallery of Canada, 1989.⌘

———. *Video: New Works: Recent Acquisitions/Nouvelles oeuvres, acquisitions récentes* [Video and Film by Artists Series/La série de vidéos et de films d'artistes]. Ottawa: National Gallery of Canada, 1990.⌘ With introduction and lengthy discussion of individual works.

———. "A Work in Progress — An Interview with Colin Campbell." In *Colin Campbell/Media Works 1872–1990*, ed. Bruce Ferguson. Winnipeg: Winnipeg Art Gallery, 1991.⌘

Documenta 6. Kassel: 1977.⌘ Includes video by Colin Campbell.

Documenta 7. Kassel: 1982.⌘ Includes video by General Idea.

Documenta 8. Kassel: 1987.⌘ Video-related text by Ian Carr-Harris; video by Monty Cantsin, Norman Cohn, General Idea and Lisa Steele/Kim Tomczak.

Documenta 9. Kassel: 1992.⌘ Video installation by Vera Frenkel.

Dolan, Frederick. "David Askevold/Political Modernism and Postmodernity." *Vanguard* 17:1 (February/March 1988): 19–22

Dompierre, Louise, and Vera Frenkel. *Likely Stories: Text/Image/Sound Works for Video and Installation*. Kingston: Agnes Etherington Art Centre, 1982.⌘

Dorland, Michael. "15th International Festival of Nouveau Cinema and Video: Musings on Video." *Cinema Canada* 137 (January 1987): 27–9

Dormeyer, James. "Le monteur vidéo: raccordeur de scènes ou fabricant d'images?" *Copie Zéro* 14 (January 1983): 27–31

"Dossier: Le videoclip." *24 Images* 48 (March/April 1990): 18–53

Dossor, Dinah. "Our Own Story: The Video Work of Sara Diamond." *Independent Media* 88 (April 1989): 4–5

Douglas, Stan, ed. *Vancouver Anthology: The Institutional Politics of Art*. Vancouver: Talonbooks, 1991.

Dowler, Kevin. "Interstitial Aesthetics and the Politics of Video at the Canada Council." In *Mirror Machine: Video and Identity*, ed. Janine Marchessault. Toronto: YYZ Books/Montreal: Centre for Research on Canadian Cultural Industries and Institutions, McGill University, 1995.

Doyle, Judith. "222 Warehouse/A Space at Harbourfront." *Parachute* 20 (Fall 1980): 50–1

Doyon, Jacques, ed. *Vidéo: Sexualité et politique/ Sexuality and Politics*. Montreal: Galerie Optica, 1987.⌘ With essays by Jacques Doyon, Clive Robertson and Jean Tourangeau.

Dragu, Margaret. "'Delicate Issue' by Kate Craig." *Centerfold* 4:2 (January 1980): 12

———. "'TV Hertz 2', March 15 & 16, 1979 [an interview by Marcella Bienvenue]." In *Video Net*, ed. Brian Dyson. Calgary: Syntax Art Society, 1980.⌘

Druick, Don. "3,2,76." In *Video By Artists*, ed. Peggy Gale. Toronto: Art Metropole, 1976.

———. "Towards Location Marking: A Video Script." *Video Guide* 1:2 (April/May 1978): 7

———. "Disorderly Characters Day 3." *Vanguard* 7:5 (June/July 1978): 19

Dubois, Philippe. "L'ombre, le miroir, l'index." *Parachute* 26 (spring 1982): 16–29

———. "Passages de l'Image [cinema/video]." *24 Images* 47 (January/February 1990): 34–40

Duchaine, Andrée. "Fifth Network/ Cinquième Réseau: conférence vidéo à Toronto [includes texts by Lisa Steele, René Blouin, Clive Robertson, Renee Baert, Terry McGlade, Pierre Falardeau, Brian MacNevin and Claude Gilbert]." *Parachute* 13 (Winter 1978): 5–10

———. "'Chaperons Rouge'/vidéo primé par le Second Annual Canadian Video Open." *Parachute* 18 (Spring 1980): 38–41

————. "Chambres à Louer: Installations vidéo, Powerhouse." *Parachute* 22 (Spring 1981): 42–3

————. *Vidéo du Québec*. Montreal: Musée d'Art Contemporain, 1982.✑ With essay and notes by Andrée Duchaine, for Quebec video 1967–81.

————. "Rückblick auf die Entwicklung des Mediums Video in Quebec/Historique de la vidéo au Québec." In *OKanada*. Berlin: Akademie der Künste, 1982.✑

————. "Evolution des avenues de la distribution au Canada." In *3e Manifestation internationale de vidéo et télévision*. Montbéliard: Centre d'action culturelle, 1986.✑

Dufour, Gary, ed. *Sara Diamond: Patternity*. Vancouver: Vancouver Art Gallery, 1991.✑

————. *Out of Place*. Vancouver: Vancouver Art Gallery, 1993.✑ With essays by Gary Dufour, Agnaldo Farias, Charlotte Townsend-Gault, Claudia Cuesta/Robin Laurence, Eugenio Dittborn/Roberto Merino, Peter Culley, Barrett Watten and Keiji Nakamura.

Dumoulin, Nicole. *Lea Deschamps*. Hull: Axe Néo–7, 1991.✑ With an untitled essay by Nicole Dumoulin.

Dunn, Marty. "L'art vidéo et ses constituantes esthétiques." In *Art <–> Vidéo: les oeuvres vidéographiques de douze artistes canadiens*. Montreal: Véhicule Art, 1977.✑

duPont, Chantal. "L'installation vidéo à l'ère du théâtre électronique." *ETC Montréal* 12 (Autumn 1990): 51–2

————. *La vidéo, un art pluriel*. Montreal: Galerie Graff, 1991.✑ Includes Mario Côté: 'Parabole 78 – avec Louise Robert'/Gabrielle Schloesser: 'La manifeste de l'inconsciente'/Diane Tremblay: 'L'abîme'/Suzan Vachon: 'Palimpseste sentimental'.

————. *Chantal duPont: sous surveillance à Paris, Montréal, New York, Paris*. Montreal: UQAM et duPont, 1993. With an essay by Christine Ross.

duPont, Chantal, ed. *Evènement universitaire d'art vidéo 1993*. Montreal: Maison de la Culture Frontenac.✑ The fifth edition of this exhibition/installation/screenings event.

Durand, Guy. *Interscop/Pologne 1990*. Quebec: Les Editions Intervention, 1991.✑ Discussion of performance, installations and video by 30 artists from Canada and the Eastern Bloc.

Dwyer, Anna. "TV Project Meeting/Video Alternatives or Just How Alter Can Video Be?" *Video Guide* (November 1978 – January 1979): 5

Dyson, Brian, ed. *Video Net*. Calgary: Syntax Art Society, 1980.✑ "The 8th International Video Exchange Directory." *Video Guide* 3:5 special issue (May 1981)

E Eckhert, Connie. "Art and Community." In *Art and Community*, eds. Jane Northey and Connie Eckhert. Toronto: A Space, 1987.✑

Elgear, Sandra, and Robyn Hutt."Some Notes on Collective Production." *Video Guide* 10: 3/4 (November 1989): 20–1

Elliott, George. "A Warning to Artists." *Canadian Art* 10:3 (Spring 1953): 105–6

Ellison, Jane. "Elizabeth Chitty/'Telling Tales'." *Video Guide* (June 1979): 6

Epstein, Judith Anne. "Paysages urbains: contrôle, surveillance et perceptions directes [Chantal duPont and Robert Lepage]." In *Paysage(s) de la vidéo,* ed. Monique Langlois. Montreal: Galerie UQAM, 1994.✑

Espinet, Ramabal. "My Mother's Place." *Fuse* 14:3 (Winter 1991): 37–9

Eyland, Cliff. "Dada Data: A Revival or What [Jan Peacock and 'Corpus Loquendi (Body for Speaking)']." *Arts Atlantic* 13:2 (Autumn 1994): 28–30

F Falk, Lorne. "Characterization of Movement/La représentation du mouvement." In *Noel Harding. Enclosure for Conventional Habit*, ed. Lorne Falk. Banff: The Walter Phillips Gallery, 1980.✑

————. "A Video Prologue." *Open Letter* 8:7 (Summer 1993): 36–45

Falk, Lorne, ed. *Noel Harding. Enclosure for Conventional Habit*. Banff: The Walter Phillips Gallery, 1980.✑ With essays by Peggy Gale, Vera Frenkel and Lorne Falk.

———— *The Second Link. Viewpoints on Video in the Eighties*. Banff: The Walter Phillips Gallery, 1983.✑ With essays by Lorne Falk, Peggy Gale, Kathy Huffman, Carl Loeffler, Barbara London, Brian MacNevin, Dorine Mignot, Sandy Nairne and Gene Youngblood.

————. *Berliner Aufzeichnungen/Berlin Notes*. Banff: Walter Phillips Gallery, 1985.✑

With essays by Lorne Falk, Rolf Langbartels, Jürgen Schweinbraden, Emmett Williams and Thomas Wülffen. Includes video by Michael Morris and Vincent Trasov.

Falk, Lorne, and Barbara Fischer, eds. *The Event Horizon. Essays on Hope, Sexuality, Social Space and Media(tion) in Art.* Toronto: The Coach House Press/Banff: Walter Phillips Gallery, 1987. Note essays by Heather Allin, Renee Baert, Manon Blanchette and Vera Frenkel.

Falling, Patricia. "The Pacific Northwest: Sex, Landscape, and Videotapes." *ARTnews* 90:10 (December 1991): 88–93

Farah, Mary Anne. "Machines in the Garden: Interactive Video Art/La technologie au jardin: la vidéo interactive." *Parallelogramme* 18:4 (Spring 1993): 48–54

———. "Telematic Performance Loops/Toronto and Quebec." *Fuse* 17:1 (Fall 1993): 41–2

Farrell-Ward, Lorna, ed. *Joey Morgan/Almost Dreaming.* Vancouver: Vancouver Art Gallery, 1987. With essays by Lorna Farrell-Ward and Greg Snider, plus artist's texts.

Farrow, Jane. "Vintage Dogma ['Aboo' by Rodney Werden]." *Fuse* 11:5 (April 1988): 33

———. "We Are Amused: Lesbian Laughter and Transgression." *Fuse* 11:6 (July 1988): 43

Fatona, Andrea. "Black Male Sexuality." *Video Guide* 11:2 (Fall 1991): 4

Ferguson, Bruce. *Canada Video.* Ottawa: National Gallery of Canada, 1980. Catalogue for Venice Biennale: video by Campbell, Falardeau/Poulin, General Idea, Sherman and Steele.

———. "Fernsehen bedeutet — Video ist/Television Means, Video Is." In *OKanada.* Berlin: Akademie der Künste, 1982.

———. "Television Means Video Is/La télé est là, donc video existe." *Parallelogramme* 8:3 (February/March 1983): 16–18, 34–6

———. "Making Airwaves/Rémous sur les ondes." In *Prime Time Video,* ed. Allan MacKay. Saskatoon: Mendel Art Gallery, 1984.

———. "Video 84." *Vanguard* 14:1 (February 1985): 24–6

———. "Ernie Kovacs: A Good Look (And Listen)." *C* 7 (Fall 1985): 14–23

———. "Notes on a Local History." In *Toronto: A Play of History (Jeu d'histoire).* Toronto: The Power Plant, 1987.

———. *On Track: An Exhibition of Art in Technology/Une exposition de l'art à l'heure de la technologie.* Calgary: Olympic Arts Festival/Festival olympique des arts, 1988. With an essay by Bruce Ferguson. Canadian video includes Norman Cohn, Tomiyo Sasaki and Barbara Steinman.

———. "The Art of Memory/Barbara Steinman." *Vanguard* 18:3 (Summer 1989): 10–15

———. "Colin Campbell: Otherwise Worldly." *[Activating the Archive]2.* Toronto: Art Metropole, 1991.

———. "Colin Campbell: Otherwise Worldly." In *Colin Campbell/Media Works 1972–1990,* ed. Bruce Ferguson. Winnipeg: Winnipeg Art Gallery, 1991.

———. "Left Beholding the Promised Land: Ardele Lister in America." In *Four Visions of Television: Daniel Dion, Ardele Lister, Robert Morin, Jan Peacock,* ed. Brian Rusted. Banff: Artists Television Workshop, Banff Centre for the Arts, 1991.

Ferguson, Bruce, ed. *1984 Ottawa International Festival of Video Art.* Ottawa: SAW Gallery, 1984. With preface by Wayne Rutherford and introduction by Bruce Ferguson. Canadians include Joyan Saunders, Lynda Craig/Jean-Pierre St-Louis, Robert Morin/Lorraine Dufour, Rodney Werden, Michael Balser, Elizabeth Vander Zaag, Shawn Sutherland, Marion Barling, Nida Home Doherty, Edward Mowbray and Maryanne Yanulis/John Greyson/Eric Schultz.

———. *Colin Campbell/Media Works 1972–1990.* Winnipeg: Winnipeg Art Gallery, 1991. With essays by Bruce Ferguson, Stuart Marshall, Sue Ditta and Dot Tuer, and text/script by Colin Campbell.

Fischer, Barbara. *Decalog YYZ 1979–1989.* Toronto: YYZ, 1992. Includes documentation of exhibitions and events (including video) over first ten years of YYZ gallery operations, plus historical essay by Barbara Fischer.

Fischer, Barbara, ed. *Tanya Mars: Pure Hell.* Toronto: The Power Plant, 1990 .

Fischer, Hervé. "L'Art et nouveau technologie/Art and New Technology." *Vanguard* 15:2 (April/May 1986): 37–42

Fisette, Serge. "L'espace, qui prend de l'ampleur [installation by François Girard at PRIM Video Gallery]." *Espace* 7:3 (Spring 1991): 24–7

Fisher, Gordon. "HIV+/– [tape review]." *Video Guide* 10: 33/4 (November 1989): 5

Fiske, John. "Art Agency: Ad Agency." In *Stan Douglas: Monodramas and Loops,* ed. Scott Watson. Vancouver: UBC Fine Arts Gallery, 1992.

Fleisher, Pat. "Videoscape in Toronto: An Interview with Ian Birnie." *Art Magazine* 6:19 (Fall 1974): 36–7

Fleming, Kathleen. "Norman Cohn/Banff Centre." *Parachute* 53 (Winter 1988–9): 47–8

Fleming, Marnie. "Sylvie Bélanger: Toward a New Body Language/Vers un nouveau langage du corps." In *Sylvie Bélanger: The Silence of the Body,* ed. Marnie Fleming. Oakville: Oakville Galleries, 1995.ᔕ

Fleming, Marnie, ed. *Sylvie Bélanger: The Silence of the Body.* Oakville: Oakville Galleries, 1995.ᔕ With a foreword by Francine Périnet and essays by Marnie Fleming, Scott Mackenzie and Andy Patton.

Fleming, Martha. "Orwell Lost in Videocab Staging." *Centerfold* 3:6 (September 1979): 319–22

———. "Colin Campbell." *Artforum* 19:5 (January 1981): 78–9

———. "Television By Artists." *Video Guide* 3:4 (March 1981): 14

———. "New Video: Sequence and Denial." In *Canada in Birmingham.* Birmingham (England): Ikon Gallery, 1981.ᔕ

Fleming, Martha, and Doug Durand. "Video is not television, Performance is not theatre." *The Body Politic* 64 (June/July 1980): 29–32

Foisy, Suzanne. "Correspondences inter-loquées [Gabrielle Schloesser]." In *Paysage(s) de la vidéo,* ed. Monique Langlois. Montreal: Galerie UQAM, 1994.ᔕ

Folland, Tom. "Deregulating Identity: Video and AIDS Activism." In *Mirror Machine: Video and Identity,* ed. Janine Marchessault. Toronto: YYZ Books/Montreal: Centre for Research on Canadian Cultural Industries and Institutions, McGill University, 1995.

Folland, Tom, and Kathryn Walter. "Vera Frenkel/The Power Plant [on '. . .from the Transit Bar']." *Parachute* 79 (Summer 1995): 50–1

Forget, Claude. "La Vidéographie de A à W: une entrevue avec Claude Forget." *NEX* 1 (1985): 10

———. "La troisième fenêtre, portative." Introduction to *A–Z. Répertoire.* Montreal: Vidéographe, 1986.

———. *Video Untamed: Passages and Stolen Memories, The First Ten Years of Vidéographe, 1971–1981/Un animal sauvage: traversées du discours et mémoires volées, les dix premières années du Vidéographe 1971–1981* [Video and Film by Artists Series/La série de vidéos et de films d'artistes]. Ottawa: National Gallery of Canada, 1990.ᔕ

———. "Absolute Dispersion, Infinite Dissonance." In *Tenth Anniversary Showcase: The Independent Film and Video Alliance,* ed. Michael Balser. Toronto: IFVA 1990.ᔕ

Fortin, Pierre. "La rhétorique du bruit." *Spirale* 57 (December 1985): 5

49th Parallel Gallery of Contemporary Canadian Art, New York. A series of guest-curated video presentations with accompanying essay was introduced by gallery director France Morin in 1982–7, each lasting for a one-month period. Artists included Rhonda Abrams, Susan Britton, Colin Campbell, Norman Cohn, Kate Craig, Tom Dean, Marc De Guerre, Gathie Falk, General Idea, François Girard, John Greyson, Bernar Hébert, Lily Lack, Marshalore, Jan Peacock, Tomiyo Sasaki, Ed Slopek, Lisa Steele/Kim Tomczak, Ewa Turska, Elizabeth Vander Zaag, Michèle Waquant, John Watt, Rodney Werden and Paul Wong.

Fox, Charly. "To TV or Not TV." In *Art, Artists and the Media,* ed. Richard Kriesche. Graz: AVZ Books, 1978.

Fox, Ted. "High Tech Art." *Cinema Canada* 109 (July/August 1984): 13–14 On exhibition and distribution facilities in Toronto.

Fraser, Edith. "Interview with Michael Hollingsworth." *Impressions* 24/25 (Spring 1980): 10–13

Frenkel, Vera. *String Games: Improvisations for Inter-City Video.* Montreal: Galerie Espace 5, 1974.ᔕ

————. "Lies and Truths." *Vanguard* 7:4 (May 1976): 12–14

————. "Art, Love and Politics Part I: a Preamble." *artscanada* 212/213 (March/April 1977): 32–5

————. "Art, Love and Politics Part II: Benign Ignorance." *artscanada* 214/215 (May/June1977): 27–30

————. "Art, Love and Politics Part III: On Collusion: Deals." *artscanada* 216/217 (October/November 1977): 39–43

————. "Notes on String Games" and "No Solution – A Suspence Thriller." In Gary Michael Dault and Vera Frenkel, *Lies & Truths by Vera Frenkel*. Vancouver: Vancouver Art Gallery, 1978.

————. "Art, Love and Politics: After Dignity." *artscanada* 218/219 (February/March 1978): 73–4, 78

————. "Signs of a Plot." *Only Paper Today* 5:4 (May 1978): 9–11

————. "Clive Robertson: A Beuys-Shaped Frame." *Centerfold* 3:1 (December 1978): 23–8

————. "Between Options/Alternative." In *Noel Harding. Enclosure for Conventional Habit*, ed. Lorne Falk. Banff: The Walter Phillips Gallery, 1980.

————. "Discontinuous Notes on and after a meeting of critics, by one of the artists present." *artscanada* 240/241 (March/April 1981): 28–41

————. "Stranger in a Strange Land." *Impressions* 28/29 (Winter 1982):13–19

————. "'. . . And Now, The Truth (A Parenthesis)' by Vera Frenkel [audio script]." In Louise Dompierre and Vera Frenkel, *Likely Stories: Text/Image/Sound Works for Video and Installation*. Kingston: Agnes Etherington Art Centre, 1982.

————. "The Cornelia Lumsden Archive: Can Truth Prevail? by R. Austen-Marshall, as presented by Vera Frenkel." In *Museums by Artists*, eds. A.A. Bronson and Peggy Gale. Toronto: Art Metropole, 1983.

————. "Ruling Fictions: The Small & Large Betrayals that Haunt us Once Again." In *Vestiges of Empire*. London: Camden Arts Centre, 1984.

————. "Ruling Fictions: The Small & Large Betrayals that Haunt us Once Again." *C* 4 (Winter 1985): 31–5

————. "The Art of Denial/the Practice of Pain." In *Issues of Censorship*. Toronto: A Space, 1985.

————. [transcript of symposium with Brian Boigon, Ian Carr-Harris, Stan Denniston, Bruce Grenville, 12 May 1985, Ontario College of Art, Toronto]. *Artists/Critics*, ed. André Jodoin. Toronto: YYZ Books, 1985.

————. "Lost Art: A Cargo Cult Romance." *Video Guide* 8:2 (1986): 12–13

————. "Lost Art: A Cargo Cult Romance." In *Luminous Sites/Ten Video Installations*, eds. Daina Augaitis and Karen Henry. Vancouver: Video Inn/Western Front, 1986.

————. "The Lumsden-LeCaine Letter [text for public-access telephone]." In *Footnotes* , an exhibition on Glenn Gould, Marshall McLuhan, Hugh LeCaine and Cornelia Lumsden. Vancouver: Canada Pavilion, Expo 86, 1986.

————. "Single Meaning, Double Text." In *Toronto: A Play of History (Jeu d'histoire)*. Toronto: The Power Plant, 1987.

————. "I Can Tell You Simply." In *The Event Horizon. Essays on Hope, Sexuality, Social Space and Media(tion) in Art*, eds. Lorne Falk and Barbara Fischer. Toronto: The Coach House Press/Banff: Walter Phillips Gallery, 1987.

————. "The Business of Frightened Desires: Or the Making of a Pornographer." In *Edge '88*. London: A.I.R. Gallery, 1988.

————. "Berlin's Beuys." *Art Monthly* (London), June 1988, 12–14, and *Art Monthly* (Australia/International), June 1988, 3–5

————. "The Place, the Work, the Dilemma." In *Nine from Toronto*. Newcastle upon Tyne: Newcastle Polytechnic, 1990.

————. *From the Transit Bar* 1:1 (June/ September 1992)

————. "From the Transit Bar — Part of the Story." *C* 34 (Summer 1992): 31–4

————. "Dysfunction, Gaps in the Chain of Evidence, and Other Teaching Stories [text of performance/lecture]." In *Akademie zwischen Künst und Lehre: Künstlerische Praxis und Ausbildung — eine kritische untersuchung*. Vienna: Institut fur Gegenwartskünst, Akademie der Bildenden Künste, 1992.

————. *The Bar Report*. Toronto: Art Gallery of York University, 1993.ᐧᐧ

————. "Recovering Memory II: The Bar Report." *Descant* 83, 24:4 (Winter 1993–94): 95–107

————. "Journey." *Border/Lines* 3 (December 1993–January 1994)

————. "from the Transit Bar." In *Public* 9: Reading Our Rights (1994): 78–81

————. "This Is Your Messiah Speaking." In *Queues, Rendezvous, Questioning the Public*, eds. Mark Lewis and George Baird. Banff: Walter Phillips Gallery, 1994.

————. "The Place, the Work, the Dilemma." In the *Harold Innis Centenary* publication, eds. Shelley Hornstein and Jody Berland. Toronto: York University, 1994.

————. *Body Missing, Andere Körper*. Linz: Offenes Kulturhaus, 1994.ᐧᐧ

Frenkel, Vera, and Dot Tuer. "Interview/Entretien." In *Raincoats Suitcases Palms*, ed. Loretta Yarlow. Toronto: Art Gallery of York University, 1993.ᐧᐧ

Vera Frenkel ... from the Transit Bar/ ... du transitbar. Toronto: The Power Plant/Ottawa: National Gallery of Canada, 1995.ᐧᐧ With essays by Jean Gagnon, Irit Rogoff, Lydia Haustein and Jeanne Randolph, plus bio-bibliography.

Friis-Hansen, Dana. "Visionary Apparatus: Points of View and the Power of the Imagination." In *Visionary Apparatus: Michael Snow and Juan Geuer*, ed. Dana Friis-Hansen. Cambridge: Hayden Gallery, Massachusetts Institute of Technology, 1986.

Friis-Hansen, Dana, ed. *Visionary Apparatus: Michael Snow and Juan Geuer*. Cambridge: Hayden Gallery, Massachusetts Institute of Technology, 1986. With an intro-duction, conversation with the artists and essay by Dana Friis-Hansen, plus an essay by Jeanne Randolph.

Frise, Heather. "Healing Images: Film and Video Programme." *Fuse* 15: 1/2 (Fall 1991): 42–3

Frohwerk, Ron, and Gerry Kisil, eds. *Off the Beaten Track/Hors des sentiers battus*. Winnipeg: Ace Art, 1989.ᐧᐧ

Fry, Jacqueline. "'We Are Still Alive' de Les Levine, ou 'La provocation ratée'," *Parachute* 3 (Spring 1976): 19–22 A critique of Levine's

show of photos, text and video from Cape Dorset, at Galerie Gilles Gheerbrant, Montreal.

Fukui International Video Biennale: "Video: Spirit of the Time." Fukui City, Japan, 1985. With essay by Michael Goldberg, works by Bernar Hébert/Michel Ouellette, Byron Black, Helen Doyle, Michael Goldberg, Paul Wong and Pierre Falardeau/Julien Poulin.

2nd Fukui International Video Biennale: "Discovery of Resources of Our Time." Fukui City, Japan, 1988. Video installations by Vera Frenkel, Jan Peacock, Barbara Steinman and John Watt.

3rd Fukui International Video Biennale: "Expansion and Transformation." Fukui City, Japan, 1989. With essay by Peggy Gale, and works by François Girard, Gary Kibbins, Susan Rynard and Lisa Steele.

Fung, Richard. "TV Dinner in 24 Languages." *Fuse* 4:4 (May 1980): 188–9

————. "Everyday People [on Paul Wong]." *Fuse* 13:1/2 (Fall 1989): 55–6

————. "Multiculturalism Reconsidered." In *Yellow Peril Reconsidered*, ed. Paul Wong. Vancouver: On Edge, 1990.ᐧᐧ

————. "Historical Relations: Sex, Gender and the Past." *Fuse* 16:2 (Winter 1992–3): 38–9

————. "Colouring the Screen: Four Strategies in Anti-Racist Film and Video"/ "L'écran coloré: cinématographie et vidéogra-phie — quatre stratégies antiracistes." *Parellogramme* 18:3 (1992–3): 38–52

Fung, Richard, and Shani Mootoo. "Dear Shani, Hiya Richard." *Felix: Landscape(s)* 2:1 (1995): 26–35

G Gagnon, Jean. "La vidéo canadienne et les procédés de l'ironie." *24 Images* 22/23 (Fall 1984–Winter 1985): 26–7

————. "Vidéo: Un bien petit mot pour un objet multiple." *Possibles* 9:4 (Summer 1985): 43–53

————. *TV or Not TV*. Montreal: Le Vidéographe, 1985.ᐧᐧ

————. "Video 84 Installations/Montreal." *Vanguard* 14:2 (March 1985): 36–7

————. "Vers un art télévisuel?" *Le téléspec-tateur*, May 1985

————. "Le chien de Louis et Salvador ou l'ironie de la surface." *Citeren in de Kunst*, Bruxelles, 1986.ᐧᐧ

バイ

———. "Ne manquez surtout pas le train de la vidéo." *Qui fait quoi?* 24 (March/April 1986): 11–12

———. "Trajectoires torontoises." *Toronto Montréal Echange vidéo/Toronto Montreal Video Exchange*. Montreal: Le Vidéographe/Toronto: A Space, 1986.∾

———. *Video and Orality/Vidéo et oralité*. Ottawa: National Gallery of Canada, 1992.∾

———. "Les installations de Sara Diamond/ The Installations of Sara Diamond." In *Sara Diamond: Mémoires ravivées, histoire narrée/ Memories Revisited, History Retold*. Ottawa: National Gallery of Canada, 1992.∾

———. "Entanglement: Video Art and TV." *Open Letter* 8:7 (Summer 1993): 46–56

———. "A propos performance/About Performance." In *Daniel Dion: Parcours/ Paths*. Ottawa: National Gallery of Canada, 1993.∾

———. "The Space to Say/L'Espace de dire ...." In *Vera Frenkel ... from the Transit Bar/ ... du transitbar*. Toronto: The Power Plant/Ottawa: National Gallery of Canada, 1995.∾

———. "Paradox in Paul Wong's Work/Paul Wong, ou la valeur du paradoxe." In *Paul Wong: On Becoming a Man/Paul Wong: Un homme en puissance ...*", ed. Jean Gagnon. Ottawa: National Gallery of Canada, 1995.∾

Gagnon, Jean, ed. *Paul Wong: On Becoming a Man/Paul Wong: Un homme en puissance ...*" Ottawa: National Gallery of Canada, 1995.∾ With artists' satements and essays by Jean Gagnon, Monika Kin Gagnon and Elspeth Sage.

Gagnon, Jean, and Nancy Paterson. *Toronto Montréal Echange vidéo/Toronto Montréal Video Exchange*. Montreal: Le Vidéographe/Toronto: A Space, 1986.∾ With texts by Jean Gagnon and Nancy Paterson.

Gagnon, Monika Kin. "How to Search for Signs of (East) Asian Life in the Video World." In *Mirror Machine: Video and Identity*, ed. Janine Marchessault. Toronto: YYZ Books/Montreal: Centre for Research on Canadian Cultural Industries and Institutions, McGill University, 1995.

———. "Go On, Push My Discursive Limits: The Ambivalence of Paul Wong's Video Works/Vas-y, fais reculer les limites de mon discours: l'ambivalence dans l'oeuvre de Paul Wong." In *Paul Wong: On Becoming a Man/Paul Wong: Un homme en puissance ...*", ed. Jean Gagnon. Ottawa: National Gallery of Canada, 1995.∾

Gale, Peggy. "A New Medium." In *Videoscape*. Toronto: Art Gallery of Ontario, 1974.∾ Additional texts by Marty Dunn and Garry Neill Kennedy.

———. "Video Art in Canada: Four Worlds." *Studio International* 191:981 (May/June 1976): 224–9

———. "Lisa Steele: Looking Very Closely." *Parachute* 2 (Winter 1976): 30–1

———. "Colin Campbell — Windows and Mirrors" and "Lisa Steele — Looking Very Closely." In *Video By Artists*, ed. Peggy Gale. Toronto: Art Metropole, 1976.

———. "Turtles and Champagne: Paul Wong at A Space." *Only Paper Today* 4:3 (February 1977): 8–9

———. "Vidéo: regard introspectif/Toronto Video: Looking Inward." *Vie des Arts* 21:86 (Spring 1977): 17–19, 85–6

———. "Video has captured our imagination." *Parachute* 7 (Summer 1977): 16–18 This essay reprinted in *In Video* (Halifax: Dalhousie Art Gallery, 1977).

———. *In Video*. Halifax: Dalhousie Art Gallery, 1977.∾

———. "Public and Private Spaces: Dance and Video in Canada." In *Dance and Film,* ed. Selma Odom. Toronto: Art Gallery of Ontario, 1977.∾

———. "I Am Here, This Is Real." In *Autobiography: Film/Video/Photography*, ed. John Stuart Katz. Toronto: Art Gallery of Ontario, 1978.∾

———. "Erschliessung von Neuland: künstlerisches Video in Canada." In *Kanadische Künstler*. Basel: Kunsthalle, 1978.∾

———. "Temporal Realities: Eric Cameron and Noel Harding." *Parachute* 10 (Spring 1978): 12–14

———. "Videoview 1. Susan Britton." *Centerfold* 2:4 (April 1978): 14–15

———. "Videoview 2. Rodney Werden." *Centerfold* 2:4 (April 1978): 16

———. "Elizabeth Chitty/Demo Model." *Centerfold* 3:1 (December 1978): 8–12

445

———."Quality and Public Appeal." In *Art, Artists and the Media,* ed. Richard Kriesche. Graz: AVZ Books, 1978.

———. "Explaining Pictures to Dead Air: The Robertson/Beuys Admixture." *Parachute* 14 (Spring 1979): 4–8

———. "Room to Manoeuvre/Une marge de manoeuvre." In *Noel Harding. Enclosure for Conventional Habit*, ed. Lorne Falk. Banff: The Walter Phillips Gallery, 1980.∾

———. "A Response to the Basic Text." In *Video, el temps i l'espai*. Barcelona: Col.legi d'Arquitectes de Catalunya, 1980.

———. "Earlier Askevold." In *David Askevold*. Eindhoven: Stedelijk van Abbemuseum, 1981.∾

———. "History Lesson." In *Performance and Multi-Disciplinarity: Post-Modernism*, ed. Chantal Pontbriand. Montreal: Les Éditions Parachute, 1981.

———. "Les femmes, il me semble . . ." *La Chambre Blanche/Bulletin No. 11* (September 1982): 6–7

———. "Colour Video/Vulgar Potential." *Parachute* 29 (Winter 1982–3): 18–23

———. "Interview: Colin Campbell." *Parachute* 29 (Winter 1982–3): 24–6

———. "Video's Voices." In *The Second Link. Viewpoints on Video in the Eighties*, ed. Lorne Falk. Banff: The Walter Phillips Gallery, 1983.∾

———."Learning to See." In *Norman Cohn: Portraits*, ed. Peggy Gale. Toronto: Art Gallery of Ontario, 1984.∾ Includes biographical information and discussion of works by Gale, plus essays by Norman Cohn and Gillian Robinson. Preface by David Burnett.

———. "The Use of the Self to Structure Narrative/L'utilisation du moi comme struc-ture de la narration." In *Western Front: Vidéo*. Montreal: Musée d'Art Contemporain, 1984.∾

———. "Talking, Television, Audience." In *Talking Back to the Media*, eds. Sabrina Kamstra, Sebastian Lopez and Rob Perrée. Amsterdam: Talking Back to the Media, 1985.∾

———. "A Tableau Vivant." *Parachute* 39 (Summer 1985): 33–5

———. "Narratives." *Parachute* 41 (Winter 1985–86): 20–3

———. "The Problem of Description [work by David Askevold]." In *Vidéo*, ed. René Payant. Montreal: Artextes, 1986.

———. "Narratives." In *Video By Artists 2*, ed. Elke Town. Toronto: Art Metropole, 1986.

———. "On/Off." In *Luminous Sites/Ten Video Installations*, eds. Daina Augaitis and Karen Henry. Vancouver: Video Inn/Western Front, 1986.∾

———. "Memory Work." *Descant* 60 19:1 (Spring 1988): 91–108

———. "Il Nuovo Video in Canada/ Individuals: New Video from Canada." In *Aspetti e Tendenze della Ricerca Video Canadese*. Ferrara: Centro Video Arte and L'Immagine Elettronica, 1989.∾

———. "Three Heads Are Better: The Videos of General Idea/Trois têtes valent mieux: les bandes vidéo de General Idea." In *Images 89/Festival of Independent Film & Video*. Toronto: Northern Visions, 1989, 30–4 ∾

———. *Electronic Landscapes*. Ottawa: National Gallery of Canada, 1989.∾ Introductory text and programme notes/descriptions.

———. "Separate Voices." In *3rd Fukui International Video Biennale: "Expansion and Transformation."* Fukui City, Japan, 1989.∾

———. "Avanzando Deprisa/Reaching Stride." In *Bienal de la Imagen en Movimiento '90*, ed. Jose Ramon Perez Ornia. Madrid: Museo Nacional Centro de Arte Reina Sofia, 1990.∾

———. "Tom Sherman: There's something perverse about this relationship." *Parachute* 58 (Spring 1990): 24–7

———. "Lorraine Dufour and Robert Morin: Another Kind of Anthropology." *Parachute* 62 (Spring 1991): 12–17

———. "Au commencement des temps/The Beginning of Time." In *Robert Morin and Lorraine Dufour. A decade of video production*, ed. Brendan Cotter. Toronto: A Space, 1991.∾

———. *Northern Lights. An Exhibition of Canadian Video Art*. Tokyo: International Videoworks, 1991.∾ With introductory essays by Peggy Gale and Akihiko Morishita.

———. "Sulla narrazione." In *Vedute tra film video televisione*, ed. Valentina Valentini. Palermo: Sellerio editore, 1992, 123–7.

———. "Eric Metcalfe: Performing the Self." In *Return to Brutopia/Eric Metcalfe/ Works and Collaborations*, ed. Scott Watson. Vancouver: UBC Fine Arts Gallery, 1992.

———. "To Tell the Truth . . ." *Texts* 9 (Winter 1993): 4–13

———. "Video and Orality/National Gallery of Canada." *Canadian Art* 10:2 (Summer 1993): 79–80

———. *Colin Campbell: Invention*. Toronto: Art Metropole, 1993.

———. "A History in Four Moments." In *Mirror Machine: Video and Identity*, ed. Janine Marchessault. Toronto: YYZ Books/Montreal: Centre for Research on Canadian Cultural Industries and Institutions, McGill University, 1995.

———. "Stan Douglas: *Evening* and Others." *Parachute* 79 (Summer 1995): 20–7

———. *Videotexts*. Waterloo: Wilfrid Laurier University Press/Toronto: The Power Plant, 1995. Selected essays 1977–92, revised and updated.

Gale, Peggy, ed. *Video By Artists*. Toronto: Art Metropole, 1976. With essays by David Askevold, Jean-Pierre Boyer, A.A. Bronson, Peggy Gale, Dan Graham and Les Levine, and artists' statements, scripts, bio-bibliographies.

Gallagher-Shuebrook, Fran. "Images 90/Euclid Theatre Toronto." *C* 28 (Winter 1991): 57–60

Garneau, David. "Interview: Wyn Gelenyse and Tom Sherman." In *Interior Presence: Projecting Situations*, ed. Donna McAlear. Calgary: Nickle Arts Museum, 1989.

Garneau, Michèle. "Un nouveau pacte avec la fiction." *La Revue de la Cinémathèque* 8 [Montreal] (October–November 1990) (n.p.)

Gault, Charlotte Townsend. "Seeing Art in Nova Scotia/Ecphore and Inniva." *Vanguard* 15:2 (April/May 1986): 23–6

Gauthier, Guy. "Télédistribution et animation urbaine." *Communications* 21 (1974) (n.p.)

———. "Expériences au Québec: le bloc [on Vidéographe]." *La Revue du cinéma: Image et Son* 267 (January 1973): 2–9

Gauthier, Lise. *Espaces-Femmes*. Saguenay/ Lac St-Jean, 1982. Commentaries on series of performances and video presentations by women from the region.

Gendron, Louise. "À qui appartient l'image?" *Circuits Vidéo/Art* 1:1 (Winter 1981): 16

Gendron, Louise, and Diane Poitras. "A qui appartient l'image?: du macramé électronique." *La Vie en Rose* 4 (December 1980/February 1981): 10

General Idea. *Ménage à Trois*. Toronto: Art Metropole, 1978.

———. "General Idea's 'Open Line'." *Video Guide* 1:4 (September/October 1978): 12–13

———. "General Idea's Press Conference." In *Art, Artists and the Media*, ed. Richard Kriesche. Graz: AVZ Books, 1978.

———. "Towards an Audience Vocabulary [with Jo-Anne Birnie Danzker]." *Centerfold* 3:1 (December 1978): 13–18

———. "General Idea: Performance und Austellung." In *Zur Definition eines neuen Künstbegriffes*. Innsbruck: Galerie Krinzinger, 1979.

———. "Cornucopia [illustrated script]." In *Fiction*, ed. Elke Town. Toronto: Art Gallery of Ontario, 1982.

———. "'How our mascots love to humiliate us . . .': Revelations from the doghouse [with video scripts]." In *General Idea 1968–1984*, eds. General Idea and Jan Debbaut. Eindhoven: Stedelijk van Abbemuseum, 1984.

———. "Exposé." In *Vidéo*, ed. René Payant. Montreal: Artextes, 1986.

———. "Test Tube." In *Video By Artists 2*, ed. Elke Town. Toronto: Art Metropole, 1986.

———. *Les vidéogrammes de General Idea/Videotapes by General Idea*. Ottawa: National Gallery of Canada. With unsigned text outlining issues for General Idea since 1978.

General Idea and Jan Debbaut, eds. *General Idea 1968–1984*. Eindhoven: Stedelijk van Abbemuseum, 1984. With essays by Jean-Christophe Ammann, Tim Guest and General Idea.

Gentleman, Ross. "Hardwear Notes." *Video Guide* 1:1 (February/March 1978): 8

———. "Hardwear Notes." *Video Guide* 1:2 (April/May 1978): 4

———. "Hardwear Notes." *Video Guide* 1:4 (September/October 1978): 14

———. "Vancouver Video Works at the VAG." *Video Guide* (November 1978–January 1979): 6

Gever, Martha, John Greyson, and Pratibha Parmar, eds. *Queer Looks: Perspectives on Lesbian and Gay Film and Video.* Toronto: Between the Lines, 1993.

Giguère, Nicole, and Michèle Pérusse. "Vidéo femmes." *Copie Zéro* 6 (1980): 35–6

Gilbert, Gerry, and Taki Blues Singer. "Videofreerainforest — August 73/a survey of video arts in Vancouver." *artscanada* 30:4, 182/183 (October 1973): 45–51

Gilbert, J.P. "Leonardo da Vinci: L'envers du récit [Serge Tousignant: video installation]." *ETC Montréal* 1:1 (Autumn 1987): 46–8

———. "Fétichisme et image télévisée: Le regard abuse." *ETC Montréal* 6 (Winter 1988): 24–5

Gilbert, Sylvie. *Noise Under the Tongue.* Banff: Walter Phillips Gallery, 1992.∾ With video by Nelson Henricks and Brian Rusted.

Gillies, Mary. "'Video Bag' at Burnaby." *Criteria* 1:3 (March 1975): 7–8

Gingras, Nicole. "Voir entre les lignes." *24 Images* 41 (Winter 1988–9): 22

———. "Vidéo québécois." *24 Images* 41 (Winter 1988–9): 23

———. "La photographie au cinéma: réverie mobile ou mobilisatrice/Photography in Cinema: A Mobile or Mobilizing Reverie." In *Le mois de la photo.* Montreal, 1989, 180–207 ∾

———. "Michèle Waquant: Histoires en réserve." *Vie des Arts* 37:149 (Winter 1992–3): 34–7

———. *Les Absences de la photographie/The Absence of Photography.* Montreal: Cinema Libre, 1994.∾

Giocondi, Lise. "Du désir de suicide au suicide de désir [on Diane Poitras: 'Pense à ton désir']." *Ciné-Bulles* 4:6 (April–May 1985): 18–19

Gitanjali. "Lexicon of the Inevitable." In *Brave New (Virtual) World — The challenge of change in the Media Arts/A Discussion Paper on Operations & Project Grants Evaluation Process and Proposed Program Changes.* Toronto: Ontario Arts Council, 1994.

Glassman, Marc. "Introduction: A New Showcase." In *Images 88/A Showcase of Contemporary Film & Video.* Toronto: Northern Visions, 1988.∾

Godmer, Gilles. "La vidéo." *Ateliers* (April/May 1979): 13–15

———. *Michèle Waquant: impression débâcle.* Montreal: Musée d'Art Contemporain, 1993.∾

Goldberg, Michael. "Some Thoughts on the Stanley House Colloquium." *Only Paper Today* 4:1 (October 1976): 4

———. *The Accessible Portapak Manual.* Vancouver: The Satellite Video Exchange Society, 1976.

———. *La Vidéographie à la portée de tous.* Vancouver: The Satellite Video Exchange Society, 1977.

———. "Freelance Producers Approach CBC-TV." *Video Guide* 1:1 (February/March 1978): 5, 8

———. "Paul Wong: Videoview 3." *Centerfold* 2:5 (June 1978): 53–6

———. "Video — A Review." In *Rétrospective Parallelogramme 2 Retrospective 1977–1978,* ed. Barbara Shapiro. Montreal: ANNPAC, 1978.

———. "Free Expression." *Video Guide* (June 1979): 8–9, 14

———. *Broadcasting small-format video and audio: a survey.* Hull: Supply and Services Canada, 1979.

———. "Free Television." In *Transcript from The International Video Art Symposium 1979.* Kingston: Agnes Etherington Art Centre, 1979.

———. "Developing Audiences for Video/Le développement d'un public pour le vidéo." *Parallelogramme* 7:5 (June/July 1982): 7, 17

———. "Video Roma." *Video Guide* 5:2 (April 1983): 15

———. "The 6th Tokyo Video Festival." *Video Guide* 6:2 (March 1984): 14

———. "Hong Kong International Video Art Festival." *Video Guide* 6:2 (March 1984): 15

———. "Thinking Back and Looking Forward." *Video Guide* 7:3 (May 1985): 14–15

———. "Video Art and TV (A Canadian Viewpoint)." In *Fukui International Video Biennale: "Video: Spirit of the Time,"* Fukui City, Japan, 1985.∾

———. "Tape Wars." *Video Guide* 11:2 (Fall 1991): 16

Goldberg, Michael, and Crista Haukedal. "Pay TV Intervention: BC Media Alliance." *Video Guide* 4:3 (1981): 11

Goldberg, Michael, and Peter Lipskis. "Crossing the Line: Film & Video." *Video Guide* 3:2 (October 1980): 6

Golden, Anne. "Romance?/La romantique?" In *Body and Soul/Corps et Ame: The Independent Film and Video Alliance*, ed. Michael Balser. Toronto: IFVA, 1994.ɷ

Goldman, Saul. "Video: The Image." *Art Communication Edition* 5 (1977) (np)

Goodes, Donald J. "1984 Ottawa International Festival of Video Art." *Arts Atlantic* 5:4 (Summer 1984): 8

Goodwin, Jackie. "Spawning Sockeyes/Tomiyo Sasaki." *Video Guide* 8:2 (1986): 8

Goodwynne, Annie. "Video as a Social Tool." *Video Guide* 9:1 (October 1987): 4

Gordon, Jane. "My Father Was an Englishman [review: Peter Karuna]." *Fuse* 16:1 (Fall 1992): 34–5

Gosselin, Claude, ed. *Michael Morris: Photographies*. Montreal: Musée d'Art Contemporain, 1980.ɷ With texts by Claude Gosselin and Michael Morris.

———. *Semaine de la vidéo féministe québécoise*. Montreal: Musée d'Art Contemporain, 1982.ɷ

Gould, Trevor. "Tom Sherman/National Gallery of Canada." *Parachute* 32 (Fall 1983): 37–8

Goulet, Denis. "Contribution à une archéologie du regard [on René Lemire]." In *Paysage(s) de la vidéo,* ed. Monique Langlois. Montreal: Galerie UQAM, 1994.ɷ

Gourlay, Sheena. "Electronic Valentine: A Story about a Storyteller telling a Story." *Fuse* 8:3 (Fall 1984): 41–3

Graff, Tom. "The Midden Heap Can Also Be the Cornucopia." *Video Guide* 5:1 (January 1983): 4–5

Graham, Robert. "Aurora Borealis: Meliorist Underground." *C* 7 (Fall 1985): 92–3

Grande, John K. "Retrospective Hooykaas-Stansfield." *Vie des Arts* 33:133 (Winter 1988): 69–70

———. "The Production of Time/Le production du temps." In Jean-François Cantin. *La Production du temps/Travaux vidéo-graphiques 1977–1994*. Montreal: Paje Editeur, 1994.

Gravel, Claire. "Waiting for Lancelot [on Lisa Steele]." *Circuits Video/Art* 1:1 (Winter 1981)

———. "Montréal-Berlin." *ETC Montréal* 7 (Spring 1989): 60–1

Grenville, Bruce. "Vera Frenkel/The Agnes Etherington Art Centre." *Parachute* 27 (Summer 1982): 44–5

———. "Vera Frenkel/Trinity Square Video at A Space." *Parachute* 36 (Fall 1984): 57–8

———. "Is It Happening?" In *Vera Frenkel: The Videotapes*, ed. Robert McFadden. Ottawa: National Gallery of Canada, 1985.ɷ

———. "Toronto: A Play of History (Jeu d'histoire)." *Parachute* 48 (Fall 1987): 61

Greyson, John. "Initial Response: Event 1 – Performance and Video at TPS." *Centerfold* 3:5 (July 1979): 272–3

———. "Miniature Theatre: Nancy Nicol." *Centerfold* 4:1 (November 1979): 51–2

———. "In the Cultural Ejector Seat: Steel and Flesh." *Fuse* 4:5 (July/August 1980): 290–1

———. "Breathing Through Opposing Nostrils." *Video Guide* 4:5 (Issue 20, 1982):6

———. "No Confusion about Censorship: The VAG Cancels Sexuality Show." *Fuse* 7:6 (Spring 1984): 245

———. "Homo Video." *Jump Cut* 30 (March 1985): 36–8

———. "Two Men Embracing: Gay Video Images." *Video Guide* 8:4 (December 1986): 10–11

———. "Sir Gay Visits the New City: A Video Script." In *Toronto: A Play of History (Jeu d'histoire)*. Toronto: The Power Plant, 1987.

———. "The Passionate Queer Documentary." *Video Guide* 10:5 (November 1990)

———. "Double Agents: Video Art Addressing AIDS/Agents doubles: l'art vidéo vise le SIDA." *Parallelogramme* 15:2 (Fall 1989): 22–31

———. "Requiem for Gaetan." *Video Guide* 10: 3/4 (November 1989): 8–9

———. *Urinal and Other Stories*. Toronto: Art Metropole and The Power Plant, 1993. Includes complete film/videography.

Greyson, John, and Lisa Steele. "The Inukshuk Project/Inuit TV: The Satellite Solution." *Fuse* 4:4 (May 1980): 203–6

Grimal, Paul. "L'exemplaire défi de 'Vidéographe'..." *Le Journal de l'audiovisuel* (Paris) 88 (September–October 1972): 19–22

Grundmann, Heidi, ed. *Art Telecommunication.* Vienna: BLIX/Vancouver: Western Front, 1984.∾ With essays by Eric Gidney, Roy Ascott, Tom Sherman and Robert Adrian X, and documentation of 'Telefonmusik' and 'Wiencouver' projects.

Guest, Tim. "Modern Love: the recent videotapes of Colin Campbell." *Centerfold* 3:4 (May 1979): 196–7

———. "Intolerance (The Trouble with Social Realism)/"L'intolérance (les problèmes avec le réalisme social)." *Parallelogramme* 8:1 (October/November 1982): 15–19, 27–31

Guilbert, Charles. "Michèle Waquant/Musée d'art contemporain." *Parachute* 71 (Summer 1993): 29–30

Guimond, Daniel. "Anaphores." *Circuits Vidéo/Art* 1:1 (Winter 1981): 15

———. "The Taste of Dying Lips." *Video Guide* 3:4 (March 1981): 6

Gumpert, Lynn, and Ned Rifkin. *Persona.* New York: The New Museum, 1981.∾

H Haar, Sandra. "Working [Sara Diamond]." *Vanguard* 17:4 (September/October 1988): 31

———. "Self-lessness." *Fuse* 13:5 (June/July 1990): 45–6

Hadeed, Hank. "Will Gutenberg Do?" *Fuse* 6:6 (March/April 1983): 371–3

Hall, David, ed. *In the Picture — and Lawn: A Video Installation by Eric Cameron/Dans le tableau — et pelouse: Une installation vidéo par Eric Cameron.* London: Canadian High Commission/Haut-Commissariat du Canada, 1980.∾

Hallas, Nancy. *Nora Hutchinson: Dick & Jane (Spot and Puff).* Guelph: Ed Video Media Arts Centre, 1990 .∾

———. *Elyakim Taussig/Catatonics: A Video Opera.* Guelph: Ed Video Media Arts Centre, 1990.∾

———. *Between Open and Closing Heart/Within These Walls: Two Experimental Video Productions by Pauline Sinclair.*

Guelph: Ed Video Media Arts Centre, 1992.∾

———. *Birthdays: A Documentary Video by Teri Chmilar.* Guelph: Ed Video Media Arts Centre, 1993.∾

Handforth, Robert. "James Collins Talks to Peggy Gale: A Video Interview." *Only Paper Today* 4:3 (February 1977): 12

———. "Test Tube." *Fuse* 4:3 (March 1980): 145–9

Hanhardt, John G. "Notes on Video/Television: Prime Time Video / Remarques sur la vidéo/télévision: Prime Time Video." In *Prime Time Video,* ed. Allan MacKay. Saskatoon: Mendel Art Gallery, 1984.∾

Hanley, JoAnn, ed. *The First Generation: Women and Video, 1970–75.* New York: Independent Curators Incorporated, 1993. With essays by JoAnn Hanley and Ann-Sargent Wooster. Includes video by Lisa Steele.

Hanna, Myrna. "Out of the Closet and Into the Factory: Ed Video, Developing an Artist-Run Co-operative." *Video Guide* 7:2 (March 1985): 10–11

Harding, Noel. "Once Upon the Idea of Two/Une fois à l'encontre de deux." In *Eric Cameron/Noel Harding: Two Audio-Visual Constructs/Deux installations audio-visuelles,* ed. Ted Lindberg. Vancouver: Vancouver Art Gallery, 1978.∾

Noel Harding/Bill Viola: Two Video Installations. Toronto: The Art Gallery at Harbourfront, 1983. With artists' biographies and text excerpts about their work.

Noel Harding. Middelburg: De Vleeshal/Toronto: Art Gallery of Ontario, 1988.∾ With essays by Eric Cameron, Claude Gosselin, Richard Rhodes, and Ritsaert Ten Cate.

Harris, Mark. "Survival Strategies [Feature Length Video]." *Vanguard* 17:5 (November 1988): 36

———. "Cannes, Capitalism & Commercials." *Video Guide* 9:5 (December 1988): 14–15

———. "Orpheus in Oedipal Brossard." *Video Guide* 10:2 (September 1989): 5

Harry, Isobel, and Joe Bodolai, "Decentral-ization of the means of visual production." *artscanada* 30:4, 182/183 (October 1973): 66–72

Harvey, Andy. "Clearwater B.C./Videotape Being Produced on Proposed Mine." *Video Guide* 1:1 (February/March 1978): 4

Hassan, Jamelie. "Reclaiming Home/ Réconquérir sa patrie." *Parallelogramme* 17:1 (Summer 1991): 16–23

Hassan, Salah Dean. "Food for Thought." *Fuse* 13:5 (June/July 1990): 37–9

Hastenteufel, Dieter. *Them Is Us Now. Now Us Is Them.* Guelph: Ed Video Media Arts Centre, 1991.

Haukedal, Crista Johnson. "Chris Creighton-Kelly [interview]." *Video Guide* 4:1 (1981): 10

Haustein, Lydia. "Displacement: Vera Frenkel, Ilya Kabakov, Michelangelo Pistoletto und Royden Rabinowitch auf der Documenta IX." *Künst und Unterricht*, Heft 164 (1992): 38–42

———. "Hyperrealität: Joan Quick-to-See Smith and Vera Frenkel." *Artis* (March 1994) (n.p.)

———. "The Transformative Power of Memory: Themes and Methods in the Work of Vera Frenkel/Le Pouvoir transformateur de la mémoire: thèmes et méthodes dans l'oeuvre de Vera Frenkel." In *Vera Frenkel... from the Transit Bar/ ... du transitbar.* Toronto: The Power Plant/Ottawa: National Gallery of Canada, 1995.

Hayden, Elke, and Ed Fitzgerald. "Video Ring." *artscanada* 30:4, 182/183 (October 1973): 65

Healey, Julie. "'Sacrificial Burnings [Nancy Nicol].'" *Video Guide* 4:2 (1981): 3

———. "Paul Wong: 'Prime Cuts'." *Video Guide* 4:3 (1981): 5–6

———. " 'Electronic Totem' by Mike MacDonald." *Video Guide* 6:2 (March 1984): 6

Hebert, Pierre. "Les enjeux de l'art à l'ère des machines. Effacement et résistance du corps." *24 Images* 42 (Spring 1989): 22–7

———. "Critique de l'idéologie hypermédiatique." *24 Images* 54 (Spring 1991): 8–12

Heffernan, Diane. "Le Réseau Vidéo des femmes devient Le Réseau Vidé-elle des femmes." *Cahiers de la femme/Canadian Women's Studies* 3:2 (1980): 104–5

Heinrich, Theodore Allen. "Biennale 1980/A View from Venice." *Vanguard* 9:8 (October 1980): 10–13

Helwig, Maggie. "Dance on Tape." *Cinema Canada* 149 (February 1988): 13

Henderson, Clark. "Recent Works." In *Video as Diary: Recent Works,* eds. John Morgan and Clark Henderson. Saskatoon: AKA Gallery, 1988.

Hennessey, Sean. "Art-Vidéo: une introduction." In *Art <–> Vidéo: les oeuvres vidéographiques de douze artistes canadiens.* Montreal: Véhicule Art, 1977.

Henricks, Nelson, and Katherine Liberovskaya. "Programme canadien: images d'une collection de solitudes." In *Première Manifestation Internationale Vidéo et Art Electronique.* Montreal: Champ Libre, 1993. With introduction by François Cormier and Laurent Lavoie, and text on Gary Hill by Christine Van Assche.

Henry, Karen. "Michael Goldberg: 'A Couple of Changes'." *Video Guide* 4:4 (Issue 19, 1982): 4

———. "Randy & Berenicci: 'Unbashed Heroics'." *Video Guide* 4:5 (Issue 20, 1982): 3

———. "Women Speak Out: Amelia Productions/3 Labour Issues." *Video Guide* 5:1 (January 1983): 3

———. "Video Shorts III." *Video Guide* 5:3 (Summer 1983): 6

———. "As the Petals Fall [on Terry Ewasiuk]." *Video Guide* 5:5 (Winter 1983): 6

———. "Community Telidon Network of the Pacific." *Video Guide* 6:1 (January 1984): 4

———. "Prime Time Moves On." *Video Guide* 6:1 (January 1984): 10

———. "Television Interference." *Vanguard* 6:3 (May 1984) (n.p.)

———. "Interview: Doris Chase." *Video Guide* 6:3 (May 1984): 3

———. "Video Culture — Cafe Video." *Video Guide* 6:4 (August 1984): 8

———. "The Words and Wounds of Silence/Helen Doyle." *Video Guide* 7:2 (March 1985): 6–7

———. "Video and Culture." *Video Guide* 7:3 (May 1985): 2

———. "Video Vancouver." In *Canadian Video Art,* ed. René Coelho. Amsterdam: The Holland Festival, 1985.

———. "Asian New World/Video Art and Documentary." *Video Guide* 8:5 (1987): 9–12

———. "Infermental VI: Western Front." *Video Guide* 9:1 (October 1987): 18–19

———. "Stan Douglas/Artspeak." *Parachute* 51 (Summer 1988): 35–6

———. "In These Times of Diminishing Visual Returns . . . [Michael Morris and Vincent Trasov]." *Video Guide* 10:1 (March 1989) 3, 18

———. "Beyond Seduction: The Videos of Norman Cohn." *Video Guide* 10:2 (September 1989): 15

———. *Angela Grauerholz, Michèle Waquant: Timeframe.* Vancouver: Presentation House Gallery, 1991.◌

———. "Grande Barrière: Daniel Dion." In *Four Visions of Television: Daniel Dion, Ardele Lister, Robert Morin, Jan Peacock*, ed. Brian Rusted. Banff: Artists Television Workshop, Banff Centre for the Arts, 1991.◌

Henry, Karen, et al. "Video '84: Oppositional Aesthetics." *Video Guide* 7:1 (January 1985): 6–13

Henry, Karen, and Paul Wong. "Vancouver Video Perspective." In *October Show*, Vancouver 1983.◌

Henry, Karen, ed. *Phosphorus Diode.* Vancouver: Satellite Video Exchange Society, 1985 ◌

Herbert, Lisa. "Interview: Sara Diamond." *Video Guide* 7:5 (January 1986): 3

Hezekiah, Gabrielle. "Nation Language in Translation/Traduire la langue nationale: 'Maigre Dog' by/de Donna James, 'English Lesson' by/de Shani Mootoo." *Parallelogramme* 20: 4 (Spring 1995): 30–7

Hoet, Jan. *Prospekt 80/2: CCMC, David Askevold, Colin Campbell, Dan Graham, Noel Harding, General Idea, Michael Snow.* Ghent: Museum Van Hedendaagse Kunst, 1980.◌ With untitled essays by Jan Hoet and Michel Baudson.

Hogan, Molly. "Video on the Trans-Siberian Railroad." *Video Guide* 8:1 (Issue 36, 1986): 12–13

Holmes, Willard. "Here Our Look Sees Itself: Rodney Graham/Tom Sherman/ Jochen Gerz." *Parachute* 60 (Fall 1990): 20–3

Holtz-Bonneau, Françoise. "L'art infographique: entrée des artistes." *Cahiers des Arts Visuelles du Québec* 9:33 (Spring 1987): 16–21

Houghton, Nik. "Sex, fleas and Or-phelia: Vera Frenkel and Ulrike Rosenbach at AIR." *Independent Media,* London (November 1988) (n.p.)

Huffman, Kathy, ed. *California Video.* Long Beach: Long Beach Museum of Art, 1980.◌ Includes Jan Peacock.

———.*Video: A Retrospective 1974–1984.* Long Beach: Long Beach Museum of Art, 1984.◌ Includes David Askevold, Colin Campbell, Vera Frenkel, Ernest Gusella, Noel Harding, General Idea, Jan Peacock, Lisa Steele and "The Second Link" exhibition.

Huffman, Kathy Rae, and Dorine Mignot, eds. *The Arts for Television.* Los Angeles: Museum of Contemporary Art/Amsterdam: Stedelijk Museum, 1987.◌ Essays by Rosetta Brooks, Anne-Marie Duguet, Kathy Rae Huffman, Dorine Mignot, Bob Riley, Janet Sternberg and Ernie Tee. Includes General Idea in exhibition.

Hume, Vern. "Another Look at the Plot for the Western Re: Placing the Satellite: Media Culture on the Plains." *Video Guide* 9:1 (October 1987): 6–7

———. *Film and Video from the Heart of the Heart of the Regions: A Country?/Le film et la vidéo du coeur du coeur des régions: Un pays?* Calgary: Inter-Disciplinary Artists Promotion and Production Society of Alberta, 1989.◌ With texts by Vern Hume and Leila Sujir, plus annotated documentation of 72 works.

I Induni, Roberto. "A mille lieux, un parcours électronique de Montréal." *ETC Montréal* 20 (November 1992/February 1993): 61–3

Infermental I. Berlin, 1981–2. Eds. Gabor Body and Astrid Heibach.◌ Supervisor: Gustav Hamos. 37 contributors, 8 countries, 4 hours.

Infermental II. Hamburg, 1983. Eds. Oliver Hirschbiegel and Rotraut Pape.◌ Supervisor: Vera Body. 77 contributions, 15 countries, 6 hours.

Infermental III. Budapest, 1984. Eds. Laszlo Beke, Peter Forgacs, Peter Hutton, Malgorzata Potoka. Supervisor: Rotraut Pape.◌ 99 contributors, 18 countries, 6 hours.

Infermental — Special Issue for Canada Berlin 1984 . Eds. Gabor Body and Egon Bunne.◌ 88 contributions, 16 countries, 6 hours.

Infermental — Extra-Ausgabe NRW Wuppertal 1985 .ↄ Eds. Werner Nekes, Egon Bunne, Marcel Odenbach, Ursula Wevers. Supervisor: Laszlo Beke. 34 contributions, 7 countries, 4 hours.

Infermental 4. Lyon, 1985. Ed. FRIGO.ↄ Supervisor: Astrid Heibach. 102 contributions, 14 countries, 7 hours.

Infermental 5. Rotterdam, 1986. Eds. Leonie Bodeving, Rob Perrée, Lydia Schouten.ↄ Supervisor: Egon Bunne. 39 contributions, 13 countries, 5 hours.

Infermental 6. Vancouver, 1987. Eds. Hank Bull, Vera Body.ↄ Supervisor: Gerard Couty (FRIGO). 59 contributions, 25 countries, 6 hours. Special feature: "Cross-Cultural Television", eds. Hank Bull and Muntadas.

Infermental 7. Buffalo, 1988. Eds. Chris Hill, Tony Conrad, Peter Weibel.ↄ Supervisor: Rotraut Pape. 58 contributions, 17 countries, 5 hours.

Infermental 8. Tokyo, 1988. Eds. Keiko Sei, Alfred Birnbaum.ↄ Advisors: Mike Hentz, Hank Bull. 73 contributions, 15 countries, 5 hours.

Infermental 9. "Herz von Europa." Vienna, 1989. Eds. Ilse Gassinger, Graf + ZYX.ↄ Supervisor: Chris Hill (Buffalo), 45 contributions, 15 countries, 5 hours.

Innis, Harold. *The Bias of Communication.* Toronto: University of Toronto Press, 1951.

Insell, Maria, ed. *In Absentia: IFVA National Film/Video Showcase/AVCI Rencontres nationales cinéma/vidéo.* Vancouver: Robson Square Media Central, 1988.ↄ With essays by Maria Insell and Paul Wong.

In Visible Colours, Film/Video Festival and Symposium. Vancouver, 15–19 November 1989.ↄ Essay by Yasmin Jiwani.

J Jackson, Chris. *Passion(s) by Colleen O'Neill.* Calgary: Stride Gallery, 1989.ↄ With an essay by Chris Jackson.

Jacques, Marie-Claude. "La vidéo, l'art vidéo à bout de souffle?" *24 Images* 33 (Spring 1987): 21–2

Japan 87 Video Television Festival/Electrovisions. Tokyo: Video Gallery SCAN, 1987.ↄ Canadians include Byron Black, Ernest Gusella, François Girard, Bernar Hébert, General Idea and Tomiyo Sasaki.

Japan 89 Video Television Festival/Delicate Technology. Tokyo: Video Gallery SCAN, 1989.ↄ Canadians include Luc Bourdon, Dennis Day/Susan Rynard and Paulette Phillips/Geoffrey Shea/Dalaibor Martinovic.

Jean, Suzanne. "Le regard activé." *24 images* 19 (Winter 1983–84): 18–20

———. "Eléments de lecture de l'art vidéo: traitement de texte de l'oeil," *Intervention* 23 (Spring 1984) (n.p.)

———. *Art Vidéo Québec.* Quebec: College F.-X. Garneau, 1985.ↄ

Jenkins, Sue. "'Now Playing': a conversation with David MacLean." *Video Guide* 10: 3/4 (November 1989): 7

Jiwani, Yasmin. "In Visible Colours: A Critical Perspective." *In Visible Colours, Film/Video Festival and Symposium.* Vancouver, 15–19 November 1989.ↄ

Johnson, Nancy. "Feminist Film and Video." *Fuse* 5:6/7 (August/September 1981): 207–10

Jones, Faith. "Awakening to the Power of the Union." *Kinesis* (June 1988): 15

Joyner, J. Brooks. "In V. Traction." *Centerfold* 5/6 (1977): 7

Juhasz, Alexandra. "Constructing Authority: Documentary Form and AIDS." *Video Guide* 10:3/4 (November 1989): 10–11

Jutras, Pierre, and Pierre Véronneau. "D'un syndrome à l'autre: des professionels ont la parole." *Copie Zéro* 26 (December 1985): 7–17 Analysis of effect of video art on film industry via exchanges between directors, producers, technicians; audience trends towards TV and rentals.

K Kalinovska, Milena, and Dierdre Summerbell, eds. *Rhetorical Image.* New York: New Museum of Contemporary Art, 1990.ↄ Includes Barbara Steinman video/photo installation and text.

Kamstra, Sabrina, Sebastian Lopez, and Rob Perrée, eds. *Talking Back to the Media.* Amsterdam: Talking Back to the Media, 1985.ↄ With essays by Dara Birnbaum, Rosetta Brooks, Max Bruinsma, Victor Burgin, Janny Donkers, Peggy Gale, Raul Marroquin, Jan Simons and Ernie Tee.

Kaplan, Nomi. "Bill Nemtin [interview]." *Video Guide* 1:1 (February/March 1978): 6

Katz, John Stuart, ed. *Autobiography: Film/Video/Photography*. Toronto: Art Gallery of Ontario, 1978.ᴄᴠ With essays by Peggy Gale, John Stuart Katz, Jay Ruby and Dennis Wheeler.

Kawaja, Jennifer. "Process Video: Self-Reference and Social Change." In *Mirror Machine: Video and Identity,* ed. Janine Marchessault. Toronto: YYZ Books/Montreal: Centre for Research on Canadian Cultural Industries and Institutions, McGill University, 1995.

Kealey, Susan. "Taxi sans detour." *Fuse* 12:6 (August 1989): 37

———. "Film & Video News." *Fuse* 16:4 (May/June 1993): 9

———. "Film & Video News." *Fuse* 17:1 (Fall 1993): 3

Kean, Shelly. "Wanted: One Door for the Unit/Pitt Gallery." *Video Guide* 4:4 (Issue 19, 1982): 3

Kearns, Gloria. "La septième art, au feminin." *Ciné-Bulles* 7:1 (August–October 1987): 35 On the Festival international de films et vidéos de femmes, Montreal 1987.

Keating, Lulu. "Paul Wong Can't Be All Wrong." *Parallelogramme* 7:2 (December 1981): 17–18

Keeshig-Tobias, Lenore. "Images 90." *Fuse* 14:1/2 (Fall 1990): 48–9

Kennedy, Garry Neill. "Video at NSCAD." *artscanada* 30:4, 182/183 (October 1973): 62–3

Keziere, Russell. "Video in Vancouver: PUMPS on Cable 10." *Centerfold* 3:1 (December 1978): 63–4

———. "Video and Values/Vancouver Video Works [Jo-Anne Birnie Danzker and Nelson Becker interview]." *Vanguard* 7:9 (December 1978–January 1979): 17–18

———. "Anarchy and the Square [Paul Wong interview]." *Vanguard* 8:1 (February 1979): 29–31

———. *Cyber Ethics*. Self-published, Toronto, 1992.

Kibbins, Gary. "Love Means Never Having to Tell a Story ['Hygiene' review]." *Fuse* 9:5 (February/March 1986): 39–42

———. "Elizabethan Video [Tanya Mars]." *Fuse* 9:6 (May/June 1986): 14–17

———. "Doing the Documentary." *Fuse* 11:1/2 (Summer 1987): 50–5

———. "How the West Was Wonderful [on 'Buck']." *Fuse* 12:1/2 (September 1988): 42–3

Kisil, Gerry. "The State of Video Distribution in the Canadian Mid-West." *Video Guide* 9:1 (October 1987): 8–9

———. "Independence: An Interview With Claude Ouelette." *Video Guide* 11:2 (Fall 1991): 6–7

———. "Harsh Light: Prairie Video." *Video Guide* 11:2 (Fall 1991): 10

Kivisild, Emma. "The Heat Is On: Ways of Seeing Sex [includes analysis of video 'In the Dark' by Steele and Tomczak]." *Fuse* 9:5 (February/March 1986): 7–9

Kivland, Sharon. "Trois contes." In *Sylvie Bélanger: Topologies du regard,* ed. Sharon Kivland. Herblay (France): Les Cahiers des Regards, 1991.ᴄᴠ

Kivland, Sharon, ed. *Sylvie Bélanger: Topologies du regard.* Herblay (France): Les Cahiers des Regards, 1991.ᴄᴠ With essays by Jean Attali, Sharon Kivland and Michèle Thériault.

Klonaris, Maria, and Katerina Thomadaki, eds. *Technologies et imaginaires / art cinéma, art vidéo, art ordinateur.* Paris: Dis Voir, 1990.ᴄᴠ Canadians include Vera Frenkel, John Porter, David Rimmer, David Rokeby and Michael Snow.

Kleyn, Robert. "The Lack of Video Form/La Mancanza di una Forma di Video." In *Video 79. Video — The First Decade. Dieci Anni di Videotape,* ed. Alessandro Silj. Rome: Kane Editore, 1979.

Knights, Karen. "Under 5." *Video Guide* 6:5 (October 1984): 4–5

———. "Present Tense: In Conversation with Edward Mowbray." *Video Guide* 7:2 (March 1985): 3–4

———. "'Not Dead Yet': Celebration or Obituary?" *Video Guide* 7:2 (March 1985): 8–9

———. "War in Flowerland: A Personal Video Documentary by Marlin Oliveros & Byron Black." *Video Guide* 7:3 (May 1985): 3

———. "Video Works: Western Front Video." *Video Guide* 8:1 (Issue 36, 1986): 4–5

———. "'Rune'/Randy & Berenicci." *Video Guide* 8:2 (Issue 37, 1986): 10–11

———. "Political Equations for the Porn Wars." *Video Guide* 8:3 (September 1986): 14–15

———. "Explicit But Equal: Toward a New Pornography." *Video Guide* 8:4 (December 1986): 6–7

———. "Exploring the Space Between Heaven and Hell: The Work of Rodney Werden." *Video Guide* 8:4 (December 1986): 9, 19

———. "In His Own Image." *Video Guide* 8:5 (Issue 40, 1987): 18–19

———. "In Absentia Video." *Video Guide* 9:4 (Issue 44, Fall 1988): 4

———. "Independent Film and Video Alliance/Annual General Assembly." *Parachute* 52 (Fall 1988): 64–6

———. "It Works: Labour and Video." *Fuse* 12:3 (September/October 1988): 45–6

———. "Betwixt and Between: Finding a Place to Re/Act From." *Video Guide* 10:2 (September 1989): 3

———. "Imager le feminin: l'art vidéo de Sara Diamond/Imaging the Feminine: The Video Art of Sara Diamond." In *Sara Diamond: Mémoires ravivées, histoire narrée.* Ottawa: National Gallery of Canada, 1992.ꝏ

———. *Distinguishing Features: 15 Years of Artists' Video at Ed Video Media Arts Centre 1976–1991.* Guelph: Ed Video Media Arts Centre, 1993. With introductory texts by Nancy Hallas, Lynne Jenkins and Don Richardson.

———. "The Legacy of our Polymeric Progeny." In *Whispered Art History: Twenty Years at the Western Front,* ed. Keith Wallace. Vancouver: Arsenal Pulp Press, 1993.

Konyves, Tom. "Video Poetry." *Circuits Video/Art* 1:1 (Winter 1981): 12

Kriesche, Richard, ed. *Art, Artists and the Media.* Graz: AVZ Books, 1978. Contributions by Jo-Anne Birnie Danzker, Charly Fox, Peggy Gale, General Idea and Marshall McLuhan.

Krizan, Sam, and Tony McAulay. "Turbulence." *Video Guide* 5:4 (Fall 1983): 7, 15

———. "Turbulence." *TKO* 2 (1983): 22–6

———. "Turbulence 2." *TKO* 3 (1983): 8–11

Kroker, Arthur. *Technology and the Canadian Mind: Innis, McLuhan, Grant.* Montreal: New World Perspectives, 1984.

Kroker, Arthur, and Marilouise Kroker. "Excremental TV." *Mediamatic* 7:2 (Summer 1993): 147–53

Krumins, Andrew. "Banff Television Festival." *Video Guide* 5:4 (Fall 1983): 4

Kunard, Andrea. "Vera Frenkel/Western Front." *Vanguard* 10:8 (October 1981): 33

———. "Byron Black/Vancouver Art Gallery." *Vanguard* 10:9 (November 1981): 39–40

Künst Bleibt Künst / Projekt '74. Cologne: Wallraf-Richartz-Museum, Kunsthalle, Kunstverein, 1974.ꝏ Major overview of conceptual/media-based works, including international history of video (Eng/German text). Canadians include Robert Arn, David Askevold, Colin Campbell, Murray Favro, Michael Goldberg, Michael Hayden, Marien Lewis, Bruce Parsons, David Rabinowitch and Michael Snow.

Künstler aus Kanada: Räume und Installationen. Stuttgart: Württemburgischer Kunstverein, 1983. Introduction by Tilman Osterwold, catalogue essays by Ulrich Bernhardt, Bruce Ferguson, Glenn Lewis and Philip Monk. Includes video by Susan Britton, Colin Campbell, General Idea, Les Levine, Ardele Lister, Eric Metcalfe/Hank Bull/Dana Atchley, Anne Ramsden, Ed Slopek and Rodney Werden.

Kureishi, Hanif. "The Buddha of Suburbia." *Video Guide* 8:5 (Issue 40, 1987): 13–15

Kwinter, Kerri. *Videotape by Colin Campbell.* New York: 49th Parallel Centre for Contemporary Canadian Art, 1986.ꝏ

———. "'Modern Love' by Colin Campbell." *Centerfold* 4:2 (January 1980): 8–9

———. "Barriers." *Paralellogramme* 8:2 (December 1982/January 1983): 17–20. French translation by Mario Campo as "Limites," *Paralellogramme* 8:3 (February/March 1983): 37–40

———. "Ontario Open Screenings, Six Days of Resistance Against the Censor Board, April 21–27, 1985." *Fuse* 9:1/2 (Summer 1985): 26–34

L   La Chance, Michaël. "Les spectres vidéo, thèmes dans la vidéo internationale récente." *Cahiers des Arts Visuels au Québec* 9:33 (Spring 1987): 30–8

———. "Le renard, les chiens et leur méduse." *Ciné-bulles* 8:3 (April/May 1989): 12–14

———. "Arrêts sur l'image. Freeze et moirés dans l'aliénation télévisuelle."

Cahiers des Arts Visuelles du Québec 10:37 (1988): 41–7

———. "L'image est un artifact ['L'encyclopédie Claire-Obscure' by Luc Courchesne]." *Spirale* 88 (May 1989): 3

Lachapelle, François. *Un nouveau monde.* Rimouski: Musée Regional de Rimouski, 1991. With text by François Lachapelle on Richard Purdy and François Hébert.෴

Lachapelle, Gilbert. "Feedback instantante et codage digital." In *Art <-> Vidéo: les oeuvres vidéographiques de douze artistes canadiens.* Montreal: Véhicule Art, 1977.෴

Lachapelle, Lise, and Thomas Waugh, eds. *Sélection vidéo/Video Selection.* Montreal: Le Vidéographe, 1989. Distribution catalogue with essays by Lise Lachapelle and Thomas Waugh.

Lacy, Daryl. "Drawing the Lines. A Videotape by Andy Harvey." *Video Guide* 4:4 (Issue 19, 1982): 5

Lafrance, Jean-Paul. *La télévision: un media en crise.* Montreal: Québec-Amérique, 1982.

Lai, Larissa. "The Site of Memory." In *As Public As Race.* Banff: The Walter Phillips Gallery, 1993.෴

Lai, Larissa, and Jean Lum. "Neither Guests nor Strangers." In *Yellow Peril Reconsidered,* ed. Paul Wong. Vancouver: On Edge, 1990.෴

Laing, Carol. "Whitewash: More News From In Between." In *Four Visions of Television: Daniel Dion, Ardele Lister, Robert Morin, Jan Peacock,* ed. Brian Rusted. Banff: Artists Television Workshop, Banff Centre for the Arts, 1991.෴

Lalonde, Joanne. "Kate Craig, Dialogues, intimité et corps à corps." *ETC Montréal* 19 (Summer 1992): 72–5

———. "Bill Viola et Adrian Piper Vidéo: mise en scène du quatrième mur." *ETC Montréal* 20 (November 1992/February 1993): 61–3

———. "Sohet Philippe: 'Vidéoréalite, une installation mediatique'." *ETC Montréal* 22 (May/August1993): 26–8

———. "Daniel Dion: La fascination des universaux." *ETC Montréal* 23 (August/ November 1993): 17–21

Lamarre, Jean, and Jean-François Leclerc. "Comment on fait l'histoire: vidéo et histoire." *Cahiers d'histoire* 4:1 (Fall 1983) (n.p.)

Lamarre, Louise, Jules Lamarre and Luc Bourdon assisté de Katherine Liberovskaya. *Le Prix de la Liberté: rapport sur la production indépendante vidéo.* Montreal: l'Institut Québécois du Cinéma, April 1992.

Lamoureux, Johanne. "On coverage: performance, seduction, flatness." *artscanada* 38:1 240/241 (March/April 1981): 25–7, 51

———. "General Idea: Le 'conte' du temps." *Parachute* 25 (Winter 1981): 4–9

———. "Les filles de vues [On Vidéo Femmes, Quebec City]." *Resources for Feminist Research:/Documentation sur la recherche féministe* 15:4 (December 1986–January 1987): 28–30

———. "Entre le programme et l'énigme: Horror Autotoxicus." In *Nell Tenhaaf: Horror Autotoxicus, Videodisc Installation.* Vancouver: Western Front, 1991.෴

Landry, Pierre. *Le geste oublié.* Montreal: Musée d'Art Contemporain, 1987.෴

Landry, Roselyne, and Diane Poitras. "Les femmes du Groupe d'Intervention Vidéo de Montreal." *Cahier de la femme/Canadian Women's Studies* 3:2 (1980): 109–11

Langlois, Monique. "Chantal duPont, une archéologie en images." *Espace* 6:4 (Summer 1990): 46–7

———. "Festival Mondial de la vidéo. Histoire(s) selon la vidéo [on World Wide Video Festival, The Hague]." *Espace* 7:2 (Winter 1991): 35–7

———. "L'éclatement des genres ['Parabôle 78' by Mario Côté, Galerie Graff, Montreal]." *ETC Montréal* 15 (Summer 1991): 76–9

———. "Chantal duPont, parcours entre ciel et fleuve / Le Lieu, Centre d'art actuel." *Vie des Arts* 36:144 (September 1991): 64

———. "L'installation Audio-Visuelle et son spectateur." *Espace* 18 (Winter 1992): 45–7

———. "Paysage(s) de la vidéo: paysage de l'interdisciplinarité." In *Paysage(s) de la vidéo,* ed. Monique Langlois. Montreal: Galerie UQAM, 1994.෴

Langlois, Monique, ed. *Paysage(s) de la vidéo.* Montreal: Galerie UQAM, 1994.෴ With texts by Jody Berland, Mario Côté, Judith Anne Epstein, Suzanne Foisy, Denis Goulet, Monique Langlois, Martin Pigeon, Louise Poissant, Jacques Schroeder and Jean Tourangeau, plus artists' statements and biographies.

Langlois, Yves. "Arts visuels: manifeste d'un vidéomane." *Le Temps Fou* 23 (November–December 1982): 52

———. "Le documentaire vidéo ou la nostalgie de la claquette." *Ciné-Bulles* 5:4 (May–July 1986): 18–19

Lapham, Lewis. "Prime-Time McLuhan," *Saturday Night* (September 1994): 51–6 Prepared as an introduction to Marshall McLuhan, *Understanding Media* (Cambridge: MIT Press, 1994).

Larivée, Suzie. "Suzanne Giroux: Le temps mauve, Giverny mediatisé." *ETC Montréal* 14 (Spring 1991): 78–9

Larkin, Jackie. "In the Dark: Talking Sex." *Video Guide* 8:4 (December 1986): 3

Larouche, Michel. "14e festival international du nouveau cinéma et de la vidéo." *Parachute* 42 (Spring 1986): 33

———. "La surréalité des images de synthèse." *24 Images* 42 (Spring 1989): 28–9

Larsen, Anne-Marie. "New Tools for Imaging." *Arts Atlantic* 10:3 (Winter 1991): 5–6

Larsen, Ernest. *Joint Ventures*. New York: Artists Space, 1990.ↄ Canadians include Balser/Fabo and Steele/Tomczak.

Larson, Doris. *Women in Politics*. Saskatoon: A.K.A. Gallery, 1984.ↄ Includes video by Sara Diamond, Laura Hackett, Nancy Nicol and Diane Poitras.

Laskey, Heather. "The Atlantic Film and Video Festival 1983." *Arts Atlantic* 5:2 (1984): 4–5

Laurence, Robin. "Paul Wong: Chinaman's Peak." *Fuse* 16:4 (May/June 1993): 43–4

Laurette, Patrick Condon. *Nova Scotia: Four Channels*. Halifax: Art Gallery of Nova Scotia, 1980.ↄ With a foreword by James Riordan, plus artists' statements: installations by Eric Cameron, James Goss, Robert Hamon and Ed Slopek.

Lawrence, Monica Holden. "Mad About the Crazy Lady." *Video Guide* 1:2 (April/May 1978): 10–11

"La vidéo s'en va . . ." *Parachute* 42 (Spring 1986): 49–50 Several letters signed to protest the end-of-contract for video curator Rob McFadden at the National Gallery of Canada.

Le Baron, Philippe. "Vidéo-Chartier." *Mediart* 13 (January 1973): 20

Lebredt, Gordon. "Once living . . . ." In *Art is Communication*, eds. Paul Petro and Geoffrey Shea. Toronto: A Space, 1985 .ↄ

Lee, James-Jason. "Cornelia Wyngaarden/Presentation House." *Parachute* 72 (Fall 1993): 63–4

Lee, Helen. "Safe Sexual Imagery [on Images '88, Toronto]." *Cinema Canada* 155 (September 1988): 33

Lee, Stephen. "Yellow Peril: Reconsidered." *Fuse* 15:1/2 (Fall 1991): 47–8

Lee-Nova, Gary, and Al Razutis. "Hybrid." *artscanada* 30:4, 182/183 (October 1973): 25–6

Legentil, Danielle. *Giverny, le temps mauve: Suzanne Giroux, Recent Works*. Montreal: Musée d'Art Contemporain, 1990.ↄ

Legris, Françoise. "Les mirages de l'Anticipation [on Chantal duPont]." *ETC Montréal* (September 1990): 30–2

Leitch, Terry. "A Personal Statement." *Video Guide* 10:3/4 (November 1989): 4

L'Espérance, Denis. "Ajustements vers l'art opto-électronique." In *Art <–> Vidéo: les oeuvres vidéographiques de douze artistes canadiens*. Montreal: Véhicule Art, 1977.ↄ

Lessard, Denis. "Cinéma, vidéo, performance." *Vie des Arts* 27:109 (December 1982/January 1983): 22–3

———. "Bons baisers du Québec/From Quebec with Love." *Parallelogramme* 8:2 (December 1982/January 1983): 6–9, 11–14

Levi. "Profile: Shawna Dempsey/Lorri Millan." *Fuse* 17:1 (Fall 1993): 43–4

Levine, Les. "One Gun Video Art." In *Video By Artists*, ed. Peggy Gale. Toronto: Art Metropole, 1976.

———. "We Are Still Alive." *Parachute* 2 (Winter 1976): 23–6 Discussing issues surrounding his work in Cape Dorset, N.W.T. (1974) for later exhibition.

———. "One Gun Video Art." In *Les Levine: Diamond Mind*. Antwerp (Belgium): Internationaal Cultureel Centrum, 1978.

Les Levine: Diamond Mind. Antwerp (Belgium): Internationaal Cultureel Centrum, 1978. Video, photo and installation work by Les Levine. Includes essays by Jack Burnham, Catherine Levine and Les Levine.

Lewis, Glenn. "Dennis Tourbin: in Conversation with a Diplomat." *Centerfold* 3:1 (December 1978): 33–5

———. "We All Sing the Same Song." *Video Guide* (November 1978–January 1979): 10

———. "Western Front, Vancouver." In *Künstler aus Kanada: Räume und Installationen.* Stuttgart: Württemburgischer Kunstverein, 1983.

———. *New Video Realities.* Cologne Art Fair, 1986.ↄ

Lewis, Glenn, Kim Tomczak and Paul Wong, eds. *Living Art Vancouver.* Vancouver: Western Front/Pumps/Video Inn, 1980. With an introduction by the curators and essays by Alvin Balkind, Bruce Barber, René Blouin and Jo-Anne Birnie Danzker, and documentation of 22 performances and 51 videotapes.

Lewis, Marien. "Norman Cohn: Portraits/London Regional Art Gallery." *Canadian Art* 2:1 (Spring 1985): 92–3

Lewis, Mark. "UMAS Videos: Rousseau Redux." *C* 9 (Spring 1986): 62–3

Lewis, Rebecca. "Video Interruptus." *Afterimage* 11 (April 1984): 4 On legal and moral questions in the cancellation of Paul Wong's 1984 exhibition at the Vancouver Art Gallery.

Lindberg, Ted, ed. *Eric Cameron/Noel Harding: Two Audio-Visual Constructs/Deux installations audio-visuelles.* Vancouver: Vancouver Art Gallery, 1978.ↄ

Lippert, Werner, ed. "David Askevold." *Extra* 4 (April 1975) [entire issue]

Lomholt, Niels. "A Journey through Videoland." *Circuits Video/Art* 1:1 (Winter 1981): 20

London, Barbara. "Delicate Technology." In *Delicate Technology: 2nd Japan 89 Video Television Festival at Spiral.* Tokyo: Video Gallery SCAN, 1989.ↄ

Lord, Barry. "Video in Venice." *Canadian Forum* 41 (August 1980) (n.p.)

Lord, Catherine. "60 vidéos entre l'humour et la rage." *L'Actualité* 4:2 (February 1979): 18

Lord, Susan. "Up Against the Law." *Fuse* 16:3 (Spring 1993): 29–31

———. "Outliving Apollo's Kiss." In *Cornelia Wyngaarden/The Fragility of Origins,* ed. Brice Canyon. Vancouver: Western Front Society, 1994.ↄ

Love, Karen, ed. *We Want Moschiach Now! — Portrait of a Chassidic Community: An Installation by Paula Levine.* Vancouver: Presentation House Gallery, 1985.ↄ With

introduction by Karen Love, essay by Marian Penner Bancroft, plus artist's statement.

———. *Timeframe.* Vancouver: Presentation House Gallery, 1991.ↄ Works by Angela Grauerholz and Michèle Waquant.

Lovett, Sharon, ed. *The 6th International Video Exchange Directory.* Vancouver: Satellite Video Exchange Society, 1978. Includes a Letter from the Editor plus articles by Andy Harvey and Shawn Preus.

Lower, Mary Ellen. "We Interrupt You For This Message: A review of 'A Retrospective of Canadian Feminist Production' Workshop by Renee Baert." *Video Guide* 8:3 (September 1981): 6–7

Lowndes, Joan. "The Canadian presence in Paris." *artscanada* 30:4, 182/183 (October 1973): 73–80

Lynch, Peter, and Renya Onasick. "Prime Time Video: Breaking Ground/Prime Time Video: Innovation." In *Prime Time Video,* ed. Allan MacKay. Saskatoon: Mendel Art Gallery, 1984.ↄ

Lypchuk, Donna. "Images '89." *Cinema Canada* 166 (September 1989): 23

M Mabie, Don, ed. *The First Ten, 1975–1985: The Catalogue.* Calgary: Off Centre Centre, 1985.ↄ With documentation and texts by Marcella Bienvenue, Charles Mitchell, Grant Poier, Chuck Stake, Nancy Tousley and Hector Williamson.

McAlear, Donna. *Striving for Ideal Resolution/Tendre vers une solution idéale.* Calgary: Nickle Arts Museum, 1988.ↄ Includes video by Lisa Steele and Kim Tomczak.

———. *Elemental Instincts: a matter of course.* Calgary: Nickle Arts Museum, 1988.ↄ Includes video by Nelson Henricks, Colleen Kerr and Stephen Peterson.

———. "Focus on Lani Maestro." *Canadian Art* 6:1 (Spring 1989): 102

McAlear, Donna, ed. *Interior Presence: Projecting Situations.* Calgary: Nickle Arts Museum, 1989.ↄ With an essay by Robert Milthorp and interviews with Wyn Geleynse and Tom Sherman. Includes video by Jan Peacock and Tom Sherman.

MacCallum, Peter. "'Casting Call' by Susan Britton." *Artists' Review* 11:19 (June 1979): 7–8

MacDonald, Mike. *Mike MacDonald: Interview by Tom Sherman* [Interviews With Artists Series]. Toronto: Mercer Union, 1991.

McElroy, Gil. "Doug Porter: Time Signals." *Arts Atlantic* 12:1 (Winter 1993): 12–14

———. "Tradition and Desire: Recent Video by Buseje Bailey & Donna James." *Arts Atlantic* 12:3 (Autumn 1993): 22–3

McFadden, Robert. *Identifying Tracks: An Introduction to Recent Canadian Video/Une introduction à des récentes vidéos canadiens.* Ottawa: Galerie SAW, 1988.ᘏ

McFadden, Robert, ed. *Vera Frenkel: The Videotapes.* Ottawa: National Gallery of Canada, 1985.ᘏ With essays by Bruce Grenville and Lisa Steele.

McGee, Robert. "Barbara Steinman: 'Icon'." In *Bienal de la Imagen en Movimiento '90,* ed. Jose Ramon Perez Ornia. Madrid: Museo Nacional Centro de Arte Reina Sofia, 1990.ᘏ

McGrath, Jerry. "Vera Frenkel and AGYU." *Parachute* 73 (January 1994): 48–9

McGregor, Gwen. "In the Realm of the Senses ['Quartet for Deafblind' by Norman Cohn]." *Fuse* 12:1/2 (September 1988): 37

McIntosh, David. "Second Decade: AIDS + Community + Television." *C* 39 (Fall 1993): 13–18

———. "Cyborgs in Denial: Technology and Identity in the Net." *Fuse* 17:3 (Spring 1994): 14–22

MacKay, Allan, ed. *Prime Time Video.* Saskatoon: Mendel Art Gallery, 1984.ᘏ With essays by Renee Baert, Bruce W. Ferguson, John G.Hanhardt, Peter Lynch/Renya Onasick and Robin F. White.

MacKay, Gillian. "Barbara Steinman." *Canadian Art* 9:3 (Fall 1992): 38–43

Mackenzie, Scott. "On Bélanger, Virilio and the Limitations of a Global Surveillance Regime/Sylvie Bélanger, Paul Virilio et les limites d'un régime global de surveillance." In *Sylvie Bélanger: The Silence of the Body,* ed. Marnie Fleming. Oakville: Oakville Galleries, 1995.ᘏ

Maclean, Jay. "Reel Life — From Us to Us." *Fuse* 4:4 (May 1980): 194–6

McLeod, Kathy and Nancy Shaw. "On Signs and Sex: 'Visual Evidence'." *Fuse* 11:3 (Fall 1987): 33–8

McLuhan, Marshall. *The Gutenberg Galaxy.* Toronto: University of Toronto Press, 1962.

———. *Understanding Media: The Extensions of Man.* Cambridge: MIT Press, 1994. (Originally published in 1964 by McGraw-Hill, New York.)

———. "Classroom Without Walls" and "Media Log." In *Explorations in Communications,* eds. Edmund Carpenter and Marshall McLuhan. New York: Beacon Press, 1966.

———. *Verbi-Voco-Visual Explorations.* New York: Something Else Press, 1967.

———. "Biennale Seminar on Video/Venice 1977." In *Art, Artists and the Media,* ed. Richard Kriesche. Graz: AVZ Books, 1978.

MacNevin, Brian. ". . .Viewpoints on Video . . . ." In *The Second Link. Viewpoints on Video in the Eighties,* ed. Lorne Falk. Banff: The Walter Phillips Gallery, 1983.ᘏ

McSherry, Frederick. "More Waves." *Circuits Video/Art* 1:1 (Winter 1981): 23

Madill, Shirley. "Winnipeg Perspective. 1985 — Video." *The WAGMAGazine* (February 1985): 4–7

———. "Comment Video Pool: An Interview with Gerry Kisil." *The WAGMAGazine* (February 1985): 12–13

———. *1987: Contemporary Art in Manitoba.* Winnipeg: Winnipeg Art Gallery, 1987.ᘏ A 75th anniversary survey of painting, sculpture, photography, performance, video, ceramics, architecture and interior design.

Madill, Shirley, ed. *Winnipeg Perspective 1985: Video.* Winnipeg: Winnipeg Art Gallery, 1985. With foreword by Terrence Heath and additional texts on artists' works.ᘏ

Maitland-Carter, Kathleen. "Colin Campbell Interviewed." *CineAction* (Summer 1987): 32–7

Majka, Christopher. "Out of the Centre/Centre for Art Tapes." *Parachute* 59 (Summer 1990): 41–2

———. "Eastern Wave [on the facilities of Centre for Art Tapes, Halifax]." *Cinema Canada* 130 (May 1986): 44

2e Manifestation internationale de vidéo. Montbéliard: Centre d'action culturelle, 1984. [proposé et animé par Jean-Paul Fargier,

Saint-Denis France] ∾ Includes text by Andrée Duchaine and historical essay by Shirley Madill. Canadians include Norman Cohn, Jean-Pierre St-Louis/Lynda Craig, Eric Metcalfe/Hank Bull, Luc Bourdon/Marc Paradis, Helen Doyle, Louise Gendron, General Idea, Suzanne Girard, Laurin/Lajoie/Demeczuk/LaCasse/Peers, Jean-Guy Michaud, Robert Morin/Gilbert Lachapelle, Miguel Raymond/Bill Vorn/H. Blanchard and Norman Thibault.

3e Manifestation internationale de vidéo et télévision. Montbéliard: Centre d'action culturelle, 1986.∾ With an essay by Andrée Duchaine and programmes selected by Susan Rynard, Joe Sarahan, Bruno Jobin (many titles). Additional works in competition by François Girard, Bernar Hébert, Ardele Lister and Suzanne Giroux.

4e Manifestation internationale de vidéo et TV. Montbéliard: Centre d'action culturelle, 1988.∾ Canadian selections and essay by Robert Morin.

Mann, Ken. "'Are We Going Backwards?' [David Tuff interview]." *Video Guide* 10:3/4 (November 1989): 3

Marchand, Rick. "AIDS Vancouver." *Video Guide* 10: 3/4 (November 1989): 4

Marchand, Sandra Grant, ed. *Eric Cameron: Exposer/Cacher.* Cameron's text trans. by Thérèze de Celles. Montreal: Musée d'Art Contemporain,1993.∾ Introductory text by Sandra Grant Marchand.

Marchessault, Janine. "Reach out and touch someone: Interactive reality at the end of history." *M5V* 2 (Winter 1991/2): 18–24

———. "Incorporating the Gaze." *Parachute* 65 (Winter 1992): 24–8

———. "Amateur Video and the Challenge for Change." In *Mirror Machine: Video and Identity,* ed. Janine Marchessault. Toronto: YYZ Books/Montreal: Centre for Research on Canadian Cultural Industries and Institutions, McGill University, 1995.

Marchessault, Janine, ed. *Mirror Machine: Video and Identity.* Toronto: YYZ Books/ Montreal: Centre for Research on Canadian Cultural Industries and Institutions, McGill University, 1995. With essays by Kay Armitage, Renee Baert, Marjorie Beaucage, Ron Burnett, Kevin Dowler, Tom Folland, Monika Kin Gagnon, Peggy Gale, Jennifer Kawaja, Janine Marchessault, Christine Ross, Nancy Shaw and Dot Tuer.

Marineau, Jean-Claude. "17ème festival international du nouveau cinéma et de la vidéo de Montréal." *Parachute* 54 (Spring 1989): 71

———. "Vidéo: la consécration par la bande." *Ciné-Bulles* 12:3 (Summer 1993): 22–3

———. "Journal vidéo." *Ciné-Bulles* 13:3 (Summer 1994): 40–1

———. "Passage à l'acte." *Ciné-Bulles* 13:4 (Autumn 1994): 42–3

———. "Journal vidéo II." *Ciné-Bulles* 14:1 (Winter/Spring 1995): 46–7

Marks, Laura U. "Sexual Hybrids / From Oriental Exotic to Postcolonial Grotesque." *Parachute* 70 (Spring 1993): 22–9

———. "Packaged for Export, Contents Under Pressure. Canadian Film and Video in a U.S. Context." *Fuse* 17:1 (Fall 1993): 12–23

Marshall, Stuart. "Strategies of Dissemblance." In *Colin Campbell/Media Works 1972–1990,* ed. Bruce Ferguson. Winnipeg: Winnipeg Art Gallery, 1991.∾

Marshalore. "Album." In *Vidéo,* ed. René Payant. Montreal: Artextes, 1986.

Marshy, Leila. "Through Her Eyes." *Cinema Canada* 144 (September 1987): 32–3

Martin, Chris. "Delinquents With a Difference." *Fuse* 48, 11:4 (Winter 1987–8): 41

Martin, Jean-Louis. "La télévision à l'heure des clochers." *Tilt* (December 1973): 36–42

Matrix Festival Book. Vancouver: Satellite Video Exchange Publishing, 1973. With self-introductory essays by Peter Berg/San Francisco, Bob Stilger/Vancouver-Washington, Nancy Hughes/Canada Council, Leigh Sigurdson/Winnipeg, Steve Hannon/Edmonton, L.A. Access Project, Audrey Bronstein/London England, Media Rites/San Francisco, Robert Forget/Le Vidéographe Montreal, Walter Wright/The Kitchen New York and Connexions/Vancouver.

Mays, John Bentley. "Lines on Video Art." *Only Paper Today* 4:3 (February 1977): 6–7

———. "Should Karen Ann Quinlan Be Allowed to Die? [VideoCabaret]." *Only Paper Today* 5:1 (February 1978): 18–19

———. "'The Truth About the USSR'/ Geoffrey Shea." *Vanguard* 15:5 (October/November 1986): 30–2

Metcalfe, Reece. "Topsy vs Autopsy." *Video Guide* 8:4 (December 1986): 18

Metcalfe, Robin. "Life Like It: Some Halifax Video [review]." *Video Guide* 8:3 (September 1986): 13

———. "Life Like It: Some Halifax Video [review]." *Arts Atlantic* 7:2 (1986): 20

———. "Women and Video Exploration: A Premiere Screening." *Arts Atlantic* 7:4 (1987): 8–9

———. "Women and Video Exploration: Three Halifax Videos." *Video Guide* 9:5 (December 1988): 8–9

———. "Joyan Saunders: Interview." *Video Guide* 9:5 (December 1988): 10–11

———. "Secret Sharer [Tom Sherman]." *Vanguard* 17:6 (December 1988 – January 1989): 35

———. "Joyan Saunders: Tongue Tied and Twisted." *Arts Atlantic* 10:3 (Winter 1991): 14–15

Miles, Geoff. "The Vraisemblable of Television." *Fuse* 6:6 (March/April 1983): 376–8

Miller, Earl. "Life Like It: Some Halifax Video." *Canadian Art* 3:4 (Winter 1986): 97–8

———. "Jan Peacock/A Space." *Vanguard* 17:1 (February/March 1988): 28–9

Miller, Janet. "Dance Scan." *Video Guide* 1:4 (September/October 1978): 10

Milne, Anne. "Sometimes I feel like I'm talking to Myself: Notes on Pay TV in Canada." *Impulse* (Fall 1981): 40–1

Milthorp, Robert. "Interior Presence: Projecting Situations." In *Interior Presence: Projecting Situations,* ed. Donna McAlear. Calgary: Nickle Arts Museum, 1989.ॐ

———. "Interior Presence: Projecting Situations [review]." *Parachute* 56 (Fall 1989): 69–70

Mitchell, Jeannine. "Manzana por Manzana/Tiempo de Guerre [review]." *Video Guide* 6:2 (March 1984): 4–5

Mitchell, John, and Vincent Trasov. *The Rise and Fall of the Peanut Party.* Vancouver: Air, 1974.

Mongeau, Michel. "Mais comment vous dire ça." *Mediart* 16 (April/May 1973): 20–1

Monk, Philip. "Television By Artists." *Canadian Forum* 61:709 (May 1981)

———. "Agit-Prop/International Performance Art Series, Mercer Union." *Parachute* 28 (Fall 1982): 42–4

———. "A Space in Toronto: A History." In *Künstler aus Kanada: Räume und Installationen.* Stuttgart: Württemburgischer Kunstverein, 1983.

———. "Tom Sherman Presenting Text / animals, weather, car crashes and communication." *Parachute* 30 (Spring 1983): 26–32

———. "Disclosure." In *4 Hours and 38 Minutes: Videotapes by Lisa Steele and Kim Tomczak,* ed. Philip Monk. Toronto: Art Gallery of Ontario, 1989.ॐ

Monk, Philip, ed. *4 Hours and 38 Minutes: Videotapes by Lisa Steele and Kim Tomczak.* Toronto: Art Gallery of Ontario, 1989.ॐ With essays by Philip Monk and Dot Tuer.

Moore, Mavor. "To Be More Visible, You Have to be Able to Be Seen." *Video Guide* 8:5 (1987): 6

Mootoo, Shani, et al. "Visible Difference [Review of 'In Visible Colours' Film and Video Symposium]." *Fuse* 13:4 (Spring 1990): 31–3

Moreau, Yvan. "Les mirages de l'anticipation [Chantal duPont, 'Archéo-Sites' installation]." *ETC Montréal* 12 (Autumn 1990): 30–3

———. "Laval: Mario Côté, voir autrement." *ETC Montréal* 22 (May/August 1993): 50–1

Morf, André. "Télévision/idéologie: les media communautaires au Québec." *Chronique* 24–5 (December 1976–January 1977): 130–45

Morgan, John. "Video as Diary." In *Video as Diary: Recent Works,* eds. John Morgan and Clark Henderson. Saskatoon: AKA Gallery, 1988.ॐ

Morgan, John, and Clark Henderson. "Playback Cabaret: Video as Diary/Recent Works." *Video Guide* 9:5 (December 1988): 13

Morgan, John, and Clark Henderson, eds. *Video as Diary: Recent Works.* Saskatoon: AKA Gallery, 1988.ॐ With essays by John Morgan and Clark Henderson.

Morgan, Marie. "The New Narrative: Video in the 80's." *Banff Letters* (Winter/Spring 1984)

Morin, Albanie, Diane Poitras and Nicole Hubert. "Les femmes ont-elles peur de la technique?" In *Femmes et Cinéma Québécois.* Montreal: Boréal Express, 1983.

———. "Tour du monde en 40 heures." *La Vie en rose* 36 (May 1986): 44–5 On Festival de Vidéo Femmes, Quebec, March 1986.

Morin, Robert. "Faire des portraits." In *Ethique & télévision/4e manifestation internationale de vidéo et TV.* Montbéliard: Centre d'action culturelle, 1988.

Morin, Robert, and Lorraine Dufour. "'La femme étrangère': script." In *Robert Morin and Lorraine Dufour. A decade of video production*, ed. Brendan Cotter. Toronto: A Space, 1991.◌

Morris, Michael. "Blueprint for Video Agreement." In *Rétrospective Parallelogramme Retrospective 1976–1977*, ed. Barbara Shapiro. Montreal: ANNPAC, 1977.

Morris, Michael, and Vincent Trasov. "Video Narcissus." *Video Guide* 9:3 (1988): 15

Morris, P. "Private Addresses." *Video Guide* 11:2 (Fall 1991): 8–9

Morrison, Ken. "Video and the Vth International Conference on AIDS: Accessibility or Abstraction?" *Video Guide* 10:3/4 (November 1989): 14–15

Moser, Mary Anne. "Video Artifact: A Video Journal." *Fuse* 13:3 (Winter 1989–90): 10–12

———. "Cut and Paced." *Fuse* 13:3 (Winter 1989–90): 48

———. "Inevitable Tension: art in electronic culture." In *Angles of Incidence: Video Reflections of Multimedia Artworks*, ed. Sara Diamond. Banff: The Banff Centre for the Arts: The International Council for Computer Communication, 1993.◌

Mossop, Rowley. "Sex in Venice [John Greyson]." *Fuse* 48, 11:4 (Winter 1987–88): 30

Mowbray, Ed, and Nancy Paterson. "Music/Rock/Video/Television: A Nice Neat Package?" *Video Guide* 5:3 (Summer 1983): 4

Mulvihill, Bryan. "Grande Barrage/Great Divide." *Video Guide* 10:5 (November 1990) (n.p.)

Murchie, John. "Luc A. Charette: Mémoires (sté/reo) Mémoires [video installation]." *Arts Atlantic* 11:3 (Spring/Summer 1992): 5–6

Murphy, Sarah. "At the Limit of Narrative: Two Tapes from Em/Media, Calgary." *Video Guide* 9:5 (December 1988): 6–7

———. "My Two Grandmothers, Her Great Grandfather, & Me [Leila Sujir]." *Fuse* 15:4 (Spring 1992): 38

Murphy, Serge. "Michèle Waquant." *Vanguard* (May 1984) (n.p.)

Murray, Ian. "Support Structure for Artists working with Videotape: Notes." In *Transcript from The International Video Art Symposium 1979*. Kingston: Agnes Etherington Art Centre, 1979.

Mushet, Mark. "Digicon 83: Screens to Replace the Canvas?" *Video Guide* 5:4 (Fall 1983): 3

———. "Subterranean Television: an interview with Madame Samantha and Bruce A." *Video Guide* 7:4 (Issue 34, 1985): 4–5

———. "Phosphorus Diode: Review." *Video Guide* 7:5 (January 1986): 4–5

Musiol, Marie-Jeanne. *Images en transit.* Pro-Arts (Ontario), 1989.

N Nelson, Joyce. "The Sweetening Machine." *BorderLines* No. 1 (Fall 1984): 8–9

———. "CRTC Asleep at the Wheel." *Fuse* 10:4 (Winter 1986–7): 11–21

———. *The Perfect Machine: TV in the Nuclear Age.* Toronto: Between the Lines Press, 1987.

Nemiroff, Diana. "Rethinking the Art Object." In *Visions: Essays in Contemporary Canadian Art*, ed. Robert Bringhurst. Vancouver: Douglas & McIntyre, 1983.

"The New Work Show [programme/catalogue]." *Fuse* 10:3 (Fall 1986): 27–30 ◌

Nichols, Miriam. "Habeas Corpus: Stan Douglas' 'Television Spots'." In *Stan Douglas: Television Spots.* Vancouver: Contemporary Art Gallery, 1988.◌

Nickel, Michelle. "Some Perspectives on Women's Alternative Art Centres." *Video Guide* 5:1 (January 1983): 9

Nicol, Nancy. "Women and Video: Vera Frenkel." *Fireweed* 1:1 (Autumn 1978) 13–19

———. "Marshalore: Another State of Marshalore." *Centerfold* 3:1 (December 1978): 36–9

———. *Intervention Productions Presents 'Let Poland Be Poland'.* Toronto: ARC Artculture Resource Centre, 1982.◌

————. "Concepts of Heroism/Heroineism – A Different Definition." *Rites* 1:8 (February 1985) (n.p.)

Northey, Jane. "Lisa Steele/Kitchen Sync [Ottawa/Paris]." *Vanguard* 11:4 (May 1982): 43–4

Northey, Jane, and Connie Eckhert, eds. *Art and Community.* Toronto: A Space, 1987.◌ With artists' and curators' statement, plus essays by Lillian Allen, Karl Beveridge/Carole Condé and Connie Eckhert. Video by Michael Baynger, John Greyson and Regent Park Video Workshop.

O *Obscure, 1982–1988.* Quebec: Galerie Obscure, 1989. Essays by Gilles Arteau, Richard Martel, Réjean Perron and others.

The October Show. Vancouver: Contemporary Art Gallery, 1983.◌ With video programme descriptions, and essays by Daina Augaitis, Barbara Daniel, Todd Davis, Mary Gingerich, Steve Harris, Josie Kane, Russell Keziere, Avis Lang, Robert Linsley , David MacWilliam and Helga Pakasaar.

O'Day, Ellie. "Stokely Seip's Nash the Slash." *Video Guide* 5:3 (Summer 1983): 3

Oille, Jennifer. "A Question of Place 2." *Vanguard* 10:9 (November 1981): 12–17

————. "Kim Tomczak/'Paradise Lost'." *Vanguard* 11:9/10 (December/January 1982–3): 18

————. "Peter Wronski/Rodney Werden/ARC." *Vanguard* 12:9 (November 1983): 47

————. "Vera Frenkel/A Space." *Vanguard* 13:8 (October 1984): 39–40

OKanada. Berlin: Akademie der Künste, 1982.◌ Essays on Canadian video by Renee Baert, Andrée Duchaine, Bruce Ferguson and Clive Robertson.

O'Neill, Colleen. "Robert Milthorp/Nickle Arts Museum." *Vanguard* 17:1 (February/March 1988): 38

O'Neill, Mark. "Hybrid TV: Feature-Length Video." *Cinema Canada* 158 (December 1988): 21–2

On Line. Kunst im Netz. Graz: Steirische Kultur Initiative, 1993. "Zero — the Art of Being Everywhere" Symposium ed. Robert Adrian X and Gerfried Stockerj. Catalogue ed. Jutta Schmiederer and Robert Woelfl.◌

Osborne, Stephen. "'Individual Release': Tom Sherman at the Western Front." *Centerfold* 3:3 (February/March 1979): 136–8

Ouvrard, Hélène. "Une carte, pourquoi?" *Medium-Media* (n.p., n.d.)

Owen, Timothy. "Videotext in Canada: Promises and Problems." *Fuse* 6:6 (March/April 1983): 354–9

P Pakasaar, Helga. *VoiceOver.* Vancouver: Contemporary Art Gallery, 1985.◌

Pakasaar, Helga, ed. *Revisions.* Banff: Walter Phillips Gallery 1992.◌ With essays by Deborah Doxtater, Jean Fisher and Rick Hill. Canadian video includes Zacharias Kunuk and Mike MacDonald.

Pallain, Marc. "Vidéo, Québec, dix ans d'âge [on Vidéographe and G.I.V.]." *Le Journal des cahiers du cinéma* 321 (March 1981) (n.p.)

Paquet, Suzanne. *Le cinéma expérimental et la vidéo des femmes.* Montreal: La Centrale/Main Film, 1991.◌ Includes introduction by Suzanne Paquet and proposals for discussion by Kitty Scott.

Paradis, Marc. "Conversation." *Video Guide* 9:1 (Issue 41, October 1987): 12

Parsons, Bruce. "Listening to VTR." *artscanada* 30:4, 182/183 (October 1973): 27–9

Paskal, Merrily. "Réflexions sur un festival vidéo." *Main Mise* 13 (May 1972) (n.p.)

Passages de l'Image. Paris: Musée National d'Art Moderne, Centre Georges Pompidou 1990.◌ Includes video elements by Jeff Wall.

Paterson, Andrew. "Rodney Werden/ARC Toronto." *Parachute* 33 (Winter 1983–4): 51

————."Four Redheads: Four New Toronto Videotapes." *Fuse* 11:3 (Fall 1987): 31–3

————. "Cold Snaps: Images '88, Northern Visions showcase of new film and video." *Cinema Canada* 155 (September 1988): 31–3

————. "Focus on Michael Balser." *Canadian Art* 6:1 (Spring 1989): 101

————. "Paulette Phillips/Geoffrey Shea/YYZ."*Vanguard* 17:1 (February/March 1988): 30–1

————. "(Many Different) Images 91." *Fuse* 15:1/2 (Fall 1991): 5–7

————. *Time, Space & Realities.* Toronto: A Space, 1995.◌

Paterson, Nancy. "Contemporary Art and Technology: the new ecological era." In *Art is Communication*, eds. Paul Petro and Geoffrey Shea. Toronto: A Space, 1985.ᴄᴡ

———. "Montreal Video Now." *Toronto Montréal Echange vidéo/Toronto Montreal Video Exchange*. Montreal: Le Vidéographe/Toronto: A Space, 1986.ᴄᴡ

———. "Curating Video." *Cinema Canada* 139 (March 1987): 14

———. "Art, Technology and Public Policy 1990/L'art, la technologie et la politique en 1990." *Parallelogramme* 16:2 (Fall 1990): 38–42

Pattanayak, Chandrabhanu. "Daniel Dion [review]." *Parachute* 78 (Spring 1995): 51–2

Patton, Andy. "Snow on the Screen/De la neige sur l'écran." In *Sylvie Bélanger: The Silence of the Body*, ed. Marnie Fleming. Oakville: Oakville Galleries, 1995.ᴄᴡ

Paul, Marie Hélène. "Vidéographe, Montréal." *Motion* (July–August 1973): 36

Payant, René. "Sites de complexité/Sites of Complexity." In *Vidéo*, ed. René Payant. Montreal: Artextes, 1986.

———. "La frénesie de l'image: vers une esthétique selon la vidéo." *Vidéo-vidéo, Revue d'esthétique*, nouvelle série 10 (1986): 17–23

———. *Vedute: Pieces détachées sur l'art, 1976–1987*. Laval: Editions Trois, 1987.

Payant, René, ed. *Vidéo*. Montreal: Artextes, 1986. Papers from the International Video Conference in Montreal, 1984.

Payne, Andrew. "From Tragedy to TV." *M5V* 1 (September 1991): 30–7

Peacock, Jan. "Wallace + Theresa." *Video Guide* 8:3 (September 1986): 11

———. *Corpus Loquendi (body for speaking)*. Halifax: Dalhousie Art Gallery, 1994.ᴄᴡ

Peeters, Ger. "The Perfect Machine: TV in the nuclear age [review]." *Mediamatic* 4:3 (Spring 1990): 154

Perez Ornia, Jose Ramon, ed. *Bienal de la Imagen en Movimiento '90*. Madrid: Museo Nacional Centro de Arte Reina Sofia, 1990.ᴄᴡ With essays by Christine van Assche, Eugeni Bonet, Peggy Gale, Barbara London and John Wyver. Canadian video includes Daniel Carrière/Richard Angers, Paula Fairfield, Zacharias Kunuk, Robert

Morin/Lorraine Dufour,Marc Paradis, Tom Sherman/Jean Piché and Barbara Steinman.

Perrée, Rob. "Water Video." *Mediamatic* 5:4 (Winter 1991): 238–40

Perrier, Patrice Hans. "La trame vidéo/ matrice multidisciplinaire." *Cahiers des Arts Visuelles du Québec* 7:26 (Summer 1985): 21–4

Perron, Mireille. "A Western View on Power, Language aqnd Women." In *Four Visions of Television: Daniel Dion, Ardele Lister, Robert Morin, Jan Peacock*, ed. Brian Rusted. Banff: Artists Television Workshop, Banff Centre for the Arts, 1991.ᴄᴡ

Perry, Bill. "Computerese." In *Art is Communication*, eds. Paul Petro and Geoffrey Shea. Toronto: A Space, 1985.ᴄᴡ

Pétillat, Gérard. "Bernard (sic) Hébert, canadien et perfectionniste heureux," *Cinéma 88* 450 (October 1988): 23

Petro, Paul. "To be decoded/à dechiffrer." In *Art is Communication*, eds. Paul Petro and Geoffrey Shea. Toronto: A Space, 1985.ᴄᴡ

Petro, Paul, and Geoffrey Shea, eds. *Art is Communication*. Toronto: A Space, 1985.ᴄᴡ With essays by Gordon Lebredt, Nancy Paterson, Bill Perry, Paul Petro, Geoffrey Shea and Nell Tenhaaf, plus interview with Doug Back and letter from Glenn Howarth.

Petty, Sheila. *Inventions of Nation*. Regina: Mackenzie Art Gallery, 1993.ᴄᴡ

Petty, Sheila, ed. *Identity and Consciousness: (Re)Presenting the Self*. Regina: Dunlop Art Gallery, 1991.ᴄᴡ With an essay by Sheila Petty, and Homi Bhabha interviewed by Jonathan Rutherford. Includes video by Leila Sujir.

Pevere, Geoff. "Collision in the Capital: Politics and Art Hit Head-On in Video Festival." *Fuse* 9:1/2 (Summer 1985): 47–50

Philp, Andrea. "Video Pool Inc." *Video Guide* 5:5 (Winter 1983): 10–11

———. "Home Street: Videotape by Gerry Kisil." *Video Guide* 9:5 (December 1988): 5, 15

Picard, Jean. "Le vidéo clip québécois: une nécessité culturelle." *Qui fait quoi?* 2:5 (June 1985): 22–4

Pigeon, Martin. "La salle de bain: un lieu d'*extrémité* [Huguette Miron]." In *Paysage(s) de la vidéo*, ed. Monique Langlois. Montreal: Galerie UQAM, 1994.ᴄᴡ

Poier, Grant. "Video." In *The First Ten, 1975–1985: The Catalogue*, ed. Don Mabie. Calgary: Off Centre Centre, 1985.◌

———. "I Woke Up This Morning — In a Cold Sweat." In *Media Blitz 2*, ed. Sandra Tivy. Calgary: The New Gallery, 1989.◌

———. "Rapids." In *Showcase/Rencontres: Independent Film and Video Alliance*, eds. Marcella Bienvenue and Nelson Henricks. Calgary: IFVA, 1991.◌

Poissant, Louise. *Machinations*. Montreal: La Société d'Esthétique du Québec, 1989.◌

———. "Archéo-Sites de Chantal duPont." *Vie des Arts* 35:140 (Autumn 1990): 71–2

———. "Televisions: Des installations d'art mediatique." *Vie des Arts* 36:145 (Winter 1991): 61

———. "La vidéo, écriture d'histoire." In *Paysage(s) de la vidéo*, ed. Monique Langlois. Montreal: Galerie UQAM, 1994.◌

Poitras, Diane. "Portrait of the Practice and Trends Among Feminist Videomakers in Quebec." *Video Guide* 6:5 (October 1984): 11

———. "Pornographie alternative." *La vie en rose* (July–August 1987): 58

Pollack, Jill. "Appropriate/Distraction." *Video Guide* 7:5 (January 1986): 10–11, 13

———. "Everyday Events: A Discussion on Video Exhibitions and Video Screenings." *Video Guide* 8:1 (Issue 36, 1986): 6–7

———. "'Cénotaphe'/Barbara Steinman." *Video Guide* 8:2 (Issue 37, 1986): 14

———. "Lost Art: A Cargo Cult Romance." *Video Guide* 8:3 (September 1986): 8

———. "After Photography Before Computers: Video Criticism." *Video Guide* 9:1 (October 1987): 3

———. "Segue Ways, or Everything in its Time and Place." *Video Guide* 9:5 (December 1988): 3

Pollack, Jill/Shona Rossel. "Women in Focus Distribution." *Video Guide* 9:1 (October 1987): 5

Pollock, Anne. *From This Point of View*. Vancouver Art Gallery, 1977.◌ Includes video by Cathy Charlton, Kate Craig, Don Druick, Ross Gentleman, Gregg Simpson, Sheera Waisman.

Poloni, Philippe. "Pour une défonce video." *Circuits Vidéo/Art* 1:1 (Winter 1981): 18

———. "Super Naturel." In *Vidéo*, ed. René Payant. Montreal: Artextes, 1986.

Pontbriand, Chantal. "Matrix: première famille globale." *Mediart* 14 (February/March 1973): 4–9

———. "L'animation ou comment faire des amis." *Mediart* 15 (March/April 1973) (n.p.)

———. "Pierre Falardeau: Sur le film et le vidéo au Québec." *Parachute* 3 (Spring 1976): 32

———. "Notion(s) de performance/Notion(s) of Performance." *Parachute* 15 (Summer 1979): 25–9 Discusses direct (live) performance and deferred performance (via video, film, photography, sound recordings).

Pontbriand, Chantal, ed. *Artistes canadiennes/Canadian Women Artists: Tomiyo Sasaki, Sylvie Bouchard, Susan Scott, Shelagh Alexander*. Paris: Centre Culturel Canadien, 1985. Catalogue essays by Bruce Grenville, Denis Lessard, Philip Monk and Christina Ritchie. Introduction by Chantal Pontbriand. Includes video by Tomiyo Sasaki.

Porter, Doug. "Luc Courchesne: Portrait Number 1." *Arts Atlantic* 10:4 (Spring/Summer 1991): 15

Poser, Carol. "Michael Morris/Nova Gallery." *Vanguard* 9:5/6 (Summer 1980): 49

Pottie, Lisa. "Confusing the Script." *Fuse* 53, 12:4 (January/February 1989): 45–6

Preus, Shawn. "Vancouver Women's Video & Film Festival." *Video Guide* (November 1978–January 1979): 4

———. "Hardware Notes: Tape Survey." *Video Guide* 6:3 (May 1984): 2, 5

———. "A Report Video '84." *Video Guide* 6:5 (October 1984): 2

———. "Distributing the Distributors." *Video Guide* 7:4 (Issue 34, 1985): 2

Preus, Shawn, and Andy Harvey. "European Flashback" and "Travelling Video Festival." In *The 6th International Video Exchange Directory*, ed. Sharon Lovett. Vancouver: Satellite Video Exchange Society, 1978.

———. "European Tour Report, Part 1: England/Netherlands." *Video Guide* 1:2 (April/May 1978): 6–7

———. "European Tour Report, Part 2: Switzerland and West Germany." *Video Guide* 1:4 (September/October 1978): 8–9

Preus, Shawn, and Paul Wong "Applebaum Hebert Intervention." *Video Guide* 4:1 (1981): 9

Prinn, Elisabeth. "Video as an organizing tool for poor people." *Newsletter: Challenge for Change/Société Nouvelle* 7 (Winter 1971–2): 14–16

Prospect 80/2: Canada. Ghent: Museum van Hedendaagse Kunst, 1980.⌒

Public Information: Desire, Disaster, Document. San Francisco: Museum of Modern Art, 1994.⌒ Includes two video installations by Stan Douglas. Essays by Gary Garrels, Jim Lewis, Sandra S. Phillips, Christopher Phillips, Robert R. Riley and Abigail Solomon-Godeau, plus artists' biographies and bibliography.

Q Quadflieg, Claus. "In der Transit Bar: Auf der Suche nach Raum und Zeit." *documenta IX Spezial* (August 1992): 3–4

Quinn, Cathy. "Life Like It: Some Halifax Video." *Video Guide* 8:3 (September 1986): 10–11

Quinn, Stanley F., "The Film Challenge: Transcript of the panel discussion held on 7 May 1977 in Toronto." *SMPTE Journal* 86:10 (October 1977): 733–8 A lengthy discussion of the new importance of video technology in television broadcasting, and comparison of film and video for ease, accessibility, collaboration, cost and portability. Suggests that film would continue to be used in television production, but that video would replace film for news programming, documentaries, and some entertainment shows. Programmers are advised to suit system to each project.

R Racine, Danielle. *Album Magnétique.* Montreal: Zone Productions, 1989.⌒

Racine, Danielle, ed. *A Mille Lieux.* Montreal: Zone Productions, 1992.⌒ With an essay by Danielle Racine; installations by Luc Bourdon, François Girard/Miguel Raymond, Suzanne Giroux, Joanna Kotkowska, Michel Lemieux/Victor Pilon, Katherine Liberovskaya and Miguel Raymond.

———. *A Mille Lieux: Une expo vidéo.* Montreal: Zone Productions, 1992 ⌒ With introduction by Danielle Racine, and untitled texts by Denis Filion for each work.

Racine, Rober. "Tele-performances/Toronto." *Parachute* 13 (Winter 1978): 11–13

———. "Festival de performances du MBAM." *Parachute* 13 (Winter 1978): 43–7 Includes use of video in performances by Marc Cramer and Louise Guay, among others.

———. "Jean-François Cantin: Propos Type." *Centerfold* 3:1 (December 1978): 40–2

Racine, Yolande. "La vidéo, au delà du récit." In Jean-François Cantin, *La Production du temps/Travaux vidéographiques 1977–1994.* Montreal: Paje Editeur, 1994.

Racine, Yolande, ed. *Tendences actuelles au Québec.* Montreal: Musée d'Art Contemporain, 1980.⌒ With essays by Louise Letocha, René Payant and Yolande Racine.

Rahn, David. "Barbara Steinman: 'Le couple dormant'," *Video Guide* 3:1 (Summer 1980): 8

Ramsden, Anne. *Anne Ramsden: Urban Geography: A Video Installation.* Vancouver: UBC Fine Arts Gallery, 1990.⌒

Ramsey, Ellen. "VoiceOver." *Vanguard* 14:10 (December 1985–January 1986): 46–7

Randolph, Jeanne. "Paul Wong 'Confused Part III: The Videotape'." *C* 3 (Fall 1984): 54–5

———. "Illusion and the Diverted Subject: A Psychoanalysis of Art and Entertainment." *Parachute* 48 (Fall 1987): 28–32

———. "Truth Disguised As Lie/La Vérité déguisée en mensonge." In *Vera Frenkel . . . from the Transit Bar/ . . . du transitbar.* Toronto: The Power Plant/Ottawa: National Gallery of Canada, 1995.⌒

Randy and Berenicci. "Rune." In *Luminous Sites/Ten Video Installations,* eds. Daina Augaitis and Karen Henry. Vancouver: Video Inn/Western Front, 1986.⌒

Rans, Goldie. "Video Refractions." *C* 3 (Fall 1984): 24–26

Ratnam, Premika. "Uncharted Territories/Territoires inexplorés." In *Body and Soul/Corps et Ame: The Independent Film and Video Alliance,* ed. Michael Balser. Toronto: IFVA, 1994 .⌒

Raymond, Miguel. "Plate-forme-Vidéo-Platform." In *Vidéo,* ed. René Payant. Montreal: Artextes, 1986.

Razutis, Al. "Le vidéo pictographique." In *Art <–> Vidéo: les oeuvres vidéographiques de douze artistes canadiens.* Montreal: Véhicule Art, 1977.⌒

Realism: Atructure and Illusion: Towards a Definition of Representational Art Guelph: MacDonald Stewart Art Centre, University of Guelph, 1981. Catalogue essay by David Nasby. Includes video by Noel Harding, Nora Hutchinson and Tom Sherman.

Régimbald, Manon. "La Quinzaine de la vidéo [Rétrospective: Josef Robakowski]." *ETC Montréal* 11 (Spring/Summer 1990): 59–61

———. "Théatralité et installations vidéo, des faits divers." *ETC Montréal* 12 (Autumn 1990): 47–50

Reinhardt, Jeanette. "Kim Tomczak: Interview." *Video Guide* 3:2 (October 1980): 5

———. "Affirmative Action: Humour in Documentary/L'Action positive: l'humour dans le documentaire." In *Tenth Anniversary Showcase: The Independent Film and Video Alliance,* ed. Michael Balser. Toronto: IFVA, 1990.ᴄᴠ

Renaud, France. "Vidéo-Québec-USA-Canada." *Mediart* 1:31 (February 1972): A2–A4

Richard, Alain-Martin, and Clive Robertson, eds. *Performance in/au Canada 1970–1990.* Quebec: Editions Intervention/Toronto: Coach House Press, 1991.

Richards, Catherine. "Virtual Bodies: what a blow that phantom gave me." In *Angles of Incidence: Video Reflections of Multimedia Artworks,* ed. Sara Diamond. Banff: The Banff Centre for the Arts, The International Council for Computer Communication, 1993.ᴄᴠ

Riley, Bob. "Comic Horror: The Presence of Television in Video Art." In *The Arts for Television,* eds. Kathy Rae Huffman and Dorine Mignot. Los Angeles: Museum of Contemporary Art/Amsterdam: Stedelijk Museum, 1987.ᴄᴠ

———. "Leave Proof." In *Public Information: Desire, Disaster, Document.* San Francisco: Museum of Modern Art, 1994.ᴄᴠ Includes brief discussion of Stan Douglas' video installations.

Ritchie, Christina. "Forms and Methods." In *Signal Approach.* Toronto: The Funnel, 1984 ᴄᴠ

———. "Visual Facts: Photography and Video by Eight Artists in Canada." *Canadian Art* 3:1 (Spring 1986): 90–1

———. "David Askevold: Double Agent." *[Activating the Archive]4.* Toronto: Art Metropole, 1995

Ritchie, Christina, ed. *Evidence of the Avant-Garde Since 1957: Selected Works from the Collection of Art Metropole Including Audiotapes, Records, Videotapes, Film, Multiples, Kitsch, Manuscripts, Stamps, Buttons, Flyers, Posters, Correspondence, Catalogues, Porn, T-Shirst, Postcards, Drawings, Poems, Mailers, Books, Photographs and Ephemera.* Toronto: Art Metropole, 1984.ᴄᴠ With essays by A.A. Bronson, Peggy Gale and Christina Ritchie.

Robertson, Clive. "W.O.R.K.S. in Progress." *Art and Artists* 9:8 (November 1974): 30–35

———. "Paul Wong." *Centerfold* (August 1976): 4

———. "An Interview between Clive Robertson and Willoughby Sharp." In *Video By Artists,* ed. Peggy Gale. Toronto: Art Metropole, 1976.

———. "Postface: Video." *Centerfold* 5/6 (1977): 6

———. "Backstage at the Pavillion with General Idea/Rehearsing the Receptionist." *Centerfold* 7/8 (1977): 2–3

———. *Clive Robertson: Television: Adjusting the Hold.* Calgary: Alberta College of Art Gallery, 1977. With an essay by Robertson and discussion of his tapes.

———. "Adjusting the Hold." *Only Paper Today* 4:4 (May 1977): 4

———. "From the Journals of Melvin Blank: Concerning 'In Video Traction'." *Only Paper Today* 4:4 (May 1977): 5

———. "Western Front Video [interview with Kate Craig]." *Centerfold* 2:2/3 (January 1978)

———. "Cloning closes the gap between Clones." *Centerfold* 2:4 (April 1978): 30–1

———. "Randy and Berneche (sic): Centre of a Tension." *Centerfold* 3:1 (December 1978): 46–9

———. "Mainly Smoke: 'As the World Burns'." *Centerfold* 3:4 (May 1979): 197–8

———. "Lisa Steele: recent tapes." *Centerfold* 3:5 (July 1979): 248–54

———. "TV Art in the Home." In *Transcript from The International Video Art Symposium 1979*. Kingston: Agnes Etherington Art Centre, 1979.

———. "The Second Independent Video Open 1979: Introduction." *Centerfold* 4:2 (January 1980): 2

———. "Editorial: CRTC and Pay-TV." *Fuse* 5:8/9 (November/December 1981): 239–42

———. *"Video/Video." Fuse* 5:8/9 (November/December 1981): 266–70

———. "And Now, the Truth [Vera Frenkel]." *Fuse* 5:8/9 (November/December 1981): 270

———. "Intervention." In *OKanada*. Berlin: Akademie der Künste, 1982.∾

———. "V/Tape Service: Comprehensive Model." *Fuse* 7:4 (November/December 1983): 141–3

———. "Three's Company: CBC-Telefilm-CFDC." *Fuse* 10:4 (Winter 1986–7): 27, 29

———. "Habits en retrospective." In *Vidéo: Sexualité et politique/ Sexuality and Politics,* ed. Jacques Doyon. Montreal: Galerie Optica, 1987.∾

———. "Video Structures: Back to Basic Memory/La vidéo au Canada: des origines à aujourd'hui." *Parallelogramme* 12:5 (Summer 1987): 39–42, 25–30

Robertson, Clive, and Justin Wonnacott. *Time and Distance/Tijd en Afstand*. Ottawa: Galerie SAW/den Haag: Kijkhuis, 1987.∾

Robinson, Gillian. "Conversations with Joseph Verge," "Mothers," "You Are Only a Stranger to Me" and "The Women Speaks Seven Tongues." In *Norman Cohn: Portraits,* ed. Peggy Gale. Toronto: Art Gallery of Ontario, 1984.∾

Rogoff, Irit. "Moving On: Migration and the Intertextuality of Trauma/En Transit: La Migration et l'intertextualité du traumatisme." In *Vera Frenkel . . . from the Transit Bar/ . . . du transitbar*. Toronto: The Power Plant/Ottawa: National Gallery of Canada, 1995.∾

Roque, Georges. "Une autre dimension." *Parachute* 9 (Winter 1977–8): 22–4

Rose, Peter. "NAMAC: On the Edge." *Video Guide* 9:4 (Issue 44, Fall 1988): 12–13

Ross, Becki. "Having the Last Laugh [Margaret Moores and Almerinda Travassos]." *Fuse* 13:5 (June/July 1990): 26–9

Ross, Christine. *Semaine de la vidéo féministe québécoise*. Quebec: Ministère des Affaires Culturelles du Québec, 1982.∾ Catalogue of the video section for the "Art and Feminism" event organized by the Musée d'Art Contemporain de Montréal. Essay by Christine Ross.

———. "Vidéo '84/Montréal." *Parachute* 37 (Winter 1984–85): 38

———. "T.V. or Not T.V." *Parachute* 40 (Fall 1985): 35–5

———. "Festival international du nouveau cinéma et de la vidéo/Montréal." *Parachute* 46 (Spring 1987): 117–18

———. "Troisième festival international de films et vidéos de femmes/Cinéma de l'ONF." *Parachute* 48 (Fall 1987): 56–7

———. "Vidéo: Vers un rénouvellement vidéographique de la critique d'art/Video: Towards a renewal of art criticism." *Parallelogramme* 14:3 (Winter 1988): 13–16

———. "5e festival international de films et vidéos de femmes de Montréal." *Parachute* 56 (Fall 1989): 53–4

———. "Le féminisme et l'instabilité de son sujet." In *Instabili,* eds. Marie Fraser and Lesley Johnstone. Montreal: Artexte 1990.

———. "Le corps, la video/Notes sur la souffrance," *Parachute* 64 (Fall 1991): 37–40

———. "Video and the Amorous Displacement of Being." *Open Letter* 8:7 (Summer 1993): 65–79

———. "La vidéographie de la défaillance, ou l'esthétique du lien chez Daniel Dion/ Breakdown Video or The Link Aesthetic in the Work of Daniel Dion." In *Daniel Dion: Parcours/Paths*. Ottawa: National Gallery of Canada, 1993.∾

———. "Evidements et territoires." In *Chantal duPont: sous surveillance: à Paris, Montréal, New York, Paris*. [Exhibition at Galerie J. & J. Donquy, Paris, April 27–May 26, 1993]. Montreal: Université du Québec à Montréal et Chantal duPont, 1993.∾

———. *Dispersions identitaires: vidéogrammes récents du Québec/Identity Dispersions: Recent Videos from Quebec*. Toronto: Art Gallery of Ontario, 1994.∾

———. "The Lamented Moments/Desired Objects of Video Art: Towards an Aesthetics of Discrepancy." In *Mirror Machine: Video and Identity,* ed. Janine Marchessault. Toronto: YYZ Books/Montreal: Centre for Research on Canadian Cultural Industries and Institutions, McGill University, 1995.

———. "Conflictus in Video." *Parachute* 78 (Spring 1995): 20–7

———. *'Je vais vous raconter une histoire de fantomes': vidéos de Nelson Henricks.* Montreal: Oboro, 1995.

———. *Images de surface: L'art vidéo reconsidéré.* Montreal: Editions Artexte, 1996.

Ross, Rodger J. "The film-Video Debate." *Cinema Canada* 36 (March 1977): 42–3

Rossignol, Iolande. "Le fluide magnétique: Sommes nous en train de perdre le nord?" *Copie Zero* 26 (December 1985): 24–7

Roth, Lorna. "(De)Romancing the North: Reflections on absences, misrepresentations and stereotypes of the Canadian North and its peoples." *BorderLines* No. 36 (April 1995): 36–43

Rousseau, Yves. "La question du support est un faux problème [Interview with François Girard]." *Ciné-Bulles* 9:1 (September–November 1989): 37–9

Rovere, Pierre. "Cinématographie/kinema graphein écriture du mouvement." *Circuits Video/Art* 1:1 (Winter 1981): 3

Roy, André. "Le clip à l'usage des jeunes générations." *Spirale* 87 (April 1989): 4

Royoux, Jean-Christophe. "Le conflit des communiations/Kommunikations-konflikte/The Conflict of Communications." In *Stan Douglas,* ed. Christine van Assche. Paris: Editions du Centre Pompidou, 1993.

Ruebsaat, Norbert, and Peg Campbell. "Pay TV: Interview with Liora Salter." *Video Guide* 4:3 (1981): 9

Ruhe, Monique. "Fukui Video Biennale." *Mediamatic* 2:4 (June 1988): 218–21

Rusted, Brian. *Vern Hume and Robert Milthorp: Personal Territories.* Calgary: The Nickel Arts Museum, 1991. With essays by Grant Poier and Brian Rusted, plus transcripts and descriptions of tapes.

Rusted, Brian, ed. *Four Visions of Television: Daniel Dion, Ardele Lister, Robert Morin, Jan Peacock.* Banff: Artists Television Workshop, Banff Centre for the Arts, 1991. With essays by Bruce Ferguson, Karen Henry, Carol Laing, Mireille Perron and Brian Rusted.

Rynard, Susan. "International Festival of Video Art: SAW Gallery." *Video Guide* 9:1 (October 1987): 14

———. "Tested Fictions and Twisted Fragments." *Fuse* 13:4 (Spring 1990): 42–4

Sage, Elspeth. "Asian New World Video." *Fuse* 11: 1/2 (Summer 1987): 17–19

———. "Video Out: A Short Course." *Video Guide* 9:1 (October 1987): 10, 13

———. "Artropolis Video." *Video Guide* 9:3 (Issue 43, 1988): 3

———. "The Colour of Money: Whatever Happened to Women In Focus?" *Video Guide* 11:2 (Fall 1991): 3

———. "Anatomy of a Thriller/Anatomie d'un extremiste." In *Paul Wong: On Becoming a Man/Paul Wong: Un homme en puissance . . ."*, ed. Jean Gagnon. Ottawa: National Gallery of Canada, 1995.

S Salloum, Jayce, and Molly Hankwitz. "Occupied Territories: Mapping the Transgressions of Cultural Terrain/On the Recent Videotapes of Jayce Salloum." *Felix: Landscape(s)* 2:1 (1995): 113–22

Samuels, Barbara. "Video Culture Off to Promising Start." *Cinema Canada* 103 (January 1984): 35

Sanders, Douglas, et al. "4th World/A Report." *Video Guide* (November 1978–January 1979): 16–17, 23

Sandqvist, Tom. "Transitbarens Architektur." *M.A.M.A. (Modern Architecture Magazine)* Stockholm (March 1993): 20–5

Sarrazin, Stephen. "Festival international du nouveau cinéma et de la vidéo." *Parachute* 46 (Spring 1987): 116–17

———. "Festival international du nouveau cinéma et de la vidéo." *Parachute* 50 (Spring 1988): 57–8

Sasaki, Tomiyo. "Spawning Sockeyes." In *Luminous Sites/Ten Video Installations,* eds. Daina Augaitis and Karen Henry. Vancouver: Video Inn/Western Front, 1986.

Savageau, Martine. "Vidéo Femmes: 'Les dames aux caméras' [Discussion with Lise Bonenfant, Nicole Giguère, Louise Giguère and Hélène Roy]." *Copie Zéro* 26 (December 1985): 26–9

Schade, Sigrid. "Vera Frenkel: 'Body Missing'." In *Andere Körper.* Linz: Offenes Kulturhaus, 1994.

Schjeldahl, Peter. "The Documenta of the Dog." *Art in America* (September 1992): 88–97

Schneider, Ira, and Beryl Korot, eds. *Video Art: An Anthology*. New York: Harcourt Brace Jovanovich, 1976. Canadians include Eric Cameron, John Fleming, Ernest Gusella, Les Levine, Bill Ritchie and Michael Snow.

Schroder, Elizabeth. "A Context for Strength: Historical Struggles, Contemporary Heroics [review: Emma Productions, Sara Diamond]." *Fuse* 8:6 (Spring 1985): 47–8

———. "Private Eyes." *Fuse* 11:1/2 (Summer 1987): 37–8

———. "Independent Images." *Fuse* 12:6 (August 1989): 32–3

Schroeder, Jacques. "L'art, le paysage, la géographie: une promenade dans la culture [Installation: Emmanuel Avenel et Marie-France Giraudon]." In *Paysage(s) de la vidéo,* ed. Monique Langlois. Montreal: Galerie UQAM, 1994.∾

Scott, Andrew. "Networks and the Eternal Frame." *Vanguard* 7:8 (November 1978): 14–15

———. "Susan Britton/VAG Videospace." *Vanguard* 8:3 (April 1979): 30

Scott, Jay. "Going through the notions." *Canadian Art* 1:1 (Fall 1984): 78–83

———. "Vera Frenkel: Canada'a pre-eminent video artist, stroyteller and mischief-maker hits her stride." *Canadian Art* 9:2 (Summer 1992): 46–51

Seaman, Brian. "Canadian Film and Video: The Distribution Dilemma [on the annual meeting of Independent Film and Video Alliance, Montreal, May 1988]." *Performing Arts in Canada* 23:2 (September 1986): 39

Semaine de la vidéo féministe québécoise. Quebec: Ministère des Affaires Culturelles, 1982.∾

1ère Semaine Internationale de Vidéo. Geneva: Saint-Gervais mjc, 1985.∾ Includes François Girard.

2e Semaine Internationale de Vidéo. Geneva: Saint-Gervais mjc, 1987.∾ Includes Dennis Day.

3e Semaine Internationale de Vidéo. Geneva: Saint-Gervais mjc, 1989.∾ Includes Michael Balser/Andy Fabo, Luc Bourdon, Bernar Hébert and Vern Hume.

4e Semaine Internationale de Vidéo. Geneva: Saint-Gervais mjc, 1991.∾ Includes Mike MacDonald, Jayce Salloum/Elia Suleiman and Esther Valiquette.

Sénécal, Michel. "La vidéographie au Québec: d'abord une industrie culturelle." *Copie Zéro* 26 (December 1985): 4–6

Sénécal, Céline. "L'image en plus." *Focus* 45 (October 1981): 44–5

Shapiro, Barbara, ed. *Rétrospective Parallelogramme Retrospective 1976–1977.* Montreal: ANNPAC, 1978. Includes annual documentation on 18 artist-run centres, plus essays by Peter Anson, Martin Bartlett, Marcella Bienvenue, Victor Coleman, Francine Couture/Esther Trépanier, Tom Gore, Marien Lewis, Allan Mattes, Michael Morris, Clive Robertson and Dennis Tourbin.

———. *Rétrospective Parallelogramme 2 Retrospective 1977–1978.* Montreal: ANNPAC, 1978. Includes annual documentation on 18 artist-run centres, plus essays by Miriam Adams/Victor Coleman, Peter Anson, D.M. Fraser, Gerry Gilbert, Michael Goldberg and Dennis Tourbin.

Sharp, Willoughby. "How I Lost My Video Virginity to the Hummer Sisters." *Centerfold* 3:1 (December 1978): 51–3

———. "Toward the Teleculture: The New Television in the Information Revolution — or, How Will the Current Battle Between 'Free' TV and 'Feevee' Effect Programming in the 80s?" In *Video/Vidéo.* Toronto: Video Trade Forum, Festival of Festivals, 1981.∾

Shaw, Nancy. "The Lull Before the Storm/Robson Square Media Centre." *Parachute* 62 (Spring 1991): 44–5

———. "Expanded Consciousness & Company Types: Collaboration since Intermedia and the N.E.Thing Company/La conscience élargie et les genres d'entreprises: la collaboration depuis Intermedia et la N.E.Thing Company." *Parallelogramme* 17:3 (Winter 1991–2): 48–57

———. "Cultural Democracy and Institutionalized Difference: Intermedia, Metro Media." In *Mirror Machine: Video and Identity,* ed. Janine Marchessault. Toronto: YYZ Books/Montreal: Centre for Research on Canadian Cultural Industries and Institutions, McGill University, 1995.

Shea, Geoffrey. "Art is communications: on curating this show." In *Art is Communication,* eds. Paul Petro and Geoffrey Shea. Toronto: A Space, 1985.∾

———. "Critical Distance or Two Chances to Look Back." *C* 7 (Fall 1985): 75–7

———. "The 1986 New Work Show." *Cinema Canada* 135 (November 1986): 33–5

———. [on Robert Morin and Lorraine Dufour]. *Cinema Canada* 137 (January 1987): 35

———. "Video Tales."*Cinema Canada* 139 (March 1987): 33

———. "Video Tales."*Cinema Canada* 142 (June1987): 34–5

———. "Video Tales."*Cinema Canada* 144 (September 1987): 42 Critiques productions by the Toronto collective 698515 (Rhonda Abrams, Dennis Day, Tess Payne and Susan Rynard).

———. "Video Tales."*Cinema Canada* 147 (December 1987): 34 On video rental fees at VTape, YYZ, CAR/FAC and Center for Art Tapes/Halifax.

———. ". . .et de la vidéo at the new film fest." *Cinema Canada* 148 (January 1988): 23–4

———. "Film/Video Interface." *Cinema Canada* 149 (February 1988): 12

Shea, Geoffrey, and Ilse Gassinger, eds. *Les Lieux de Vidéo. (Diderot* 4) Durham (Ont.): UMAS 1993.∾

Sheridan, Rick. "Dictionary of Innovative Media Projects." *Video Guide* 9:1 (October 1987): 15

Sherman, Tom. "The Art Style Computer Processing System." *Journal for the Communication of Advanced Television Studies* (London, England) 2:2 (Fall 1974) (n.p.)

———. "Introduction." In *Video By Artists,* ed. Peggy Gale. Toronto: Art Metropole, 1976. Includes "How to Adjust a Colour Television," printed separately in *Cultural Engineering,* Ottawa: National Gallery of Canada, 1983.

———. "The Art Style Computer Processing System." In *Videation,* ed. Bob Martin. Richmond, Virginia: Commonwealth University, 1977.

———. "The Artist Attains Ham Radio Status in an Era of Total Thought Conveyance." *Centerfold* 2:6 (August 1978)

———. "Larry Dubin: a video portrait." *Centerfold* 3:5 (July 1979): 240–2

———. "My Brand of Video Aesthetics." *Article* (Halifax) 1:2 (June 1980) (n.p.)

———. "Communication is the Goal, The Media are the Means." In *222 Warehouse Show.,* ed. Robin Collyer. Toronto: A Space, 1980 ∾

———. "Television as Art in Toronto." *Community Television Review* (Minneapolis) (1981) (n.p.)

———. "Transvideo." *Fuse* 5:2/3 (March/April 1981): 97–9

———. "Television by Artists in Canada: Ten Years of Cable Experience." *Community Television Review* (Minneapolis) 4 (April 1981): 13–15

———. "Ma perception de l'esthétique de l'art vidéographique (no. 2)," "My Brand of Video Aesthetics #2," "La théorie du lapin et la transformation psychologique des données," and "The Rabbit Theory of Data Transformation." In *Tom Sherman: Vidéogrammes et écrits/un aspect différent de la télévision,* ed. Manon Blanchette. Montreal: Musée d'Art Contemporain, 1982.∾

———. "Videoactivity in Canada Generates a New Breed of Timekillers." In *Beyond Video Art.* San Francisco: Contemporary Arts Press, 1982.

———. *Cultural Engineering.* Ottawa: National Gallery of Canada, 1983. Ed. and with introduction by Willard Holmes.∾

———. *Ingénierie culturelle.* trans. Hélène Papineau, ed. Willard Holmes. Ottawa: National Gallery of Canada, 1983.∾

———. "Canada Council: A New Medial Arts Section." *Video Guide* 5:4 (Fall 1983): 5

———. "Excerpts from an interview: Telecommunications and Art Subsidy." In *Art Telecommunication,* ed. Heidi Grundmann. Vienna: BLIX/Vancouver: Western Front, 1984.∾

———. "Message to Electro Culture." *LAMP Media Journal,* Syracuse University, 1986.

———. "Appearance, Memory and Influence" and "Message to Electro Culture." In *Video By Artists 2,* ed. Elke Town. Toronto: Art Metropole, 1986.

———. "The Value of Privacy." *Parachute* 48 (Fall 1987): 12–14

————. "Media Arts Criticism?/Critiquer les arts médiatiques?" *Parallelogramme* 14:2 (Fall 1988): 19–23

————. "Equidistant Relationships" [excerpt] and "Interview with Wyn Geleynse and Tom Sherman." In *Interior Presence: projecting situations*, ed. Donna McAlear. Calgary: The Nickle Arts Museum, 1990.ᴄᴠ

————. "From a Reservoir of Predictions." *[Activating the Archive]1*. Toronto: Art Metropole, 1990

————. *Mike MacDonald: Interview by Tom Sherman* [Interviews With Artists Series]. Toronto: Mercer Union, 1991.

————. "Primary Devices: Artists' Strategies for Using Video, Computers and Telecommunications Networks." *Leonardo, Connectivity: Art and Interactive Telecommunications Issue*, 24:2 (Winter 1991) (n.p.)

————. "Democratizing Video [a review of Thede/Ambrosi: *Video the Changing World*]." *Canadian Forum* 71:814 (November 1992) (n.p.)

————. "Reflecting on the Future of Video." *Texts* 9, Winter 1993 (inside cover)

————. "3 Machines in One." *Texts* 9, Winter 1993 (inside cover)

Sherman, Tom, and Clive Robertson. "The Government: Electric Eye." *Centerfold* 3:1 (December 1978): 54–7

Shinhat, Molly. "Speaking of Colour." *Fuse* 13:4 (Spring 1990): 10–12

Shuebrook, Ron. "Appearances, N.S." *Vanguard* (April 1984): 21–5

Sicotte, Louise-Véronique. "Mieux vaut une grosse gaffe qu'une petite réussite." *Ciné-Bulles* 13:2 (Spring 1994): 52–4

Silj, Alessandro, ed. *Video 79. Video — The First Decade/Dieci Anni di Videotape*. Rome: Kane Editore, 1979. With essays by Peter Chow, Fred Forest, Don Foresta, Alberto Grifi, John Howkins, Robert Kleyn, Richard Kriesche, Giuseppe Richeri, Andrea Ruggeri, Giuliano Scabia, Alessandro Silj and Martha Stuart.

Silverthorne, Jeanette. "Vera Frenkel: . . . from the Transit Bar." *BorderLines* No. 36 (April 1995): 44–7

Slopek, Ed. "'Miniature Theatre' by Nancy Nicol." *Centerfold* 4:2 (January 1980): 6–7

————. "Plato/Non-A (A Videotext)." In *New Uses for Television*, ed. David Craig. Charlottetown: Confederation Art Gallery and Museum, 1981.ᴄᴠ

————. "Television, Techne, and Ecological Fitness/ Télévision, techné, et opportunité écologique." *Parallelogramme* 8:3 (February/March 1983): 19–25, 46–9, 91

Snider, Greg. "The Space Between the Studies and the Gallery." In *Joey Morgan/Almost* Dreaming*, ed. Lorna Farrell-Ward. Vancouver: Vancouver Art Gallery, 1987.ᴄᴠ

Snoek, Sonja. "Visual Culture as Alibi." *Mediamatic* 5:4 (Winter 1991): 241–4

Snow, Michael. "De La 1969–1972." In *Video Art*, eds. Ira Schneider and Beryl Korot. New York: Harcourt Brace Jovanovich, 1975.

Somers, Eric. "Video as Art at Banff: An Experiment in Electronic Colour and Space." *Art Magazine* 6:19 (Fall 1974): 38–9

Sonne, Harriet M. *Altered Situations Changing Strategies/The Canadian Worker in the Art of the 80's*. Toronto: A Space, 1984.ᴄᴠ Includes video by Lisa Steele/Kim Tomczak.

Sorfleet, Andrew. "Scarlet Fever [John Greyson]." *Fuse* 13:3 (Winter 1989–90): 44–7

Spaner, Karen. "Monitor/Alice, Who Did That to Your Face?" *Video Guide* 1:1 (February/March 1978): 7

Stange, Ken. "Felicity Redgrave: In Search of the Sacred." *Arts Atlantic* 10:3 (Winter 1991): 13–14

Starko, Janice. " 'Currents' Controversial Video in Calgary." *Video Guide* 6:3 (May 1984): 7

————. "Em-Media: The State of Video Art in Calgary." *Video Guide* 6:3 (May 1984): 8–9

Steele, Lisa. "Birthday Suit," and "Facing South" [scripts]. In *Video By Artists*, ed. Peggy Gale. Toronto: Art Metropole, 1976.

————. "Letter to John B. Mays on Video." *Only Paper Today* 4:4 (May 1977): 6

————. *The Ballad of Dan Peoples*. Toronto: Art Metropole, 1978.

————. "Rodney Werden's 'Baby Dolls'." *Centerfold* 2:6 (September 1978): 95–6

————. "Susan Britton: New Tapes." *Centerfold* 3:3 (February/March 1979): 116–20

———. "To the Audience: Tapes and Performance at YYZ." *Centerfold* 3:5 (July 1979): 273–4

———. "The Second Independent Video Open 1979: catalogue [descriptions and discussion of 24 artists' tapes]." *Centerfold* 4:2 (January 1980): 13–24

———. "On Video Distribution." *Fuse* 4:4 (May 1980): 186–7

———. "The Lure of the 'Public'." *Fuse* 4:4 (May 1980): 226–9

———. "Oppositional Television (Canada)." *Fuse* 5:2/3 (March/April 1981): 74–83

———. "Changeless Channels." *Fuse* 5:10 (January/March 1982): 358–60

———. "Talking Tongues: Lovespeak." *Image Nation* 25: Cost of Living/Le cout de la vie, (Summer 1982) (n.p.)

———. "Snakes and Ladders: Feminism in the Media." *Fuse* 7:3 (September/October 1983): 80–2

———. "Snakes and Ladders: Music Notes/Inconolatry in Motion (Part I)." *Fuse* 7:5 (February 1984): 193–7

———. "Snakes and Ladders: Music Notes/Inconolatry in Motion (Part II)." *Fuse* 7:6 (Spring 1984): 249–54

———. "Who Minds the Gate?/Que fait le tri?" *Paralellogramme* 9:5 (October/November 1984): 15–16, 22–3

———. "Committing Memory." In *Vera Frenkel: The Videotapes*, ed. Robert McFadden. Ottawa: National Gallery of Canada, 1985.

———. "Committed to Memory: Women's Video Art Production in Canada and Quebec." In *Work in Progress: Building Feminist Culture*, ed. Rhea Tregebov. Toronto: The Women's Press, 1987.

———. "Shake It Up, Baby: Works of Intervention by Ardele Lister/Allez ma chérie, fais-moi bouger tout ça: oeuvres interventionnistes d'Ardele Lister." In *Images 92/Festival of Independent Film & Video*. Toronto: Northern Visions, 1992.

———. "Finding the DIFFEREN(t)CE/looking for the self and the other in the work of John Orentlicher." *[Activating the Archive]3*. Toronto: Art Metropole, 1993.

Steele, Lisa, and Kim Tomczak, "See Evil." In *Issues of Censorship*. Toronto: A Space, 1985.

———. "Statement of Intention." In *Toronto: A Play of History (Jeu d'histoire).* Toronto: The Power Plant, 1987.

Steinman, Barbara. "1980 Tour de '4'." *Video Guide* 3:1 (Summer 1980): 9

———. "Chambres à louer." In *Vidéo*, ed. René Payant. Montreal: Artextes, 1986.

———. "Cénotaphe." In *Luminous Sites/Ten Video Installations*, eds. Daina Augaitis and Karen Henry. Vancouver: Video Inn/Western Front, 1986.

———. *Echoes of Earlier Appearances.* Montreal: Barbara Steinman and Galerie René Blouin, 1990. Artist's texts and documentation of installation works, including video.

Steltner, Elke. "Video Dream: But I Only Have Eyes For You." *Only Paper Today* 4:33 (February 1977): 12

Sterbak, Yana. "Information: film/video." *Parachute* 8 (Fall 1977): 49

———. "Information: film/video." *Parachute* 9 (Winter 1977–8): 39–40

———. "Information: film/video." *Parachute* 10 (Spring 1978): 51

———. "Information: film/video." *Parachute* 12 (Fall 1978): 62

Steven, Peter. *Brink of Reality: New Canadian Documentary Film and Video.* Toronto: Between the Lines, 1993.

Stewart, Sandy. *Here's Looking at Us: A Personal History of Television in Canada.* Toronto: CBC Enterprises, 1986.

Stoesser, Elise. *Tomiyo Sasaki: Four Video Installations.* Regina: Dunlop Art Gallery, 1986.

Stuart, Martha. "Meditation on the Screen." *Video Guide* 4:2 (1981): 7

Suerta, Leonardo. "Travelling/Travelo." *CinemAction* 15 (Summer 1981): 54

Sujir, Leila. "The Video Work of Sara Diamond/Les vidéos de Sara Diamond." In *Images 90/Festival of Independent Film & Video/Festival du film et de la vidéo indépendents*. Toronto: Northern Visions, 1990.

Sunderburg, Erika. "Towards a Representation of 'Human'." *Video Guide* 9:4 (1988): 14–15

Swartz, Jill. "Sabotage: A Video Installation Performance." *Video Guide* 4:4 (Issue 19, 1982):6

T *A Tale of Two Cities: Video Art in Alberta.* Edmonton: Ring House Gallery, 1986 ⌒

Tallman, Susan. "General Idea." In *Vedute tra film video televisione.* Palermo: Sellerio Editore, 1992.

Talve, Merike. "Wallflower Order [Marion Barling]." *Video Guide* 5:2 (April 1983): 5

———. "The October Show." *Video Guide* 5:5 (Winter 1983): 3–4

———. "Television Interference." *Video Guide* 6:3 (May 1984): 4–5

———. "Street Culture: A Video Series." *Video Guide* 6:4 (August 1984): 4–5

———. "Vestiges of the Avant-Garde in Installation." In *Luminous Sites/Ten Video Installations,* eds. Daina Augaitis and Karen Henry. Vancouver: Video Inn/Western Front, 1986.⌒

Tan, Sid. "Kwan Kung: Patron of Video?" *Video Guide* 8:5 (Issue 40, 1987): 4–5

Tate, Peter. "There's a Mutant in the Garden." *Video Guide* 1:4 (September/October 1978): 3

Teag, Jan. "The Victory of Video: Montreal's 14th International Festival of New Cinema and Video." *Cinema Canada* 125 (October 1985): 24–6

Telfer, Gary. "Gisèle Trudel: The Theory of IT; Putting IT into Practice, Art I." *Parachute* 49 (Winter 1987–8): 45–6

Tenhaaf, Nell. "Re-telling Pandora: technology and myth." In *Art is Communication,* eds. Paul Petro and Geoffrey Shea. Toronto: A Space, 1985.⌒

———. "Simorg Culture." *Parachute* 72 (Fall 1993):41–3

———. "Of Monitors and Men and Other Unsolved Feminist Mysteries"/"Des moniteurs et des hommes et autres mystères féministes non-résolus." *Parellogramme* 18: 3 (1992–3): 24–37

Testa, Bart. "Cultural Engineering by Tom Sherman." *BorderLines* No. 2 (Spring 1985): 35–6

Théberge, Pierre, ed. *About 30 Works by Michael Snow/Autour de 30 oeuvres de Michael Snow.* Ottawa: National Gallery of Canada, 1972.⌒ With texts by Jonas Mekas and Pierre Théberge. Includes video installation 'De La'.

———. *Greg Curnoe.* Montreal: Musée des Beaux-Arts, 1981. Includes an essay by Théberge, plus Curnoe's videotape *Springbank Road Race* (1975).

Thériault, Michèle. "La quête d'un lieu/The Quest for Place." In *Sylvie Bélanger: Topologies du regard,* ed. Sharon Kivland. Herblay (France): Les Cahiers des Regards, 1991.⌒

Thezé, Ariane. *Ariane Thezé: Interférences.* Self-published, Montreal, 1992. With a text by Louise Poissant.

Tivy, Sandra, ed. *Media Blitz.* Calgary: The New Gallery, 1988.⌒ With introductory essays by Marcella Bienvenue and Sandra Tivy, plus descriptions of works.

———. *Media Blitz 2.* Calgary: The New Gallery, 1989.⌒ With an introduction by Sandra Tivy and essay on video by Grant Poier.

Todd, Kim. "The Nine Tape Test/New videotapes at Pumps, Vancouver." *Centerfold* 3:6 (September 1979): 331–2

Todd, Loretta. "Native Video in B.C." *Video Guide* 9:2 (Fall 1987): 6

———. "Curatorial Statement." In *Artropolis 90/Lineages & Linkages.* Vancouver: A.T. Eight Artropolos Society, 1990.⌒

Toillefer, Helene. "Loly Darcel, Indices d'une rupture vers la credibilite." *ETC Montréal* 17 (Winter 1992): 68–70

Tomas, David. "Through the Eye of the Cyclops." *Video Guide* 8:2 (Issue 37, 1986): 15

———. "Through the Eye of the Cyclops." In *Luminous Sites/Ten Video Installations,* eds. Daina Augaitis and Karen Henry. Vancouver: Video Inn/Western Front, 1986.⌒

Tomczak, Kim. "Susan Britton/Casting Call." *Video Guide* (June 1979): 3

———. "Video Cabaret." *Video Guide* (November 1978–January 1979): 9

———. "'In Ten Sity': Paul Wong at the Vancouver Art Gallery Videospace." *Centerfold* 3:3 (February/March 1979): 135

———. "Modern Times/A Review." *Video Guide* 6:5 (October 1984):10

———. "Video News." *Fuse* 9:6 (May/June 1986): 45

———. "Video News." *Fuse* 10:1/2 (Summer 1986): 15

———. "Video News." *Fuse* 10:4 (Winter 1986–7): 10

———. "Video News." *Fuse* 10:5 (April 1987): 13

———. "Video News." *Fuse* 10:6 (Spring 1987): 4

———. "Video News." *Fuse* 11:1/2 (Summer 1987): 10

———. "V/Tape." *Video Guide* 9:1 (October 1987): 11

———. "Video News." *Fuse* 11:4 (Winter 1987–8): 6

———. "Video News." *Fuse* 11:5 (April 1988): 14

———. "Video News." *Fuse* 11:6 (July 1988): 8

———. "Video News." *Fuse* 12:1/2 (September 1988): 10

———. "Video News." *Fuse* 12:3 (November/December 1988): 12

———. "Video News." *Fuse* 12:4 (January/February 1989): 8

———. "Video News." *Fuse* 12:5 (April/May 1989): 11

———. "Video News." *Fuse* 12:6 (August 1989): 14

———. "Video News." *Fuse* 13:1/2 (Fall 1989): 17

———. "Video News." *Fuse* 13:3 (Winter 1989–90): 25

———. "Video News." *Fuse* 13:4 (Spring 1990): 25

———. "Video News." *Fuse* 13:5 (June/July 1990): 9

———. "Video News." *Fuse* 13:6 (Summer 1990): 19

———. "Video News." *Fuse* 14:1/2 (Fall 1990): 24

———. "Video News." *Fuse* 14:3 (Winter 1991): 9

———. "Video News." *Fuse* 14:4 (Spring 1991): 12

Tomlins, Colin. "A Revolutionary Effort [on Julien Samuels]." *Video Guide* 9:2 (Fall 1987): 19

Tooby, Michael. *Visual Facts. Photography and Video by Eight Artists in Canada.* Glasgow: Third Eye Centre, 1985.◐ Includes video by Vera Frenkel, Anne Ramsden and Paul Wong.

Toronto: A Play of History (Jeu d'histoire). Toronto: The Power Plant, 1987.◐ Includes essay on video by Bruce Ferguson and video works/statements by Colin Campbell, Vera Frenkel, John Greyson, Lisa Steele/Kim Tomczak and Rodney Werden.

Toupin, Gilles. "L'alternative du Groupe Véhicule." *Vie des Arts* 17:70 (Spring 1973): 58–61

Tourangeau, Jean. "Export 80." *Vie des Arts* 25:102 (Spring 1981): 70–1

———. "Chambres à Louer [Barbara Steinman]." *Circuits Vidéo/Art* 1:1 (Winter 1981): 6

———. *Sélection de vidéo canadienne.* Saint-Etienne (France): Maison de la Culture et de la Communication de Saint-Etienne, 1982.◐

———. "Vidéo du Québec/Musée d'art contemporain." *Parachute* 27 (Summer 1982): 40

———. "In Video Is Canada Visible?" *Vanguard* 12:7 (September 1983): 26–30

———. "Vidéo identification et fantasme."*Vie des Arts* 28:112 (September 1983): 65–6

———. "12e Festival International du Nouveau Cinéma/Section Présence Vidéo." *Vanguard* 13:2 (March 1984): 37–8

———. "Vidéo 85 à Montréal." *Vie des Arts* 30:120 (Fall 1985): 79

———. "John Mingola, ou l'art de l'emprunt." *Vie des Arts* 30:120 (Fall 1985): 78

———. "Seront questionnées les limites (troisième temps)." In *Vidéo,* ed. René Payant. Montreal: Artextes, 1986.

———. "Sexualité et représentation." In *Vidéo: Sexualité et politique/ Sexuality and Politics,* ed. Jacques Doyon. Montreal: Galerie Optica, 1987.◐

———. "La Vidéo au Québec." *Vie des Arts* 33:134 (Spring 1989): 27–9

———. "La Vidéo." *Vie des Arts* 34:138 (Spring 1990): 70–1

———. "Production et analogie en vidéo/ Transition and Analogy in Video." In *Robert Morin and Lorraine Dufour. A decade of video production,* ed. Brendan Cotter. Toronto: A Space, 1991.ℚ

———. "Words and Images in Video." *Open Letter* 8:7 (Summer 1993): 57–64

———. "Paysages/visages de la vidéo — ou comment inverser le genre en nous laissant voir [Suzan Vachon]." In *Paysage(s) de la vidéo,* ed. Monique Langlois. Montreal: Galerie UQAM, 1994.ℚ

———. "Montréal: Joanna Kotkowska, Prélude, No. 5, Opium, Egoïste, Tabou . . ." *ETC Montréal* 27 (August/November 1994): 16–18

Tourangeau, Jean, ed. *Aventure/Venture.* Montreal: Saidye Bronfman Centre/Centre Saidye Bronfman, 1987.ℚ With essays by Danielle Leger and Jean Tourangeau.

Town, Elke. *Fiction.* Toronto: Art Gallery of Ontario, 1982.ℚ Includes "Cornucopia" script by General Idea.

———. "Tom Dean: 'Disharmony and Its Charms'." *C* 3 (Fall 1984): 27–32

———. "Consolidation and Resistance: Video in Toronto, An Overview." In *Canadian Video Art,* ed. René Coelho. Amsterdam: The Holland Festival, 1985.ℚ

———. "Video: Territory of Limits." In *Vidéo,* ed. René Payant. Montreal: Artextes, 1986.

———. "The Emperor's New Clothes/Art Metropole." *Vanguard* 15:2 (April/May 1986): 52–3

———. "Luminous Sites." *Vanguard* 15:3 (Summer 1986): 12–16

Town, Elke, ed. *1986 SAW Gallery International Festival of Video Art/Festival International d'Art Vidéo.* Ottawa: SAW Gallery, 1986.ℚ With Introduction by Elke Town and articles by Stephen Kolpan (on Gary Hill), Jeremy Welsh (on British work), Greta Van Broeckhoven and Albert Wulffers (on Marie André).

———. *Video By Artists 2.* Toronto: Art Metropole, 1986. With essays by Judith Barry, Raymond Bellour, Klaus vom Bruch, Colin Campbell, Chris Dercon, Jean-Paul Fargier, Helmut Friedel, Peggy Gale, General Idea, Dan Graham, Barbara London, Stuart Marshall and Tom Sherman.

Townsend, Charlotte. "The Mezzanine/ Nova Scotia College of Art and Design." *artscanada* 166/167/168 (Spring 1972): 78–81

Townsend, Doug. *A Delicate Time/Recent Videotapes.* St. John's: Memorial University Art Gallery, 1985.ℚ

Transcript from The International Video Art Symposium 1979. Kingston: Agnes Etherington Art Centre, 1979. Peggy Gale, Curator. Contributions by Maria Gloria Bicocchi, Susan Britton, Kate Craig, Jaime Davidovich, Michael Goldberg, David Hall, Wulf Herzogenrath, Ian Murray, Clive Robertson and Paul Wong.

Tregebov, Rhea, ed. *Work in Progress: Building Feminist Culture.* Toronto: The Women's Press, 1987. With essays by Lisa Steele, Rhea Tregebov, Wendy Waring and others.

Trinity Square Video 1982–1991 Collection of Independent Video. Toronto: Trinity Square Video, 1991. With transcript of panel discussion "A Critical Perspective" with Colin Campbell, Richard Fung, Bill Lee, Clive Robertson, Dot Tuer and b.h. Yael.

Trott, Jamirte. "'Impossible Love': Videotape by Candace Reckinger." *Video Guide* 7:2 (March 1985): 5

———. "Video as Personal Expression." *Video Guide* 8:1 (Issue 36, 1986): 8

———. "Big Screen/Small Screen." *Video Guide* 8:2 (Issue 37, 1986): 19

———. "Sex on the Video Screen." *Video Guide* 8:4 (December 1986): 8

Tuer, Dot. "Going Public." *Vanguard* 14:1 (February 1985): 40

———. "Lisa Steele/National Gallery of Canada." *Parachute* 38 (Spring 1985): 50

———. "Artists' Television." *Parachute* 47 (Summer 1987): 46–8

———. "New Video/A 698515 Inc. Presentation." *Vanguard* 16:5 (November 1987): 38

———. "The CEAC Was Banned in Canada." *C* 11 (Fall 1986): 22–37

———. "Video in Drag: Trans-sexing the Feminine/Lorsque la vidéo se travestit: la transgression du féminin." *Parallelogramme* 12:3 (February/March 1987): 24–9, 37–43

———. "From the Father's House: Women's Video and Feminism's Struggle with Difference." *Fuse* 48, 11:4 (Winter 1987–8): 17–24

———. "Utopias of Resistance/Strategies of Cultural Self-Determination." In *4 Hours and 38 Minutes: Videotapes by Lisa Steele and Kim Tomczak*, ed. Philip Monk. Toronto: Art Gallery of Ontario, 1989.⌒

———. "John Watt/YYZ." *C* 27 (Fall 1990): 58–9

———. "Requiem for a Modern Love." In *Colin Campbell/Media Works 1872–1990*, ed. Bruce Ferguson. Winnipeg: Winnipeg Art Gallery, 1991.⌒

———. "Perspectives of the Body in Canadian Video Art." *C* 36 (Winter 1993): 29–37

———. "All in the Family: An Examination of Community Access Cable in Canada." *Fuse* 17:3 (Spring 1994): 23–30

———. "Worlds Between: An Examination of the Thematics of Exile and Memory in the Work of Vera Frenkel/Mondes intermédiares: Examen des thèmes de l'exil et de la mémoire dans l'oeuvre de Vera Frenkel." In *Raincoats Suitcases Palms*, ed. Loretta Yarlow. North York: Art Gallery of York University, 1993.⌒

———. "Worlds Between: An Examination of the Thematics of Exile and Memory in the Work of Vera Frenkel." *Matriart* 4:3 [Women and Technology Issue] (1994): 6–13

———. "Mirroring Identities: Two Decades of Video Art in Canada." In *Mirror Machine: Video and Identity*, ed. Janine Marchessault. Toronto: YYZ Books/Montreal: Centre for Research on Canadian Cultural Industries and Institutions, McGill University, 1995.

———. "From Xerox PARC to the Kitchen Table: Playing the Artistic Stakes in Cyberspace." *BorderLines* No. 37 (August 1995): 14–20

Turrel, Mark. "'The World is Sick (Sic)' [review]." *Video Guide* 10:3/4 (November 1989): 9

V Vachon, Suzan. "La vidéo est-elle légère?" *Catalogue Evènement interuniversitaire d'art vidéo*. Montreal, 1993.⌒

van Assche, Christine, ed. *Stan Douglas*. Paris: Editions du Centre Pompidou, 1993.⌒ With Introduction by Christine van Assche and essays by Peter Culley and Jean-Christophe Royoux.

van Barneveld, Aart. "Generating a Dialogue." In *Canadian Video Art*, ed. Rene Coelho. Amsterdam: The Holland Festival, 1985.⌒

Vancouver: Art and Artists 1931–1983. Vancouver Art Gallery, 1983.⌒ Includes an essay on video by Paul Wong plus chronology, biographies, and "Personal Perspectives" by Kate Craig, Michael Goldberg, Sandra Janz, Chris Reed, Barbara Steinman, Kim Tomczak and others.

"Vancouver Video Perspective/October Show." *Video Guide* 5:4 (Fall 1983): insert ⌒

Vander Zaag, Elizabeth. "Articulate Video." *Video Guide* 9:1 (October 1987): 3

———. "Artropolis Video." In *Artropolis/Exhibition of Contemporary British Columbia Art*. Vancouver, 1987.⌒

Van Dijck, Leen (trans.). "Hetero-geneous." *Anna R. Part One* (1980–1) (n.p.)

Van Steenburgh, Phil. "'Habits' by YYZ, Toronto: Invitation to a Screening." *Cinema Canada* (July/August 1986): 26–7

Vazan, Bill. "Lines." In *Video By Artists*, ed. Peggy Gale. Toronto: Art Metropole, 1976.

Verjee, Zainub. "Going All the Way: a panel on recent work and approaches." *Fuse* 11:3 (Spring 1992): 37

———. "The Colours of Culture: Film and Video by People of Colour/Les couleurs de la culture: les films et les vidéos réalisés par des artistes de couleur." *Parallelogramme* 17:4 (Spring 1992): 38–47

Vestiges of Empire. London: Camden Arts Centre, 1984.⌒ Includes text by Vera Frenkel.

Video Alliance. "Proposed Guidelines for Video Events, Festivals, Exhibitions and Broadcast." *Parallelogramme* 8:5 (June–August 1983): 19–20

Video Circuits: An Exhibition on the Theme of Videotape as Art. Guelph: McLaughlin Library, University of Guelph, 1973. Preface by Judith Nasby, catalogue essay by Eric Cameron, appendix by Ian K. Easterbrook.

Vidéo 84/Rencontres vidéo internationales de Montréal. Montreal, 1984.⌒ Lecture abstracts for conference and programme book for installations in Montreal.

Video, el temps i l'espai. Barcelona: Col.legi d'Arquitectes de Catalunya, 1980. With essays by Eugeni Bonet, Juan Downey, Peggy Gale, Dan Graham, Wolf Kahlen, Shigeko Kubota, Muntadas, Joaquim Dols Rusinol, plus artists' projects.

Vidéo et après/La collection vidéo du Musée national d'art moderne. Paris: Editions du Centre Georges Pompidou, 1992. With a "history of video" by Christine van Assche; Canadians include Stan Douglas, General Idea and Zacharias Kunuk.

La Vidéo Fameuse Fête, ou les 10 ans de Vidéo Femmes. Quebec: Vidéo Femmes, 1984.↷

Vidéo Femmes. "La Vidéo Fameuse Fête, ou les 10 ans de Vidéo Femmes." *Video Guide* 6:2 (March 1984): 11

Video Inn. "Invitation to Exchange." *Video Guide* 1:4 (September/October 1978): 4

4. Videonale in Bonn. 18–23 September 1990.↷ With essays by Marga Bijvoet, Jean-Paul Fargier, Micky Kwella, Michael Maziere and Danijela Puresevic. Includes Dennis Day, Paula Fairfield, Robert Hamilton, Tess Payne and Susan Rynard.

Videoscape: An Exhibition of Video Art. Toronto: Art Gallery of Ontario, 1974. Introduction by Marty Dunn, catalogue essay by Peggy Gale, additional texts by Marty Dunn and Garry Neill Kennedy.

The Video Show. London: Serpentine Gallery, 1975.↷ Includes Noel Harding.

Video/Vidéo. Toronto: Video Trade Forum, Festival of Festivals, 1981.↷ With essays by Renee Baert and Willoughby Sharp, and excerpts from a brief submitted by Trinity Square Video to the Federal Cultural Policy Review Committee, March 1981.

Vipond, Mary. *The Mass Media in Canada*. Toronto: James Lorimer and Company, 1989.

Vision in Disbelief: The 4th Biennale of Sydney. Sydney (Australia): Biennale of Sydney, 1982. Preface by Elwyn Lynn. Includes video by Colin Campbell, Norman Cohn, Nancy Nicol, Lisa Steele, John Watt and Rodney Werden.

W Wallace, Keith. "Body Fluid (1986)/Paul Wong." *Video Guide* 8:2 (Issue 37, 1986): 6–7

Wallace, Keith, ed. *Whispered Art History: Twenty Years at the Western Front*.

Vancouver: Arsenal Pulp Press, 1993. With introduction by Keith Wallace and essays by Peter Culley, Karen Knights, Judy Radul, Alexander Varty and William Wood.

Walworth, Dan. "La cascade/Cascadage." In *Robert Morin and Lorraine Dufour. A decade of video production*, ed. Brendan Cotter. Toronto: A Space, 1991.↷

Wanyeki, Lynne. "Twenty Bold, Brash and Beautiful Years: Video In's Twentieth Anniversary." *Fuse* 17:3 (Spring 1994): 32–3

Ward, Rick. "No Masters Yet." *Video Guide* (June 1979): 4–5, 14

Warhol, Cindy. "TBA/TV [interview]." *Video Guide* (June 1979): 6

Wark, Jayne. "Corpus Loquendi/Body for Speaking, Dalhousie Art Gallery [review]." *Parachute* 76 (Fall 1994): 58–9

Watson, Scott. "Luminous Sites/Vancouver." *Parachute* 43 (Spring 1986): 38–9

———. "Stan Douglas' Uncertain Subjects." In *Stan Douglas: Monodramas and Loops*, ed. Scott Watson. Vancouver: UBC Fine Arts Gallery, 1992.↷

———. "Cornelia Wyngaarden/Mike MacDonald." *Canadian Art* 10:3 (Fall 1993): 88

———. "Cornelia Wyngaarden's Queer Subjectivities." In *Cornelia Wyngaarden/The Fragility of Origins*, ed. Brice Canyon. Vancouver: Western Front Society, 1994.↷

Watson, Scott, ed. *Stan Douglas: Monodramas and Loops*. Vancouver: UBC Fine Arts Gallery, 1992.↷ With essays by John Fiske and Scott Watson.

———. *Eric Metcalfe: Return to Brutopia/Works and Collaborations*. Vancouver: UBC Fine Arts Gallery, 1992.↷ With essays by Peggy Gale, Brice MacNeil and Scott Watson.

Waugh, Thomas. "Les formes du discours sexuel dans la nouvelle vidéo masculine." *Communication Information* 9:1 (Summer 1987): 45–6

Werden, Rodney. "'The Typist': a videotape [script]." *Only Paper Today* 4:3 (February 1977): 10

———. *Pauli Schell*. Toronto: Art Metropole, 1978.

———. "Rodney Werden talks with Peggy Gale." In *The 1978 Canadian Video Open*. Calgary: Artons/Parachute Center for Cultural Affairs, 1978.↷

———. [untitled videotape transcript for "Call Roger"]. *Im(pul)se* 4:4/5:1 (1976) (n.p.)

———. "Aboo." *Impulse* 12:3 (Spring 1986): 6–9

———. "Money talks bullshit walks: a statement regarding technique, motivation and intent, and some analysis." In *Toronto: A Play of History (Jeu d'histoire).* Toronto: The Power Plant, 1987.⌥

Western Front Vidéo. Montreal: Musée d'Art Contemporain, 1984.⌥ With essays by René Blouin and Peggy Gale.

White, Peter. "Fairly Reasonable Paintings" and "Introduction." In *John Will: Triple Threat Artist,* ed. Peter White. Regina: Dunlop Art Gallery, 1988.⌥

White, Peter, ed. *John Will: Triple Threat Artist.* Regina: Dunlop Art Gallery, 1988.⌥ With essays by Eric Cameron, Nancy Tousley, Peter White and John Will.

White, Robin F. "Is It Prime Time Yet?/L'art vidéo aux heures de grande écoute?" In *Prime Time Video,* ed. Allan MacKay. Saskatoon: Mendel Art Gallery, 1984.⌥

Wilde, Virginia. "Test Tube: Some General Instructions for Media Artists." *Parallelogramme* 7:2 (December 1981): 16–17

Will, John. "Triple Threat." In *John Will: Triple Threat Artist,* ed. Peter White. Regina: Dunlop Art Gallery, 1988.⌥

Williams, Carol. "Sites of Intervention/ Visual Evidence." *Vanguard* 16:4 (September/October 1987): 14–16

Wilson, Pat. "Through the Holes: Structuring a Passage for Meaning." *Fuse* 8:1/2 (Summer 1984): 66–7

———. "Broadcasting & Bureaucracy: New Television." *Fuse* 10:4 (Winter 1986–7): 24–32 On Art and Television Symposium (Toronto) with Susan Crean, mediator, and panelists Barbara Osborne (Media Alliance, New York), Jean Gagnon (Vidéographe), Michel Ouellette (Agent Orange, Montreal), Stan Fox (TVOntario) and John Dimon and Jim Burt (CBC)

Windwraith, Karen. "First National Lesbian Conference [review]." *Video Guide* 1:4 (September/October 1978): 7

Winzen, Matthias. "International oder Nicht? Zu Arbeiten der kanadischen d9 Teilnehmerin Vera Frenkel." *Das Kunst-Bulletin,* Geneva (March 1993): 16–19

———. "Internationalism at Documenta 9 [letter and editorial correction]." *Art in America* (November 1992): 35

———. "A Bar in Kassel/Un buffet de passage à Kassel." In *Raincoats Suitcases Palms,* ed. Loretta Yarlow. North York: Art Gallery of York University, 1993.⌥

Women in Focus. "The Fifth Annual Vancouver International Film Festival." *Video Guide* 8:2 (Issue 37, 1986): 3

Wong, Paul. "Video." In *From This Point of View: 60 British Columbia Painters, Sculptors, Photographers, Graphic and Video Artists,* ed. Alvin Balkind. Vancouver: Vancouver Art Gallery, 1977.⌥ With work by Cathy Charlton, Kate Craig, Don Druick, Ross Gentleman, Gregg Simpson and Sheera Waisman.

———. "Peggy Gale [interview]." *Video Guide* 1:2 (April/May 1978): 9

———. "In ten sity." *Video Guide* (November 1978–January 1979): 11, 23

———. "Daniel Dion and Daniel Guimond: Valeur Extra Règle/Extra Rule." *Centerfold* 3:1 (December 1978): 43–5

———. "Kingston Symposium." *Video Guide* (June 1979): 7

———. "Making Video: Cable Access, Artists Cooperatives, Fees and Rights." In *Transcript from The International Video Art Symposium 1979.* Kingston: Agnes Etherington Art Centre, 1979.

———. *Export 80.* Montreal: Prime Video, 1980.⌥ With a brief essay by Wong on 8 Montreal video artists.

———. "Export 80." *Video Guide* 3:2 (October 1980): 9

———. "Ed Mowbray/Excerpts and Euphoria." *Video Guide* 4:1(1981): 3

———. "Void Space New Media (Out of Context)." *Video Guide* 5:5 (Winter 1983): 8–9, 14

———. "Void Space — New Media (Out of Context)." In *Vancouver: Art and Artists 1931–1983.* Vancouver: Vancouver Art Gallery, 1983.⌥

———. "Sexual Views: An Installation." *Video Guide* 6:2 (March 1984): 8–10

———. "The Market Is the Medium: Introduction." *Video Guide* 8:3 (September 1986): 18–19

———. "Body Fluid (1986)." In *Luminous Sites/Ten Video Installations,* eds. Daina Augaitis and Karen Henry. Vancouver: Video Inn/Western Front, 1986.◌

———. "True Enough." *Video Guide* 8:4 (December 1986): 12–13

———. "Jim Wong-Chu: Paper Son." *Video Guide* 8:5 (1987): 3, 19

———. "In the Vernacular/Four Window Installations." *Video Guide* 9:3 (1988): 4

———. "Self Winding: A Performance." *Video Guide* 10:1 (March 1989): 5

———. "Feature Length Video — Is Longer Better?" *Video Guide* 10:2 (September 1989): 4

———. *Chinaman's Peak: Walking the Mountain.* Banff: Walter Phillips Gallery, 1993.◌

Wong, Paul, ed. *Yellow Peril Reconsidered.* Vancouver: On Edge, 1990.◌ With essays by Anthony Chan, Richard Fung, Monika Kin Gagnon, Larissa Lai/Jean Lum, Midi Onodera and Paul Wong.

Wood, William. "Cornelia Wyngaarden/UBC Fine Arts Gallery." *Parachute* 63 (Summer 1991): 45–6

Woodrow, Paul. "W.O.R.K.S.: A Conceptographic Reading of Our World Thermometer." *artscanada* 30:4, 182/183 (October 1973): 54

Wooster, Ann-Sargent. "The Way We Were." In *The First Generation: Women and Video, 1970–75,* ed. JoAnn Hanley. New York: Independent Curators Incorporated, 1993.

World-wide Video Festival 1982. The Hague: Kijkhuis, 1982.◌ Canadians include Michael Goldberg, Noel Harding, Nora Hutchinson, Ardele Lister, Nancy Nicol, Tom Sherman, John Watt and Paul Wong.

World-wide Video Festival 1983. The Hague: Kijkhuis, 1983.◌ Canadians include Helen Doyle, Vera Frenkel, Noel Harding, Ed Mowbray, Nancy Nicol, Kim Tomczak and Peter Wronski.

World-wide Video Festival 1984. The Hague: Kijkhuis, 1984.◌ Canadians include Noel Harding, Eric Metcalfe/Hank Bull, Jayce Salloum and Geoffrey Shea.

World-wide Video Festival 1986. The Hague: Kijkhuis, 1986.◌ Canadians include Michael Balser, Doris Chase, François Dugré/Johanne Fournier, François Girard, Bernar Hébert, Susan Rynard and Geoffrey Shea.

World-wide Video Festival 1988. The Hague: Kijkhuis, 1988.◌ Canadians include Luc Bourdon and Jayce Salloum.

World-wide Video Festival 1989. The Hague: Kijkhuis, 1989.◌ Canadians include Balser/Fabo, Dennis Day, Bernar Hebert, Marc Paradis, Susan Rynard, Jayce Salloum and Michèle Waquant.

World-wide Video Festival 1993. The Hague: Kijkhuis, 1993.◌ Includes special section on performances, documentaries, TV programmes, cooperative video projects, plus index of artists and works from the 11 years of the festival to date.

Wronski, Peter. "Festivals: What's in it for you?" *Video Guide* 5:4 (Fall 1983): 8–9

Wyngaarden, Cornelia. "As a Wife Has a Cow." *Video Guide* 7:4 (Issue 34, 1985): 14

———. "As a Wife Has a Cow." In *Luminous Sites/Ten Video Installations,* eds. Daina Augaitis and Karen Henry. Vancouver: Video Inn/Western Front, 1986.◌

———. "Vera Frenkel [interview]." *Video Guide* 8:3 (September 1986): 3–5

———. "Curatorial Statement." *Artropolis 90/Lineages & Linkages.* Vancouver: A.T. Eight Artropolis Society, 1990.◌

Y Yael, B.H. "Film and Video: On the Level." *Fuse* 11:3 (Fall 1987): 8–9

Yarlow, Loretta, ed. *Raincoats Suitcases Palms.* North York: Art Gallery of York University, 1993.◌ With essays by Dot Tuer and Matthias Winzen, and a Tuer/Frenkel interview.

Youngblood, Gene. "The Future of Desire/The Art and Tech of Video in the 80's [excerpt from Video Inn lecture]." *Video Guide* 4:1 (1981): 13–15

———. "A Medium Matures: Video and the Cinematic Enterprise." In *The Second Link. Viewpoints on Video in the Eighties,* ed. Lorne Falk. Banff: The Walter Phillips Gallery, 1983.◌

Z Zemans, Joyce. "Video Activity of N.E. Thing Co. Ltd." *artscanada* 30:4, 182/183 (October 1973): 61

Zemel, Carol. "Women and Video, an introduction to the community of video." *artscanada* 30:4, 182/183 (October 1973): 30–40

Zippay, Lori. "New Imagery." *Video Guide*
4:5 (Issue 20): 7

Newspapers/journalism:

There are copious references to video projects, programmes and artists in daily and
weekly newspapers, beginning in the early
1970s. None are listed here, as the sheer volume and the popularizing tone combined
to make their collection and annotation
inappropriate to the present bibliography.

Video centres in Vancouver, Calgary,
Winnipeg, Toronto, Montreal and Halifax
all have selections of these materials on
file.

INDEX

VIDEO re/VIEW

THE (best) SOURCE FOR CRITICAL WRITINGS ON CANADIAN ARTISTS' VIDEO

For more information contact:
Art Metropole
788 King Street West
Toronto, Ontario M5V 1N6
tel (416) 703-4400
fax (416) 703-4404
e-mail: ART_Metropole@intacc.web.net

Published by
Art Metropole & V tape, Toronto
Distributed by
Art Metropole
Edited by
Peggy Gale & Lisa Steele
New translations by
Jean-Luc Svoboda
Research & Selection by
Peggy Gale & Lisa Steele
Text entry by
Judy Mintz, Art Metropole
Bibliography by
Peggy Gale, with supplementary French entries by Maria Cristina Martinez
Index by
Peggy Gale & Cheryl Rondeau-Hoekstra
Bibliographical editing/proofreading by
Beverly Endersby & Karen MacCormack
Text proofreading by
Peggy Gale, Lisa Steele, Kim Tomczak & Susan Wheeler

Cover image:
Twinitron (1992) by David Buchan
Book design by
Julie Gibb & Christian Morrison, GreenStreet Design, Toronto
Typeset in
Thesis serif by Luc(as) de Groot
Printed in Canada by
Premier Printing Limited, Winnipeg

Art Metropole and V tape wish to acknowledge the financial support of: the Canada Council; the Museums Assistance Program of the Department of Canadian Heritage; the Government of Ontario through the Ministry of Citizenship, Culture and Recreation; the Ontario Arts Council; the Culture Division of Metro Parks and Culture; and the Toronto Arts Council.

Canadian Cataloguing in Publication Data
Main entry under title:
VIDEO re/VIEW: The (best) Source for Critical Writings on Canadian Artists' Video
Co-published by V tape.
Includes bibliographical references and index.
ISBN 0-920956-37-8
1. Video art – Canada. 2. Video art – Canada – Bibliography.
I. Gale, Peggy, 1944-   . II. Steele, Lisa, 1947-   . III. Art Metropole.
N8545.5.V53V53 1996   709'.71   C96-930422-6